A GENERAL HISTORY OF EUROPE
EDITED BY DENYS HAY

EUROPE IN
THE HIGH MIDDLE AGES
1150–1309

JOHN H. MUNDY

LONGMAN

LONGMAN GROUP LIMITED
Longman House, Burnt Mill,
Harlow, Essex CM20 2JE, England
and Associated Companies throughout the World

First published 1973

First issued in paperback 1975
Third impression 1983

ISBN 0 582 48194 5

Phototypeset by Filmtype Services Limited, Scarborough, England

Printed in Hong Kong by
Wah Cheong Printing Press Ltd

To C.W.M.

Contents

Maps

Abbreviations

AA.SS.	*Acta sanctorum*
BIMA	*Bibliotheca iuridica medii aevi*, ed. Augusto Gaudenzi et al., 3 vols. (Bologna, 1888–1901)
BGPM	*Beiträge zur Geschichte der Philosophie des Mittelalters*
BuF	Ludwig Rockinger, ed., *Briefsteller und Formelbücher des eilten bis vierzehnten Jahrhunderts*, 2 vols. (Munich, 1863–4)
CICan	Emil Friedberg, ed., *Corpus iuris canonici*, 2 vols. (Leipzig, 1879–81)
CICiv	*Corpus iuris civilis*, ed. Mommsen, Krueger, et al., 3 vols. (Berlin, 1912–20)
MGH	*Monumenta Germaniae Historica*
Const.	*Constitutiones et acta publica*
Epp. sel.	*Epistolae selectae*
LL	*Leges*
Ldl	*Libelli de lite*
SS	*Scriptores*
FIG in usum scholarum	*Fontes iuris germanici antiqui in usum scholarum*
SS in usum scholarum	*Scriptores rerum Germanicarum in usum scholarum*
Staatschriften	*Staatschriften des späteren Mittelalters*
PL	J. P. Migne, ed., *Patrologia latina* (Paris, 1844–64)

RIS	*Rerum italicarum scriptores,* in new edition of 1900 onward
Rolls Series	*Rerum britannicarum medii aevi scriptores*
TUJ	*Tractatus universi juris*

Preface

This general history is written for undergraduates: young men and women whose natural faculties have matured and who hope to acquire rather more learning than is needed by the mass of their peers. Such young people are capable of understanding everything known by their elders. But the young also differ from the old. Because of their innocence, or ignorance, they often have an advantage: if at all open-minded and unspoiled, they are more capable of ready comprehension. Burdened by experience and learning, the minds of older persons often seem to peer in order to judge instead of merely looking in order to understand. 'The old', said Giles of Rome, 'are naturally sceptical and ungenerous; the young generous and credulous.'[1] But, aside from this and other differences, all adults share a certain equality. A general history addressed to the young is therefore inadvertently one addressed to all men, that is, not only to students, but also to their parents and teachers.

As readers will see, a difficulty of this book is that the expository text has been interlarded with many quotations from primary sources. Because these quotations often contain matter that goes beyond the points I am trying to make, they sometimes disrupt the even flow of argument and throw a reader off. This hardship may be borne, however, because there is no other way to give a reader a taste of how the men of the time spoke and felt. Yet another difficulty of this extensive use of primary sources is that, although usually easy to read and understand as wholes, specific words and phrases are often not easy to translate into modern terms.

This is one of the reasons why I leave occasional Latin words

[1] *De regimine principum* 1, 1, 2 in Rome 1607, 7.

xiii

and phrases in my translations or place them in brackets. This practice is especially frequent in the sections devoted to institutional history for the obvious reason that few medieval institutions have an exact modern equivalent, but it is also frequent in the case of technical or highly charged words in passages concerning intellectual history. An example is the word *curiosus*, a pejorative term that was applied both to the wealthy and leisured and to certain intellectuals by the moralists of the time. Other words are left in Latin in order to emphasize the measure of uniformity obtaining in the culture of this age and the tendency of its thinkers to employ generic and abstract terms for specific institutional entities. An example of this is the use of the word *potestas* (in place of the more familiar Italian *podestà*) to describe the highest magistracy of the Italian town republics. The reason for this modest departure from normal practice is to remind the reader that *potestas* or its vernacular derivatives like *podestà*, *poosté*, etc. were widely used in western Europe to describe urban magistrates and seignorial authority, and therefore represents the degree to which political power was decentralized in this period.

The employment of a Latin word also reminds the reader of something that is obvious but all too easily overlooked in an age of national states and national languages. The Europe treated in this book was a region principally divided between the Latin-speaking peoples and the Germanic peoples. Although the latter had once invaded and momentarily subjected the Latins, the attraction of the latters' originally Mediterranean culture had conquered the invaders. The universal language of western Europe had become Latin, and French, a language of Latin stock, was the most developed and widely spread literary vehicle of its vernacular tongues. In spite of the great importance of the Germanic peoples (and of the lesser, and, for the time being, declining importance of the Slavic peoples and those on the Celtic fringe), there is no doubt that Latin and its derivatives so dominated the cultural life of Europe that, if one were obliged to find a single adjective with which to qualify the word 'Europe' for this period, one would choose 'Latin', and describe the whole as 'Latin Europe'.

How to choose and how to cite primary sources is also not without difficulties. The general principle has been to use the

most easily available modern edition in order to enable a reader
to look it up as speedily as possible. The majority of texts cited
and translated derive from printed editions of the original texts,
but this rule is not infrequently waived. This is because I have
not had time to read everything and must therefore have recourse
to documents and tracts cited in other writers' books, something
especially noticeable in the sections on institutional history.
Sometimes, however, a text or document that I have myself
studied is cited as being in someone else's work. This is because
the author has not only used the text or document itself, but has
also explored its context. See, for example, the citations in the
forthcoming footnotes of texts and documents used by such as
Hermann Fitting and Ernst Kantorowicz. No matter what their
source, however, the translations of the texts used are my own.

The method of citation is deliberately regularized in order to
be understandable to those who are not specialized in the specific
part of the history being treated. Partly because they enjoy the
sense of possessing a higher gnosis or of belonging to a school,
historians of the Middle Ages often use recondite systems of
reference deriving from special traditions or appearing to offer
the maximum of economy or accuracy in communication with
other specialists. These systems are eschewed here. As an example, the conventional abbreviations of canon and civil law are
avoided. Justinian's *Codex* is referred to as *Code*, not as C. The
only exception is that the *Decretals of Gregory IX* are referred to
as the *Liber extra*, partly because the longer title explains only
under whose aegis this book was published and not what it contains, and partly because the brief title records the fact that it was
compiled of materials that had not hitherto been assembled
systematically—a *liber extravagantium*. But the conventional
citation with the sign X is avoided as being meaningless to the
general audience of the literate. In spite of differing special
traditions, also, the subdivisions of medieval works are given as
much as possible according to the rule *optima est citatio a maiore
ad minus in omnibus*. For brevity's sake, also, early modern editions
of medieval texts are often referred to in this manner: 'in Venice
1582', meaning the edition published at Venice in that year. For
series with lengthy titles, a page of conventional abbreviations
has been provided.

Special thanks go to those who read parts of this volume—

PREFACE

J. M. W. Bean, Marshall Clagett, R. W. Emery, Werner Gundes-heimer, Denys Hay, Julius Kirshner, P. O. Kristeller, P. N. Riesenberg, K. M. Setton, R. E. Somerville, K. M. Woody, and especially to Beatrice Gottlieb. The book was written at the Institute for Advanced Study, Princeton, New Jersey, and time free from teaching was subvented by a National Endowment of the Humanities fellowship and by Columbia University.

John Mundy
15 November 1971

xvi

I

The Sources

Public records, administration, and law

The shape and quantity of the sources in this period was determined by two factors. The first of these was the growth of the economy and the consequent growth of government, both ecclesiastical and secular. This required an ampler and more

BIBLIOGRAPHY. Other than examining the bibliographical lists recorded in both Christopher Brooke's and Denys Hay's volumes in this series, perhaps the best introduction to the sources is to read the manuals. In English, the standard manual is L. J. Paetow, *A Guide to the Study of Medieval History* (2nd edn., New York 1931). More succinct is Louis Halphen's *Initiation aux études d'histoire du moyen âge* (3rd edn., Paris, 1952). A good and very technical manual is Heinz Quirin's *Einführung in das Studium der mittelalterlichen Geschichte* (Braunschweig, 1961). The best annual bibliographical survey for all subjects is to be found in the *Revue d'histoire ecclésiastique*, and brief reviews of value are available in another periodical, the *Erforschung des Mittelalters*.

After this the student may turn to the general histories, especially to volumes five, six, and seven of the *Cambridge Medieval History*, 8 vols. (1911–36), now available in an abbreviated two-volume edition (1952). Even better—for those who read French—are volumes IV (in two parts) and VIII of Gustave Glotz, ed., *Histoire générale*. From there the reader might turn to somewhat more specialized general histories. An example is the three volumes of the *Cambridge Economic History* (1942–60; vol. I re-edited 1961) on agrarian life, trade and industry, and economic organization. Another is the indispensable *Histoire de l'église* edited by A. Fliche, V. Martin, and E. Jarry—a series that is being translated—especially vols. VIII to XII.

In regard to the materials being discussed in this chapter, the best guides are the general surveys devoted to these fields. A list of those dealing with philosophy and theology will be found in the bibliographical note to chapter XIII below. In regard to Latin letters, one consults H. de Ghellinck, *L'essor de la littérature latine au XIIe siècle* (2nd edn., Brussels, 1954). What the clergy and literate laity were reading can best be seen in Ch.-V. Langlois, *La Vie en France au moyen-âge du XIIe au milieu du XIVe siècle*, 5 vols. (Paris, 1908–28), an invaluable collection. To these may be added R. R. Bezzola, *L'origine et la formation de la littérature courtoise en occident: 500–1200* (Paris, 1944–63) and the magnificent book by E. R. Curtius, *European Literature and the Latin Middle Ages* (New York, 1953, trans. from the German of 1948).

I

specialized documentation than had been needed before. The second was the beginning—in reality, it had begun in the eleventh century, or even the late tenth—of the secularization of legal documentation and of letters, a process far more advanced in law than in literature and philosophy in this period. The social and ideological roots of this change will be introduced in chapter II and discussed at more length in subsequent ones. In spite of the secularization, it is important to remember that, for reasons both obvious and to be rehearsed later in this book, the documentation of ecclesiastical government and law was especially rich in this time. On the most basic of all levels, the economic, the principal need was for an enlarged and increasingly flexible documentation of property right and contractual obligation.

Other than the ecclesiastical, the largest single literate profession by the thirteenth century was that which provided scribal services. Because of its traditions, commercial power, and rapidly growing urbanism, Italy was ahead of the rest of Europe in the appearance of the public scribe. At first closely linked to the judicature, the notariate emerged as an independent institution during the twelfth century. Certain judicial elements remained attached to it, however, in that notaries informed the parties about the law in the acts they wished drawn and were obliged to refuse to record illegal transactions. As Italian towns gained their freedom in this period, also, the controls over the notaries by princely courts diminished. By about 1200 the most significant affiliation for an Italian public scribe was with the town-licensed guild or college of notaries, which examined him for entry into the profession and protected his interests. All the same, both

---

Translations pose a problem simply because there are so many. A partial guide is provided by C. P. Farrar and A. P. Evans, *Bibliography of English Translations from Medieval Sources* (New York, 1946), a book that is currently being updated. Among the scholarly collections of translations are the Columbia University *Records of Civilization*, *Nelson's Medieval Text*, and *Les Classiques de l'histoire de France au moyen âge*. There is much available in translation. The whole of Thomas Aquinas is translated and much by such key figures as Bonaventure and Roger Bacon is also available in English. Many paperback versions are also to be found. Almost all of the poems and romances and not a few of the histories cited in these pages are in paperback.

To turn to the material discussed in the first part of this chapter, the best introductions to legal studies are A. M. Stickler, *Historia iuris canonici latini* (Turin, 1950), Hermann-Kantorowicz, *Studies in the Glossators of the Roman Law* (Cambridge, 1938), and, for an excellent survey of Europe's legal history, Paul Koschaker, *Europa und das römische Recht* (Munich, 1953).

the imperial and papal appointment of notaries remained useful because scribes who were granted the right to draw up instruments by these theoretically ecumenical institutions could service an 'international' clientele. Some or all of these historical accretions were therefore often a part of a notary's claim to attention. Thus one sees mention in 1216 of 'Peter, notary of the commune of Rimini, notary of the sacred palace of Milan, and judge (*missus*) of the lord Otto emperor'.[1]

Since a notary was a public person licensed by public authority, his subscription or signature was sufficient to authenticate an act. Furthermore, since a written act recorded the decisions of a party or parties, it soon became customary to consider the notary's register, in which the wishes of the party or parties were first recorded in abbreviated form, as a proof equal in value to the enlarged charters requested by them for their private collections. Among the earliest extant notarial registers is that of the Genoese, John the Scribe, of 1155. As social regulation became more intense in the thirteenth century, the ancient Roman practice of recording or 'insinuating' documents in public archives was revived. The private registers of the notaries were therefore supplemented by public ones housed in municipal offices containing records of important transactions. The jurist Albert of Gandino described this in his *Questions on Statutes* of 1289: 'It was enacted at Bologna that legal instruments ought to be inserted or placed in the public register, if valued at more than twenty-five pounds.'[2]

The Italian system spread to neighbouring areas during the course of the twelfth century. By the early fourteenth century, there were also attempts to have it adopted in northern France and elsewhere, but its real expansion in those regions took place only in the later Middle Ages. This was partly because the economic immaturity of northern Europe did not yet require extensive documentation. As John of Bologna put it in a *summa* of the notarial art written for John Peckham (d. 1292), archbishop of Canterbury: 'Although tracts on instruments are necessarily widely diffused in Italy, because Italians, being cautious, wish to have a public record of everything they contract mutually, and because almost the opposite is true in England, namely, that, unless absolutely necessary, an instrument is requested only very

---

[1] Cited in Harry Bresslau, *Handbuch der Urkundenlehre* (Berlin, 1912) I, 629.
[2] *Quaestiones statutorum* 69 in *BIMA* III, 189.

3

rarely', he will write only about those documents required for judicial business and decisions.[3]

But things were also changing even in northern Europe. In the thirteenth century, there were town notariates as far apart as Lübeck and Metz and the towns in southern Germany and Flanders. The difference from Italy was largely one of the degree of development. The customs of Rheims of 1269 attempted to reduce the numbers of scribes who drew acts for private parties, but notaries were nothing like as numerous in the north as in the south. In 1293 the guild of notaries at Pisa, a substantial but not gigantic town, had at least 232 members. Many northern towns were still in the stage of developing notarial services for private persons out of the group of scribes associated with town government whereas in Italy the college of notaries, although licensed by communal authority, already had an independent existence. Furthermore, since, as we shall see, northern towns were not as free of princely authority as were those of Italy, the scribal services of princely and episcopal courts were expanded to take care of the burgeoning need. Since princes, bishops, some towns, and even some lesser nobles had seals representing their degree of importance or independence, scribal service together with the authentication of the prince's seal was sold to private clients. Northern documents were therefore usually sealed whereas those of Italy, unless emanating directly from public authority, were usually merely signed by the notary or marked with his 'manual seal' or mark. Both of these forms of authentication were accepted in major jurisdictions. Alexander III (d. 1181) instructed the bishop of Worcester that 'it seems to us that authentic documents have no authority if the witnesses have died unless they have been drawn by a public hand [of a notary], so that they are public documents, or unless they have an authentic seal'.[4]

A change in the nature of documentation accompanied the growth of scribal service, one paralleling the rise of the economy and the expansion of the state. Before the Gregorian age, other than privileges and other documents emanating from occasional ecclesiastical or secular princely courts, the principal evidence of property right was to be found in ecclesiastical archives. Most of the documents contained therein, moreover, were drawn by

[3] *Summa notarie*, prologue in *BuF* II, 603.
[4] *Liber extra* 2, 22, 2 in *CICan* II, 344.

4

churchmen attached to the institutions receiving the gifts or privileges described on the parchments, and it was often found convenient to compile the charters into books called cartularies. By 1300 cartularies had become far rarer, and, more significantly, the documentation had become laicized, in that laymen collected their own documents and almost all instruments were written by lay notaries. At least, this was so in areas like Italy where the notariate early flourished. There, indeed, the notarial and public registers described above soon became the weightiest body of materials. This change, it has been seen, was slowly occurring elsewhere throughout much of Europe. Nevertheless in the thirteenth century the church of northern France still provided much of the public scribal service needed in that region by the sale of the seals and services of the episcopal courts. In short, the process of secularization was slower in the north than in the south. However that may be, it is fair to say that, by 1300, the overwhelming bulk of documentation concerning economic and social matters was to be found in the notaries' registers and the acts drawn by them.

Although less prepossessing in bulk, governmental records obviously give more information about political and ecclesiastical institutions. It is usually and correctly said that the chanceries of secular princes did not reach maturity until about 1200. From that time are to be dated the first extant registers or rolls of letters sent from the court, from the reign of John (accession 1199) in England, for example, and of James I (accession 1213) in Catalonia–Aragon. Before that time, most governmental agencies and princely courts entrusted the preservation of the privileges and grants they issued to those who received them, and, just like monasteries and private families, mainly concentrated on recording their rights and revenues. Thus Catalonia–Aragon possessed a celebrated *Book of Fiefs* dating from the reign of Alphonso II (accession 1162). The famous tally of what was owed the king by fiefholders and communities called the *Domesday Book* (1086) was constantly used by the English treasury, but was early supplemented by a record of its actual income called the *Pipe Rolls*, a series that is continuous from the beginning of the reign of Henry II in 1154. But the growth of chancery registration was an advance over that, not only because it provided an orderly and chronologically arranged record of governmental activities, but

5

also, in the long run, provided a public record to be consulted by others than the prince and his officers for the definition and protection of their rights.

The model for the secular chanceries was surely ecclesiastical and the greatest of the Church's chanceries was that of Rome. The Roman tradition of registering the acts of a prince (the *res gestae*) had never ceased there. When Cardinal Deusdedit compiled his legal code for the use of the Gregorians in 1087, he cited materials from the registers of the ancient pope Gelasius I. Although, with the exception of some fortuitously preserved fragments of the registers of John VIII of the ninth century and Gregory VII of the eleventh, the whole of this immense archive was lost in the Roman wars of the thirteenth century and the continuous series begins only with Innocent III (accession 1198), everybody knew that Rome had continued this practice. The canonist Stephen of Tournai (d. 1203) remarked that 'it is the custom of the Roman church that, when a letter about a matter of importance is sent to anyone, it retains a copy, which copies are compiled into a book which is called a register', thus implying that such was not the case elsewhere.[5] Although we know that Stephen's comment was somewhat belated and that others were already adopting the practice, it is certain that the papal chancery was the most advanced in western Europe, a fact that is illustrated, among other things, by the sheer bulk of its correspondence. In the eighteen years of John XXII's pontificate (d. 1334), about 65,000 papal letters, or bulls, were registered. A result of this immense amount of paper work was that popes could sometimes slip up. In 1183 Lucius III reversed his own decision in favour of the chapter of Sainte-Geneviève of Paris against Rosny-sur-Bois. He apologized to the serfs of Rosny for his earlier judgment, stating frankly that 'because of the great quantity of business referred to the apostolic see, it is impossible to recall the tenor of all our letters and other actions so that the trickery of certain parties can sometimes circumvent us, and we can unknowingly be induced to write contradicting things we have written before'.[6]

Once initiated on a grand scale, registration spread everywhere. Court decisions were especially suited for this kind of record, and

[5] Cited in H. Bresslau, *op. cit.* I, 121.

[6] Cited in Marc Bloch, 'De la cour royale à la cour de Rome', *Studi in onore di Enrico Besta* (Milan, 1937) II, 153.

so were the acts of bishops and other people of prelatial and princely grade. A peculiar example of an episcopal register is that of the visitations or inspections of his archdiocese by Odo Rigaud, archbishop of Rouen. Stretching from 1248 to 1269, this record contains a mine of information on the behaviour of the parish clergy and the religious (as the regular clergy were called). Still others were the registers of the inquisitors when the Inquisition was instituted to hunt out and pursue heretics in the 1230s. Some of the extraordinarily variegated sources of this kind will be cited in forthcoming chapters.

The growth of scribal culture produced an extensive literature, both in the chanceries and in the notariate. Most common was the genre called the *ars dictaminis,* or art of letter writing. A type firmly established by the time the period treated in this volume begins, it was well represented throughout the thirteenth century. Connected to this genre were formulary books or collections of letters, some for general use (as in the case of Pons the Provençal cited below) and others specific to a given chancery. An example of the latter is a formulary book composed in the papal chancery around 1270 that contains nearly three thousand model letters. There were also contrasting styles derived from the differing institutional bases that produced this literature. Linked with the Church and with princely courts, the northern schools of the *dictatores* were marked by elegant, often heavy, Latinity. Trained in one of the most celebrated northern schools, that of Orléans, Pons the Provençal (fl. 1236–52) taught at Toulouse, Paris and Orleans and his collection of letters and *Summa dictaminis* had a continuing vogue in the later Middle Ages. As we shall see, Italian Latin was often simpler. Although producing ornate Latinists such as Peter of Vinea (d. 1249), the imperial chancellor whose style even influenced the papal chancery, Italy was dominated by the practical needs and styles of the professional notariate. It was there also that the *ars notaria,* or notarial art, was invented.

Differing careers will illustrate the different types of literary material and styles. Peter of Blois (d. 1205) wrote a celebrated *ars dictaminis* in the elegant Latin of the north. An author of worldly and amatory poetry, he tutored a Norman-Sicilian prince in 1167, and, on returning north in 1173, entered the secretarial service of Henry II of England and his wife. He closed his career

7

as archdeacon of London and chancellor of the archbishop of Canterbury. While serving in these offices he wrote on the crusades, ecclesiastical discipline and the sacraments, as well as producing sermons and a spate of letters full of classical allusions. Quite different was the life of the Bolognese Rolandino Passaggeri. A notary in 1234, Rolandino entered the town chancery in 1238 and became the notary of the bankers' guild in 1245. Again in the town chancery in 1249, he penned a celebrated response to the threats against Bolognese liberty contained in a letter of Peter of Vinea, the chancellor of the Hohenstaufen emperor, Frederick II. In 1255–56, he issued his *Summa artis notarie*, the principal textbook for this discipline during the rest of the Middle Ages. In the 1280s, he was busy teaching at the university and redacting legislation for the Guelph, or popular, party, including the famous *Most Sacred Ordinances* of 1282, the crowning monument of popular legislation. Heard of until 1297, this veritable chancellor of the republic closed his life in retirement.

The governmental materials described above were not usually legislative enactment. What principally appears in the registers are privileges, administrative orders, and judicial decisions by the prince and his officers, and the justification for these actions was that they were reestablishing or maintaining the right order of things, applying the ancient principles of a theoretically good law to new circumstances. That there were legislative enactments in this period, however, there is no doubt. When the popes promulgated the canons decided on by themselves and the fathers assembled in council, they legislated in both the Roman and modern senses of that term. Embodied in the *Liber augustalis*, also, the constitutions of Melfi of 1231 promulgated by the Emperor Frederick II exemplified the prince's right to issue laws (*ius legis condendae*) when meeting with a general assembly of his realm. Furthermore, as governmental functions were defined with greater clarity, the role of judicial precedent in making new law became clearer. The function of precedent was known to the English jurist Henry of Bracton (d. 1268) who himself collected a celebrated *Case Book*. Designed to protect town liberty against the encroachments of princely power, the thirteenth-century *Cartularies of the City and Bourg of Toulouse* not only included princely grants, or privileges, and legislative enactments of the town's magistrates (*constitutiones* or *stabilimenta*), but also collected their decisions in law in order to prove their extensive jurisdiction. It must be confessed, however, that only Italy's learned lawyers and town councillors fully understood the distinction between legislation and judicial precedent in this period.

The multiplication of administrative and judicial functions led to the appearance of manuals. One of the earliest and best of these was the *Dialogue of the Exchequer* written by Richard FitzNeale, a second generation civil servant—if the term is not too anomalous —whose father, then bishop of Ely, had bought him the office of the treasurer in 1169 and who died in that office and as bishop of London in 1198. His was a manual that treated the history, practice, and legal implications of the activities of the English treasury. Of a different kind was the *Ordo judiciarius* completed and revised by the canonist professor Tancred of Bologna in 1216, a work that speedily became the standard manual for canon law courts. Still another type was the Florentine *dictator* Buoncompagno of Signa's (fl. 1200–35) *The Cedar*, a frankly humorous manual on how to write founding charters and to issue legislation or statutes.

Of wider range because they contain much private law were the codes published in this period. These were roughly of two kinds: codifications of local customary law and general, or common, law codes. The former ranged all the way from simple village and town customals to positive monuments of jurisprudence such as the *Mirror of the Saxons* written by Eike of Repgow from 1220 to 1235 and the *Customs of Clermont-en-Beauvasis* finished in 1283 by Philip of Remi, lord of Beaumanoir, both of which contain much more than their names imply. The law common to a whole kingdom is exemplified by England's two great treatises on her laws and customs, the first of about 1187 attributed to the then chief justiciar Ralph of Glanville, and the second written by Henry of Bracton between 1235 and 1259. Although it only gradually won general currency, another example of this kind of common law of a realm is the *Book of the Laws* (commonly called *Las siete partidas*) written from 1256 through 1263 by a commission for the king of Castile, Alphonso X.

More ecumenical than the law of any one kingdom was the law of the Church. It was also a more learned law because it early gave rise to commentary and found an immediate place in the schools.

Of special importance here were the collections of this law. The most significant of these was the *Concordance of Discordant Canons*, or *Decretum*, compiled around 1140 by the Camaldolese monk Gratian. Although not formally authoritative, this great assemblage of conciliar canons, papal letters, and patristic sources became the basic text of canon law and speedily spread everywhere. Those who glossed it and commented upon it were called 'decretists'. Soon, recent papal letters and conciliar canons were also amassed into collections. Finally, at the request of the pope, the Dominican Raymond of Peñafort (d. 1275) compiled and issued in 1234 a collection called the *Decretals of Gregory IX*, or the *Liber extra*, that superseded all other collections and was legally authoritative. Since there were five books in the Gregorian collection, the next publication of similar materials, that of Boniface VIII issued in 1298, was called the *Sixth Book*. Those who commented upon or glossed these collections were called 'decretalists'. The ordinary gloss on the *Decretum* was by John Teutonicus (Zemeke) around 1215–17. The Gregorian decretals were glossed by Bernard of Parma from 1241 through 1266, and the *Sixth Book* by John Andreae from 1294 to 1303. Apart from the explicatory glosses, the jurists wrote *summae*, or general and epitomized surveys of the whole field. In the twelfth century, the most celebrated of these was that of Huguccio of Pisa (d. 1210), to which the thirteenth century added the commentaries of Innocent IV (d. 1254) and the *Golden Summa* and *Lectura* of Hostiensis (Henry of Susa, cardinal of Ostia, d. 1271). As we shall see when treating law more generally, certain particular problems soon merited special commentary. An example, though by no means the earliest, is the *Tract on Usury* by Alexander Lombard written shortly before 1307.

The most universal of all the laws was Roman law or, rather, the work of learned jurists to draw jurisprudential principles from what was later called the *corpus juris civilis*, the Justinianic compilation of Roman law, all of which except for some 'novels' was studied at this time. As we shall see, what gave Roman law its presidency was that it was enforceable in no place on earth save in the minds of the legal professors and lawyers who taught or used its normative principles (*norma juridica*). It ruled, as the tag had it, 'not for reason of empire but because of the empire of reason', and the civilians proudly asserted that even canon law depended upon Roman procedures and norms 'as upon a staff'.

Much of the work on Roman law was in the form of exegetical glosses. Of these, the standard work was the compilation by Accursius (d. 1260) called the great or *Ordinary Gloss.* There were other types of literature as well. The Bolognese professor Azo (d. about 1230) wrote glosses on the whole of the *Code* and *Digest*, dogmatical *summae* on the *Code* and *Institutes*, elaborations (*brocarda*) on the *regulae juris* or principles of law, and *quaestiones* in which the authorities were listed on particular points of law, their opinions contrasted, and their disagreements resolved. Furthermore, Azo's students and contemporaries compiled his *lecturae* and followers extracted from his writings sections on specific problems, such as usury or arbitration, and published them separately. Although not altogether new, a specialized literature of this kind grew apace from just before 1200. A treatise on criminal law (*De maleficiis*) and one on statute law by Albert of Gandino (d. about 1310) may be cited as examples. Disagreements naturally abounded, and compilations of the *dissentiones doctorum* soon became part of this literature. Other than *responsa* or *quaestiones* on points of law, individual jurists rendered their opinions in specific law cases, thereby creating yet another branch of literature, the *consilia*, sometimes also called *responsa.* An early example is a consultation of John Bassianus in the late twelfth century. What individuals could do, groups could also. Faculties, such as those at Bologna and Toulouse, frequently produced *responsa.* Naturally, not everyone was happy at this multiplication of literature and opinion. Buoncompagno not only made fun of the obscurities of the first glossator Irnerius (d. before 1118), but also said citing the great Azo that 'when a gloss requires a gloss . . . the sense [of the law] is being contemned and drowned in a labyrinth of double meaning.'[7]

To conclude this section, it is obvious that to read private charters, administrative manuals, and even court records is rarely entertaining and just about as intellectually stimulating as reading formal logic, theology, or other technical literatures. At the same time, there are alleviations. As we shall see, the jurists of this time were moved by a very real sense of progress and advancement. Testaments are sometimes moving; court cases sometimes

---

[7] *Rhetorica novissima* 10, 1 in *BIMA* II, 292.

amusing and even exciting. King John of England, to name but one prince, was a witty man even in his official correspondence. Lastly, a kind of Rabelaisian humour—perhaps a necessary consequence of so much dull work—was already a distinctive mark of the legal and scribal professions. The Bolognese jurist Bulgarus (d. about 1166) cracked his students up when, himself a widower and marrying a widow, he resumed his course on the morrow of his bridal night with the text from the *Code*: 'Rem non novam neque insolitam aggredimur—I have entered a thing neither new nor unaccustomed.'[8] A notable example of this spirit is Buoncompagno of Signa, the Florentine *dictator* who wrote in the period between 1200 and 1235 and who taught briefly at Bologna. Other than his old and new rhetorics—the latter of which is partly an *ars concionandi*, or manual for public speakers, Buoncompagno wrote tracts on grammar, testaments, friendship, and the art of writing love letters. All of his works are intentionally funny as well as instructive. He was in fact the medieval equivalent of a professional humorist. The quality of this wiseacre's (*truffator*) wit is shown by his teaching of how *not* to use sacred Scripture:

> A fellow who carnally knew a nun said: 'I have not violated the divine bed, but, because the Lord delighted me in his creature, I have striven to exalt his horn.' Again, a nun could say to her lover: 'Thy rod and thy staff, they comfort me.' Or wives may say to their lovers: 'Give us of your oil, for our lamps have gone out.'[9]

And there was ideology in this humour too. Proud of their school-taught Roman law, Bologna's jurists maligned the Lombard law that had been systematized at Pavia on the model of the *Institutes* and *Code* in the late twelfth century. To the jurists, as Buoncompagno and others tell us, this law of Charlemagne's (!) was the 'German stain' or 'blot', a law that should not be called *lex*, but instead *fex* (dung). Hostility to the *Longobarda* and *Libri feudorum* was animated partly by the anti-German feeling of the Italians and partly by the hostility of the popular parties in the

[8] A free translation of *Code* 3, 1, 14 which incipit was later used in a bull of Boniface VIII (see p. 322 below). Lawyers used *res* in this sense, as in the phrase *habere rem cum ea*.

[9] *Rhetorica novissima* 8, 1 in *BIMA* II, 284a. The scriptural passages are 1 Samuel 2:10, Psalm 23:4, and Matthew 25:8. Buoncompagno's version of Samuel reads *cornu eius studui exaltare*. The Vulgate has *et sublimabit cornu christi sui*.

towns to the knightly aristocracies who lived there and whose fiefs and service were usually regulated by this law. But the *Longobarda* of the gentlefolk survived these thrusts, and it, or its derivatives, still ruled the duelling field in nineteenth century Europe.

Ecclesiastical and secular letters

The court of conscience supplemented the court of law. Indeed, a mark of the Church's leadership at this time, this court may be said to have penetrated even more deeply into the mind of the time than did the coercive tribunal of man's justice. Culminating in the work of the circle of Peter Cantor (the precentor of Nôtre-Dame, d. 1197) at the university of Paris and in the insistence of the Lateran council of 1215 upon at least one annual confession for all Christians, a renewed emphasis on the penitential system began to result in the production of *summae* or manuals of conscience to guide the clergy in their work. Among the earliest of those specifically directed to the lay apostolate was one written by Alan of Lille toward the end of the twelfth century. In the same period Peter Cantor issued his *Summa on Sacraments and Advices to the Soul*, whose third book was devoted to cases of conscience. The greatest of these works in our period was the *Summa of Penitential Cases* written between 1220 and 1234 by Raymond of Peñafort. This literature speedily branched out to produce epitomes or *summulae* useful for daily work. Specialized literature also soon appeared. A late example is a little tract called *Rules for the Merchants of Toulouse*, a compilation concerning usury and related topics culled by a Dominican named Guy from the much larger *Summa of Confessors* of John of Freiburg written between 1290 and 1298.

As Peter Cantor said, preaching was perhaps the most essential part of the Church's work. There had always been great preachers in the Church. Bernard of Clairvaux's (d. 1153) preaching tours to southern France, the Rhineland, and elsewhere illustrate how famous preachers were sought after by the local clergy. There is no doubt, however, that preaching reached new heights in the period we are examining. Around 1200 Paris produced an astonishing roster of successful preachers, many of whose sermons were collected for the use of the clergy. Among these were the revivalist Fulk (d. 1202), a parish priest of Neuilly and student of

Peter Cantor; Robert of Curzon (d. 1218), professor at Paris and
cardinal; Stephen Langton (d. 1228), professor there and later
archbishop of Canterbury; and James of Vitry (d. 1240), who
died as archbishop of Acre and cardinal. The mendicants of
later generations were even more active. An example is Berthold
of Regensburg (d. 1272), a Franciscan spellbinder who the exaggerated local chronicles of southern Germany say was capable of
attracting crowds of a hundred thousand or more, and whose
extant vernacular sermons fill two substantial modern volumes.

Closely connected with preaching—indeed, with all the intellectual work of the Church—were biblical studies. Already richly
commented upon during the earlier Middle Ages, Holy Scripture
was given its great or ordinary gloss by a series of students from
Anselm of Laon (d. 1117) through Gilbert the Universal, a canon
of Auxerre and later bishop of London (d. 1134). Thereafter
followed questions, commentaries or postils on specific parts of
the Bible. A principal centre of this study was Paris, where the
work of two canons regular of St Victor, Hugh (d. 1141) and
Andrew (d. 1175), was further advanced by the circle of Peter
Cantor mentioned above. In the thirteenth century, leadership
passed to the mendicants, who brought to this subject not only
the Aristotelian methods then penetrating the schools but also
much traditional Jewish commentary, especially that of Rashi
of Troyes (Solomon ben Isaac, d. 1105). Including postillators as
radical and distinguished as the Franciscan Peter John Olivi
(Peter, the son of John Olivi, d. 1298), the mendicants produced
the greatest commentator of all, the Franciscan Nicholas of Lyra
(d. 1340). Naturally, these studies evoked much discontent with
the quality of the biblical text itself. Forever swinging wide, the
extremist Franciscan Roger Bacon (d. 1292) attributed the
imperfections of the contemporary Bible to the fact that the Paris
bookmakers were laymen, and married ones at that.

Biblical studies were also partly historical ones. This is illustrated by the *Historia scholastica* of the onetime chancellor of
Paris, Peter Comestor (d. about 1179), which presents a much
read abbreviated version of the Bible story with legendary
accretions. In fact, the tradition of universal history running from
the beginning of the world to the end still dominated historical
writing in this period. Although the concision and artistic unity
of an Otto of Freising (d. 1158) was not equalled in this period,

universal history was well represented. Other than the English historians who shall be mentioned shortly, the genre was continued by Godfrey of Viterbo (d. 1191) in his *Pantheon*, or *Memoria saeculorum*; the Dominican encyclopedist Vincent of Beauvais (d. about 1259) in his *Speculum historiale*, or *Historical Mirror*; and William of Nangis (d. 1300), a historian connected with the royal monastery of St Denis that, from about 1274, was beginning to produce the official vernacular annals of the French monarchy, the *Great Chronicles of France*. There were also specialized versions of this kind of history like Martin of Troppau's (d. 1278) history of the popes and the emperors, a version of which was finished by 1258.

When the historians spoke about their own times, they were not only more original—in fact, the universal history parts of most chronicles were hastily copied from earlier sources—but also more accurate. Perhaps the best school was that of England's monastic chroniclers. Among these were William of Newburgh (d. 1198), Roger of Hoveden (d. 1201), and the great monk of St Albans, Matthew Paris (d. 1259). Although usually having a clear bias—Matthew Paris, for example, was hostile both to Rome and the monarchy of Henry III and he loved fraudulent miracles—these historians attained a degree of excellence that owed much to the international quality of England's French-speaking aristocracy and also to the strong empirical tradition already exemplified in England's ecclesiastical academies at Oxford and Cambridge. They illustrate not only how open monastic life was to outside events, but also how information could be transmitted with relative accuracy from one part of Europe to another.

Each important European movement evoked its historians. An illustration is the history of the Slavs written by the German monk Helmhold (d. 1177), replete with stories of the German expansion. The crusades in the Holy Land and the Near East had their historians. Among the best was William, archbishop of Tyre (d. about 1186), gifted in Arabic and Greek, who wrote a history of the crusades and a lost, although much cited, history of the oriental monarchies. That *historia* did not always mean simple history, however, is shown by the preacher and archbishop of Acre, James of Vitry. His *Historia orientalis* is a combination guidebook and history of the Holy Land and adjacent regions and his *Historia occidentalis* discussed the orders, divisions, and sacraments of the Latin church. His was a *vade-mecum* for a parish priest or a pilgrim.

Almost any major event is covered reasonably well in histories either devoted to the event itself or to the region in which it took place. As we shall see, furthermore, local history and the recording of particular events were perhaps the favoured forms of historical writing among the laity at this time. As an example of coverage, the Albigensian crusade of 1209 and the introduction of the Inquisition into Languedoc in the 1230s were recorded not only in the general French chronicles, but also in the English ones mentioned above. Furthermore, readers are presented with almost every possible point of view. Peter of Vaux-de-Cernay, a Cistercian who accompanied the crusaders, wrote a detailed polemical history favouring the crusade, full of magnificent details, spurious miracles, and propaganda. A long and anonymous rhymed history, titled the *Song of the Crusade*, expressed with vigour the attitudes of the southerners who fought the crusaders. Although orthodox, a reasonably impartial account of the spread of heresy was given by the chaplain of the counts of Toulouse, William of Puylaurens. Puylaurens is one of those who did not write for the public taste, and he therefore never adverted to the miracles or fantastic natural happenings that were the stock in trade of medieval popular writing. A brief but remarkably accurate account of the entry of the Inquisition into Toulouse in the 1230s is to be found in the chronicle of the Dominican William Pelisson. Lastly, there is the unpublished but extensive history of the Dominican order itself written by the noted inquisitor and historian Bernard Guy (d. 1331) in which particular attention was paid to western Languedoc and to Toulouse, where the mother house of the order was founded.

This last work reminds us of the histories of the various new orders of the Church, a type that was inmixed with the lives of their founders and their notable saints and men of letters. Related to this genre was the chronicle of Salimbene of Parma (Salimbene de Adam, d. about 1290), surely one of the most astonishing documents of the Middle Ages. A running account of Italian history from 1167 to 1287, Salimbene's history not only treats the Franciscan order from immediately after the life of its founder, its internecine struggles and its battles with the Dominicans, but also includes the author's tract on ecclesiastical government, *On Prelatry*, of much significance for our understanding of the organization of the Church in the thirteenth century. To this Salimbene added the intensely personal history of his own entry into the order, a colourful account of the war between the Italian towns and the Hohenstaufen, and wonderful details on every conceivable kind of heretical, extremist and devotional sect.

As is evident, biography was close to history. The tradition represented by Abbot Suger of Saint-Denis's (d. 1152) life of Louis VI of France and Otto of Freising's and his continuator's *Deeds of Frederick I Barbarossa* was continued in a work like the life of Philip II Augustus of France by William the Breton (d. about 1225–26). To these may be added saints' lives, a genre that was becoming more and more historical in the period we are traversing. Large collections of saints' lives appeared. Of these, the most widely read was James of Voragine's (Varazze, d. 1298) collection of semi-biographies and tales called the *Golden Legend*. Related to this kind of literature were such exemplarist semi-historical, semifictional books as the *Dialogue of Miracles* by the Cistercian Caesarius of Heisterbach (d. 1240), designed to explore the hazards, joys, history, and teaching of the life religious.

To history, biography, and related genres must be added philosophy and theology, so necessary for the ideological and institutional developments mentioned above. During the middle and later years of the twelfth century substantial segments of Greek theology by such as John Chrysostom (d. 403) and John of Damascus (d. 749) were translated. This was accompanied by the continuing translation of scientific and philosophical works from the area of Arabic culture, including the recent figures of Averroes (d. 1198) and Maimonides (d. 1204). Along with this came the work of Aristotle and other Greek writers on philosophy and the sciences, much of which natural philosophy had been introduced to the Latins by the 1160s by means of direct translations from the Greek and by means of Arabic treatises on this subject and astronomy. The best known translators from the Arabic were Gerard of Cremona (d. 1187) and Michael Scot (d. before 1235), and the most widespread translations from the Greek of Aristotle and his ancient commentators were by James of Venice (fl. 1140s) and the Dominican William of Moerbeke, who died in 1286 as archbishop of Corinth. This body of new

17

knowledge obliged contemporaries to recast the Neoplatonic and Augustinian traditions that had ruled the early Middle Ages.

The form in which this knowledge was presented also changed. The first three-quarters of the twelfth century were marked by the production of essays, biblical commentaries, and summary textbooks, all except the latter characterized by elegant Latinity. The names of those who set the tone for the twelfth century have already been seen in Mr Brooke's volume: Abelard (d. 1142), Bernard of Clairvaux (d. 1153), and Gilbert of La Porée (d. 1154) being among the most notable. To these may be added the elegant Latinity and broad interests of John of Salisbury (d. 1180) of the following generation, whose *Policraticus* was an encyclopedia of the institutional and intellectual imperatives of the time. The earlier period had also seen the completion of the *Four Books of Sentences* by Peter Lombard (d. 1160), a *summa* that, although somewhat uninventive, was so appealing because of its systematization of theology and Church organization that it became Latin Europe's foremost textbook after being defended at the Lateran Council in 1215.

During the thirteenth century, although essays continued to be produced, as shown by Thomas Aquinas's (of Aquino, d. 1274) tracts on *Being and Essence* and on the *Government of Princes*, work in philosophy and theology became closely bound to the educational curriculum developed in the University of Paris and similar schools. Again, although highly technical, the schoolmen's Latin was less rhetorical and elegant than that of the twelfth century essayists. One reason for this was that a commentary on Peter Lombard's *Sentences* became the dissertation or *Habilitationsschrift* of the academic theologian, so that there was little place left for the older form of the essay. To commentaries upon the whole or parts of the *Sentences*, were added other literary forms derived from the academic exercises of examinations and disputations. During the later thirteenth century, therefore, commentaries and questions (*quaestiones quodlibetales* and *quaestiones disputatae*) became a principal branch of philosophical and theological literature, and the syllogistic form of the *quaestio* influenced the writing of such textbooks as Thomas Aquinas's *Theologica Summa*.

It is worth remarking that the work of the Church in the world was not serviced only by the schoolmen of the universities, nor was it dominated by them. The great mendicant preachers or collectors of saints' lives were rarely academics. And one may add to this the encyclopedist tradition, perhaps best exemplified by Vincent of Beauvais's *Great Mirror*, a work subdivided into three parts, the *Speculum naturale*, the *Speculum doctrinale*, and the *Speculum historiale* mentioned above. Although interminable— but much medieval writing was that: try reading the *Divine Comedy*—and often tiresome, such works of the thirteenth and early fourteenth centuries represent an effort to give churchmen and literate laymen alike a coherent body of knowledge on a somewhat popular level.

Apart from the literature produced by the lay professions, verse initially predominated in lay letters or in the letters directed to a lay audience, and, as we shall see, the French language was everywhere dominant. Naturally, a principal topic was human love. Influenced by the 'religious' thought of men like Abelard, Bernard of Clairvaux, and the Victorine mystics, themes of spiritual ascent or progress were explored in poems such as *Perceval*. Other verse expressed the feeling or passion of being in love; troubadour poetry, for example, delineating for all time the lover's longing or thirst. The actions educed by love's passion and the tests to be overcome by lovers were investigated in the Arthurian literature, especially through the figure of Lancelot. This subject will be further examined in the chapters of Parts Two and Three below, but the reader is reminded that there was an enormous literature on it, much of it playful, humorous and earthy.

Love was only one of the activities of the social elite that set the tone for medieval society. Another was career and advancement. The two subjects could be interwoven. In his *Erec and Enide* Christian of Troyes (fl. 1150–80)—incidentally, a poet greatly admired by Dante—taught that love only flourishes in those who strive to advance in the world. To this type of didactic romance must be added the great songs in praise of war. Some of these, like the twelfth-century *Ralph of Cambrai*, preached the virtue of moderation (*mésure*) and the punishment meted out to those ruled by rage. Others, like the earlier and ever popular *Song of Roland*, provided a hero whose almost suicidal and Christlike sacrifice provided the very model of the winning of eternal fame by arms. There were also humorous take-offs on the martial virtues, complete with anti-heroes who did everything badly without a shred of virtue.

Especially in the areas of French culture where the *mores* of the aristocracy flourished best, gentlefolk were interested in having recorded the histories of their families or those of their famous ancestors. The history of the counts of Anjou and lords of Amboise by the canon Breton of Amboise (fl. 1155–73) is an example of this, and so is that of the lords of Ardres and counts of Guines by the clerk Lambert of Ardres (1194–1203). A chaplain composed a fine vernacular verse biography of William, marshal of England and earl of Pembroke (d. 1219). By the thirteenth century, laymen were in this business themselves, writing both biographies and autobiographies in the vernacular. Among the most celebrated of these were the memoirs of Philip of Novara (d. 1261–64), seignior, jurist, and historian of Cyprus and of France d'Outremer, and the biography of the sainted Louis IX, king of France, finished in 1309 by John, lord of Joinville, surely one of the great gentlemen of all time. As Novara shows, vernacular history had also begun to make its appearance. An outstanding work was the history of the Fourth Crusade and of the Latin empire of Constantinople by Geoffrey of Villehardouin, marshal of the Champagne and of Romania (d. about 1213). In Italy, where lay literacy in Latin was most extensive, town history was an early speciality of laymen. A late example but one notable for the richness of its ideological perceptions was the history of the March of Treviso written by the son of a notary, the grammarian Rolandino of Padua (d. 1276). To this may be added a literature in praise of individual cities. The one to be cited in these pages is the curiously statistical praise of Milan by Bonvesino of Riva in the 1280s.

To these types of literature may be added a spate of increasingly specialized tracts on the ages of man, manners, chivalry, and social and political theory, much of it written by laymen such as Philip of Novara mentioned above, Brunetto Latini (d. 1294–95), and that wonderful polymath Raymond Lull (d. about 1315). The name of this Catalan also reminds us that, by 1300, laymen were even writing treatises on theology and philosophy. Another Catalan theologian was Arnold of Villanova (d. 1313), a medical doctor, utopian, and ardent defender of the radical Franciscans. Add to this the fact that one of the most widely circulated pieces of literature in western Europe was the *Romance of the Rose*, the larger part of which was written by John Clopinel of Meung-sur-Loire somewhere between 1270 and 1285. Not only a lively description of love, of the unavoidable combat between woman and man, of manners and behaviour, John's work also constituted a veritable vernacular encyclopedia of philosophy and theology, moral and even systematic, principally drawn from the writings of the theologian Alan of Lille, the great Cistercian intellectual who died in 1202. It ought also to be mentioned that Dante Alighieri began work on his *Divine Comedy* in about 1307. During the ten or more years he spent on this immense encyclopedia, he took time off to draft a celebrated politico-ecclesiological tract called *On Monarchy* (*c.* 1313), a work that insisted upon the moral, though not spiritual, equality of the state and the Church.

PART ONE

Latin Europe

II

Christendom

Social frontiers: the two peoples

Impelled by motives described in Mr Brooke's earlier volume and occasionally reviewed in this one, the inhabitants of western Europe elevated the Church to lead Latin society during the Gregorian age, a period of social crisis and internal warfare that extended from about the mid-eleventh century until the end of the first quarter or so of the twelfth. During this gradual revolution, a new structure of social and governmental power that had been emerging since the far away days of late antiquity came into being, and remained to characterize Latin Europe's apogee in the twelfth and thirteenth centuries. This power structure differed from that obtaining in the earlier Middle Ages and from the one that

BIBLIOGRAPHY. The books that set the tone for the socio-political history in this volume and for the relationship between the clergy and the other social orders are the following: Alois Dempf, *Sacrum Imperium: Geschichts- und Staatsphilosophie des Mittelalters und der politischen Renaissance* (Munich, 1929), E. H. Kantorowicz, *The King's Two Bodies: a study in medieval political theology* (Princeton, 1957), Georges de Lagarde, *La naissance de l'esprit laïque au déclin du moyen âge*, 5 vols. (2nd edn., Louvain, 1962), Gustav Schnürer, *Kirche und Kultur im Mittelalter*, 3 vols. (Paderborn, 1924–30, now available in both French and English translation), and the study by Jean Rivière cited in the bibliography for chapter XV. Another useful work for the theme treated in this chapter is Justus Hashagen, *Staat und Kirche vor der Reformation: Eine Untersuchung der vorreformatorischen Bedeutung der Laieneinflüsses in der Kirche* (Essen, 1931). Other works that rarely treat subjects directly handled in this volume but that are important for its *mise en scène* are Ernst Bernheim, *Mittelalterliche Zeitanschauungen und ihrem Einfluss auf Politik und Geschichtsschreibung* (Tübingen, 1918, rprt.), Konrad Burdach, *Reformation, Renaissance, Humanismus* (2nd edn., Berlin, 1926), Friedrich Heer, *Aufgang Europas: Eine Studie zu den Zusammenhangen zwischen politischer Religiosität, Frömmigkeitstil und dem Werden Europas im 12. Jahrhundert* (Vienna, 1949), Eugen Rosenstock-Huessy, *The Driving Power of Western Civilization: the Christian revolution of the Middle Ages* (Boston, 1950, an excerpt from his *Out of Revolution: the Autobiography of western man* of 1938), and Gerd Tellenbach, *Church, State and Christian Society at the time of the Investiture Contest* (Oxford, 1940, a translation of his *Libertas* of 1936).

25

appeared in the later Middle Ages or early modern times. In the earlier period, Europeans were primarily governed—except on the local and familial levels best investigated by historical anthropologists—by empires and quasi-national states, aided by often rebellious and restive but always subordinate churches. In the later Middle Ages, large units of political and social power again dominated as the people began to create the nation-state or other substantial units of government, such as the Italian principates and the major German principalities. Here again, although in a quite different form, these secular powers were to rule a subordinate clergy, eventually, indeed, largely to replace them by the secular levites or philosophers of recent times.

In the twelfth and thirteenth centuries the structure of power was different. Although great monarchies lingered from the past and although, as we shall see, some of the governments that were to become the nation-states of modern times were already beginning to appear, the greater measure of real power had been entrusted to the ecumenical or general government exercised by the Church of Rome and to the local governments of town and countryside throughout the west. These, whether seigniorial or republican in constitutional form, were governed by an aristocracy of both rural and urban origins, and, under this aegis, were as free as they were ever to be from the authority of central government. From the days of the Gregorians until the turmoil of the fourteenth and fifteenth centuries, what led Europe was an inadvertent, rarely conscious, but very real alliance between Europe's aristocracies and the see of Peter.

I am surprised to recognize my debt to a largely German cast of scholars because I sometimes find myself in agreement with W. F. P. Napier, that admirer of French rationalism, who, when annoyed by a German officer, angrily asserted in his *Peninsular War* that the Germans, although 'regular and plodding even to a proverb, . . . possess the most extravagant imaginations of any people on the face of the earth'. This may be so, but, in the study of medieval history, there is no doubt that the German contribution to the relationship of ideas to institutions has been greater than that of any other people.

On the institutional and intellectual history of the crusades, see Paul Alphandéry and A. Dupront, *La chrétienté et l'idée de croisade*, 2 vols. (Paris, 1954–59), Carl Erdmann, *Die Entstehung des Kreuzzugsgedankens* (Stuttgart, 1955), and Michel Villey, *La croisade : essai sur la formation d'une théorie juridique* (Paris, 1942). On the crusades themselves see Steven Runciman, *A History of the Crusades*, 3 vols. (Cambridge, 1951–54), K. M. Setton ed., *A History of the Crusades*, 2 vols. (2nd edn., Madison, 1969), and René Grousset, *L'empire du Levant : histoire de la question d'orient* (Paris, 1946).

In this circumstance the Church everywhere created agencies or mechanisms to fortify the sense of cultural identity of Latin Europe and to lead the citizens of its *respublica christiana*. Although war within Europe still continued, Christendom's great war became the crusade, a series of expansionist wars waged at the expense of neighbouring cultures and religions. The needs of this war and the hope of realizing at home the ideal of a truly Christian republic moved the Church to police the peace and to regulate society. Europe's military élite was restrained at home by the idea and law of the just war and by such mechanisms as the peace or truce of God. The doctrine of the just price and the rigoristic condemnation of usury were employed to police the marketplace, and the accent upon brotherhood among the citizens of the republic served as the foundation for the building of a social corporatism that weakened the unregulated and grasping hands of the rich, both old and new. In every field of human activity, the expansion of the penitential system and of the jurisdiction of canon law testified to the capacity of the clergy to regulate and harmonize the life of man on earth. The Church may be said to have replaced or supplemented the state in many functions.

Although not always harmoniously, the hierarchy and the secular clergy were aided in this work by the monastic or regular clergy. Indeed, the monks were often ahead of the rest of the Church. The Cistercians and other orders were famed for clearing Europe's forests and marshes. The west's best soldiers served in the ranks of the military orders. New orders and foundations appeared everywhere to house the aged, the sick, the destitute and the fallen. The thirteenth century saw the fulfilment of earlier efforts in education: the building of the university system. The monks and parish clergy combined to enhance the role of sacerdotal authority by glorifying the miracle of the mass and by expanding the penitential system. In regard to penitence, the theoretical culmination was reached at the time of the Franciscan Alexander of Hales (d. 1245) and the Dominican Thomas Aquinas who expounded the doctrine of the treasury of the saints, that reservoir of superabundant grace upon which the priest could draw for the indulgences granted fallible man. In regard to the mass, the cup having been withdrawn from the laity during the later eleventh and early twelfth centuries, the theory of the priestly miracle of transubstantiation was finally codified at the

Lateran Council in 1215, and the feast of the *corpus Christi* was generalized by papal edict in 1264. So important did the function of the priesthood (*sacerdotium*) seem that the great canon lawyer Hostiensis did not blush to state that the priestly dignity was 7,644½ times greater than the royal (*imperium*), paralleling the difference in the brightness of the sun and moon as stated in Ptolemy's *Almagest*. The role of the priest as the confector of the miracle of the mass and as the judge in the court of conscience fortified Latin man's confident sense that there existed a direct link between God's eternal ordinance and human institutions, between heaven and earth.

Circumstances justified this sanguine attitude on the part of western man and his clergy. At a time of growing population, newly cleared fields, new towns, expanding personal freedom, and the conquest of foreign lands, nature herself seemed beneficent, and man's institutions seemed to enable him to achieve a happy end. But this demanded a difficult adjustment on the part of churchmen themselves; indeed, it caused a basic change in the very ethos of the Christian Church. Many, it is true, were still attracted by what had once given men freedom in the days of pagan and Christian Rome and at the time of the state-dominated churches of the earlier middle ages: the accent on the other world —the world of heaven against earth, of spiritual against material values, of things felt but indemonstrable as against things demonstrable. But now, corrupted perhaps by their successful leadership of the world, ecclesiastical thinkers and leaders increasingly turned to examine and manipulate the world in which they lived. The west's new receptiveness to Aristotelian and Arabic scientism or naturalism was an expression of this. Another was a heightened interest in both the ideal and practical forms of ecclesiastical and secular government. Moved by such perceptions, as we shall see, the utopian wing of the clergy and their lay followers tried to remake the world on the model of the supernal Jerusalem, to make a heaven on earth. This Europe-wide movement around 1200 attracted such varied groups as the professors at Paris headed by Robert of Curzon (d. 1218) and others taught by Peter Cantor and the humble craftsfolk brigaded in the mass movement of the Italian Humiliati.

Such being the inspiration of churchmen, the Austin Friar Giles of Rome asserted about 1285 that government should have three objectives. One was to defend the people and keep them in peace. Another was to give the people the material means of living well. The ultimate objective was to provide education:

A king ought therefore see to it that the study of letters flourishes in his kingdom, and that there be many learned men and scholars there. For where wisdom and the fount of letters flourish, surely the whole people will thence draw a measure of learning. . . . Indeed, if the ruler of a realm does not promote education and does not wish his subjects to be learned, he is not a king but rather a tyrant.[1]

The objective here was the advancement of the faith: material well-being, peace, and education were necessary to help man attain salvation. This educational teleology was well expressed in the *Brief Discourse*, a manual designed to instruct preachers and teachers written by Peter Cantor. There the chanter likened teaching to the building of a house. Its foundation is reading; disputation and discussion compose its walls; 'preaching which the two former serve, is as a roof protecting the faithful from the heats and tempests of the vices'.[2] Peter's scholars were to be preachers remaking the world in the image of a Christian society.

So great an emphasis upon working in the world necessarily led to a gradual shift not only in the values of churchmen but also in the institutions of the Church. In the past, when the state had dominated the Church, the contemplative and cloistered life of the monks had seemed more consequential than the active life. Because it contained a basic reality, this conviction never died. An abbot like Rupert of Deutz (d. 1135) claimed that the apostles were all monks, and that the Saviour did not make them preach, baptize or perform miracles but instead exalt themselves by exemplifying virtue and by humbling themselves before others. And this is also what the later Francis of Assisi (d. 1226) believed he stood for. On the other hand, Francis himself and his own Franciscans speedily went to work to animate the Church's mission by preaching and stimulating penance at the world's crossroads.

---

[1] *De regimine principum* 3, 2, 8 in Rome 1607, 417. The translation of *industres* as 'scholars' used above is modelled upon the French translation of Giles's treatise (*Li livres du gouvernement des rois*, ed. S. P. Molenaer [New York, 1899], 314), where the text reads 'mult de sages hommes et de sages clers'.

[2] *Verbum abbreviatum* 1 in *PL* CCV, 25.

A clerical generation convinced of the validity of working in the world was also capable of applying to the inner spiritual life of a man no matter what his activity the peculiarly intense sense of vocation that had marked only the withdrawn religious in the past. It is the sense of this inner asceticism, this inner progress in self-discipline and self-realization, that is explored in the tract of the Franciscan scholar and general Bonaventure (John of Fidanza, d. 1274) variously called *The Three-fold Way* or the *Itinerary of the Mind*. In short, although men were still attracted by spiritual withdrawal, physical withdrawal into the cloister faded as an ideal before the appeal of an active engagement in the world's life. It was therefore but a short step to assert that the various clerical professions fighting evil in the world or improving it were actually superior to the monks confined to the quiet of their cloisters. A utopian activist such as Robert of Curzon found it perfectly natural to claim that a teacher explaining holy Scripture in the schools deserved a higher reward than any Cistercian. Hostiensis referred in his *Summa aurea* to 'just judges leading the active life without duplicity, a life which, if well conducted, would be more fruitful than the contemplative'.[3] And, before 1235, canonists were flattered to hear Buoncompagno of Signa borrow from Roman law to liken doctors of canon law to soldiers in arms. In fact, this example permits one to see the paradox of clerical leadership: the more the priests led, the more they had to respect the world's professions. Reluctant though they were to admit it, there were times when soldiers were more necessary to the Church than monks. Had not Gregory VII bitterly complained in 1079 to Abbot Hugh of Cluny, who had received a Burgundian duke into his cloister when the papacy needed every ally against the Empire, 'You have taken away or have received the duke into the quiet of Cluny, and thereby have caused one hundred thousand Christians to lack a protector'?[4]

Were it merely necessary to provide soldiers, there is no reason why the clergy could not have expanded to provide that function themselves. To some extent they did, indeed, as in the military orders. The reason that the clergy did not do so was something else. To elevate priestly power to lead or direct the life of men in the world was only one side of the clerical ambition. The other

[3] Cited in Kantorowicz, *The King's Two Bodies*, 122n, along with much else.
[4] *Registrum* 6, 17 in *MGH*, *Epp. sel.* II, 351.

was defensive: the defence of ecclesiastical liberty by freeing the clergy from secular authority. It will be remembered that, from of old, there were two peoples, two nations, often abrasively rubbing shoulders in the Christian republic. Writing in the early fourteenth century, Alberic of Rosate summed up the doctrine of earlier jurists: 'For there are two peoples, one of the clerks and the other of laymen . . . and they are two types of diverse nature, one superior and the other inferior. . . . And it may be said that there are two governors in Milan, the archbishop who rules the clerks and the temporal lord who rules the laity.'[5] Superior though the clergy may have been after the Gregorian age, they could not but remember that earlier on they had been inferior to lay power in a real or institutional sense. To be free from lay oppression, therefore, churchmen wished to be judged only by themselves and not by laymen, whose princes, they thought, had often repressed them and corrupted their spiritual standards. Since lay government was not likely to favour employing officers who claimed the right to be examined only in ecclesiastical courts, their desire for freedom required them to withdraw from the service of princes and governments. More generally, their liberation from lay jurisdiction required them to give up secular offices of all kinds and the exercise of professions involving them in the lay world. Nevertheless someone had to fill these offices and professions. However paradoxical it may seem, then, the Gregorian enthusiasts' ambition to free the clergy from lay power resulted not only in churchmen temporarily leading western Europe, but also in the creation of lay literacy and a lay sense of profession that, in the long run, enabled laymen to take the leadership of Europe from the clergy itself.

But the transformation did not happen overnight. As shall be seen, the division between lay and clerical was long obscured by the lack of trained laymen and by the persistence of the old patterns of the state-dominated churches of the early Middle Ages. Besides, lay literacy in Latin had never entirely vanished in western Europe. That princes should be literate had always been urged, and there were lay notaries and lawyers in a few parts of Italy before the Gregorian age. But these are merely the exceptions that prove the rule. As the Premonstratension Philip of

---

[5] *De statutis* 2, 2, 17 in *TUJ* II, 29a.

Harvengt (d. 1182) said, the word 'clerk' was applied to any literate person, and, on the whole, 'clerk' meant 'churchman' in this period. It may also be argued that the rise of lay literacy and of the lay professional sense is nothing other than a reflection of the fact that an increasingly mature society requires the services of more literate men. But what is important is that the clerical order did not expand to provide these services itself in the twelfth and thirteenth centuries. Instead, the layman's desire for officers who could be held to account in lay courts and the clerical ambition to be free of secular authority combined to provoke a 'purge' of the old clerical cadres by a 'reforming' laity and clergy. This purge helped create the beginnings of the secular literate or clerical professions during the Gregorian troubles. Not a few early jurists and scribes were onetime clerks who had been married or charged with simony.

The new legislation of the Church on the clerical involvement in the professions pointed in two directions. Starting in the early twelfth century and culminating in the canons of the Lateran Councils of 1179 and 1215, churchmen were forbidden to serve as officers, lawyers and notaries for secular officers and persons. Furthermore, the exercise of certain professions was altogether closed to them, such as that of surgeon because it involved the shedding of blood. The second effort of Church law was to limit the education of the clergy in secular pursuits. By 1163 monks were prohibited from studying civil law and medicine, and in 1219 this prohibition was extended to clergy with the grade of priest and to archdeacons, parish rectors, and other such full-time officers. The lower clerical grades were left free to learn all of the secular professions except surgery, but clerks were not usually permitted to exercise them except within the Church or, occasionally, for the protection of the poor.

As this legislation implies, the first secular professions were those of medicine, law, and scribal services. To these may be added the teachers of the liberal arts, such as grammarians, and of the practical arts, such as mathematics. Related to the greater professions was a whole range of artisan quasiprofessions such as the druggists and surgeon-barbers associated with medicine, and the stationers and book copiers who sprang up around the universities. Nor were the frontiers ever very clear. Master builders, for example, ranged from simple masons and carpenters to the masters of the works (*magistri operum*) employed by cathedrals and towns. As will be seen in later pages such artists or architects were soon considered to be members of the higher or liberal arts. Another matter treated in more detail later is also worth recording here. Because of the great numbers who were in lower clerical orders in this period, and because of the frequency with which middle-aged people moved into the clergy, the frontier between ecclesiastical and lay was not as sharp as these paragraphs may imply. The history of the master mason Gerhard of Rile, master of the works (*rector* or *provisor fabrice*) of the new cathedral at Cologne begun in 1248, is a case in point. In 1257 Gerhard became a canon and his wife entered a Cistercian nunnery. By 1268 he had become a priest in the cathedral's service. Other than his architectural gift, the only remarkable thing about Gerhard was that his four grown children followed him into the clerical order.

Although, in the long run, the medical doctors were probably more important for the development of an earth- or human-centred philosophy, the jurists—being members of a larger profession and one directly involved with cases involving morality—were those who had most to do with the growth of lay self-consciousness in the professions of this period. Roman law had always maintained that the empire and its law were sacred things, and it was derived from this that those who practised law and sought to prevent evil in the world were themselves sacred. In a phrase similar to one used in an assize of about 1141 in the Norman kingdom of Apulia and Sicily, a gloss on the early twelfth-century code called *Peter's Excerpts* expressed this idea: 'For what is sacred is partly human, like the laws, and partly divine, like the church (*res ecclesie*). Some priests are therefore divine priests, like presbyters, and others are human, like magistrates, who are called priests because they administer sacred things (*dant sacra*), that is, the laws.'[6] This self-congratulatory theme was repeated by all the jurists. Nor need it cause surprise that the eventual development of this argument elevated the civilian jurist to equality with the priesthood of the church and above the contemplative religious. Alberic of Rosate (d. 1354) summed up earlier teaching by asserting 'that judges who judge justly are not only to be called

---

[6] For this and the Roman texts from which it derives, see Kantorowicz, *op. cit.*, 121n.

priests, but even angels of God, and deserve more than monks (*religiosi*)'.[7] And, in saying this, Alberic was merely echoing the famous canonist Hostiensis. Indeed, circumstances obliged the Church to admit the equality of lay jurists. As early as 1252, the layman Giles Fuscararius (d. 1289) taught canon law at Bologna, and not a few of the judges sitting at the Roman court and in those of the bishops were laymen.

The lay spirit speedily vaulted beyond the narrow professionalism of the jurists. If lawyers could be called priests, so also could soldiers, a notion repeated in Raymond Lull's (d. 1315) *Order of Chivalry*, the most popular manual of knighthood and nobility in the later Middle Ages. Moreover, however exalted the role of the clergy—and we know that it was very high indeed—the obvious truth of the proposition made even churchmen tell the laity that, in God's eyes, all men were equal. In his book on *The Building of God*, Gerhoh of Reichersberg (d. 1169) reminds us that, whether rich or poor, noble or servile, merchant or farmer, every man who has renounced the devil, 'even if he never becomes a clerk or a monk, can be shown to have renounced the world. . . . For every man has his place (*ordo*), and every profession without exception has a rule in the Catholic faith and apostolic doctrine suitable to its quality, under which, by fighting well, a man can attain the crown.'[8] Implicit in this is the idea that the layman belongs to an order, just as does a monk, an idea made explicit by James of Vitry in his survey of the western Church:

> We do not judge only those who renounce the world and enter an order to be monks (*regulares*), but instead can call *regulares* all faithful Christians who serve the Lord under evangelical rules and live ordained under the one highest abbot [i.e. God] . . . Similarly, there is an order of the married, of the widowed, and of virgins. And soldiers, merchants, farmers, and artisans and all the other multiform types of men have rules that are peculiar to them and mutually different . . .[9]

Two things gave this doctrine power. To the implicit priesthood of those who worked in the world to eradicate evil was added what the clergy themselves had developed, the monastic vocation of all truly faithful Christians. The spread of the monastic ethos

[7] See *ibid.*, 122n.
[8] *Liber de aedificio dei* 43 in *PL* cxciv, 1302d.
[9] *Historia occidentalis* 34 in Douais 1596, 357.

to the lay world, at first in the Gregorian age and then again in the mendicant movements of the thirteenth century, will be treated in later chapters. Here it may be noted that this combination of the *sacerdotium* of the *vita activa* with the monastic *vita contemplativa* of the inner spiritual life had begun to give laymen an increasing sense of their ideological—that is, religious—equality with the clergy. But, truth to tell, this equality would have meant little or nothing without the growth of lay literacy.

That literacy was of two kinds, Latin and vernacular. Anent Latin, although there were always exceptions, the principal vehicles of lay literacy were the professions of medicine, law, and that of the public scribes or notariate. Just as the academic jurists and other professors stole their black robes of honour from the clergy, so had they taken Latin to be their language of learning. And there was more to it than that. As taught by the jurists, notaries, and grammarians, a somewhat simplified Latin developed as a juristic and literary vehicle and found a place between the high Latinity of the past that still continued in use and the rising vernacular culture beneath. What this meant in practical terms is easily seen. Around Toulouse in Languedoc, for example, not only did the Latin in the documents improve in the decades around 1200, but also the vernacular was driven out of the documents by Latin as the notariate penetrated villages and small towns in the decades after 1200. In the same region, furthermore, ordinary businessmen habitually collected their own files of Latin documents from the notaries who drew them. The businessmen were surely rarely able to compose the documents, and many could not understand them when they were read; but it is very probable that they could read them.

Although somewhat defensive, the proponents of this Latin were aware of its character and role. Introducing his history of the March of Treviso, the grammarian Rolandino of Padua (d. 1276) explained why he chose Latin instead of the vernacular:

> I write prose because I know that I can say what I want more clearly in it than in verse, and because nowadays Latin prose is more understandable among readers than poetry. ... And perhaps it is more useful and pleasing to some, especially to the literate, to discover written in Latin the sufferings and labors of modern men than to hear in the vulgar of the deeds of the noble ancients.[10]

CHRISTENDOM

The relationship of this Latin to the elegant Latinity of classicism or the earlier Middle Ages may be seen in Buoncompagno of Signa. Buoncompagno felt that his own simple latinity was something altogether new. He detested the authority of the ancients, especially what he thought was Cicero's needlessly obscure style: 'Besides, in the rhetorical works that he wrote, the construction is inept and the position of words is intricate, whereby he most clearly contradicted his own instructions, because he there required that the narrative be brief, lucid and clear.'[11] Although his prophecy was roundly in error, Buoncompagno argued that Ciceronian Latin would never recover its ground because the students no longer studied it. Who would, he thought, study with the learned *dictatores* or professors of rhetoric with their artificial exercises in Latin composition? Who in his right mind would address a fellow named Papa as 'Mr *Servus servorum dei*?' Only a *dictator!*

Although statistics are lacking for this period, it is not hard to estimate the currency of this vulgar Latin—if such a phrase may be used. The overwhelming bulk of Latin literature in the late twelfth and thirteenth centuries was written in it. This was not only because it was used by jurists and notaries but also because it became the language of the schools for the clergy itself. As may be judged from some of the examinations recorded in Odo Rigaud's register of visitations in his archdiocese of Rouen from 1248 to 1269, the lesser clergy—especially in the countryside—were only gradually attaining literacy in Latin, and vulgar Latin was easier to learn than the high modes of classical discourse or those of a Peter Damian, a Bernard of Clairvaux, or a John of Salisbury. Partly because of the educational background of the students, also, and partly because of its extraordinary flexibility, vulgar Latin was eminently suitable for technical discourse in philosophy and theology among the schoolmen in the high schools or universities of the west, and it therefore caught on in spite of the lamentation of such as John of Salisbury about the decline of Latin style.

Another way of judging the currency of vulgar Latin is to look at individual communities. An assessment of taxes in the upper

[10] *Cronica in factis et circa facta marchie Trivixiane (AA 1200–62)* in *RIS* (ed. 1905) VIII, i, 7–8. By the ancients, Rolandino was probably referring to Roland and the other French heroes.
[11] *Rhetorica novissima*, prologue in *BIMA* II, 252.

36

and lower towns of Carcassonne for the Flemish war in 1304 affords a glimpse of the professional services typical of town life. Estimated on the basis of four persons per taxable hearth, the population of this modest city was around 9,500 souls. Including nine *plebani*, or parish rectors, some 260 clerks lived there. This figure included monks, friars, the canons and priests of the cathedral chapter, and those in lesser clericality, such as hospital workers and inmates, schoolteachers and domestics. The legal professions were represented by forty-three public notaries and fifteen advocates or lawyers. Twelve Lombards and thirty Jews offered their economic services. Lastly, forty-three gentlefolk and forty police or soldiers inhabited or were stationed in this military and administrative capital.

Of these groups, we may assume that, because their business required correspondence with their homeland and other Lombards, the Lombard males were somewhat literate in vulgar Latin. Most of the Jews were literate in the vernacular and many in Hebrew, but few, if any, in Latin. That the notaries and lawyers were literate in Latin goes without saying, but there were differing degrees of this competence. Having *patrocinium*, or the right to represent clients in the courts, the lawyers of this southern region were all university-trained by this period. Notaries, on the other hand, were probably taught by being apprenticed locally to others of their profession. This would not have been the case in a great centre like Bologna, where the notaries usually went through the faculty of arts at the *studium* or university.

Nine medical doctors were also counted in Carcassonne. There, because of the town's proximity to the medical faculty at Montpellier, it is to be presumed that most of the medical doctors were *phisici*, that is, those who had studied natural science at the university. These undoubtedly had Latin. Farther to the north, it is likely that most doctors would be simple *medici*, men trained by practitioners, just a cut above simple surgeons. The matter was almost one of geographical distribution at this time. Although, as Bonvesino of Riva tells us for Milan in the 1280s, *phisici* were common enough in Italy's urbanized areas, there were few in the north, even in the Low Countries, where they were largely to be found among the clergy who did not practise medicine in the lay world. Along with the legal and medical elites at Carcassonne went the clergy, especially those among the secular and regular clergy who had taken higher orders, an unknown percentage of whom had seen the inside of a university. And, as has been argued above, not a few town gentlemen and burghers also had some competence in Latin letters.

Literacy in the vernacular was equally important. Most gentle-folk, if literate at all, were literate only in the vernacular. This also goes for certain groups in the Church, such as the female religious and even secular canons, those whose birth was so elevated that they were damned if they would learn Latin. This does not mean that such people were uncultivated. The poetry of the age—for vernacular literature was at first primarily poetic—treated almost every conceivable theme of interest to an alert mind. Further-more, gentlemen of means usually had readers or scribes in their households to whom they dictated their letters and who read to the family at dinner or other times. A rather exaggerated example of this is Baldwin, who in 1169 became count of Guines and lord of Ardres, towns not far from Boulogne in northern France. According to the family chronicler, a priest of Ardres named Lambert, Baldwin collected romances and heroic *chansons* and had translated and read to him parts of sacred Scripture, sermons, a commentary on the mystical sense of the Song of Songs, Alfred's life of Saint Anthony, 'a great part of the physical art', Solinus's *De naturis rerum*, and selections from Augustine, Denis the Areopagite, and Thales of Miletus (?!). Dinner must have been a pretty heavy affair at this gentleman's house. The count's secretary was a layman who translated and collected books for his patron's edification.

The range of vernacular letters increased during the thirteenth century. A basic text for soldiers such as Vegetius's *Epitome on War* was widely circulated in its original Latin, but parts were paraphrased and incorporated in the Spanish 'mirror' of govern-ment and legal code called the *Siete Partidas* of Alphonso X in 1260. The whole was finally translated into French by the poet John Clopinel of Meung (d. 1305). Indeed, quite as much as his immensely popular continuation of the *Romance of the Rose*, John's translations testify to the audience for vernacular works. These included Boethius's *Consolation of Philosophy*, the life and letters of Abelard and Héloise, Ailred of Rievaulx's *Spiritual Friendship*, written about 1160, and Gerald of Wales's *Topography of Ireland* of about 1188. This work of translation into French was to continue unbroken and increasing until after the mid-fourteenth century. To John's contribution of the *Romance of the Rose* one may add the work of Dante Alighieri (d. 1321), the wide circulation of whose vernacular works reminds us of Italy's many literate burghers and gentlemen.

As significant as the evidence of lay literacy in the vernacular was the spirit of the times. 'An illiterate king is a crowned ass', went the tag. This doctrine was gradually extended to all gentlefolk during the centuries studied in this volume. There was schoolteacher's special pleading in this: could one be a soldier and also an amateur of letters? Writing the history of the counts of Anjou, the canon Breton of Amboise (fl. 1155–73) defended Fulk the Good, who had celebrated mass in clerical garb on the feast of St Martin of Tours, by saying that, 'although this very intelligent man had been expertly instructed in the rules of letters and the grammatical art as well as in Aristotelian and Ciceronian reasoning, he was considered the best among the greater, better and more vigorous knights'.[12] The later Gerald of Wales (d. 1220) went so far as to assert that the more a man knew of the liberal arts the better he was as a soldier, a point he proved by adducing Greece under the Macedonians, Rome under the Caesars, and the Franks under the Carolingians! By the time John of Meung wrote his part of the *Romance of the Rose* the idea that the perfect gentleman was to be as lettered as he was expert in arms had become a commonplace.

Ideals aside, it is obvious that literacy was not widely spread among the laity by 1300. Dated no later than 1324, a manual of the faith called the *Mirror of Human Salvation* tells us that 'literate people can have knowledge of God from the Scriptures, but ignorant ones ought to be instructed by books for laymen, that is, by pictures'.[13] Besides, not a few of those who wrote for the lay market were clergy. A number of troubadours, for example, were clerical or ended their lives in clerical garb. In 1184–86 Andrew, a chaplain, wrote a celebrated tract on love, an amusing sociophilosophical discussion of this theme or occupation that enjoyed

[12] Louis Halphen and René Poupardin, eds., *Chroniques des comtes d'Anjou et des seigneurs d'Amboise*, 140.
[13] *Speculum humanae salvationis*, prologue, ed. J. Lutz and P. Perdrizet (Leipzig, 1907), 2. The presumed author is the Dominican and then Carthusian Liudolph of Saxony.

wide circulation. The author of the most significant part of the *Romance of the Rose*, John of Meung, is believed to have been a Parisian clerk.

Reservations aside, lay literacy in the vernacular penetrated far below the aristocracy and even the patrician bourgeois of the towns. Our modern imagination has done a disservice to medieval popular culture by the employment of the term 'courtly love'. It is true that there is something aristocratic about medieval love poetry and tales, but that derives from simple things. Who would think of a public notary as the ideal lover? The soldier was naturally the lover: by risking his life on the field of honour, he proved his competence to take the risk of love with all its needed loyalty, frequent obloquy, and difficult tests. And the beloved was also aristocratic. Not only did she risk childbirth—no easy thing in those times—but also the lover did not have to bother helping her servants raise her children. But that does not mean that there was any necessary class affiliation for the different genres of love literature, ranging from the courtly fancies of Arthurian romance to the so-called 'bourgeois' earthiness of the *fabliaux*. The lives of the troubadours compiled in the fourteenth century show us that not a few of the most spiritual and courtly poets were burghers and merchants. And gentlemen both enjoyed earthy verse and wrote it. The famed 'first' troubadour, William IX, duke of Aquitaine (d. 1127), composed some of the raunchiest stuff on record, and the English chronicler William of Malmesbury (d. about 1143) reports with mock horror that the duke had a mistress 'whom he so loved that he had the girl's picture painted on his shield, saying often that he wished to bear her in battle as she bore him in bed'.[14]

Evidence of the popularity of this literature and its themes is everywhere to be seen. A Bolognese statute of 1288 ordered that singers of French songs (*cantatores Francigenorum*) may not perform in public places when preaching was underway. In an early fourteenth-century moral guidebook for Toulousan businessmen a Dominican author wagged his finger at his audience: 'I advise each one of you to read or at least to listen to [the *Rule of Merchants*] in place of those useless fables and romances that are

[14] Cited in Reto R. Bezzola, *Les origines et la formation de la littérature courtoise en occident* (1960) II, ii, 272.

40

customarily read in workshops and stores.'[15] As significant as the circulation of this literature was the penetration of the vernacular into legal documentation. Generalized everywhere by about 1300, the use of the vernacular for business documents testifies to the literacy of the business classes and even of certain groups of artisans or workers. In Italy, Brunetto Latini (d. 1294) even wrote a vernacular rhetoric in Ciceronian style for the use of town notaries and chancellors.

The profound effects of the invasion of religion by the vernacular in the thirteenth century will be discussed in chapter XIV. What is significant in the present context is that the clergy often reacted against the growth of the lay spirit and of lay competence in letters and thought. Sometimes, one feels, their doubts about lay efforts in philosophy and theology were partly justified. The great clerks were better at these subjects than were Raymond Lull, for example, Arnold of Villanova, and even Dante. But the reaction was greater than the stimulus justified, and the clerks obviously wished that they could put the genie back in the bottle. Besides, specialists are often hostile to those in other fields. Churchmen, for example, fell heir to an easy way to attack the greatest of the secular professions, that of the jurists. Sharing the intellectuals' usual prejudice against lawyers, Giles of Rome observed that

all jurists are political idiots. For, just as laymen and plebeians are called dialectical ignoramuses by the Philosopher . . . because they do not argue with artifice and dialectical skill, so lawyers, because they speak of politics narratively and without reason, can be called political ignoramuses. For this reason it is obvious how much more highly those who know the political and moral sciences are to be regarded than those who know law.[16]

Nor were these opinions merely those of a conservative. Word for word they are to be found in the work of the Franciscan zealot Roger Bacon. Although inviting wonder about how men invariably make their own knowledge into the universe's only yardstick, these conflicts between lay and clerical intellectuals are good evidence of the power of secular intellectualism at this time.

[15] Oxford, MS Lincoln Coll. Lat. 81, f. 34 and Cambridge, MS Add. B. 65, f. 1.
[16] De regimine principum 2, 2, 8 in Rome 1607, 309.

In conclusion, somewhat before but principally in the period with which this volume deals, churchmen rose to lead western Europe. Turning towards the world they seemed to rule, they tried to discover what it was composed of and to create agencies to make it better. In so doing the clerks themselves helped to build lay literacy and the lay spirit. And, as we know, these were things that were to reduce clerical power and authority later on. In the meantime, however, the two peoples, the clerical and lay, were relatively harmoniously balanced. The scales were to tip toward the lay or secular principle only in the later Middle Ages and the utter inanition of the Church was only to become obvious in recent times.

Internal frontiers : France, Italy, and Europe

When looking at western Europe during the twelfth and thir-teenth centuries, what first strikes the eye is the predominance or leadership of France and Italy. Until towards the end of the eleventh century, the Germans and their great state, the Empire, had been both culturally and militarily preponderant, and the memory of this circumstance still influenced the perceptions of those living around 1200. Although many already knew better, Frederick I Barbarossa, the Hohenstaufen emperor (d. 1190), could still assert that all Europe's kings were mere kinglets (*reguli*) in comparison with him. Only about 1250 or even 1268, with the extinction of the Hohenstaufen imperial line, were con-temporaries finally and indisputably aware of the extraordinary importance of France and Italy. This is because men's eyes are attracted by the pontiffs and princes and by the great institutions they appear to direct. Although many knew that the movements of the peoples and of the many smaller institutions in which they were brigaded controlled great men and great institutions, it is in the nature of things that the others are more visible. What struck men in the thirteenth century was the astonishingly rapid success of the Capetian monarchy and the invasion of much of Europe by papal power and its affiliated Lombard merchant-bankers—and, of course, the defeat of the Hohenstaufen Empire. But there were some who shared our later view and who knew that the founda-tions of French and Italian leadership had been laid much earlier. It did not escape them, as it cannot us, that the basic victories of the Roman Church, the fundamental rise of Italian commercial and industrial power, and the vast emigration of Frenchmen and of French culture took place in the latter half of the eleventh century and the first half of the twelfth, in short, during the Gregorian age. It is also curious to note that, as we shall see, the generality of men had no sooner realized the true dimensions of French and Italian grandeur than these began to fade. Preaching and writing in Florence, the Dominican Remigio de' Girolami could say that all of Europe's other princes were mere *roguli* when compared to France's king. *Antonomastice*, her king was the King, just as Aristotle was the Philosopher and Mary the Virgin. Barely half a century after he died in 1319, even the most loyal Frenchman would have smiled sadly on hearing such a remark.

To turn to France, it is certainly true that French greatness was not coterminous with the frontiers of the French royal state. It can indeed be argued that the growth of Capetian power never enclosed all the areas of French speech and culture and coincided with the loss of others that had traditionally been part of that linguistic and cultural group. Along the northern frontier with the Empire, it is certainly true that French speech was penetrating maritime Flanders at the expense of Flemish, that French culture had come to dominate in a Germanic region like Luxembourg, and that Capetian political influence was dominant from Flanders to Lorraine by 1300. On the eastern frontier with the Empire Capetian success was even more marked. The definitive absorption of the great county of Champagne into the royal domain in 1284 reminds us that a territory whose princes had several times looked toward the Empire in earlier days had become irrevocably French. By 1245 the old imperial territory of Provence had fallen to the house of Anjou, a cadet line of the Capetians. The occupation of Lyons by France in 1312 completed the loss of the lower Rhône valley by the Empire, and French influence had penetrated into the Burgundies and the Lorraines and, behind them, into the German Rhineland and Swabia. All in all, one can understand why King Philip IV the Fair (1285–1314) at Paris and Pope John XXII (1316–34) at Avignon believed that the French prince had a good chance of becoming the German emperor. Still, one may not forget that the loyalty of Flanders was doubtful, that Walloon regions like Brabant and the Liègeois were not part of the kingdom, and that other French-speaking areas such as most of the

43

Lorraines and the Burgundies and all of Savoy lay beyond Capetian control.

The history of the Iberian frontier is not dissimilar. From Carolingian times onward Catalonia was part of France, and, until the 1220s, public scribes there occasionally dated their documents with the regnal year of the French king. During the twelfth century period of feudal decentralization in southern France a loose confederation under the house of Saint-Gilles-Toulouse, extending from eastern Provence on the Rhône to western Languedoc and the Agennais on the Garonne, began to break up. It looked for a time as if the Catalans and Aragonese (who unified in 1162) would take over the region from Provence through maritime Languedoc to the little Pyrenean counties and that the rest would fall to the Poitevins and Aquitanians—groups that were joined to the Plantagenet (or Angevin)[17] northern French and English monarchy in the reign of Henry II (1154–89). As we shall see, the Plantagenets lost their northern French domains, including Poitou, during the reign of Philip II Augustus (d. 1223), and were in no position to have any further ambitions to the south. Beginning with the launching of the Albigensian Crusade in 1209, northern French crusaders and eventually the Capetians themselves intervened with vigour in the southland. Already failing in Provence, the Catalan-Aragonese hold in Languedoc was smashed by the crusader Simon of Montfort with the death of King Peter II of Aragon on the battlefield of Muret in 1213. By 1300, although Languedoc and the mountain counties were restive throughout the century and Montpellier was not lost by Aragon until 1349, most of southern France had been absorbed into the Capetian domain. In the meantime, however, a treaty signed at Corbeil in 1258 had split this once unified linguistic and cultural area. There the Catalans renounced all claims to Provence, Languedoc and the mountain counties, while France surrendered its ancient claim to Catalonia and Roussillon. The only breach of the Pyrenean frontier in favour of France came about as a result of the union of Navarre with Champagne in 1235. In 1284, the Capetians collected this kingdom along with the inheritance of the

[17] In order to avoid confusion with the Angevin cadet line of the Capetians which spread from Provence to Naples and eventually to Hungary, the term Plantagenet will be used to describe the house descended from Geoffrey of Anjou, whose nickname was Plantagenet.

44

counts of Champagne.

Far more important than the history of the Capetian monarchy were the movements of the French people and their culture. It is known—so well indeed that it need not be repeated—that the French, rivalled but not quite equalled by the Italians, were Europe's greatest crusaders. And leadership in the crusades meant excellence in warfare. Certainly, others also exemplified martial vigour. Although the Germans often granted the French preeminence in learning, they reserved for themselves the gift of making war. And, in fact, the vehemence of German chivalry was much feared. Noted for their ability in naval warfare, the Italians were also not bad on land. During the later twelfth century, they popularized the crossbow, whose bolts made necessary the introduction of horse armour and the beginnings of plate armour at this time. By about 1300, indeed, warfare's future course could be dimly discerned in the successful combination of bowmen and men-at-arms by the English in their Scottish wars and in the seemingly fortuitous defeat of Habsburg chivalry by the Swiss mountaineers in 1295.

For the time being, however, chivalry ruled the battlefield, and French chivalry, especially that of northern France, was undoubtedly Europe's best. William of Newburgh reports that Richard Coeur-de-Lion believed that French knights were 'sharper' than English because of exercise in frequent tournaments. Englishmen, he said, 'should learn the art and use of war so that the Gauls should not insult English knights, as being rude and less expert'; and the way to improve them was by introducing the tournament.[18] It is not surprising that the most expert soldiers of the age, the Templars and Hospitallers, were largely recruited from France, and that northern France produced the two most brilliant commanders of the age, Richard Coeur-de-Lion and Simon of Montfort of Albigensian fame. Late exceptions apart, the military orders that sprang up in Spain and Germany followed the rule of the Temple, itself inspired by that of the Cistercians. The Teutonic Order (founded 1190; military in 1198) derived its general rule and military usages from the Temple and the rule for its hospitals from the Hospital.

Along with soldiers went emigrants. The great age of French

[18] Cited in Léon Gautier, *La chevalerie* (1884), 675.

emigration precedes the time treated in this book and lies between 1050 and 1150. Soldiers and settlers flooded from Poitou, Aquitaine, Languedoc and the Burgundies into Spain. Many Spanish towns had French quarters in the twelfth century. In 1118 Alphonso VII granted Toledo's citizens their *fuero*, describing them as Castilians, Mozarabs, and Frenchmen. In successive waves, also, Cluniac monks and then Cistercians penetrated everywhere. For a time, almost every southern French monastery or church of any size had affiliates south of the Pyrenees. The first major victory over Islam won by Spaniards alone—although French crusaders had participated in the earlier stages of the campaign—was Las Navas de Tolosa in 1212.

Much the same was true on the German frontiers: the earlier age witnessed the deeper penetration. Although contacts continued (witness the meeting in 1253–55 at the Mongol capital at Qaraqorum in central Asia of the Franciscan missionary William of Ruysbroek and four French-speaking individuals who appear to have been swept up in the Mongol raid on Hungary in 1242, one Lorrainer, one Parisian, one Londoner and a Cuman Turk), French settlement in Hungary's nascent towns was at its peak around 1100. German towns also admitted these immigrants, especially French Jews. The school of Rashi of Troyes, the celebrated Talmudist and biblical commentator, influenced those of Mainz, Worms and Speier, and French Jews penetrated not only the Rhineland and the valley of the upper Danube but also eastern Saxony. Even in the thirteenth century, French was still occasionally spoken by German Jews and left a mark upon German Jewish speech from Cologne to Regensburg.

The other Germanic frontier was England. That her conquest in 1066 made her a province of French culture is obvious. Nor did French pressure or settlement cease at that date or even at the accession in 1154 of the Plantagenets from Anjou. Although declining in force, settlement went on well into the thirteenth century. The last and unsuccessful French invasion was that of Philip II Augustus's son in 1215–17 during John's unhappy reign, but French penetration continued throughout most of the century, as is shown by the constant importation of continentals from as far away as Provence and Savoy into English service. Given the traditions of those of us of English speech, it is important to emphasize that these successive invasions were French. Even the first of 1066—although led by Normans who clung to a sense of quasi-Nordic identity that set them apart from both the Gauls and the Franks, as the mythopoeic historian Dudo of St Quentin of the 1020s so clearly shows—drew volunteers from all the north-eastern provinces of French culture from Brittany to the Liègeois, and the Anglo-French almost indifferently referred to themselves in their documents as *Normanni* or *Francigeni*. As to the French of France, there is no doubt that they believed that the French had conquered the English. Abbot Suger of Saint Denis reasoned in his life of Louis the Fat that William Rufus of England failed in an attempt to invade France because 'it is neither right nor natural for Frenchmen to be subject to Englishmen, but rather for English-men to be subject to Frenchmen'.[19] Not long after about 1274 when this sentiment was incorporated into the vernacular *Great Chronicles of France* it was to appear somewhat anomalous.

Being a relatively more populous land, Italy received fewer French. The earlier tenth and eleventh century movements of the Burgundians and Savoyards were followed by a relatively small number of Normans and other French who created the Norman kingdom of Sicily and the mainland principalities around Naples in southern Italy from about 1060 to 1091. The only other pene-tration of importance was that of the Angevins in the thirteenth century, a subject to be treated later. It is worth noting in passing, however, that the French were at no time able to do in Italy what they had done in England, Spain, and, to a lesser extent, in Germany, that is, to influence and even recast city life. In the Mediterranean area, indeed, French success was greatest in the Near East where they not only nearly monopolized the seigniorial grade in society, but also rivalled the Italians in sending urban settlers, especially to the Holy Land, Cyprus, and even to parts of mainland Greece. When in 1224 the Latins in Constantinople were threatened by Greek and Bulgar counterattack, Pope Honorius III addressed the French monarch to ask aid for the Emperor Robert of Courtenay. God, he said, 'has given into the hands of the Gauls the empire of the Romania . . . and there a New France, as it were, has recently been created'.[20]

---

[19] *Vita Ludovici grossi regis*, prologue, ed. Henri Waquet (Paris, 1864), 10–12. The learned editor mistranslated this passage.

[20] Raynaldi, *Annales ecclesiastici* XIII, 341a-b. I owe this reference to Kenneth Setton of the Institute for Advanced Studies.

One of the results of this astonishing explosion was the spread of the French language. French was the language of the crusaders and, with its long domestication in the Near East, soon became a secondary or even primary tongue for many who lived in a wide arc from Greece to the frontiers of Egypt. The Cypriote historian Leontios Makhairas told no more than the truth when he wrote in the fifteenth century that 'after the Lusignans conquered the island, we began to speak French and Greek became barbaric'.[21] The best example of the advance of French at the expense of the Germanic tongues is to be seen in England. There French—though Latin played a role also—suppressed a lively Germanic administrative and literary dialect until well into the fourteenth century. And, once it had gained its full recognition beside Latin in the ever conservative language of law, French held its place in England for ages. Praised by Fortescue in the fifteenth century, by Coke in the seventeenth, its recent demise was still mourned by Blackstone in 1758. One recalls the unhappy defendant at the Assizes of Salisbury in 1631, 'qui puis son condemnation ject un brickbat a le dit Justice que narrowly mist, et pur ceo fuit indictment drawn par Noy envers le prisoner, et son dexter manus ampute et fix al gibbet sur que luy mesme fuit immediatement hange in presence de Court'.[22]

Latin apart, French was also Europe's premier literary language. No matter whence they derived, authors who sought wide audiences wrote in it. In his famous encyclopedia, *Li Livres dou tresor* of 1260–66, Brunetto Latini remarks that 'were anyone to ask, since I am an Italian, why this book is written in Romance, in the French tongue, I reply that it is for two reasons, one, that I am in France, and the other, that this language is the most delectable and the most widespread of all tongues'.[23] These remarks do not imply that strong vernacular literatures other than French did not exist. Both Spain and Germany boasted vigorous native traditions. Even in Italy, where Latin did so much to retard the easy development of Italian, and where French, either Provençal or northern, quickly became the language of courts and urban aristocracies, a popular vernacular poetry persisted. On the other hand, poets of the stature of Alphonso the Wise of Castile

[21] Cited in Grousset, *L'empire du Levant*, 379.
[22] F. W. Maitland, *English Law and the Renaissance* (Cambridge, 1901), 68.
[23] *Li livres dou tresor* I, 1, ed. F. J. Carmody (Berkeley, 1948), 18.

(d. 1284), Walter von der Vogelweide (d. 1240), and Wolfram of Eschenbach (d. about 1225) owed much to French authors. Although the French were immensely indebted to earlier literatures—Arabic, both Muslim and Jewish, early German and Celtic, as in the Matter of Brittany, and to classical letters—they led the world in this period. No poets in other languages equalled Christian of Troyes (fl. 1150–80), Bertrand of Born (d. 1208/10), Bernard of Ventadour (fl. 1180s), William of Lorris (d. about 1240) and John of Meung until the great Tuscans, Guido Cavalcanti (d. 1300/01), Cino of Pistoia (d. 1336) and Dante, appeared.

Music at this time was closely related to poetry, much of which was sung. Although, except for a few tunes, little is known about secular music, ecclesiastical music is better known, and there the French undoubtedly led in the introduction of polyphonic forms into the plainsong of the time. Leadership in this enrichment and quasi-secularization of church music was to be found at Saint-Martial in Limoges until about 1150 and thereafter at Nôtre Dame of Paris in the latter twelfth century, with Leoninus and Perotinus (d. 1220). By the mid-thirteenth century the Rhineland and France's eastern counties were forging ahead.

The attractiveness of French culture was based on more than the arts of sensibility. To men of this age, France was the home of manners, style and elegance. Englishmen and others visited Paris to stock their wardrobes—for gentlemen at arms then dressed as fancily as women. Both the Italians and Germans berated the arrogance and sexual libertinism or freedom of the French but eagerly adopted the manners and dress of those who, as Coluccio Salutati truthfully recorded much later on, were 'the fathers of all urbanity'. And the French were arrogant about their culture. The youthful poems of the jurist Philip of Remi, lord of Beaumanoir (d. 1296), poked fun at the insular accent of his Anglo-French employers. And one of the reasons French songs were frowned upon by Italian town fathers was their lasciviousness. Envy combined with anger to caricature the French, their cuisine and private lives. At the time of the conflict over Maimonidean ideas, in which the French rabbis represented the conservative party, the writer of a letter attributed to Maimonides himself warned: 'Beware of the works of the French because they think they have the best chance of knowing God when they eat beef marinated in a sauce (*saulce*) of vinegar (wine?) and garlic. . . .

Most of them anyway have two women and their thoughts are incessantly on intercourse with them.'[24] Besides, Frenchmen usually lived well in the relatively peaceful thirteenth century. Latini complained that the Italians, warring among themselves, built crabbed country homes enclosed by walls and towers. The French, however, 'build grand and ample houses with large decorated rooms to have joy and delight without war and disturbance', homes surrounded by lawns and fruit trees.[25] No wonder that John of Salisbury called France 'the most gentle and civil of all nations'.[26]

There was more to it than creature comforts and chic. French styles and engineering dominated architecture, both military and civil. Among the most inventive monuments of castrametation were the Hospitallers' Krak des Chevaliers in Syria, completed around 1205, and Richard Coeur-de-Lion's astonishing castle, Gaillard-des-Andeleys in Normandy. Better known is the northern French invention of Gothic, probably in the Ile-de-France, a style and engineering technique that had spread throughout northern France and the Plantagenet domains on either side of the Channel during the twelfth century. Replacing or refurbishing older monuments, Gothic began to penetrate Languedoc and Italy around 1220, and Germany by 1263. If Peter of Montreuil, the probable designer of the Sainte-Chapelle, busied himself largely around Paris, his relative Eudes accompanied his patron Louis IX to Cyprus and there designed several churches. Author of a famous architectural sketchbook but an architect of modest fame, Villard of Honnecourt was employed from Hainault to Hungary. In 1287 Stephen of Bonneuil left Paris with a team of builders for Sweden. John des Champs brought Gothic to Toulouse and Narbonne. In 1266 Peter of Agincourt accompanied Charles I of Anjou to southern Italy, where, after introducing the French style, he was rewarded by a knighthood.

At this time, also, curiosity or the love of learning was customarily described as a natural characteristic of the French mind. Although assigning the Empire to the Germans and the Church to the Italians, the popular cliché gave the university to the French,

[24] Moritz Güdemann, *Geschichte des Erziehungswesens und der Cultur der Juden* I, 73.
[25] *Li livres dou tresor* 1, 129, ed. F. J. Carmody, 126.
[26] *Ep.* 225 in *PL* CXCIX, 253.

by which was meant, of course, the *studium generale* of Paris. French law was also important. It influenced England profoundly and penetrated into the western regions of Germany. It was also imported into southern Italy under its twelfth-century Norman kings and became predominant in the Latin colonies along the coasts of the eastern Mediterranean and Aegean Seas. There its most notable monument was the *Assizes of Jerusalem and Cyprus*, a collection of laws and tracts on government compiled in the thirteenth century, one of whose authors was Philip of Novara, a typically active memoirist, soldier and statesman of *France d'Outremer*.

If France was the great success story of the twelfth and thirteenth centuries, Italy was not far behind. Her fleets swept the Mediterranean and her sons joined the French in the settlement of that sea's eastern shores. In the Fourth Crusade of 1204, when Constantinople fell and the Latin Empire was established in Greece and the Aegean, one-quarter of the territory was given to the emperor—a Frenchman—and the other three-quarters were divided equally between the principal crusaders and the Venetians who had provided the fleet. This effectively gave the latter the upper hand in Bosporan and Greek commerce. Moreover, the Piedmontese house of Monferrato was granted the major fief of the new Latin emperor, the kingdom of Thessalonica. More lasting was the settlement of Italians along the coasts of the Mediterranean and Black Seas in cities or quarters of cities enjoying the privilege of extraterritoriality. Some of these *fondachi*, like Genoa's Pera, a suburb of Constantinople, soon became self-governing communities.

Italian arms never gained victories comparable to those of the French, however, largely because they were employed at home. There the purpose was to weaken the traditional power of the German Empire in the peninsula. Although imperial suzerainty never wholly disappeared, it gradually faded to a point in political theory, admittedly significant in polemics, as is instanced in Dante's *De monarchia*, but relatively unimportant in the practical politics of Italy's states and urban republics. As the jurists—even French ones like Peter Dubois—recognized, these little states admitted 'no superiors in the world'. Their decisive victories over transalpine power were won in the late twelfth century, from the defeat of Frederick I Barbarossa at Legnano and the subsequent

Peace of Constance in 1183 to the struggle over the succession between the Guelfs and the Hohenstaufen after the death of Henry VI in 1197. After these events, although German intervention continued to play a significant role in Italy, the great wars of the time of Frederick II Hohenstaufen were primarily struggles of southern Italy against the Guelf towns of the north and centre.

Although, from today's perspective, it may seem that Italy would have done better to have unified under the Apulian or Sicilian Frederick Hohenstaufen, contemporary Italians felt no sense of failure. They were proud of their newly won liberty, and their freedom was the quality that impressed the foreigners who observed them. James of Vitry described the Italians as being sober but talkative,

> circumspect in council, diligent and zealous in managing their government, prescient and tenacious about future matters, refusing to be subject to others, defending before all else their liberty, issuing their own laws and customs under one common captain whom they elect, and observing them faithfully.[27]

Besides, if Italy's maritime enterprise ruled the eastern Mediterranean by the end of the twelfth century, the next hundred years saw its rise in the western part of that sea and its penetration into the Atlantic as far north as Bruges in the period between 1271 and 1317. As will be shown in later chapters, also, the spread of the Italian merchant-bankers and money lenders beyond the Alps was a notable characteristic of the economy of the thirteenth century.

Equally significant was the wedding of the Italian towns' interests to those of the Church and particularly of the papacy. Exceptions apart, the popes and the townsfolk stood together against the emperors. Not only was liberty to be gained from this alliance, but also profit. By 1200, during the pontificate of Innocent III, Rome was the diplomatic capital of the Latin west, and by 1300 western princes were well advised to retain ambassadors at the papal court, of whom many, if not most, were also officers of the Italian merchant-banking houses, especially Florentines. Playing on the classical division of Europe into the four great nations of the French, Germans, Italians and Spaniards, Boniface VIII once looked around his court and observed that

---

[27] *Historia orientalis* 67, in Douai 1596, 124.

the Florentines verily constituted a fifth nation. Besides, the papacy was itself closely bound to Italy. From the death of the Englishman Adrian IV in 1159 until the accession of Urban IV in 1261, the popes were all Italians and so were most of the curial personnel. These remarks should not convey the impression that Italian participation in the life of the Church was limited to administrative direction or to profit. Two of the four larger mendicant orders of the thirteenth century were Italian in origin, including the Franciscan, the largest of all. Again, if the French seemed to contemporaries to exemplify the intellectual life with their University of Paris, the penetration of that institution's faculty of theology by the mendicant orders was initially an Italian invasion. The first Dominican to teach there was Roland of Cremona, and the names of John of Fidanza (Bonaventure) and Thomas of Aquino speak for themselves.

The Italians were not without their own intellectual specialities. Although rivalled by the graduates of Montpellier and, in Mediterranean regions, by the Jews, Italians were pre-eminent in medicine. Besides, if France had philosophy, Italy had law. To moderns, Italians are best known for studies of Roman law in Bologna and other centres. But there was more to it than that. By modernizing Roman law, as we know, the professors created the most influential *ius commune* of the medieval period. And although the Gallic spirit dominated feudal law, the Lombard *Libri feudorum* of the twelfth century, as later glossed and systematized by the professors, became a normative feudal code for much of western Europe by 1300, its authority being accepted directly within the Empire and indirectly elsewhere. As indicative of Italian leadership in legal studies was the growing authority of her jurists (or those who taught in Italy) in expounding and creating canon law, the other great *ius commune*. It may be recalled that, although this law was Roman or Mediterranean in origin and character, the ecclesiastical chancelleries of northern Europe had led in its development since Carolingian days. By the mid-twelfth century this had changed: the great canonists now learned their business in Italy. Lastly, all of these learned studies were firmly based upon practical legislative and judicial experience. The statutes and codes of Italy's urban republics and other states constitute the largest and most articulated body of constitutional materials to be found anywhere in western Europe during this period.

Finally, the arts of Italy, although still deeply under trans-alpine and French influence, were beginning to evolve independently. Among the influences that stimulated Italy's artists were, first, their hostility to the Germans who had ruled them for so long, and then, after the honeymoon years of the thirteenth century, their reaction against the French. The Italians therefore naturally sought for sources of inspiration that did not come from beyond the Alps. For a brief time, one such source was Byzantine art. In the long run the most fruitful and seemingly independent source was that of classical antiquity. The turn toward a renewed classicism may be already discerned in the twelfth century. Its effects are to be seen in the spacious independence of the buildings placed in the cathedral complex of Pisa, for example, as well as in specific works, such as the reliefs in the cathedral and baptistry of Parma executed by Benedict Antelami in 1198. Ancient themes reappeared; for example, the equestrian statue or relief of Oldrado of Tresseno, *potestas* in 1233, that graced the Palazzo delle Ragione in Milan. In the baptistry pulpit of Pisa, completed in 1260, the famous Apulian architect and sculptor Nicolas Pisano employed classical models for the figures decorating a basically Gothic monument. What this means for the emergence of Renaissance art cannot be overlooked. Giotto of Bondone, later the official architect for the republic of Florence, was a well-known painter and sculptor by 1300.

But the Italians did not come by their classicism easily or without borrowing from their neighbours. An example is the history of Latin style. In the twelfth century, the best Latin was usually written north of the Alps, as the prose and verse of Bernard of Clairvaux and John of Salisbury attest. Until well into the thirteenth century an elegant if sometimes affected Latinity marked composition there, as is shown by the school of *dictatores* at Orleans. Influenced by the practical needs of the legal profession and the notariate, the Italians generally favoured simpler styles and found their counterparts north of the Alps only among the academic theologians and scholastics whose lack of style had so offended John of Salisbury. As we know, one illustration of this practical or vulgar spirit may be seen in the works of Buoncompagno of Signa.

There is no doubt that, in the long run, Buoncompagno's case for vulgar Latin was a lost one. The growing use of the vernacular for legal documentation—a reaction perhaps of the laity against both the ecclesiastics and the learned and their desire to read more easily what concerned their property—was to weaken irreparably the base of popular Latin culture. A lesser reason was the influence of transalpine Latinity so useful for the pomp and ceremony of monarchy. This is shown in the orotund style of Peter of Vinea, Frederick II's chancellor of Sicily. Naturally the lawyers did not appreciate this new development—in fact they never quite gave in to it. The Bolognese professor Odotredus (d. 1265) referred scathingly to those who wish to 'speak obscurely and in a pompous style as do the most exalted doctors and as did Peter of Vinea'.[28] Still, the self-conscious classicism of many of Italy's *dictatores* and intellectuals in the later thirteenth century shows that they were about to make classicism their own. What may be admitted, however, is that the high style of Petrarch and Boccaccio in their Latin works had had a long period of gestation and that one of its parents was probably not Italian.

To sum up these two sections of this chapter, France and Italy led Europe during the twelfth and thirteenth centuries. This seems strange. Their cultural and military pre-eminence and their capacity to influence other parts of western Europe seem odd when their internal constitutions are examined. During the twelfth century French law spread far beyond her frontiers, yet France herself boasted no monarchy or state comparable to that of Plantagenet England, Norman southern Italy, or even the declining German Empire. To illustrate the machinery of French government, or lack of it, we learn that a few wagons containing all the archives and the treasury of the Capetian monarch were captured on the battlefield of Fréteval by Richard Coeur-de-Lion in 1194. The typical Italian state that produced Europe's *ius commune* and published its most elaborate statutes was an urban republic, tiny when compared to the states of Spain, to England, and to Germany's provinces, not to speak of the Empire.

But the size of political units was not the principal criterion of inventiveness or importance in this period. Having implanted Latin civilization throughout northern and eastern Europe, the

[28] Cited in Helene Wieruszowski, *Vom Imperium zum nationalen Königtum* (Munich, 1933), 67n.

great states and quasinational kingdoms that marked the early Middle Ages from the days of the Carolingians weakened in the eleventh and twelfth centuries. The age of the empires was over, although few could yet see it. In spite of the Hohenstaufen revival, the German Empire had been irreparably weakened by the alliance of the Roman Church, the German nobility and the Italian towns in the time of Gregorian enthusiasm. Conquering the Moors, the kings of Castile-Leon tried to forward a Spanish idea of empire long ago borrowed from the Carolingians. In 1139 Alphonso VII of Castile was termed emperor, ruling in New Castile, Leon, Aragon, Navarre, Castile, Galicia (Portugal), Catalonia and Provence, and in 1159 the northern annals of Cambrai spoke of three empires—the Byzantine, the German, and that of Galicia (St James of Compostella). But, defeated by geography and by papal and French encouragement of separatism in Portugal, Catalonia-Aragon and elsewhere, this reminiscence of Spanish nationhood and unity soon faded.

In regard to the nations, the princes of Europe's peripheral powers, from the Kiraly (king = Charlemagne) of Hungary to the kings of Norway, governed quasinational states that resembled those of the early Middle Ages. In terms of institutional and social structures, they might be described as 'late Carolingian'. Although their churches were invaded by Roman 'reform' or interference, and their civil institutions were transmuted by French feudalism and immigration, England, the states of inland and western Iberia, and northern and eastern Germany, had, and partly retained, an identity and unity that marked them off from France and Italy. Although conquered by the French, for example, England never disappeared as a nation.

Significant though these retentions were, it was in France and Italy and the parts of Europe hard against their frontiers that the institutions most characteristic of the medieval epoch reached the peak of their development in this time. On the local level, these institutions were the seigniories of the countryside and the 'collective seigniories' of the towns, both jealously seeking a measure of independence from regional princes or kings. Both types of communities were generally governed by aristocracies, aristocracies of wealth, both new and old, of lineage, both newly ascending and traditional, and of experience in government. Although representing local interests, this aristocracy was usually

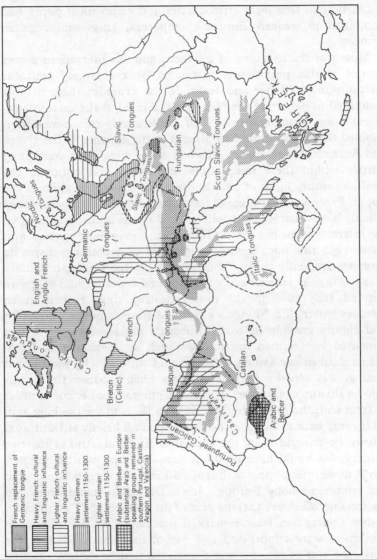

1. *Europe's languages and patterns of settlement about 1300.*

allied with the Church, especially with the ecumenical authority of the papacy. To simplify the complex social structure of the age, it can be said that local aristocracies and ecumenical popes had combined to weaken Europe's emperors, kings and regional princes.

Moreover the harmony of northern and Mediterranean power typical of this period was instanced by the largely amicable relationship of France and Italy. In the crusades these nations combined to penetrate the Near East. Aimed at the eastern continent's westernmost nucleus of civilization, this penetration enabled the Latins to find fulfilment at the expense of the Greek and Arabic cultures. Again, although there were many conflicting parties within these much divided nations and although the twelfth-century kings of France were not always the allies of the popes, France—'the refuge of the popes' was the commonplace— usually buttressed Rome's policies, and Rome in turn represented the interests of the majority of the Italians, save those of the south. After 1250 this once flexible alignment of seemingly disparate interests gradually became more formal as the Capetian dynasty rose to rule the larger part of France and its cadet line of Anjou entered Italy to help the popes destroy their Hohenstaufen enemies. After this, France's kings and Rome's popes were often and rightly considered to be Europe's greatest princes, a fact lamented by German imperialists such as Alexander of Roes. When Rabban bar Sauma, a Nestorian Christian who was born at Peking, was sent by Persia's Mongol khan to draw the Latins into an alliance against the Muslims, he first visited Rome in order to treat with the pope. He then went to Paris to see the king and, on his way back to Rome in 1288, stopped off briefly at Bordeaux, a town he thought to be the capital of England. And of the two princes, few could have doubted that the pope was the greater. To Rabban, the pope was Europe's king of kings, a notion that was common among Europe's Jews. Dating his commentary on the tractate *Nazir* in 1321, the year of the rising of the Pastoureaux, Rabbi Todros ben Isaac remarked that it was 'at the time when the lepers were suppressed and evil men appeared before the pope, the king of nations, and demanded that he destroy the true Law'.[29] But we shall see that the lesser of the two princes was able

[29] Cited in Salo W. Baron, *A Social and Religious History of the Jews* XI (2nd edn. [New York, 1967]), 251.

to defeat the greater.

One may not, however, exaggerate the importance of the French and Italians. They did not advance by means of their own power and wealth alone; they were also blessed by a happy circumstance. One reason that their leadership was relatively easily accepted was that their principal neighbours were busy expanding Europe's frontiers. The Spaniards fought Islam to the south, their crusades and military orders remaining in the Iberian peninsula. The English were busy at home and along their Celtic fringe, and their gallicized nobility was known to be far less enthusiastic about the crusades than their brothers across the Channel. England's greatest crusader, Richard Coeur-de-Lion, was the most French of all her kings. Although not so in the case of the Swabians and other Alpine Germans, the inhabitants of Germany's northern and eastern provinces fought their wars and crusades on their home frontiers. If the Teutonic Knights began in the Holy Land, they won their fame on the Vistula and beyond. Latin Europe's centre therefore profited from the fact that, in this expansionist age, the powers and peoples on the periphery looked outside Latin culture for advancement, not within. It was there, on their home frontiers, that the English, Germans and Spaniards could confess that they emulated the French. Around 1108 the eastern Saxon princes summoned the Germans against the Slavs:

> Wherefore, O most famous Saxons, Franks, Lorrainers, and Flemish, conquerors of the world, here you can both save your souls and, if it pleases God, acquire and settle a beautiful land. [Christ], who has summoned the French to set out from the furthest reaches of the west to triumph by the arm of their virtue against his enemies in the furthest east, will give you the will and power to subjugate these nearby inhuman gentiles and to prosper in everything.[30]

Christendom's frontiers: the crusades

The late years of the twelfth century witnessed a resurgence of Islamic resistance to Christian attack. The Byzantine attempt to recover central Anatolia from the Seljuk Turks failed decisively when the Emperor Manuel was defeated at Myriokephalon in

[30] Rudolph Kötzschke, *Quellen zur Geschichte der ostdeutschen Kolonisation* (Leipzig, 1912), 10, No. 3.

1176. To turn to the Latin territories, the unification of the Muslims of Syria and Egypt under Nureddin and Saladin caused the loss of Jerusalem in 1187 and threatened the coastal cities. In the western and central Mediterranean, where the rigorist sect of the Almohades rallied Muslim strength, the picture was much the same. Moving eastward from Morocco, these Berbers regained by 1160 the coast from Bone to Tripoli that had been lost to the Norman kings of Sicily. Profiting from the division of the Castilian empire also, the Almohades momentarily unified Spanish Islam and administered a severe defeat to Castile as late as 1196.

During the first two-thirds of the thirteenth century, however, the Muslim counterattack came to a halt and the Christians resumed their march. In the Iberian peninsula the progress of the Almohades had already been slowed by the activity of five recently created Christian military orders and frequent French crusades. A temporary alliance of Spain's Christian powers finally crushed the Almohade host at Las Navas de Tolosa in 1212. Thereafter the Spaniards advanced rapidly. By 1238 the loss of the Balearic Islands and Valencia to Aragon cost Islam its command of the central reaches of the western Mediterranean. By mid-century Portugal had taken the Algarve, and Islam had lost half-empty Cordova and populous Seville to Castile. Cadiz fell in 1265. In the meantime the Italians turned their attention to the economic penetration of North Africa. Missionaries and merchants from France and Italy were active from Senegal on the Atlantic to Tunis near Sicily. Europe's geographical knowledge grew apace. The Canary Islands were settled from Spain in 1270. In 1291 the Genoese merchant prince and soldier Benedict Zaccaria joined with the brothers Vivaldi to equip two ill-fated galleys that set out past Gibraltar in order to circumnavigate Africa. The Azores were marked on a portolan map of 1350.

In the eastern Mediterranean the Latins took few new territories from Islam, but they shattered the remnants of Greek power. Beginning with the conquest of Cyprus by Richard Coeur-de-Lion in 1191, Latin arms gradually won their way to the mainland. The French and Venetian Fourth Crusade captured Constantinople in 1204, creating a Latin Empire that, although it lasted on the Bosporus only until 1261, left French principalities and Venetian possessions extending in mainland Greece from Thessaly and Attica to Achaea and Naxos in the Peloponnesus.

Like the French and Italian rule of the islands of the Aegean Sea and of Rhodes, Crete and Cyprus, these Latin dominions were to last until the fifteenth century. The Latins had not won so much territory in the Near East since the days of the First Crusade. In Syria and the Holy Land the deterioration of the Latin position was arrested, principally by the efforts of Coeur-de-Lion. Thereafter, in spite of occasional disasters like that of the Egyptian campaign of Louis IX of France in 1249, Christian expeditions together with the divisions between the Ayyubid dynasts of Saladin's Kurdish line kept the eastern frontier more or less stable. Indeed, led by the Emperor Frederick II, the Christians recovered the administration of Jerusalem in 1229 and held it until 1244.

A further reason for the stabilization of the Christians' frontiers was the irruption into the Near East of the Mongols from Asia. Although the two power blocs worked directly together only in Armenia, the Mongols strengthened the Latins by weakening the Muslims. Basing themselves in conquered Iran, Mongol armies took Baghdad in 1258 and ruined Irak. From here they raided Syria and the Seljuk principalities of Anatolia. Furthermore, the unification of central Asia and China opened up great opportunities to westerners. Trade flourished under the Mongol peace. The khans also preferred to rule their heterogeneous subjects by means of foreigners. When Marco Polo retraced his father's steps and arrived at the Mongol court in 1275, he and his party immediately enlisted in the khan's service, serving as provincial governors and ambassadors until their departure nearly twenty years later. The khans also favoured religious heterogeneity and therefore encouraged Latin missions. From 1245 until 1340 missionaries, principally Italian Franciscans, were despatched eastward. By the end of this period forty Franciscan establishments, extending from Iran and Turkestan to China, had been heard of. An example is the mission of the Apulian Franciscan John of Monte Corvino in 1294. John translated the New Testament into the Mongol tongue, erected a monastery and two churches in Peking, and delighted the khan by buying 150 boys to chant the Latin mass. In 1307 Clement V named him archbishop of Peking.

Merchants and adventurers accompanied the Latin missionaries. Fifty years after the Polos, the Franciscan Odoric of Pordenone tells us that the Chinese port of Amoy contained a *fondaco*

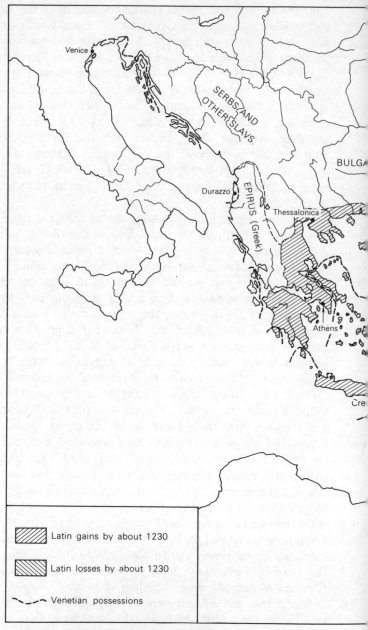

Venice

SERBS AND
OTHER SLAVS

BULGA

Durazzo

EPIRUS
(Greek)

Thessalonica

Athens

Cre

///// Latin gains by about 1230

Latin losses by about 1230

–·–·– Venetian possessions

2. The Latins in the Eastern Mediterranean in the 1230s.

62

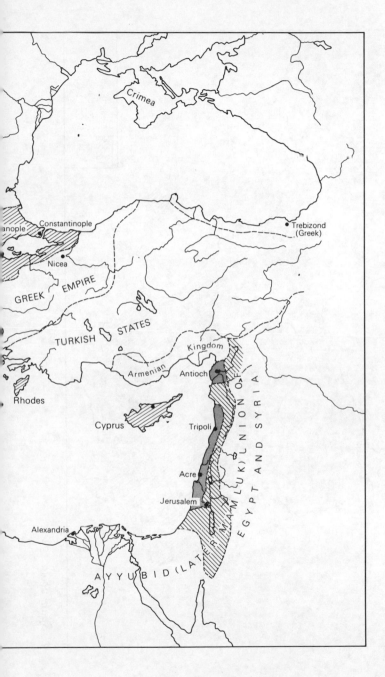

Crimea

anople
Constantinople
Trebizond
(Greek)

Nicea

GREEK EMPIRE

TURKISH STATES

Rhodes

Armenian Kingdom

Antioch

Cyprus

Tripoli

MAMLUK) UNION OF

Acre

EGYPT AND SYRIA

Jerusalem

Alexandria

A Y Y U B I D (LATER

63

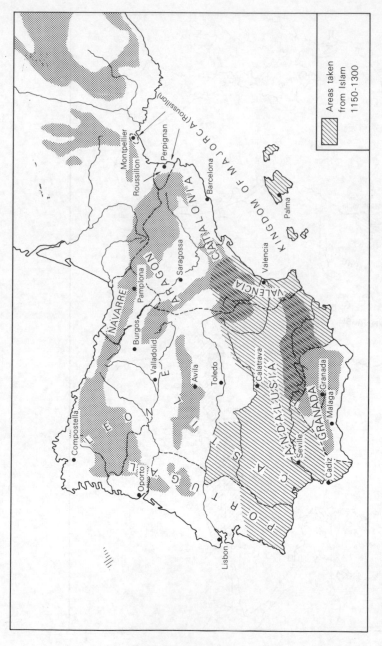

Areas taken
from Islam
1150-1300

Montpellier
Roussillon
Perpignan
(Roussillon)
CATALONIA
Barcelona
KINGDOM OF MAJORCA
Palma
NAVARRE
Pamplona
ARAGON
Saragossa
Valencia
VALENCIA
Burgos
Valladolid
Avila
Toledo
Calatrava
LEON
ANDALUSIA
GRANADA
Granada
Malaga
Compostella
CASTILE
Seville
Cadiz
Oporto
PORTUGAL
Lisbon

3. *Spain about 1310.*

64

for Christian merchants, a settlement equipped with its indispensable public bathhouse and church. The fastest route to China ran from the Genoese towns in the Crimea-Azov region of the Black Sea, where the Franciscan had established two archdioceses, across the Caspian Sea by Genoese vessel, and thence through Tatary. Writing early in the fourteenth century, Francis di Balducci Pegolotti, a director of the Bardi firm of Florence, reported that the route to Peking was quite safe. Italians were also busy in Iran, then in the control of a friendly Mongol khanate. In 1321-24 a Dominican missionary observed that Genoese merchants sailed their own vessels from the Persian Gulf to India and Ceylon, recruiting sailors locally but preferring Abyssinians for armed marines. Noting, as most Latins did, that Egypt was the principal enemy of the Christian cause, the missionary William Adam from Languedoc suggested around 1313 stationing a squadron off Aden —a town he had visited—to intercept Red Sea traffic.

During the last years of the thirteenth century and the first half of the fourteenth, however, these alluring prospects vanished forever. The subdivision and weakening of Mongol power was rapid; Persia eventually returned to Islam, and China to a native dynasty. Islam rose again. The great Muslim state that was destined to play a major role in western history during modern times was already showing its strength, an Ottoman expedition having briefly crossed the Dardanelles to Europe in 1300. Farther south the Mamluks, erecting a state built around an élite of slave soldiers and officers, replaced the Ayyubids in Egypt and Syria. Their famous commander Baybars not only repulsed the Mongols in the 1260s but also re-established the Abbasid caliphate in Cairo. His successors then went on to push the divided Christians from their coastal holdings in Cilicia, Syria and the Holy Land, where in 1291 Acre was the last town to fall. In the western Mediterranean also, Islam again advanced. There a new Moroccan dynasty, that of the Berber Merinids, unified the whole coast of North Africa, repulsed the Franco-Italian attack of Louis IX on Tunis in 1270, and stabilized the Islamic frontier around Granada in Spain by successful raids from 1261 to 1285.

On only one frontier, that of the north and east, did Latin expansion continue well into the fourteenth century. There, too, a momentary recession had marked the late twelfth century. In Hungary, for example, the Byzantines made and unmade kings at the height of the Comnenian dynasty and had even briefly weakened the hold of the Latin Church. After the death of the Emperor Manuel in 1180 and the subsequent collapse of the Greek Balkan empire Byzantine pressure was no longer to be feared. Greek and Slavic Orthodox Christianity was everywhere in retreat. In Russia the Mongol assaults of the 'thirties and 'forties of the thirteenth century all but obliterated the southern principalities from Kiev to the Carpathians, and subjugated all the rest of Russia save the republic of Novgorod the Great.

Among the Latin Christians it was the Germans who derived the greatest profit from eastern Europe, partly because there was no strong or well-developed state to stand against them. Once potent and unified, Hungary's government weakened throughout the thirteenth century, and was not pulled together again until the accession of a Neapolitan-Angevin dynasty in 1308. Poland was divided among rival princes and did not unify until well into the fourteenth century. Of the pagan peoples near the Baltic, only the Lithuanians showed signs of developing a real state. Even the disasters afflicting these regions were profitable to the Germans. The Mongol raids on Poland and Hungary from 1241 on increased the already lively desire of the princes of these areas to import Germans and German institutions to organize their lands, build their cities, and modernize their courts and armies on the model of western chivalry.

In general, the German penetration of eastern Europe was peaceable. Around the shores of the Baltic, however, where the native populations long remained pagan, it was warlike. The wars against the Wends came early in the German resumption of the push over the Elbe. By the thirteenth century the Germans had penetrated to the Vistula and had thrown outposts along the Baltic shore as far north as Riga, founded by them in 1198. From 1208 on, leadership was taken by the Teutonic Knights, who absorbed the two military orders already pioneering in Livonia and Prussia. The knights' Baltic towns joined the general expansion of German commerce in the Baltic and North Sea region. There, in that northern Mediterranean, the forerunners of the later Hanseatic League were already making their appearance. Coming from towns as far apart as Cologne or Utrecht in the west and Reval in the east, the merchants of the Gothland Society already dominated the trade of the once Scandinavian port of

Wisby. By 1229 they had won rights to settle in Novgorod, rights similar to those of an Italian *fondaco* in the Mediterranean. Led by the merchants of Lübeck, Cologne and Hamburg, Germans had established similar *Kontore* in Bruges, Bristol, London and England's east coast ports by the 'fifties and 'sixties. By 1293 Lübeck's leadership among these northern German towns was already beginning to make itself felt, and the great days of the German Hansa were just around the corner. Up to the north the last Danish maritime empire succumbed to German attack in 1227, and Scandinavia was thereafter opened to German trade and settlement. Invited by the Nordic princes, German merchants settled everywhere, monopolizing trade but also building towns. The Scandinavian kings hastened to modernize their government, importing German cadres and modelling their institutions on German feudalism.

With the exception, then, of what may be called German Europe—where expansion continued well into the fourteenth century—the advance of Europe's frontiers seems to have halted before or around 1300 and to have begun to retreat thereafter. This was not all to the bad, if only because it inspired a redeployment of resources. The Teutonic Order, for example, whose grand master remained in Acre to 1291 and then retired to Venice, removed this officer to Marienburg in 1308. To some degree, chivalry followed this movement, Prussia becoming the land of crusading derring-do after 1300. On the whole, however, the failure of the Latin effort against Islam disturbed Europe deeply.

What made it worse was that the defeat could not wholly be attributed to renascent Muslim power. As an examination of her wars shows, there was also a change within Latin Europe itself. In the past, war had generally moved toward Europe's frontiers. French culture and arms, for example, invaded England until into the thirteenth century. Until the early 1300s, in turn, the Anglo-French expanded at the expense of Britain's Celtic fringe. By 1284 the remnant principality of north Wales had been irrevocably crushed. From 1152 onward the English penetrated Ireland, conquering Leinster and the Pale and raiding throughout the island. By 1307 England's attack on the curious Anglo-Celtic and even quasi-French power called Scotland seemed about to result in the annexation of that kingdom.

In the course of the thirteenth century there was a shift in

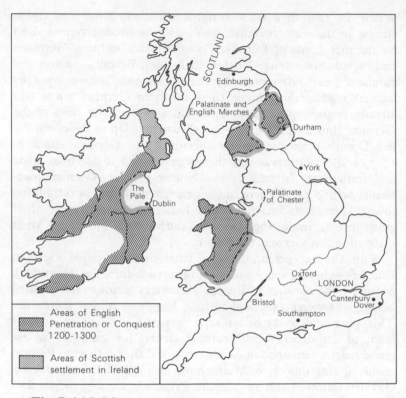

4. The British Isles about 1300.

direction. If the campaigns of Henry III in France during the
forties and fifties were military flops, they nevertheless secured
Capetian recognition by 1258 of Guienne and adjacent territories
as legitimately held fiefs of the English king, thus bringing to a
halt the Capetian conquest of the Plantagenet domain on the
continent. From the 'nineties onward the English—for whom, by
now, this term seems increasingly suitable—began to intervene
again on one of the traditional frontiers of French cultural expansion, that of Flanders and the Low Countries. A step towards the
Hundred Years War, the intermittent combats from 1292 through
the first third of the fourteenth century were not English victories.
The county of Flanders remained nominally French long after
these first skirmishes. By the peace of Athis in 1305, the French
crown acquired Douai, Béthune, Lille, and Saint-Omer, and it

also avenged its chivalry's defeat at Courtrai in 1302 by crushing the Flemish townsmen at Cassel in 1328. But France's hope of incorporating the rest of Flanders in the royal domain was forever finished. In sum, although the English had yet to invade the continent in force and to lay claim to the French Crown, France had been stopped. Meanwhile, in the British Isles the English had been set back. If Wales was too far gone to raise its head again, Ireland was not. In spite of several major efforts, English expansion there ceased in the later thirteenth century and English holdings gradually shrank. The successful rising under Robert Bruce from 1307 to the victory of Bannockburn in 1314 began the restoration of Scottish independence that was to cause the English so many headaches during their long wars with the French.

Before the thirteenth century, furthermore, Europe's great war had been the crusade, in spite of the importance of lengthy conflicts at home such as those between the German emperors and the Italian towns or the Plantagenets and Capetians over France's Atlantic provinces. This may be seen in the numbers of effectives in the field. Richard Coeur-de-Lion won his spurs in France and lost his life there, but he won his laurels as a Great Captain in the eastern Mediterranean, where he commanded heterogeneous armies two or three times the size of those he ever led at home. By the thirteenth century, however, the largest armies and most interesting campaigns were to be found at home, notably in Italy, at the time of the Hohenstaufen wars.

War, it seems, was coming home to roost. An example may be seen in the wars in the Mediterranean. By the early twelfth century, the happy age of the crusades, the Italian maritime cities had swept the waters of the eastern Mediterranean, and the crusaders, largely French, had occupied its easternmost shores. Between the Italian maritime cities and the Holy Land lay two substantial powers, the Greeks at the height of the Comnenian revival and the Norman state of southern Italy and Sicily, whose mutually destructive battles over Epirus, Macedonia and Antioch were almost unremitting. The first of these two powers to fall was Byzantium, beset not only by the Seljuks in Anatolia, but also, from 1186, by the Balkan revolts of the Bulgars. At about the same time the Latins began to attack the Greeks, an attack that culminated in the catastrophe of the Fourth Crusade in 1203–04, from which the Byzantine state never really recovered. About the same time, the Italian maritime republics aided the Hohenstaufen invasion of southern Italy and Sicily, profiting from their participation in the ensuing wars from 1190 to 1215 to win substantial trade concessions and rights of extraterritoriality there. During the thirteenth century, the struggle between the more industrialized and urbanized north and centre of Italy against southern Italy—a Latin state but one containing important Greek and Muslim components—intensified. In general the victory went to the north, resulting not only in the defeat of the Hohenstaufen in 1268, but also in the splitting off of Sicily from the mainland part of the south Italian state between 1282 and 1302.

The victory of the popes and of their Lombard allies was won only at the cost of increased foreign intervention in Italy. Beset at Rome, Innocent IV fled to Lyons on the Rhône. Although he later returned and his successors usually resided in Italy if not in Rome, it is noteworthy that, from 1245 to 1312, the general councils that had formerly been summoned to the Lateran were held in the valley of the Rhône. Northern Italian strength having proved insufficient to defeat the Germans of the Empire and the southerners of Apulia and Sicily, Innocent invited the French to settle the question. From 1261—the year in which a French pope, Urban IV, was elected—to 1268 the Angevins spearheaded the final assault on Hohenstaufen Italy.

Nor were the French the only invaders of Italy. As the Germans failed, others came to fill the imperialist or Ghibelline ranks. A weak Castilian intervention preceded the entry of the Catalans and Aragonese at the time of the Sicilian revolt against the Angevin French in 1282, known as the Vespers. These new interlopers did not stop with building a kingdom in Sicily but pushed on into the Aegean, establishing a Catalan duchy in Thebes and Athens in 1311. The struggles among Italy's maritime powers became increasingly intense as the century wore on, further weakening the Latins in the Near East. The Greeks retook Constantinople in 1261 partly because of Genoese hostility to Venice's monopoly of Bosporan commerce, and the continuing combat between these two republics was instrumental in causing the loss of the Syrian and Palestinian coasts to Islam. Besides, only the larger naval powers could hope to compete any longer. Genoa crushed Pisa's fleet at Meloria in 1284 and weakened her commercial empire thereafter. Marseille's flourishing trade and

THE CRUSADES

marine suffered the same fate during the Angevin and Catalan struggles over Sicily.

In brief, by fighting among themselves with ever increasing vehemence, the Latins helped the Muslims halt western expansion by the end of the thirteenth century. And the slowing of Latin expansion was accompanied by a profound change in western ideology. An example may be seen in the ideas of Christendom and the crusade as these had been formulated during the Gregorian age. Upon the failure of the Empire and the general weakening of secular government at that time, the conception of Roman Christianity—the *respublica* or *civitas christiana*—rose above that of membership in nation or state. And, when Urban II launched the crusade to 'recover' Jerusalem from infidel hands, he weakened the moral justification for wars within Europe, even surrendering or relaxing the sanctions against heretics or schismatics that had marked the full flight of the Gregorian war against the Empire and against the secular domination of the Church. From the point of view of winning that war, Urban's step was a compromise, even a retreat, but one that enabled the papacy to assume the leadership of Europe in its renewed expansion after the great civil wars of the Gregorian epoch. This does not mean that the holy war did not continue to find application within Europe itself. The popes used the crusade indulgence against Roger II of Apulia-Sicily in 1135, against Ireland in 1152, against the king of Leon in 1197, and against the Hohenstaufen regent in Sicily, the Markward of Anweiler, in 1199. The historian Matthew Paris even assumed that the campaign of the French crown prince Louis against John of England in 1213 was a papal holy war. But all this was secondary. The great holy war was the crusade against Islam and other non-Christian peoples: the *pax dei* at home and the *bellum romanum* abroad.

Sometime around 1200 the crusade began to come back home to the west. The Fourth Crusade against the schismatic Greeks was an early example, one that the pope initially deplored but rapidly accepted because of his hopes for the union of the Churches. A second was the crusade launched in 1209 against the Albigensian heretics, which soon developed into a war of the northern French against Languedoc. The return to the old Gregorian pattern of religious or moral wars at home awaited the final struggle between the popes and the Hohenstaufen from 1240

71

onward. Innocent IV prohibited the preaching in Germany of the crusade for the Holy Land in order to draw troops to the Italian front. The Angevin attack on the Hohenstaufen was declared a crusade, as were the successive Capetian and Angevin wars against the Catalans and Sicilians from 1282 on. Indeed, the popes had become so used to calling their wars crusades that Boniface VIII launched one in 1297 against the Colonna family, his enemies in the college of cardinals and the papal states. For this, an often cited passage of Dante derided him, calling him 'the prince of the new Pharisees, whose every enemy was Christian, waging war near the Lateran, not with Saracens or Jews'.[31]

Nor were Dante's complaints unique: they derived from a long polemical tradition. Many were disturbed by what they thought to be the perversion of the crusade. Matthew Paris accused Innocent IV with sabotaging the crusade of Louis IX of France in order to advance his Italian policy. In 1265, when in France, an archbishop of Tyre observed that it was bad enough when the pope redirected to Sicily those who had sworn to go to the Holy Land, but even worse when money raised for Jerusalem was used to support the Angevin interest in Italy without the consent of the donors. What these polemists forgot was that the popes, including Boniface VIII, all wanted to resume the crusade, but thought that Hohenstaufen-Ghibelline ideology had first to be eradicated in order to stop Europe's internecine wars. Besides, rigorists like Peter Cantor had always argued that the old Adam of man's sinfulness could not be eradicated by conquering others, but only by a purification—forceful or not—of one's own soul and society.

Related to this idea was the fact that the failure to defeat Islam encouraged an always latent and often expressed belief that corruption and sin impeded Christian leadership. Doubts about the leadership of Latin society made some believe that, to succeed, the holy cause must be entrusted to the just, 'the poor', or the poor in spirit. Already evident in the First Crusade, this idea eventually assumed all sorts of forms. One of these was the Children's Crusade of 1212. Probably designed initially to stir adolescent faith, popular preaching from Vendôme on the Loire to towns on the upper Rhine evoked a curious youth movement and march toward Jerusalem. Greeted by Innocent III and others

[31] *Inferno* 27, 85.

as praiseworthy, in that fervid youth was shaming the cold indifference of age, the movement petered out with several thousands of displaced youths, and charges that usurious merchants
or Jews had sold them into Muslim slavery.

Not dissimilar ideas about the force of innocence were expressed by the Pastoureaux, who rose to crusade for Louis IX
during his captivity in Egypt in 1251. Initially encouraged by the
authorities, including the Queen Mother, the Holy Innocents of
this movement were no longer 'little children', but rather 'the
poor'. As could be expected, the Pastoureaux largely remained at
home, roughing up townsmen, the well-to-do and the Jews.
Movements of this type had been known in the west before 1251.
One similar in its social overtones was that of the Capuciati of Puy
in 1182. Also encouraged at first by the pope and other authorities, the Capuciati were organized to defend the peace threatened
by the bands of soldiers left unemployed when fighting ended
between the Capetians and Plantagenets. Like the Pastoureaux, the
Capuciati went too far, became rebellious or revolutionary and
were suppressed. A difference between the two movements, however, is well worth underlining. The Capuciati mobilized to
restore the *pax dei*, that necessary counterpart of the crusade:
God's peace at home, God's war abroad. The Pastoureaux and
their many successors who merged into the peasant and artisan
revolutionaries of the fourteenth century were different. They
were interested in God's war at home.

Finding scapegoats for western defeat was no monopoly of the
poor. All society played that game. Blaming the fall of Acre on the
misbehaviour of its defenders was a case in point. The accusa-
tions were principally directed against the Templars. Their order
was the object of popular dislike for a variety of reasons. Their
houses served as treasuries for kings, for example, whereas their
rivals, the Hospitallers, preserved themselves from unpopularity
by running public hospitals. The principal reason the Templars
were chosen for obloquy, however, was that, being the earliest
and the largest of the military orders, they were the very symbol
of Christendom's defeat. They were blamed for the fact that most
of their members were to be found at home, not at the front—
something they had in common with any self-supporting military
organization. In France the prestige of the order had been falling
consistently, as is reflected in the fact that the monarchy, from

1287 onward, at first limited its right to acquire property and then began to attack it. In the persecution that started in 1306 and resulted in the abolition of the order in 1312 and the execution of the grand master and his associates in 1314, the full extent of western escapism was disclosed. Like other groups attacked by religious passion in this period, the knights were charged with every possible crime: heresy, materialism, sorcery, and sodomy with both man and beast.

The abolition of the Templars was the first important and successful attack since antiquity on an order of the regular clergy by lay power. Moreover, it coincided with the beginning of the Avignonese 'captivity' of the Roman pontiffs in 1309. Part of what was happening was that, under the stress of failure, secular princes found popular support for taking over the command of the crusades from the popes. As the head of what appeared to be Europe's greatest power and as the heir of Louis IX, canonized in 1297, the king of France thought of himself as the natural leader of the west. The councillors of King Philip IV of France believed that the military orders should be united and that, on becoming grand master of the single new order, Philip himself should assume the crown of Jerusalem and lead a united Europe in a great crusade. Moved by this idea (and by others that we shall see), it is not surprising that the French came to believe that the interests of France were identical not only with those of the Holy Land but also with those of the Christian faith. The secular notion that the nation is the Holy Land was in the process of being born.

III

Latin, Muslims, Greeks and Jews

Missions

Even if the crusades were failing, Latin Christians were not entirely deprived of hope of gaining the day. Opposition to the crusade had always existed among those who believed that the problem of the Christian lay within his own soul and not in the souls of others. Some had always held that religion and secular government were so far separated that infidels or pagans enjoyed natural rights and even that pagan civil dominion over Christians was justifiable. Lastly, a belief that religion was a voluntary affair not to be imposed by force had always persisted in the minds of churchmen. Partly because of the failure of the crusades, all these themes were reinvigorated during the thirteenth century. According to the chronicler Salimbene, Franciscan enthusiasts predicted the failure of Louis IX's crusade and were happy when

BIBLIOGRAPHY. For several topics treated in this chapter, the reader is referred to the bibliography of the previous chapter. The standard general history of the Jews is that of S. W. Baron, *A Social and Religious History of the Jews*, vols. III to XII inclusive (New York, 1957–67). An interesting debate over the nature and origin of English anti-Judaic legislation in this period is to be seen in H. G. Richardson, *English Jewry under the Angevin Kings* (London, 1960) and the comments on this work by G. I. Langmuir, 'The Jews and the archives of Angevin England: Reflections on Medieval Anti-semitism', *Traditio* XIX (1963), 183–244. The legal history of the Jews is perhaps best seen in J. E. Scherer, *Die Rechtsverhältnisse der Juden in den deutsch-österreichischen Ländern* (Leipzig, 1901) when balanced by the information given by Vittore Colorni, *Gli Ebrei nei sistema del diritto comune fino alla prima emancipazione* (Milan, 1956) and Guido Kisch, *The Jews in Medieval Germany* (Chicago, 1949). See also such specially excellent studies as R. W. Emery, *The Jews of Perpignan in the Thirteenth Century : an economic study* (New York, 1959), G. G. Scholem, *Major Trends in Jewish Mysticism* (3rd edn., New York, 1954), and Joshua Trachtenberg, *The Devil and the Jews : the medieval conception of the Jew and its relation to modern antisemitism* (New Haven, 1943). Moritz Güdemann's *Geschichte des Erziehungswesens und der Cultur der abendländischen Juden während des Mittelalters und der Neueren Zeit*, 2 vols. (Vienna, 1880–84) is still both indispensable and charming in spite of more recent work.

their prophecy was fulfilled in the disaster of Damietta in 1249. Roger Bacon argued that the moment the Church supported a crusade it became involved in secular wars. As proof, he pointed to the French crusade against Catalonia-Aragon. Besides, he said, crusades simply do not work. Even when the Christians are victorious over the unbelievers, they do not have enough troops to hold the conquered area. War is self-defeating: infidels and pagans 'are not converted by war, but instead are slain and sent to hell'. And

> Christian princes who labour for [the unbelievers'] conversion, especially the Teutonic Knights, really wish to reduce them to slavery, as Dominicans, Franciscans and other reliable men throughout Germany and Poland have clearly ascertained. And therefore the pagans defend themselves, not because they have a better religion, but simply because they are resisting violence.[1]

These and similar ideas encouraged a new emphasis on missions directed not only toward Islam but also toward other Christian sects and the Jews. Setting the style for the mendicant orders, Francis of Assisi preached to the Egyptians in 1219. The missionary type was often fantastically energetic. After his conversion to religion in 1265, the Majorcan nobleman and mystic Raymond Lull lectured all over Europe to interest the authorities in missions and in the language studies to make them possible. He attended the council at Vienne in 1311 when the universities of Oxford, Paris, Bologna and Salamanca were directed to teach Greek, Hebrew, Arabic and Syrian. He visited Armenia and Cyprus and voyaged frequently to North Africa, where he was slain by the Muslims at Bougie in 1315. Nor was Lull ahead of his time. The founding of sees and of mendicant houses throughout the Near East has already been mentioned. The third general of the Dominicans, Raymond of Peñafort, urged Thomas Aquinas to write his *Summa contra gentiles* in 1261/64 for use in missions and requested the kings of Aragon and Castile to finance schools for teaching Arabic. His efforts echoed the decision of the general chapter of the Preachers in 1250 that Dominican *studia* should teach Arabic, Hebrew and Greek. Careers were built around the new missionary techniques. The Dominican Raymond Martin

---

[1] *Opus maius* 3, 3, 13 and 4, 2, 1, ed. J. H. Bridges (Oxford and London, 1897–1900), II, 121 and 200.

was employed in Aragon investigating Jewish texts in 1264. In that year and again in 1269 he preached against Islam in Murcia and Tunis. In 1281 he had retired as lector in Hebrew at his order's school in Barcelona. Missionary organizations were formed. The Preachers created a Society of Missions for Christ in 1312 which, together with the United Brethren, a group of one-time Greek Basilians following the Dominican rule, ran Catholic missions in Persia and Armenia in the early fourteenth century.

During the thirteenth century, then, missions replaced the crusade in the emotions of many Latin Christians. Older patterns of behaviour persisted, however—even forced conversion. The treatment of the pagans on Germany's eastern frontier, for example, recalls not only the early days of the crusade in Spain and the Holy Land but even Charlemagne's conquest of the Saxons. According to the *Chronicle of Livonia* of 1227, the Germans there summoned a village with the words: 'If you want peace, renounce idolatry, and receive the true peace, which is Christ, in your fort', and the pagan defenders of another village replied: 'We know your God to be greater than ours, who has forced our minds to worship him by conquering us. Whence we beg that, sparing us, you mercifully impose on us . . . the yoke of Christianity.'[2]

If such candour was both condemned and infrequent, church-men could rarely refrain from twisting the arms of those they wished to bring into the *via veritatis*. The relationship of Rome and the eastern Churches illustrates this. During the missionary age hopes for the reunion of Christendom were very much in the air. Part of the Armenian Church joined Rome in 1198. During the late twelfth century Roman influence rose in Bulgaria, cul-minating in a momentary unification of the Bulgar Church with the Roman in 1204. Greatest achievement of all, Constantinople united with Rome at the second council of Lyons in 1274.

Given the strength of this movement and its obvious advantages for the war with Islam, one wonders why it failed. So unpopular among the Greeks was the union with Rome that it lasted for only eight years. Part of the reason for this failure was the memory of what had happened to the Greek clergy when ruled by the Latins. At the conquest of Constantinople in 1204 Thomas Morosini was installed in place of the Greek patriarch of that city and, importing

[2] *MGH. SS. in usum scholarum*, 48 and 80.

Venetian canons, planned to replace all the Greek bishops with Italians. Although appalled by Morosini's plan, Innocent III forced the Greek bishops to subscribe to Latin beliefs—so vigorously that soon only one remained in his see—and actively fostered the settlement in this region of the missionary monastic, especially Cistercian, and mendicant orders of his own Church. Even harder was the fate of the Greek Church in Cyprus after the Lusignan dynasty was established in 1192. By 1220 the Greek clergy were obliged to take an oath of obedience to the Roman Church. Two years later the four Greek prelates of the island were told to remove their sees from the towns into the countryside. A violent attack by the Latins in the 'fifties led to papal 'arbitration' in 1260. The pope settled the question by abolishing the Greek metropolitanate, entrusted its functions as head of the island church to the Latin archbishop of Nicosia, and assigned the clerical tithe wholly to the Latins!

Nor can one expect the relations between religions or sects to have been otherwise. Latin Christianity had increasingly become the basis of western man's definition of citizenship during the Gregorian and crusading ages, and it was difficult for him to view other religions or sects dispassionately. It is true that there was some practical tolerance. Peter Cantor proposed that it was better to give charity to an indigent pagan or Jew than to a Christian who could get along. His was a religious motive. Nor should the effect of simple unbelief or indifference towards religion in many on either side of Christendom's frontiers be underestimated. The Latins living in the Holy Land or Spain tended to be more understanding than those at home. And gentility was almost as much prized by gentlefolk as was religion. Saladin was something of a hero to western chivalry, and Dante reserves a pleasant place for him in hell. In Wolfram of Eschenbach's popular romance Parzifal, the heathen Feirefiz fully equals the Christian hero on the battlefield and in good manners. Besides, they happen to be relatives. The scholars' assessment of religions often put the Muslims fairly high up, below the Jews but above idolators and pagans. Peter Cantor even praised them because they adored one god, so hated idolatry that they had no images in their 'temples', and made no sacrifices there but only prayed. But his was an especially rigorist voice in the Latin Church.

On the other hand, the Christians' understanding and tolerance of Islam was not deep. Examining the Trinity, the Muslims claimed that Christians were polytheist. In turn, many Christians —including distinguished lawyers such as Innocent IV (d. 1254) and Hostiensis—found their best defence against this charge to be an assertion that Islam was naught but idolatry and polytheism. As Dante reminds us, a shrewd guess had long ago told Christians that Islam derived from Judaism and Christianity, but this only made it worse, as being a heresy. The celebrated collector of saints' lives, James of Voragine, archbishop of Genoa, tells that a Jacobite archdeacon or a Nestorian monk converted Mohammed from his idolatry into Christian heresy. Gerald of Wales explained why Muslims eschewed pork: the fellows were simply judaizing. To this prohibition was added that of wine because Mohammed, when 'drunk, since he had preached filth and smut, fell one night in the street and was bitten by pigs, which are considered dirty beasts'.[3] Of course, many praised Muslims for their relative sobriety. Peter Cantor remarked that Saladin considered the drunken Christians unworthy to live on earth.

With few exceptions, also, the relationship between Christians and Muslims was hostile. Captured in war, Muslims could be enslaved. Describing the capture of Damietta in 1220, one of James of Vitry's letters records what happened to the prisoners. Four hundred of the wealthiest were kept to exchange for captured Christians. Too numerous to keep, the rest were sold as slaves, only the children being retained at great expense by the good bishop to be converted to the true faith. A German formulary book for letter writers dated around 1302 contains the following model for a salutation:

> Eugene bishop etc. to a king or sultan of the Saracens. We do not greet you, not because we do not wish your health, but because you do not believe in the true health, that of Christ Jesus crucified for the salvation of humankind, and because you do not cease to injure those who profess the Christian name.[4]

The fact that cultural allegiance or citizenship was defined by the faith in the crusade era weakened what may be described as the implicit tolerance of secular monarchy. Conqueror of Toledo

[3] *De principis instructione* I, 17 in *Rolls Series* LXXXI, viii, 68.
[4] Baumgartenberg, *Formularius de modo prosandi, BuF* II, 731. The pope in the letter is Eugene III (1145–53).

in 1085, Alphonso VI of Castile found it useful to be described as emperor of the two religions (Islam and Christianity) when addressing Muslims, and a successor, Ferdinand III (1217–52), had four languages inscribed on his tomb: Arabic, Castilian, Hebrew, and Latin. Old laws like the *Usatges* of Barcelona contained clauses wherein the prince promised to maintain the law loyally for all citizens: Christian, Saracen, Jew and 'heretic' (those, one guesses, who still adhered to the Mozarabic rite). All these titles and laws derived from periods when the Christians were invading Muslim territories, when alliances and revolts of the Muslim and Jewish populations were of much use to Christian wouldbe conquerors. But there was more. 'Divide and rule' is good counsel for a monarch, and national-religious minorities often provided useful and loyal officers and troops. Alphonso VIII of Castile (1158–1214) was criticized by his Christian subjects and by Innocent III for using Muslims as officers and granting them church tithes. Similar censure fell on Andrew II of Hungary for using the Ismaelites (Asiatic Muslims settling in Hungary) in order to dampen the opposition of his feudal magnates, and were repeated against most of his successors of the Arpad dynasty. The Sicilian Muslims who were settled in the military colony of Lucera on the mainland by Frederick II Hohenstaufen are another famous example.

In spite of princely resistance, legislation barring Muslims from public office, prohibiting them from owning Christian slaves or domestics, against publicity for their cult, and against social intercourse with Christians slowly spread from the late twelfth century, inspired by laws issued by the popes in Rome. By the early fourteenth century the same types of legal impediments were imposed on the 'schismatic' Greeks in Sicily by the Catalan Frederick III. The attitudes behind this law even affected the tone of courtly literature in these regions. Alphonso X of Castile's poetry and even his famous code, the *Siete partidas*, were remarkably intolerant, compared to the older tradition of Spanish letters.

In fine, like the Greeks, the Muslims who lived under Latin rule could not have viewed the missionary efforts of the Latin clergy as other than an aspect of the social persecution to which they were increasingly subjected. And their religious brethren beyond the frontiers of the west must have been alerted to what their fate would be were they to submit to Latin domination. This is significant because, in the past, the Muslims had often been tempted to call in the Latins to help them solve their own internecine squabbles. By 1300, however, they had learned better— for a time.

Jews in Latin Europe

The law dealing with Muslims under Christian rule was a medieval adaptation of late Roman and Visigothic legislation on the Jews. The history of this people—the foreigners residing at home, as it were—will illustrate the failure of the Latin missionary movement and the relationship of this failure to the intense social pressures engendered in western society by 1300.

In numbers and cultural wealth, western European Jewry reached its peak in the later twelfth century and early thirteenth. Although there had been serious attacks on Jews residing in the Rhineland and adjacent regions during the early crusades and almost equally severe assaults in Muslim Spain in the first half of the twelfth century, these crises were successfully weathered. Both in the north and in the Mediterranean, Europe's Jews flourished as never before until the grim years of the later thirteenth century and early fourteenth initiated a new and much more lasting period of persecution and impoverishment. Obviously, the greater centres of Jewish life were to be found outside of the Latin west in the area of Arabic culture. This was beginning to change, partly because the Latins conquered Sicily and the larger part of Spain, and partly because the power of Arabic culture was fading in comparison with that of the Latins. In spite of this, a rich effluvium from this multinational and multireligious culture still emanated northward to Europe's Jews.

Not that northern Jewry, especially that of France and the Rhineland, was insignificant. From Carolingian days the Jews there had the memory of being richer and more learned than the relatively barbarous peoples with whom they lived. As intermediaries between Islam and Christendom they had helped transmit the teachings of a richer southern culture to these northerly regions. Although this wealth was fading, and although northern Jewry was itself becoming somewhat parochial in comparison to the Latins, the memory of past greatness lingered. Furthermore, the fact that Jews, however retarded by the vicissitudes

81

visited upon them by their Christian neighbours, were largely townsmen and therefore more literate than most of their Christian neighbours fortified their sense of cultural superiority. The northern Jews were also very influential, even in Spanish Jewish circles. They had devised a way of living with the Latins that the Jews once under Islamic rule could now use. They had adopted Jewish *mores* to the norms of Latin Christian life. An early example was the abrogation of polygyny by the celebrated ruling of Gershom of Mainz (d. 1028), a ruling echoing the earlier ban on polygyny for citizens under Roman law. They were also peculiarly rigid in their insistence on religious practices and law. One senses that this love of the letter of the law has to do with the fact that the Jews were the only group permitted to hold a faith other than Christian in the whole of the Latin west, except a few peripheral and recently acquired regions. Although far more numerous under Islam, Jews were not so unique in the multinational and multireligious area of Arabic culture.

Most historians seem agreed that Mediterranean Jewry enjoyed an ampler and deeper culture than that of the north. From the south—one thinks of Maimonides, an Andalusian who mostly lived in Cairo in Egypt—came the Aristotelian naturalism that influenced the rest of Jewry. It is to be noted that the rabbis of France and Germany did little more than condemn this way of thinking at the very moment Latin thinkers were tumbling over themselves in their eagerness to read and use it. In Italy, Languedoc and Spain, things were different, although there were ideological battles there too. The history of natural philosophy was paralleled in the practical art of medicine. Whereas there are only rare references in the north to Jewish surgeons, and Jews themselves are known to have consulted Christian doctors, the same was not true in the south. Jewish medicine had long been famous in Spain and was known around Montpellier in Languedoc. The Hohenstaufen and Angevin dynasts of southern Italy and the popes of the late thirteenth century regularly employed Jewish doctors.

Ahead in natural philosophy and science, Mediterranean Jews also seem superior in messianism and mystical thought. Although Eleazar Rokeah (E. ben Jehudah, d. 1223-32) of Worms produced an encyclopedia of quietist ethics, *mores*, messianic numerology, folklore and superstition called the *Book of the Devout* (*Sefer*

Hasidim), it is known that the author was one of a succession of notable rabbis of the originally Italian family of the Kalonymides active in Speyer, Mainz and Worms. Besides, if German or Ashkenazic Jewry could vaunt its Hasidic mysteries, Spanish or Sephardic rabbis, together with those of Languedoc, led in the not dissimilar tradition of the Kabbalah. The author of the *Zohar*, Moses (ben Shemtob, d. 1305) of Leon, was an inhabitant of Guadalajara, and, although he voyaged all over the Mediterranean from Syria to Italy, the Yoga, prophet and messianist Abraham (ben Samuel, d. after 1291) Abulafia was raised in Saragossa and Tudela. The name of Abulafia also recalls the different quality of the messianic and prophetical traditions in north and south. Although there was much speculation in the north about the date on which the Messiah would come, the general tendency was to put it off to the remote future. In the area of Arabic culture or adjacent to it, the messianists were more confident and, in spite of the hostile attention they elicited from Muslim or Christian governments, sometimes swept whole communities. Inclined toward prophetical messianism, for example, Abulafia determined to plead the case of Jewry before the pope in 1280. He was probably inspired by a belief common among the Jews and expressed by the Kabbalist Nahmanides (Moses ben Nahman or Rambam) of Barcelona and Gerona in his debate with Paul Christiani, a Dominican convert or apostate from Judaism, in 1263: 'When the end of time will come, the Messiah will go to the pope at God's command and ask him to liberate his people.'[5]

If their radicals were bolder, the southern Jews were also more open to foreign and secular influences than northern. This is not to say that northern Jewry was hermetically sealed off from the world around it. There was a Jewish minnesinger, Süsskind of Trimberg. No sooner had Walter of Metz finished his verse encyclopedia called *Ymage du monde* in 1245 than it was translated into Hebrew by the Londoner Chaim ben Deulecret or Deulecresse, and it is suspected that the Neoplatonic mystic naturalism of John Scotus Erigena influenced the Hasidim. On the whole, however, Mediterranean Jewry was more open and much franker about it. There, a secular and erotic love poetry flourished among the Jews just as it did among the Muslims, and,

---

[5] Cited in Scholem, *Jewish Mysticism*, 128.

just as did Muslim poetry, probably influenced Christian verse. Writing a book on ethics in 1278 the Roman Jehiel ben Jekutiel cited not only Scripture and the Talmud, but also various pieces of Christian wisdom literature, the philosophers Aristotle and Porphyry, and a saying of Frederick II Hohenstaufen. In the early fourteenth century, Leo Romano (Judah ben Moses, b. 1292), the companion of the Angevin Robert I (1309–43), not only continued the old tradition of translating Arabic treatises, but also prepared a Hebrew version of selections from Augustine, Albertus Magnus, and Aquinas because, as he said, he believed that intelligent Jews were 'of the opinion that truth and real knowledge are going to other peoples, especially to the Christians', and that Jews should therefore have this wisdom available.[6]

Leo's older cousin Immanuel ben Solomon (ben Jekutiel of the Roman Zifroni family, d. 1330) represents another side of southern Jewry. A poet in Hebrew and Italian, a friend of Boso of Gubbio of the circle of Dante and Cino of Pistoia, he wrote a mystical commentary on the Song of Songs and a famous collection of satirical verses on religion, love, and Jewish life called the *Mehabberoth*. His sceptical spirit shows in his Italian works. He is a bad Jew, he tells, no Saracen, and not a Christian. Take the best from each religion: Christian eating and drinking is good, Moses required few fasts, and one can debauch with Mohammed. Love is the only complete lordship, knowing no law, no belief, no mass. In line with this, southern Jewry seems to have been less resistant to conversion. In Toulouse in Languedoc, for example, Pons David, the son of a mint master, usurer, and generous donor to the Hospitallers in his testament of 1208, was related to Jews, and Yspaniol, comital vicar of the town from 1164 to 1176, appears to have derived from a Jewish family. In the north, Jews rarely converted voluntarily. And, although not being aggressively messianic like the southerners, their Hasidic quietism appears to have strengthened their resolve to suffer martyrdom when attacked by Christians.

In spite of these differences, all Jewish communities had many similarities. Every substantial settlement had a school supported by the members of the synagogue (*scola Judaeorum*). From recommendations about class size and about the role of the senior

[6] Cited in Güdemann, *op. cit.*, II, 157.

teacher and his semi-student assistants, Jewish lower schooling, although far older and initially involving all male children, was similar to Christian parish education. Like parish ones, Jewish lower schools were certainly day schools, and most youths left school either at the age of thirteen, the age of religious majority, or at sixteen. What took place thereafter is describable as higher education. Not a few students must have been dropped even before the ages of thirteen and sixteen. Evidence on this is given in the *Hukke ha-Torah*, a tract on education produced in thirteenth century Languedoc. If a pupil proves unsatisfactory, the teacher is to take him to his father and say: 'God may enable your son to do noble things, but, for learning, he's too stupid.'[7] Unlike Christian but like Islamic education, no provision is made for female schooling, although a few girls were trained by their rabbinical fathers.

The course of studies is fairly well known. From the age of five, the student began with languages (the vernacular, Hebrew and Aramaic). Examples were drawn from the Bible, itself the subject of study for the next years. From ten to sixteen, parts of the *Mishnah* were read. Then higher education began, to be spent on the large tractates with material drawn from the whole of the Talmud, that is, both the *Mishnah* and the *Gemara*, and, no doubt, readings in the innumerable commentaries of the medieval rabbis. This period was to last for seven years during which the student lived at school and not at home.

The description of this seven-year period in the *Hukke ha-Torah* has led some to think of a kind of Jewish university, and it seems possible that the idea could have been fathered by seeing a Latin university. The fact that most rabbis came from rabbinical families or married into them, however, shows that Jewish higher education was conducted in the homes of learned rabbis. This form of education was normal in the area of Arabic culture and was also characteristic of the non-celibate professions and ways of life among the Latin Christians, where apprentices (*discipuli*) were sent to live with master artisans or artists, and young gentlemen learned manners, arms, and sometimes letters in the courts of local magnates. Other than the natural tendency of institutions to specialize in a mature society, what made the university so

---

[7] Güdemann, *op. cit.*, I, 96. In Güdemann's translation the phrase is *schwer von Begriff*.

different from Islamic, Jewish, and Latin lay education was ecclesiastical celibacy. In so far as is possible in human society, this practice or ethos freed the life intellectual from bondage to family, and so strong was this clerical impulse that it even affected the secular professions of law and medicine in which most teachers and practitioners were married.

Jewish formal education and learning were essentially limited to sacred Scripture and the Talmud. Philosophy and natural science flourished among the Jews in Arabic culture, of course, but it is to be noted that, like similar attempts in Islam, Maimonides's attempt to graft philosophy on the law, as in his famous code the *Mishneh Torah* (1180), was neither particularly successful nor well received. The situation was different in Latin education where, by 1300, every university student had had formal instruction in natural philosophy. Another measure of this difference is to be seen in the fact that northern European rabbis did not much read Maimonides's *Guide for the Perplexed* (1190), but Thomas Aquinas wrestled with it constantly, and the Dominican Neoplatonist Master Eckhart (d. before 1329) swore by it. In Jewish education, then, everything centred on the law and the observances, and the dominant tone of rabbinical literature was therefore analogous to that of Latin legal writing. Abraham of Posquières (ben David or Rabad, fl. 1150s–70s) not far from Montpellier wrote commentaries—extended glosses, really, analogous to what the Latins called *scholia*—on five of the tractates of the *Mishnah*, on twenty-four from the Talmud, and pioneered in commenting on the legal side of the Midrashim exegesis of the Scriptures. He also criticized and commented on Maimonides's *Mishneh Torah* and on the works of other authorities. Lastly, he published his *responsa* on particular questions about the law.

Abraham's interests seem narrow until it is remembered that an immense work like the Talmud contained not only law and religious observances, but also a host of observations on, and examples of, ethics, *mores*, magic, prophecy, indeed all sorts of subjects. The unification of such a mass of heterogeneous material into a number of texts like the Talmud fitted Near Eastern and Arabic Mediterranean culture, where society was divided into national-religious castes, and was of obvious use to the Jews as a minority under the Latins. This urge toward unification contrasted sharply with the Latin bent in the opposite direction.

Although, as we shall see, there was a real attempt to unify all knowledge into one grand Christian scheme, a unified *corpus* of tradition and law never really emerged. This is probably because, among the Latins, a religious definition did not sufficiently define a nation or a people. There were several nations under the aegis of Latin Christianity, and, within each of these, the separation and even mutual hostility of Church and state encouraged a sense of institutional autonomy. In line with this, when maturity and wealth made it possible to develop specialization, the different disciplines—theology and law, for example, or theology and philosophy—tended to produce specialized institutions such as university faculties, and to become autonomous intellectual specializations.

Another characteristic of all Jewish communities was the possession of a limited right of autonomy or self-government. This meant that civil litigation between Jews was settled by Jewish judges, the *dayanim*. Civil cases between Jews and Christians usually went to the defendant's court, although as in England and France, there were often arbitrative tribunals in that the prince's presiding officer appointed a panel composed half of Jews and half of Christians. Criminal cases, especially those involving the shedding of blood in commission or punishment, usually came before the ordinary courts, as was proposed by most Italian town statutes and by John of England's legislation of 1201. This meant an invasion by Christian police and judges of the Jewish community even in the case of adultery between two members of the community—a crime hard to prove but profitable because involving confiscation of property—as in the law granted the Jewry of Cologne in 1252.

The institutions of self-government among the Jews were similar to those of Latin guilds and small communities. Given the importance of the learned and the wealthy, there was a natural tendency toward government by elders, and the judges and community councillors frequently chose their own successors. There was nothing rigid about this, however, and, in theory, the people—that is, the adult male members of the *scola Judaeorum*—chose their rulers. Writing to the Jewish community in Saragossa in 1264, Solomon ben Adret (Rashba) of Barcelona remarked about the canonical number of seven councillors that a community is not legally obliged to choose the wise or the rich. Any good man will do. He further stated that constitutional form varied. There are

> places where affairs are entirely run by the advice of the elders
> and councillors, others where the majority [of such councillors
> and elders] can do nothing without consulting all the people
> and obtaining their consent, and still others where individuals
> are given the authority to do as they see fit in all general
> affairs.[8]

One function of such councillors was to raise the taxes required by government. Here too practices differed because of the differing relationships of large Jewish communities to small satellite ones in nearby villages and small towns. Answering a question posed by the Jews of Montpellier, Rashba remarked that the senior community sometimes dominated, but that elsewhere, as at Tarragona, Villafranca and Montblanch, the larger centre was obliged to consult the lesser ones on the repartition of taxes.

According to jurists trained in Roman law, Jews were Roman citizens. They therefore profited from the protections afforded to citizens and bore the burdens of citizenship, but, as an inheritance from the days of the Christian Empire and Visigothic Spain, were prohibited from holding public office and from owning real property. Except under Islam, individual Jews were rarely permitted to own land, that is, to have *ius dominii* over it. Just as they were permitted to lend money, they were allowed to hold land pledged to them for debts, and were often granted by a magistrate the *ius utile* or right to use or rent land. Thus in 1239 Frederick II Hohenstaufen granted the Jews from the island of Gerbi settling in Palermo a portion of the royal date groves—whoever heard of an Arabic-speaking towndweller without a date-palm?—and the right to rent lots for houses with leases of from five to ten years. Unlike these Africans who had been encouraged to settle in Sicily in order to help introduce the cultivation of indigo and henna, Jews under Latin government were never—save in Spain or Italy— permitted to become farmers or landlords. On the other hand, being townsmen, they were often allowed to lease vineyards, dairies and other facilities for domestic consumption and ritual needs.

Roman citizens they were, but they were citizens of an empire that did not exist and, for reasons to be surveyed later, the sense of

[8] Haim Beinart, 'Hispano-Jewish Society'. *Cahiers d'histoire mondiale* XI (1968), 227.

peculiar liberty that this term conveyed in medieval literature was not extended to them. What was emphasized was their service or servitude to Christian princes and magistrates. And lesser princes had succeeded the emperors. In England, Sicily and Spain's kingdoms Jews were the possessions—*servi nostrae camerae speciales* as they were called in Sicily, chattels as in England—of the kings, who jealously guarded their monopoly. The mid-twelfth century *Laws of Edward the Confessor*—a fictional title—tell us that 'all Jews, wherever they are in the kingdom, must be under the guardianship and protection of the king; nor may any of them be subject to any richman [baron] without the licence of the king, because Jews and all their property are the king's.'[9] In such strong and relatively centralized monarchies, the prince often appointed the heads of the Jewish communities—as Frederick II acceded to the request of the Palermitan Jews of Gerbi and ordered his governor to appoint an Elder from among them—or even appointed a head of the national Jewry like the *episcopus Judaeorum* in England. This officer was sometimes aided by an elected national synod. An example is a royal order to England's Jews to choose six delegates from each large community and two from each small one to meet at the Worcester parliament in 1241 in order to negotiate the subsidy owed the king.

In countries where political power was decentralized, the Jews came under local authorities. In France, for example, the Capetian effort to monopolize the Jews was only partially successful by the end of the thirteenth century. The typical older pattern may be seen in a series of royal treaties from 1198 to 1210 with the counts of Champagne and those of Saint-Pol and Nevers as well as in the royal legislation of 1230 on the subject. These documents stipulated that no one should lure Jews from another's Jewry, and that Jews who voluntarily moved should be returned by extradition. So powerful were local seigniors that in 1235 a count of Boulogne blandly willed to *his* people the property of *his* Jews in reparation for *his* sins. Small wonder that, writing in the late twelfth century, Isaac ben Samuel of Dampierre referred rather enviously to the fact that 'in the countries around us Jews have had the right to reside wherever they wished, like the nobles'.[10]

The Empire was not quite so decentralized. Although Frederick

---

[9] Felix Liebermann, *Gesetze der Angelsachsen* (Halle, 1901), I, 650.

II gave rights over the Jews in their dominions to the princes, he still issued a general privilege for the Jews in 1236. Until late in the century, also, German Jews rightly insisted that they were not primarily citizens of local communities, but instead of the whole Empire or at least of a substantial principality. A rabbi who had served all over Germany, Meir ben Baruch of Rothenburg ob der Tauber (d. 1293), reported that the Jews 'are not dependent and obliged to pay taxes wherever they happen to be, as the Gentiles are, but they are like freemen who have lost their possessions but have not been sold into bondage'.[10]

Princes wished to profit from 'their' Jews. Forced loans, ransoms (to avoid confiscation of property) and taxes were the principal sources of this profit and, because of their need for money, princes often exploited the Jews excessively or even expelled them and took their property. Hard pressed financially because of the war with the Plantagenets, Philip II Augustus first ransomed his Jews and then drove them out in 1182. This desperate expedient failed because the royal Jews merely migrated to France's greater feudatories and enhanced the revenues of the Capetian's rivals. They were therefore readmitted sixteen years later. In short, Jews were used or abused by princes according to need. Matthew Paris's wisecrack about the pledging of the Jews by Henry III of England to his brother Richard of Cornwall in 1255—to the effect that those whom the king had skinned the count would eviscerate—expresses this side of the relationship.

Predatory though they were, the princes were not those who initiated attacks upon the Jews, although they tried to make sure that, if they took place, they reaped the profits. On the whole, they had little desire to kill the goose that laid the golden egg. And there was more than money in this symbiotic relationship. Jews were useful as officers, especially as tax collectors. And the functions of licensed usury were many. Since Jewish loans were supposed to be registered by public authority, a prince's officers, although often defrauded and as frequently defrauding, roughly knew what the taxation possibilities of a Jewish community were and, for the protection they offered in upholding the sacredness of contracts, drew a percentage of the take into the treasury. Besides, a prince could sometimes buy the loyalty of a recalcitrant magnate

[10] Baron, *op. cit.*, XI, 18–19.

or ecclesiastical institution by cancelling their debts or coerce their obedience by insisting on their payment. Facing a somewhat hostile Christian population, the Jews were therefore loyal to, or dependent on, their princely masters.

Almost every movement against princely or seigniorial power attacked Jews. In England from Magna Carta's clauses in 1215 until the expulsion in 1290, the baronial opposition to the kings fought the Jews. The expulsion from France in 1315 coincided with the gentlemen's league (*liga*) of France and the Champagne against the arbitrary government of the king. What was true of baronial opposition was also true of towns. The movement for town liberty was usually anti-Judaic, and towns often attacked their Jews when they rose against their lords. Otto of Freising tells us that in 1146 Bernard of Clairvaux was called in to silence a wandering monk at Mainz who had a history of stirring up revolts of the people in the cities on the pretext of attacking the privileges of the Jews. The statutes of Arles in 1215 had the Jews elect three consuls—an honourable title in those days—who swore on the Mosaic law when they took office, just as the Christian consuls swore on the Gospels. Faced with the hostility of the Arlesians, later Jews must have looked back on the days when the archbishop-lord promulgated these statutes as the good old days. Once princely or seigniorial power was reduced and the urban aristocracies began to build oligarchies, as we shall see, they made peace with 'their' Jews. It was then the turn of the people. As the plebs rose to gain a measure of political power around 1300, the worst trials of medieval Jewry began. Rural gentlefolk and town patricians then often professed shock at the depth of anti-Judaic feeling among the farmers and artisans.

Accompanying this evolution of political and social power was a kind of economic expropriation. Even in the expanding economy of the twelfth century, Christian merchants replaced Jews in commerce except in the Arabic Mediterranean and along Europe's eastern frontiers. Paced from of old by maritime Venice, Italy's northern towns led the world in this type of exclusionary legislation. This, combined with the prohibition of the ownership of land, obliged Jews who wished to advance to lend money to Christians. The more developed and mature society became, the more the Jews were pushed into this economic function. The ecclesiastical attack upon Christian usury may have had something to do with this increase. The fourth Lateran Council of 1215 required the restitution by Jews of 'grave and immoderate usuries', explaining the need for this law as follows: 'The more the Christian religion curbs the taking of usury, the more does Jewish perfidy become used to this practice, so much so that, in a short time, the wealth of Christians will be exhausted.'[11] But the picture had long since been clear. Writing in the early twelfth century, Abelard put into the mouth of a Jew the sentiment that Jews cannot escape the hatred of the people. Not being permitted to own land, 'what remains to us is usury, that we sustain our miserable lives by taking interest from strangers, which makes us most hateful to them'.[12]

Usury was not, however, enthusiastically adopted by all Jews. Although it sometimes occurred, it was forbidden among the brethren, that is, among Jews. Moreover, the Jews' right to collect usury from Christians was actively debated. Although usually permitted in Christian law, many, including Thomas Aquinas, asserted that it had no colour of moral or legal right. When asked why Jews, since they had no other way of making a living, should be punished by having to make restitution for their usuries, Aquinas said that they could not be allowed to profit from their crime. Not in the position to do otherwise, the Jews tended to justify taking usury from Christians. Around 1204 Moses of Paris (ben Jehiel ben Mattathiah) permitted it on the grounds that the brotherhood of the Jews with Christians had been sundered, but Joseph the Zealot (ben Nathan Official) of Sens straightway dismissed this opinion as without merit. The great Maimonides permitted usury, but only in the way that some Christians allowed usury to be taken from Muslims—in order to defeat the enemies of the faith. In 1246 Meier ben Simon of Narbonne appears to have adopted what we shall see to be the familiar Christian expedient of trying to pass usury off as interest.

There is no doubt that Jews had largely become usurers in much of western Europe. Notarial registers from late-thirteenth-century Perpignan in Roussillon record a total of fourteen acts showing Jews active in commerce and local trade whereas 1,643 transactions record loans to Christians. Of the 220 Jewish adults mentioned in these acts, at least eighty per cent were money-

[11] *Liber extra* 5, 19, 18 in *CICan.* II, 816.
[12] *Dialogus inter philosophum, Judaeum et Christianum* in *PL* CLXXVIII, 1618.

lenders, and, of those mentioned twice, ninety-three per cent were in the business. But the evidence from Perpignan also corrects a traditional misapprehension about the function of usury in this period, namely that it was always what we today call consumer credit. Economically speaking, Perpignan was a new town in the second half of the thirteenth century, and most of the loans made by the Jews there were not consumer loans. The Jews' debtors were those who directed growing and successful business enterprise. Several conclusions may be drawn from this. One is that Jews were wanted in growing but relatively underdeveloped areas. The Jews accompanied the Germans in their drive toward the east and were genuinely welcome there. Once a region was built up, however, a different cycle began in which Christians replaced Jews in the 'big money' business, as we shall see the Lombards did in France and England. In this circumstance, Jews were limited to humble trades and to petty usury or pawnbroking which, although profitable and economically necessary, evoked much bad feeling on the part of the people. Roussillon is an example of this. While numerous suits against Jewish usurers were brought into ecclesiastical courts from about 1261 on, the Catalan monarchs stoutly protected the right of the Jews to lend at interest and to collect their debts. In the early fourteenth century the monarchy's secular courts began what eventually grew into a systematic economic persecution of the Jewish community, leaving it reduced and impoverished in the fifteenth century.

The pages above and those that follow may leave the impression that the only enemies of the Jews or of the Muslims within Christendom were the people and the churchmen. This was partly so. Churchmen were the ideologues of medieval society, and it is not surprising that they voiced the passions of western man. In the long run it was the people, the humble many, who paid the debts and suffered the full intensity of economic pressures, and anti-Judaism therefore appeared in virulent form each time they reached for a measure of power. Reversing the expulsion of 1306, the French Crown readmitted the Jews in 1315 and made a vigorous effort to protect them. Like so many of the French monarchy's fiscal policies, this one failed before the opposition of France's urban and rural aristocracies. But what impelled these was the vast popular movement of the Pastoureaux of 1319 through the early 1320s that, beginning in Languedoc, swept the whole of France. Shouting their utopian slogans, these mobs of deracinated workers, farmers and others, massacred Jews, lepers, and a few aged in the hospitals before turning against their rulers and towards inevitable repression. Such was the backdrop for the royal expulsion of the Jews in 1322.

But there is more to this history. The torment of the Jews had much to do with the growth of the centralized state in this period and of the monarchical institutions that accompanied it, a fact suggested by their early expulsion from England and northern France. As these regions sought to become nations, so to speak, they expelled their Jews. Moreover, a desperate need of princes for money made them squeeze their Jews hard at this time. As shall be seen, their lack of money was caused by the resistance to princely power of the aristocracies that mobilized their strength to refuse the needed subsidies. Even had he no wish to expel his Jews or impoverish his Muslims, the prince had little choice but to profit from this expulsion or impoverishment. And men often take pleasure in doing what they cannot help but do.

The ambivalence of Latin princes towards the Jews is therefore worth examining, as are the pressures to which they were exposed. The exponents of Christian brotherhood and of economic and social utopias had harsh words for princes who tolerated Jews and profited from their usuries. Of course, rigorists such as Peter Cantor were even more hostile to Christian usurers licensed by princes. Such fellows are rightly called Jews, he said, 'because the princes who protect them do not permit them to be charged with any crime, saying "These are our Jews." But they are worse than Jews' because the Jew is permitted by Deuteronomy 23:19, to take usury from a foreigner, but not from a co-religionist, which is what Christian usurers do.[13]

But perhaps there were ways to solve this quandary. Always moderate although not always kind, Aquinas held that Jews were obliged to restore usuries to specific persons whose claims could be proved (*certae personae*), and that, if a prince lost revenue because of this, he had only himself to blame. 'For it would be better for princes to compel the Jews to earn their living by working, as they do in Italy, rather than allow them to live idly being

---

[13] *Verbum abbreviatum* 50 in *PL* CCV, 158.

enriched by usury alone.'[14] But the Dominican was exaggerating the possibility: in southern Italy, especially Sicily, Jews were often artisans and even farmers, but that was very rarely true in northern Italy, and then only in the least favoured occupations. Besides, Aquinas's was not a new idea: the western utopian tradition had long since argued for it. James of Vitry disguised this programme as a description of the difference between the Saracens and Latins:

> The Saracens among whom they live, hold them in greater hatred and contempt than do the Christians. For while the detestable avarice of Christian princes supports them because of material profit, permits them to have Christian servants, and allows them to despoil their Christian subjects by immoderate usuries, they are permitted to live among the Saracens only when they work with their hands at the most abject and vile professions, are servants and slaves of the pagans, and generally live in the lowest possible conditions.[15]

Being men of their time and pressed hard by their society's most popular spokesmen, few princes publicly defended their relationship with the Jews. What they did was to argue that imperfect things necessarily exist in this imperfect world, or claim, as did Otto III, duke of Burgundy, in 1205, that papal law against the employment of Jews in public office was an invasion of the secular sphere. But when, as they sometimes did, they went over to the popular ideal, it was a bad day for the Jews. Writing a biography to forward the canonization of Louis IX of France, the dead king's chaplain, William of Chartres, described his sainted prince:

> As hateful to God and man, Jews he so detested that he could not even see them, nor did he wish to turn any of their property to his own use, saying that he did not wish to keep their poison, and that he did not want them to exercise usury, but instead to gain their livelihood in licit professions or commerce. . . . When many of his councillors tried to persuade him to the contrary, asserting that the people could not live without loans, or cultivate the land or exercise professions or commerce, and that it was better that the Jews, who were already damned,

[14] *De regimine iudaeorum ad ducissam Brabantiae* 2 in R. M. Spiazzi, *Opuscula philosophica* (Turin, 1954), 250a.
[15] *Historia orientalis* 82 in Douai 1596, 160.

should perform this damnable function than Christians who would, for this very reason, oppress the people with even heavier usuries, he answered this as a Catholic man, saying, 'Concerning the Christians and their usuries, that pertains to the prelates of the church. To me pertain those of the Jews, because they are under the yoke of my servitude. . . . Let the Jews give up usury or leave my land.'[16]

And Louis was probably the most popular of all medieval kings.

Although there is evidence that Christian and Jew often lived happily together in Latin Europe, Abelard's Jew had long since rightly complained that 'we are thought worthy of such contempt and hate by all that whoever injures us in any way believes that action to be the highest justice and the greatest sacrifice to his God'. After sleepless nights, each day the Jew rises and goes fearfully among his enemies. Even the princes 'who rule us and from whom we buy protection at such cost desire our deaths all the more because it is then more permissible to seize our possessions'.[17]

Jews and the failure of missions

There had always been a polemical literature by Jews against Christians and by Christians against Jews. To judge from such different writers as Abelard and Raymond Lull, even somewhat sympathetic Christians believed that the Jews had been punished for their rejection of the Saviour. God had made them the only people without a prince, everywhere humiliated and oppressed. Having refused the Lord's 'my yoke is easy, and my burden is light' (Matthew 11:30), they were left bearing the burden of the old law, a heavy law, superstitious (taboos on food, menstrual blood, etc.) and materialist (compare circumcision with baptism). Abelard makes his Jew say: 'Everyone who obeys it knows that the precepts of this law are so tangled with difficulties that we are crushed as intolerably by the yoke of our law as by the oppression of other men. Who, for shame and pain, does not abhor or fear to receive this sacrament of our circumcision?'[18]

---

[16] *De vita et actibus . . . Ludovici noni* in Francois Duchesne, *Historiae Francorum scriptores* v (Paris, 1636), 471.
[17] *Dialogus inter philosophum, Judaeum et Christianum* in *PL* CLXXVIII, 1617.
[18] *Ibid.*, 1618.

The view that the Jews had caused their unhappy fate by their obdurate reluctance to accept the Christian dispensation had implicit in it an idea of Jewish character. This was not yet defined in racist terms. Just as in Islam, of course, racial awareness and racist concepts were known in the Latin west. That there was a sense of national characteristics or bents will be shown later. Colour and appearance were also much commented on. Blond, white and blue-eyed are the usual heroes and heroines of medieval literature. It will be recalled that the physical appearance of Negroes was used in the *Song of Roland* to symbolize the last foul attack upon the hero, and that even so ecumenical a fellow as the hopelessly imaginative Marco Polo, who was entranced by Chinese women, described Negroes as being ill-favoured and looking like demons. Naturally, these notions of race were applied to the Jews. Such was the precedence of religious distinctions, however, that, except perhaps in the popular imagination, racial ones were secondary. Caesarius of Heisterbach's book for novices in the Cistercian order several times refers to the Jewish stench (*foetor judaicus*), of which, however, according to him, the body can be washed clean by conversion.

That the Jews hated the Christians was a common Christian suspicion, and that envious malevolence was a mark of the Jewish character had always been thought. These ideas developed new manifestations during and after the Gregorian and crusading periods when Latin Europe's sense of Christian citizenship and cultural definition was strengthened. England, for example, is thought to have invented around 1141 the theme of the Christian boy, the Holy Innocent, murdered by the Jews. So popular was this tale that, in 1181, Abbot Samson of St Edmunds managed to conjure up his own boy martyr. In spite of the condemnation of this libel by popes and princes alike, it continued to flourish. In 1255 England's justiciars said that the murder of Hugh of Lincoln —a pure fabrication—implicated all Jewry. Written for a king of a partially Jewish society whose forebears had been notably tolerant, the *Siete partidas* of Alphonso X of Castile blandly noted that it had been heard said that Jews crucified Christian boys on Good Friday.

Equally important was the fact that, as in the case of the Muslims, the distinction between Jews and Christians became a matter of great interest to legislators and jurists. As shall be seen later, this parallels a movement for a more precise definition of civil and social status among Christians themselves. Leadership in the formulation of this new law was taken by the Church that borrowed it from Late Roman and Visigothic legislation. Although the first laws derived from the Gregorian age, the most active pontificates were those of Alexander III and Innocent III, especially at the fourth Lateran Council of 1215.

The intention of the legislators was mixed. It was in part protective. The Jews' right to keep their faith and property was early asserted by Calixtus II (1119–24) and repeated by pope after pope. Anti-Jewish libels, like the ritual murder of Christian boys, were repeatedly attacked by the pontiffs, especially by Innocent IV in 1247 and 1253. In Rome, where the pope was the prince, the Jews were issued a constitution enshrining their liberties by each pontiff on his accession. On the other hand, the intention was to keep the Jews in their place. During the twelfth century the custom developed at Rome of the Jews exhibiting their scrolls of the law at the pope's solemn entries or coronation parades, a practice soon adopted by Europe's secular princes. Commending the law, the pope would add that the Jews had failed to observe it by refusing to recognize the Christ. The theme of Jewish servitude to the Christian was revived in a papal letter of 1205: Alphonso VIII of Castile was reminded that, in appointing Jewish officers, he was putting the handmaid before the mistress, the Synagogue before the Church. And, in the same year, Innocent III noted that he had requested France's princes to repress the excesses of the Jews 'lest they should presume to lift up their necks, submitted to the yoke of perpetual servitude, against the reverence due the Christian faith'.[19] By 1215 a whole battery of laws prohibited all kinds of social relations between Jews and Christians, the employment of Christian servants by Jews, the building of new synagogues, and the holding of public office. Imitating the harsh Muslim law on this point, they were also to be visible: 'Jews and Saracens of either sex living in Christian lands should wear clothing such that they can be distinguished from Christians, and on Easter they should not go out in public.'[20] In 1215, also, as has been seen, Jewish moneylenders were required to restore 'heavy and immoderate usuries' under pain of 'indirect excommunica-

[19] *Liber extra* 5, 6, 13 in *CICan* II, 776.
[20] *Ibid.*, 5, 6, 14 in *CICan* II, 776.

tion'—a means of cutting Jews off from any commerce with Christians first mentioned in a papal letter of 1198.[21] Here were laws opening a whole new field of enforcement to the ecclesiastical courts.

As missions among Jews and other non-Christians began to assume more importance, the historical record of the faith was investigated ever more intensely. Among the sources for this history were those of the Jews. Unfortunately, the Talmud and the rabbinical commentaries upon it contained passages hostile to Christ and the Christians. And even silence could be held against the Jews. A Benedictine prior at Oxford, Robert of Criklade (d. about 1161) believed that the silence of the ancient historian Josephus about Christ had been caused by a Jewish plot to tamper with the text to hide the evidence that would condemn them. Much indulged in by converted Jews, the study of Jewish texts led to the famous attack on the Talmud by Gregory IX in 1239. In the next year a 'debate' between the converted Jew Nicholas Donin and northern French rabbis took place at Paris before the queen mother, a debate in which the Jews merely had the right to answer charges against their faith. Two years later several wagon-loads of copies of the Talmud were burned. Much excited by these scenes and preferring, as his biographer Joinville tells us, to run the Jew through, Louis IX ordained in 1254 that Jews should cease from usury, blasphemy and sorcery, and that their books should be burned.

Similar events took place in the kingdom of Aragon. Paul Christiani of Burgos, a converted Jew who became a Dominican, petitioned Clement IV against the Talmud. In 1267 the pope requested the king to establish a commission. The commission went to work but, fortunately, the Talmud and other texts were merely 'corrected' and not burned because the missionary friar Raymond Martin said that they were useful for Christ's cause. A debate similar to that in Paris took place in Gerona in 1263. The intellectual quality of these exchanges is shown by the fact that the Jewish leader at Paris, Rabbi Jehiel, and his peer at Gerona, Nahmanides, took refuge in Palestine shortly after the debates. Furthermore, in 1242, the crown of Aragon obliged its Jews and Muslims to hear Christian preaching, and, in 1263, to give Christ-

[21] *Ibid.*, 5, 9, 12 and 18 in *CICan* II, 814–6.

ian missionaries free entry to their mosques and synagogues. In 1278 the popes granted the Lombard Dominicans the same right. In this context, the growing knowledge of each other's beliefs had had the effect of increasing the hostility of the members of the different religions.

These laws and ideas influenced the parts of Europe where they had not been known or applied before, such as Germany. The ritual murder accusation was first heard of there in 1235. Written in 1221–24, Eike of Repgow's law code, the *Mirror of the Saxons* does not mention the Christian conception of Jewish servitude but the Swabian *Mirror* of 1275 speaks of it at length. Whereas Jews had usually been treated in the same way as Christian merchants in older practical law, a new tone crept in. Promulgated in 1265 by the archbishop of Mainz, the statutes of a confederation of seigniors and towns in the region of the Rhine, Main and Lahn rivers stated that the peace should be upheld for all inhabitants, no matter what their status, adding, *immo eciam et Judeis*—'even for Jews'.[22] Although he protected Jews against his troublesome townsmen, Frederick II Hohenstaufen, having to be more Christian than the pope because of his wars with Rome, seems to have been the first to introduce the notion of the perpetual servitude of Jews into imperial law. Confirming Vienna's liberties in 1237, he excluded Jews from holding public office 'since, from the earliest times, imperial authority has proclaimed perpetual servitude to be the perpetual punishment of the Jewish crime'.[23] In Germany as elsewhere, however, secular law only reluctantly followed ecclesiastical. While churchmen derived Jewish servitude from their crime against Christ, secular law often preferred one of the traditional explanations for the origin of all servitude, that of their having been captured in war: the captor of the Jews had been the Emperor Titus, hence the emperor's right to their service.

In spite of the reluctance of princes, the tenor of western law on the Jews became ever more hostile. Civil legislation may be exemplified by the early fourteenth-century statutes of the town of Avignon. Jews were to be locked in the *Juzataria*, or ghetto, on Christian holy days and were not permitted on the streets

---

[22] *MGH, Constit.* II, 612, No. 444.
[23] J. L. A. Huillard-Bréholles, *Historia diplomatica Friderici secundi* (Paris, 1852–61), V, pt. 1, 57.

when the *corpus Christi* was being carried. The town fathers further ordained 'that Jews or whores should not dare to touch fruit or bread exposed for sale; if they do, they must buy what they have touched'.[24] Ancient law similar to modern *Rassenschande* was also revived. A paragraph dealing with treason, adultery and arson in the late-thirteenth-century compilation of English law called *Fleta* included the following: 'Apostate Christians, witches and others of that kind are to be drawn and burned. Those cohabiting with Jews and Jewesses, those engaged in bestiality, and sodomites are to be buried alive.'[25] Nor was this only secular legislation. A provincial council of Arles meeting at Avignon in 1337 listed among the crimes that no confessor could absolve without episcopal permission the act of cohabitation with Jews, Muslims or beasts.

In these circumstances it is not surprising that the tendency to live on the same street or in the same quarter of a town became more advisable and more obligatory for the Jews. This was not a radical change. Except for the wealthy who preferred more ample housing, who enjoyed just being different, and who could always buy their way out, there was a natural impulse among Jews to live near their work, synagogue and school. Besides, contemporary society provided models. Juridically and geographically defined quarters were characteristic of the national-religious caste structure of Islamic society and were known elsewhere in the Mediterranean. Special town quarters were also common in Latin society as long as the movement for town freedom had not taken the reins from the hands of a prince or seignior. For a time, northern Spanish towns had French quarters with their own law and walls or ditches, and the Slavs and Germans did not initially live together pell-mell like rats in the straw in their new towns. At the start, furthermore, the formalization of Jewish quarters had more to do with providing protection and pleasant surroundings than anything else. Thus the Jews—many of them French—who were invited to settle in Speyer by the archbishop-seignior in 1084 were delighted by his provision of a walled area, and the German Jews who were settling in the new towns of the Polish regions of the Oder and Warta rivers, while certainly not happy about

[24] M. A. R. de Maulde, *Coutumes et règlements de la république d'Avignon* (Paris, 1879), 200, tit. 137.
[25] *Fleta* I, 35 in *Selden Society* LXXII (London, 1955), 90.

the rhetoric of the pronouncement, were probably not offended by the insistence of a provincial council of Gniezno held in Breslau in 1267 that they live apart from the Christians, German or Polish. Nevertheless, relations had worsened. The fathers at Breslau wanted the Jews set apart so that their faith and *mores* would not corrupt the Christians; the bishop of Speyer had wanted them protected from the insolent 'animal herd' of their Christian neighbours. In short, what made the quarter into a ghetto in the later Middle Ages was not the demarcation so much as the impoverishment and imprisonment of the Jews who lived within it.

As things worsened for the Jews in the later thirteenth century, their condition varied. In Spain and other Mediterranean regions, notably the islands, they were somewhat protected by being numerous and only one of several religious minorities. In eastern Europe, where their economic services were still so much in demand, Jews were not only protected but even highly privileged by their cameral servitude to princes. Serfs were subject to particular lords; Jews, like the nobility, held of the prince alone. Even town law was still beneficent. In 1297 the Brandenburger lord of the town of Stendal ordered 'that the said Jews shall enjoy the common law of the city and are to be treated by the consuls [town councillors] just as their own burghers [*burgenses*]'.[26] In the more mature regions of France and northern and central Italy, and in areas under their economic and cultural domination, however, cameral servitude failed to offer protection and the Jews were impoverished, as in Italy, or expelled, as permanently from England in 1290 or temporarily from royal France in 1306 and again in 1322. Driven toward Europe's frontiers by the severity of expropriation and expulsion, the already long-established distinction between northern Jewry and that of the Mediterranean was further reinforced.

The gradual deterioration of their position inspired various reactions among the Jews. One of these was rage against the Christians. Although the polemic between the two faiths had always been crude, it reached new heights at this time. Compiled from earlier French sources, especially the work of Joseph the Zealot in the 1260s, the anonymous German *Nizzahon vetus* of the late thirteenth or early fourteenth century exemplifies this. The apostle

---

[26] Cited in Otto Gierke, *Deutsche Genossenschaftsrecht* (Berlin, 1868), I, 261.

Peter is there called Peter the Ass—a teaching not without parallel on the Christian side, where Peter, because he represented the active life and the hierarchical structure of the Roman Church, was sometimes portrayed as a bumbling fellow when compared to the apostle John, the symbol of the contemplative life, of apocalyptic understanding, and of intellectualism generally. Few Christians, however, would have enjoyed the *Nizzahon's* repetition of the old notion that Christ was a common criminal, the Hanged One, or the story of his bastardy from the whore Mary, referred to throughout this text as Haria (from the Aramaic word meaning ordure).[27] Not that such things were unknown among Christians. 'God's bastardy' was a medieval oath. According to a text of 1308 probably written by the French jurist and publicist Peter Dubois, Boniface VIII, when dying, was urged to give his soul over to the Virgin. To this he replied: 'Silence, fool, I don't believe in that she-ass or her foal.'[28]

What was bad in a Christian was unforgivable in a Jew. As they came to know how the Jews doubted the Saviour, mocked the Virgin Birth and the Trinity, and questioned the Christian interpretation of the Old Testament, the inquisitors not only went after the Talmud, but all sorts of books. In his famed inquisitors' manual of 1323–24, Bernard Guy listed to be destroyed books by Rashi of Troyes, Maimonides, and the rationalist and violent polemist David Kimhi (ben Joseph, fl. 1160–1235) of Narbonne. Apropos of the latter's praise of Saladin for liberating Jerusalem in 1187, it is worth noting that, unlike the stand that Islam's Jews took in Spain around 1100 and 1150, Latin Europe's Jews generally favoured the side of Islam from the later twelfth century onward.

On the other hand, the sorrows of the Jews also inspired self-hating narcissism. By their failure to teach the law, and by irreverent noise in synagogue, etc., said Isaac of Corbeil in 1277, the Jews had brought it all on themselves.

We must learn from the Christians who, although they do not have the right faith, stand silently dumb in their houses of prayer. . . . And our fathers have told us and we have indeed

[27] See David Berger's soon-to-be-published Columbia dissertation, containing an edition and translation of this text.
[28] Text No. 34 in Mollat's edition of Etienne Baluze, *Vitae paparum Avenionensium* (Paris, 1917), III, 162.

seen it with our own eyes that many synagogues have been destroyed or changed into churches because they have not been treated with due respect.[29]

A preacher like Berthold of Regensburg would have been struck dumb by this description of the pious decorum of the Christian faithful. Now they, according to such tongue-lashing preachers on their Lenten tours, really made noise, even interrupting the elevation of the host with their flirting and gaming.

So marked a deterioration of their onetime position caused a number of Jews to be attracted by Christian missions. This seemingly happy solution appears merely to have raised new problems for the ecclesiastical or secular legislator. The Jews reacted strongly against those who converted voluntarily, and they helped those who had been converted by force to escape. Under such pressures, converted Jews relapsed not infrequently. By the mid-thirteenth century the laws applying to heretics had been applied to relapsed Jews. By 1271 the inquisitors had been charged with hunting them and their abettors down. Although in principle opposed to forced conversion, Nicholas III answered a question of the French inquisition in 1278 by stating that even forcibly converted Jews must remain Christian. Those who aided relapsed Jews were in better case. According to a *responsum* of about 1280 by the university doctors of Pavia, Bologna and Ferrara, fautors were liable to the death penalty only if they had actually aided the Jew to escape. Those who provided food, etc., were to be corrected more mildly, that is, by fines, exile, prison or indirect excommunication.

Nor was conversion the answer. An illustration is the treatment accorded the numerous *neofiti*, or New Christians, in the kingdom of Naples—a history paralleled elsewhere, as in Spain. A royal decree of 1311 required *neofiti* to leave their old communities and integrate with the ordinary Christian population. Later legislation reversed this, ordering them to live in their own quarters. The ostensible motive for this was that their traditional observances might judaize the Christians, but one suspects that, in an ever more competitive and mature economy, the Christian majority wished to keep for itself the better sources of wealth. In fine, although the full measure of discrimination against 'quasi-

[29] Güdemann, *op. cit.*, I, 84–5.

Christians' awaited later times, it seems clear that conversion was only a partial solution, one that could not appeal to many Jews.

Utopian dreams

As Latin society matured during the thirteenth century, the missionary movement failed just as the crusades had. By 1300 more effort was spent on trying to regulate and profit from religious minorities than upon the crusade or upon missions. An essentially defensive objective had replaced the grand aggressions of an earlier era. Then the crusader had gone to fight the unbeliever abroad; now he chased Jews and Muslims around at home. Not that the enthusiasts of the age gave up their dreams; they merely developed them all the more. Roger Bacon proposed to recast the whole educational system and society generally to the end that 'all the nations of the unbelieving predestined to the life eternal should be converted to the efficacy and glory of the Christian faith'.[30] Like his contemporary Raymond Lull, he sought to find a universal science that would enable the missionary to explain Christ's truth to unhearing ears. Developing a thought to be found in one of Aquinas's *quodlibets*, namely that when you argue with Jews, you centre on the Old Testament, with Manichaeans on the New, and with others who use neither of these authorities, you have to use natural reason, Bacon declared that natural philosophy was common to all men. And, since philosophy accorded with Christianity, he was convinced that a proper use of it would suffice to bring the heathen to Christ. To effect this teaching, however, languages were necessary. Because of the Christian ignorance of Hebrew Bacon said, 'an infinite number of Jews among us have perished because no one knew how to preach to them, or to interpret the Scriptures in their tongue, or to confer or to dispute with them. . . . O! ineffable loss of souls, when it would be so easy to convert innumerable Jews.'[31]

But the idea that it would be easy was not long held by those who worked in the field. Lull had once had much the same conviction and had lectured audiences from Paris to Rome on the key to universal knowledge. Moreover, he had learned Arabic and

[30] *Compendium studii philosophiae* 1, in *Rolls Series* XV, 395.
[31] *Opus maius* 3, 13, ed. Bridges III, 120.

served as a missionary in the field. Experience, however, taught him a measure of wisdom. By 1295 he had become an advocate of the need to conquer the Muslims by arms in order to assure Christian missions a fair hearing and by 1308 he had a plan of campaign worked out. His idea for a crusade for free speech appears to owe something to a book of 1291 by the missionary Fidenzio of Padua, a Franciscan provincial in the Holy Land. And the canonists Hostiensis and Innocent IV stated that the Muslims contravened natural law by refusing free entry to Christian missions.

The eventide of the crusade and missionary movements produced not a few intellectuals who shared with the Pastoureaux and other popular movements the apocalyptic vision and vehemence of the utopian mind. Some of the utopians were wonderfully materialist or practical. Writing his *Recuperation of the Holy Land* in 1306, Peter Dubois tried to lure Christians to conquer the Near East by telling them that spices and other goods would be cheaper if they did. Although he briefly alluded to the great religious commonplaces, his method of conversion was based upon ideological packaging. An élite of western girls and boys could show the Muslims how good it could be and would intermarry with them. The Mamluks' Egyptian subjects were enslaved; they would rise in revolt were the Latins but to wave freedom's banner. Dubois's programme for Europe was equally interesting. The Church was to be reorganized and to help finance and direct a comprehensive educational system designed to prepare young women and men for the eastern settlement. To end war in Europe Dubois elaborated a political organization whose commander was to be the king of France and whose highest judge was to be the Roman pontiff. He also proposed a European congress and a permanent system of international arbitration. Others played war games. The Venetian senator Marino Sanuto, in his *Secrets of the Faithful of the Cross* of 1321, proposed to mobilize Europe under the pope and the French king. Like others, he thought in terms of an alliance between the Tatars and the Latins, urged an attack on the strategic base of Islamic power in Egypt, and looked forward to the eventual conquest of the Indian Ocean.

All these schemes for renewing the crusades shared the idea that coercion was necessary for the advance of the faith. In earlier and happier days, one had not had to face that, but Latin history had clearly shown that, apart from Mongol Asia, Latin missions had succeeded only where Latin power dominated. Even the professedly voluntary union of Constantinople and Rome in 1274 was largely motivated by the Emperor Michael VIII Paleologus's fear of Charles I of Anjou and Naples, and of his plan to restore the Latin empire on the Bosporus. The Sicilian Vespers of 1282 and the consequent loss of Sicily to the Catalans enabled the Emperor Andronicus II to withdraw obedience from Rome and drive the unionists out of his Church.

Intelligent and often genuinely prophetic though those who called for crusades and missions were, few listened to them. The Latins were far too busy making war on other Christian Europeans and pursuing Europe's own religious minorities to pay much attention to the foreigner outside. And much of their utopia had faded even back at home. The vision of Paul's Colossians 3:9–11 was beautiful. The Christian will put off the old man with his sins and put on the new in the image of the God who created him. Then, there will be no gentile or Jew, circumcised or uncircumcised, barbarian or Scythian, slave or free, but Christ will be all and in all. This was to happen in history, here on earth.

The earlier utopian and founder of the Order of Fiore, Abbot Joachim (d. 1202), believed in this hope and prophesied its fulfilment. At the end of time, the vision would become real and the Jews would show this by converting. Being an intellectual, however, the great abbot thought of this event as being in the future and therefore merely wrote a book against the Jews. The members of such popular movements as the Pastoureaux, however, could not wait for God's angel to sound the trumpet. Urged by their mental haste and material poverty, these humble eschatologists looked for signs of the coming time and, if the Jews had to be converted to provide these signs, they would be. But the member of a minority traditionally domiciled among a hostile majority was an unlikely candidate for conversion. Individuals apart, the social functions and circumstances of the Jewish people had made its inner harmony dependent upon being apart or even hated. When threatened by the Pastoureaux, then, the Jews were rarely converted, and this increased the rhythmic cycle of pogroms, expulsions and forcible impoverishment that marked the later Middle Ages.

At first destructive because it encouraged attacks upon the Jews and Muslims, the knowledge Christians obtained of their writings was to bear great fruit. Rashi, whose commentaries on the Talmud were condemned by Bernard Guy, influenced Christian biblical studies through the work of Nicholas of Lyra, and Maimonides, whose *Mishneh Torah* was also condemned, moved the whole of scholasticism with his *Guide for the Perplexed*. The period around 1300 saw the high point of the reception of Muslim and Jewish learning. It is impossible to imagine the Catalan Arnold of Villanova's mixture of eschatological immediacies and medical mysticism except in terms of an intellectual background not dissimilar to that of Abraham Abulafia. The even more influential Catalan Raymond Lull openly modelled himself and his hero Blanquerna on the Muslim mystic hermits or sufis. That express hostility could stimulate or mask learning is shown by the curious history of the *Mi'rag* (*The Stairway* or *Ladder*), a lengthy piece describing Mohammed's voyage into heaven and hell. Translated into Castilian by a Jewish doctor at the court of Alphonso X, it was done into Latin and French in 1264 by an Italian, Bonaventure of Siena. Bonaventure translated it, he said, that Christians might 'know that the rash assaults against Christ by Mohammed were as wrong-headed as they were ridiculous, and that, when compared with these lies, the truth of the Christian faith will be seen to be all the more appealing'.[32] And yet it is known that, without this work and others like it of Muslim popular piety and learning, Dante's *Divine Comedy* would not have had its distinctive architecture. In retreat for a time, then, Latin Europe was still hungrily devouring the wisdom of other cultures, thus renewing a power that would burst out over an astonished world at the dawn of modern times.

But the retreat was real; indeed, it was sometimes a self-induced rout. There was more to the failure of Christian missions than can be explained by examining the relationship between the missionaries and those they sought to convert. In 1332–33 those—largely Italians—attending a service in the Franciscan church of Tabriz in Persia were horrified to hear a radical friar, George of Adria, describe Pope John XXII as the antichrist. The Latins were exporting their schisms, not only their faith, and these schisms show that, at home as well as abroad, the mission of the Latin Church was failing. Aspects of this failure are examined in the last three chapters of this volume.

[32] Cited in Francesco Gabrieli, 'New Light on Dante and Islam', *East and West* IV (1953), 175a.

PART TWO

Economy

IV

The Economic Base

The land

The growth of western agriculture moved into high gear in the early twelfth century and continued through the thirteenth. Expansion was accompanied by the improvement of technology: the use of the horse in farming, improved harnesses for traction animals, the introduction of water- and windmills, and the spread of the three-field system. Most of these innovations had appeared long before 1150; only the employment of the horse for ploughing and the spread of windmills may be assigned to the twelfth century. In agriculture, as in so much else, the men of this age perfected and spread a technology bequeathed to them by their fathers.

BIBLIOGRAPHY. A preliminary sketch of the relationship of technology to society may be found in Lynn White, *Medieval Technology and Social Change* (Oxford, 1962). In his *L'économie rurale et la vie des campagnes dans l'occident médiéval*, 2 vols. (Paris, 1962—translated in 1968), Georges Duby provides a fine general survey of medieval agrarian history. A more general history is B. H. Slicher van Bath, *The Agrarian History of Western Europe—A.D. 500–1850* (London, 1963—from the Dutch original of 1960). The best one-volume survey of general economic history is that of Josef Kulischer, *Allgemeine Wirtschaftsgeschichte des Mittelalters und der Neuzeit*, vol. I (Munich, 1958). English readers will do well to consult *The Cambridge Economic History of Europe*, vols. II: *Trade and Industry in the Middle Ages*, ed. Michael Postan and E. E. Rich (1952), and III: *Economic Organization and Policies in the Middle Ages*, ed. Michael Postan, E. E. Rich, and Edward Miller (1961). The views of Henri Pirenne are widely diffused in numerous English translations—an example being his *Economic and Social History of the Middle Ages* of 1936. Much of his best writing on economic history has been brought together by Emile Coornaert in a recent volume entitled *Histoire économique de l'occident médiéval* (Paris, 1951). Fritz Rörig's little *Mittelalterliche Weltwirtschaft* (Jena, 1933) is stimulating and imaginative. Demographic studies rarely contain much information for this early period. See J. C. Russell, *British Medieval Population* (Albuquerque, 1948), K. J. Beloch, *Bevölkerungsgeschichte Italiens*, 3 vols. (Berlin, 1937–61), and Roger Mols, *Introduction à la démographie historique des villes d'Europe du XIVe au XVIIIe siècle*, 3 vols. (Gembloux, 1956).

The expansion of agriculture was especially noticeable along the frontiers of the Latin society from Spain to Slavdom. Although first settled by westerners in an earlier age, central Spain's high plateaux were still filling up. In Germany the movement toward the east was resumed around 1150 after the agonies of the Gregorian age. Aided by Dutchmen or Flemings, German peasants pushed across the Saale-Elbe frontier toward Transylvania and the Tatra range. To the north, the line of settlement remained in western Bohemia, the Lusatias, and central Brandenburg and Mecklenburg up to about 1200. After that, bypassing most of Bohemia and Moravia, it moved forward through Pomerania, down into Silesia and into the northern reaches of the Vistula River.

More important was the increase in the area under cultivation within western Europe itself. Along the English and continental coasts of the North Sea and the German reaches of the Baltic, tidal marshes were drained. By about 1300 cultivation in the delta of the Rhine, Meuse and Scheldt Rivers had advanced at the expense of the sea almost as far as it has today. Monasteries often pioneered in this work. Over two-thirds of the Abbey of the Dunes' land at Hulst near the mouth of the Scheldt consisted of polders, land reclaimed from the sea. River valleys had also been opened. The Milanese led in building dikes and clearing the central stretches of the Po valley, a task accomplished by about 1300. The deforestation of valleys and flood control not only increased the area under cultivation but also transformed shallow and swampy streams into navigable rivers.

The clearing of the forest was part of the same effort. Although important stands of timber were found in the Alps, the Pyrenees and the other mountains bordering the Mediterranean basin, Europe's great forest lay to the north. There, bounded by the Arctic's icy seas and tundras and by the mountains and steppes of the south, a vast wood extended from England into Russia. By 1300 this belt had been broken into, the plains·opened to cultivation and the western reaches of the forest split into identifiable segments. These woods were far larger than their remnants today and played a correspondingly greater part in the life of the time. Although not all the royal forest was ever wooded, England's king could claim that the whole county of Essex lay within his forest and, indeed, his forest monopoly constituted a major economic and constitutional problem for his people. Reservations aside, the great forest had been invaded by somewhat intensive agriculture for the first time in its history. The significance of man's effort was already apparent. The region from the Rhine to the Loire, centring in Flanders, had become the most urbanized section of northern Europe, presenting the first example in world history of an inland urbanism not based on irrigated river valleys. As we have already seen, part of this region was also the centre of the most widely spread national culture of this age, that of the French.

So richly had nature endowed the northern European plain that it is somewhat surprising that the Mediterranean basin could equal this area in the power balance of the Middle Ages. There is no doubt that the southern region was naturally poorer. Its dry climate and light soils made for less cereal production than in the north. Nor could the utilization of land be as intensive there as in the north, where a system of using two-thirds of the arable land each year could be more commonly adopted. Further evidence of northern agricultural superiority was the use of the horse for ploughing. Although this animal cost more to feed than the ox, its advantage lay in the fact that it was faster and, for certain tasks, stronger. Although Morocco, Lombardy, and the Castilian plateaux were famous for their horses, only the damper soils of the north could feed enough horses to use them extensively in agriculture. Indeed, the horse was not even much employed for transportation in the south, where the almost universal beast of burden was the ass, supplemented by the mule. Besides, the greater natural resources of the north had long enabled its farmers to live in larger villages than those of the south, except for the inhabitants of favoured regions such as Lombardy and parts of central Italy, Catalonia and Navarre in Spain, and certain rich alluvial valleys in southern France.

The north's advantages were not fully realized at this time, nor were they to be until modern times. The full measure of the region's natural resources were not yet tapped; too many forests remained to be thinned, too many swamps to be drained. Intensive agriculture had as yet penetrated only the most favoured regions, such as the alluvial soils of northern France and parts of western Germany. Even in England, the three-field system had spread only to certain heavy soils of the southern and eastern counties. The use of the horse for ploughing was still in its infancy, being adopted extensively only in northern France, the westermost parts of the Empire, and sections of southern England. Furthermore, Mediterranean agriculture was still able to hold its own against the underdeveloped north. Geography made it possible to use what was produced there more fully than in the north. Transportation in the north was chiefly overland, whereas the indented coasts of the Mediterranean's many peninsulas and islands offered the advantage of cheap sea transportation. The inadequacy of food preservation and storage in this period combined with the demand for variety of diet also aided Mediterranean agriculture. The north depended on the south's specialities of dried fruits, rice and sugar, and it was across the inland sea that preservative spices came to Latin Europe.

The peoples of the Mediterranean had also developed their agricultural techniques highly. Dry soil cultivation by means of irrigation was common, not only in the Near East but also in Africa and Spain, where Valencia stands out as an example. Lacking moisture in the summer, the upland plain round Milan was irrigated by the waters of the Ticino, brought about forty miles in the greatest canal of the time, the Muzza, built between 1179 and 1257. Ranching in the dry savannahs or high plains of the Mediterranean basin produced horses, beef and wool. Such production was important in Castile, where from the 1260s on there functioned under royal sponsorship an organization of ranchers and merchants called the Mesta. Its wool was able to compete with that of England and Burgundy not only in Florence and Pisa but also in Flanders by the early years of the fourteenth century. Most important, perhaps, was the fact that, because of the relatively small urban development of the 1200s, the Mediterranean area was still able to supply its needs for basic agricultural products, with the exception of timber. Sicily and Apulia produced a sufficient surplus of cereals to help feed northern Italy's mercantile and industrial towns; Apulia alone exported 688,000 bushels in good years during the early 1300s.

As the cultivated area expanded and town markets grew, agriculture developed in much the same way in both north and south. By the late 1200s specialization had appeared everywhere. By 1300 wine production was concentrated in the Bordelais, Poitou, Burgundy and adjacent regions, and in the valleys of the

Moselle and Rhine. Coming from an area of more diversified agriculture, the Italian Salimbene was astonished to see that the peasants of Auxerre in 1245 raised nothing but wine, buying whatever else they needed with the money from the sale of this commodity. Regional specialities frequently involved relationships that were international in scope. The wool for the cloth manufactured in Flemish shops came largely from England, though Brabant, Burgundy and Spain also contributed. The dyestuff woad initially came from the Rhineland and Picardy, but by 1300 the area from Agen to Toulouse on the Garonne competed in this market. Most of the wine sold in the towns of Flanders came from the Rhineland and the Bordelais, though some came from Poitou. Enough has been said to show that England, Flanders and the valleys of the Rhine and Garonne had interlocking economic interests, a fact that helps to explain the struggle over Flanders between England and France.

Largely because of the strong regional particularism of this age, the growth of markets did not always result in agricultural specialization. Towns were usually surrounded by areas of mixed production. Humbler citizens exploited a field or two to produce vegetables or wine for household consumption. The wealthy possessed substantial farms providing not only produce but also storage facilities, summer recreation, and centres for rural investment. The greater the urban centre, the larger such areas were. The 9,000 acres around early-fourteenth-century Mantua were divided into 5,500 acres for arable and pasture, 2,500 for vineyards mixed with other crops, 500 for wines alone, and 500 for stands of timber. Government intervention increased. Messina's town fathers twice prohibited the importation of wine, in 1272 and 1294, because this community could make do with its own but had to spend money on importing other commodities.

Expanding agriculture required intellectual effort. In part this involved new forms of investment contracts whose terms contain much information on fertilization and other technical matters. The thirteenth century also saw the beginnings of an agronomic literature. Other than copies of the ancients—Palladius, Varro and Columella—the most notable tracts were those of Walter of Henley in the early 1200s and the Bolognese lawyer Peter Crescenzi at the start of the next century. Even important thinkers busied themselves with this subject, including Robert Grosseteste, the bishop of Lincoln. Of course, agronomy was still in its infancy. Crescenzi was mainly interested in law, and his agronomy was hardly more than an epitome of Columella. Grosseteste really wrote about household management. Most practical of all, Walter of Henley was principally interested in estate management and not in agricultural innovation. He was opposed to using horses 'because the malice of ploughmen will never allow the team of horses to go faster than that of oxen'.[1]

Medieval agriculture was capable of supporting a very considerable population. Tentative though they are, figures for the decades around 1300 indicate a population in western Europe that was not to be materially surpassed until the agricultural and industrial revolutions of modern times. The area within the frontiers of modern France probably contained over twenty million souls. Naturally rich though undeveloped, England supported around three million. Italy boasted about eight million of which about two and a half million were in southern Italy and Sicily. Some areas are known to have had high densities of population. In 1281 the town and *contado* of Padua contained about 90,000 souls, about a third of the total being domiciled in the town itself. The density of the overall population was about a hundred per square mile, that of the countryside alone about sixty-five. In 1255 the countryside around Pistoia supported an even denser population, about 114 per square mile. Parts of northern France and Flanders certainly surpassed these figures and so did sections of Lombardy.

This large population rested on a rather fragile agricultural base. Fertilization was primitive, and the alternation of crops was rare. Metal tools were in relatively short supply and so was traction, that is, animal power. Even in crowded thirteenth century Italy, a team of good oxen equalled in price the value of a typical family farm or allotment. The result was that the yield per acre was very low. Cereal production on the lands once owned by the bishop and chapter of Winchester, for example, was about five times higher in the decades before 1914 than in the 1200s. On the other hand, yield per acre was not quite so important to medieval man as to us because a larger percentage of his labour went into farmyard agriculture, the raising of fowl, small beasts and garden crops, than is true today. Nor was the need for export production as great, since urban population was relatively small,

[1] *Le dite de Hosebondrie*, ed. Elizabeth Lamond (London, 1890), 10.

that of France in this period being only a seventh or a tenth of the whole. Besides, unlike today, the forest was an important source of food. In 1269 Alphonse of Poitiers ordered a round-up of boars in his Auvergnat forests to provide salt meat for the soldiers he contributed to his brother Louis IX's crusading host.

Furthermore, to compare the well-developed agriculture of modern England with that of medieval England is to lose perspective. The modern period admits of wide variations, an acre in the Po valley producing about twenty-six bushels of grain in the early twentieth century, for example, a sharp contrast with the twelve bushels of poorer Sicily. For this reason, other statistics may be more useful. In 1879 the yield of grain per acre in the rich but technologically backward region around Mantua had only doubled since the thirteenth century. An inquiry in the prefecturate of Marseilles in 1812 indicated that the return on seed grain planted over a ten-year period was about four and a half to five, only a trifle higher than that expected by the Hospitallers in that region five hundred years before. In short, it is probable that thirteenth-century agriculture could stand comparison with that of not a few of modern Europe's regions before 1850.

Indeed, it may be argued that production sufficed for men's needs in the 1200s. A study of famine and disease cycles in western Germany and the Low Countries shows that, while the twelfth century suffered about five general crises, there were only local difficulties for a century after the hardships of 1215–16, which were alleviated by importing grain from eastern Germany. Not that hunger did not occasionally strike. England underwent six years of shortages or famine in this period and three of them falling together (1257–59) constituted a major crisis. Still, diet schedules show that food was usually in sufficient supply, and that quantities were improving until toward the end of the century. Hospital regulations provided for meat thrice a week and eggs or fish on other days. In 1300 workers building a bell tower in Bonlieu-en-Forez were provided liberally with bread, beans for soup, eggs, cheese, meat and wine. A canon's basic ration other than bread in the house at Maroeuil-en-Artois in 1244 consisted of three eggs each morning, and three more eggs or three herrings or a portion of salt meat each evening.

To assert that man could often eat well enough, however, does not describe the standard of living. In spite of spicing, salting and smoking, the storage of food surplus was in its infancy. The cold wave of the early 1300s was to show the extent to which society was at the mercy of a change in climate that reduced food production for more than a year. Besides, full bellies do not alone determine health; dentistry and medical care are also needed. Excepting cures for minor ailments, care with diet and some surgery, medicine helped little until the revolutionary innovations of modern times. The result was that the death rate was high, particularly among the lower classes. Statistics from the Winchester estates indicate that in 1245 the life expectancy of a twenty-year-old rural worker who had escaped the high mortality risk of childhood was only twenty-four years. Moreover, the age distribution of population was quite unlike today's. Although longevity was not infrequent, infants and children died like flies. The overall ratio of women to men seems to have been not too dissimilar from today's, but age made a difference here too. There were more girls than boys but more adult men than women, a reflection of the fact that women frequently died in childbirth.

Population pressure became acute even before 1300, and untilled land of good quality became rare. This affected the forest. In heavily settled northern France, even by the early 1200s, landlords sought to protect their woods from overcutting and to diminish the villagers' rights to pasture their beasts there. By 1300 the mountains around the Mediterranean basin were threatened with the loss of their forest mantle. From England to Italy grain had been planted in marginal, easily exhausted soils. Although the number of new villages founded in areas of old settlement in the 1200s hardly surpassed and perhaps did not equal the foundations of the 1100s, the villages themselves were bursting at the seams. In 1241 the inhabitants of Origgio near Milan cultivated fifty-five per cent of their land; by 1320 only sixteen per cent was left untilled. The population of nine villages in the vicariate of Nice rose from 414 households in 1263 to 722 in 1315. Farmland was dangerously subdivided. At Weedon-Beck (Northants) the number of tenants rose from 81 to 110 between 1248 and 1300, with no increase in land.

Gentlemen suffered, too; an inheritance of about 240 acres at Rozoy in the Ile-de-France was subdivided into seventy-eight parcels. Excessively subdivided farms both blocked the rational use of the land and prevented the individual farmer from raising sufficient capital for technological improvement. Government regulation of the rural economy grew apace. This is best seen in urbanized northern Italy, whose republics regulated in minute detail the labour, forms of contract, and type of production and marketing in order to assure their towns balanced and regular supplies of food and raw materials. The tightening caused by population pressure was paralleled by an increasing litigiousness within communities and by big social movements like the Pastoureaux of France and the peasant risings of the 1280s in the Low Countries that foreshadowed the violent social upheavals of the fourteenth century.

Although historians estimate that by 1300 the tempo of agrarian growth was slowing down, the continued increase in population until shortly before the disasters of the 1340s makes it seem likely that contemporaries were unaware of it. Their expectations were those inculcated in them and in their fathers by the experience of earlier and happier ages. Besides, the turn of the century was not without evidence of continued progress. Germany, as we know, continued to expand. Pomerania was settled in the thirteenth century. Heavy German peasant settlement in East Prussia and adjacent regions did not begin till after 1280. Opened to colonization in the late 1200s, Silesia by 1350 boasted around 1,500 new settlements. Furthermore, a process of rounding out kept alive a feeling of continued growth even in areas of older settlement. In southwest France in the thirteenth century the founding of new villages played almost as much of a role as it had in northern France in the twelfth. As the emigration to Spain from the valleys of the Garonne and its confluents gradually ceased, a great new village movement got under way. Starting slightly before 1230 and continuing almost until 1350, well over four hundred *bastides* were founded, though not a few failed to fulfil their founders' hopes.

The towns

During the 1320s the medieval town reached its apogee. Towns were not large; a population of 5,000 souls was not to be scoffed at in this period. There were bigger towns, however, and indeed two regions in which the big town was typical. One of these regions was centred in north and central Italy and the other was in and around the county of Flanders. In the northern centre, Ghent and

Bruges were the great cities, the population of the latter rising to about 35,000, of the former perhaps to 60,000; Ypres had about 15,000 to 20,000. In the large area roughly enclosed between the Rhine and Loire valleys and extending over the Channel to southern England there were other important towns and groups of towns. One such group was that of the Rhine–Meuse area, whose biggest town was Cologne with perhaps 30,000 inhabitants. Set in a region of modest towns and surrounded by rich plains and forests, Paris was northern Europe's greatest city. Capital of the Latin west's intellectual life and of her most prepotent state, her population rose to about 80,000 in 1328. England represents the less developed side of Europe's urbanism, as do much of Germany and Spain. Of England's nine large towns, only one vaunted more than 10,000 inhabitants: London with her 30,000 to 40,000 souls.

Lombardy, Liguria, Tuscany and adjacent territories constituted the most heavily urbanized region of the Latin west. There lay Venice, the west's largest town, with a population of about 90,000 in 1338. Milan appears to have been of almost the same magnitude, Genoa and Florence somewhat smaller. The patriotic chronicler John Villani estimated Florence's population at 90,000 before the plague. Pisa had 50,000 in 1315. What makes Italy impressive is that a large number of towns ranging in population from 10,000 to 30,000 were located in a rather small area. Other than Florence and Pisa, for example, Tuscany boasted no less than four towns in this range—Siena, Lucca, Pistoia and Arezzo—and similar statistics can be derived from other areas in Lombardy. This contrasted sharply with the rest of the Mediterranean area, where occasional large cities like Naples and Palermo (50,000 inhabitants) and the ancient metropolises of Alexandria and Constantinople were the focus of the economic life of regions not notable for other important centres.

The medieval town may be defined as a centre of communication and production. It was the hub of a network of communications serving the interrelationships of the regions beyond its walls. These interrelationships were many faceted and included government, warfare or defence, education and transportation. As a productive centre, the town created industrial goods for use at home and abroad. Providing these services, towns were useful to princes interested in developing their territories. In 1174, the charter for Jüterbog in Brandenburg stressed the fact that this town was expressly founded in order to build up the region. Indeed, the phrase *ad edificandam provinciam* was a commonplace in documents of this kind. The grand duke of Poland valued towns so highly that in 1253 he gave Posen's *locator*, or town planner, jurisdiction over seventeen nearby villages. As at the founding of Leipzig in 1160, the burgher immigrants to Posen were encouraged to acquire and exploit extensive rural properties. When Aquila was founded in the Abruzzi around 1254, its episcopal prince provided 'that a city of one body be constructed from outlying villages and lands, which, as dispersed members, however much moved by shining loyalty, were unable to resist the attacks of our enemies and were incapable of affording each other mutual aid'.[2]

Awareness of the town's importance should not be taken to mean that town and countryside were rigorously separated in this period. Because of the town's relatively small size, it was much closer to a village than is the case today. Many town dwellers either worked on the land or invested in it. In the second half of the thirteenth century, almost two-thirds of new loans by Jews to Christians in Perpignan were made to country folk, and in the late 1200s the Lombards regularly lent money in the countryside from Normandy to the Lorraines and from Hainault to Dauphiné. At his death in 1229 Pons of Capdenier, Croesus of the town of Toulouse and donor to the Dominicans, left over 300 documents listing his rent rolls in town and country, and testifying to his interests in lumber, animal husbandry and agriculture generally. Even great cities were somewhat rural. Florence's industrial proletariat worked seasonally in the fields. Nearly a third of the debts occasioned by the crash of the Peruzzi merchant-banking firm of Florence in 1347 were paid off by selling landed property. Typical was the Champagne town of Provins, which in the early 1300s had a population of 8,000 to 10,000 in the town itself and in eight villages outside. During a plebiscite 1,741 votes were cast by townsmen and 960 by villagers; 900 voters were in the textile industry, 450 in other technical professions, and 500 worked in the vineyards and fields. Everywhere, most burghers and many artisans owned a bit of land.

If towns were somewhat rural, villagers were somewhat urban.

[2] Cited in Emile Lousse, *Société d'ancien régime* (Louvain, 1943), 208–9.

The social and political aspects of this will be discussed later; here village industrial and commercial activity may be stressed. Mining was a village industry in the Middle Ages, as was woodwork. Villagers were also busy in some of the great export industries. In the 1200s woollens for export were manufactured not only in Flemish cities but also in villages like Dixmuiden and Poperinghe. Indeed, technology combined with geography sometimes benefited the village more than the town. During the late twelfth century the introduction of the fulling mill into England weakened the urban industry and moved it to the countryside in Yorkshire, Wales, etc., where the millers found ample waterpower. In 1233 Castelfigline near Florence was proud of its guild of tailors. Early fourteenth-century Fabriano in the March of Ancona was famed for its production of writing paper. Not a few fortunes were made by villagers acting as creditors and merchants, even if only part-time. Around 1180 the tavern keepers of Ferrières-en-Gatinais were obliged by the seignior to close their shops during his annual wine sale because they served as brokers for foreign buyers.

In spite of similarities there were differences between commerce and industry in town and village. Industrial specialization was more developed in town, and innovation was more frequent there. This is not to say that city folk were more inventive than rural, but rather that a larger industrial establishment is usually more inventive than a smaller one, and that, living at the hub of a communication network, the townsman had the advantage of being in more frequent contact with innovation elsewhere. This advantage could be erased by many things. The need of England's fulling mills for waterpower ruined an urban industry. Restrictive legislation, such as that of artisan guilds, could prevent the reception of innovation and force the exponents of a new process into the less organized countryside. As long as the economy was expanding, however, the advantage in commerce and industry generally lay with the town. This advantage was, furthermore, strengthened by other town functions. Villages were invaded not only by the products of town industry and by its merchants but also by the jurists and clergy trained in its educational centres. In spite of rural monasteries and granges the clergy were more heavily concentrated in towns than the distribution of urban and rural population warranted. Secular government usually had its seat in towns.

As a result of these differences, the temperament of the townsman differed from that of the villager. To his good or ill, he was more informed than the rustic, more talkative, more easily moved, more ambitious. In spite of the security offered by town walls, there were also risks in living packed together. The public services owed by property holders in town and country differed, as the customs of Milan in 1216 show. Rustics were obliged to maintain public roads, irrigation canals and the like; the townsman busied himself with the paving and illumination of the streets, and with cesspools. On the whole townsmen lived better and more interesting lives than countrymen. But there were members of the rural population who cannot be described as simple villagers, notably the clergy and the rural aristocracy. Even when gentlemen actually inhabited villages, their horizon was larger because they travelled. Most tournaments, most litigation, most festivals, most archidiaconal synods, were held not in remote provincial backwaters but in or near the larger centres of population. Chivalry's poet, Christian of Troyes, introduces his hero Erec to society with a duel in a bourg, and has him complete his habilitation with a combat in a city. As in all civilizations, the town's function was that of leadership, a leadership justified by the wider contact with the world possessed by its citizens than by villagers. In 1202, when the burghers of Tournus in Burgundy requested the abolition of the seigniorial tax on marriage, they did so not only because they found it heavy but also 'because it appeared infamous and strange to foreigners'.[3]

Because each sought the maximum return for its type of activity, the interests of towns conflicted with those of the countryside. Almost equally important in intensifying this struggle was the jealous particularism of medieval society, a characteristic to be defined later in this book. In urbanized Italy, and to some extent in Flanders, the towns were victorious and reduced the countryside to subservience. Elsewhere they were not so successful. The combat was fought on every level. A vexing but typical question was that of tolls on bridges, rivers and overland routes. Often initiated to finance the improvement of transport facilities, tolls once established were rarely voluntarily abolished or reduced and easily multiplied to excess. Those along the Rhine increased

---

[3] Cited in Georges Duby, *La société aux XIe et XIIe siècles dans la région Mâconnaise* (Paris, 1959), 400.

from about nineteen in 1200 to about fifty-four in 1300, thereby becoming an international scandal.

The urban merchants' seemingly praiseworthy desire for un-trammelled trade was only one side of the picture. Townsmen imposed tolls just as much as village seigniors. Besides, tolls were a way by which rural society and small towns siphoned off some of the profits of interregional commerce and also, often inadvertently, protected local industries and even local independence. This may be illustrated by the wars the consuls of Toulouse waged against twenty-three seigniories and local communities from 1202 to 1204. The consuls fought to limit or abolish tolls, but what they really wanted, and in a few cases achieved, was the subjection of the villages, opening them to economic and political exploitation by Toulouse's citizens. Italy's urban republics had a similar policy, although there thirteenth-century legislation was also concerned with planning for the cheap and sufficient provisioning of the town by its *contado* (the region under its government outside its walls).

Partly because of the economic context, one of continued expansion until after 1300, these conflicts should not be exaggerated. Economic growth cushioned rivalries by expanding areas of mutual interest. If urban moneylenders sometimes hurt the villagers, they often implemented the farmer's search for economic freedom from the domanial system. Besides, the matter is too complex to be described as a simple struggle between town and countryside. It is sometimes better to define the struggle in terms of changes in the relative size and importance of great cities, modest towns, villages and hamlets. By the thirteenth century the growth of commerce and the revival of the centralized state had created the pattern typical of the late Middle Ages. In Europe's central regions great cities were growing while middling towns stabilized or shrank, villages amalgamated and small hamlets withered.

And the combat between regions is often best seen by exploring the relationship between areas of heavy urban development and those of relatively light urban development. Italy gives an example of this. Sometime after 1200 most of northern Italy's important towns were faced by the problem of an adequate grain supply, and by 1300 most of them had created permanent bureaux to assure a regular supply at fixed prices—bureaux that precede by about fifty years the first such agency known in the north, at Ghent. The population of Italy's towns was evidently outrunning the cereal production of their own *contados*. Siena's *dogana blade* or grain bureau dates from the early 1200s and was not the first of its kind. In 1261, 2,200 tons of Sicilian grain entered the port of Genoa alone. By the early fourteenth century, a reliable grain merchant opined that Florence's *contado* could feed her for only five months of the year. In 1320 the republic owed the Acciajuoli firm 40,000 gold florins for Sicilian grain. The Hohenstaufen and Angevin wars paralleled a radical change in the relationship of southern to north Italy. In the late 1100s Apulia–Sicily was an active maritime power; some of her industries, such as silk, were world famous; and her state was the most powerful one in Italy. By 1300 all this had changed. Sicily and Naples had been divided between the Catalans and the French. The sea had been wholly lost to the northerners. Luccan and Florentine silk was better known than that of Palermo, and northern bellies were full of Sicilian and Apulian grain. The economy of the south—to use too modern a term—had been 'colonialized'.

It comes as a shock to realize just how small the largest European towns were in this period. No western city in 1300 came near the size of ancient Rome (300,000 to a million). In ancient and medieval times, furthermore, both the Near East and China boasted megalopolitan centres with as many as a million inhabitants. Obviously, the relationship of technology to geography plays a role here. Ancient and medieval alike, the great cities were either seaports or located in irrigated valleys like that of the Tigris and Euphrates. The inadequacy of overland transportation prevented the rise of the great city in inland areas until the invention of the railroad. Yet neither geography nor technology explains the smallness of the medieval town. In 1300 Venice and Bruges were great ports but neither equalled ancient Rome or medieval Baghdad.

Another comparison is useful here. About 1500 Paris was over three times as large as it had been about 1300, yet France's overall population was probably about the same or even smaller. This change, this new capacity to support the great city, was not primarily caused by technological advance. True, Atlantic traffic had increased, carting was more common, and the first canals had just begun to supplement medieval river routes. Basic techniques, however, had not much advanced, the innovations of the late Middle Ages—gunpowder, printing, new types of sailing vessels, etc.—having only a gradual or indirect influence upon living standards. Indeed, it is likely that the Frenchman of 1500 lived scarcely any better than, if as well as, his forefather of 1300.

There was one change, however, in the life of late medieval man to which the inventions mentioned above give a clue. They were all connected with warfare and the growth of the apparatus of government. It is probable that the growth of larger and more successfully coercive states and the concomitant concentration and mobilization of resources and manpower in the later Middle Ages were the principal conditions that made the great city possible. The existence of unitary states also explains why the Romans, Near Easterners and Chinese had been able to maintain great cities in spite of their backward technology. The relative smallness of the medieval town may therefore be partly explained by the absence of centralized states and the particularism of social and political life.

Industry and commerce

At its peak in the early fourteenth century, Latin Europe possessed a fairly large industrial capacity. A few examples will suffice. In 1313, 92,500 seals were stamped in the town of Ypres to be affixed to bolts of woollen cloth. With 20,000 inhabitants, Toulouse produced 1,000 mail coats, 3,000 gorgets, 3,000 helmets and 600 crossbows for the king's army in 1295. In the mid-1300s Ghent boasted a minimum of 5,200 weavers and fullers out of a total population that may have reached 60,000, a specially significant figure when it is remembered that these crafts were only a part of the woollen industry. In 1292 in Paris, a less specialized town, a breakdown of roughly 130 regulated professions showed eighteen guilds dealing in food supply and consumption goods such as firewood, five in building and related arts, twenty-two in metallurgy, twenty-two in textiles and leather, thirty-five in clothing and personal equipment, ten in furniture, three in medicine and sanitation, and fifteen in miscellaneous specialities, including banking, brokerage, bookmaking and the public baths. What is striking about these figures is the number of industries producing consumer goods. The much smaller

town of Poitiers registered only nineteen guilds in the early
1300s. Represented by three organizations, the manufacture of
riding equipment and harnesses was the most developed industry.
There were also ropemakers, locksmiths and tinsmiths. Four
guilds prepared leather goods and textiles. No less than six sold
foodstuffs and fuel, to which may be added the two guilds of
publicans and innkeepers. Doubling as bankers or moneylenders,
the goldsmiths led the financial life of the town.

A relatively large industry together with a considerable population required a commensurately lively commerce in basic commodities. Figures of Italy's trade in cereals have already been
given, but other commodities were almost as important. In
occasional years around 1300, England was able to export as
much as fifteen million pounds of raw wool. In the early 1300s a
maximum year's export of about twenty-five million gallons of
wine from the Garonne valley was recorded. French wine was
exported everywhere. In 1229 it had won a place in supposedly
abstemious Tunis, and in 1291 we hear of quantities shipped to
the Genoese towns on the Black Sea. A capacity to move quantities of perishable and exotic commodities may be illustrated by
the accounts of a Hanseatic merchant at Stockholm in 1328.
Faced with the doleful prospect of a wake, a family of notables
bought one and a half pounds of saffron, twelve pounds of cara-
way, ninety pounds of almonds, one hundred and five pounds of
rice and four of sugar, all from the Mediterranean, especially
Spain and Italy. Asia contributed four and three-quarter pounds
of ginger, a pound of cinnamon, three pounds of galingale, while
Africa provided half a pound of grains of paradise, good for hot
toddies. The shopping list included three large barrels of wine,
one from the Rhineland and two from Bordeaux. One is reminded
of the observation of Buoncompagno of Signa who, while sourly
castigating the mock grief of his compatriots at funerals, remarks
that the English and other northerners customarily 'mix drink
with their tears until they're drunk, and are thus consoled by
being happier than usual'.[4]

A lively and growing commerce was accompanied by improvements in transportation. Mediterranean sailors adopted northern
Europe's rudder and square sail in the late twelfth century. The
compass was introduced about the same time, Alexander Neckham

[4] *Boncompagnus Boncampagni, BuF* I, 141–2.

having mentioned its use in navigation at Paris as early as 1180/87. It was subsequently improved and by the early 1300s the compass had come to resemble the instrument we know now. *Portolani*, or sea guides, accurately mapped the whole of the Mediterranean's coast. With these and other improvements, point-to-point sailing was not only possible but frequent, although, as was true in the Mediterranean until the nineteenth century, most shipping hugged the coast. Until the great galleys of the 1300s, the ships were generally small, although large vessels are also mentioned. Genoa and Venice boasted *nave* 83 or 110 feet long, ships with a cargo capacity of 600 to 630 tons. Contact by sea between the Baltic and North Sea area and the Mediterranean, the two most developed maritime regions, had only begun, initiated by sporadic expeditions of ships from northern waters to the south, such as the crusading fleets of Richard Coeur-de-Lion's time. Exemplifying Italy's rise, the direction of these sailings was reversed in the thirteenth century. The first Italian voyages to Flanders and northern waters are recorded in 1277, and by about 1314 regular sailings to Flanders and England of great galleys from Genoa and Venice were scheduled. Along with this, Italian sailors and captains began to take service in Spain and France and to encourage the diffusion of Mediterranean maritime law.

Inland transportation likewise improved, in part because of the increased use of rivers, especially downstream. That river routes were vital for medieval transport is shown by the fact that, with notable exceptions like Milan and Florence, no inland cities not on navigable rivers grew to a large size. France's major inland towns were all situated on navigable rivers—Paris, Rouen, Orléans, Lyons and Toulouse. Rivers were used for the slow moving transfer of bulky and basic commodities. The Italian Salimbene noted how the peasants around Auxerre shipped their wine to Paris via the Seine. Those around Toulouse used the Garonne to get their wine, wool and woad into the Atlantic market. Meaningful for individual communities, river routes affected whole regions as well. Germany, where the rivers flow from south to north, is an example. There the rivers drew the eastward moving German immigrants toward the north, causing them to exert their greatest pressure not upon the peoples of central and eastern Europe, but rather upon those of the north, towards the shores of the Baltic. One suspects that the relative indifference of the northern and eastern Germans to the affairs of the Lorraines and of Swabia, not to speak of the old imperial lands on the Rhône and in Italy has something to do with the northerly direction of the communication grid in which they lived.

Roads were of more general significance. Customarily of packed earth, medieval roads were rarely paved, save in a few towns and elsewhere where there was heavy pedestrian traffic or carting. Unpaved roads marked Europe until the automotive age, and a primary reason for this seems to have been the use of horses and asses, whose hooves are not helped by paving. The thirteenth century witnessed a growing use of cartage, the four-wheeled wagon with pivoted front axle supplementing the two-wheeled cart from about 1250. Cartage, however, still had a long way to go. Even the famous Septimer pass in the Alps did not have a road suitable for carts until after the mid-1300s. Still, the need for heavy and year-round cartage in heavily urbanized areas had already resulted in careful road planning and maintenance. Muddy stretches were planked or paved, and, as around Pisa, roads were raised on embankments to avoid spring floods. The high-road between Florence and Pisa was paved in 1286. Among the triumphs of the time was the opening of the Saint Gotthard pass in the Alps in 1237, a dangerous route soon to be equipped with a stone bridge, a fine engineering feat for the time. Villages, towns and princes legislated on road maintenance, minimum sizes of different types of routes, and the provision and protection of shade trees. While roads were protected by the public peace and their maintenance was a duty of the communities or lands in which they lay, bridges had more positive attractions. Although the Order of the Bridging Monks is a modern fiction, bridges were often financed by the clergy and the builders sometimes formed temporary societies or fraternities until the work was done. Classified as 'pious places' in canon law, bridges were customarily given small donations in private testaments. They were also made to serve social ends. While partly assigned to maintenance, tolls collected on bridges often went to support hospitals or other charitable institutions associated with them or even built on them.

Overland transport had improved vastly since antiquity, an improvement that made it possible to urbanize the inland reaches of western Europe. It has been estimated that in Roman times overland haulage of bulky goods doubled the price about every hundred miles. In the 1200s the increase over the same distance was about a third. Shipping was still the cheapest form of transport. In 1283, for example, the *nave San Niccolo* carried grain from Sicily to Pisa at an increase on the original price of only about eight per cent per hundred miles. With all this, transport and travel were relatively slow. Including stopovers, five to ten miles a day was common for pack trains. Unhurried mounted parties made eighteen to twenty miles a day. Though less sure, transport by sea could be more rapid. In good weather the whole length of the Mediterranean from west to east could be traversed in one to two months. These estimates do not illustrate maximum speed, nor how fast news was transmitted. We hear of a galley that made Pisa from Sardinia at an average of a hundred miles per day in 1313. In the early 1300s the papal couriers, largely borrowed from the Tuscan merchant-banking firms, counted five days from Avignon to Paris, eight to Bruges, thirteen to Venice and ten to Valencia. In short, all Europe could be informed of an event within about a month.

Transport and travel were also seasonal. Dirt roads do not weather well, and what could be carted in summer often had to be sledged in winter. Storms all but shut the North Sea and the Baltic for three months a year. The Mediterranean was better off. Venice's statutes of 1284 forbade the sailing of her great convoys (*mudae navium*) to the east from the end of November to the first of March. On the other hand, the Venetian senator Marino Sanuto proposed stationing a permanent squadron of warships off Alexandria to interrupt the year-round commerce of that port. Still, there was a seasonal rhythm and the result was that, although industry did not cease, commerce dropped off during the winter. Merchants and notaries spent the bad season catching up with the business of the year before and preparing for the one to come. This rhythm was also reflected in the fair, the most important medieval commercial institution. Although local markets continued uninterrupted, most small towns came alive commercially only during their summer fairs. A more substantial community like Toulouse had fairs that ran from mid-Lent to early December. Only great cities or ports like Genoa and Venice were commercially active the year round, though even there the tempo slowed somewhat. Even the great fairs of Champagne and Brie, where the Lombards met the merchants of all of Europe and thrashed out the exchange of commodities and the primitive balance of payments, submitted to the same rule. The cycle of six fairs held in the towns of Troyes, Provins, Bar-sur-Aube and Lagny-sur-Marne petered out from November to January.

Town and village

In town, as in the countryside, most homes and workshops were humble. Except in the older towns, they were small, rarely over two stories, and usually not made of stone. In regions rich with timber they were built of wood or of wood and stucco, often being roofed with straw. In the Mediterranean area brick construction was common, and so was adobe. What first struck the eye, however, were the town's towers and spires—the immense development of monumental architecture and fortification. A memory of past ages of turmoil and now a mark of jealousy guarded indeppendence, walls were a principal investment of both town and village. In Florence's *contado* there were about eleven fortified villages or *castella* in 1100; by 1200 there were 205. The third wall around Florence contained no less than fifteen gates and seventy-three towers. To keep up with population growth was a major problem, Ghent's walls being successively enlarged five times between 1160 and 1300. Little needs to be said about monumental architecture save that most of the greater western churches had been built by the early 1300s. By that time Toulouse, a town with the population of modern Wisconsin's Neenah-Menasha boasted five great churches, one fully the size of Chartres, not to speak of many less significant monuments. So lovely were these communities that one understands why Henry II, witnessing the burning of his natal city of LeMans, cried out that, since God had stolen from him the town he loved most in all the world, 'I'll pay You back as much as I can by taking from You what You love most in me!'[5]—namely, his soul.

This emphasis on building led to the exaltation of all the arts. As the careers of John Pisano and Giotto indicate, architects were not specialized in that craft alone; they were also painters and sculptors. Their virtuosity had begun to be recognized, Master Ventura of Bologna, for example, being acclaimed a 'noble and famous architect' in 1234. The services of such men were eagerly

[5] Gerald of Wales, *De principis instructione* 3, 24 in *Rolls Series* XXI, viii, 283.

sought and often richly rewarded. The Florentine master mason who undermined the walls of Poggibonsi in 1220 was recompensed by exemption from taxes. When Orvieto employed Lawrence Maitanis in 1310 he was given a salary of twelve gold florins, the privilege of having as many apprentices (*discipuli*) as he wished, citizenship for self and family, fifteen years exemption from military service and taxes, and the right of a noble to bear arms in town. This contract reminds one that art had been assimilated to letters in the Italian town, because, following Roman law, privileges of this kind had previously been granted only to professors of the liberal arts. Furthermore, in the arts and architecture professional instruction of disciples by distinguished masters was already the rule. A contract in 1294 provided that an apprentice would reside with a Florentine master painter and that he would 'faithfully and zealously perform whatever the said master ordered him to do in the theory or practice (*dottrinam et exercitium*) of the said art'.[6]

Even professionalism did not prevent occasional disasters, largely derived from an excess of ambition. The choir of Beauvais cathedral collapsed in 1284. Too grand for the town's means, it took nearly forty years to rebuild and the nave was never completed. It may be noted, however, that the choir rose to a height of 150 feet, the highest hall in the world until the introduction of steel construction. The building of churches and bridges was often pretty slow, though rapid work was not unheard of. Richard Coeur-de-Lion constructed Gaillard-des-Andeleys in just over a year in 1197–98. This was a work of engineering genius. Even though the castle was taken in 1204, it amply justified Richard's boast upon hearing that Philip of France was planning to besiege it: 'By God's throat, even if that castle were all built of butter and not of iron and stone, I've no doubt it would defend me against him and all his forces.'[7] In towns where citizens could be drafted for emergency work, astonishingly speedy construction could result. In 1159 the Genoese are reported to have built a wall of 5,520 feet including four towers in fifty-three days.

The need to erect town and village fortifications strongly encouraged the impulse to plan for town betterment. To this may

[6] Published in Wolfgang Braunfels, *Die Staatsbaukunst in der Toskana* (Berlin, 1959), 225.
[7] Gerald of Wales, *loc. cit., Rolls Series* XXI, viii, 290.

be added another motive, to keep the community healthy and clean. Both village and town statutes regularly accent the need for cleanliness and orderliness in the disposition of rainwater, garbage and slops. Slaughterhouses and dirty industries were either placed outside the town or on the downstream end. Street sweepers were common, San Gimignano having two for each quarter. The medical theory current at that time that impure air induced illness provided an excellent motive for the paving of streets. In 1237, when the *potestas* ordered all streets paved in Florence, he did so that the town might be 'cleaner, more beautiful, and healthier', and similar motives inspired Philip Augustus with regard to the streets of Paris in 1198, though with less immediate results. Such regulation was part of viewing the town as a whole. In Siena the first street map for planning purposes is heard of in 1218, and the first comprehensive building code was dated 1262. As in road building, this legislation was initially modelled on late Roman law but gradually grew to surpass its model, determining the width of streets, uniformity and ornamentation of façades, and the like. Old laws, such as those permitting the destruction of buildings for nonpayment of taxes or as punishment for grave crimes, were rescinded, lest, as a statute of Lucca said in 1309, 'the appearance (*aspectus*) of the city of Lucca should be deformed by the destruction of houses and towers'.[8]

Overtones of social class are also to be perceived in the approach to town planning. In Tuscany, for example, the relatively aristocratic Ghibellines seem to have been somewhat lukewarm about public building. They were more interested in private houses, in their own commodious and defensible palaces within the towns, of which the famous towers of San Gimignano are a reminder. Because the humbler burghers and the people lived so much in the streets and needed the convenience of public buildings, the popular, or Guelph, party was more active in widening streets, enlarging public squares, and building ecclesiastical and other public buildings. It was largely men of this political commitment who wrote the *Laudes* of their citics, of which literary genre Bonvesino of Riva's praise of Milan of 1288 is the most famous example.

In older centres town planning was largely limited to the

[8] Cited in Braunfels, *op. cit.*, 45.

amelioration or beautifying of the existing plant. Sometimes, however, the enlargement of a town was carefully planned. In the Neustadt, which was added to Hildesheim in 1215, the rectangular grid of its street layout contrasts sharply with the unplanned or radial pattern of the older parts of town. The same was true of the new, or lower, town added to Carcassonne in 1247. A variety of types of plan were favoured for town and village alike. The most popular plan was the simple rectangular or square grid, sometimes adapted to a more or less circular exterior wall pattern, as in Neubrandenburg in 1248. Planned cities were often slow in building. Perhaps designed by the artist Eudes of Montreuil, Aigues-Mortes was begun in 1244 and its walls were still being constructed in the 1270s. What had been set down at the start was simply the general layout. In 1290, when the king and the Cistercians planned the huge bastide Grenade-sur-Garonne (a new town named after Grenada in Spain), the emplacement for the fortifications was laid out and places set aside for a central market, church and public hospital.

Two observations must be made about this planning. The first is that there was no specialized profession of town planning. Artists of all types engaged in it. Although closely controlled by the town fathers, John Pisano served as the town planner in Siena and Pisa. The clergy, knights, notaries and simple burghers who served eastern German princes as *locatores* not only planned towns and villages but also laid out jurisdictional areas and published customary law codes. The second is that villagers sought to enjoy the convenience of town life, and that there was therefore no distinction between village and town planning in this period. Towards the end of the movement of the founding of *bastides* around Toulouse, the seigniors and planners of Revel in 1342 determined that there should be several public mills, a prison, and a square, arched and colonnaded on all sides, on which the town hall was to be located. It was further ordained that

> 'the consuls and the university of the said town may construct and perpetually keep free [of rent] two houses of piety [hospitals] in two suitable places wheresoever they see fit to build them, each containing a half *arpent* of land in which the poor of Christ shall be received, . . . free from all tax.'[9]

[9] J. Ramière de Fortanier, *Chartes de franchises de Lauragais* (Paris, 1939), 576.

Further evidence of this is to be seen in the flexible terminology of the time. In southern France and much of Italy, the jurists thought they had it taped by saying that a *civitas* was a city of some size housing an episcopal see and that it could be contrasted with a *villa* (unfortified village or small town) or *castellum* (fortified village). But *villa* was also the generic term to describe a jurisdictional area and was therefore applied to towns as well as to villages. Furthermore, since settlers wanted the amenities of town life, mere villages were often called towns and granted the privileges of urban law. In England and France a new town was often built in a less desirable location than that in which an old village was already standing. The lord who founded it was not likely to advertise a village. Many a new thirteenth-century town in hilly Cornwall remained smaller and had fewer conveniences than old villages in the great plains of East Anglia. In eastern Germany and Poland, a new village was sometimes grandly called a *civitas*.

Planning directed attention to public health. Urban sanitary regulations have already been mentioned and village custumals often included provisions on the same matter. To this may be added provision for public bathing, as the twenty-six public bathhouses listed in the tallage of Paris of 1292. As important was the attack on the problems of sickness, old age, and other social needs like burial costs. Although the Church led the way in this work, individual laymen and municipalities also founded hospitals and other charitable agencies. All hospitals were under the jurisdiction of canon law, but they were extraordinarily diverse in their institutional organization, some being attached to monasteries or cathedral chapters and others being private or municipal. Leper houses and private old folk's homes were often self-governing. Hospital orders also appeared. Although also military orders, the Hospitallers and the Teutonic Knights were famed for their hospitals. Founded in 1198 the Trinitarians devoted one-third of their budget to the repurchase of captives from Islam and the other two-thirds to the maintenance of hospitals.

With the obvious exception of leper houses, hospitals rarely specialized. In 1232 St Catherine's in Esslingen received the poor, passing strangers, needy women in labour, and orphans, as well as the sick. The aged were customarily looked after in hospitals, constituting the principal body of inmates in the smaller ones. Specialized institutions, however, were known. Such was

Metz's famous maternity hospital of the early 1300s. Most hospitals were very small, housing the apostolic number of twelve or thirteen inmates. Not a few were larger. Strassburg's St Leonhard's had fifty prebends for the aged, besides offering other services. Nürnberg's Holy Ghost housed about 250 patients in 1341. Towns were able to offer considerable facilities. In 1262, for example, the population of Toulouse was 25,000 to 30,000. In that year there were seven leper houses and fifteen hospitals. One hospital contained fifty-six beds, another was surely much larger, and most housed about a dozen aged folk. Villages were not too far behind. In 1210 L'Isle-en-Jourdain near Toulouse possessed two small hospitals and one leper house. The larger Jewish communities also had hospitals: a *domus hospitale Judaeorum* existed in Regensburg in 1210 and a similar institution was to be found in Cologne. The Latins were very proud of their hospitals. Writing in 1308 about the presumed superiority of Christian charity to that of the Saracens, Raymond Lull crowed that 'the Christians build hospitals in which they receive the poor, the sick, and travellers, and in each city they have one, two or even three hospitals. But I never heard that the Saracens have more than two hospitals, one at Tunis and the other at Alexandria.'[10]

Given the state of medical knowledge at the time—in 1308, when he suddenly fell ill, no less a prince than Albert I of Habsburg was hung by his feet from the ceiling—hospital care consisted principally of rest, regular bathing and wholesome diet. Medical diagnosis was usually provided by lay doctors. Roger of Molins's statutes for the Hospitallers in 1181 states that a doctor 'who knows the quality of excrements, the diversity of the sick and can administer the remedy of medicines' should be hired in each hospital.[11] Private medical help was supplemented by the state; in Milan around 1300 the town paid doctors to give free medical care to the poor. Hospital staffs usually consisted of clerical administrators and nursing personnel, who together often formed a chapter with voting rights. In 1220 the great Hôtel-Dieu of Paris was staffed by four priests, four lesser clerics, twenty-five sisters and thirty lay brothers. Ideally, hospital staffs were to treat the sick and the poor as living embodiments of the

[10] *Disputatio Raymundi christiani et Hamar saraceni* 2, 25 in *Beati Raymundi Lulli opera* (Mainz 1729, reprt), IV, 474b–75a.
[11] Léon Le Grand, *Statuts d'hôtels-dieu et de leproséries* (Paris, 1901), 12.

Christ. Sometimes this Christian image was given a social over-
tone. The Hospitallers called their patients *seignors malades*, and
the statutes of the hospital of Aubrac in 1162 instructed its staff
that they 'should take most particular care that . . . the poor should
always precede as lords, while they themselves should follow as
serfs'.[12]

Much of the service provided by hospitals and religious houses
was not directed to the poor. Medieval convents had always
looked after the young or the aged in return for gifts of real
property or rents, and this form of social insurance continued
throughout the period being studied here. The forms of insurance
were immensely varied. In 1248 a married couple gave the monastery of Val-Dieu, not far from Maastricht, a piece of land in return
for an annual pension of eight barrels of wheat and eight shillings.
The survivor was to receive half the annuity. At Toulouse donations were frequently made to the Hospitallers by individuals who
wanted to be guaranteed care and residence in the hospital when
sick or old. Old folk arranged for their retirement. In 1233 a
gentleman entered the hospital, stipulating that he could remain
a layman as long as he wished, that he was to receive bread and
water as a brother—he would provide the *companaticum*—and
that the Hospitallers 'should keep him well dressed and shod,
including Stamford cloth, and equipped with breeches and shirts
in summer and winter' for all his days.[13] Presumably sick, a
cutler retired into the hospital in 1242, leaving two houses and
other property to his heir, a minor son. Under the guardianship of
fellow craft members, the boy was to reside at the hospital for ten
years, there to be educated in *studium litterarum*. Expenses for
teachers, books and clothing were to be borne by the estate. Were
the young man to cease study within the stipulated term or be
unwilling to enter the order at its expiration, the estate was to pay
the Hospital a hundred shillings for its service. As will be shown
later, there were also other systems of social insurance.

Enough has been said to show that the expanding economy of
the twelfth and thirteenth centuries brought with it a better
standard of living for western man. Since economic growth is not
always pleasant and is not usually uniform among social classes,

---

[12] *Ibid.*, 17.
[13] J. H. Mundy, 'Charity and social work in Toulouse', *Traditio* XXII (1966),
263–4n.

THE ECONOMIC BASE

however, some members of every group had something to complain about. An explosion of rage against economic individualism and new wealth marked the turn of the twelfth and thirteenth centuries. The results of this anger will be investigated in chapters VI and XIV below. In the meantime, it suffices to point out that contemporary literature abounded in criticism of wealth, the commonplace being that gold dictates everything. The rich castigated themselves for excessive luxury. Writing in the 1220s, the biographer of William the Marshal of England contrasted the spartan beginnings of his champion—he travelled with only two servants—with the luxury of the lowest squire of his own times, voyaging with a pack animal laden with clothing and creature comforts. The rich also castigated the humbler classes, the prior Geoffrey of Vigeois in the Limousin lamenting that

> our old barons used to wear common cloth, so that Bishop Eustorge and the viscount of Limoges and Comborn when travelling sometimes wore lamb skins and fox furs that an artisan would be ashamed to wear today. Since then, rich vestments of divers colours have been invented, strangely cut in spheric figures with little pendant tails and tassels. . . . Now boots, which had once been rare and reserved for gentlefolk, are worn by any kind of person. Once, men shaved their heads and grew a beard; now peasants and workers grow long hair and shave their beards. As Merlin remarked, the walk of women has come to resemble the undulations of a serpent because of the insane length of their trains. . . . With all this, cloth and furs cost twice what they used to. Nowadays men of the most humble condition wear clothing that would have suited only the greatest lords of past times. But [in contrast to these modern men] the oldtimers daily found something left on their tables with which to nourish the numerous poor to whom, moreover, they gave abundant alms. Today, these onetime hosts of the castles are often obliged to go afar, begging aid themselves.[14]

Writing in the mid-1100s, the good prior obviously exaggerated, but his complaint is characteristic. Both the new poor and the old rich found a common enemy in the new rich. The nouveaux who were noticed were often townsmen, especially bourgeois. Around 1200 John of Flagy's romance *Hervi* records the marriage of the daughter of a duke of Lorraine to a rich provost and bourgeois of

[14] *Chronique* I, 73 in *Recueil des historiens des Gaules et de la France* XII, 450.

Metz. Her complaints are silenced by her father who begs her to give way lest she cause the loss of his debt-ridden lands. Fortunately for the aristocracy's opinion of itself, the poet saw to it that Hervi, the issue of this union, had nothing to do with trade but preferred hunting, fighting and making love, as became a gentleman.

Complaints notwithstanding, by 1300 everyone's lot had improved. Throughout Europe new village emplacements and new town walls were being planned to absorb the projected increase of population. Past experience had misled the planners, however; anticipation had lost touch with reality. Many of those walls were not to be filled until well into modern times. But who could be expected to know what the future was to bring? It is true that the men of the twelfth and thirteenth centuries had had the experience of economic cycles and periods of crisis. From the 1170s through the mid-1220s the economy seems to have faltered with the usual accompaniment of wars and famines. After 1250 a series of moments of difficulty culminated in the crisis of 1278–85. Renewed troubles appeared just before 1300 and were not exorcized until about 1320. But all of these troubles had been repaired by rapid economic increase and a continually growing population, so that even the most alert minds could not have dreamed of what the disasters of the 1340s would bring.

Sometimes, also, what seemed to be decline was really growth. An instance may be seen in the rapid withering of the fairs of Champagne and Brie during the early 1300s. Although partly weakened by the French wars over Flanders, these fairs failed principally because of Europe's economic growth. The meeting place for the merchants of Europe's two main urban areas—that between the Rhine and the Loire with its centre in Flanders, and that of Italy—Champagne was admirably located as long as the main route of commerce between these two areas was the Rhône valley. As has been seen above, however, the sea route between Italy and Flanders came into use in the early 1300s. During the thirteenth century the rise of Vienna and the opening of the new Alpine passes illustrates the growth of German urbanism and the consequent multiplication of new routes between Germany and Italy. Italian merchants visited Champagne during the early 1200s, but by 1300 they resided permanently in all important northern cities, including Paris, the great town that had drawn away so much of Champagne's business. In short, the decline of the fairs of Champagne and Brie was a sign of the economic maturity of the Latin west and could not be construed as an indication of future economic crises.

V

Economic Organization

Rural enterprise

The manor, or great farm, was a complex economic organization requiring a careful balance of labour and land. Excluding forests, pastures and land used in common by the village community, the territory of the manor was traditionally divided into two categories: the strips or fields assigned to the domain, or demesne, and those held by the tenantry. Supervised by the landlord or his agent, the domain was the main farm of the manor. Those who worked this farm were in two categories. The first of these was the landlord's *familia*, a household group that, on a large farm, ranged from gentlemen managers to servile domestics. The second were the free or servile tenants who differed from the *familia* in that they were largely maintained by produce from the land alloted them by the lord of the manor in return for labour on the domain

BIBLIOGRAPHY. The discussion in this chapter of the problem of coercion and labour is designed to serve to correct the well-known view of Henri Pirenne to the effect that an expanding economy prompted by mercantile growth is necessarily accompanied by a growth of human freedom. The section on commerce and the capitalization of industry is built as a commentary and occasional criticism of Max Weber's 'Zur Geschichte der Handelsgesellschaften im Mittelalter', *Gesammelte Aufsätze zur Sozial- und Wirtschaftsgeschichte* (Tübingen, 1924, 312–443, first published in 1889), on the basis of the works cited in the footnotes of this chapter and the survey of recent literature to be found in Germain Sicard, *Aux origines des sociétés anonymes : les moulins de Toulouse au moyen âge* (Paris, 1953). Other works useful for readers are the volumes of the *Cambridge Economic History* cited in chapter IV and R. L. Lopez and Irving Raymond, *Medieval Trade in the Mediterranean World* (New York, 1955). On commerce, see also E. H. Byrne, *Genoese Shipping in the Twelfth and Thirteenth Centuries* (Cambridge, Mass., 1930), Armando Sapori, *The Italian Merchant of the Middle Ages* (New York, 1970, translated from the French of 1952), Adolf Schaube, *Handelsgeschichte der romanischen Völker des Mittelmeergebiets bis zum Ende der Kreuzzüge* (Munich, 1906), Philippe Dollinger, *The German Hanse* (London, 1970, translated from the French of 1964), and Yves Renouard's *Les hommes d'affairs Italiens du moyen âge* (Paris, 1949).

and other obligations. The size of the domain as against that of the land held by the tenants varied. In twelfth-century Bavaria a typical lord granted his tenants three or four times more land than he retained in demesne.

When large and efficiently operated, the manor provided a balanced and harmonious economic setting for landlord and tenant alike. Members of the *familia* often specialized in handicrafts, as did some of the tenants, and rural artisans were frequently held in bondage long after the field hands had been freed. On the other hand, the quasi-industrial workshops of the early medieval villa had long since evolved into villages or small towns, paying fees in kind or money. Many essential commodities—salt, metalware, millstones, stock animals—had to be imported. Even in big manors, there was little or no economic autarky. If landlords disliked buying commodities outside, they undoubtedly enjoyed selling their surplus produce. In the thirteenth century Glastonbury, Peterborough, Ramsey, and most of the other large English monasteries busily pushed the export of their wool and grains, as the transport service demanded of their tenants indicates. The peasants of Ramsey abbey near Ely performed carting services as far south as London and Canterbury.

The great farm was not the only kind of exploitation known in Europe, nor had it ever been. In part, this was because the size of manors had always varied widely. Manors that englobed whole villages were rarely in the majority, even in the parts of Germany or England famed for manorial exploitation. Over half the villages of Leicestershire contained more than one manor, and one village had as many as five. Many smaller farms had always existed in the shadow of their greater neighbours. Besides, much of Europe's geography was inimical to the rhythmic community farming typical of the real manorial system. The dry soils of the Mediterranean basin did not require the heavy ploughs and community provision of traction needed on the richer but heavier soils of the north. Although vast estates with dependent peasantries existed in the south, open fields were rarer than in the north and the domain was less important as a source of income for landlords than the income from tenant farmers. Mountainous and hilly areas, broken terrain such as bocage, and recently drained areas were also more suitable for independent than community farming. Lastly, certain types of crops—dyestuffs, wine and olives—did not lend themselves to manorial farming.

By 1200, moreover, the great manor had begun to weaken and the old demesnes were breaking up, though not precipitately. In England and in central Germany, for example, the system persisted strongly, and its slow weakening was punctuated by occasional revivals. How slowly it declined may be illustrated by figures drawn from eight manors depending on the bishop of Winchester: thirty-seven per cent of Winchester's land was in demesne in the second half of the thirteenth century and no less than twenty-four per cent remained so in the early fourteenth. Where export markets for grain, wool or hides expanded, the manorial system was able to grow again. In England this took place during the thirteenth century. In Sicily *latifundia* based on sharecropping flourished. In northern England, central Spain, Pyrenean France, and parts of southern Italy, ranches, sheep runs and rights of way for the transhumance of flocks and herds increased during the 1200s.

In general, however, the new farms of the twelfth and thirteenth centuries differed substantially from the old manors. They were smaller. In Bavaria, for example, the great monastic and seigniorial demesnes were slowly broken up into a number of smaller units rented or farmed out to lesser knights or estate bailiffs (*Meier*), some of whose farms (*curiae, Hofen*) were substantial. A second stage occurred during the later 1200s, when a wealthy yeomanry holding under *Meierrecht* exploited farms averaging about fifty acres. Somewhat earlier a similar process had taken place in France, where modest knights, substantial bailiffs, burghers and well-to-do peasants built up semi-independent farms.

Although many such farms were composed of strips and parcels of land mixed among the allotments of the villagers in the large open fields, others were more concentrated, particularly when carved out of newly cleared land adjacent to an old community. The result was that parts of the northern European plain began to look the way they do in modern times. The era of the country house was also starting. In thirteenth-century Burgundy, gentlefolk left the villages inhabited by their forefathers and built modest manor houses in the midst of their own farms, or *domaines*, as they preferred to call them. These smaller exploitations were more specialized and less self-sufficient than the large manors of the past. Handicrafts played a small part in their economy, and to pay for the importation of industrial goods from nearby towns and villages the types of crops had to be tailored to fit market needs.

The new farm was more self-contained than the old in that, except in the peak seasons of hay-making and harvesting, the landlord could rely more on salaried or familial labour than upon the village community. One result was that the labour service of the villagers was no longer so necessary and was therefore either commuted into money payments or rents, or sold. The nature of the new farming is illustrated by the records of the monastery that owned the fortified village (*castellum*) of Pasignano near Florence in the thirteenth century. The monastery housed fourteen monks; it was maintained and its domain farmed by nearly forty lay brethren, the equivalent of the dependent domestics and hired hands of a lay landlord's *familia*. The rest of the monastery's land was rented to about sixty-nine households, whose remaining labour services were thought of so little value that the abbot undertook to sell or mortgage them all in 1242. Naturally some services were long retained. Although the Alsatian monastery of Marmoutier had replaced field work by a rent early in the twelfth century, transport services and help at harvest and hay-making time were required until well into the thirteenth.

The effect of this change—which had started long before the period discussed here and continued long afterwards—was to transform the relationship of the tenant to the landlord. Outside of seigniorial or governmental rights which he may or may not have possessed, and outside of what were, in effect, commutation charges for the abolition or reduction of old services, the landlord's right was now best expressed in terms of land rent. Reflecting this shift, documentation changed. The complicated registers balancing the allotments given to tenants against their services were no longer necessary; other than proof of ownership, all a landlord needed was copies of current leases, to be discarded when new ones were issued. As long as his rent was not threatened, it mattered little to him who used his land, and tenant changes were even welcome because he usually received a percentage of the sale price of his property. In short, instead of being the responsible master of a community enterprise, the landlord was becoming a rentier.

Like the semi-independent farm, this relatively flexible system of land tenure gradually spread through western Europe, especially where urbanization was strong, for instance in Flanders, parts of northern France, and large reaches of north and central Italy. It was also important on Europe's frontiers. East of the Elbe River, field labour was not required of settlers from the mid-twelfth century onward. Indeed, by the end of the century, variations of the same general type of tenure appeared everywhere, ranging from England's burgage tenure to Languedoc's commoner's fief. Furthermore, as we have seen, town and village were not far apart at this time. Most of England's boroughs were like the *villeneuves* of north France—mere villages, that is. Typical of the Low Countries was the settlement of Herenthals, newly founded by the duke of Brabant in 1209. The new village (*burgesia nova*) was inhabited by farmers called bourgeois (*burgenses*) invited to hold their lands on terms similar to those described above.[1]

Dying hard, old manors often briefly recovered their health. We have seen that in thirteenth-century England the larger monasteries, assured of steady markets, resumed the direct management of their lands, expanded the quantity held in demesne, and even increased the labour owed them by their peasants. This effort was only temporarily profitable, and the late 1200s witnessed a renewed decline. Besides this manorial revival did not ruralize handicrafts or industries, as had happened during the building of the manorial system in the very early Middle Ages. In any case, the fact that the manorial economy weakened very grudgingly indeed must be underlined again and again. Although sales, exchanges, and other contracts relaxing tenurial restrictions were widespread in thirteenth-century England, they were more usual in recently settled areas and around the larger towns of the south-east than in the manorial regions of the Midlands. *Meierrecht* and other types of tenure evidencing the disintegration of old manors were common enough along the Rhine and in Bavaria, but they began to penetrate north-west Germany only during the late 1200s. The difference between the later and earlier ages may be viewed as one of degree and not of kind. The great manor had never entirely dominated rural life, and the new smaller units still partly relied on traditional manorial services owed by the village tenantry.

Many historians have argued that the settlement of unoccupied

[1] Cited in Léo Verriest, *Institutions médiévales* (Mons, 1946), I, 162.

and frontier lands, together with urbanization, is enough to explain the emergence of semi-independent farms and the weakening of a manorial system based on forced labour and community enterprise. Up to a point their argument is correct. The eastern Germans were free of manorial services until the late thirteenth century. Urbanization certainly encouraged a more specialized division of labour between town and countryside. Manorial and village workshops increasingly surrendered industrial production to the town, and farmers raised commodities geared to the market needs of a somewhat urbanized world. An expression of this gradual change was the increase in the use of money among countryfolk, a phenomenon closely related to the spread of export crops. In 1245 on farms of the Bavarian monastery of Baumberg ordinary cultivators paid fifty-eight per cent of their rents and charges in money while those with vineyards paid ninety-eight per cent. Independent operators of smaller farms may have had an advantage over the old community exploitations because they could more easily switch to the new crops demanded by a market economy.

On the other hand, the frontier and urbanization are insufficient explanations. Everything depended on general movements of the economy and society. The settlement of the eastern German frontier was channelled through newly founded towns, and the services and tenures known in the older western manorial economy did not penetrate there at that time. Later on things began to change as the economy came to a standstill and then began to retreat. During the later Middle Ages and early modern times the eastern town—save for a few ports—slowly weakened, and a new manorialism came into being. In short, the eastern European city of around 1300, like that of the early modern Spanish America, seems to have served a premanorial function, that of encouraging settlement. Too precocious to last, most of these towns were displaced or reduced by the rise of the great eastern manor with its semi-industrial workshop. In times of social and economic growth, however, the evolution seems to have been different. In early medieval Europe, the spread of the *villa* or manorial structure—itself the heir of Rome's fading urbanism—may be viewed as a pre-urban stage. At a later stage of more rapid economic growth, whose high point is being treated in this volume, larger centres (i.e. towns) moved to the fore, and both the great manor and village industry declined.

Again, one wonders if the settlement of new lands or frontiers and economic growth or its aspects such as urbanization were the only causes for the diminution in labour services on the land and the lessening of coercion in the economy generally. All these things happened at the same time and were characteristic of the twelfth and thirteenth centuries. But the proposition that economic expansion necessarily increases freedom is open to question. It does not hold for the earlier period when the manorial system spread into north-west Europe, an expansion that signified a very considerable economic advance in the regions beyond Rome's ancient frontiers. Nor does it serve for other periods of antiquity (the post-Punic Roman republic) and modern times (Europe's colonial expansion) during which an increase of forced labour or even formal slavery accompanied the settlement of new lands, economic growth and urbanization. The question we must ask ourselves is why coerced or slave labour did *not* grow in our period, the age of the Latin west's most rapid economic growth and urbanization.

The answer to this question is complex. As we have seen, the medieval town was relatively small and therefore did not draw so heavily on the resources of the area supplying it as did the megalopolitan centres of antiquity and modern times. The reasons were surely not only technological and economic but also social, in that this fact reflected the particularism of medieval life. Again, both the circumstances and social habits of the age opposed a fully rational use of men as machines. Men could be depressed and oppressed, as various forms of the manorial system clearly show, and they could also be mercilessly exploited, as were the sharecroppers on Sicilian *feudi* (*latifundia*). Although possible in theory, however, really efficient slave enterprise was not practicable at this time.

This may have been because the interests of the clergy led them to insist on the moral responsibility of all individuals, slave or free, and therefore on marriage and some kind of family life. Although this did not prevent servitude, it impeded the efficient use of the human animal. As for the aristocracy that constituted the principal group of landlords, their martial activities and their profits from seigniorial or governmental functions distracted them from the purely economic use of their dependants. It has been suggested that the renewal of the manor in thirteenth-century England may have been partly owing to the fact that the king's near monopoly of the right to govern pushed England's seigniors to exploit more fully the economic side of their enterprises. In these circumstances, a relatively strong central government was better than seigniorial decentralization for keeping servile folk in their place. In England the king's justice was widespread, and hungry for cases; in France a rival jurisdiction often lay just over the next hill. Perhaps most significant of all, an efficient slave economy requires plentiful and cheap recruits. Unlike his counterparts in conquering Rome and early modern times—when the rich resources of Africa were tapped—the thirteenth-century entrepreneur had no easy way to replace superannuated human machines. The Church forbade the enslavement of Christians, and except for a few Baltic peoples who were anyway being rapidly converted, Europe had no large non-Christian groups. There were such groups around the Mediterranean, but they were there protected by Muslim powers, still able to hold their own against Latin Europe. Save for a few bonanzas like the conquest of the Balearic islands, a thin trickle of expensive domestic slaves from Africa and the Black Sea was all Europe could afford at this time. And where the increase of servitude was impracticable, it became profitable to sell freedom.

That peasants sought freedom—of that there is no doubt. One side of this was personal freedom, a matter to be discussed later. The farmer also found that he could use his time more profitably on his own land than on that of his lord, and was willing to pay for the privilege. The commutation of services into money spelled freedom for the peasant because the real value of money shrinks in the price rise characteristic of expanding economies. The change to money payments was gradual. In 1181, of the twenty manors constituting the patrimony of St Paul's of London, six offered their dues in kind, eight in kind and money, and six wholly in money. The landlord's own farm became more important to him than the vestigial dues and rents collected from peasants. In 1267 the *domaine* of a seigniory near Macon in Burgundy gave its lord an annual income of about one hundred pounds; the villagers holding tenures from him contributed only five.

The peasant was even better off if he held his land permanently, by hereditary right. Pasignano in Tuscany illustrates the situation in favoured communities. Of the sixty-eight families holding of the monastery in 1233, eight knights or otherwise well-to-do folk may be excluded. Of the remaining villagers, six were humble non-hereditary tenants while fifty-five were designated as perpetual tenants paying fixed quit-rents for farms (*poderi*) that were both hereditary and alienable at the tenant's will. Ideally, farmers wanted even more—to have land in freehold, as an allod (*in iure proprio*). This ambition was rarely realized except in areas like Frisia, where the manor had never taken root, or where, as in parts of southern France, free property had always been common. Sometimes around towns, also, especially those of Italy, an urban republic's abrogation of all seigniorial rights together with the depreciation of rents gave well-to-do peasants an opportunity to free their farms almost completely.

But one should not overstate the peasant's gain. If he advanced, it was often because it was useful to those who had power. Admittedly the commutation of services into money meant a loss for landlords, and improved conditions in one village induced agitation in neighbouring communities, agitation that was usually successful where political power was decentralized. This is to look at only one side of the coin, however. Landlords often insisted on changing to money payments and farmers, being short of cash, were not always happy about it. In a growing economy where much land remained to be cleared and cultivated, an alert entrepreneur wanted capital, that is, money. Although there might be an eventual loss of income from older parcels of land, the money rent received from them could be used to develop profitable new ones from which little or no income had come in the past.

The process of land development was complex and, while the majority of landlords profited, some lost out. In the mid-twelfth century the old Cluniac monastic houses, deeply committed to areas of older settlement, suffered an economic crisis, while the Cistercians, whose monks sought the 'deserts', or new lands, flourished. The advantages to be gained from new exploitations were many. For one thing, there were the fees derived from the governmental function of the seignior, a subject to be treated later. Furthermore, new rents were not the only new economic source of income. During the late 1200s farmers eager to settle in eastern Germany usually paid an entry fee. Even more important were the fees collected for the use of mills, winepresses and other common facilities built by the entrepreneur. In brief, as long as land remained to be settled or could be exploited more intensively, rent fixing and the commuting of rents and services into money was like selling old investments in order to buy new and more profitable ones.

As the process went on, the value of the landlord's *dominium*, or right to the land, sank in comparison to the value of the tenant's right to its use, and the jurists began to stress the legal right of the tenant to his property. Long-term rent contracts, like the *emphiteusis* of Italy, were described as sales, as *venditiones et investiturae*. Although long impeded by older law and feudal practice, much the same change was spreading elsewhere in Europe. To play upon the jurists' use or misuse of the Roman categories of *proprietas* (ownership) and *possessio*, it might be said that, as the right to use the land became economically more important, possession was really coming to be nine-tenths of the law. This does not mean that landlords' rights became meaningless. On the contrary, the purchase of customary rents could and did serve as a safe and predictable investment for rentiers.

More enterprising landlords preferred to acquire the use right (*dominium utile*) themselves and then lease it for a sum that represented a true return on its value. In 1281 only fourteen per cent of the revenues of the monastery of St Peter in Ghent derived from hereditary leases, while eighty-six per cent came from properties leased for short terms. The acquisition of use right was also a way of introducing new crops. For example, land could be rented on the condition that the tenant planted vines or woad. In areas with plentiful labour the main advantage of acquiring use right was that landlords could insist on non-hereditary or short-term leases, or on rents in kind, or both.

What this meant in economically mature regions may be seen by comparing Pasignano of the early thirteenth century with the same village at the beginning of the fourteenth. In the early 1200s the vast majority of the villagers held their farms of the monastery in hereditary tenure upon payment of quit-rents and services. By 1300 the situation had altered radically. Whatever services survived the abbot's alienation in 1242 had disappeared when the town of Florence abolished them in 1289. The population was therefore entirely free. Meanwhile the monks had been busy acquiring the use right to their lands. Of about fifty farms, twenty-four were rented on short term leases to farmers who paid as much as one-half of their grain crop and other lesser dues. Twenty-six farms were partly lost to the monastery, being leased perpetually by individuals whose patrimony they constituted. These were gentlemen or bourgeois domiciled in Florence, whose factors subleased them to sharecroppers. The lease (*mezzadria*) was one whereby owners provided the equipment, supervised the cultivation, and collected a large percentage of the crop. When one adds to this the fact that many other types of contracts were known, by means of which urban and rural investors provided herdsmen with sheep or ploughmen with oxen or horses in return for a share of the profits, it is clear that in regions like Tuscany agriculture had moved far from the manorial system of the past. What had been a 'paternalistic' relationship between a lord and his dependant had turned into a relationship between capitalist and worker.

It is tempting to think that a system closer to today's is a happy one, and it is true that, in terms of the time he could devote to his own advancement, the economic freedom of the farmer had been enlarged by the weakening of the manorial system. On the other hand, he found this profitable only as long as the economy boomed. Around 1300 economic growth slowed and the peasant's nakedness began to be apparent. He was exposed to the ups and downs of the market as never before. No longer inhibited by manorial laws, alienation and division among heirs split up the peasant's farm, making it less viable in an increasingly competitive economy. The farmer could get seed, animals and capital from an investor but, as we have seen, the terms of such investment often reduced him to the level of a labourer.

As the economy matured the older common interests of landlord and farmer were threatened. As the supply of new land ran out and the acreage already under cultivation was not made more productive by technological change a rentiers' crisis became inevitable. Some landlords had always been hurt in this way, but the problem does not seem to have become general until well into the thirteenth century. Then, as we have seen, new investors and alert older landed families pushed short-term leases and sharecropping. In parts of France and south-west Germany obligations reminiscent of manorial service were imposed. On the whole, however, in regions of dense settlement the problem was rather to rationalize and expand the unit of production by getting the peasants off the land. Assuredly this had often been done in the past, but it only became serious when the ejected farmer no longer had anywhere to go.

In this circumstance the price of liberty sometimes seemed too high, and servile peasants whose land was more or less hereditary became increasingly disinclined to change their status. An example of this may be seen in the history of French royal taxation around 1300. The kings of France had been slow to convert the serfs on their own domain into free tenants. Royal enfranchisement was expensive: for it the serfs of Pierrefonds paid Louis IX (d. 1270) five per cent of the value of their real property and those of Paray ten per cent of the value of their movable property. During the fiscal crises of the Aragonese and Flemish wars from the 1290s on, the treasury avidly hunted for money. Under Philip IV the Fair (d. 1314) the government stepped up its efforts to sell liberty to its peasants, and under Louis X (d. 1316) it tried to force them to buy it. The farmers resisted stoutly. The royal serfs in the Toulousain, from whom the Crown had dreamed of getting as much as a third of the value of their total goods, held back. In the early 1300s, the best the Crown could hope to get was six to thirteen per cent, and even then most of the serfs refused to buy freedom. Liberty had become too costly.

To conclude, during the later thirteenth century a new age began, in which the relationship of landlord and tenant was no longer so happy. Growing litigiousness and bitterness marked rural life. Competitiveness was not yet, however, so destructive as it was to be later on. During the thirteenth century, indeed, it had stimulated invention more than it did social war. As an example, a basic change in the rural credit system took place in this period. In the past, a form of mortgage called the *pignus* had been a common type of contract. By it, one who needed capital pledge a piece of property in return for a loan, and until repayment surrendered the income from the pledged property which served as interest on the loan. Involving a temporary or sometimes permanent cession of real property, a contract of this kind was practical when land was cheap and available. As land became rarer and correspondingly more expensive, economic circumstance joined with ecclesiastical censure of what was clearly a usurious contract to push the *pignus* out. It was soon discovered, however, that capital could be provided by other means, without involving usury or threatening the loss of land. For instance, one who needed capital could sell a rent on his land—indeed, on any means of production—thus assuring his creditor anywhere from five to fifteen per cent annually. First seen in the twelfth century, this flexible contract spread through most of France by about 1250 and thence slowly throughout Europe, illustrating the happy and inventive side of a mature economy. What could not be foreseen was that, in the difficult economic circumstances of the later Middle Ages, rents would tend to become perpetual and burden the land with irreparable debts.

Commerce

Compared to the later age of the national state, the medieval period was at once universalist and particularist, a fact that deeply affected commerce. By the thirteenth century, save among the humble ranks of rural tinkers, the wandering merchant of Europe's primitive past had all but disappeared. The typical merchant of this age was an inhabitant of a particular community, sharing the intense loyalty of its citizenry. He was not an Italian so much as he was a Luccan or a Pisan. When harmed by the inhabitants of another town or region and refused redress by it, he recited his complaint to a court of fellow citizens who might empower him to collect reparation from any denizen of the other town or region. Although rarely seen in the quasi-national state of England or the royal lands of France, this use of the law of marque and reprisal was seen not only in the independent cities of Italy, but also in towns like Toulouse in Languedoc, Arles in Provence, and Cologne in the Rhineland where, at different times, the decentralization of political power gave these communities political freedom and forced them to protect their own interests. The overlapping of general and local political authority sometimes made trade a rather chancy affair. In 1303, for example, a Milanese merchant on his way to Flanders was held for ransom by a Rhenish seignior on the grounds that the emperor, theoretically the sovereign of both parties, owed the good Rhinelander money.

But although local, the merchant was also universal. A reason for this was that, communications being what they were, few merchants were sedentary. A Lombard would travel to Flanders and back and a German to Barcelona and back in the course of a season. Once out of his home region, the merchant was among foreigners. A great gentleman like Benedict Zaccaria of Genoa (d. 1307), who owned industrial shops in Genoa and Florence, raised mastic on Chios, mined alum in Phocaea, and, as a merchant and corsair, ranged from England to the Holy Land, could look after himself, but ordinary merchants had to be protected against the hostility or ignorance of local society.

A series of institutions had therefore long since appeared to protect merchants. Foremost among these was the fair. Not only an occasion for business, a fair was also a time and a place under a special law of the peace designed to protect all honest merchants. Those from warring communities abode together under the fair's peace, and marque and reprisal were in abeyance. A special jurisdiction ruled the merchants under a law suited to their needs, a *ius mercatorum*. Furthermore, in both the ecclesiastical and secular law of the peace, the merchant was a protected individual, supposedly neutral in the wars of local society. Bartholomew of Exeter's (d. 1184) penitential records papal legislation censuring those who harassed travelling clerics, pilgrims and merchants, and even those who molested the latter with unwarranted tolls or tariffs. By threatening exclusion from the all-important fairs of the Champagne, the counts of that region and their successors, the kings of France, were able to issue safe-conducts to Lombards on their way to the fairs that were effective not only in France but even in much-divided, warring Italy.

Besides, merchants protected themselves by association. Lombards visiting the Champagne usually travelled in caravans. On the sea, the Venetian convoys (*mudae*) and analogous state-regulated flotillas of the other great Mediterranean ports were famous. Associations spawned to control and maintain routes. Formed in the early fourteenth century, the hanse, or company, of the Loire River consisted of twenty-two guilds, towns and seigniors interested in promoting the traffic on this artery. Other associations were designed to control a particular trade. By the early 1200s the London hanse had grown to include fifteen towns in Flanders whose merchants imported English wool. Another hanse united the merchants of seventeen cities who handled the sale of manufactured cloth at the Champagne fairs.

Merchants found it advantageous to present a united front to strangers. Italians at the Champagne fairs created an agency (*universitas*) with police power prohibiting any of its members from charging another before a foreign judge or court. So strong was the desire to govern oneself and have a sort of home away from home that the Pisans captured by the Genoese at Meloria in 1284 formed a *universitas* with its own seal in their prison camp. When domiciled abroad, merchants often lived in a kind of jurisdictional enclosure, a *fondaco* (from the Arabic *funduk*), as it was called in the Mediterranean. These were sometimes ghettoes. The two large Venetian settlements in Mamluk Alexandria enjoyed limited self-government but were also locked at night from the outside. Sometimes they were much more powerful; for example, the Genoese community of Pera across the Golden Horn from Constantinople established in 1261. In commerce, self-governing Pera soon outstripped the capital, and grandly offered citizenship in Genoa's overseas empire to Greek, Near Eastern, and Latin applicants. Ideally suited to the particularism of the age, such institutions spread in the west. Around 1300 the merchants of Lucca had consulates (*loggie*) in Paris, London, Bruges, Rome, Naples, Venice, Genoa, Avignon and Montpellier. Quite as important were the installations (*Kontoren*) of the Germans, such as the Stalhof, or Steelyard, in London. Extraterritoriality was granted to the Germans in London as early as 1250, and similar privileges were extended to those in Bruges two years later.

Common economic interests bred common political designs, that is, leagues of cities. In areas with strong central governments such leagues remained essentially alliances of traders. Such were the Cinque Ports in England, with their commonly elected *maire* and *jurats*, whose power was confirmed by the crown in 1278, though it had existed long before. In regions where central power was weaker, leagues were more vigorous. Of these, the most famous was the Teutonic Hanse. It began around 1230 with a temporary alliance between the merchants of Hamburg and Lübeck. By 1265 the merchants of several towns agreed to be subject to one maritime code, that of Lübeck, and in 1293 representatives of twenty-six communities met at Rostock to confirm this agreement. By 1300, when its constitutional development really got under way, the Hanse dominated all long-range commerce in the North and Baltic seas and within much of northern Germany.

By the thirteenth century the growth of urbanism and the increase in the frequency of commercial contacts had begun to weaken the sharp contrast between universalist and particularist elements in medieval commerce. Townsmen became used to foreigners and prized the profits that could be made from them. Hotels and restaurants were regulated to assure pilgrims—that is, tourists—and merchants of honest treatment. Innkeepers often mediated between foreigners and native businessmen, and soon a special profession emerged. Runners or brokers (*coraterii*) appeared in southern Germany, the Rhineland and Flanders during the first four decades of the thirteenth century. Italy was typically more advanced: an official schedule of brokers' fees had been published in Genoa as early as 1204. In 1323 Pisa counted over 165 of these specialists. Exemplified by the courier service founded by the Lombards at the Champagne fairs, better communications made it possible to run a business from a distance. As a result, the sedentary merchant had become fairly common by 1300. The best examples were the Italian merchant-banker firms. The Florentine Acciajuoli had a total of forty-one factors abroad in 1341, of whom the majority were in Italy, but others were stationed from London to Nicosia and Tunis. The great Peruzzi firm boasted 150 factors spread even more widely through Europe, Africa and the Near East.

Growing trade also led to more uniform commercial law. An example is maritime law. By the late twelfth century Italian codes had so influenced each other that one may speak of a common Mediterranean maritime practice. The Plantagenets spread their *Rolls of Oleron* from the Bay of Biscay to the narrow seas, where they served as a source for the sea laws of Flanders. As we have seen, the code of Lübeck came to rule the North and Baltic seas. These codes were no longer rudimentary. Lübeck's senate sent the Teutonic Order a collection containing no less than 250 articles in 1254. The history of maritime law reflects the movement of an intellectual current. Itself derived from Byzantine and Italian models, Barcelona's code influenced legislation throughout northern Europe. And all the codes militated against the rampant particularism of the age. The customary law of salvage gave landsmen the profits of storm or navigational error, sometimes even allowing the ransoming or enslavement of shipwrecked foreigners. By 1200 the law of wreck and wrack had been abolished in the

Mediterranean, save on the frontier between Islam and Christendom and save for a politically inspired momentary revival by Charles of Anjou in southern Italy in 1272. In the north, progress was slower, and intellectuals like Gerald of Wales contrasted the barbarity of local English practice with that of the Romans. The Hanseatic towns had to be granted exemptions from wreck and wrack by special treaties with England in 1228 and Flanders in 1253.

On land as on the sea. The law of marque and reprisal continued in force—indeed, the jurist Alberic of Rosate, summarizing the teaching of the thirteenth century, remarked that, although opposed to natural law, this practice was nevertheless permissible where there was no superior authority or state to whom recourse could be had. But the old law had been robbed of much of its sting in Italy. The right of an individual to avenge himself at the expense of the inhabitants of another community had become so hedged about by lawyers' cavils and the provisions of treaties between Italy's various states that the practice became rather like modern international reprisal. Although slower, a similar evolution was taking place north of the Alps. In 1271 Deventer pleaded successfully with Cologne for the abrogation of personal marque and reprisal on the grounds that the occasional malice of an individual should not be permitted to upset regular traffic. The twelfth-century code of Magdeburg, which legislated against the practice, was gradually adopted in Brandenburg, the March of Lausitz, Silesia and Pomerania.

Reinforcing the movement toward uniformity were dual citizenship and domiciliary rights, both derived from the increasing frequency of contact between people from different regions. Dual citizenship was sometimes initially associated with a particular traffic. In 1149 the citizens of Cologne and Trier agreed to be one people (*unus populus*) in promoting the sale of their wine. By the late 1200s dual citizenship, although usually limited to non-political rights, was not only common in Italy but was also known in most of France and Flanders and in parts of Germany. Closely related to it was the right of domicile, of which the most famous example was the Lombard Privilege. Although Italians, or Lombards, as the rest of the Latins called them, had begun to settle in France early in the 1200s, the privilege itself did not develop until the latter half of the century. In Germany the oldest

Lombard Privilege was that of Trier in 1262, and, reflecting the weakening of the Champagne fairs, the first Flemish one dates from 1281. By about 1325 most Rhenish, Swiss and south German towns had accorded Italians this residence right. The tallage roll of 1292 tells us that Lombards were the wealthiest inhabitants of Paris. In fact, two Italians had taxable incomes nearly twice that of the richest French patrician clan, that of the Marcel. There were difficulties, however. French law for foreigners (*droit d'aubaine*) still claimed their inheritances for the king, and exemptions were dearly bought. After the death of Gondolfo, Paris's greatest Lombard, in 1300, it took four years of litigation before his heirs could free what remained of his fortune from royal custody.

The invasion of Europe by Italians or, as they were called in the north, the Lombards, was a distinctive mark of the economy of the thirteenth century. Lombard success was partly due to Italy's geographical position in the centre of the Mediterranean basin. Italy also stood midway on the great axis of trade running from Flanders to the Middle East. In addition to these commercial advantages, Italy's industry was at least equal in size and development to that in the area between the Rhine and Loire Rivers. A further stimulus to Italian enterprise was the close connection of the Italian, and especially Tuscan, merchant-bankers with the Church. As the popes rose in spiritual and political presidency in Europe, the Tuscans became their principal collectors and creditors. A partial schedule of papal collectors published by Martin IV (1281–85) shows this clearly. Tuscany and Liguria were assigned to the Buonsignori of Siena. England, Scotland, and most of Germany and Slavonia were given to eight Florentine houses. Portugal and parts of Spain went to three firms at Pistoia and Lucca. The humble Squarcialupi of Lucca drew the consolation prize, the northern islands, including Greenland, where hides, whalebone and similar commodities substituted for money.

The rise of the Italians resulted in several profound changes. One of these concerned the Church and the decline of the ecclesiastical orders that had played a direct economic role in the past, a matter to be discussed further on. Another concerned the Jews, a minority which, as we have seen, was being pushed out of the more lucrative and respectable branches of business by Christians during this period. The Italians almost wholly replaced them, thus making their explusion from England and France possible. In the records of the archdiocesan visitations of Odo Rigaud of Rouen from 1248 to 1269, most debts owed by the monasteries were to Jews. Rigaud himself borrowed from Lombards, and by 1300 most French monasteries were in debt either to local folk or to Lombards. By 1291 resident Lombards paid the French Crown a revenue twice that paid by the Jews.

Lombard success should not leave the impression that Italians were everywhere victorious. Jews remained economically important in the Iberian peninsula and in central and eastern Europe. If Lombards were able to invade both England and Flanders, they never successfully penetrated the Germans' northern seas. By 1300 the frontier between German and Italian mercantile enterprise had been fixed in Flanders, where it was to remain for centuries. What eventually hurt the Lombard most was the slow maturing of local economies and the emergence within them of substantial merchants and businessmen. Not so far-ranging as the Lombard, these local cadres reflected the growth of medium-range commerce and the intensification of local investment and industry. By 1300 the multiplication of men of this stripe in France enabled, and possibly compelled, the kings occasionally to expropriate and expel the Lombards. Such actions were sporadic—1268–69, 1274, 1277, 1291, for instance—and soon rescinded, but they show a desire and even the beginnings of a capacity to do without the foreigner. When we recall that the Pastoureaux and other popular revolutionary groups hated Lombards almost as much as they did Jews, the meaning of these occasional acts of xenophobia becomes obvious: local society was beginning to arm itself against the agents of medieval universalism. The maturing of local economies paralleled the start of the rise of the national state and the beginning of the decline of papal authority in Latin Europe.

In the meantime and for a long time to come, the Lombard was necessary to the economies and to the rulers of the west. A curious example may be seen in the careers of the Florentines Albizo and Musciatto Guidi who, together with their brother Niccolo, entered French royal service in 1289, where they did much to modernize the fiscal administration. It was *Biche et Mouche*, as the French called them, who raised 10,000 florins from the Peruzzi firm with which were hired Raynald of Supino's soldiers who attacked Boniface VIII at Anagni in 1303.

Business and credit

Business is a marriage of labour and capital. By the twelfth and thirteenth centuries, the forms of marriage had multiplied enormously and had produced astonishingly complex and varied types of contracts. The question naturally arises as to where these contracts came from. One answer is Roman law. As modernized by the jurists of Bologna and other centres of study, Roman law had the advantage of bypassing the vagaries of local custom and of reintroducing forms that had fallen out of use in the early Middle Ages. On the other hand, the sales, leases, and renting and hiring contracts used in this period did not find their exact models in the Justinianic corpus. Matured by economic growth and legal study, these forms largely derived from earlier manorial or feudal practice.

Some have argued that manorial and feudal systems militated against the individual's right to alienate property and therefore against freedom of contract, that hereditary right was the norm under these systems, and that the arrangements of a landed economy must be entirely different from those of a money economy. The first part of the argument is certainly correct because any regulatory or policed economy is opposed to freedom of contract. The other two parts of the argument are meaningless. At no time were all landed arrangements or contracts of service hereditary. Nor did the benefice or fief necessarily imply land; it was simply a kind of salary. As the economy grew and money became available, salaries could again be paid in cash. Writing on the office of the Italian urban *potestas*—or head of state—in the 1240s, John of Viterbo echoed the town statutes of the previous century by calling the pay given public officers a 'salary or fief'.[2] This use of the word fief was rare in most of northern Europe, where it was still firmly associated with military or feudal service. Even there, however, a prince's need for fighting men or political allies was increasingly being served in the thirteenth century by a form of pension known as the money fief (*fief-rente*).

Examples of the carryover of manorial practice may be seen in many contracts—both rural, where we would expect them, and urban, where we would not. In a typical sharecropping contract (*metayage*), the party providing land and equipment was often

---

[2] *Liber de regimine civitatum, passim* in *BIMA* II, 13 and 21 (for example).

termed the lord (*dominus*), and the tenant was obliged to deliver the lord's share of the crop to his home or shed, there to be weighed on his scales. An urban parallel may be seen in the statutes on clothmaking promulgated in Toulouse in 1227. The supplier of raw wool was there described as the lord (*dominus*), quite without regard to the fact that he may have been a smaller operator than the artisan. The raw materials were to be collected from and delivered to the lord's home, there to be weighed on his scales. The antique overtones of this statute do not mean that it was primitive. The law described above was common in Europe, and, in industrial terms, implied the use of the putting-out or domestic system.

A common method of joining capital to labour was the *societas*. Roughly analogous to a modern partnership, the society or company was characterized by the sharing of profits and risk by the partners. The *societas* cannot be clearly separated from the various types of contractual relationships mentioned above. Sharecropping contracts, for example, were often described by Italian jurists as 'quasi-societies' in that risks were shared because the contract insured the leaseholder against losses caused by weather, warfare, or other act of God. Several types of contractual relationships evolved into partnerships. In Languedoc, for example, the *gazanha* enabled an investor to place money or animals with a farmer or herdsman in order to receive a share of what was produced. By the mid-1200s parties to this type of venture were often termed associates (*socii*) and the entity itself a *societas*.

There was also an influence from feudal and family law. Sharing—*pariage* in French, *parage* in Anglo-Norman law—was an obvious way of exploiting and developing seigniorial rights. Most of the many *bastides* erected by Alphonse of Poitiers in Languedoc after 1250 were done in partnership with local seigniors. In 1198 a *pariage* treaty ended a long conflict between the bishop of Viviers and the count of Toulouse over the silver mines of Largentière. Close to these arrangements were family communities in which relatives shared the profits and duties of a common inheritance. How closely all of these forms were related may be seen in Beaumanoir's famous compilation of the customs of the Beauvaisis where commercial partnerships, *pariage*, family societies, and even the community of man and wife are all lumped together in the chapter on *compagnies*. If Italian jurists had gone beyond that stage, they nonetheless loved to discuss the Lombard communitarian family, and always insisted that the essence of a commercial *societas* was its law of brotherhood (*ius fraternitatis*). Still, jurists like Azo and Accursius did not look back to Lombard institutions for inspiration as much as they did to Roman law. There they read that the *ius fraternitatis* made all partners brothers; they were equally exposed to risk and equally and wholly responsible. Lacking this quality, a society—like a contract, for that matter—was termed leonine, reflecting the myth of the lion who ate the shares of the other beasts with whom he had agreed to hunt.

Partnerships were almost infinitely flexible, even in relatively backward areas. In Toulouse the canons of the cathedral sued the armed guards of a farm in 1191 because they had fled when an enemy appeared, thus breaching the *societas*. In a testament of 1218 a father placed the care of the capital left his minor son in the hands of a company erected for seven years. His executors were to receive yearly written accounts and the active partners were threatened with sanctions if their administration was faulty. Although most partnerships were small, there were notable exceptions. Among these were maritime societies, because ships and their cargoes were expensive. Ships and mercantile ventures were financed by being divided into a number of shares. As early as 1197, the capitalization of a Venetian vessel was divided into a hundred such shares (*sortes*). Mining also required more capital than most enterprises, and the sale of shares spread from the Mediterranean to northern Europe, the first shares of the famous Swedish copper mine of Stora Kopparberg being mentioned in 1288. Other large-scale business enterprises used the same methods. Although the average number of partners in a Tuscan merchant-banking firm (*firma*) was from four to five, some firms had as many as twenty-five. Shares were employed here, too. In 1331 the capital of the great Florentine firm of Bardi consisted of fifty-eight shares, a little over thirty-six per cent of which was held by six members of the family and the rest by five outsiders.

Many societies were shortlived, charters often specifying as little as a year's term, thereafter renewable at the will of the partners. Maritime ventures were often for one voyage only, and even the great merchant-banking societies were not firms in a modern sense, but rather constellations of transitory partnerships. In certain industries things were different. Large-scale milling or mining required companies of longer duration. An example is the Bazacle mills in Toulouse. These water mills were operated separately, each being owned by a group of partners (*parierii*), some of whom were millers and some simply investors, clerical or lay. Gradually the operators of all the mills joined to face common threats and carry out common designs. In 1177 they combined to build a barrage across the Garonne River to increase the flow of water. In 1193 one *socius* acted as spokesman for all the Bazacle associates in a court of law. These were the beginnings of a corporation that ended its existence only in the twentieth century. Other businesses did not possess this degree of stability, but continuity was often lent to them by family tradition. Although there are many humbler cases, the most striking instances were the Lombard merchant-banking firms. When the Florentine firm of the Scali crashed in 1326, the Scali family had been in business for well over a century.

As companies grew, their personnel became specialized. Salaried workers are first heard of at the Bazacle mills in 1291. Management could also be salaried at this time. In 1307 the Florentine merchant-banking firm of the Alberti gave their factors maintenance, a percentage of the annual profit, and a yearly salary of twenty-five pounds. Their assistants (*discipuli*) were paid fifteen pounds plus keep. Practical business required a combination of partnerships, contractual relationships, and hired labour. Florence's Peruzzi not only employed factors all over Europe but were also investment partners in sixteen industrial and commercial companies. What was true of family firms was also true of individual operators. Big for his town, John Boine Broke (d. 1286–87) of Douai joined partnerships for merchant ventures, put his wool out for manufacture, and ran his own dye works and drying house with hired labour.

There were often different types of partners in the same company, though the primitive idea of a brotherhood of equals sharing the same work was still strong, particularly in certain industries. According to the thirteenth-century statutes of the Tuscan silver mines at Massa the shareholders elected a master of the company (*magister montis*) to direct operations at the pits. A partner who neither worked nor sent a satisfactory replacement could be compelled to surrender his share to the company (*communitas fovee*). Similar restrictions were imposed on investors by the millers at Douai and elsewhere. It was, however, already normal in most small business partnerships for one partner to provide capital and the other labour, and this was slowly introduced into mines and mills, simply because they needed capital. When, in 1294, the abbot of Admont held shares in the Steirmark iron industry called the Bergwerk, it is obvious that neither he nor his monks were miners or smelters.

The distinction between active and inactive partners was gradually accepted. An early instance was in the maritime company, because the capital needed often exceeded that possessed by those aboard the vessel, whether merchants or seamen. Shares (*loca, sortes*) were sold to sleeping partners, and were soon treated as simple investments that could be sold, pledged, willed and divided like other property. In the case of large and successful family merchant-banking firms investors often became partners on the condition that they would have little or nothing to do with management.

The difference in types of partners posed many problems, among which was that of responsibility. As we know, a *societas* was a brotherhood, whose members were wholly responsible for the actions of their associates. The incidence of this responsibility had therefore to be controlled. In small partnerships, a partner's principal protection derived from the fact that this business community was a small world whose denizens he knew well. There were also significant legal protections included in the terms of partnerships. In 1256 Rolandino Passaggeri's manual of the notarial art tells us that each partner must agree 'not to contract debts or give credit without the agreement and consent of both partners, and to show, see, and give accounting of the partnership whenever the other partner should require it'.[3] In larger companies, the junior partners sometimes demanded a voice in order to protect themselves. When, after a period of financial difficulty, the Buonsignori rebuilt the Magna Tavola of Siena in 1289, they stated that, as senior partners, they would conduct the business according to the decision 'of the majority of us [the family] and of the other partners of the said firm'.[4] Government intervened by requiring the public registration of the partners' names and the

[3] *Summa artis notarie* I, 6 in Venice 1583 I, 141v.
[4] Cited in Armando Sapori, 'Compagni mercantili toscane', *Studi in onore di Enrico Besta* (Milan, 1937), II, 126.

company statutes. In 1303 a suit in Paris charging a firm for the debts of a presumed associate failed when it was found that the individual in question was not listed as a partner in the register of the Florentine chamber of commerce (*consules mercantie*).

These controls did not suffice for many partnerships in which an investor could not check the actions of the active partners, for example in a maritime society when an investor did not take part in the voyage. In practice, therefore, his responsibility was limited to the amount of his share. This did not satisfy the civilian jurists, still less the canonists. As a result, we cannot speak of a legal conception of limited liability, but only of restrictive clauses like those mentioned above, which protected investors. In private companies, the nearest thing to a modern conception of limited liability is to be found in the late thirteenth century, when firms became larger and their directors more clearly separated from the investing partners. Then, new and stronger mechanisms were needed to protect the firm against the actions of individual share-holders and the shareholders against those of the firm. This was accomplished by the gradual recognition that a company was something other than the sum of its partners. The jurists came to describe it as a whole (*universitas*) or body (*corpus*), and thought of it as a fictive person—fictive, to use their phrase, because it did not have a soul. This made it possible to distinguish between the capital of a *corpus* and the private fortunes of the partners. In 1301 the statutes of the Florentine woollen guild (*Calimala*) provided that the creditor of an insolvent partner could not molest the other partners or attack the *corpus* itself, although he could take over his debtor's shares. When the Buonsignori were in difficulties in 1298, the junior partners petitioned the Sienese government to intercede on behalf of the firm at the papal court and request a moratorium on payments. They specifically asked that 'no partner of the company should or ought to be obliged [by public authority] to pay the debts of the said company above or beyond his share of the capitalization'.[5] Although special arrangements were worked out, the principle of limiting liability to the sum invested by the partner was rejected. In a constitution of 1310, however, the Sienese government accepted the notion that a partner, although liable for all debts of a company, should pay them only according

[5] Cited in *ibid.*, II, 127. This is a simplified translation of a complex text: '. . . ultra sive pro parte maiori sibi contingente pro modo capitalium eorundem.'

to his percentage of ownership. The authorities went on to insist that in the future merchant-banking firms should maintain a sufficient reserve of specie.

As can be seen, a characteristic of Italy's economy after 1250 was the growth of state regulation. State intervention exercised a particularly inventive influence on the development of the company. Governments actively sponsored companies, as is illustrated by the Venetian senate's order to its merchants in Alexandria in 1283 to form a cartel in order to corner the cotton and pepper trade. More significant, in view of later developments in northern Europe, were the Genoese chartered companies. An early case was the Maona of Ceuta in 1234–35, in which a group of investors armed a fleet in return for a share of the booty. By 1346 the form had developed so that, in the Maona of Chios-Phocea—a huge operation divided into 2,013 shares valued at a hundred pounds each—the shareholders were to be given possession of the conquered islands and the right to govern them. The Venetians, so much more successful in the long run, preferred direct state operation. Just before 1300 the senate sponsored the building of the great galleys and instituted a regular convoy system for these special vessels. Given a monopoly of carrying spices, silk and other light and valuable goods, they were not only commanded by state-appointed officers but were also increasingly owned and operated by the government.

The chartered company appears to have been closely related to the organizations (*montes* or *compere*) created by the state to raise money. *Montes* are heard of in Italy from the 1160s. Their origin seems to have been twofold, namely, the assignment of state revenue to pay debts owed by the government to private parties and the use of forced loans, a characteristic of early urban and seigniorial public finance. An early example may be seen in Genoa in 1164, where a *mons* of seven shares was created by the assignment of specific revenues for eleven years. The shares were divided among six creditors, who purchased anywhere from two full shares to a quarter of a share, each of which was alienable and negotiable. The system was capable of almost infinite expansion. Shares in harbour duties, in the state salt monopoly—indeed, in anything—could be assigned to raise money to pay state creditors. By about 1180 shares were assigned for life and thereafter gradually became permanent and heritable, though government retained the right to repurchase them and not infrequently cut the rate of return. They were still forced loans in formal law, but governments soon found it advantageous to advertise the annual return the shares (*partes* or *loca*) would pay, and investors began to clamour for them. In short, a system roughly analogous to the funded debt of modern public finance had been created. Here again, her love of free enterprise led Genoa to differ from the other Italian towns. By 1323 her *compere* had become autonomous companies, with directors who were elected by the shareholders. This freedom was not to be won in Venice, where the old *montes* composed of forced and voluntary loans were consolidated as a state-managed funded debt, later called the *Monte vecchio*, as early as 1262.

The emergence of the state as a major economic operator in thirteenth-century Italy is of great historical significance. It reminds us again of the superiority of Italian fiscal techniques over those seen elsewhere in the Latin west. No northern ruler was able to establish a *mons* in this or the next century. Around 1300 even the largest northern European towns had only begun to sell *rentes*, which were analogous to the system described above for twelfth-century Genoa. The erection of state-chartered, state-regulated, and state-managed companies and funds also introduced something close to the modern conception of limited liability. It is evident that participants in *maone* or state *montes* risked nothing other than the sums they had invested.

Just as useful as the companies described above for accumulating capital and providing credit were loans, mortgages, and a whole range of related contracts. Because these contracts were involved in the clerical attitude toward usury, they will be discussed later. Suffice it to say now that, although urban and princely governments regularly issued schedules of permissible interest rates, pure loans became less important as the thirteenth century progressed. Besides, while monasteries and the military orders of the Church were still deeply involved in land credit in the twelfth century, the shortage of land, the enforcement of the clerical ban on the *pignus*, and the rise of secular enterprise drove them out of this business in the thirteenth. Jews and lay Christians still lent money, however, and, as we have seen, the Lombard invasion of ultramontane Europe signalled the slow relegation of the Jews to the lower levels of moneylending. Not that Christians did not push in here too. The petty usurers of Asti and Chieri, so busy in France, and many local businessmen throughout Europe, began their race to economic glory from this sordid starting line. But the distinction between petty usury and real business was widely recognized in Italy's mature economy. In spite of clerical censure, Pistoia and Florence collected special taxes from little moneylenders in the thirteenth century but never thought of touching their great merchant-bankers, who were, as John Villani called them, 'the columns of Christianity'.[6]

Another method of providing capital for enterprise was an outgrowth of the habit of placing valuables—money, jewels, or documents—in safekeeping. Churches, monasteries, and the houses of the Templars and Hospitallers were first used for this purpose but—except for safe deposit—were gradually replaced by secular businessmen. The advantages possessed by laymen was that they were able to invest the money deposited with them and to offer their clients a profit on their deposits as well as a measure of protection. Although churchmen could invest money, they were not able actively to direct businesses lest they be liable to prosecution in secular courts. In 1198 the papal rule for the Trinitarians forbade this order from receiving precious metals and specie in deposit. The Templars and Hospitallers were allowed to do so, but were not permitted to pay interest on private deposits made in their houses.

The variety of deposits may be seen in the comments of Buoncompagno of Signa in 1215:

> Some deposit their property with the religious, others with laymen who are believed to be good, others with innkeepers of whom they have heard report or with whom they are staying for a time, and still others with merchants or moneychangers. Some then deposit only for safekeeping, others for both safekeeping and profit.[7]

Shortly thereafter deposit contracts had become an ordinary method for investments by businessmen, widows, gentlefolk, and ecclesiastical institutions. An act from Perpignan may serve as an illustration. In 1286 an entrepreneur there received money from a gentlewoman

[6] Cited in Sapori, *op. cit.*, II, 136.
[7] *Boncampagnus Boncompagni,* in *BuF* I, 173.

in deposito . . . on the condition that I may do business with the said monies together with my own, either personally or by my agents in France, Flanders or elsewhere, from this date for a year or thereafter as long as it pleases both you and me, and I will faithfully give you three parts of the profit etc., retaining the fourth for myself

for his labour (*pro labore*), as other similar acts record.[8] Deposits were also taken by the Italian merchant-banking firms and were expected to produce a profit, at rates which, though rarely stated, were known in the market.

The advantages of deposits of this kind were many. Although they did not altogether escape ecclesiastical censure, they were not looked upon with as much disfavour as were loans or leonine societies. In the civil courts the investor did not share responsibility for the actions or debts of those with whom he deposited his money. Indeed, if they failed, they became his debtors. As a result, the deposit for gain expanded enormously during the thirteenth century, replacing loans (*mutua*) and various kinds of partnerships. What this meant for capitalization may be illustrated by the larger Tuscan companies. From 1300 to 1303 over one million gold marks (137,000 florins) were deposited with the Spini firm by the papacy. By 1318 the great Florentine house of the Bardi had accumulated assets of over ten million gold marks, a sum eight times larger than its own original capital or *corpus*.

The deposit could be adapted to the needs of an expanding banking system. A Genoese lawsuit of 1200 indicates that most businessmen in that active port had bank accounts. Theirs were call deposits, meaning that the depositor received no interest but could withdraw his money at will, the banker meanwhile having the use of it. Bankers soon encouraged reputable depositors to overdraw their accounts, thereby introducing a system of bank investment in short-term loans. Lacking statistics until the late fourteenth century, we cannot estimate the quantity of credit created by this method, but it must have been considerable.

Even though bankers' associations and government regulation were already combining to produce a separate banking profession, economic enterprise was still not very highly specialized. The Tuscan firms were only partly banks, being also or principally mercantile houses that invested in commerce, industry, and land.

[8] Richard W. Emery, *The Jews of Perpignan* (New York, 1959), 194–5, No. 147.

There were also smaller operators who were on the local level what the Tuscan merchant-bankers were on the universal. Possibly once a serf, Arnold of Codalet became one of Perpignan's richest men in the period from 1276 to 1287. As a depositor, he invested in trading ventures from Seville to Flanders, but he made his fortune by speculating in local seigniorial and ecclesiastical rents and revenues. In his small town, he received both call deposits and investment deposits from local businessmen and rentiers, thus serving as a one-man banking and investment house. Nor was Arnold unique in his age; his analogue was to be found throughout the west.

It is difficult to discover the price of capital or the rate of profit, but *per annum* interest rates seem to have been high around 1300. In the domains of the kings of Aragon the legal maximum was $12\frac{1}{2}$ per cent for Christians and 20 per cent for Jews. Although common in western law, these figures appear to have been unrealistically low. On commercial credit, Genoa permitted 25 per cent, and Venice set the maximum at 20 per cent, as did the ordinances of the Champagne fairs in 1311. For what moderns would describe as consumer credit higher rates were allowed. Under the Flemish Lombard Privilege of 1281, Italians were permitted $43\frac{1}{2}$ per cent. Moneylenders exacted their highest rates from the poor or profligate. At Nîmes in 1289 a Lombard was charged with having extorted 202 per cent. Even state finance involved rates that are staggering today. Not only had the Emperor Frederick II promised to pay his Roman bankers anywhere from 36 to 48 per cent, but also, after his death, his gold throne was pledged in 1251 to secure a Genoese loan. At the same time, several caveats must be entered. Medieval interest was not what interest is today; it was a penalty for nonpayment within a stipulated period. More moderate returns upon investments were also common. On the whole, however, high interest rates reflected the immaturity of national and state finance as well as the risks taken by businessmen in a society split into many independent political entities.

Overall rates of profit were not so great, perhaps because the high cost of capital was partly compensated for by a high rate of gain in individual transactions. Around 1300 land rents appear to have brought an annual return of anywhere from 5 per cent (in Narbonne) to 10 per cent (along the Rhine). Those who deposited for gain with businessmen in Perpignan seem to have expected about 10 per cent. Genoese state *compere* offered subscribers from 7 to 10 per cent while Florence's *montes* gave anywhere from 10 to 15 per cent. After paying off the 7 or 8 per cent owed on their depositors' investments, the partners of the Peruzzi firm averaged a profit of just under 16 per cent in the period from 1308 to 1324, a time of unusual economic expansion. The usual percentage on deposits with mercantile firms in Florence ranged from 6 to 10 per cent yearly, and, to judge from the books of the Del Bene firm, the return of those investing in partnerships in the wool industry oscillated between 7 and 15 per cent.

The developed business of this age required ancillary agencies. Some were still ecclesiastical, although, as we have seen, the direct participation of the Church was rapidly declining. The Templars and the Hospitallers continued to serve as deposit bankers. In France the Crown used the Paris Temple as a treasury continuously until 1295. But laymen made even the Templars unnecessary. Although papal revenues had been deposited with the Templars into the early 1200s—for example, the Languedoc hearth tax raised during the Albigensian crusade in 1212—the Tuscans had taken this business by mid-century. Although the decline of the Templars and Hospitallers was related to the decline of the crusade in the Near East, the Tuscan merchant-bankers also won out because they offered better service. They were happy to serve as revenue collectors and, besides, deposits placed with them yielded a return. Furthermore, they operated on as grand a scale as did the military orders. Whereas the Scoti of Genoa had aided the northern crusaders rather modestly during the Albigensian crusade, by 1266 a combine headed by the Buonsignori advanced Charles of Anjou no less than 160,000 pounds of Paris, a sum considerably larger than the total debt of the French Crown to the Templars in 1286.

Equally important was the fact that great quantities of specie no longer had to be transported. A reason for this was that, imitating the earlier methods of the Templars and Hospitallers, merchants and bankers had devised a variety of paper transfers. A primitive bill of exchange moving credit from Genoa to Alexandria is known of as early as 1155. In the 1200s papal collectors in London used bills of exchange (*facere cambium*) with the Bardi to carry the credit to Rome. Non-negotiable promissory notes were speedily generalized, a collection of 7,000 such for the period from 1249 to 1291 being discovered in the archives of Ypres alone. As early as 1200 interbank transfers were common in Italy, and by mid-century Italian merchants at the Champagne fairs paid for their purchases by such transfers. So important were these business mechanisms that, when imposing his embargo on the export of goods and money to Italy at the time of the conflict with Boniface VIII in 1301, Philip the Fair took care to prohibit the escape of credit by means of merchants' letters and deposits.

The growth of commerce was reflected in the improvement of coinage. There was a general stabilization of the value of coins because of the successful pressure upon princes by business communities, and coinage slowly became more uniform as the state developed its economic powers. By 1300 England had reduced the number of its mints from over forty to twelve, and even France, initially burdened by the almost incredible number of three hundred mints, was able to cut this to thirty by 1315. Since increased trade demands bigger payments, larger coins became more common. The various types corresponded to western Europe's principal economic areas. Before 1200 the English minted the great silver penny (sterling) that served as a model for the various coinages in the Hanseatic region of the North and Baltic seas. In 1192 the Venetians issued their great penny (the matapan or *grossus Venezianus*), whose weight and style, though only slowly received in Venice itself, was rapidly adopted by the rest of Italy's towns, replacing even the Norman coinage of southern Italy. Reflecting the power of Italian enterprise in the late 1200s, coinages like the Italians' spread everywhere. The great penny of Tours imitated Italy's model in 1266, and was itself copied for most of the coinages in the Rhineland by 1300. About the same time the king of Bohemia invited Florentine mintmasters to introduce their model in his realm.

The maturity of the Latin economy was most clearly revealed, however, by the regular issuance of gold coins—the first since Carolingian times. As early as 1149 the Genoese minted the *genofino d'oro*, a type that never caught on. From time to time in the 1200s the greater western princes stamped a few gold coins of little importance save as collector's items. Even the *augustales* of the Emperor Frederick II had no real economic significance. As could be expected, it was the northern Italians who really took the market with the Florentine florin, first coined in 1252, and the

Venetian ducat of 1284. Writing in the late thirteenth century, the Florentine Dominican preacher Remigio de' Girolami praised his city's coin:

> Note that the nobility of this money is shown in three ways: first, by its metal, because the gold in Sicily's tarena is good, that in the augustalis better, but that in the florin best; second by its engraving, because on one side it has the lily, which is a thing of great excellence . . . ; [and third,] by its currency, because it circulates throughout the world, even among the Saracens.[9]

All was not bliss, however. Although the economy generally continued to flourish, a major crisis in public finance was apparent around 1300. Trying to extend their power without adequate support from a still decentralized society, princes ran into debt, sometimes ruinously. By 1290 Guy of Dampierre, count of Flanders, owed the Lombards a sum equalling nearly a quarter of the annual take of the French royal treasury, and his resulting powerlessness intensified the struggle between France and England over industrial Flanders. The weakness of public finance gradually affected the economy at large. Undertaken for profit, the famous mutation of 1295 was the first significant breach of the stability of France's royal coinage since the start of the century. In spite of howls of rage by individuals whose savings had been wiped out, like Peter Dubois, and in spite of the solemn protestations of the clergy in the *Declaratio prelatorum* in 1303–04 and those of the nobility in 1314 and 1316, the devaluation of coinage soon became normal state policy in France and throughout much of northern Europe. In short, a crisis in public finance, one reflecting the immaturity of national and regional institutions, seems to have preceded the more general economic difficulties of the fourteenth century.

[9] Cited in Charles T. Davis, 'An early Florentine political theorist: Fra Remigio de' Girolami', *Proceedings of the American Philosophical Society* CIV (1960), 688.

VI

Regulation and Corporatism

The Church and usury

Dealing with the marketplace, the churchman was of two minds. In part, he was inspired by utopian hope. From each according to his means and to each according to his needs—the Platonic ideal configured in the Acts of the Apostles 3:32–5 moved him deeply. As the Church rose to lead the Latin Christians during the Gregorian age, many of its spokesmen called for remaking the world over into a truly Christian society, one in which all men, like the ancient monks, would live without individual property and practise economic brotherhood. This teaching of social and economic utopianism expanded enormously around 1200 and, as will be seen, paralleled the rise of social and economic corporatism with

BIBLIOGRAPHY. My design here is to use the definition of the conception of usury advanced by B. N. Nelson in his *The Idea of Usury: from tribal brotherhood to universal otherhood* (2nd edn., Chicago, 1969) and to tie it to the social movements of the time, especially to the development of social corporatism and ecclesiastical utopianism—matters treated from a different perspective in chapters XIV and XV below. Other works of interest on this subject are J. W. Baldwin, *The Medieval Theories of the Just Price* (Philadelphia, 1959), J. T. Noonan, *The Scholastic Analysis of Usury* (Cambridge, Mass., 1957), Franz Schaub, *Der Kampf gegen den Zinswucher, ungerechten Preis und unerlautern Handel im Mittelalter von Karl dem Grossen bis papst Alexander III* (Freiburg, 1905), and T. P. McLaughlin, 'The teaching of the canonists on usury (XII, XIII, and XIV centuries)', *Mediaeval Studies* I (1939), 81–147, and II (1940), 1–22. The latter study is a masterpiece of clarity.

The treatment of the guilds and their relation to other forms of social corporatism derive their basic definitions from Gunnar Mickwitz's perceptive and systematic *Die Kartellfunktionen der Zünfte und ihre Bedeutung bei der Entstehung des Zunftwesens* (Helsinki, 1936) and Fr. Olivier-Martin, *L'organisation corporative de la France d'ancien régime* (Paris, 1938). Another useful work is that of Emile Coornaert, *Les Corporations en France avant 1789* (Paris, 1941).

When this book was finished I read J. W. Baldwin, *Masters, Princes, and Merchants: the social views of Peter the Chanter and his circle*, 2 vols. (Princeton, 1970). It is especially valuable for giving the reader large segments of Robert of Curzon's unpublished *Summa*.

its hostility to new wealth and economic individualism, the beginnings of the secularization of the monastic ethos, the weakening of the crusades, and other great impulses that moved the *respublica christiana*. Practical statesmen and great prelates were enticed by the utopian dream. A student of Peter Cantor, Cardinal Robert of Curzon, professor at the university of Paris and papal legate in 1213, proposed a way to bring the world back to bliss:

> It does not seem to me that so many evils can be purged unless a general council of all bishops and princes is convoked under the lord pope, where the church and the princes together will instruct all, under penalty of excommunication and condemnation, that all should work either mentally or physically, and that each should eat his own bread, that is, the bread won by his own labour, as the apostle has commanded, and that there be no idle or pushing fellows (*curiosi aut otiosi*) among us. Thus would be removed all usurers, all factious men and all robbers; thus would charity flourish and the fabric of the churches again be builded; and thus would all be brought back again to its pristine state.[1]

On the other hand, like other Christians, the clergy knew that the ideal could never be wholly realized. Robert of Curzon's legatine mission was ended abruptly by Innocent III in 1216 because of the French Crown's opposition to his violent attack on usury, the opposition of the clergy to the utopian rhetoric in his councils, and the indifference of the well-to-do to his appeals for a crusade directed over their heads to the poor, to children, and even to the sick. To practical reservations were added theoretical ones. If the common possession of all things was sanctified in divine and natural law according to Gratian's *Decretum*, this jurist and monk also admitted that in this imperfect world we are forced to choose between two evils, that of private right as against the even greater evil of violence or anarchy. Caesarius of Heisterbach told his Cistercian novices stories about Ensfrid, dean of Saint Andrew's in Cologne, famed for seizing food from the rich to give to the poor. He hastened to warn them, however, that 'many things are allowed the saints that are not permitted to those who are not holy. Where the spirit of God is, there is liberty'.[2] As long

---

[1] Georges Lefevre, 'Le traité *De usura* de Robert de Courçon', *Travaux et mémoires de l'université de Lille* x (1902), 33. The biblical passage is 2 Thessalonians 3:10–12.

[2] *Dialogus miraculorum* 6, 5, ed. Joseph Strange (Cologne, 1851), I, 352.

as the poor were aided, wealth was permitted, and so was private property. Indeed, some justified private property more than others. It was only postlapsarian to Duns Scotus, but according to Thomas Aquinas it was found even in the state of innocence. An even more vigorous justification is to be found in Giles of Rome's rehearsal of Aristotle's arguments against Platonic communism. Giles states that we have more incentive to do well with what we own ourselves, and he argues that, since brothers of the flesh often fight among themselves, economic brethren would fight even more fiercely.

The clergy were further obliged to admit that the merchant or businessman performed a necessary social function because he transported and handled goods. Often copied afterwards, an early twelfth-century passage by Honorius of Regensburg defines the merchants' honour: 'You are ministers of all nations because you bring them whatever they need through the perils of rivers, of thieves, of the road and the dangers of solitude. All men are therefore your debtors to render prayers for your labour.'[3] Nor should the businessman be gratified only by prayers. Giles of Rome's ample schedule of salaries or remuneration *pro labore* includes that to be gained from special techniques or knowledge. He even applauded the ancient if morally dubious case of the philosopher who cornered all the olive presses in the off season and then rented them at high rates when they were needed.

Compromises aside, the clergy were inspired by their utopianism to have a rather sour, if often sound, perception of the vices to which the members of other social orders were exposed. They also clearly had an interest in accenting such vices, if only because moral censoriousness is a kind of usury that the religious mind customarily exacts from the rest of the world's inhabitants. Texts to prove this point abound in the penitential literature, from Bartholomew of Exeter in the twelfth century to the great *summa* of Raymond of Peñafort in the thirteenth. Although more severe than most, a passage from a council at Rome of 1078 contained in Gratian's *Decretum* will give an idea of the rigoristic tone of this literature:

If a soldier or trader or one devoted to any profession that

---

[3] *Speculum ecclesiae, Sermo generalis, Ad mercatores*, in *PL* CLXXII, 865. Honorius is also thought to have been from Autun, but the matter is of no importance here.

cannot be exercised without sin should come to penitence when snared in serious sin, . . . he should know that he cannot possibly perform a true penitence by which he may obtain eternal life unless he leaves business or gives up his profession . . . that he should nevertheless not despair, we urge him to do whatever good he can in the meanwhile, in order that omnipotent God may light his soul to penitence.[4]

The last sentence is significant not only because it mitigates the rigour of the rest but also because it shows how the clergy operated to police the marketplace. Primarily this was in the court of conscience.

Ecclesiastical legislation dealt with many aspects of the economy, but of these only one will be treated here because it expresses in extreme form the churchman's hope for economic brotherhood and his tendency to press too hard upon the layman's conscience. Following the Jewish law of brotherhood (Deuteronomy 24: 19–20), Christians were not to lend at interest to other Christians, a practice then termed usury. As Gratian's *Decretum* put it: 'Usury exists when more is asked than is given; for example, were you to give ten shillings and seek more, or one measure of grain and require something above it.'[5] Seemingly simple, this could be extended to include a vast number of activities. *La Somme le Roi*, a vernacular tract of 1279, lists moneylenders, mortgagers, heirs who refuse restitution of usury by penitent relatives, helpers of Jews or other usurers, businessmen taking advantage of the market or of buyers, and lenders exploiting those in their debt. Indeed, few relationships escaped the jurist's or casuist's eagle eye. A commonplace of this literature refers to the professor who does favours for his students so that they will study with him.

Exceptions were made, especially in favour of the poor (*pauper*), a very inclusive term at this time. Minors' inheritances and women's dowries were favoured. The consuls of Genoa's chamber of commerce were not too bold when they promised to uphold all sentences rendered by the archiepiscopal court except those 'concerning usury given to minors from money invested by the consuls or that guardians have placed to advantage'.[6] In a decretal

---

[4] *Decretum* 2, 33, 3 de penitencia, 5, 6 in *CICan* I, 1241.

[5] *Decretum* 2, 14, 3, 4 *CICan* I, 735.

[6] Cited in Benjamin N. Nelson, 'Blandardo the Jew', *Studi in onore di Gino Luzzato* (Milan, 1949), I, 115n.

usually cited to justify the deposit contract, Innocent III instructed the archbishop of the same town to permit a poor and worthy citizen to invest his wife's dowry with a merchant in order to sustain the burdens of matrimony. Besides, the Church was also the *pauper*. When the mortgage was forbidden, churchmen were expressly allowed to use it to redeem Church property from lay hands. A curious example of clerical self-interest, this was soon extended to include the recuperation of patrimonies wrongly lost to lay families. But in the large the exceptions were neither many nor important.

This law did not spring up overnight. The basic principles were known in classical antiquity and the early Middle Ages, but the legislative activity of the Church did not seriously invade the lay world until the age of the crusades. The need to protect the crusader then elicited a flood of papal and conciliar legislation. In the later years of the twelfth century, the accent began to shift. As though following the introversion of the crusade idea itself, churchmen, exemplified by Robert of Curzon at the Council of Paris in 1212–13, moved from regulating their own order and protecting crusaders to the conversion of the whole world to their idea of a truly Christian economy. This not only affected secular business but changed clerical practice as well. Although mortgages had long been suspect because the creditor collected as interest the fruits of the property pledged to him, monasteries, military orders, and chapters had regularly invested in these contracts. After the formal condemnation of the *pignus* by the pope in 1180, they no longer did so save in exceptional cases. Legislation became increasingly comprehensive, every type of contract and partnership being investigated with meticulous care. Rigorism was the order of the day. In 1163 when Alexander III wrote to an archbishop of Rheims asking him to protect a debtor against excessive usury, it seems likely that, as in Roman law, moderate usury was permitted or, at least, tolerated. After the Lateran Council of 1215, however, the excuse of allowed and moderate usury could be pleaded only by Jews. The lengths to which the clerical legislator went is shown by the canon *Naviganti* of 1236, wherein Gregory IX refused any profit to those who lent money to merchants even if they shared the risk. Even though, as Cardinal Geoffrey of Trani argued in 1245, this may have referred only to maritime loans, rigorists were not slow to use it against any and all business.

To enforce the new law, the Church developed new punitive agencies. There was a general change in the form of episcopal tribunals from synodal bodies of laymen and clergy to the purely clerical court of the bishop or his judge (*officialis*) during the later twelfth century, and the new courts actively prosecuted usurers. Judicial action was reinforced by the development of coercive measures. At the Council of Toulouse in 1229, testaments not witnessed by a churchman were declared invalid, thus indirectly insisting upon deathbed restitution of usury. At the Council of Lyons in 1274 notorious usurers were denied Christian burial until restitution was made. At the Council of Vienne in 1311–12, the famous canon *Ex gravi* crowned this edifice by condemning princes or town fathers who protected or permitted usury, declaring that those who pertinaciously defended this sin were heretics.

Enforcement of this law changed business practice. In the twelfth century open loans (*mutua*) were common, and the jurists frankly mentioned usury. Widely used in southern France and Italy, the code called *Peter's Excerpts* regulated the relationships of creditor and debtor in, among others, the following chapter: 'If anyone owes a sum to his creditor, that is, capital (*caput*) and usuries, and pays any part of the debt, he may choose at the time of payment whether he wishes it to count for the usuries or for the principal.'[7] Writing in 1215, Buoncompagno of Signa casually recorded a type of letter form requesting intercession to obtain a loan at usury, which included the following debtor's promise: 'Moreover, we will give satisfactory security to the creditor with suitable pledges and our oath for both capital and usury.'[8] Furthermore, a lax interpretation of the *ius fraternitatis* of the business partnership appears to have been current. The glossator Alberic of Porta Ravennate (d. early 1190s) proposed that partnerships in which one partner bore most of the risk and the other shared equally in the profits were perfectly licit. Later on, such opinions were rare: if the great canonist Hostiensis echoed Alberic's argument on the business society, his was a minority voice. The rigour or even preciosity of contemporary practice is shown in Rolandino

---

[7] *Exceptiones Petri* 2, 29 and 31, and also 1, 5, ed. Carlo G. Mor, *Scritti giuridici preirneriani* (Milan, 1938) II, 115 and 54.

[8] *Boncompagnus Boncampagni*, in *BuF* II, 167.

Passaggeri's *summa* of the notarial art, in which he warns notaries that they condone usury when they draw up leonine contracts or partnerships 'because where the fourth part of the gain or loss [of the capitalist] is spoken of, you only write the fourth part of the gain'.[9] Jurists no longer mentioned usury save to condemn it, and town statutes, like those of Saint-Gilles in 1233, warned notaries to have nothing to do with it. Sometimes, as in Toulouse, the change occurred with dramatic rapidity. A common contract for a long time, the *pignus* vanished in the 1190s. The *mutuum* or loan was more durable, disappearing only during the Albigensian crusade, a period of intense factional strife within the town. From 1206 to 1215, Bishop Fulk, once a merchant and troubadour in Marseilles, sought to evoke popular support for the crusade and against heresy by attacking usury. He modernized the episcopal court and created a popular organization called the White Confraternity, both of which hunted usurers. Although the heretics were scarcely touched and the Whites were speedily countered by a Black Confraternity, Fulk's effort against usury was successful. During this time the first open testamentary restitutions were seen and the *mutuum* disappeared from documents drawn up by public notaries. In barely twenty years, the *pignus* had vanished and the *mutuum* had gone underground.

As the juridical aspects of the prohibition of usury became important, so also did the penitential ones, especially the restitution of usury. The basis of this practice was as ancient as the Church itself, and was tied to the Church's conception of the role of the rich. Honorius of Regensburg had said:

> Now, O men of wealth, I warn you that God wanted the rich to be the fathers of the poor. Remember that you came naked into the world, and that naked you will leave it. And because you must leave your riches to others, hasten now to build up heavenly treasures through the hands of the poor. . . . Decorate churches with books, robes, and other ornaments, restore those that have been destroyed or deserted, enlarge the prebends of God's servants, . . . build bridges and highways (*plateae*) thus preparing your road to heaven, and provide lodging, food and clothing for the poor, sick, and wandering thus buying eternal riches for yourselves.[10]

[9] *Summa artis notarie* I, 5, *de locatio et conductio*, Venice 1583 I, 123v.
[10] *Speculum ecclesiae, Sermo generalis, Ad divites* in *PL* CLXXII, 864.

The rich were therefore always urged to build and decorate pious places and to receive strangers and the poor. Systematic testamentary restitution, however, does not appear to have begun much before the 1180s. Thereafter the practice grew enormously. Rolandino listed the various types of restitution, both *certa* and *incerta*, under the following rubrics:

1. Open or public restitution to known people (*certa*).
2. 'In fear of infamy', covert restitution by the penitent's confessor to known victims whose names were listed in a closed codicil externally authenticated by two witnesses (*certa*).
3. General restitution by the penitent's executors to those who can prove usury against him—*suis conquerentibus*, as the documents so often say (*certa*).
4. Distribution of a sum of money by the executors to pious causes for the souls of those whom the usurer has harmed (*incerta*).

Rolandino's fourth case was implicitly dangerous for the moral life of the clergy because it meant that they could get their hands on tainted money. This is why our author insists that gifts to pious causes of this kind 'are to be made only with the consent of an important authority, such as the pope or a bishop'.[11] Everyone was aware of this problem. From of old, the clergy were forbidden to receive oblations or gifts of tainted money. In his biography of Louis IX of France, John of Joinville repeated a commonplace when he complained that the devil invented the system of restitution in order to corrupt the clergy.

The moral calculus involved was indeed extraordinarily complex. Restitution was a rendering of accounts made by an individual in the sweat of his deathbed; gifts *pro anima* during a life of unrepentant crime could not replace it. The attempt to avoid restitution by what moderns call philanthropy was condemned as one of the seven deceptive types of restitution by the Council of Ravenna in 1317. But such gifts could not be rejected and, in fact, had to be encouraged. Few conscientious confessors could wholly deprive of hope those who thus expressed an intention, however imperfect, of healing the wounds they had dealt the body social,

---

[11] Rolandinus Passagerii, *Flos testamentorum* in his *Summa artis notarie* (Venice, 1583) I, 226v–27r. The *Flos* is usually published among Rolandino's works and appears to be a contemporary work, but there is a question about its authorship.

that is, the *pauper* or the Christ. Hence rich men and great firms customarily gave annual gifts to charity. In 1310, when their capital stood at 147,000 pounds, the Florentine Peruzzi gave 2,500 pounds for pious causes. This does not mean that, if guilty of usury, the partners of this merchant-banking firm were excused from deathbed restitution. On the other hand, there were ways an individual could clear his balance-sheet during his lifetime. In 1254, for example, a pope gratified the Austin Friars of Todi:

> Inclining to your prayers, we permit . . . you to receive for the erection of your church up to five hundred small Sienese pounds from those of the city and diocese of Todi who have extorted usuries or acquired other things illicitly and cannot find out to whom restitution of the said usuries should be made. We do not wish, moreover, that those who have granted you the said usuries should be held to make any other restitution for them, but they should nevertheless remain obligated for the restitution of other acquisitions, if such there be.[12]

And restitution was sometimes treated rather cynically. An example is found in a manual of cases of conscience written by Claro of Florence between 1254 and 1262. This Franciscan asks whether those who have invested in town revenues bought cheaply during the risks of a war and have profited tenfold from them in the subsequent peace are obliged to restitution. No, he answers, 'they are to be excused for reason of risk and danger and are therefore not held to make restitution to the commune, but they ought to give very fat charities from their profits'.[13]

These examples illustrate the morally usurious quality of clerical action, and this, in turn, leads one to attempt to explain the persistence and even growth of moral rigorism in the thirteenth century. Ecclesiastics, we know, were forbidden to participate in economic life in any other role than that of rentier (although labour was also sometimes permitted). This self-restraint was powerfully reinforced, if not imposed, by the division of power between clerical and secular society characteristic of Latin Europe, a division that compelled ecclesiastics to sur-

[12] *Bullarium OESA*, No. 116 in *Augustiniana* 13 (1963), 499. This refers only to *usurae incertae*, not to *usurae certae*.
[13] *Casus conscientie Fr. Clari de Florentia* 30 in Bibl. Naz. Flor. MS B. VII. 1166 (Conv. Soppr.), 35r. I owe this reference to Julius Kirshner of the University of Chicago.

render functions for which they could be held responsible by civil power. The pure rentier, however, is at a disadvantage in a rapidly burgeoning economy. To subsidize its own growth and mission, then, the Church had to multiply the means of eliciting lay charity. Quite inadvertently, the employment of moral rigorism combined with economic and social utopianism was— if not overdone—a good way of getting a share of the profits.

The effect of this legislation and practice was to stimulate charity and public-spiritedness. Testamentary and other restitution and gifts made the medieval town the jewel it became by paying for the building and refurbishing of *pia loca*, a term that then included not only churches and cloisters but also bridges and public places (*plateae, fora*). The expansion of education and of hospital care for the sick and aged during this period also reflects the same impulse. Furthermore, the overall effect of ecclesiastical legislation was not harmful to the economy. As we know, the mortgage was replaced by the sale of rents and similar contracts. This had two advantages. Since it was a simple sale (*emptio et venditio annui census*), the rent contract was not usurious so long as it could be repurchased at the original price. It also suited the evolution of the economy, since relative to the value of land, it reduced the price of capital. The banning of the *mutuum* with usury multiplied the use of business partnerships, and, most important of all, encouraged the growth of the deposit contract. This, too, fitted in with the growth of economic maturity, in which the price of capital tended to diminish as risk declined.

Obviously, however, these benefits for business were by-products unintended by ecclesiastical legislators, and the rigorists among the clergy did not intend to let businessmen escape so easily. During the late thirteenth century Henry Goethals of Ghent declared the *rénte* usurious. The deposit contract was even more frequently attacked. The canon *Naviganti* of 1236, we recall, refused profit to lenders in mercantile ventures even when they shared the risk. But stark rigorism did not always have its way. The more general opinion was that earlier advanced by Peter Cantor: even were a man to seek avidly for profit, 'were he to give money to anyone to be invested and share both the loss and the gain and in the expenses . . . that would not be usury'.[14] Still,

[14] *Summa de sacramentis et animae consiliis* 3, 3, III, 2a: *Liber casuum conscientiae* ed. J.-A. Dugauquier (1963), 181, paragraph 213.

REGULATION AND CORPORATISM

even this intelligent doctrine could be formulated in a very hard way. Preaching in France before he became archbishop of Canterbury in 1207, Peter's student Stephen Langton likened the life of the Christian to a business partnership: 'for just as among merchants it is not a just society if one member always wishes to be a sharer in the profit and never in the loss or inconvenience— if by chance it happens, thus it is not a true partnership if we wish to live with Christ, and refuse to die with him or for him.'[15]

The banishment of usurious contracts from public records did not mean that moneylending ceased. A variety of surrogates took the place of the old *mutuum* or converted it into a loan without usury. Among these methods was one described by Bernard of Pavia in his *Summa decretalium* of 1198. As long as the creditor put no pressure on his debtor and no breach of the law was intended, the latter could gratify the former with a gift. This and other devices have been described as mere tricks; and so they sometimes were. What may be missed by this interpretation is that Bernard's formulation involved the intention of the parties to the contract. The emphasis on intention implied that money-lending had become, as it were, an aspect of penitential discipline. That this encouraged economic inventiveness, there is no doubt. As usury faded, interest became more important. Interest was naturally penitential because it was a penalty for nonfulfilment of contract. As *Peter's Excerpts* put it in regard to a fraudulent sale, the deceived purchaser 'should recuperate the price together with the interest, that is, the loss that he has suffered because of that sale, and the gain that he could have made with his money'.[16] To the clergy a bad debtor was almost as much of a problem as an evil creditor, and those to whom money was owed did not hesitate, therefore, to plead their cases before ecclesiastical tribunals. Besides, the interest or putative penalty (*poena*) could be formally stated in loan contracts. Echoing the jurist Bernard of Pavia, Raymond of Peñafort wrote in his penitential manual: 'If indeed the penalty be contractual (*conventionalis*), that is, placed in the contract by the common consent of the parties, to the effect that,

---

[15] Cited in Phyllis B. Roberts, *Stephanus de Lingua Tonante* (Toronto, 1968), 155n.
[16] *Exceptiones Petri* 2, 15, ed. Carlo G. Mor, *Scritti giuridici preirneriani* II, 108. Note that this twelfth-century text mentions the two famous extrinsic titles, *damnum emergens* and *lucrum cessans*. The third is the factor of risk, *periculum sortis*, one mentioned elsewhere in this chapter.

through fear of the penalty, the debt will be paid on a certain day, usury is not committed, just so long as the intention is good.'[17] Not a few clergy also understood the real risks of business. An example is Peter John Olivi, the famous radical Franciscan. Perceiving that entrepreneurs who risked lending money to towns or persons were foregoing a probable profit, Peter suggested compensation for this loss (and, in so doing, rejected the familiar Aristotelian argument about 'barren money'):

> For since money or property which is directly managed by its owner is put to work for a certain probable gain, it not only has the simple quality of money or goods, but, even beyond that, a certain seminal quality of generating profit, which we commonly call capital (*capitale*), and therefore not only does the simple value of the object itself have to be returned, but also an added value.[18]

As is obvious, the examination of the merchant's intention took place in the court of conscience, where the hot urges of the market were either cooled by the rigour or fanned by the laxity of the confessor. In reality, however, more was involved than the opinion of the clergy alone. The consensus of the business community or of society at large had to be taken into consideration. The size of the penalty—that is, as moderns would say, the rate of interest—and the terms of its application were matters determined by the custom or circumstance of the market. Until Calvin, this had nothing to do with the clerical prohibition of usury itself, but it was closely related to the practical efforts of the confessional and to the prosecution of usurers in Church courts. One cannot help but be struck by the fact that the texts of this period usually describe those who are to be prosecuted or denied burial as 'manifest and notorious' usurers. The constitutions of the archbishop of Pisa of 1323 defined such individuals as 'those of whom it is notorious *de jure* in that they have confessed or have been condemned for usury, or notorious *de facto* because they have given evidence of involvement in this business in a way which no subterfuge can hide, as when they have a counter or

---

[17] *Summa* 2, 7, 4 as cited and misconstrued in H. G. Richardson, *English Jewry*, 139.
[18] *De contractibus usurariis* in a manuscript of the *Biblioteca Communale of Siena*, Cod. U. V. 6, f. 307rb. Julius Kirshner was kind enough to point out this passage to me and to provide a microfilm copy of the MS.

table ready for this kind of business'.[19] It is evident that usurers of this kind suffered from *mala fama*, a bad reputation in their communities.

A final question posed by Church law is that of its relationship to secular government. The successful penetration of the market-place by the Church reflects the failure or at least the weakness of secular government in the post-Gregorian epoch. As the state began to renew its powers, however, conflicts of jurisdiction arose. In 1205, for example, Philip II Augustus of France questioned the right of church tribunals to prosecute usurers without the consent of secular authorities. He was defending a profitable practice of the Capetian monarchy. In 1143 the saintly Louis VII had sold a privilege to the burghers of Tours for 30,000 shillings, promising 'that neither we nor any of our successors . . . will seek money from them or sue them for usury, ill-gotten gain, or any multiplication of their money'.[20] On the other hand, princes and seigniors were sometimes inclined to favour the Church's stand. With undeveloped secular tax agencies, they were happy to derive whatever material gain they could from the efforts of churchmen. As we know from the *Dialogue of the Exchequer* (1176–79) and the treatise on the laws and customs of England traditionally attribu-ted to Ralph of Glanville (d. 1190), England's kings quickly 'received' Church law, reserving the prosecution of living usurers to the ecclesiastical courts but claiming the inheritance of dead and unrepentant ones for the Crown. In France reception was slower, but, if the late-thirteenth-century code called the *Establishments of Saint Louis* represents actual practice, the re-ward for secular rulers was even greater: 'When a usurer is found in the territory of a baron or elsewhere, and it is proven against him, his property is to go to the baron. And then he must be puni-shed by holy church for his sin, because it belongs to holy church to punish each sinner for his sin.'[21]

The Church had most difficulty with the towns. This is not because townsmen were more usurious than others; they were no more so than millers, rich peasants or estate bailiffs. Besides,

[19] Emilio Cristiani, 'Note sulla legislazione antiusuraria Pisana (secolo XII–XV)', *Bollettino storico pisano* XXII (1953), 13.
[20] Cited in Heinrich Büttner, 'Frühmittelalterliches Städtewesen in Frankreich', *Studien zu den Anfängen des europäischen Städtewesens* (Lindau, 1958), 186.
[21] *Etablissements de Saint Louis* I, 91, ed. Paul Viollet (Paris, 1881), II, 148–9.

substantial urban elements, both rich and poor, were deeply moved by the utopian hope for economic brotherhood. But townsmen were not as willing to accept the full rigour of the Church's position as were princes. Towns were financial centres, and the urban officers necessarily pushed the interests of those who had selected them. If clerical rigorists often berated the Italian merchant-bankers, the urban republics protected them. Rigorists questioned the state loan or debt societies (*montes*), but the authorities defended the subscribers by insisting on the legal fiction of the forced loan. There was also an inner dynamic that derived from the interplay of the economy and the republican form of government. Those who led government were generally the well-to-do, a group constantly changing as newly wealthy men moved into positions of command. Because the poor were preserved for virtue by their incapacity to do evil and the old rich by their lack of need or their antipathy to new economic methods, the rigorist's censure was largely directed against the new rich. Usury was therefore a political issue in urban republics. It sometimes led to extreme violence, as in Toulouse during the Albigensian crusade and frequently in the Italian cities. Although the principles on which the canons were based were rarely questioned, town fathers generally tried to limit their application and to put a brake upon prosecution.

Because of economic necessity, the position taken by town governments eventually was adopted by the state everywhere. Early in the thirteenth century the great jurist Azo noted the conflict between divine and civil law over the *mutuum*. Although admitting the inferiority of civil to divine law he argued that, for the common good or public need, an inferior officer may discriminate in the application of his superior's law. Because of the world's evil, the *lex humana* could not forbid usury completely but merely attempt to moderate it.

God, went the commonplace, demands nothing impossible from man and, in his influential *Summa confessorum*, the Dominican John of Freiburg (d. 1314) followed Hostiensis in saying that, where there are divergent opinions and contradictory laws, the more humane or more rational ones are to be preferred. Even the severe canon *Ex gravi* could be sidestepped, it being argued that a secular officer or prince who permitted usury was not heretical so long as he did not assert that his action was without sin. And moderate churchmen were accommodating. Thomas Aquinas opined that Jews are to make restitution of their usuries if the wronged debtors are known (*certae persones*). The vast majority of debtors, however, were *incertae*—for what borrower would ruin his credit in the money market unless the whole business community had it in for his particular creditor? For *incertae persones*, Aquinas went on, the prince may tax the Jews for the common good of the land—which is to say, in effect, that government may license Jewish usury and derive a profit from it. The learned professor then added: 'And what has been said of the Jews is to be understood of the Cahorcins and of all others who busy themselves in usurious pravity.'[22] And, by the time Thomas wrote, Cahorcin no longer meant a man from Cahors but instead any usurer, especially a Lombard.

The impulse toward relaxation was strengthened by the fact that the Church was itself the greatest government or state in Latin Europe. As a result, although the utopian hopes of such as Peter Cantor, Stephen Langton, Robert of Curzon, and James of Vitry were heard and even shared in Rome, they were in fundamental conflict with the financial needs of ecclesiastical government. Examples of what the latter meant in the forum of conscience are easy to find. In 1297 Boniface VIII wrote to six members of the Florentine merchant-banking family of the Franzesi noting that,

> because as you state, much ecclesiastical property is known to have come into your hands by means of usury and otherwise by evil and illicit contracts as well as much property of laymen by means of usuries for which restitution cannot be made, we, benignly considering that you are uncovering your guilt in this matter by a humble and spontaneous confession for the exoneration of your consciences, and wishing because of this to provide for you of the great clemency of the apostolic see, remit and concede to you that, by the authority of this see, you may licitly and freely have and retain all the property you have acquired in this way and even other properties acquired by these methods.[23]

---

[22] *De regimine Judaeorum ad ducissam Brabantiae* 3 in R. M. Spiazzi, *Opuscula philosophica divi Thomae Aquinatis*, 250b.
[23] *Registres de Boniface VIII* I, 627, No. 1661. The 'usuries for which restitution cannot be made' is a free translation of *per usuras incertas*.

And among the Franzesi mentioned were the Mouche and Biche who did so much to harm Boniface's cause in the conflict with the French king. But before one mocks the moral casuistry or the lack of prevision of this pontiff it is useful to recall that the text the clergy learned and expounded is hard to live by on this earth: 'But love ye your enemies, and do good, and lend, hoping for nothing again; and your reward shall be great, and ye shall be the children of the Highest: for He is kind unto the unthankful and to the evil.'[24]

Economic corporatism

The fact that the *pignus* and the *mutuum* were driven out of circulation is puzzling. Historians have attempted to explain it by saying that twelfth-century *pignora* and *mutua* provided capital for consumption only and not for economic growth; loans, it is said, being made principally to the poor, to improvident gentlemen or to declining monasteries. But this seems doubtful. A study of Jewish loans in late-thirteenth-century Perpignan shows that borrowing at interest—usury, that is—was engaged in by all classes and that the most successful businessmen of the community were among the borrowers. Evidence from Toulouse before the Albigensian crusade tells us that members of every class were creditors and debtors and that the income from *pignora* was often a substantial part of a landed family's inheritance. Documents from Narbonne, Marseilles, Pisa and other Italian towns show that the magistrates of these commercial cities were in the habit of financing the state by borrowing at usury until just after 1200. Furthermore, as we have seen, these contracts were so necessary that, when banned, they were soon replaced by all sorts of substitutes. Where the *mutuum* could not be replaced, it was permitted a half-life in the form of licensed usury and its punishment reduced by papal or episcopal penitential relaxations. And, from the point of view of economic function, it would certainly have sufficed to have policed the *mutuum* or the *pignus* by means of the traditional conception of the just price. One therefore wonders why such efficient contracts were driven underground and partly destroyed.

[24] Luke 6:35. In modern English, the 'nothing again' of the King James version is 'nothing therefrom' and hence refers to avoiding usury.

Significant though the moral rigorism of churchmen was, it could not alone have effected this change. Nor could the clergy have imposed this inconvenience upon an unwilling society. Lay adherence to the rigorists' programme was linked to two things: the idea of the crusade and the ethos of social and economic corporatism. Because crusaders borrowed money to finance their expeditions the attack on usury had always been part of crusade propaganda, just as the protection of debtors was part of the crusaders' privilege under canon law. In 1214 Innocent III defended his radical legate Robert of Curzon against French opposition by telling Philip II Augustus that a crusade could not be mounted unless usury was suppressed. Since, as we have seen, the crusade was a principal expression of the Latin desire to expand at the expense of neighbouring societies and religions, the importance of this link between usury and the crusade cannot be overestimated. But what most attracted men to the rigorists' cause was their express appeal to the law of brotherhood and to the utopian ordering of human society. It is noticeable that the reception of the clerical programme by laymen coincided with the rise of trade and craft guilds, of professional associations, and even of formally demarcated social orders and groups. It is therefore likely that the growth of a corporatist ethos in the economy and society of the Latin west during the late-twelfth and thirteenth centuries provided the basic popular support or even impulsion for the clerical programme. It is to the economic side of this corporatism that our attention shall first be turned.

Called by many names, the guild or corporation expressed the desire of medieval men to pool their strength to attain common objectives and to protect and increase the rewards of their labour. Even the poor takings of casual charity could be made the most of by organization. The town of Tours had a beggars' guild in the late twelfth century. Pleasure too can be maximized by joining in a group. Buoncompagno of Signa tells us in his *Cedrus* that private clubs and gangs of youths were common in Italy. Their names did not underestimate the value they put on themselves—the Falcons, the Lions, the Round Table Club. Before going further, however, it is best to remind ourselves that neither the desire to associate nor its intensity of passion was peculiar to the Middle Ages. It had been known before in antiquity, and the guilds described below were the forerunners of a corporatism that grew in France through the seventeenth century and dominated German labour as late as the revolution of 1848. Our problem is to define the characteristics of the corporatism of the late-twelfth and thirteenth centuries.

The guilds and associations of this time were relatively new. Around 1200 Paris had a powerful merchant guild and four or more trade and craft organizations. From 1261 to 1270, the *Livre des mestiers* of the provost of Paris registered the statutes of 101 trades and crafts. In 1292 there were 130, and in 1313 no less than 157. The rapidity of this expansion gave guildsmen of that time a sense of adventure that never again marked Europe's corporate structures. A second characteristic of this corporatism was that it still retained many primitive features. In much of northern Europe the impulse to associate had first been expressed in brotherhoods providing protection to traders and others whose itinerant occupations placed them outside of normal social communities or groups. The merchant guild was initially an organization of this kind. The guild, or hanse, combined economic functions with jurisdictional or governmental rights over a settlement (*Wik, portus*) adjacent to an older town or community, and thus membership in it was similar to citizenship.

Several of these primitive elements were still alive in 1200. The statutes of the Danish protection guild of Flensburg even included a provision whereby the brethren were obligated to aid the flight of a *congildus* who had slain a stranger. Even in the thirteenth century the merchants of Bedford, near London, claimed that the definition of community citizenship was membership in their association. In general, however, northern urban institutions had gone beyond this early stage. As towns grew, their once somewhat independent geographical parts fused together, and associations of crafts and trades took their places beside the merchants' guild. As a result, the merchants' guild lost many of its political functions to the larger political community and—and/or, really—its conception of membership became that of the whole community or *universitas*. This was a process of scission or increasing specialization, in which political functions were separated from economic ones. Not that merchant guilds lost all leadership. The nearest Paris ever came to self-government was when her merchants' association (*Marchands de l'Eau*) farmed, or bought the right to exercise, the royal office of provost in the late 1100s.

In Italy and adjacent regions things were different. There merchant associations had also played a very important role in the early history of towns, but by the thirteenth century they had become more analogous to modern chambers of commerce with a degree of economic jurisdiction than to medieval guilds. In the custom of Milan of 1216 the chamber of commerce (*consules negotiatorum*) was assigned jurisdiction over the town mint and markets, and its statutes and judicial decisions were to be recited annually in the general assembly of the citizenry. On the other hand, the custom expressly stated that the *consules negotiatorum* were not government officers and could therefore be elected to judicial or other public posts.

It is not easy to distinguish between what is primitive and what is mature. The domination by a merchants' guild of the financial life or politics of a Flemish town reflects the past. On the other hand, when the town fathers of Bruges announced in 1240 that no one but a member of the Hanse of London could hold high public office, this indicates the formation of a firm oligarchy or plutocracy. The members of the Hanse were not simple merchants as much as they were entrepreneurs in the wool industry, and membership in the Hanse was more or less restricted to patrician families. Much the same may be said about the political policies of Florence's entrepreneurial associations, especially the wool and silk guilds and that of the bankers. The difference between these later merchant or entrepreneurial associations and the earlier primitive ones is that, although political office was sometimes limited to their members, town citizenship was not confused with guild membership.

Another example of maturation is the evolution of the guildsman's public duties. All men owed service to prince or community and at first the terms of this service reflected those of manorial or feudal service. A charter of 1158 tells us that the tanners of Toulouse owed both the count and the town help in building siege artillery in time of war. Twenty years later the master stonemasons of Nîmes confessed an obligation to work for the count at fixed wages and to service his artillery. For each castle destroyed, they were to be paid one hundred shillings. During the Albigensian war, the butchers of Toulouse's Great Market were to accompany the army and sell meat at fixed prices on credit. The Garonne boatmen stated in 1231 that they owed the count transport services in return for an annual dinner. Customs of this kind were long remembered, but the maturing of the economy soon led to greater flexibility. In late-thirteenth-century Florence, although construction guilds provided experts to help the republic's officers draft building codes and make inspections, the government let contracts to individual builders and masons. As may be seen in the *Book of Montaperti's* description of the Florentine army in 1260, the guilds provided many of the engineers and artillerymen, who were, appropriately enough, under the command of officers titled masters, but these special companies were not directly connected with the guilds.

A guild was usually associated with a particular trade or craft. This was an obvious and suitable arrangement for tradesmen, such as butchers and bakers. Industrial crafts were sometimes more complex. As an industry grew, a process of scission took place. In 1227, for example, Toulouse's woollen industry was ruled by one association; shortly before 1300 five associations shared the industry, each devoted to a different part of the manufacturing process. A principal reason for such scission was that, because of the small size of machinery, a system of household workshops was compatible with efficient production. The guild system reflected the organization of industry into small workshops each containing, besides sleeping partners who may have capitalized it, a master or owner, several workers (journeymen), and a few apprentices—perhaps a dozen workers at most. Only the mining and water-milling industries seem to have surpassed these limits by 1300. As for the shops or tables of tradesmen, they were naturally small, and remained so until the recent revolutions of packaging and distribution.

One result of the smallness of the productive unit was that the idea of economic fulfilment for the craftsman and tradesman was not unlike that of a shopkeeper in the nineteenth century. An independent shop with a small, paternalistically ruled staff was his idea of heaven. This was true even of entrepreneurs in large industries, like cloth-making. The capitalist did not think in terms of factories. Instead, he invested in others' shops by means of partnerships, or sent his goods to be manufactured in a shop by means of the putting-out or domestic system. In short, a principal difference between the medieval guild and today's industrial organizations is the importance of the intermediary grade between the capitalist and the worker, that of the guild master or shop owner.

This middle element encouraged an economic policy that was both regulatory and restrictive. Guilds suffered from a small-business bias, and their laws sought to make the mean the norm of the profession. Trade guilds, for example, customarily prohibited any member from owning more than one or two tables or shops. The guilds' meticulous regulation of the purchase of raw materials, production methods and prices reminds us that mutual suspicion is the price of economic brotherhood. Guilds were also monopolistic, in that they tried to exclude foreigners from membership and early exhibited a trend towards hereditary membership. This was especially true in the trades. In the late 1100s the Parisian butchers were already attempting to limit the ownership of tables to members of families enrolled in the corporation. Similar motives in industry led to a gradual multiplication of training stages and an increased accent upon the 'mystery' or 'mastery' of a craft, and eventually to production of the obligatory masterpiece. In thirteenth-century Paris masterpieces were required only by the saddlers and the silk workers' guild; the practice did not become general till the next century. As the guild built its hierarchy around craft techniques, a certain technical conservatism soon became apparent. There was a futile struggle against water-powered fulling mills by the old guilds based on hand mills in both France and England. Just before 1300 German cloth guilds fought the introduction of the spinning wheel. As the rate of economic growth slowed down around 1300, also, the division between masters and workers gradually became more rigid, especially in the larger industries. This was obviously hard on the workers because they found themselves unable to achieve the normal ambition of the medieval artisan, that of becoming a master with his own shop.

The guilds' technological conservatism and desire for monopoly (*monopolium*) excited resistance by consumers and by import-and-export interests. Town governments refused to close guild membership to immigrants and fought the guilds' attempts to regulate sources of raw material and prices of finished goods. Only by the end of the thirteenth century can the corporate impulse be said to have won out. The victory reflected not the failure of consumer or even export–import interests so much as the maturing of the economy. The guilds had won their place in the sun, but they found themselves operating under ever more intense state regulation. The appearance of state-chartered or owned companies, the spread of protectionism (Pisa, for example, in 1303 prohibited the import of semifinished woollens to protect local industry), and the delineation of various navigation acts, like that of Barcelona in 1286, were entirely compatible with the growth of guild corporatism. As long as the cartel aspect of guild legislation was subordinated to the common good, the guild was one of several means by which society mobilized itself for economic battle. The economic idea that was already being limned around 1300—especially in the countries of the Mediterranean basin—was that of the mercantilist state.

Corporatism and society

The process of guild scission mentioned above was not simply a response to technological circumstances. It was also social. In larger industries, a split between entrepreneurs and artisans generally took place. This was partly because of the guilds' own levelling legislation. In the English town of Beverley around 1200, for example, the weavers excluded any members who became rich enough to qualify for the drapers' or merchants' guild. In general, however, the split was caused by the resistance of lesser shop owners and craftsmen to exploitation by the wealthy. The issues were many. They included the form of partnerships between entrepreneurs and artisans, the terms of putting-out contracts, and wages and hours. There was also the problem of debt. Town statutes often prohibited artisans from pledging their tools to secure loans, showing that much of their equipment was supplied by capitalists. On the other hand, there was legislation to protect debtors against imprisonment. Although more advanced law may be found, Beaumanoir's custom of Clermont-en-Beauvaisis may be taken as typical. Imprisonment was to be mitigated by allowing debtors to provide for their own needs, if they had the means, and 'if they have nothing, he who holds them in prison must give them bread, wine and soup as much as they can use at least once a day'. Imprisonment was to last only forty days, a longer term being called 'a thing contrary to humanity'.[25]

[25] *Coutumes de Clermont-en-Beauvaisis* 51, 1539, ed. Am. Salmon (Paris, 1899–1900), II, 279–80.

Sometimes conflicts between groups took place within a single company, if it was a sizeable one. In 1291 the workmen employed at the Bazacle Mills of Toulouse were forbidden to form a union lest they harm the mill owners and the public. Struggles within a guild between masters and workers were common. A burgo-master of Provins was slain in 1281 when the clothworkers rose in protest against a projected increase in hours. Twelve years later laws against journeymen's associations were again promulgated. Frequently an entrepreneurs' association, or 'guild merchant', fought with the guilds of the artisans. At Leicester the weavers and fullers attempted to form guilds in 1264 and 1275 and to bargain with the drapers of the guild merchant. Some of the issues are revealed by the complaints of London's merchants against the weavers in the late 1200s. The artisans, they claimed, had raised prices without notice, cut the number of looms, engaged in a slowdown, and gone on strike, in effect, by extending their Christmas holiday through January.

These conflicts were sometimes complex and had far-reaching consequences. The Florentine wool industry is a case in point. Whereas one hears only of weavers, dyers and finishers around 1200, the picture was altogether different by the 1290s. Then two principal organizations headed this industry, the Arte di Calimala, whose members specialized in importing unfinished cloth, and the Arte della Lana, whose members were importers of raw wool. The Lana had no less than fourteen different crafts under its direction, some in established guilds, like the weavers and finishers, and others, like dyers and carders, employed on the basis of putting-out. In regard to the latter labourers, the entrepreneurs of the Lana not only had the advantage of providing the raw material and equipment on their own terms but also won from the town government the right to exercise a limited police jurisdiction. The workers reacted by trying to organize, and their efforts to do so invariably involved the government. As moral regulator of the marketplace, the Church, too, was interested. The bishops generally favoured the Lana, while popular preachers and the Franciscans, true to their urge toward apostolic poverty, favoured the lesser folk.

And things were still more complex. The Lana policed entrepreneurs as well as artisans because, by using workers not under its controls, unscrupulous members or interlopers could profit from substandard labour. This in turn involved the relationship of town and countryside. It was principally in outlying villages that a black market labour supply could be found. In this context things became very casuistical indeed. The bishop stood to the right, the Franciscans to the left. When, preaching in 1304, the friar Jordan of Rivalto excoriated an episcopal condemnation of peasants for weaving illegal cloth he intended to aid the poor, but was inadvertently also giving comfort to the most voracious of the entrepreneurs. Since Florence's merchant-banking firms not only dealt in international public finance but also imported wool and invested in Lana partnerships, the struggles within this corporation could affect Europe at large. Conversely, the French embargoes on the export of wool to Italy during the battle between Philip the Fair and Boniface VIII had repercussions upon the stability of Florentine political and economic institutions.

In the urbanized parts of northern Europe, there were similar relationships between domestic and foreign policy. Patrician merchants and entrepreneurs in Flanders had long battled with artisans and labourers. Although prohibited, strikes were frequent. As early as 1242 patrician-ruled towns had combined to prevent the emigration of workers seeking better conditions. From the 1280s into the early 1300s grave social and political troubles, both rural and urban, shook the whole area. In the towns the crafts tried to organize and then to take over the government. This involved foreign intervention. England, the enemy of France, Flanders's overlord, was in it up to the hilt, especially since she supplied the bulk of the raw wool used there. Opposed by the patricians who ruled his all but independent towns, the count of Flanders reluctantly allied with the people and the English. In 1297 a shortage of English raw wool sparked risings in Douai and Bruges that toppled the patrician governments and led to the great victory over the French at Courtrai in 1302. Although a semblance of French authority was soon re-established, these events introduced an age in which the crafts pushed in to share political and social authority with the entrepreneurial and patrician elite.

These violent conflicts of the rich, the middling and the poor were the beginnings of the persistent social warfare that marked late medieval life, but men in 1300 could not perceive that frightening prospect. Occasional violence aside, things seemed to

197

be moving in the right direction. If government increasingly intervened in the economy, the guilds invaded government, thus giving the simple artisan a larger part in the management of his community.

Economically speaking, corporatism clearly benefited the masters and even the journeymen. Although presumably a higher percentage of the total population than today was poor, fragmentary figures from Paris in 1292 and Toulouse in the 1300s indicate that there was no great gap between the rich and the poor. An effort to improve conditions of employment and salaries is evidenced in guild ordinances. According to the Parisian *Livre des mestiers*, the mistreatment or firing of workers among the swordmakers could be protested before the six guardians of the craft, four of whom were masters and two journeymen. The proportion of journeymen among the officers of the bronzeworkers was even higher, two out of five. Journeymen fullers were still better off. Two of the four fuller guardians were journeymen, and the annual election was so arranged that the journeymen chose the master guardians and the masters the journeymen guardians. Government was often called on to intervene in these matters. At Douai a dispute between the merchant drapers and the shearers—highly trained artisans like most of those mentioned above—was settled in 1229. In return for concessions, the shearers agreed to forgo using the strike as a weapon. Kickbacks were prohibited and wages (actually, prices for work done) were to be fitted to the general price pattern by a simple device. When prices rose, the shearers were to petition the town-appointed inspectors of the industry to present their case to the town council. Were prices to fall, the merchant drapers were to do the same.

Craftsmen also tried to reduce the hours of work, and, aided by the Church, their efforts seem to have been successful. The *Livre des mestiers* forbade night work in all but eighteen of the 101 crafts registered, the reasons given ranging from the need for good lighting to the need for repose. The role of the Church is difficult to appreciate because it was partly inadvertent. Holidays tend to multiply in any society, and the Middle Ages was no exception. In Paris by about 1300 obligatory religious holidays and feasts had risen to twenty-eight or thirty, giving, when Sundays are counted, about eighty days of rest each year. To this could be added anywhere from twenty to thirty half-holidays (*jours de commun de foire*) for lesser feasts. During the thirteenth century the clergy insisted on the Saturday half-holiday, in which the devout were to prepare themselves for Sunday's observances. Doggerel verse on this theme was widespread, in which the confessor asks, for example: 'Let your conscience tell me/If indeed you have on Saturday/Left work at the time you ought?'[26] The Saturday half day was often included in guild ordinances. To these general religious holidays may be added those traditional in the crafts. In the early 1200s the shearers at Arras took four days at Christmas, eight at Easter and eight at Pentecost. All in all, it has been estimated that in the region from Paris to Artois the average work week was four or five days. This should not give the reader the idea that the year 1300 was labour's time of bliss. The work day ran from dawn to dusk, with anywhere from an hour to an hour and a half off for meals. Naturally, the work day varied with the seasons, from seven or eight hours in winter to fourteen in summer. Salaries were adjusted accordingly. In late-thirteenth-century Brussels wool spinners earned $2\frac{1}{2}d$ a day in winter, $3d$ in spring and autumn, and $4d$ in summer.

Guilds provided social services. Annual banquets, parades, ceremonial inductions of new masters, and ostentatious gifts to charity were customary. Many guilds paid for the funerals of their members, and it was usual to give free training to sons of impoverished masters. Social services were tailored to the needs of particular professions. Many of Modena's smiths served as wandering tinkers, and the statutes of their guild in 1244 therefore tell us that 'if anyone of the said association should fall sick from the Alps to the Po [valley] and from Bologna to Parma, guild officers (*massarii*) must bring him home, and, if he is poor, . . . they must do this at the expense of the profession (*ars*)'.[27] As time went on, such services became more structured. The ordinances of the Parisian furriers of vair in 1319 provide for an entry fee of 10s 6d plus an additional charge of 1d per month. Among the services offered in exchange was sick pay. A sick member received 3s per week, another three for a vacation week following convalescence, and a further three upon earning his first pay.

The social services of the guilds were supplemented by special

[26] Cited in Emile Coornaert, *Les corporations en France*, 78.

[27] Cited in Piero S. Leicht, *Storia del diritto Italiano: Le Fonti* (2nd edn., Milan, 1943), 322.

confraternities created both for this purpose and for devotional activities. They were sometimes more able to resist entrepreneurial pressure than the guilds themselves. When, in the late thirteenth century, the Florentine dyers' guild had been quashed by the Lana, their charitable association still remained. One reason for their strength was that confraternities were invariably associated with the Church. The Church's attitude toward such groups was mixed. Moved by the Gregorian excitement, it supported them in the early twelfth century; by the late 1100s it often questioned them. A council at Rouen in 1189 complained about the crowding of churches with altars associated with guilds and pious confraternities. Similarly, groups expressing ideas of apostolic poverty as a labour ideology were often repressed, a notable example being the suppression in 1178 of the Humiliati in northern Italy. By 1201, however, papal policy changed, and the Church opened its arms to the Humiliati and similar groups. Propagating a kind of Christian utopianism, the Humiliati were immensely successful for a time, especially among the labouring classes in the cloth industry. In Florence they acquired an island in the Arno in 1239 and there erected an industrial community of brothers and sisters. A similar movement began in northern Europe about the same time, and communities of women (Beguines) and men (Beghards) spread like wildfire through Flemish, French and Rhenish towns. In 1250 Cologne alone boasted about a thousand Beguines.

As time went on the original impetus of these movements weakened. Secular guilds objected to their competition, and the vast growth of secular associations removed part of their reason for being. Although the papacy and the new mendicant orders favoured the growth of economic corporatism and stimulated the foundation of charitable agencies to aid artisans and labourers, the Church was not wedded to any one social group. The main effort of both the mendicant orders and local parish groups was to create charitable confraternities that included on their rolls men of every social class, though obviously the poorer parts of the population were the principal beneficiaries. The result was that the Christian utopian labour movement began to fail. By 1277 the Florentine Humiliati had sold their business and retired from industry. In the north, the organizations of the Beghards disappeared or became part of the lunatic fringe, although Beguinages remained characteristic of the Rhineland and Low Countries well into modern times. A quiet commentary on the fading of utopian hope and on the position of women in industry may be seen in a petition of 1295 to the town council by the Brussels Beguinage requesting the same return for their labour as the members of secular guilds.

As the Church responded to the rising power of artisans and shopkeepers, so also did the state. This is a subject of some complexity. On the whole, princes actively encouraged the creation of guilds—so much so, in fact, that some towns in backward regions had more developed corporate structures by the mid-thirteenth century than did great urban republics. One reason for this was fiscal, in that the right to constitute guilds was sold by the prince. Another was the aristocracy's love of the poor and dislike of the new rich. To Joinville, the oppression of the poor by the rich amply justified Louis IX's removal of the provostship of Paris from the *Marchands de l'Eau* and its assignment to a royal officer, Stephen Boileau. This action was heartily applauded by the craftsmen and tradesmen who had been fighting the patrician merchants since 1250, and their loyalty was rewarded by Boileau's publication of their guild ordinances in the *Livre des mestiers* in 1261. So usual was this type of action among princes that it might be described as a formal espousal of the corporate principle, which was soon extended to cover the political order as well. Thus in 1257 the king of Aragon divided the two hundred seats of Barcelona's great council among the town's social groups; eighty-nine seats went to the patrician bourgeois (*cives*), twenty-two to the merchants, and eighty-nine to the arts and trades (nine carders, four weavers, three tailors, etc.). No urban republic, however great, was yet willing to grant the lesser elements of its population such extensive representation.

On the other hand, princes were not mainly actuated by love of the poor or even by desire for money. Princely government has a quality of social opportunism, since a prince loves no social group but only himself. When merchant aristocracies dominated towns, princes generally supported the people; when the situation was reversed, they favoured the patricians. When the commons (*vils homens*) seemed about to take control of Barcelona in 1285, the king of Aragon had no hesitation in crushing them with the utmost brutality. During the period under discussion, however, kings were able to play *bon prince* more consistently than in later times because the merchant aristocracies were the traditional leaders of the towns in their search for independence. It is worth noting that the withdrawal of the right to farm the provost's office from the *Marchands de l'Eau* obliterated forever whatever modicum there had been of Parisian self-government.

In urban republics corporatism advanced more slowly but eventually attained the same heights. Every profession and craft formed its own association, and corporatism became the constitutional basis of the state. In Florence this principle was not recognized until 1282, when the seven greater guilds (the medical and legal professions, the bankers, and the entrepreneurs' associations of the silk and woollen industries) dominated the government. By 1292 the middling guilds, like those of the butchers and masons, and even some lesser artisan corporations had pushed into the government, only dyers, carders and other proletarian groups being excluded. Economically exploited and politically disenfranchised, these humble folk tried to organize in order to share the advantages already won by the middling crafts.

The time was not propitious, however. Around 1300 a curious balance had been established, in which a majority of the population had obtained a substantial part of what they desired. On the other hand, a significant minority, sometimes swollen by immigration from the countryside, was still deprived of economic and political fulfilment. Over a hundred years of intermittent social war were to pass before these latecomers, educated in a century-long tradition of rising lesser social groups, abandoned their hopes. Add a tightened economy to this social and ideological tragedy, and some reasons for the turmoil of the unhappy but inventive fourteenth century may be glimpsed.

PART THREE

Society

VII

Laboratores (Workers)

Men and women

Although complex in reality, the social orders of the Latin west were often described in simple terms. There were three great orders: the clergy, the warriors, and the labourers. As a sour old Dutch saying put it, the spokesman of each order advanced to describe his function, saying

Ik bid voor U—I pray for you,
Ik strijd voor U—I fight for you,
Ik leg eieren voor U—I lay eggs for you.[1]

These were social categories and are investigated as such later on. In the meantime, one might pause to consider the fact that those who really lay eggs for mankind are the women.

[1] An old folksaying cited in Emile Lousse, *La société d'ancien régime* (Louvain, 1943) I, 103.

BIBLIOGRAPHY. Except in the history of law and *mores*, the Germans seem to have led the way in examining the history of women. See Karl Bücher, *Die Frauenfrage im Mittelalter* (Tübingen, 1910) and such specific studies as Wilhelm Behagel, *Die gewerbliche Stellung der Frau im mittelalterlichen Köln* (Berlin, 1910). This is somewhat unfortunate because, since German towns were rarely much developed until after 1300, the record of women's participation in economic life is wanting for this earlier period. Legal studies may be represented by the fine book by Adhémar Esmain, *Le marriage en droit canonique*, 2 vols. (2nd edn., Paris, 1929–35), and G. H. Joyce, *Christian Marriage* (2nd edn., London, 1948). The literature on love and related topics is vast. A stimulating popular history is that of Denis de Rougement, *Love in the Western World* (2nd edn., New York, 1956), but the reader should not take his view of Christian marriage or of love as a heresy seriously. A recent review of ideas of love is to be found in F. X. Newman, ed., *The Meaning of Courtly Love* (Albany, 1969), in which, however, one should examine but query the curious literalism of D. W. Robertson, the distinguished authority on Chaucer. The ideal physical and moral qualities for both woman and man is shown in Georg Weise, *Die geistige Welt der Gotik und ihre Bedeutung für Italien* (Halle, 1939). See chapter XIV below for women's participation in heresy.

The basic view of the seigniory and its relationship to the rural classes used here

205

derives from Fustel de Coulanges, *L'alleu et le domaine rural* (Paris, 1889) whose famous remark that the large landed proprietor became 'dans les limites de son domaine, une sorte de chef d'Etat' (p. 458) has been modernized or put into the context of general social history by Marc Bloch, *Feudal Society*, 2 vols. (Chicago, 1961, translated from the French of 1949) and updated by works such as that of Georges Duby, *La société aux XIe et XIIe siècles dans la région Mâconnaise* (Paris, 1953). Earlier statements of his views by Bloch were discussed and sometimes corrected by Léo Verriest, *Institutions médiévales*, vol. 1 (Mons, 1946), who also offered a devastating criticism of Pirenne's famous contention concerning the total separation of the classes and populations of town and countryside. Other interesting studies are J. A. Raftis, *Tenure and Mobility: studies in the social history of the medieval English village* (Toronto, 1964), Geoffroi Tenant de la Tour, *L'homme et la terre de Charlemagne à Saint Louis: essai sur les origines et les caractères d'une société —Le Limousin* (Paris, 1942), Philippe Dollinger, *L'évolution des classes rurales en Bavière depuis le fin de l'époque carolingienne jusqu'au milieu de XIIIe siècle* (Strasbourg, 1949). Lastly, much of the discussion of peasant emancipation and classes is built upon Marc Bloch's *Rois et serfs: un chapitre d'histoire capetienne* (Paris, 1920), but other sources enable me to accent the connection of the idea of liberty to ecclesiastical and other conceptions of progress and the restoration of a primal bliss, topics to be taken up again in later chapters. Bloch's strong laicism resulted in a mild ideological myopia about the Church.

In line with the remark made above on the work of Verriest, the treatment of the social classes in the medieval town is designed to correct the assertion by Henri Pirenne—expressed in his *Medieval Cities* (New York, 1925) and other works— that the town was separate from the countryside (save in Italy) and that nobles, churchmen, and peasants were not among the 'progressive' economic elements of the time. Pirenne's view finds a counterpart in German historiography, notably in Max Weber, *The City* (Glencoe, Ill., 1958, an indifferent translation of chapter 8 of part two of his *Wirtschaft und Gesellschaft* [2nd edn., Tübingen, 1925]) and Edith Ennen, *Frühgeschichte des europäischen Stadt* (Bonn, 1953), wherein it is claimed that there was an original and primal difference between northern European urbanism and that of the Mediterranean. The latter is said to have preserved the classical or Roman tradition whereby the city was the centre of a province and housed rural landowners as well as urban folk whereas the northern (especially German) city developed the new sense of the bourgeois town separate from the nobility and peasantry of the countryside. A mixing of the two traditions is to be seen in Fritz Rörig, *Die europäische Stadt im Mittelalter und die Kultur des Bürgertums* (2nd edn., Göttingen, 1955—translated as *The Medieval Town*, London, 1967). Pirenne's position has been questioned as early as Niccolà Ottokar, *Le città francesi nel medio evo* (Florence, 1927) and the close relationship between town and countryside has been outlined by one of his pupils, Johann Plesner, *L'émigration de la campagne à la ville libre de Florence au XIIIe siècle* (Copenhagen, 1934). My position is not quite the same as that of these critics, but is that the difference between northern and southern urbanism is not one of original essences and that it developed only in the course of the eleventh and twelfth centuries for reasons that have nothing to do with purported Germanic and Roman traditions. On the close relationship between town and countryside, see Maurice Beresford, *New Towns of the Middle Ages: town plantation in England, Wales, and Gascony* (New York, 1967) and Walter Kuhn, *Siedlungsgeschichte Oberschlesiens* (Würzburg, 1954). Other interesting and contentious works on the town are Charles Petit-Dutaillis, *Les communes françaises: caractères et évolution des origines au XVIIIe siècle* (Paris, 1947) and Hans Planitz, *Die deutsche Stadt im Mittelalter von der Römerzeit bis zu den Zunftkämpfen* (Graz-Cologne, 1954).

In the most intimate sense, society is divided into two peoples, the women and the men. What caused the many divisions of function between men and women and also the subordination of women to men appears to have been twofold: woman's weaker muscular endowment and her capacity to bear children. Women rarely went to war except to urge their men on, help them plan for it, and to bewail or rejoice in their departure. Although women laboured in the fields and in industry, they did not plough, hunt, mine, or do heavy metalwork or building. Also, being larger, men could threaten to, and did, beat women. Although not markedly different from those obtaining within recent memory, the conditions of childbearing differed from those of today. In a time of high infant mortality, the capacity of a woman to have children was prized in a way now scarcely imaginable. But childbearing also enslaved women. The exposure of unwanted children was prohibited by law and voluntary abortion was not only forbidden but risky and relatively inefficacious. One thinks, for example, of an abortifacient such as that made of ergot. In short, birth-control—as was the case until yesterday—was almost reduced to being a function of the ages at which marriage took place, sexual practices such as onanism (Genesis 38:9), or the casual brutality of parents and servants to the very young. A second hardship for women was the prevalence of accidents at birth and the incidence of childbed fever which caused a higher death rate among young adult females than among young men in spite of the hazards of war, hunting, heavy labour, and riding.

Having noted the fundamental inequality of the sexes, it comes as a surprise to realize that the ideal of the time stressed their equality. The marriage sacrament, for example, required no institutional sanctions, being simply the free and voluntary agreement of a woman and a man before witnesses, something posing obvious difficulties for parents with nubile daughters. In the Pauline texts repeated by churchmen and glossed to a point far beyond what they had meant to the Hellenized Jew Paul himself, if the husband owned his woman, the wife owned her man. And, because it contravened the theoretical equality and responsibility of all souls, the Church had done away with those primitive German laws that had placed a higher value on a woman of child-bearing age than on one past her prime. Because she was the very kernel of the family, the married woman was especially protected by the lawyers. For the recuperation of her dowry and her husband's marriage gift, a woman had precedence over all her husband's other creditors. Judgments about marriage based upon the intentions of the parties usually favoured the woman. A curious case may be seen in a *responsum* of the professors of law at Toulouse around 1300. Was a young woman who, under the influence of wine and pleasant company, played the 'game of man and wife' complete with mock marriage ritual and not so mock consummation, legally married? No, she said, having subsequently married another. And no, the doctors found, although consideration was to be given to her condition.

It is to be noted that much of this law did not reflect a high estimate of woman's worth. In a sense, women, especially mothers, were almost children to the lawyers. But here it is worth remembering—to speak only of the norms of Roman law embodied in so much medieval jurisprudence—that, although the *patria potestas* was indeed great, it was hedged about with corresponding responsibilities. The disinheritance of children and the loss of a mother's rights required public legal action and not merely the will of the father. As is evident, the right of children to support and education by their father is almost as important to a mother as her own rights. The lawyers confessed that a prince or magistrate could adjust the details of both divine and natural law, but were also sure that they could not change their essence. A pope, the commonplace said, could never dispense from the Old and New Testaments, nor a legislator from the natural duty of a father to educate his children. And on this principle were built real protections for women and mothers in canon and civil law.

Certainly, in comparison with Islamic and Jewish women, Christian European women seemed better off. Divorce on the initiative of the male was far more difficult in Christendom than on the other side of the frontier. In both Islam and Jewry scarcely any attention was given to the education of women, partly because they played a very small 'religious' role in these two cults. Although not allowed entry into sacred orders, women were active participants in all the movements that livened the western Church. Between 1245 and 1251 no less than thirty-two convents of women were incorporated into the Dominican Order within the German province alone. At Strassburg in 1257, twelve cloisters housed about three hundred sisters, and, as we shall see in chapters IX and XIV below, there were many more laywomen associated with the new devotions of the mendicant orders. And convents, although controlled and open to inspection by prelates, were self-governing institutions with elected abbesses. Although, unlike the monks who usually had Latin, nuns often had only the vernacular, some sisters were distinguished in Latin letters. An example is Hildegard of Bingen, famed for prophetic visions, an indefatigable traveller and correspondent with theologians, emperors, and popes, who died in 1179 as abbess of Rupertsberg.

Out in the world, the daughters of gentlefolk and wealthy burghers often learned vernacular letters at home or in selected convents, institutions analogous to modern finishing schools. So important was this to the gentry that the historian of the Dominican order, Jordan of Saxony (d. 1237), claimed that one of the reasons why Dominic of Osma founded the monastery of Prouille in 1206 was because the rural families of southern France, unable to meet the costs of orthodox convents, were sending their daughters to be raised and educated at heretic houses. Concerning ordinary burghers, it is worth noting that in 1320 four of Brussels' ten lower schools were for girls. It is therefore not surprising that one of the major poets of the age was Mary of France who wrote her *Lays* at the Angevin court from 1165 to 1190.

Women were, of course, restricted. Writers on manners often advised against too much education for women. It was a waste of time in view of their duties around the crib and the hearth, duties that, except among the wealthy, must have been far more difficult and time-consuming than they are today. Another argument against education was that learning inclined women toward insubordination. On the whole, women were excluded from the literate and clerical professions, partly because, one imagines, these professions had evolved out of the clergy, and long retained a clerical ethos, if not celibacy. There were exceptions. According to a reliable report, the celebrated canonist John Andreae who died at over seventy years of age in 1348 had his daughter Novella lecture his students when he was sick, although he thought it best to hide her from them by a veil. More seriously, female teachers of vernacular letters are heard of in the towns and so are scribes, but women did not attend the university and guilds of notaries did not include them. They were very active in medical and hospital work. There too, not being trained at a university, women were excluded from the art and profession of medicine, but were frequent practitioners of the craft, midwives having a near monopoly of childbirth. In hospital work women were almost as important as men. This was because university trained doctors were not part of the hospital staff in this period and because many hospitals were organized like monasteries, that is, run by the assembly of their administrators and nurses and sometimes even inmates. The quality of such arrangements as well as the relationship of man and wife may be illustrated by some charters concerning the small hospital of Saint-Antonin at Toulouse in 1202:

> I, the hospitaler John, marry you Sibil; and I, Sibil, marry you John; and I, Sibil, give and concede my body to . . . the said hospital to serve God and the poor, present and future . . . [Sibil then gave property to the hospital in lieu of a dowry] . . . And Raymond Calvet [master or *dominus* of the hospital] receives the said Sibil as sister and participant in the said hospital and all its properties . . . [and pledges to John and Sibil] that he will receive no man or woman in the said hospital without their advice and consent, and that John and his wife Sibil are to be the masters of the said house after [his] death and that of his wife Ricarda . . .[2]

Westerners were proud of the high position of their women relative to those in Jewry and in Islam, and were convinced of the superiority of their system. Although there is another obvious motive for its creation, a theme of popular literature well represented in the sometimes brutal stories of Caesarius of Heisterbach was that of Jewish girls wishing to marry Christian boys or to have them as lovers. In his scheme for the conquest of the Near East, Peter Dubois argued that eastern potentates would be delighted to marry the educated and lively girls of the west. More significantly and more dubiously, he also asserted that eastern women, held in the bondage of polygyny and purdah, would welcome the western soldiers. Here, Peter was one of several crossing lances in the long battle between Heleno-Roman monogyny and Near Eastern polygyny, an institution that had won many victories in the Mediterranean in late antiquity and the early middle ages, and that was only in this period again beginning a long decline.

[2] Cited in my 'Charity and social work in Toulouse', *Traditio* XXII (1966), 248n.

Certainly, on the ideal level of love literature, the equality of the lover and the beloved, of the man and the woman, was always insisted on. Here reference is not made to the love of the unattainable woman, the love from afar of troubadour poetry. As in the parallel literature of Christian mystic love, this was a device enabling a poet to concentrate upon describing the feeling of being in love and especially of love's overwhelming longing. What is meant here is that the beloved woman cannot be passive: she must come to her love as much as he goes to his. In woman's work such as grooming and healing, Iseult is as competent as is Tristan in man's work, hunting, singing and making war. She sacrifices as much and commits as many crimes for her love as does he. A principal theme in *Aucassin and Nicolete* is that the Saracen maiden Nicolete proves that a woman's love and fidelity are equal to a man's. Men love only one woman at a time, went the ancient commonplace, but women desire men indiscriminately—any useful or passable candidate will do. Nicolete proved the ancients wrong. Even in Christian of Troyes's *Erec and Enide*, a story about the rebuilding of mutual respect and love by a young married couple by means of accomplishment and fulfilment in their careers, Enide undergoes and passes tests of her loyalty, courage, and social graces just as does her husband—one of which was that, having once told him to put aside sloth and get going, she must not nag or officiously intrude any further.

This ideal equality was contradicted by reality, a reality imposed by childbearing, its relationship to the holding and division of property, and the power of family or lineage conceptions in this period—a matter to be studied later. Not only in princely lines, but, to a lesser extent, in those of the gentlefolk and burghers, marriages were arranged by parental agreement. Although this had the advantage of protecting a woman after her husband's death and enabled women of good family to play almost independent roles when married, it emphasized family advantage at the expense of individual choice. It is therefore no wonder that adultery was a more significant theme in medieval love literature than it is today and that Andrew the Chaplain could state in the 1170s— referring to a purported decision of a court of love headed by the Countess Mary of Champagne—that true love could not exist in marriage and that marriage was no excuse for not making love. Of course, family interests and their relation to childbearing and property did not always have this effect. Although sources are exiguous and not much studied, it is known that, among the farming population, the need for extra hands even encouraged the institution of trial marriage—to see if the pair could have children —and one wonders how many of the propertyless poor could afford to be married at all. On the whole, however, family solidarity and the wealth and power bound up with it impeded the freedom of lovers, indeed, of men almost as much as women. Even so mighty a prince as Henry II of England was driven to marry Eleanor of Aquitaine in order to resist or defeat Capetian power. She was not only a woman ten years older than Henry, but also one who, although very intelligent and loyal to her children, was both wilful and even treasonous. Not that Henry was a saint. . . .

The second impediment to the attainment of the ideal was imposed by servitude and the ethos of service. Although it accented uterine succession and may therefore have had something to do with the importance of women in the servile household, servitude obviously impeded freedom because neither a male nor female serf could marry without the permission of the lord and the payment of a fee. The moralists fought this. Peter Cantor denounced servile restrictions upon marriage because they contradicted his somewhat exaggerated interpretation of 1 Corinthians 7:39: 'If any woman wishes to marry, let her marry in the Lord' —freely, that is, and without tax. On the level of aristocratic service, much the same was sometimes true. A woman fiefholder was sometimes nearly as disposable as was her fief. When, after many famous services to both Henry II of England and to his son the young Henry, William the Marshal's suit was pleaded before Richard Coeur-de-Lion on the grounds that Richard's father had given William the heiress to the county of Pembroke, Richard exclaimed: 'By God's legs, he did not give her to him! He only promised to. But I'll give her to him all free, both the girl (*la meschine*) and the land!'[3]

A third impediment was that women often married older men. Although the only reliable evidence dates from later times and although economic circumstances have much to do with the age of marriage, it is likely that men of middling means, especially townsmen, waited until they had inherited property or had

[3] *Histoire de Guillaume le Maréchal*, ed. Paul Meyer (Paris, 1891–1901), v. 9368ff.

established themselves in business before marrying. At that point such men were not likely to marry women who had reached their own age without being betrothed. Parenthetically, one may conjecture that, far more than poor public health, this was one of the reasons why town populations had to be replenished from the countryside throughout the Middle Ages. The high mortality of childbearing also made it probable that men of reasonable means would have more than one wife in their lifetimes, and this would affect the gentlefolk and humbler people who often appear to have married women near their own ages in their first marriages. The result was that not a few girls were married to men ten or twenty years their senior in their first marriages. This helps to explain why women were considered to be 'in subjection' to men, but it was not all to the bad. Unattractive and mentally or economically insecure young women could hope to do better in the market of the overaged than among the young and strong. Such marriages could lead to a kind of equality between a strong young woman and a failing older man, a marriage between the generous credulity or ignorance of the youthful bride and the sceptical carefulness of the experienced older husband. Besides, at the worst, there was always a propertied widowhood to be looked forward to.

In spite of this and in spite of the fact that it existed everywhere, this kind of marriage did not attract the idealist. No romantic poem is known in which the lover and the beloved are not both exquisitely young. And there were elements of fear here: an old man will be cuckolded by a young wife—a theme seen as early as the eleventh century poem *Ruodlieb* where an old man sits in a privy to watch his wife and a young man through a knothole. The matter could be put more elegantly, as by Philip of Novara. He disliked this kind of marriage not only because it was risky—'for if he has the wish, he certainly does not have the capacity'—but also because it was distasteful. He even advised against marriage between those of equal age when old: 'Two rotting bodies in one bed are simply unbearable.'[4]

As among men, but more exaggeratedly, one feels the picture is describable in terms of a balance between servitude and freedom. The servile side of a woman's mentality or her compensatory reaction to her 'subjection' is illustrated in the literature of the time. This was sometimes plaintively humorous. An example is

[4] *Des quatres tenz d'aage d'ome* 4, ed. Marcel de Fréville (Paris, 1888), 95.

the *Lamentations of Mahieu*. Writing before 1292, the author argues that marriage is a harder and worthier state than celibacy. Women are impossible: they talk too much. Why, do you suppose, did the Saviour first show himself to women after his resurrection? Because he wanted everyone to know about it as fast as possible. Why did Jesus not marry? He knew better. Bachelors made the laws of marriage, including the prohibition of divorce, which is simply incredible. Mahieu asked the Lord: your daughter Eve betrayed you; can you imagine what your wife would have done? In short, this law is unfair: the Lord ordained what he did not dare try himself. The Saviour gently replies that married men will have a higher place in heaven because they have suffered more. He also confesses that he had sanctified the married state and allowed his mother to marry, 'But I did not tonsure the monks/Nor constitute any monastic order.'[5]

Some of this literature had little to do with women, but much to do with men, their attraction and repulsion, their conflict between sweetness and gall, perfume and stench. Focused by the celibate ethos of the monks, this ambivalence toward women among men was experienced as rarely before or after. The charm of a girl's figure and the lilt of her voice tempted both Peter Damian in the eleventh century and Peter, the hermit of Murrone, who was elected Pope Celestine V in 1294 and canonized in 1313. And both converted their attraction into scatological rages and fancies. Damian also repeated the ancient charge that the end-product of heterosexual carnality was homosexuality. Philip of Novara put this more subtly. Easy carnality led older men, prompted by fear of ageing and death, to seek avidly all sorts of unnatural vice and perversions. Just as pride is the vice of the poor and covetousness that of the rich, so lust is the vice of the old. Where these themes relate to women is the conjuring up in the romances of the evil and witchlike woman, the sower of discord who upsets the whole world with her lying tongue. Typical of the different feeling about women in the two worlds of Islam and Christendom, however, the theme of woman as the emasculating natural traitor giving herself only to the love of the hideous and the worthless seems not as well developed in Christian as in Islamic letters. Perhaps Eve was countered by the Virgin. Muslim women may sometimes have thought that what their

[5] Cited in Ch.-V. Langlois, *La vie en France au môyen-age* II, 277–83.

menfolk called polytheism had its advantages.

The freedoms enjoyed by women are best seen at the times of their attraction for, and dominance over, men. The first of these was when they were young, the time a pretty village girl could set her sights high and when her counterpart among the gentlefolk could hope not only for a rich man but also for a blithe and handsome one. The latter naturally had advantages over the former, because the attitude of the wealthy toward village girls was ambivalent. In the opinion of the burghers and gentlefolk who tried to use them, they were not 'nice' girls—to employ a modernism. Andrew the Chaplain's recommendation as to how to approach them was analogous to the modern 'just push the "dog" over'. But, as Adam de la Hale (d. 1286–88) tells us, that rarely works. This poet's heroine was Marion, a peasant maid endowed with natural good sense, courtesy, and great taste who rejected out of hand the suit of a *miles gloriosus*, a pompous and brutish knight.

Still, youth was the period of advancement for women, and the moralists made sure to warn them to go the right way. Philip of Novara tells of a handsome woman who was so beguiled by the gifts she received when young (twenty to forty years old in his scheme) that she collected ornamented and jewelled knives from her successive lovers. In middle age (forty to sixty) she had to begin to give them away and, at that, never obtained more than a one-night stand. She ended with nothing save angry bitterness. Not that happy marriage was not known. The pieces that dealt with it usually connected love to career and advancement, and it is worth noting that there were married couples who have gone down in history as magnificent teams. Such a one was Alice of Montfort and her husband Simon, the conqueror of the Albigenses who was slain at the siege of Toulouse in 1218. A specialist in handling the clergy and a good public speaker, Alice was Simon's principal recruiting officer and fundraiser, possessing an indomitable energy that fully equalled her husband's cold rage on the battlefield.

A second age of woman's power was widowhood, when a possibly still young woman acceded to the measure of authority over her family and over the property or means of production that had been her husband's. What this, together with woman's capacity for hard work, meant for the artisan classes may be seen in the following. Although there are few figures for the period discussed in this book, statistical evidence from later ages shows that women constituted a significant part of the labour force in industry. In late medieval Frankfurt about thirty-three per cent of the crafts and trades was wholly female, as against about forty per cent wholly male, the remaining ones being more or less evenly divided. Not that women were equal to men. Evidence from France shows that women's salaries were always lower than those of men in comparable positions.

Much of this information, one feels, may be read back into the earlier period. In 1179–82 the 'brothers and sisters' had equal rights in the turners' guild at Cologne. Thirteenth-century Parisian guild statutes indicate that some crafts were wholly female and that women could be admitted to the mastership in some of the silk and woollens guilds. According to the *Livre des mestiers*, a widow usually exercised her deceased husband's profession, although if she married someone not in the craft she usually lost the mastership or at least the right to train apprentices. Although master guildswomen usually 'bought out of' the police duty of watch and ward, Wismar in 1292 boasted one woman—a *domina* Adelaide—who pledged herself 'to serve watch as long as she lives just like any other citizen'.[6] Parenthetically, it is worth noting that, around Toulouse, married women of all classes were often addressed in the documents as *domina*. Such was not the case with men: few were addressed as Mister (*dominus*). An interesting result of this participation in industry and of marriage and widowhood was that, where guilds had become the basic electoral bodies of town government, women even played a minor role in political life. Thus it could happen that, in mid-fourteenth-century Provins, twelve per cent of the voters in a political plebiscite were women.[7] And that they presumably voted against self-government for the community in favour of princely rule was a mark of their political maturity.

Among the martial aristocracy, everything about widowhood depended on the degree of liberty the class had won from princely power (a matter to be discussed later in terms of wardship, etc.) because otherwise a widow might be forced to marry an agent or

---

[6] Helmut Wachendorf, *Die wirtschaftliche Stellung der Frau in den deutschen Städten des späteren Mittelalters* (Quakenbrüch, 1934), 32.
[7] F. Bourquelot, 'Un scrutin du XIVe siècle', *Mémoires de la société nationale des antiquaires de France* XXI (1852), 455ff.

favourite, however unsuitable. But the history of burgher, gentle, and princely families is full of powerful and dominant women of middle age. This is partly because the art of directing or commanding other men does not require learning or even much practice. All it needs is intelligence, courage and decision, qualities in which women were fully the equal of men. A notable example of this was Blanche of Castile, the mother of Louis IX of France, whose long regency was a spectacular success. Her only weakness was her excess of motherhood. According to the Lord of Joinville, she so dominated her son that he could scarce call his mind his own and hardly dared lend his body to his wife.

There were also, of course, stolen freedoms, and this brings us back to the existence of love among the married. There were all sorts of these and one may believe that this theft was occasionally condoned or even encouraged. The husband who advanced not by his own efforts but instead by his wife's prowess in other's beds was a universal figure of fun, but there are many corrupt ways to advance a career. Also, it is hard to use the word 'adultery', because, as is obvious, everything depends on traditional *mores* and especially on wealth. It is noteworthy that the poets did not bother to list the names or to count the number of Iseult's children, and it is evident that what may be passed off as love among the rich and leisured is merely obvious and bare adultery among those of lesser means. Or, rather, the picture is more subtle than that. In late thirteenth-century Italian towns, for example, the people, especially the workers, often loved the French, their songs, their courtliness, and their easy-going ways. So did the knightly aristocracies and the richer burghers who 'lived nobly'. Those who did not like the French and gallicism—although they too had read the poems and heard love's siren song—were lesser gentlefolk, burghers, yeoman farmers, in a word, those with modest property and strong social ambitions for themselves and their children. It was this group that drew up the sumptuary legislation on women's clothing and jewelry and in which strong hostility to adulterous love was most often found. Indeed, even those of this social level, and somewhat above, who were moved by the freedoms of the well-to-do could not really carry it off. Although professionally ambitious, Abelard finally married Heloise, but they could not live it out. We know little about this famous pair as parents, but they had a child who, raised back at home in Brittany by Abelard's sister, marched off into history pursued by a didactic poem by his father, saddled with the appalling name of Astrolabe.

Hardly discussed by serious analysis, the relationship between love and morality is hard indeed to define. The aristocracy, it has been truthfully said, was more broadminded than the middle classes. What is wrong about this statement is that it fails to consider the grave threat posed by adultery between a lord's wife and his vassal or a member of his household. Adultery was bad enough and secular law often allowed a husband to slay those guilty of it in the heat of the moment. But, for obvious reasons, adultery with a wife who headed a household or court was far more disruptive of social order and was sometimes visited with exemplary punishment. In 1314 a scandal involving two gentlemen and two princesses rocked the court of Philip the Fair of France, and resulted in the death and mutilation of the two men and the disgrace of the women. Another weakness of this statement is that it accents the difference in sexual *mores*, but does not show that those with means were able to spend time on titillating moral problems.

An example of this kind of casuistry is to be seen in a thirteenth-century vernacular romance called *Flamenca*. Because the king has paid some attention to his handsome wife, Archibald of Bourbon falls into a jealous rage. Followed everywhere, his young wife is practically incarcerated, being allowed only to go to church. Enraged in turn by her husband's constant surveillance and invasion of her freedom, the woman eventually resists. There, in church, the inevitable happens. A young gentleman who has been to the university is serving as a clerk there, perhaps as a secular canon. He is literate, well mannered, martial in bearing and behaviour, and, most of all, deeply sympathetic. Archibald was so busy watching the king at the gate that he failed to notice that the young gentleman had slipped in the postern. But *Flamenca* is really a study in lack of moderation (*mésure*) and in the inefficacy of rage. Besides, the tormented husband had evidently overlooked the ancient lore contained in the widely read translations of the *Roman de Sidrac* that 'the hottest woman in the world is colder than the coldest man in the world', and the further teaching therein contained that wives have been unfaithful before and still brooks continue to bubble and flowers to bloom.[8] But it all worked out

8 Cited in Langlois, *op. cit.*, III, 250.

for Archibald. One day the young man blithely rode away to war, and he and his wife lived happily ever after.

Similarly, it is not enough to say that the middle classes were wholly puritan. That they were that, there is no doubt, because it was they who drew up the sumptuary laws, the statutes against noise, public entertainments, lewdness in public, too visible prostitution, gambling, and all the rest of the disorders of the streets. But it was the good town fathers who, at Toulouse, inhibited the count's right to confiscate property for adultery by making it literally impossible to catch anyone *in flagrante delicto* in spite of the severity of the promulgated law. And it was also this same group that took seriously Augustine's celebrated observation that whores were necessary lest men fall into even worse vices, and systematically planned for it. Responding to the advice of his planners, the lord of the *bastide* of Villefranche-de-Lauragais included in his founding charter of 1280 the following paragraph:

> Item, lest dissolute and shameless whoring women exercise their lust and pleasure in the houses and habitations of the said town by providing an evil example to many people to the prejudice of the republic, we grant to the said inhabitants the faculty of building in some part outside of the said town a house of prostitution, in which these said women of ill fame shall be received, and the profits from the said house shall remain and pertain to the said inhabitants for repairs that have to be made to the aforesaid.[9]

These ambivalent or alternating feelings were shared by both men and women and reflected the general attitudes of medieval man toward the flesh and the body. Here men's attitudes ranged all the way from violent flagellation to a positive cult of the body, the laity leaning toward the latter and the clergy toward the former. James of Voragine believed it edifying to tell us that, when Titus asked the apostle Peter why he had not healed his daughter Petronilla, he replied that it was because she was too beautiful to live. The reverse of this coin is shown by the lilting chant-fable *Aucassin and Nicolete* of the early 1200s, which consciously and blasphemously titillates: by lifting her skirts, the virgin Nicolete miraculously caused a sick man to leap up off his bed. Dour veterans and the clergy rarely missed an opportunity to castigate

[9] J. Ramière de Fortanier, *Chartes de franchises de Lauragais*, 576.

the banners and magnificent armour of the knights, but Dante's *Convivio* stresses the duty of men and women alike to dress elegantly and to cultivate beauty of body as well as of mind. And the clergy themselves were all mixed up. As we know, they themselves produced much of the romantic literature of the time, but were of two minds about it. Somewhat hopelessly, one imagines, a thirteenth-century penitential of the school of Peter Cantor distinguished between two types of public entertainers: 'some frequenting public drinking bouts and lascivious parties in order to sing dirty songs are damnable. . . . Others, however, . . . who sing the deeds of princes and the lives of saints, and who solace men in their sickness and distress . . . , these certainly can be borne, as Pope Alexander says.'[10]

Laymen were especially inclined to question clerical views on sexuality and the body. Writing for the lay audience, the chaplain Andrew's *De amore* of the 1170s and John of Meung's continuation of the *Romance of the Rose* a century later flatly argued the natural impossibility of celibacy, clerical or other, and the jurist Peter Dubois, a contemporary of John's, opined that the requirement had been instituted in the Church by the old and decrepit. Besides, the clerks could daydream too. In Andrew's intentionally humorous dialogue between a 'very noble' gentleman and a 'very noble' lady—not his wife, naturally—the gentleman argues that *amor purus* or heavy petting is better than *amor mixtus* because less dangerous in terms of pregnancy, though both are forgiveable because they are 'natural' and because love alone inspires man to virtue. He goes on to say that 'I will prove to you by inevitable necessity that a clerk is more to be chosen for love than a layman. For he is more cautious and prudent in everything'. Unbelievable, replies the lady, because a knight at least has warlike virility while a clerk is disfigured by his tonsure and appears 'as though clothed in a female costume'.[11] She adds that clerks can't give honest gifts because they are not supposed to have anything to give. Who wants to be a receiver of stolen goods?

In spite of the polarization of views, it is important to remember that this was not a simple conflict between ecclesiastical asceticism and secular acceptance of the body. This was a battle that tore all men apart, and nothing shows this better than the debate over the

[10] Cited by Léon Gauthier, *La chevalerie* (Paris, 1884), 656.
[11] *De amore* 1, 6, G, ed. Amadeu Pages (Castello de la Plana, 1930), 109–10.

social role of love in works directed to the lay audience and than the relationship between the women and the clergy. Anent the first, it is notable that, unlike medieval Islam and modern times, there is little literature on sex, but much on love. Perhaps because of the heroic idea of spiritual freedom taught by the clergy and the martial ethos of risk-taking loved by the gentlefolk (matters further examined in the next two chapters), medieval women and men experienced love and investigated it with a vehemence unimaginable today. A full-blown religion of love is found in *Tristan and Iseult*, where we learn that love, although necessary and even obligatory, can find no fulfilment on earth but only in heaven. Here on earth, the lovers—although perfect in moral and physical beauty—are obliged by their adulterous love to violate all the canons of society: marriage, friendship, family, and loyalty to Church and state. As seen even in so playful a piece as *Aucassin and Nicolete*, another tradition refuted this argument, although one confesses that it was based upon the easier problems of pre-marital love. Although admitting that love has its antisocial side, it is nevertheless a commitment whereby the lover shows his capacity to advance to greater things, thereby reflecting 'religious' teaching wherein the ability to experience carnal love gave evidence of a capacity to love spiritually.

The relationship between women and the clergy was also ambivalent. The clergy were of two minds about women. Giles of Rome remarked that, because of their weak endowment with reason, they surrendered to their passions more easily than did men. And, had he thought of it, Giles would have certainly used Humbert of Romans's last line of defence against women preaching, namely that the first woman, Eve, had upset the world with her teaching. Humbert had put it:

I do not permit a woman to teach for four reasons. The first is her lack of intelligence which women have in smaller quantity than men; the second is the subjection imposed upon her; the third the fact that, if she does preach, her appearance will provoke lust . . . ; and the fourth because of the memory of the first woman who . . . taught but once and turned the whole world upside down.[12]

---

[12] From his *De eruditione praedicatorum*, cited in Gottfried Koch, *Frauenfrage und Ketzertum*, 171n.

Humbert was really arguing in favour of Paul's position stated in I Timothy, 3:4: 'But I suffer not a woman to teach, nor to usurp authority over the man, but to be in silence.'

To some clerks, however, women's capacity to triumph over their weaknesses was a source of virtue. Addressing the nuns of Godstow in 1284, Archbishop John Peckham of Canterbury repeated the classical sentiment that, the more fragile their sex, the more worthy their virginal penitence. And that there was iron in women, none could doubt. Do we not read in Scripture that weeping women adhered to the crucified Christ more firmly than his fleeing disciples? The Dominican preacher Berthold of Regensburg was telling no secret when he said that women attended church more regularly and went to sermons and confession more willingly than did men. It was this aspect of the relationship between women and clerks that inspired Robert of Abrissel (d. 1117) to found the order of Fontevrault (rule adopted in 1115), whose home community was governed by an abbess who eventually supervised two convents of professed religious, one female and the other male, as well as two houses of *conversae* for those sick in body (especially lepers) and those sick in mind (fallen women). Innocent III thought it meritorious of laymen to marry fallen women, and a number of orders specializing in them, like the German sisters of Mary Magdalene (founded 1225), appeared during the thirteenth century. This was not all grisly condescension. In a very real sense, there was a working alliance between the women and the clergy.

The lives of the saints in this period and the biographies of other clergy show that mothers frequently pushed their sons toward the celibate life of the ecclesiastical order. As noted above, also, everybody knew that women were more inclined to attend church, more susceptible to the influence of priests, confessors and preachers, more devoted to the cults of the saints, and more credulous in regard to miracles than their menfolk. Men may have led the Church, but the true believers were most especially women, sometimes to the point of embarrassment as the Rhenish Dominicans found when their female houses and female tertiaries multiplied enormously in the course of the thirteenth century. But it is not enough to say that women believed more than men did. In the first place, theirs was only a specialized aspect of belief, and women, like the clergy, were famed not only for hardheaded practicality but also for their manipulativeness in personal relationships. In the second place, one must discover the function of this particular kind of belief and its effect on the clergy.

It seems probable that women gained freedom by profiting from, and even by stimulating, the hostility of the two kinds of powers they dealt with: the two worlds of men. Exercised over women, the power of the layman was immediate, sexual, expressed by greater physical strength, and practical because it involved property and the maintenance or abandonment of children. The authority of the clerk was at a remove, only occasionally sexual, and, in regard to the relationship of women to their husbands and lovers, was inclined to be idealistic, even unreal, as when it insisted on those Pauline texts that proclaimed the free right of a woman to choose her mate, and, within marriage, on her equality with her husband. The clerical standards of judgment, in fact, often transcended and even confounded those based on practical experience in the world. It is therefore not surprising that women conspired to people the clerical order with selected and specially brought-up sons, and that they enthusiastically seconded their erstwhile children's practice of winning their points in the battle with the laity by means of sentimental obfuscations or by appeals to the miraculous. To force the argument a trifle, women were never more practical than when they were at their most credulous.

The farmers

Although gentlemen and bourgeois often condescended to them, farmers, or peasants, were not disparaged by clerical and other social theorists. Early in the twelfth century, Honorius of Regensburg praised the honour of the farmer: 'What do you say about farmers (*de agricolis*)? Most of them will be saved because they live simply and feed God's people by means of their sweat',[13] a sentiment repeated by Vincent of Beauvais and Raymond Lull, the thirteenth-century encyclopedists. In his *Jeu de Robin et Marion*, the poet Adam de la Hale had a rough knight beaten in love's battle by a sweet and gentle peasant boy. To this romantic pastoral theme—one often repeated in the literature—a theologian like Peter Cantor would add that of the peasant's native

[13] *Elucidarium* 2, 18, in *PL* CLXXII, 1148–9.

223

wisdom. Who is wise, he asks, the rich man, the jurist, or the man of letters? None of these, the wise man is the farmer. But this wisdom rested on a fragile base. The preacher Berthold of Regensburg described the mutual malice of the peasants by comparing them to the naked fish who devour each other because of their poverty and helplessness.

The social status of the agricultural population ranged from wholly free to wholly slave. The origins of this inequality interested men of the time. In his compilation of the customs of the Beauvaisis, Beaumanoir catalogued the reasons for the existence of servitude. It derived in part, he said, from some men's poverty or their incapacity or unwillingness to bear arms. Some had sold or given themselves to saints to enjoy the protection of the Church, and yet others had been reduced by the oppression of powerful lords. Although simple, Beaumanoir's is a not inaccurate account of the subjection of individuals to the mighty in the early Middle Ages. Beaumanoir also states that slavery resulted from capture in war, an argument that rang true for a period when defeated Muslims, as we have seen, were often enslaved. And, although the actual events had long been forgotten, differences in the status of rural classes derived from the time of the German conquests. Some conquests were even fairly recent, and the idea of the racial or cultural superiority of the conquerors was still alive. The French conquest of England gives evidence of this. A reflection may be seen in the *Dialogue of the Exchequer*. There the master—the author—informs his disciple that a system of fines for the covert murder of Normans or Frenchmen had been imposed on English communities at the time of the conquest. By now, he remarks, the races have so fused that the fine has been extended to the murder of any freeman. For a community to avoid the fine the murdered man must be proved to have been a serf—the proof of Englishry that lasted until 1340.

Beaumanoir's belief that slavery ultimately derived from conquest not only reflected reality but also transmitted a powerful intellectual tradition, that of classical philosophy as mirrored in Roman law. Roman law had many other teachings useful to the jurists of this time. In its theory, though not necessarily in its practice, a man was either slave or free, a sentiment echoed by almost all medieval jurists. Useful in the abstract, this was not an accurate description of medieval servitude and was not usually thought to be so by men of the time. In *Fleta*, that epitome of the legal thought of Glanville and Bracton, this Roman theory is buttressed with the argument that neither services owed nor conditions of land tenure have anything to do with an individual's freedom or slavery, which is personal in nature. The author is obliged to admit, however, that this is true *de jure*, but not *de facto*. Beaumanoir, a less pedantic jurist, bluntly stated that there were many conditions of servitude, ranging from hard to light, sometimes personal in nature and sometimes attached to tenure and services.

This multiplicity of social grades and servitudes contrasts sharply with the relatively clearcut distinction between slave and free in a neighbouring society like that of Islam and also with that of Latin Europe's own past, among both the primitive Germans and the Romans. Some of the reasons for the difference have already been given, namely, the mitigating effect of the Church on slavery and the economic impracticality of acquiring slaves from the outside. Other reasons are to be found in the social organization of Europe. Since the faraway days of late Rome, the freeman and the slave had been coming closer. In part, this was because men were viewed as parts of a regulated society, each having his function or duty and his appropriate reward. All men were therefore bound to service, the rich and powerful just as much as the poor and humble. During the medieval period the advocate of this sociology was the Church. From antiquity to the days we are treating here its social commentators delighted in paralleling the heavenly hierarchies with those of this world, stressing the point that true liberty was service to God, his Church, his princes, and his people. In this service ethos the distinction between slave and free, between servitude and liberty, was understandably obscured and therefore, until well into the twelfth century, churchmen customarily described bondage to the Church as true liberty. In 1103, for example, Cluny's monks called some serfs who had been given them 'rustics who, liberated from the yoke of servitude, have been bound to the service of the blessed Peter'.[14]

To these reasons may be added a political one, namely the growth of seigniorial power. In parts of France and Italy and adjacent regions the seigniory had arisen during the period before that considered in this volume, but the institution itself with its

[14] Cited in Duby, *La société . . . dans la région Mâconnaise*, 248.

relative independence from the authority of kings and greater regional princes, was very much alive in the twelfth and thirteenth centuries. It was still being implanted in certain regions, notably in Germany. Although usually a wealthy landlord, the seignior was essentially the ruler of a community, the head of what was, in effect, a small state. Depending on time and place, this little state could be anything from one or more villages to a substantial town with its village dependencies, such as the lordship of the Williams of Montpellier. Usually it was composed of a group of villages or hamlets more or less tightly controlled by an important local family. The seignior's powers were those that extended over the whole community. In terms of the economy, he gained rights over the forest and uncultivated lands, and he built and profited from common facilities, such as mills and winepresses. His was the duty to protect the village church and often the right to collect its tithe and nominate its clergy. Most significant of all was the seignior's capacity to command and judge the community's inhabitants. If exaggeratedly, Beaumanoir described the seigniory (*potestas, poosté*) when he remarked that all barons who held fiefs in the county of Clermont had all rights of justice, both high and low.

The seigniory helped to erase the sharp line between servitude and freedom. However unconsciously, the seignior followed a policy of social levelling. To him it mattered not from whom the peasant held his land or to whom he was personally bonded. What the seignior sought was the obedience of all the inhabitants of the community. In areas where the independent seigniory was strong, therefore, words like *rustici* and *laboratores* were increasingly used to describe the farmers, replacing older terms that more exactly delineated their particular tenurial or personal situations. Characteristic of the seigniorial age were phrases such as Beaumanoir's *homes de poosté*, that is, men of the seigniory, a definition embracing both free and servile elements. Legislators felt the need to deal with the rural population as a whole. An imperial peace ordinance for Bavaria in 1152 is an example. A rustic was not to carry sword or lance, only the bow, nor, whether free or servile, was he permitted the judicial duel. His clothing was to be grey or black, and none but gentlemen of the sword were to drink wine. Partly derived from past manorial and personal duties, a variety of charges were imposed on most inhabitants of villages. Some were taxes, like the seignior's tallage. Others were services or labour for community causes. Freemen became subject to marriage taxes and restrictions (*formariage*) and were obliged to sue in seigniorial courts, losing for a time the capacity to appeal to the courts of kings or regional princes. In France, the term villein (*villanus*) came to designate any inhabitant of a village subject to the community jurisdiction, whether free or servile in personal status. In England, where seigniorial authority was not so developed, it referred only to those peasants who were members of a lord's manorial *familia*.

This levelling or fusion was never complete. More advanced in parts of France and northern Italy, it was not so usual in wide reaches of Germany, England and Spain. One reason was the relative weakness of the seigniory in areas where it was faced by vigorous central governments, whose interest was to protect the freeman's status because the profits of justice derived from him accrued to the crown. Strong central government enabled princes to police servile groups more effectively than could be done in the decentralized political world of the seigniors. The result was that thirteenth-century Europe boasted a wide variety of social structures. In Scandinavia and sections of north Germany, where the seigniorial system was only beginning to penetrate, freemen were both numerous and independent but formal slavery was still clearly demarcated. In intermediary zones like England and most of Germany these distinctions had faded. Slaves no longer existed, although many deeply servile qualities marked German peasants under *Hofrecht* (the law of the servile *familia*) and Englishmen in villenage. The parade before the master of young adult villeins for him to 'pull' for domestic service was an annual event in many English manors. On the other hand, the continued vigour and success of England's monarchy arrested the decline of freemen. For important cases freemen customarily attended the hundred court, one that was at least formally royal. Only villeins or other serfs were judged by their lord of the manor. As the continued strong distinction between *Hofrecht* and village customary law shows, much the same was true in Germany, although there the weakening of the Empire led to the depression of many freemen and the growth of seigniorial power, especially in the west and south.

Even in those areas where seigniorial authority was most developed, however, the community never embraced all the village's inhabitants. Some individuals remained in categories clearly designated as servile, and these were often excluded from full community membership. Most inhabitants at Villeneuve-le-Roi had been granted the freemen's custom of Lorris in 1163, but we hear in 1246 that Louis IX freed 326 individuals there. The seigniorial administrative officers, often recruited from the village, formed a group apart. So, to some degree, did the clergy and the local military aristocracy of the knights. Although rustics performed guard duty and went to war, they were, as the texts had it, an 'unarmed multitude' in comparison with the knights. A Bavarian peace ordinance of 1244 allowed them to bear arms only when summoned for the *defensio patrie* (*Landwehr*), when pursuing criminals, and when parading on their village's patron saint's day. Men of the higher orders tended to think of all farmers as little more than serfs—'stinking serfs' said the great poet and seignior Bertrand of Born. Even the sympathetic Beaumanoir wrote condescendingly of the free inhabitants of the seigniory in terms of 'what they have of freedom'.[15] With his usual scorn of the English race, Fitz Neale attributed the thefts, homicides, adulteries, and other crimes that plagued England's countryside to the material wellbeing and innate drunkenness of its peasants.

In spite of these limitations, there is no doubt that the achievement of relative uniformity by seigniorial pressure led to an awareness of common interests. When reinforced by the evolution of the economy discussed above, this soon led to peasant solidarity in the search for freedom. That rustics were mightily aided by a decentralized political structure is shown by the fact that the movement for liberty was most advanced in the regions of France and Italy where the seigniory had won its earliest and greatest victories. Although there was some solidarity among princes and nobles, there was also much competition. Complaints were legion that older communities were weakened by the freedoms offered in new ones. Like the greater towns, each seigniory was a jealous little state whose master sought to get the most out of its citizens and to make the most of them. However much they may have been oppressed at home, it was in the interest of their lord to protect them from outside authority. This was of particular importance for new and growing villages, some of whose settlers had escaped from the jurisdiction of other seigniors, who often wished to re-

---

[15] *Coutumes de Clermont-en-Beauvaisis* 45, 1451, ed. Salmon II, 233.

cover the fugitives. The village like the town defended its new citizens, though never quite so effectively. A Franconian Rhineland peace ordinance of 1179 provided that if any lord should claim to have 'in any village or other place . . . a man whom he claims to be his serf or under his tutelage (*advocatitium*), he must plead his case before the judge of that village or place'.[16] And it was not easy to do this. In early-thirteenth-century Alsace a protesting lord was required to bring to that court seven close relatives of the fugitive on his mother's side in order to prove his case by their oath. In short, because of mutual competition among the seigniors the old saw *Stadtluft macht frei* was almost as true of the village as of the town.

In the context of political decentralization, high authority often favoured granting freedom to those held in bondage by lesser lords. The kings of France, conservative in regard to their own serfs, intervened in favour of peasant liberty outside of the royal domain. The villages owned by the bishop and chapter of Laon had been stirred by the franchises recently won by the town of Laon and by the five villages of the nearby commune of Bruyères. Taking advantage of an episcopal vacancy in 1174, fourteen of these villages grouped around Anizy-le-Chateau bought from the king the right to form a commune on Laon's model. Shortly thereafter the newly elected bishop tried to revoke this grant. The rustics resisted and a war ensued. The town of Laon, a royal monastery, and the villagers formed an alliance but were defeated by the bishop and the local castellans, or greater barons. The king then prepared to act, and he proclaimed the sequestration of the temporal domains of the bishop. Fearful for the balance of power, the king of England and his allies in Hainault swiftly intervened and in 1179 forced France to revoke the commune. A similar course of events transpired in 1185, when Philip Augustus appears to have granted the right to a new commune. After incessant conflicts and much peasant emigration, Anizy-le-Château won her liberties in the mid-1200s, and several other villages of the group won theirs shortly thereafter.

That the French kings were not disinterested lovers of liberty is shown not only by their conservative policies in their own domains but also by their support of lords who were their loyal

[16] Cited in Heinrich Mitteis, 'Stadtluft macht frei', *Festschrift Stengel* (Münster, 1952), 352.

supporters. There was a lengthy legal battle between the royal chapter of Sainte-Geneviève of Paris and the inhabitants of Rosny-sous-Bois. It began in 1178 when the chapter obtained a royal charter asserting the farmers' servile status. The men of Rosny carried their suit to the higher authority of Rome, and in the course of years no fewer than five popes supported their claim to freedom against both crown and monastery. Too remote to be efficacious, papal power failed, and the peasants 'voluntarily' disavowed their free status in 1226. Such was the spirit of the times, however, that by 1246 the village had been freed in exchange for an annual tallage of sixty pounds.

Although townsmen were unwilling to free their own serfs, the great towns usually supported peasant liberty. The best examples are to be found in the Italian urban republics, whose citizens consciously desired nearby towns and villages to share their political and social system. Besides, it was profitable for them to disrupt any seigniorial jurisdiction that stood in the way of subordinating the countryside to the town. By the thirteenth century the partial enfranchisements of the past had been rounded out by acts of general and final emancipation like that of Vercelli in 1244 and of Florence in 1289. Typical of the religious imagery of the age, when Bologna freed the remaining rustics of her *contado* in 1256–57, six thousand names were inscribed in the citizens' registry called the *Book of Paradise*.

We have already seen what the peasants wanted in economic terms. Their social ambitions were not dissimilar. They wished to fix in law or custom, and thereby to limit, what they owed their lords. Labour and military service were among the objects of such legislation. In 1208 the new settlers (*hospites*) at Braye owed Nôtre-Dame of Paris the following armed service: '[They] ought to have suitable equipment, like the other men of the village, [and ought] to go with the lord of Braye or his sergeants on campaign (*in chevalcheiam*) . . . with this limit, that they ought to be able to return home each night'.[17] They also sought to fix or even to abolish the fiscal charges owed the lord. Among these were the fees or fines of justice, especially the lord's right to confiscate property for high crime. Taxes on the transmission of property were also of importance. Typical of this legislation was the evolution of *mainmorte* in the village of Orly near Paris. *Mainmorte* had

[17] Cited in Verriest, *Institutions médiévales* I, 157.

originally meant the seignior's absolute right to dispose of a peasant's property at his death but had long since become a tax upon inheritances. By 1252, however, a witness testified that in the custom of Orly *mainmorte* merely meant that 'if anyone were to die without an heir of his body, his property would go to the chapter [the lord], otherwise not'.[18]

The ultimate liberty was that of mobility. This was partly social, like the right of an individual to marry outside of his social group or community. The rural population therefore made a concerted attack upon marriage taxes and controls (*formariage*, *merchet*). There was also the right to leave the community—a right that, if it became widespread, could obviously weaken if not destroy the little state that was the seigniory. What the farmers wanted is shown by a clause in the liberties of Saint-Bauzeil in southern France in 1281:

> 'If, by chance, a present or future inhabitant should wish to leave the said town in order to reside elsewhere, unless he has committed a manifest crime of such enormity that he should be detained, we give and will give to him the free power and licence of going wherever he wishes with all his property.[19]

Fearing the loss of taxpayers, seigniors were very reluctant to grant this privilege. Issuing a custumal for Montgaillard in the Ariège in 1258, the lord provided that 'we enfranchise and manumit all our serfs living in the said village as long as they wish to remain in it. If, however, . . . they should leave it, by that act they revert to their pristine servitude.'[19] In Lorraine, Austria and Bavaria, seigniors of overcrowded communities encouraged serfs for whom they were economically responsible to move to nearby towns or villages in return for annual remitments, but they were extremely reluctant to let freemen escape in this way. So clear was this issue that, when founding new villages, lords frequently prohibited the reception of settlers from their own older villages and towns.

The franchises won were usually summarized or recorded in custumals or charters. Publication of village customs was known in the eleventh century and became common in favoured regions like Italy, Provence, parts of France, and the Low Countries in the

---

[18] Cited in Bloch, *Rois et serfs*, 30.
[19] Cited in Verriest, *op. cit.* I, 226.

course of the twelfth century. Even in the 1200s they were relatively rare in Germany between the Rhine and the Elbe and in England. Each area experienced its own cycles or pulsations. In the basin of the Seine, around Paris, new communities gained them during the twelfth century, but the height of the issuance of charters of franchise was not reached until the period from 1245 to 1275, when older communities also benefited. The movement was strongest around towns and in areas of new settlement, such as eastern Germany. In the mountainous and lightly populated county of Comminges no less than sixty villages won charters from 1202 to 1300. These customs or franchises were not entirely homegrown. Many, if not most, emulated town constitutions and rights. Between 1160 and 1303 the laws of Louvain were adopted by many villages in southeast Brabant, and, in their respective areas, the laws of Liège, Douai, Namur, and Saint-Pol had the same success. Although inspired by urban models, some franchises were direct products of princely legislation. Such were the liberties of Lorris of 1155, adopted by many royal foundations in the Ile-de-France, and those of Beaumont-en-Argonne of 1183, issued by the archbishop of Rheims and eventually adopted by about five hundred villages, mostly in the Champagne.

As the general level of the peasantry moved upward, so also did individuals. Some rose faster than others. An example may be seen in the village of Pasignano outside Florence. In 1233, of the seven gentlemen holding of this monastic seigniory, five were knights, and of these the most consequential was the 'noble knight' Messire Tolosano. His family is first heard of in 1130, when his grandfather, a smith, acquired property in freehold (*iure proprio*). By 1156 the rent of the family's lands held of the monastery had been fixed in money, at a sum never to be raised. In 1202 the abbot formally enfranchised Tolosano's father. In 1233 our noble knight's relatives in Pasignano included a smith and several humble peasants, and at Poggibonsi, to which a branch of the family had moved around 1200, a cousin in the legal profession. Nor was this case unusual. Durand Blanot, whose brother was a simple peasant, served as a sergeant for the monks of Cluny at Voranges in the Mâconnais. His first son, James, was wealthy enough to enfeoff some of his lands to a knight and to educate one of his children at Paris. This boy became a master and a canon of Nôtre-Dame, and finished his career as judge (*officialis*) for the archbishop of Lyons, from 1274 to 1287. Born about 1220, Durand's second son, John, had an even more spectacular rise. He was sent to Bologna to read law and returned to enter the service of the duke of Burgundy. Subsequently knighted by the duke, he acquired the liege fief of Uxelles in 1268 together with its seigniory, thereby replacing the Gros, a once great but now fading baronial family.

Although the principal way for peasants to advance was to move to town, the professions of arms, of law and the Church also provided careers to the humble. In no way exceptional, England's Church boasted at least three distinguished men of peasant origins: Robert Grosseteste, bishop of Lincoln (1235–53), Robert de l'Isle of Durham (1274–83), and John Peckham, primate of Canterbury (1278–92). Indeed, the matter was often commented on. Philip of Novara remarked that it was easy to prove that the clergy and chivalry were the most worthy and profitable professions. Through arms, one could rise to empire, and

> by the clergy it has often happened and can happen that the son of a poor man becomes a great prelate, and is rich and honored as such, and becomes the father and lord of him who was lord of him and his; and he rules and governs everyone, and can even become pope, and be father and lord of all Christianity.[20]

Some did not view this complacently. Around 1250 Werner der Gaertner, a monk of Ranshofen, composed the adventures of Meier Helmbrecht, a peasant's son who, corrupted by war, grew his hair long like a gentleman, drank only wine, and wore a sword. The poet's lesson was that pride goeth before a fall, and he made his point by depicting wealthy farmers who emulated the gentlefolk.

Nor were those who sought freedom deprived of intellectual justification. In an age when it was profitable to make men free, the clerks relegated to second place their past doctrines of service and instead looked for texts to prove the glory and usefulness of liberty. Some of these were to be found in Roman law, where the basic notion was that men were naturally equal and free. As Ulpian had long ago expressed it: 'In civil law, slaves are considered as nothing, but not so in natural law, because in natural

---

[20] *Des quatres tenz d'aage d'ome* 15, ed. Marcel de Fréville, 10.

law, all men are equal',[21] a sentiment echoed by all the jurists and publicists of our period. Men of the time were confident that they could restore man to his pristine liberty. A prologue to an emancipation in Castelsarrasin in 1268 reads: 'In nature all men are free, but the *jus gentium* made some men slaves. And because a thing returns easily to its nature, learn that we, moved by piety . . . freely manumit our serf.'[22] In this secular image, men became Roman citizens when freed. Rolandino Passaggeri describes how a master frees his dependants, remitting to them 'all right of patronage, restoring to them their ancient birthright and freedom in law, and calling them Roman citizens, and finally restoring them to the primeval law according to which all men were born free, nor had manumission been introduced at that time because servitude was unknown'.[23]

Because he was restoring the natural and right order, he who granted liberty was not to be unduly praised. As Henry of Bracton and the anonymous author of *Fleta* put it, the *ius gentium*, or civil law, had not destroyed man's natural freedom; it had only obscured it. Buoncompagno of Signa wrote: 'No one is said to confer liberty but rather to cast off a certain veil of servitude by which freedom is said to be cloaked.'[24] But enfranchisement was more than a mere restoration of a pristine state; it included the idea of innovation or of augmentation. When the Florentines freed the serfs of their *contado* in 1289, the prologue of their act read:

> Because liberty, in which the desire of each man depends upon his own will and not on that of another, and by which cities and peoples are defended from oppression and their laws protected and improved (*augentur in melius*), and because freedom is honored in many ways by natural law, we, therefore, wishing not only to maintain but also to increase it . . .'[25]

In this statement and in those of Bracton and *Fleta*, a definition of freedom is also exposed. Freedom is the natural faculty of each man to do what he wants. This was of ancient inspiration indeed,

---

[21] *Digest* 50, 17, 32 and also 1, 1, 4.

[22] Cited in Bloch, *Rois et serfs*, 150.

[23] *Summa artis notarie* 1, 7 in Venice 1583 1, 157v. See also *Digest* 1, 1, 4, and *Institues* 1, 2, 2.

[25] Cited in Pasquale Villari, *I primi due secoli della storia di Firenze* (Florence, 1905), 290.

234

being the Stoic conception expressed by Cicero: 'Quid enim est libertas: potestas vivendi ut velis.'[26]

These ideas of the Roman jurists and their medieval successors were powerfully reinforced by those of churchmen. When the priors of Florence spoke of an increase in liberty in the charter of 1289 they were referring to the notion of progress, of the *renovatio in melius* that had been a part of Christian thought since the days of Paul of Tarsus. To the theologically minded jurist God was nature in the sense that he was its creator, and man's similarity to God made him free. In his *Mirror of the Saxons*, Eike of Repgow took up and dismissed as worthless all the attempts to find a biblical justification for slavery and concluded 'that man belongs to God and anyone who takes possession of him sins against the power of the omnipotent'.[27] And Beaumanoir believed that it was shameful for any Christian to remain in a servile condition. When the king enfranchised the bondsmen of the Valois demesne in 1311, the prologue of the act observed that man 'as a being who is formed in the image of our Lord, ought generally be free by natural law'.[28] Two years previously a scribe in royal service had copied into his formula book what he took to be a model manumission, one deriving from a monastery in Soissons:

> Since our Redeemer, creator of every creature . . . wished to assume human flesh so that, by the grace of his divinity . . . he could restore us to our pristine liberty, it is well that those whom nature created free in the beginning and the *jus gentium* placed under the yoke of servitude should be restored to that liberty in which they were born by the benefit of manumission.[29]

To these juristic and churchly motives may be added others. One of these was pride of nation or race. Almost every people of this time claimed to be descended from those symbols of freedom, Aeneas and his Trojans. In addition, both the French and the Germans asserted that they were the Franks. Claiming the city of Lyons for France in 1307, the lawyer Peter of Belleperche re-

---

[26] *Paradoxa* 71, ed. Nino Marinone, 34. The text the medieval jurists used was Digest 1, 5, 4: *libertas est naturalis facultas eius quod cuique facere libet, nisi si quid vi aut iure prohibetur.*

[27] *Sachsenspiegel* 3, 42, ed. C. W. Gärtnern (Leipzig, 1732), 409.

[28] *Ordonnances de Rois de France de la troisième race* XII, 387.

[29] Cited in Bloch, *Rois et serfs*, 154, who did not notice that, word for word, the formula derived from Pope Gregory I, letter VI, 12, in *MGH Epp. sel.* i, 390.

marked that the town had been the ancient capital of the Gauls, a people whose name had been changed to the Franks when they smashed the yoke of servitude to the Romans. However this curious idea was stated, it could be used in the matter we have been examining. In the ordinance of 1315 in which the French king sought to force his own peasants to purchase their freedom, the prologue began thus:

> Although according to natural law all men are born free, by certain usages and customs which have long been introduced and maintained to the present in our kingdom, and perchance by the crimes of their predecessors, many of our common folk have fallen into the bondage of servitude and diverse conditions, which much displeases us, we, considering that our realm is called and named the kingdom of the French (*des Frans*) and desiring that the fact in truth accord with the name, . . . have ordered that . . .[30]

It was obviously advantageous to all concerned to encourage peasant emancipation in a time of economic growth and seigniorial competition. The benefits to emancipators were not merely indirect ones. Liberty was paid for, and charters of manumission sometimes mixed the motives of generosity and acquisitiveness quite wonderfully. When a count of Joigny freed a family in 1328, he did so 'in remuneration and pure guerdon of good and agreeable services, gentilities and kindnesses that they have given . . . and still do assiduously daily without ceasing, . . . in pure and special grace, by God and in pure charity and with regard to piety . . . for the sum of two hundred pounds in cash . . .'[31] But this should not make us think that money was everything: it is heaven to see others happy when one is happy oneself.

In earlier chapters the period around 1300 was characterized as one in which there was increasing friction between landlord and tenant. Similar problems afflicted the seigniory. The lords became more interested in holding on to what still remained to them after the centuries of liberation and in expanding their prerogatives whenever they could. The whole rural population was affected, but not all elements equally. In any given region, whole villages or groups of them had been so completely freed that

[30] *Ordonnances de Rois de France de la troisième race* I, 583.
[31] Cited in Bloch, *Rois et serfs*, 136.

seigniorial authority could not easily be restored. Within villages, individuals or groups had risen too far to be reduced. An illustration of this is the use of the term 'bourgeois' in both north and south France. In the twelfth century the word had often been employed to describe the settlers of newly founded villages— which were like many of the smaller thirteenth-century boroughs of England. By the thirteenth century the French usually restricted its use to the leading members of the village community, e.g. to a notary, a merchant or a particularly well-to-do farmer. Although a testimony to the achievements of past generations, this social division between villages and between inhabitants of the same village was not altogether happy. It did not much matter in areas where the distinction between free and servile folk had always been clear, like England and parts of Germany, but it intensified social divisions in those parts of the west where the triumph of the seigniory had brought about some measure of social fusion. In parts of France and northern Italy communities which, and individuals who, still owed a substantial part of the services and fees once paid by everybody were slowly separated from the free communities and individuals and tainted by the mark of servitude, an invidious distinction that helps explain the woeful lack of solidarity in the late-medieval countryside.

These distinctions were relatively rigid in comparison with those of the past. This rigidity was caused not only by the desires of the seigniors and the wish of those already freed to distinguish between themselves and their less fortunate brethren but also by an intellectual current of the age. Trained in the schools and inspired by the complexity of thirteenth-century society, the jurists tried to find comprehensive systems in which to define the place of each man. Although their writings often reflected reality very clearly, the overriding effect was formalistic. As exemplified by Bracton and others, they expatiated upon the Roman conception of the indelibility of servitude—pure theory, be it remembered, not Roman practice—and used Roman phrases like *homines de corpore* for those who owed seigniorial or familial services. Even a practical administrator like Beaumanoir who was little touched by the spirit of systematization divided the rural population into three groups, the gentlemen, the freemen of the seigniory, and the third estate, that is, the serfs.

The influence of the schools was not altogether baleful, however. Bondsmen were helped by Roman law on slavery as applied by the lawyers of this age. *Fleta's* author notes that according to the *ius gentium* a master had the right of life and limb over his slave but that the *ius civile* (Roman law) had deprived him of this. Reflecting the same tradition, the early-fourteenth-century custom of Burgundy allowed those in 'servile servitude' (*serf-servage*) to disavow their lords if threatened with death or lack of maintenance. Not that serfs had it easy. The Freising Lawbook of 1328 tells us that a master who killed his serf with a sword or club was to be executed. Flogging was different. If the man died the same day the master was liable; if thereafter, he was not, because it was rare that men died from whippings and masters had to put the fear of God into their serfs to get any work out of them.

A further beneficial result of the study of law in the schools was the gradual formulation of a distinction between what late medieval jurists were to call 'liberate servitude' and formal slavery. This idea is well expressed in a famous passage by Beaumanoir on the 'estate' of the serf:

> There are several states of servitude. Some serfs are so subject to their lords that the lords can take whatever they have both dead and alive and, rightly or wrongly, can imprison them as long as they wish, and are held to answer only to God. Other serfs are treated more gently for, as long as they live, the lord can require nothing from them unless they misbehave except the taxes for their servitude.[32]

The taxes the author meant were the rent, tallage, inheritance dues and fees for marriage. He then goes on to observe that these happy serfs are to be found in France, especially in the Beauvaisis, the others in foreign lands. Here Beaumanoir was not being inventive. Robert of Curzon had earlier contrasted the tax-paying serfs (*servi censuales*) found in France with the slaves (*servi ascripticii et empticii*) in Apulia and Sicily who were, he said, bought and sold like sheep or cattle. The term 'slave' to define this relatively rare social category was being adopted by Italian and French jurists from the Empire (*sclavus* = Slav) during the thirteenth century.

[32] *Coutumes de Clermont-en-Beauvaisis* 45, 1451–3, ed. Salmon II, 233–6.

238

The Townsmen

Townsfolk shared a measure of the servitude to which the bulk of the rural population was condemned by the opinion of gentlefolk. Even in the thirteenth century a townsman in the region around Namur was never formally entitled a freeman (*liber homo*), a term mainly applied to the nobility, and much the same seems to have been true in wide reaches of northern France a century earlier. One reason for this attitude was the hostility of the martial and clerical elements of society towards trade and manual labour. When England's William the Marshal accosted a runaway monk in company with a noble damsel, he was not perturbed by the couple's irregular liaison, but he blandly confiscated their money when he learned that the monk was going to town to put it out at usury. This attitude was reflected in law. Fitz Neale deprecated bourgeois business, proposing that a freeman who sought to trade or lend money became nothing but a merchant. Indeed, did he do so, 'the degenerate knight or other freeman should be punished by another law than the common law of the free'.[33] There was also a deeper if simpler cause, namely the pride of order that marked the martial aristocracy. Like peasants, most townsmen could not be counted among them.

Townsfolk were only gradually differentiated from villagers. Even in the period with which this book deals, the key term bourgeois (*burgensis*) did not necessarily designate a town dweller. The only word never applied to rural folk was citizen (*civis*), derived from Roman usage and initially attached to an inhabitant of a large or ancient city, especially one housing an episcopal see. The circumstances in which the town sought its liberty were similar to those of the village, in that rivalry between seigniors was instrumental in advancing their cause. A chronicler lamented that in 1152 the citizens of Vezelay, 'abjuring their legitimate lord [the abbot of Vezelay], had allied with a tyrant [the count of Nevers] ... to create an execrable commune ... in order to cast off the yoke of ecclesiastical liberty from their necks and to adhere to the count'.[34]

The ambitions of townsmen and villagers in the age of liberation were basically the same. Both tried to lessen the charges that

---

[33] *Dialogus de scaccario* 2, 13, ed. Hughes, Crump, Johnson (Oxford, 1902), 146.
[34] Cited in Guilhermoz, *L'Origine de la noblesse* (1902), 385.

weighed on them, namely, tallage and forced loans, quartering or hospitality rights, inheritance controls and taxes, *formariage*, and military service. The privilege won by Lübeck in 1163 was not unlike that of a village. Its citizens were to defend their own walls but were excused from all outside campaigns. In 1223 the countess of Nevers surrendered her *mainmorte* to the citizens of Auxerre 'so that their heirs and successors, wherever they live, should possess . . . the inheritance of their parents or predecessors without any trouble or payment'.[35] If the principle of *Stadtluft macht frei* was more vigorously upheld in towns than in villages, it was often restricted there also. In 1191, when the lord of Landrecies amplified and confirmed his town's liberties, he specified that any of his own serfs found resident there should not be retained in *bourgeoisie*. As we have already seen, town customs and laws, although more elaborate, were quite suitable for adoption by villages.

Although there were many similarities between town and village, there were also many differences. Many of these have been examined in chapter IV where it was asserted that the differences were those of emphasis and degree, not of kind. Some additional differences may be mentioned here. Reflecting a more frequent exchange of goods and services, money was more common in town, a fact that enabled towns to mobilize their resources more rapidly. The annual tallage paid by each villager at Busigny in 1201 consisted of a measure of oats, a loaf of bread, a hen and sixpence; in 1191 the citizen of Landrecies gave 16*d*: a shilling for his *bourgeoisie* and 4*d* for the lord's tolls. Everything was on a larger scale because towns were bigger. Villages of fishermen often provided small boats for a lord's service, but only towns could offer warships. In 1191 the king of Sicily granted Gaeta the right to cut its military assessment from two galleys to one, except in case of the *defensio regni*. What remained social in a village became political in a town. In Burgundy a maltreated serf had the right to abjure his lord. In 1282 the federated towns of Stendal, Tangermunde and Osterburg in the Altmark of Saxony were formally granted the right to seek another lord if harmed by their own. In short, the rights and liberties gained by town citizens were won more rapidly and were greater than those of villagers.

Although never absolute, the distinction between town and

[35] Cited in Verriest, *op. cit.* I, 223.

countrymen became more and more marked. By the thirteenth century the word *laboratores* had lost whatever inclusiveness it had ever had; it was now applied only to farmers. The term bourgeois had spread throughout Europe to describe townsfolk, being restricted in villages only to those professional or rich persons who did not live like farmers. When the jurist Alberic of Rosate posed the question 'Who are to be called citizens and who rustics?' he answered in a manner familiar to modern ears: 'They are called citizens who were born in a city. . . . And they are called urban citizens who live in a town. . . . They are called rustics who were born in a village, hamlet or castle.'[36]

Like the village, the medieval town developed a community sense, which enabled it to mobilize its powers against its enemies. The process was partly one of territorial unification. Few towns began as unified wholes but instead consisted of several nuclei— a comital or episcopal town, for example, a relatively new merchant settlement, and villages or settlements near monasteries outside the town's walls. The integration of these more or less independent segments was obviously in the interest of the community, and town fathers therefore pressed for it. This was not a simple matter of self-determination. Local princes, secular or ecclesiastical, also encouraged and even forced this unification in order to destroy enclaves of independent seigniorial authority. Once a vigorous community sense capable of advancing its own interest had grown up, however, the princes no longer found it profitable to support unification. The kings of France, faced by the danger of Parisian unity under the *Marchands de l'Eau* when they had won the right to farm the royal provostship, defended the continued independence of no less than five jurisdictional areas in that town and its suburbs, including those of the royal monastery of Saint-Germain-des-Près and the Temple.

More important for our present purpose was the formation of a social community within the town, creating a measure of equality and solidarity. What this meant was the growth of a notion of common citizenship, at first sometimes expressed in a revolutionary oath association (*commune, compagna*) of groups of inhabitants and eventually in the more refined conception of the *universitas* or *corpus* of the citizenry. The test of citizenship was birth, legal residence in the community, and participation in the common

[36] *De statutis* 2, 177, 17 in *TUJ* II, 49ra.

burdens of defence and tax. Furthermore, citizenship was soon extended to newcomers who, after a suitable period of a year or more, could prove residence and the shouldering of common duties. Formal naturalization—*citadinantia* in Italian law—was also widespread. If the community accepted new members, it also asserted the right to expel those who seemed undesirable. Citing the famous glossator Accursius, Alberic defined exile (*relegatio* or *bannum*) as a 'kind of ejection from the common good and thus, in a certain sense, a secular excommunication'.[37]

The emergence of this sense of citizenship and equality took many years and was rarely, if ever, complete. Leaving aside the clergy, most western towns began their history with three roughly demarcated social elements: an administrative group, often martial and aristocratic but rarely averse to trade; a merchant group, privileged, as were the Jews, to travel in order to serve the community and fill the seignior's purse; and artisans and other workers, even agricultural ones, who were sometimes held by the bonds of manorial servitude. All these elements owed service to prince and community but the order of the knights was more honourable and better remunerated than the others, and the status of the artisan was humbler than that of the merchant. In parts of Germany as late as the early twelfth century the relation of artisan to merchant typical of the earlier Middle Ages could still be seen. There merchants frequently derived their liberties from and owed their service to a higher lord—sometimes the emperor—than did the artisans, who were usually dependants of a local lord or ecclesiastical institution. The unification of merchant and artisan groups was often expressed by granting the latter the liberties, especially the right of mobility, possessed by merchants. As late as 1120 the founding charter of Freiburg im Breisgau specified that all inhabitants were to be merchants and to enjoy the merchant power, although it is clear that most of them were not engaged in foreign trade. Although this use of the term merchant persisted on some of the frontiers of European urbanization, it was soon replaced by either citizen (*civis*) or bourgeois (*burgensis*), terms that referred to all the members of the community, whether merchants or not.

Common citizenship, or the condition of being bourgeois, had been accepted in regions of rapid urbanization around the turn of

[37] *De statutis* 4, 1, 9 in *TUJ* II, 66ra.

the twelfth century, but elsewhere the struggle for the formation of a unified social community was still going on. We have already seen the charter of liberties won by the inhabitants of Auxerre from their lord in 1223, in which the free citizens were granted exemption from inheritance taxes. More significant for community solidarity was a further provision: 'Moreover I manumit altogether and perpetually my other citizens of Auxerre . . . who were not of free condition, so that, the opprobrium of servitude being wholly put behind and removed, they may freely leave and return to Auxerre whenever they wish.'[38] In general, however, by this date few western towns of any importance contained substantial minorities of inhabitants in manorial or seigniorial servitude. There were, of course, problems posed by the wealth of some and the poverty of others, but this was not allowed to vitiate the principle of equality before the law. Typical of legislation at this time is a provision of the statutes of Avignon in the 1240s providing that 'the good carpenters (*probi homines fustarie*) are of no worse condition than any others of this city'.[39] The employment of the term or phrase 'good men' (*probihomines, bonihomines*) in the early 1200s to designate the representatives of any group, no matter how elevated or humble, was a measure of the desire of townsmen for the kind of social equality within the town in order to stimulate community solidarity.

More difficult to assimilate into the community than humble folk were the officers of seigniorial administration, especially those who were martial. Such officers inhabited all western towns during the early Middle Ages and were remarkably varied in social status, ranging from simple toll collectors to sergeants, knights and even greater notables, like viscounts. Moreover, they often combined different functions. The 'proud knights' of Puy in central France whose towers were levelled by the bishop and the commonalty in 1102 operated the town mint. They were, in short, the business élite of the community. In line with the general evolution of the martial aristocracy, such service groups gained freedom at different times in different places. Some evolved into the knightly and eventually noble element of town society. An example of this may be seen at Worms, where in 1190 the town council consisted of twenty-eight bourgeois and twelve *ministeriales*, that is, quasiservile

38. Cited in Verriest, *op. cit.* I, 223.
39 Maulde, *Coutumes et règlements de la république d'Avignon*, 208, tit. 158.

officers dependent on the seignior or prince. In the 1200s, these ministers were called knights. Humbler ministerial groups often became bourgeois. In the early twelfth century the ministers at Cambrai claimed that their offices and emoluments were hereditary. In 1135 the conflict between the bishop and his ministers was arbitrated, and sergeants who held fiefs were assured that their offices were hereditary. Those without fiefs were denied this privilege and forthwith became bourgeois. By 1205 even the superior group of *ministeriales* was moving toward the bourgeoisie, being termed 'the sergeants of the bishop of Cambrai who are merchants'.[40] During the late twelfth and early thirteenth centuries this evolution of a service group into a free aristocracy or a free bourgeoisie is observable principally in the territories of the Empire. A similar evolution had taken place earlier in Italy and in areas influenced by the precocious development of the French martial aristocracy.

There was an important change in the relationship of the ordinary members of the town community to those of this service group who had become or were becoming knightly or noble. Acute observers in the thirteenth century, like the Franciscan Salimbene of Parma, remarked that nobles lived in the countryside in northern France, whereas in Italy they lived in town. What he said was true enough, but modern historians have sought to elevate this into a fundamental difference between the character of town life in northern Europe and that of the Mediterranean basin. Although the difference was apparent by the thirteenth century, its origins must be defined with caution. Prior to the developments around 1100, service cadres, the progenitors of future knightly aristocracies, lived in towns everywhere in the west. Even in the 1200s, not all towns in the Mediterranean basin boasted knights or nobles as citizens. It was also rare in Castile or western Iberia and in parts of Italy like Savoy. The frontier to the north was not quite as clearly drawn as historians have been tempted to believe. In the 1200s many Rhenish and south-western German towns counted knights among their citizens. Altogether typical was the council of Zürich, composed in 1127 of *ministeriales et concives*, termed *milites et cives* in 1225, or that of Oppenheim in 1287 containing sixteen knights and sixteen burghers. Although knightly citizens were rare in Flanders and the adjacent regions of northern France and the Low Countries, knights or nobles who

[40] Cited in J. P. Ritter, *Ministérialité et chevalerie* (Lausanne, 1955), 86.

were exempted from the towns' jurisdiction often resided in town, especially in the older sections as in Saint-Quentin or Bourges.

It has been argued that where towns were large and powerful, knights and nobles tended to live in them as citizens. Although this is generally so, the mere size of towns does not seem a sufficient explanation. In south-west Germany and lower Languedoc urbanization was relatively light, yet knights were citizens. In Flanders, where cities lay thick, nobles did not often live in town, and, when they did, were rarely assimilated as citizens. What may explain these differences is the strength or weakness of princely government in the decisive period up to 1200. Weak princely authority was then more characteristic of southern and eastern France than of northern and western, and within the Empire government was most feeble in a wide belt extending from northern Italy up the valley of the Rhône to the valleys of the Meuse and the Rhine. The social policy of princes in regard to towns that were striving for independence and the conquest of the regions around them was based on the ancient principle of *divide et impera*. When knights and nobles lived in a town the prince often posed as their defender and tried to bolster the distinctions that kept them apart from the rest of the citizens. The Emperor Henry VI's privilege to Florence in 1187 surrendered much but insisted on the knights' exemption from communal taxes. A similar provision was included in the Capetian privilege given to Noyon in the French royal domain in 1181. Princes also did as much as they could to prevent knights from living in town or from serving as citizens. In the statutes granted to Abbeville in 1184 the count of Pontivy stipulated that 'the bourgeois of Abbeville may not receive in their commune any of my vassals or anyone having a free fief in my domain'.[41] Nor were rural seigniors allowed to join communes, even if they wished to, which they often did. In 1179 the count of Troyes expressly ordered that 'no castellan living near Meaux may enter into that commune except with my permission'.[41] The tone of this type of legislation is shown by the Emperor Frederick I Barbarossa's comprehensive edict for the town of Trent, in which he first forbade the citizens to oblige any noble or commoner to reside in their towns and then went on to prohibit them from compelling 'those who live outside in open or

[41] Cited in Ennen, *Frühgeschichte der europäischen Stadt*, 261.

fortified villages (*in municipiis vel castellis*) to be subject to their power and jurisdiction'.[42]

In areas where towns grew rapidly and were helped by the deterioration of central government, this restrictive legislation failed. The best examples are the towns of northern Italy and Tuscany, although other regions boasted cities that shared some measure of their success. The knights domiciled in the Italian towns profited from their early release from direct service to the emperor or his agents and became their communities' leaders in the search for political freedom. The larger cities also gained sufficient power to force rural seigniors to join the citizenry. An entry in the annals of Reggio for the year 1169 illustrates this process. A great rural notable and numerous lesser knights confessed themselves to be citizens and agreed to reside in Reggio for two months out of the year in peacetime and four months in war. The submission of rural lords was on a considerable scale. A Sienese law of 1252/62 listed no fewer than one hundred families of the *contado* obliged to maintain domiciles in the town. In short, even though the knightly aristocracies of Italian towns and those like them long retained certain privileges, they had been successfully integrated into the community. In 1164, when the great Lombard League was formed against the emperor, the ambassadors pledged the support of all male citizens from their towns, excepting only clerks, criminals, madmen, the mute and the blind.

In regions where towns were not so strong, or local princes retained greater authority, townsmen's demands were necessarily more modest. In no position to assimilate the members of the service aristocracy domiciled in town, much less to oblige rural seigniors to live there, the town fathers sought either to exclude them altogether or to restrict them to certain parts of the town. As we learn from the grant to Noyon of 1181 providing that all those domiciled in the town save clerks and knights owed taxes and military service, free knights were too privileged to be citizens. Such communities, therefore, tried to deny knights or nobles the right of habitation. In the midst of his wars in France, King John of England promised the citizens of Rouen that no knight would spend more than one night in town unless at the king's express command or because of illness. Again, the founding charter of Freiburg im Breisgau in 1120 promised that 'no man or minister

[42] Cited in Ennen, *op. cit.*, 257.

of the duke or any knight will live in this city, unless by the common consent and wish of all the town's inhabitants'.[43] The effect of princely power was to stir the bourgeois to stress as much as possible the distinction between their order and that of the knights and nobles. So far did they carry this that they even made a virtue of what had once been a mark of servility by prohibiting intermarriage between their order and that of the nobles, as may be seen in the founding charter of Lübeck in 1163, the custom of Cologne, and many other laws. Community solidarity was accomplished not by including knights and nobles but by cutting them out. This considerably weakened the political action of these towns, but it was to be of great ideological importance in the future, because it created a feeling or ethos of bourgeois self-consciousness in much of northern Europe.

No sooner achieved, the unity and solidarity of the citizenry began to weaken as society matured. Among the reasons for this change must be counted the rise of the people (*populus*), with its characteristic accompaniment of increased social and economic corporatism. Although this movement had begun in the twelfth century, it was only in the thirteenth that class, guild or professional affiliation began to replace the older and simpler accent on individual citizenship. As an example, the case of Toulouse may be cited, if only because it was in no way in advance of its time. There private documents had never alluded to an individual citizen's station in life, and constitutional documents had generally referred to the body of citizens simply as the good men (*bonihomines*) of the City and Bourg, the two parts of the town. Traditionally, also, a *civis* was one who lived in the City, a *burgensis* one who lived in the Bourg. In 1226, however, a public edict divided the citizenry into knights, burghers, and 'other good men'. The author of a contemporary poem on the Albigensian crusade found it more accurate to describe the people as 'the knights, bourgeois and commonalty', and as 'the knights, bourgeois and artisans (*menestrals*)'.[44] These distinctions were introduced into private documents around 1250. Before that, knights were rarely identified as such, nor were burghers or artisans. After that, the notaries, emulating their Italian teachers, were careful to record the professions and social status of the persons for whom they drew acts.

[43] Cited in Ennen, *op. cit.*, 260.
[44] Cited in J. H. Mundy, *Liberty and Political Power in Toulouse* (1954), 378.

Something close to an obsession with social position and professional function seems to have become a mark of the time.

In part, this was a healthy recognition of real social fact. Differences in social function, style of life and wealth within a town's population had always existed even in the simple days of the twelfth century. But men of the later age were faced by such clear contrasts of class and function that they were obliged to evolve a more intricate vocabulary of social description. The word bourgeois began to take on the meaning it was to retain until late in the nineteenth century. A Catalan jurist, Vital of Canyellas, defined the term citizen (*civis*) before 1250: 'Citizens are those who live in cities or in towns equal to cities; of which group those are called bourgeois (*burgenses*) who, although they have masters and workers through whom they exercise their professions, do not work with their own hands.'[45] How elaborate the vocabulary became is shown by an Austrian formulary book of the early 1300s, where we note what was to be typical of the later Middle Ages, namely, that merchants are ranked lower than real bourgeois. The middle range of secular dignities comprises

> dukes, marquesses, counts, *Freiherrn*, barons, mayors of cities (*capitanei urbium*) and all laymen having dignities, such as simple knights, or having a certain insign title of freedom, such as solemn citizens. Minor laymen [are such as] merchants, simple citizens, workers (*professores*) in the mechanical arts, and all similar folk lacking dignities.[46]

These texts illustrate the penetration into the middle classes of the old theme that trade is demeaning and that those who do not work with their hands are more honourable than those who do—a theme that was to be part of the bourgeois ideology until well after the days of Charles Dickens. But the good burghers did not have it all their way. In the common language of the time, they were the *otiosi*, the leisured folk, as they would translate it, or, as the artisans and the clerical moral rigorists did, the idle. In late-thirteenth-century Italy and the Low Countries artisans were proud of their blue nails and rarely lost an opportunity of legislating against the *otiosi*. From the other side, the 'real'

---

[45] Cited in Ernst Mayer, *Deutsche und französische Verfassungsgeschichte* (Leipzig, 1891), 227. Vital is also called Centellas and died as bishop of Huesca.
[46] *Baumgartenberger Formularius de modo prosandi* in *BuF* II, 727.

gentlemen looked down on them. Raymond Lull remarks:

> Almost all craftsmen and tradesmen want to be bourgeois or want their children to be. But you must know that there is no office so perilous as the estate of the bourgeois, nor that lasts so short a time. . . . No man lives so short a life as the bourgeois. And do you know why? Because he eats too much and does not exercise enough. . . . And no man is so annoying to his friends as is a poor bourgeois and in no man is poverty quite as shameful as in a bourgeois. No man gains so little merit or enjoyment from the charity he gives as does a bourgeois.[47]

And if workers wanted to be bourgeois, bourgeois wanted to be gentlemen. As towns had grown, an aristocracy had emerged within them. While its members continued in trade and business, they also began to acquire rural properties and to intermarry with the local nobility, from whom, indeed, some of their ancestors had sprung. These were the urban gentlefolk who, as later medieval law expressed it, 'lived nobly' or, as described in an Avignonese document of 1251, were 'honourable bourgeois who are accustomed to live as knights',[48] and who went to war armed as knights. Such patrician families were to be found not only in the towns around the Mediterranean, but also in all the areas of heavy urbanization—in the Low Countries, northern France and western Germany. As is frequent among the wealthy, the patricians constituted themselves in extended family groups, or great lineages, that contrasted sharply with the more or less nuclear family groups of the poorer citizens or artisans, who built a substitute in their guild affiliations. A fascinating example of these great lineages were the *paraiges* of Metz, whose origins seem to be associated with particular quarters of the town as well as with blood relationships. By the late 1200s about eight *paraiges* dominated the town and were subdivisible into about 221 individual patrician families comprising a total of about a thousand members. Although aristocratic and rich, the *paraiges* were extensive enough to have numerous poor relations, particularly by marriage. A cloth finisher was a son-in-law of the distinguished Colon family of Porte-Sailly, and a daughter of the knight Gervais of Lessy had married a baker.

---

[47] Cited from his *De doctrina puerili* in Ch.-V. Langlois, *La vie en France au moyen âge du XIIIe au milieu du XIVe siècle* IV, 353.

[48] Maulde, *op. cit.*, 269, No. XVI.

The growth of an urban aristocracy posed many problems, some of which will be examined in Chapter XII when political and constitutional questions are treated. But one may be mentioned here. Patricians were not only businessmen, they were also busy acquiring land, preferably fiefs that lent them a colour of nobility. This was encouraged in an area like northern Italy, where the purchase of rural estates by bourgeois or town knights served to tie the *contado* closer to the mother city. Elsewhere, where towns had not extended their power over more than a limited *banlieue*, this practice could be financially damaging. Patricians who acquired rural properties often moved their formal residences from town, withdrew from citizenship, and, while continuing business there, contributed nothing toward the taxes and services of the community from which they derived their basic income. This practice seems to have contributed to the financial crisis that afflicted many northern French towns in the latter half of the thirteenth century, but it is clear the problem existed much earlier. In 1197 the king of France granted the town of Roye the following privilege: 'that the men of this town who are rich (*otiosi*), acquire fiefs, make themselves noble (*ingenuos*) and are not knights should either become members of the commune or vacate the town, unless they hold a fief of us.'[49] This exception became significant later on because, on the payment of a fine to the crown (*amortissement*), the rich bourgeois could proceed as before.

Faced with these marked social differences, the problem of the jurist was no longer so much to make the punishment fit the crime as to make it fit the status and means of the criminal. He therefore turned to his books to disinter the Roman distinction between the *honestiores* and the humbler folk. When answering the question if the rich and the poor should be punished equally, Albert of Gandino stated the general principle adopted in Italy and then throughout Europe. This judge and *potestas* (supreme magistrate) proposed that it depended on whether the punishment was to be pecuniary or corporal: 'In the first case the rich ought to be punished more severely, and thus [Roman] law says that, because of poverty, the penalty should be restrained and diminished, as we see being done by the *potestates* every day. . . . In the second

[49] Cited in Ennen, *op. cit.*, 257.

250

case, the poor should be more severely punished',[50] save in cases of false testimony, forgery, treason, desertion in war, and other grave crimes. One reason for this law was that, just as the growing complexity of society had produced a group well above the average burgher in its standard of living, so it had created something like a real proletariat. Composed of youths and recent immigrants, this unhappy mob could be only slowly absorbed into the rigid corporate structure of the trades, industry and the professions. Such unfortunates grew in number in the economic tightening around and after 1300, and they began to pose a perpetual threat of delinquency or civil violence. An especially severe application of corporal punishment was therefore devised for *ribaldi*, or *viles persone*—men and youths, that is, without regular employment and of bad reputation, conversation and habits.

It may be proposed that, paradoxically, the very success of the towns had created such diversification of social status and wealth that the old, simple vocabulary of equal citizenship no longer suited urban society. Furthermore, the demise of the old spirit signalled the weakening of the community solidarity that had arisen in the western town from the eleventh century to the thirteenth and that had helped its citizens to win so many liberties from reluctant princes.

[50] *Tractatus de maleficiis* 39, 22, 8, ed. Hermann Kantorowicz, *Albertus Gandinus und das Strafrecht der Scholastik* (Berlin, 1926) II, 253.

VIII
Bellatores
(Soldiers and Gentlemen)

The martial order

To churchmen, the duties of the martial order were similar to those of princes who were themselves *bellatores*. Honorius of Regensburg addressed the military thus:

> Soldiers! You are an arm of the church, because you should defend it against its enemies. Your duty is to aid the oppressed, to restrain yourselves from rapine and fornication, to repress those who impugn the church with evil acts, and to resist those who are rebels against the priests. Performing such a *militia*, you will obtain the most splendid benefices from the greatest of kings.[1]

[1] *Speculum ecclesiae*, Sermo generalis, Ad milites, in *PL* CLXXII, 865.

BIBLIOGRAPHY. The book that inspired this chapter is P. Guilhermoz, *Essai sur l'origine de la noblesse en France au moyen âge* (Paris, 1902, recently reprinted). To this one adds the work of Bloch and Duby mentioned in chapter VII and also Gaetano Salvemini, *La dignità cavalleresca nel comune di Firenze* (Florence, 1896, reprinted in 1960) and J.-P. Ritter, *Ministerialité et chevalerie: dignité humaine et liberté dans le droit médiéval* (Lausanne, 1955). Indispensable local studies are Léopold Genicot, *L'économie rurale namuroise au bas moyen âge*, vol. II: *Les hommes—La noblesse* (Louvain, 1960), Karl Bosl, *Die Reichministerialität der Salier und Staufer*, 2 vols. (Stuttgart, 1950–51), Yvonne Bongert, *Recherches sur les cours laïques du Xe au XIIIe siècle* (Paris, 1949), Walter Kienast, *Untertaneneid und Treuvorbehalt in Frankreich und England* (Weimar, 1952), Heinrich Mitteis, *Lehnrecht und Staatsgewalt* (Weimar, 1933), Otto Brunner, *Land und Herrschaft* (Baden bei Wien, 1939), and Michael Powicke, *The Military Obligation in Medieval England* (Oxford, 1962). Although there are some good books on chivalry—note Sidney Painter, *French Chivalry* (Ithaca, 1957) and especially the numerous editions of Léon Gauthier, *La chevalerie* (Paris, 1884)—there is little systematic writing on the idea of nobility. Other than primary texts, the treatment here was built by reading Guilhermoz, Salvemini, Kantorowicz (mentioned in the bibliography to chapter II), and, in regard to the related sense of profession, to Hermann Fitting, *Das castrense peculium in seiner geschichtlichen Entwicklung und heutigen gemeinrechtlichen Geltung* (Halle, 1871; rprt.), a study without which none of the later ones would have been written.

Other clerks were more censorious. The learned Alan of Lille lamented that nowadays 'they are not soldiers, but rather robbers and ravishers; not defenders but rather invaders'.[2] Exaggerated though this was, there was something to it. An order devoted to arms is naturally warlike. Bertrand of Born, enemy of Richard Coeur-de-Lion and poet and seignior of the Limousin, gloried in the flowers and fresh grass of spring because then war could begin again. Besides, he said, a baron was so much more generous when war forced him to build up his household or *mesnie*.

When there were no wars, there were tournaments. The Church questioned these group combats. Although permitting a viaticum and penitence, the first Lateran Council (1139) went so far as to deny Christian burial to the victims of such engagements. Secular princes also tried to limit tournaments. That they could be awful there is no doubt. A combat between the Burgundians and English at Chalons in 1274 was fought with such animus that it could be described as a small war. Ecclesiastical and secular legislation mitigated the violence of tournaments by encouraging the substitution of single or small group combats for really massive engagements. Any more rigoristic law would never have been received, because tournaments served two important needs. They trained soldiers in their business, and they served as a means by which young squires and knights not yet endowed with fiefs could gain reputation and profit, since the arms and horses of the defeated were surrendered to the victors. This practice was anathema to clerical rigorists but, as usual, living imposed other standards. Having begun his career winning prizes in company with an avaricious Flemish squire named Roger of Gaugi, England's William the Marshal came to his deathbed after a long and distinguished life. There he was told by his chaplain that no one attains heaven who does not return what he has taken by force. The marshal replied:

Henry, bear with me a bit. The clerks are too hard on us; they shave us too closely. For I took five hundred knights whose weapons, harnesses and horses I retained. If God's kingdom is closed to me for that, nothing can be done, for I can't give them back. . . . Either their argument is false or no man can be saved.[3]

[2] *Summa de arte praedicatoria* 40 in *PL* ccx, 186.
[3] *Histoire de Guillaume le Maréchal*, ed. Paul Meyer, v. 18480 ff.

Since the master of the Temple attended his agony and the arch-bishop of Canterbury delivered his funeral oration, William probably stood as good a chance as most.

The noble's idea of glory was not always what the clergy favoured. They were urged to eschew vainglory here on earth and to seek instead heaven's true glories. Some knightly writers were distinctly ambivalent because of this preaching. Philip of Novara, himself a seignior, believed that from arms came empire: 'for good knights, by renown, valour and deeds, have many times attained great wealth and great conquest.'[4] He hastens to add, however, that like St George, soldiers can become Christ's holy martyrs, and argues that a saint's reputation lasts longer than that of the greatest emperor because of the yearly feast inscribed on the ecclesiastical calendar! But there was one clerical idea that appealed profoundly to the brotherhood of men at arms. Each Templar swore that 'I will imitate the death of my Lord, because as Christ laid down his life for me, so am I prepared to lay down my life for my brethren'.[5] John of Salisbury extended this duty to all soldiers when he said that their final duty was, 'as the sacra-ment teaches, to shed their blood and, if need be, to give their lives for their brothers'.[6] And it was only in war that this glory could be experienced and won. A thirteenth-century treatise on town government illustrates the debate on this point. Following the ancient authority Vegetius Renatus, a young knight is made to say that wars must be found for the young in order to give them experience. He asserts that virtue in arms is mankind's highest achievement and is therefore richly rewarded:

> Indeed, the memory of those whom fame reports to be worthy in arms lives long after their passing, nor, as the histories of the poets show clearly and as the common language of French eulogizers describes in many books long since spread through-out the world, are their names lost to posterity.[7]

His opponent in the town council replies that war is no mere exercise and that it may be waged only because of clear public necessity. Somewhat fatuously, he further states that 'I'd rather

[4] *Des quatres tenz d'aage d'ome* 15, ed. Marcel de Fréville, II.
[5] *La règle du Temple*, ed. Henri de Curzon, 63. This is the rule of 1128. The pertinent biblical passages are I John: 3, 16 and John: 15, 13.
[6] *Policraticus* 6, 8, ed. C. C. J. Webb (Oxford, 1909), II, 23.

be worthy in learning (*scientia*) than in arms',[7] thus repeating an argument that was to echo throughout the centuries.

This passage reminds us that others than clerks questioned the virtues of the martial order. Good bourgeois did also, and what offended them was the nobles' pride and indifference to ordinary morality. The speed with which gentlemen rode through the crowded streets of Italian towns was a cause of annoyance and of legislation. What would a solid burgher think of Geoffrey of Bruyères, lord of Karytaina in Morea and distinguished soldier, who, just at the moment the Byzantines were mobilizing against the Latins in 1252, went off to Italy with the wife of the lord of Catavas, the prettiest woman in all Romanie, on the pretext of touring local shrines? Whatever the burgher thought, Geoffrey's peers greeted him with cheers when he returned. What was worse in the eyes of the burghers, gentlemen were so extravagant. Buoncompagno of Signa tells us why they were always in debt:

> Frequent hospitality for reason of courtliness, standing as guarantors for the debts of their friends, gifts given in praise of war, seditious plots, lawsuits, visits to courts, marriage settlements, making love to women, dicing, . . . borrowing at usury, gluttony, drunkenness, negligence, violent contentiousness (*controversiarum incursus*), and improvidence with family property.[8]

For all the world like Kwakiutl Indians and their potlatches, seigniors who gave tourneys rivalled each other in the number of harnesses (armour) and horses they could lavish on their guests. These festivals, or 'courts', were often elaborately fanciful. In the *Romance of the Rose*, John of Meung has the lover's army assault the castle of maiden chastity. Nothing but a literary device, one might say. But in 1214 nobles from Padua, Venice and elsewhere assembled in Treviso for a 'court'. Armed with golden crowns and jewellery, the maids and ladies defended a castle whose walls were cloth of gold, scarlet, silk, and velvet. Equipped with fruits, spices, perfumes and flowers, the gentlemen began their assault. Unfortunately the banner of St Mark was knocked to the ground when the Venetians and Paduans began to brawl on entering the

---

[7] *Oculus pastoralis* 6, 1, ed. L. A. Muratori, *Antiquitates Italicae medii aevi* (Arezzo, 1776) IX, 840–2.
[8] *Boncompagnus Boncompagni* in *BuF* II, 166.

first gate, thus reinforcing the already lively animosity between the two towns.

This incident reminds us of another quality of the martial order, irritability. Nobles expected to have their way and were quickly angered when they did not. This was partly because of their upbringing. An unknown thirteenth-century French preacher reports that humble folk spoiled their children, lavishing affection on them until suddenly they were put to the plough or the bench. Gentlefolk were different. They rarely saw their children, giving them over to the servants and then sending them to service in the household of some notable. But when they grew up they were raised on high. Although both bourgeois and peasants went to war, gentlemen usually had more experience of actual combat, and this made them look down their noses at the other militias. Furthermore they had to face fear more frequently than others, and, while fear lends wisdom, it also makes men edgy and touchy. It is noteworthy how frequently the subject of fear appears in the literature of this time. The accuracy of Joinville's description of the battle at Mansurah in 1249, especially of the rout of the first division, or battle, of Louis IX's army, has been rarely equalled in the history of war. Typical of his gentlemanly sense of law, Beaumanoir interpolates into the section *Des Semonses* of his customal a discourse on permissible and impermissible flight, reminding his readers that those who flee are more likely to be killed than those who stand. On the other hand, the *Roman de Sidrac*, a popular thirteenth-century translation from the Arabic, observed that 'a good flight is better than a bad remaining'.[9] In short, while gentlemen were more courteous and usually far quieter than clergymen or bourgeois, they were given to fits of anger and violence that sharply contrasted with the behaviour of the other social orders.

The martial order enjoyed certain privileges. Even in Italian towns litigation between knights or knightly families was settled by courts of their peers. In return for the expense of maintaining harness and horses they were exempted from certain taxes. In Arles in 1205, knights paid the tithe on their property, while others paid both tithe and tallage. In Pistoia during the early 1200s knights paid the usual personal and property taxes in town, but their holdings in the *contado* were exempt from the hearth tax.

[9] Cited in Langlois, *La vie en France au moyen-âge* III, 261.

But, if knights were privileged in an economic sense, they were also impeded. They not only owed an expensive and sometimes dangerous service, but, in a manner similar to a farmer under manorial law, they were not usually allowed to alienate the portion of their lands (or other income-bearing goods) held as salary for this service. In the long run, this led to a curious development. To simplify a complex history, in those areas where the manorial system was weakening and farmers and burghers were becoming free to sell or otherwise alienate their holdings, in areas, that is, of a relatively unregulated or 'free' economy, the gentleman's fief or benefice obviously posed a problem similar to that of ecclesiastical mortmain. As long as no additional service was going to be required of them (and we shall see that to have been the case), it was in the interest of the large percentage of gentlefolk whose primary occupations were war, politics, and the life of 'high' society to protect their income by extending this inalienability to all of their properties, no matter how acquired. By the early thirteenth century, therefore, clauses forbidding the alienation of property, rents and sometimes other types of income to knights or the Church began to appear in private leases and sales. Although this restriction could usually be obviated by paying special fees to landlords, urban governments or princes, it could also be established in the same way. The growth of a distinction between noble and non-noble land was therefore a mark of thirteenth-century social life, and an early expression of the social rigidities that were to be characteristic of the late medieval period.

Although the martial order was usually distinguishable from the other orders, it was also a very broad one. In addition to titled princes, it included wealthy men and those having seigniories who were set off from the rest of the order by special, if informal, titles. Such were England's barons, sometimes called rich men (*divites*), Castile's *ricoshombres*, or the *comtors* of Catalonia. In the county of Namur, a region with about 370 villages, only about twenty families were called *nobiles* in the twelfth century. At about the same time the Limousin had its *principes*, Burgundy its *castellani*, Flanders its *barones*, and Lombardy its *capitanei*. Below these were the lesser members of the order. Around Mâcon in Burgundy in the later 1100s about 150 families of knightly grade were not materially better off, though socially higher, than the fifty or so families of important ministers (provosts, stewards) of princes, castellans, and churchmen. Indeed knights were often quite unmartial. In the late thirteenth century the anonymous poem *Siefried Helbling* described the lesser Austrian knights. Tournaments were not for them; they wanted to increase the yield of milk in their cows. Instead of drinking the wine they raised, they sold it. If war broke out, it had better be over by harvest time because that was when these farmers had to be home. And much the same was true of England's rural gentry. Because the privileges of knights were justified on the basis of their special service, they could lose their status if they neglected their profession. The statutes of the town of Fréjus in 1235 state that if a knight spends the greater part of his time 'ploughing, digging, carting wood or manure, or doing other agricultural labour, he should not have the knight's liberty'.[10] And had he not assumed the duties of knighthood by the age of thirty, he would have to pay the count of Provence's tallage.

This law reminds us that there was social mobility. Lesser folk could rise into the martial order, but the movement could also be downward. By the early 1200s, about three-fifths of the *nobiles* of the Namurois had sunk to the level of ordinary knights. Eventually a new and greater nobility, called the 'peers of the castle of Namur', made its appearance during the second half of the century. Far less numerous than the *nobiles* of the earlier age, the new order contained only about five of the older families. To some members of the knightly order knighthood seemed so unprofitable or so impossible to maintain that they were quite willing to exchange it for economic advantage. In 1238 the chapter of St Cunibert of Cologne conceded a property to one Otto of Stipel, 'who does not intend to become a knight. . . . Furthermore, be it known that, if the said Otto should happen to become a knight, he must sell the said property within the year, nor may he sell it to any church, knight or son of a knight who wishes to become one.'[11]

The rise and fall of families was rarely rapid during this period. A given region would have a period of relative stability followed by one of fairly rapid change. Statistics for the knightly order in the region around Cluny in Burgundy indicate a high degree of stability in the twelfth century. Of the forty-three knightly

---

[10] Published in Ch. Giraud, *Essai sur l'histoire du droit français* (Leipzig, 1846) II, 12.
[11] Cited in Guilhermoz, *Origine de la noblesse*, 379.

families known of in 1100, only six had vanished by about 1200, having been partially replaced by three new families, one of peasant origins. The tempo then began to accelerate. By 1240, sixteen new knightly lines appeared, of whom seven were branches of old families, two had risen from the ranks of the richer ministers (provosts) and one from petty ministerial or peasant origins. Then followed an age of more rapid social change, for which, unfortunately, statistics are lacking. It seems that, in much of Europe, the twelfth and early thirteenth centuries were times of relative social stability for the martial order, a fact that may have had something to do with the rise in the status and freedom of all groups in this period. All were more or less rising together.

Knighthood and nobility

Relative stability aside, momentous changes were taking place within the martial order during this age. To explain this, we must turn back a bit. At one time, the term noble (*vir nobilis, ingenuus*) had usually meant free, and relatively few members of the martial order were *nobiles*. In the course of the tenth and eleventh centuries this had changed radically, first in France and then in Italy, so that simple knights could legitimately be termed noble. This meant that knights held their fiefs hereditarily and that they were exempt from most taxes except feudal aid, that is, ransom for their lord, dower for his eldest daughter, the knighting of his eldest son, and occasional other things. They were judged by their peers and were also able to limit the amount of court or military service they had to give, in north France and elsewhere the usual obligation being forty days of free military service. Well into the twelfth century, however, memories of the past were very much alive. When Louis VI freed his sergeants (ministers) in Laon in 1129, he specified that they were now free to become clerks, knights, or burghers. In the 1180s the English justiciar Ralph of Glanville could still argue that a peasant, when emancipated and knighted, was free (*liber*) only in relation to his master and other peasants and not in relation to men of any other order. But the great jurist of the next century, Henry of Bracton (d. 1272), maintained the contrary. Throughout much of the west, to be knighted meant to be ennobled.

Although freed earlier and more fully than peasants or burghers, the knights were held by a rein whose tightness varied vastly, even in France. In northern France, most of a knight's property was held in fief. In Burgundy, Languedoc, and elsewhere in France most knights' land was allodial, and the feudal bond was consequently much weaker. The service ethos was still strong, however. To be trained through serving, young men of knightly family were attached to the courts of princes and great lords from about the age of fourteen. When they got older, they became part of a prince's fighting household retinue, or *mesnie*. A great prince, such as the young King Henry, the son of Henry II of England, was able in a tournament at Lagny-sur-Marne in 1180 to field a *mesnie* of twenty-seven Normans, twenty Frenchmen, twenty Flemings, fourteen Englishmen, and six Angevins. The *mesnies* of barons were on a lesser scale. An exchequer account of 1166 records that Walter Waleran of Wiltshire owed the king twenty knights, eight of whom were in his *mesnie*. Not only did *mesnies* constitute the élite of a normal medieval army, they were also composed of young men who had to please their masters in order to get a suitable fief. Great nobles still depended on kings and princes, just as lesser knights did on great nobles for the transmission of their fiefs. How barons felt is shown in Magna Carta of 1215. After an initial statement on ecclesiastical liberties, the next seven rubrics deal with wardship and inheritance. There the barons tried to fix the inheritance tax (relief), insisted on suitable guardianship for minors, and sought to protect the portions allotted to widows and to shield them from forced remarriage. Similar laws may be seen in almost any feudal code of the age.

In spite of the strength of the old service ethos among the knights and nobles of Italy, France and England, even ordinary knights were considered noble, or free, in the period with which this book is dealing. There were several reasons for this improvement in the status of the knight, and one of them concerns the Church and its ideas of the *pax dei* and the crusade. Medieval churchmen had always insisted on the dignity of the function of the soldier, the *miles Christi*, and not only on the vices of the order to which he belonged. Their argument had been enhanced by the crusade and by the creation of the military orders of the Church. The influence of this may be seen in Brabant, whose nobles had never bothered to assume the knightly title until the Temple and Hospital entered the duchy around 1175. More decisive in elevating the knightly order than the direct influence of the Church, however, was the decentralization and devolution of governmental authority. During that long process it was the natural if often inadvertent policy of a prince, faced by the strivings toward independence of his magnates and officers, to build a personal *mesnie*, or *familia*, of quasiservile soldiers and domestics, and at the same time to encourage the members of the magnates' *familiae* to seek for themselves the liberties their masters had already won. Two could play at that game and the battle between the magnates and the princes offered an opportunity for simple soldiers and administrative officers to advance toward freedom.

Although this process was almost complete in many areas, it was not so in Germany, where, in spite of the shattering blows given the Empire during the Gregorian age, a quasiservile knighthood dependent on the emperor or his greater ecclesiastical and secular vassals had been more firmly established than almost anywhere else in western Europe. In the mid-twelfth-century German Empire to be a noble (*vir nobilis, ingenuus, Freiherr*) still meant to be free. Although there was already a free knighthood, to be a *ministerialis* or simple knight implied servility. Many ministers still came from servile or peasant origins. Not only was their military or court service heavy but they also paid tallage and other servile dues. They were bound by *formariage*. As late as 1263 Sophia of Velturns, the daughter of a great Swabian minister, had to be enfranchised to marry a *Freiherr*. Although her first son was to share her husband's freedom, the rest of her sons were to be ministers. Ministerial offices and benefices were not usually formally hereditary, though they were often so in practice. In spite of this, some *ministeriales*, especially those in imperial service, rose high. Werner of Bolanden served the Hohenstaufen loyally from 1160 to 1190 in their struggle with the archbishop of Mainz and the bishop of Trier. At the height of his career he governed seventeen castles and towns, almost 1100 knights owed him service, and he held lands from forty-six different lords. Yet another great minister was the seneschal, the Markward of Anweiler, on whom, in 1195, the Emperor Henry VI conferred 'freedom, and invested him with the duchy of Ravenna together with the Romagna and also with the march of Ancona'.[12] The

[12] The Ursberger Chronicle cited in Karl Bosl, *Die Reichsministerialität der Salier und Staufer* I, 593.

261

Markward died in 1202 as regent of Sicily and guardian of the future Emperor Frederick II.

That adventuring Englishman, Gervais of Tilbury, who served the Empire as marshal of the kingdom of Arles in the late 1190s, tells us in his *Otia imperialia* that Henry VI changed the German system, adopting that of the English and French, in which knightly offices and fiefs were hereditary. Although oversimplified, there is much in what Gervais had to say. It was largely in the late twelfth and early thirteenth centuries that the basic change occurred in most of the Empire, except toward the east. In Eike of Repgow's code, the *Saxon Mirror* (1224–32), an enfranchised minister, like a peasant, never became a noble. In the *Swabian Mirror* (1257–74) a freed minister owing knightly service became noble (technically a *Mittelfreier*) because of the estimation in which knighthood had come to be held. The change also may be seen in the region of Namur. There in the mid-1100s to be a *vir nobilis* was everything. By the mid-1200s the knightly title had so appreciated that, in lists of witnesses, dubbed knights preceded unknighted nobles without regard to past nobility. More, the word *messire*, once accorded only to the old nobles, was addressed to knights from about 1220 onward. This was accompanied by the slow but sure acquisition of hereditary right to office and benefice, and the disappearance of servile restrictions and charges: *formariage*, tallage, etc.

The history of the rise of knights and ministers was still more complex. In most of Germany the knightly title, reinforced by French and ecclesiastical influences, stood above that of the *ministeriales*, and therefore the members of the latter group moved toward freedom more slowly. In Austria and parts of Swabia the ministerial group ranked higher because of its close connection with the Hohenstaufen Empire. In thirteenth-century Austria a minister was a grand seignior. It was only around 1240 that the lesser knights began to rise toward freedom, and, while many made the grade, others became burghers or sank into the peasantry. There were variations in other areas. The knights were ahead in Brabant and Liège, but the ministers around Namur. This is shown by the use of seals, those symbols of jurisdiction or of the individual's capacity to act in law. At the end of the twelfth century around Namur only *nobiles* and great churchmen had seals. The ministerial cadres began to adopt them in the 1220s and 1230s, and the first example of a simple knight's seal is of 1249.

The evolution of Europe's martial order had by and large come to the point where knights were both noble and free, and to be knighted meant to be ennobled throughout most of the west. So highly thought of was knighthood that kings and princes vied to enter it. In 1248, the year of his election as emperor, William of Holland was knighted by the king of Bohemia with these words: 'To the honour of omnipotent God, I ordain you knight and joyfully accept you as a member of our college.'[13] Although knighting normally took place at the age of majority (around twenty or twenty-one), princes were sometimes dubbed earlier in order to lend them the authority of membership in this select order. An example is Henry III of England who was dubbed at the age of nine.

Unlike the nobles of the past, whose claim to freedom had been the peculiar freedom of their lineage, the knight's freedom was based partly on his office, his functioning as a soldier. The sense of a profession, or *militia*, was not new among soldiers. Indeed, it derived from Roman law. The clergy had also always possessed it and based their authority upon it. As society matured, other militias began to appear. Of these the most significant were those of the professors, especially of law but also of letters, and the judges and lawyers, those whom Placentinus (d. 1192), a jurist who taught at Bologna and Montpellier, called 'a *militia* of unarmed soldiers, that is, those militating in letters (*literatoria militantes*)'.[14] This observation echoes the introductions to both the *Code* and the *Institutes*, in which it is said that imperial majesty was not only decorated by arms but also armed by laws, in order that the emperor might be victorious not only over Rome's enemies abroad, but also over injustice and crime at home. Others than Italians had heard of this noble ideal. It was enshrined in the great texts of English law, those of Glanville and Bracton, and in *Fleta*. Alphonso X of Castile had it incorporated into his *Siete partidas*, which also went on to divide society's orders into '*ricoshomes, caballeros, maestros, cibdadanos, menestrales e labradores*', adding that 'knowledge of law is another manner of knighthood'.[15]

Indeed, the professors and jurists of the *militia litterata* or

[13] Cited in Gauthier, *La chevalerie*, 291.
[14] Cited in Hermann Fitting, *Das castrense peculium*, 551.
[15] *Las siete partidas* I, 10, 3 (Madrid, 1807), II, 90.

togata were not satisfied with mere equality with the *militia armata* but actually sought precedence. When Azo read in the *Code* that professors and jurists practising their professions for twenty years were accorded the ex-vicarial dignity, he glossed this to mean that master John the Grammarian and Accursius, the professor of law, might be said to have the rank of count or duke on retirement. The treatise on criminal law (1286–1301) by Albert of Gandino argued that, while lawyers and judges were exempt from torture in law, knights were not, unless they were in the actual service of a prince or republic. By the time Bartolo of Sassoferrato was writing in 1355 he could sum up juristic tradition on the famous text of the *Code* by blandly observing: 'In brief, it says that lawyers are said to militate in laws, as soldiers in arms, and are more necessary to the republic than soldiers.'[16] In Bologna, the fountainhead of legal studies, the doctors took precedence over the knights. A statute of 1301 provided that formal processions were to be headed by the *potestas*, the captain of the people, and other elected officers, followed immediately by the judges and doctors, after whom trailed the knights and the commonalty.

Ludicrous though some of this may sound, it reflects the developing professional sense in thirteenth-century society. This even affected warfare. A learned literature on this subject began to appear. This principally consisted in copying and translating Vegetius Renatus's *Epitome*. An early adaptation of this ancient text for a specific type of war—that of Italy's urban republics—is to be seen in the *Pulcher tractatus materie belli* of the late thirteenth century, and thus was set in motion a tradition that persisted through the time of Machiavelli to the Napoleonic wars. True to his time, the Franciscan Salimbene remarked about a *potestas* of Parma that he was 'a brave knight and learned (*doctus*) in war'.[17] In 1277/79, when Giles of Rome wrote his widely read treatise on government, he likened knights to

> the masters and doctors of the other sciences. And just as no one should be made a master in another branch of learning unless it is agreed that he is instructed in that art, so should no one be raised up to the military dignity unless . . . it be opined that he will be competent in war's work. . . . And although

[16] Cited in Fitting, *op. cit.*, 551.
[17] *Liber de prelato* in his *cronica* in *MGH. SS* XXXII, 98.

footmen and mounted men who are not knights wage war, nevertheless knights ought to be the masters of the soldiers and the organizers of the others in battle . . .[18]

And this professionalism was readily welcomed in the noble family because, owing to the service ethos, gentlemen and gentlewomen were traditionally career-minded. In his didactic romance called *Erec and Enide*, Christian of Troyes (fl. 1150–80) had long since taught that marriage, making love, wealth and high lineage were not enough. He argued, in fact, that love could only flourish in those who strove to attain a place in the world. Borrowing the Aristotelian divisions of practical philosophy (*practica*), that is, self-government (*ethica* or *monostica*), the government of groups (*economica*), and the government of society (*politica*), Christian had his married hero and heroine first learn self-respect or love, then love of others and friendship, and, finally, love of society and fulfilment within it. At that point, Erec and Enide are crowned king and queen.

The appearance of the other professions and the emphasis upon the qualifications or performance of the individual knight revived the ancient discussion of what constituted nobility. There were three principal definitions: nobility of blood, of wealth, or of virtue. The main argument for nobility of blood was given by the chaplain Andrew in his tract on love written in the mid-1180s, a wisecracking work that is a positive dictionary of social ideas. From the fact that scarlet dye holds faster in English wool than in Italian, a lady argues by analogy that virtue is more likely to be found in noble blood than in plebeian. Besides, gentlemen are handsomer; their limbs are slenderer. Nor, she continues, would God have instituted different orders of men, had there been no reason for it. Andrew's contemporary, the Abbess Hildegard of Bingen, had already developed this point when answering a query as to why she permitted only noblewomen into her monastery. She replied that God had instituted a natural order and that a man should not try, as did Satan and Adam, to vault higher than his natural place. Besides, she asks, who would stable cattle, asses, sheep and goats all pell-mell together in the barn? Just as there is a heavenly hierarchy, so also is there one on earth. Although God

---

[18] *De regimine principum* 3, 3, 1 in Rome 1607 (reprint), 558–9. The French version of 1286 is even clearer: Giles's *ordinatores aliorum in bello* is translated *ordenneors des batailles*, that is, of the battles or squadrons (ed. S. P. Molanaer, 372–3).

loves all equally, that does not mean that all are equal here below.

Although these sentiments won the plaudits of the nobility of ancient lineage, they did not attract the majority of writers in this period, partly because of the rise of knighthood and partly because most authors were either jurists or clerks whose outlook was professional and whose blood may often have left something to be desired. And blood has little intellectual appeal. After all, taught the *Roman de Sidrac*, gentlemen must remember that we are all sons of Adam. Dante developed this argument scholastically in the *Convivio*. If one asserts that a peasant (*villano*) cannot become a gentleman, he says, one implies that the *villano's* ancestors could not. One is therefore obliged to consider our origins and debate the absurd proposition as to whether or not Adam was a noble. Earlier on the good chaplain Andrew had remarked that if it were proposed that some had been ennobled through virtue in the past, one must also admit that 'there are many seminally deriving from these first nobles who are wholly declined by degeneration. And if you reverse the proposition, it's not false either,' he added, using the dialecticians' tag.[19] History amply confirmed his opinion. The chaplain and historian of the house of Anjou, Thomas of Loches (d. 1168), explained the humble origins of this house by observing that the Emperor Charles the Bald elevated commoners because

> in those days, there were *men of old stock and many family portraits* who *boasted* about the deeds of their *forefathers* and not their own, and who, when entrusted with any important office, *employed someone from the people as an instructor in their office*, so that those whom the king *ordered to command* others were seeking *another commander for themselves*.[20]

The words italicized above come from Sallust's *Jugurthine War*, a fact that reminds us that all the arguments against nobility of blood came from antiquity. Among them was another used by Thomas when he remarked that the humble origin of the Angevin line was a matter of no moment, 'for we have often read that

[19] *De amore* 1, 6, ed. Amadeu Pages, 9.
[20] *Gesta consulum Andegavorum* in *Chroniques des comtes d'Anjou*, ed. Louis Halphen and René Poupardin (Paris, 1913), 25 and 27. The latter quotation, according to the editors, is related to Cicero's *De senectute* 16, 56: 'In agris erant tunc senatores ...' followed by the story of Cincinnatus. I owe this reference to R. W. Southern of Oxford University.

senators formerly lived on the land and that emperors were torn from the plough', a point further substantiated by the biblical cases of the shepherds Saul and David.[20]

Others opted for wealth as a source of nobility. Dante discussed Aristotle's maxim—repeated by the Emperor Frederick II—that nobility consisted of old wealth combined with virtue. He dismissed the first part of the proposition because of the three imperfections of riches: 'First, the wantonness of their acquisition; secondly, the moral danger of their increase; and, thirdly, the harmfulness of their possession.'[21] In Andrew's *De amore* a noblewoman reminds her plebeian suitor that love-making is a full-time occupation; you can't spend the whole week making money and take Sunday off to court your lady. The commoner rejoins that he makes it only to spend it. By spending, he says, 'I defend the nobility of my behaviour and virtue. Besides, did I not busy myself making honest and licit profits, poverty would keep me in obscurity so that I could not perform noble acts, and thus my nobility would rest on nothing but the assertion of my own word, a type of courtliness and nobility no one believes in.'[22] Wealth meant something, therefore, as everyone admitted, just as long—as John of Meung put it in *The Romance of the Rose*—as it was made to be spent and did not deter the lover from his true business. Practical statesmen were aware of its importance. Writing before 1264, John of Viterbo in his book on the office of the *potestas* stated the case carefully. Although no head of state should be elected simply because of his wealthy family, John recommended that, if two candidates were otherwise equal, the richer should be chosen, because 'one may presume that [the poorer candidate] might be more easily corrupted. I do not deny, however, that it is quite suitable to elect someone who is not rich, if he is diligent, provident, discreet, gracious and tested.'[23]

This prudential type of argument did not please rigorists. For them, neither blood nor money counted. Since, says Andrew the Chaplain, 'virtue is more to be praised in a plebeian than in a noble', other things being equal, the commoner should be preferred as the beloved.[24] Everything came from virtue. Dante con-

---

[21] *Convivio* 4, 1, 3.
[22] *De amore* 1, 6, 2, ed. Amadeu Pages, 24.
[23] *Liber de regimine civitatum* 5 in *BIMA* III, 221b.
[24] *De amore* 1, 6, 4, ed. Amadeu Pages, 41.

cluded, 'and thus is nobility derived from virtue; and not virtue from nobility'.[25] His friend, the poet and jurist Cino of Pistoia, expressed similar ideas in his *Lectura on the Code* of 1312/14:

> Whoever deserves nobility by virtue is more worthy of being called a noble than he who descends from a noble family, because no one is noble by race, except presumptively, and even he is to be commended for what he has sought for himself rather than from what he has from his parents. . . . As Cato said: 'Learning ennobles the mind.'[26]

And Dante's teacher, Brunetto Latini, had declared in his popular *Tresor* of 1260/66 that 'ordinary folk say that courtesy results from lordship, others that its cause is riches, and yet others from nobility of blood, but the wise say that the only true reason why a man is worthy of being a prince and a lord is the virtue that he has in himself'.[27] About all such authors were willing to grant nobility of lineage was a presumption of virtue. About 1265 an anonymous Parisian Dominican declared that he saw nothing in nobility 'except that nobles are constrained by a certain need not to degenerate from the virtue of their parents', a notion derived from St Jerome.[28] The desire to live up to an honoured tradition did not always produce results. Brunetto repeated a commonplace when he observed that to be a man 'of mean spirit and high lineage is like being an earthen pot covered outside with fine gold'.[29]

But men of the time were ambivalent, and popular opinion did not really support the view of these major intellectuals. One suspects that James of Voragine's *Golden Legend* would not have been so widely read had not the life of almost every saint begun with a description of his or her noble origins—a nobility enhanced, of course, by virtue. Nor was this stereotype only the medieval equivalent of the 'society' orientation of today's popular press. Alphonso X of Castile was obliged to admit various sources for nobility, including lineage. Gentility, the king avers, derives 'first, from lineage, second, from knowledge [as of law], and,

---

[25] *Convivio* 4, 1, 19.
[26] Cited in Fitting, *op. cit.*, 552.
[27] *Li livres dou Tresor* 2, 29, ed. Carmody, 199.
[28] The *De eruditione principum* of the Pseudo-Thomas cited in Wilhelm Berges, *Die Fürstenspiegel des hohen und späten Mittelalters* (Stuttgart, 1958) 11n.
[29] *Li livres dou Tresor* 2, 29, ed. Carmody, 230.

third, from excellence in arms, customs and manners'.[30] But, although 'lineage is a noble thing, virtue surpasses and outdoes it; and whoever has both may be really called a noble (*ricohome*), because he is rich by lineage and a man completed by virtue'.[31]

The late thirteenth-century saw a recrudescence of literature defending hereditary nobility. The most famous spokesman for this point of view was Raymond Lull, whose *Order of Chivalry* of 1274–75 was widely read throughout the later Middle Ages. Not only did he repeat the old arguments, but he also adopted themes seen only in poetry or popular literature before. To Lull a knight who has children by a plebeian wife honours neither gentility nor knighthood, and—far worse!—a knight's wife who bears a child by a commoner destroys 'the antiquity of chivalry and the noble confraternity of noble lineage'.[32] Indeed, no one has sufficient power to knight a man of common lineage. Even Lull, however, had to bow before virtue and thereby contradict himself, although grudgingly. Because man is rational, transcending the beasts, 'the order of chivalry therefore consents that by many noble habits, many noble deeds, and ennobling by the prince, there can be in chivalry an occasional man of new, honourable and gentle lineage'.[33] Besides, Lull had to face reality. Although he believed that ideally judges should be chosen only from chivalry, he required them to be trained in law as well as war.

The new nobility

Why did a literature defending hereditary nobility begin to appear in the thirteenth century? One reason is that literacy among nobles had grown beyond poetry and romance and now sought to express itself in semiphilosophical discourses like those of Raymond Lull, developing ideas that had existed long before. Furthermore, these ideas reflected the strong family feeling of the medieval nobility, a quality that distinguished them from both the

[30] *Las siete partidas*, I, 21, 2 (Madrid, 1807) II, 197–8.

[31] *Las siete partidas* I, 9, 6, ed. 1807 II, 63.

[32] *Llibre que es de l'orde de cavalleria* 7, ed. Pere Bohigas, *Obres essencials de Ramon Llull* (Barcelona, 1957) I, 453b; also French translation in *Le livre de lordre de chevalerie* 8 in Columbia University, Plimpton MS 282, 104r.

[33] *Llibre que es de l'orde de cavalleria* 3, ed. Pere Bohigas, *Obres essencials de Ramon Llull* I, 535b; also Plimpton MS 282, 92v, where the chapter is four. The French has been followed here because, being later in time, it is more 'reactionary.'

clergy and the jurists. The clergy was an order of celibates, and the jurists derived their professional sense from their ecclesiastical predecessors, a fact illustrated by their habit of calling untrained judges and jurymen 'laymen' or, as the jurist Azo said in his commentary on the *Code*, 'laymen and the illiterate'.[34] The careers of clerks and jurists might be aided by their family connections, but, in theory at least, their posts and salaries were not hereditary. It is true that, like the priesthood of the clerk or the doctorate of the jurist, knighthood was something assumed or won by an individual and not by a family, but the tradition of hereditary offices and remuneration that had grown up since late Roman times enabled the knights, once they were free, to emulate in this respect the nobles and great officers of the earlier Middle Ages. The result was that, while individuals of no lineage could always be knighted, families of freemen that had produced knights and that had hereditary possession of the remuneration given knights could not be deprived of their right to lay claim to this office. In short, once freed, knightly families adopted the lineage traditions of the older nobility.

Throughout the Middle Ages the nobility organized itself into lineages or extended family groups. Without going into the involved history of Europe's family structures, it suffices to say that family links were reinforced to a degree rarely met with today. One reason for this is true even now, namely that the rich and powerful almost always have larger family groups than the poor and humble, just as flies cluster around the jam pot but care not for the salt. In both town and countryside, therefore, rising families either entered into close relationship with older lineages or constituted new and expanding families of their own. Such were the origins of patrician lines of the towns as well as of many rural families rising from ministerial cadres.

A second reason for the powerful role of the family was more particularly medieval. Family solidarity grew strong partly because government authority was weak and decentralized. Where princes were weakest, as in southern and eastern France and parts of Italy, most twelfth-century litigation between local notables was handled by arbitration, and the decisions were guaranteed by the relatives of the parties involved (*proximi*). A settlement of this kind was of such significance that it was often described in terms

[34] Cited in Guido Rossi, *Consilium sapientis judiciale* (Milan, 1958), 34.

later used in public or even international law: *pax, pactum*, and the like. The power of family solidarity encouraged the persistence of certain primitive legal customs such as compurgation, or the swearing by members of a family as to the veracity of a case presented by an individual. If two individuals involved in conflict could elicit the support of their families it was rare that the matter would not end in arbitration unless those on either side were determined on a private war, or vendetta. This was why the judicial duel, though nicely attuned to the spirit of a martial aristocracy, rarely came off. It stirred up too much bad blood and led to vendettas. How important vendettas were is easily shown. Beaumanoir's chapter on war (*guerra*) largely concerns vendettas, and, although most town statutes discriminate between 'licit and public war' and private war, the laws of Avignon of 1243 contain the following permission: 'Item, we ordain that every knight, bourgeois, good man . . . according to the ancient liberty of this city, may give aid in war to their lords and to their friends', under certain conditions designed to protect the community as a whole from direct involvement.[35] The importance of family unity is indicated by the existence of acts of formal exclusion (*forjurement*) of individuals from a family that did not wish to protect them against the consequences of their acts.

So vigorous were these family groups that they often imposed their will on the state, or what stood for the state in this period. Great wars, like those between the Plantagenets and Capetians in France and those between the Welfs (Guelphs) and Weiblinger (Hohenstaufen or Ghibellines) in Germany and Italy, were partly conflicts between rival families over offices and power. The literature of the feudal age reminds us of this. Everyone knew the *Song of Roland* and how Ganelon's family had stood by him when he was charged with the treason that caused Roland's death. Charlemagne's court had been unwilling to proceed against him because of the might of his family, and the emperor's cause had won only by means of a judgment of God through trial by battle. The drama of the thirteenth century *chanson de geste, Raoul de Cambrai,* was built around Bernier's conflicting loyalties—to Raoul, his lord, and to his own lineage, Raoul's mortal enemies.

The size and cohesiveness of families varied vastly. By the time

---

[35] Maulde, *Coutumes et règlements de la république d'Avignon,* 190, chapter 112 of the customs.

with which we are dealing, the family was usually a patrilineal group bearing a common family name and sharing the exploitation of offices and wealth. To leave it there, however, neglects the importance of women who, when married, brought to their new homes a connection with another patrilineal family. The group capable of swift cohesive action was usually the married couple and a number of their close relatives (*proximi, parentes*) who habitually acted together, although the community of brothers who shared a common inheritance was also important. The aristocratic family may therefore be viewed as a group of relatively small and tight nuclei rather loosely integrated into the grander constellations of two or more major patrilineal groups. That this system could mobilize power is beyond doubt. In 1273 at Tournai when a father renounced his son before the town fathers because the youth had breached a truce, seventy co-jurors from his own lineage joined him in this act, as did fifty-three of his wife's relatives, together with others in lesser categories of relationship or clientage, a total of 129 persons. Yet medieval men were as puzzled as we are by the obligations owed by different degrees of relationship. In *Raoul de Cambrai* the question was raised by two supporters of the principals as to whether or not they should fight: were they closely enough related to Raoul and Bernier?

Similar problems came up in the application of family controls on property. These were usually of two kinds. One was the right of family members to have first option on the property of a relative who was about to alienate it (*droit lignager*). Another was the recognition that a transaction involving loss of property was not complete without the consent of close relatives (*laudatio parentum*). The size of the group that had to be consulted or offered options varied widely from place to place and from time to time.

Thus constituted, these families were not without deep strains and stresses. One of these was the problem of marriage for family advantage examined in chapter VII above. Another was the European-wide tradition of subdividing property among all heirs. The effects of such partition were eased by the generally expanding economy of the age, at least until the *rallentando* around 1300, and besides, the loss of heirs was healthily—if that's the word—high. Of the seven sons of Henry, castellan of Bourbourg near Guines, two entered the Church, two died accidentally (one as a youth and the other as a knight), and a fifth was blinded in a tournament and was therefore rendered ineligible. The two brothers who successively acquired this rich inheritance produced no male heirs who survived beyond 1194, when the seigniory fell to Henry's granddaughter Beatrice—and what a race for her there was among the local nobility! It was normal family practice to push some children into the Church and others into the *mesnies* of semiprofessional soldiers maintained by great princes and seigniors. One can thus understand why the crusades, though harming some members of the aristocracy, were profitable to most: they reduced the partition of family inheritances. Still, long-continued subdivision was bound to weaken a family, and there are many examples of this ruinous process. Knightly and even seigniorial families sometimes fell to the level of a rather leisured yeomanry with tastes too elevated for their means.

Although not enough is known to hazard more than the most tentative generalizations, it seems that still another factor intensified this crisis within the martial aristocracy. It was associated with the spread of freedom. Among the peasantry servile holdings were less frequently subdivided than free ones, because it was in the interest of the lords to keep them as viable entities. The problem of partition, therefore, marked the age when peasants tended to be free. Much the same seems to have been true of the martial order. As long as the ethos of service was strong and the *militia armata* was somewhat ministerial, subdivision was not a serious threat. By the time nobles and knights had become wholly free, however, the problem was more pressing, and, as a result, gave rise to fitful legislation by princes in England and France from the 1180s onward in order to insure the performance of feudal military service.

Methods of single succession to the parental *heritage*, as Beaumanoir called it, particularly primogeniture, were gradually adopted by nobles in England, Brittany, Anjou and parts of the French royal domain. Gentlemen could be aware of the problem without princely pressure, however, as has been shown by a recent study of the Mâconnais. There the great nobility of the twelfth century, the castellans, were already suffering from the partition of their ample holdings. Around 1200, therefore, some lines adopted single succession, especially primogeniture. Later on in the thirteenth century, as the knights of the region rose to control smaller seigniories, they too began to adopt similar restraints.

Nobles therefore pressed their surplus offspring into the Church and into careers in law and in arms with ever greater insistence. The desire of noble families to limit inheritance rights was to be a mark of the nobility of the later Middle Ages and more than anything else indicates the pressure put on this social group by the slowing down of economic growth around 1300. Together with the failure of the crusades, this evolution helps explain the rise of mercenary companies composed of scions of knightly families. Such companies appear in growing numbers in the Italian wars of the later thirteenth century and the French wars of the fourteenth.

Economic forces acting on the martial aristocracy were joined by social ones. In many large western towns a bourgeois aristocracy aped the knights and went to war with similar equipment and something of the same martial spirit. The statute of Avignon in 1243 cited above is an instance of this. Many of the liberties possessed by nobles had been extended to large groups of commoners, not only bourgeois but also peasants. Save in the romantic imagination of poets or the fictions of backward-looking jurists, the peculiar quality of being noble was no longer defined by the use of 'noble' to mean 'free'. Here, also, the growing power of secular government made itself felt. Since knighthood was an accolade, it could be used to reward service. We have already seen that an architect had been dubbed toward the end of his career by Charles I of Anjou and Naples and a jurist by a duke of Burgundy. These individuals obviously had been honoured not for military prowess but rather for other services to the prince. The case of one William, chamberlain of the count of Namur, shows that promotion could come late in life. Already a mature man, William held his important office in 1289. Eleven years later he was raised to the grade of squire, and in 1305 to that of knight. The Italian city republics went even further. Knighting had become so common a recognition of civic worth that in 1322 the Florentines were obliged to order that no one could be dubbed after death!

Warfare became more expensive as time went on. Although mounted chivalry still dominated the field of battle, town militias, notably those of the Italians, had introduced the crossbow, the first of the new weapons that eventually changed the face of war. The crossbow made horse armour necessary in the late twelfth century and stimulated the beginnings of the replacement of chain mail with plate armour in the thirteenth. Heavier horses were needed. Better equipped and more expensively mounted, knights customarily rode at the head of formations and their death rate was consequently higher. They campaigned with larger retinues than squires, that is, non-knighted members of their own social status. In fine, to be dubbed a knight when young showed a willingness to undertake an expensive and risky career. Writing in the 1270s, Raymond Lull recommended that a squire lacking the means should forgo knighthood. Otherwise, he said, he would become a thief—or, a historian might add, a mercenary—in order to pay for his golden belt and spurs.

Faced by these manifold and increasing difficulties, the martial aristocracy began to change its character. Until about 1200—and sometimes later in Germany, not to speak of Scandinavia and the Slavic lands where knighthood had barely been introduced—the accent had been on the function of knighthood. The new concept was based on the privileges of those of knightly stock. The nature of this change may be illustrated by a rather late but unusually complete series of imperial privileges addressed to the *ministeriales* or knights of the Rhenish-Franconian town of Oppenheim. In 1226 the emperor wrote to the 'knights' of Oppenheim. In 1269 he greeted the 'knights and sons of knights', and by 1275 Rudolph of Habsburg addressed 'all the knights, their sons and grandsons (*nepotibus*) at Oppenheim possessing the *jus castrense*',[36] the latter phrase referring to the privileges accorded the military in Roman law. The result of this evolution may be seen in a charter of 1293 emanating from Manosque in Provence adverting to questions raised between 'the knights and military (*militares personas*) whose names are NN, knights, and NN, squires or military (*domicelli vel militares persone*) on one hand and the good men and commonalty (*populares personas*) on the other'.[37] These texts show that non-knighted gentlemen from knightly lines had come to equal knights in their general social status. This is confirmed by the fact that up to 1258 in the region of Namur non-knighted military were generally called sergeants (*servientes*), a term with distinctly servile or pejorative connotations in that somewhat backward area. Later, however, gentlemen's sons were invariably called squires and considered noble.

[36] Cited in Guilhermoz, *Origine de la noblesse*, 482.
[37] Cited in Guilhermoz, *op. cit.*, 479.

The dissociation of knighthood from nobility had taken place earlier and faster in the Italian urban republics. A Florentine statute of 1289 defined nobles as members 'of a house where there is a knight, or where there was one within the last twenty years, or as those who, in common parlance, are normally held to be or are called notables (*potentes*), nobles or magnates'.[38] Even in so chivalrous an area as France actual knighthood became gradually rarer, being replaced by the sense of belonging to a noble lineage. Of the sixty nobles of forty-three families in the county of Forez near Lyons who leagued together against royal fiscalism in 1314–15, four were widows, twenty-nine were knights (two of whom had lately been bourgeois), and twenty-seven were squires (*donzeaux*), of whom one was of peasant origin. Of the squires, eleven died as such, six were knighted before the age of forty, five before fifty, four before sixty, and one was knighted in his sixties. Gone were the days when one was dubbed at twenty-one or shortly thereafter.

Faced by social pressures from below and by the rigidities of an ever more mature economy, the families of knightly origin were taking on the style of the great nobility of the earlier Middle Ages. Function was about to be defeated by lineage. Instead of being defined by what it had to do in order to earn its privileges, the new nobility was eventually to be characterized by its peculiar freedom, in other words, by what it did not have to do. In some places the nobility could even be distinguished by what it was not permitted to do. In 1225 the king of England addressed 'all earls (*comites*), barons, knights and free men who are not merchants',[39] and early-fourteenth-century French legislation for Picardy distinguished between the types of commoners who acquired noble fiefs, stating that 'some live as nobles and are apt for bearing arms and others live as merchants and are not apt for bearing arms'.[40] Although this nobility, or *gentillece*, as Beaumanoir called it, borrowed much from the old *nobiles* of the past, it must be emphasized that it was still new in the thirteenth century. The first evidence of family heraldry dates from this time, as do the first serious discussions of chivalry as nobility, like that of Raymond Lull. Europe's first formal treatise on heraldry was the

[38] Cited in Gaetano Salvemini, *La dignità cavalleresca*, 398.
[39] Cited in Guilhermoz, *op. cit.*, 464.
[40] Cited in *ibid.*, 464.

posthumously published *De insigniis et armis* of Bartolo of Sasso-ferrato (d. 1357). This Italian jurist was so indifferent to the nobles' sense of lineage that he blandly opined that anyone could have coats of arms, comparing them to watermarks, trademarks, and the signs of commercial companies. The new idea of nobility was only budding. It was not to flower until the later middle ages and the early modern period.

The change posed serious problems for government, which was threatened with a loss of military service or compensatory monetary payment. On the other hand, government gained an advantage, namely, the possibility of knighting faithful subjects and thus elevating them into a privileged order. The way these matters were handled differed from one part of Europe to another.

In Italy and adjacent regions, where the towns were relatively independent, the republican spirit dominated. As early as the mid-twelfth century the imperialist historian Otto, bishop of Freising, had complained that

> in order not to lack means of oppressing their neighbours [the Milanese] are not ashamed to allow young men of low condition or even artisans of contemptible or mechanical arts, whom other peoples would reject like the plague from the more honourable and liberal pursuits, from assuming the knight's belt and grades of dignity and hence it is that they far excel all other cities in wealth and power.[41]

Italians had their usual ready answer for this type of charge. The thirteenth-century Italian poem *L'Entrée d'Espagne* said that the Lombards with Charlemagne at the siege of Pamplona were all naturally free, all knighted at war without regard to birth, and all privileged to carry bared swords before the king. In Italy, also, the difference in the style of life of a rich bourgeois and a knight was small, particularly because knights were frequently engaged in business. In spite of the opinion borrowed from Roman law by Accursius in his *Glossa ordinaria* (1220–34) stating that a soldier (*miles*—knight) may not be a merchant, almost all of the Florentine and other merchant-bankers were nobles. In 1312–14, Cino of Pistoia sourly remarked about Italian knights that 'nowadays one can rarely say of knights that they give up mercantile pursuits or

---

[41] This passage from the *Gesta Friderici I* is cited everywhere, but see Salvemini, *op. cit.*, 355.

private business, and not a few are to be found who exercise the most common crafts and do not know how to arm themselves'.[42] For these, Cino comments, it suffices to wear golden spurs and to enjoy honorific prerogatives, and they should have no other privileges. Since bourgeois were like knights and knights like bourgeois, it was appropriate that all knights, squires, and bourgeois wealthy enough to 'live nobly' should possess knights' equipment and serve as knights either personally or by means of substitutes. The easiest way to determine who owed knight service was to equate it with a certain level of personal and property taxes, a system used throughout northern Italy by the mid-1200s. As a result, the age-old rights of the knights to judgment by their peers and exemption from taxes slowly disappeared.

Knighting became for a time an accolade similar to modern British knighthood. This happened in the following way. With the rise of democratic or popular elements within the Italian republics the law identified the class of the *nobiles* or *magnates*, but deprived them not only of their privileges but also of their civil rights, notably by excluding them from public office. So severe was this persecution that nobles in Italian towns frequently sought to become commoners. In 1322, for example, four nobles of Putignono in the *contado* of Pisa stated that, 'although they have and have had the name of nobles, nevertheless they were always *effectualiter* commoners and supporters of the Pisan people and always intended to be so'.[43] They petitioned the government to make them commoners by formal enactment. In such circumstances, individuals worthy of reward would no longer accept knighthood if it implied nobility. At different times and in different places, therefore, a system of popular knighthood developed. In Florence it appeared in the 1290s and continued on and off through most of the fourteenth century. Thus Bartolo of Sassoferrato was able to remark in his *Commentaries on the Code*: 'We observe in this city of Perugia, that if any plebeian is knighted, he is considered noble; but in Florence he remains a commoner even after knighting.'[44]

Elsewhere in Europe the *militia armata's* evolution partly paralleled that in Italian urban republics. This was because of

---

[42] Cited in Fitting, *op. cit.*, 559.
[43] Cited in Emilio Cristiani, *Nobiltà e popolo nel commune di Pisa* (1962), 114–5.
[44] Cited in Salvemini, *op. cit.*, 399.

the change in the nature of warfare. Twelfth-century princes like the Plantagenets and Capetians fought their wars with their own *mesnies* and with those of the greater nobles who owed direct service for their fiefs. They supplemented these forces with mercenary bands composed largely of foot or mounted sergeants. The militia service of ordinary knights and townsmen was only occasionally called upon and then largely for the so-called defence of the realm (*defensio patriae* or *regni*) when the prince had a traditional right to the unlimited service of all freemen. Only in Germany, where ministerial cadres still existed, were ordinary knights summoned for long campaigns beyond the frontiers of their own provinces. In the thirteenth century, as the crusades wilted and warfare within Europe became more intense, armies became larger and campaigns lasted longer. In Italy's urban republics whose wars were all *defensiones patriae* because the citizenry had voted for them, paid militia service developed to an extraordinary degree. Similarly, the first instinct of Europe's princes was to make the most of the militia available at home, especially because public finance was so rudimentary. One way of doing this was to insist on the citizen's obligation to serve by identifying all wars with the ancient *defensio patriae* in order to circumvent the limitations on military service that had been won by the martial order and other militias. Militiamen had to be paid something, but not as much as experienced mercenaries.

Although all western princes sought to reinforce and use the *militia armata* in this period, the best-known effort is found in England, where it took the form of distraint of knighthood. The first distraint was in 1224, when it was ordered that those who held knightly fiefs worth twenty pounds *per annum* were to be knighted or else pay a fine. In 1241 the law was extended to anyone holding property worth that amount, whether or not his property was a fief or he of knightly stock. When this legislation was repeated in 1256, Matthew Paris, the historian of Saint Albans, observed that it was enacted 'so that knighthood should be reinforced in England as it was in Italy'.[45] It has been suggested that the principal reason for these repeated laws was fiscal, that the king wished

---

[45] *Chronica majora*, ed. *Rolls Series* LVII, v, 560. This legislation is paralleled by the earlier laws of the assizes of arms (which were also repeated in this period) that dealt with military service from the very bottom of society up to freeholds worth fifteen pounds *per annum*, but here I am concerned with knight service.

to collect the fines and not the service. This seems unlikely. Not only did Henry III and Edward I promote a lively propaganda for knighthood—no less than three hundred knights were dubbed in one ceremony in 1306—but they also made real attempts to use these troops, so much less expensive than good mercenaries or even household *mesnies*. It was amply shown at Bannockburn against the Scots in 1314, however, that—to paraphrase the ancient military writer Vegetius Renatus—multitudes of occasional and inexperienced militiamen serve only to perplex and embarrass. It was also difficult to use this militia overseas, where most of England's wars after 1300 were to be fought. The kings therefore gradually gave up their effort and depended on the increasingly professional *mesnies* of great magnates and mercenary companies of Frenchmen or Englishmen under contract or indenture. On the other hand, although paid, the infantry was raised by a kind of conscription operated by the later commissions of array.

Similar policies in France led to similar results. Among these were the logistical log-jam of the crusade against Catalonia-Aragon in 1284–85 and the uncontrollable mob scene at Courtrai in 1302 against the Flemish townsmen, both of which foreshadowed the French disasters of the Hundred Years War. The meagre or even tragic results of these policies in the military sphere should not blind us to the fact that they marked a considerable strengthening of royal power. In the twelfth century, most French knights owed service for benefices or fiefs held from local princes or great magnates, rarely from the king. With the growth in the late 1200s of the theory that all wars were *defensiones patriae* or *regni*, the king was able to summon the militia of all those of knightly origin—the *arrière-ban* (Latin, *heribannus*, from German, *Heerbann*)—and not just the greater feudatories and barons. In spite of the fact that tradition favoured the marshal of Mirepoix's protest against this extension of the military obligation, he lost his suit against the Crown in 1272 before the *parlement* of Paris. By the early 1300s all French gentlemen owed service or compensatory taxes based on their wealth and status. Although the Norman and Angevin princes had accomplished their invasions of England by the use of semiprofessional *mesnies* and even mercenaries and although Charles of Anjou's successful intervention in the Italian wars against the Hohenstaufen had been carried out by largely professional forces, France's own defence was to be based on the militia principle throughout much of the later Middle Ages, largely because the English invaded France and thus justified the call to the *defensio regni*. Militias of occasional soldiers are, by virtue of their numbers, often capable of defeating professional soldiers, but this capacity rests on the social solidarity of the militias involved, a quality notably lacking in fourteenth-century France. Because of the traditional martial pride of French chivalry, it took generations of national disaster before professionalism could triumph and the militia principle atrophy among the nobles. Paradoxically, not until that occurred could the nobility be called a wholly 'privileged order'.[46]

If the change from feudal service to general militia service in Europe's princely states paralleled the evolution in Italy's urban republics, the history of knighthood was very different, because of the weakness of the republican spirit outside of that peninsula. In western Europe in this period knighthood usually conferred nobility—Beaumanoir's *gentillece*. Western princes sought the monopoly of knighting, at first in order to control the militia and then in order to reward faithful servants. Although Roman law accorded them this right, in practice any knight could dub the son of a knight. Where the princes moved in was in the ennobling of commoners through knighthood. But even in the thirteenth century it was difficult to establish this as a royal monopoly in a large nation like France, with its semi-independent duchies and counties such as Brittany and Flanders, not to speak of England's Guienne and Gascony. In 1298 royal authority was obliged to confess that, from time immemorial, in Provence and the seneschalcy of Beaucaire 'bourgeois were accustomed to assume the knight's belt from nobles, barons and even archbishops without the authority and licence of the prince'.[47] Bit by bit, however, the rights of the prince began to prevail. From the 1270s the French kings developed a lucrative business of selling grants of nobility or rewarding service with them. An example is a charter of 1295:

Because . . . our most dear father manumitted master John of Taillefontaine, clerk, . . . we, approving this liberty, concede to

[46] Until 1347 the *arrière-ban* included commoners as well as nobles. The last time a force was raised by means of the *arrière-ban* was in 1756 to ward off an English coastal raid.
[47] Cited in Gauthier, *op. cit.*, 249.

the same John . . . that he may acquire noble fiefs and assume the belt of knighthood, whensoever he may wish, and, by that act, . . . enjoy the privileges and honour of perpetual nobility.[48]

In fine, as nobility became privileged, princes began to find means with which to control access to it.

It is worth pausing over one final point: the balance of power between a prince and his nobles, between the state and its privileged citizens. In the prince's eyes, nobility derived from virtue, and virtue from service to himself. And in his eyes nobility should ideally be non-hereditary, to be won by each man through his service. The social levelling and universal service owed to prince and country that this implies were already understood, as may be seen when Rudolph of Habsburg in 1276 greeted all of his subjects, from the peasants to the greatest nobles, as 'my ministers'.[49] So resistant was the concept of lineage among the martial aristocracy, however, and so useful an impediment to the totalitarian rationalization of society was the irrational principle that noble blood contained the essence of freedom, that the state could not level all its citizens into a common servitude at this time, nor was it to do so until both princes and nobles had bowed off the stage of history.

[48] Cited in Guilhermoz, *op. cit.*, 478.
[49] Ritter, *Ministérialité et chevalerie*, 105.

IX
Oratores
(Ecclesiastics)

Seculars and regulars

In his *Summa Aurea* (1251/2), the canonist and cardinal Hostiensis observed that the Trinity was reflected in the three orders who together made up the church: the laity, the religious, and the secular clergy. As jurists liked to express it, the tonsured, whether of the secular clergy or the religious, constituted the central core of the Church. More narrowly considered, the body of the clergy (*coetus clericorum*) included only those who were in the seven or eight orders of the medieval Church: priests, deacons, subdeacons, acolytes, exorcists, readers, porters, and psalmists. In fact, jurists often elevated the episcopate into yet another order, a perfection of priesthood, thus providing a nice parallel between the nine orders of the Church militant and the nine angelic orders of the Church triumphant. The theologians, however, never bought the canonists' idea that a bishop's administrative functions made him superior to a priest.

Only the vaguest estimates as to the number of those in holy orders are possible. Using figures from after 1300, it has been

BIBLIOGRAPHY. Along with the works mentioned in the bibliography to chapter II above, the most enlightening social history—sociology, really—of the Church is Gabriel Le Bras, *Institutions ecclésiastiques de la Chrétienté médiévale* (Books 1 to 6—all published), 2 vols. (Paris, 1959–64). To these may be added the elegant popular histories of Emile Gebhart, *Mystic Italy* (trans. 1893) and *Monks and Popes* (trans. 1907) and G. G. Coulton, *Five Centuries of Religion*, 4 vols. (Cambridge, 1929). See also the books dealing with the mendicants in chapters XIV and XV below. Especially interesting studies of the regular clergy and popular devotion are the last five essays in Georg Schreiber, *Gemeinschaften des Mittelalters: Recht und Verfassung—Kult und Frömmigkeit* (Munster, 1948), E. W. McDonnell, *The Beguines and Beghards in Medieval Culture* (New Brunswick, 1954), and Luigi Zanoni, *Gli Umiliati nei loro rapporti con l'eresia, l'industria della lana ed i comuni nel secoli XII e XIII* (Milan, 1911). One should also note David Knowles, *The Monastic Order in England* (2nd edn., Cambridge, 1963).

proposed that clerks in major orders (i.e. priests, deacons, and sub-deacons) ran to about one in ninety of England's total population. Of course, many priests were canons or professed religious and therefore did not exercise the care of souls. Parish rectors were relatively rare and important persons. In Carcassonne in the early 1300s there were nine *plebani*, or parish rectors, a number only equalling that of the university trained medical doctors who administered to this community of about 9,000 souls. A rector was rare enough to be considered the social analogue of a belted knight among the laity. This gives a somewhat distorted impression, however. By the thirteenth century, every *plebanus* had several beneficed assistants of sacerdotal grade. Besides, every cathedral supported numerous beneficed priests working with the laity, and the multiplication of chapels and churches attached to hospital and monastic orders and to chapters of canons regular, not to speak of the mendicant orders, had enormously increased the numbers of priests serving the population. So many of them were there that the problem of the underemployed priest was taken up at the council of Vienne in 1311–12.

The number of those in lesser orders was very large in comparison with modern times. Although tonsured, they were not required to be celibate—which meant that they ranged from those who intended to enter major orders to those who were satisfied to remain where they were. Besides, canon law admitted a grade of those who were tonsured but in no order at all. Such individuals filled many lesser functions in cathedrals, parishes and hospitals, and though the majority of them were humble there was no obstacle for those trained in law or the notarial art to advancing rather high in the administration of the Church. The new office of bishop's judge (*officialis*), which spread in the latter half of the twelfth century, was held by many in lower orders and even some laymen. Many of the notarial and even judicial offices of the papal court were staffed by such men. Since clergy were also privileged in secular matters, it is easy to understand why tonsure should have been sought after by those who had no ecclesiastical ambitions whatsoever. At the time of Philip the Fair about a tenth of the citizenry of Rheims were exempt from taxes because they were 'church bourgeois', busy as merchants, as artisans, and as civil notaries. Although clerks were permitted to labour as artisans and farmers in order to supplement their incomes, the fact that Church law had long since prohibited them from acting as merchants and civil scribes shows the exceptional character of this circumstance in northern France. In the same province, serfs crowded into the ecclesiastical order to benefit from enfranchisement *ad tonsuram*.

The great number of lesser clerks provides a marked contrast between the medieval Church and that of modern times. Numerous laymen employed or associated with the work of the clergy—university students, for example—were somewhat protected by canon law, and when these are added to those in lesser orders one perceives that the priesthood was cushioned from the laity in a manner unimaginable today. But the Church was already pursuing policies designed to reduce this broad intermediary group. Lower grades were being absorbed into higher ones. Innocent III completed the elevation of the subdiaconate into the higher orders, and psalmists were vanishing fast. There were two principal reasons for this, one being the constant conflict with lay authority over whose jurisdiction such people belonged in; the other, as the bishop of Olmütz complained to the council of Lyons in 1274, was the multiplication of clerks beyond the possibility of regular employment or maintenance.

The second principal segment of the clergy was the religious. Before turning to them, however, we must recall a useful distinction, that between administrative function and vocation. When a monk or a friar became a bishop he did not lose his initial vocation, though he had to be exempted from its full rigours. Moreover the penetration of the secular clergy by the monastic idea was everywhere apparent. An example is to be found in cathedral chapters, which were of two kinds, those whose members were secular and those whose members were regular. If the former, a chapter was composed of tonsured canons, each assigned a living, often inhabiting an individual house and possessing private means. Canons regular were like monks, cloistered and bound by their profession to their order, whether Augustinian (founded 1059) or Premonstratensian (founded 1120). Houses of canons regular not attached to cathedrals were common in medieval towns.

The principal definition of a monk in this period was his tonsure. He also submitted to the rule of his order and observed celibacy, claustration, and community of property. In the faraway past most monks had been 'assimilated laymen', but by this time most of them gradually advanced through holy orders to the priestly grade. The religious had also been divided into at least three groups. The first was composed of those who had professed, whether male or female, of whom the former were able to enter holy orders. These were the choir monks, or real monks. The other two groups were the lay brethren and the oblates.

Especially significant in orders like the Cistercians (founded 1098), lay brethren (*fratres conversi* or *barbati*) neither lived in the monks' cloister nor were permitted entry into holy orders; theirs was the duty of manual labour. In the image of the time, the *conversus* was Martha, the sister of Mary Magdalene and Lazarus. Martha represented the active or labouring life by which the contemplative or spiritual life of Mary was supported. The sisters did not always get on very well. Disputes between the choir monks and the untonsured lay brethren were frequent where, as in the order of Grandmont (founded early 1100s, rule composed 1143), the latter directed the fiscal administration of the monastery. The intermittent battles among the Grandmontines from 1185 to 1223 did much to prevent the spread of the order. According to James of Vitry, the issues were many.' Among these was the fact the monks wanted to sing the ordinary offices, whereas the lay brethren wanted them to sing masses to the Virgin and to the Holy Spirit, and especially commemorative masses for the dead. In short, faced by the problem of raising money, the *conversi* wanted the monks to help by keeping up with the new devotional movements in the Church, those that interested laymen, especially donors. Where orders were wholly dominated by *conversi* there were few troubles. The hospital and military brothers of the Hospitallers (founded 1099, military brothers admitted sometime before 1160) and the soldiers of the Templars (founded 1118) got on well with their priestly chaplains.

Our period witnessed a radical change in the institution of the *conversus*, largely because of the increasing opportunity of joining the religious on terms more consonant with the growing personal freedom seen among the laity both rural and urban. The Church was obliged, after all, to compete with lay vocations for its recruits. The best example is to be seen in the mendicant orders, especially the Franciscans (founded 1209, given rules in 1221 and 1223). Here lay brethren, like those in holy orders, were titled friars (*fratres*) and belonged to the First Order, the Second being the nuns of the Clares (founded 1215), and the Third the Tertiaries, or associated laymen and women. The lay brethren lived in the convents together with the brothers in holy orders and, in the early days of the order, set the tone of the house because their sacerdotal brethren were busy in the world. All was not harmony between the two groups, as we shall see, but it cannot be doubted that the status of the lay friar was well above that of the Cistercian *conversus*. As a result, by the mid-1200s, the Benedictine and Cistercian *conversi* had largely been replaced by salaried domestics. In the meantime, the mendicants, particularly the Franciscans, had secularized the grade of the *conversus*. Dominican and Franciscan writers customarily spoke of the Franciscans' male Tertiaries as *conversi* or Beghards (a term also applied to independent groups), although these continued to live in the world.

Oblates were the third group of the religious. They were persons closely associated with the order's devotion, differing from the monks only in their lack of final vows or tonsure. In practice the link was more relaxed than this, and the oblate grade shaded off insensibly into purely lay groups, such as teachers in the outside schools of monasteries or cathedral and other chapters, children entrusted to the monks for education, old folk living in or near the religious community, and even old soldiers assigned residential pensions by secular patrons. Like the lower orders of the secular clergy, the innumerable layfolk in the service or on the fringes of the religious were those over whom civil and ecclesiastical courts fought continuing battles. The inmates of hospitals—the aged, lepers, the sick—and the staffs of hospitals and educational institutions, not to speak of individual hermits (who often lived in town!), had certain similarities with the religious. When one adds to this minestrone the layfolk who banded together to emulate the life of the religious while remaining in the world, such as the Italian Humiliati, the Franciscan Tertiaries, the Beguines (female) and Beghards (male) who sometimes constituted parishes or semiregular orders wholly composed of *conversae* or *conversi*, one is astonished at the variety of semireligious groups in the thirteenth century. So also were contemporaries. The multiplication of these groups obscured the line between oblates and *conversi*—Beguines, for example, often being indifferently called one or the other—and even led to a confusion between the formally professed religious and the laymen.

In spite of this great growth, individual religious houses were not huge. At its peak in the mid-twelfth century the mother house of Cluny was said to have boasted three hundred choir monks as well as the largest basilica in Latin Christendom. In the same period the great English Cistercian monastery at Rievaulx had 140 monks and 600 lay brothers. In 1286 Bury St Edmunds had eighty monks and 122 domestics. These were unusually large concentrations. Regular or secular, French cathedral chapters ran from thirteen to eighty-four canons. The visitations of Odo Rigaud, archbishop of Rouen, from 1248 to 1269, give evidence of many small monasteries, priories, and granges housing no more than four or five religious.

What made the Middle Ages different from today was the total number of houses. The mendicants of the thirteenth century added hosts of new foundations. In 1316 a general chapter of the Franciscans at Naples estimated the number of male houses in the provinces of Germany, France, and Italy at 1,017 and the houses of the nuns of St Clare at 285. The Dominicans (founded 1215) were a smaller order, 582 male convents being catalogued in an official list of 1303. On the other hand, Dominican nunneries flourished almost as much as the Clares, there being 149 at that date. There were two other major mendicant orders, the Carmelites (brought to England from the Holy Land in 1242 and reorganized as mendicants by 1245) and the Augustinian Eremites or Austin Friars (founded 1256). At least six smaller mendicant orders were founded before 1300. To these must be added lay groups, both male and female, more or less associated with the mendicants. By 1300 the Franciscans boasted no less than 250 groups of Tertiaries. One of their provincial councils at Colmar in 1303 gathered 150 friars who were greeted by 300 local *conversi*, or Beghards. In 1288 Bonvesino of Riva tells us that in Milan, 'there are fully 220 houses [not convents but small buildings similar to private homes] of the second order [quasiregulars] of the Humiliati of both sexes in our city and *contado* in which are a copious number of individuals leading the religious life by labouring with their own hands',[1] not to speak of the third orders of the Humiliati and mendicants.

Apart from the papacy, the religious (as the regular clergy were called) led the Church in the period from 1150 to 1300. Since they

[1] *De magnalibus urbis Mediolani* 3, 7, ed. Novati, *Bullettino dell'istituto storico italiano* XX (1898), 81–2.

were nearest the laity, in the sense that it was not necessary to be in holy orders to participate in their vocation, they provided both a cushion between laymen and the sacerdotal élite and an outlet for the religious and social passions of the laity. In the history of the Latin Church there were at least two revolutionary surges when the religious recast the life of the rest of Christendom. One of these occurred in the thirteenth century and was expressed by the growth of the mendicant orders and similar devotional groups. The other had occurred during the Gregorian age and was already clearly subsiding by the mid-twelfth century.

It is worth comparing these two periods of religious renewal. In many ways they were similar. Both began with a wave of enthusiasm that, though initially repressed, eventually burst the dam that contained it. Both were greeted as revolutionary and troublesome. The Premonstratensian Anselm of Havelberg (d. 1158) defended the new devotions of the earlier time in terms similar to those used by advocates of the mendicants in the 1200s. Their calumniators, he reports, ask:

Why are there so many innovations in God's church? Why do so many new orders rise up in it? Who can even count so many orders of clerks? Who is not astounded by so many types of monks? Indeed, who is not horrified and who, amid so many and so diverse forms of mutually conflicting orders (*religiones*), is not disturbed by this infuriating scandal?[2]

Anselm answered that, in the Church as in the Synagogue before it, although there was but one belief, there had always been many ways of living.

The movements of both ages fructified both town and countryside. Although the mendicants began in towns, their mission soon spread to the villages. In the earlier time, although the Cistercians and Carthusians had settled in the wilderness, the new orders of canons regular were habitual town dwellers and, like the monks of Cluny before them, deliberately sought to reinvigorate the secular clergy as well as the work of hospitals and educational institutions. Few occupations were as vigorously worldly as those of the Templars and Hospitallers. In fact, an anonymous Premonstratensian tract divided the monks of the

[2] *Dialogi* i, i in *PL* CLXXXVIII, 1141. Anselm called the first dialogue *Liber de una forma credendi et multiformitate vivendi a tempore Abel justi usque ad novissimum electum.*

twelfth century into the following categories: 'Some being wholly separated from the crowd, lead a peaceable life in God [Cistercians] . . . ; others, being located next to men in towns and in fortified and open villages [Cluniacs], are sustained by charity from the faithful, by incomes from churches and tithes.'[3] Much the same divisions were to be found among the canons, who, however, largely lived in towns: 'Some are segregated altogether in conversation, dress and habitation from the crowd as much as possible [Premonstratensians]; others are placed next to men [Victorines]; and yet others live amongst men, whence they are called secular [canons].'[4] For a time papal authority had encouraged lay devotion and consequently the creation of lay communities that were not formally bound by a rule but renounced the world and devoted themselves to the common life (*communis vita*). In 1091 Urban II approved just such a lay group because he judged that 'it is all the more worthy of perpetual conservation because it is stamped in the form of the primitive Church'.[5]

There was one further similarity between the two movements. Both lost their impetus partly because, once established, the new orders themselves joined with older interests to brake the progress of what seemed to be dangerous enthusiasm. For the monks and canons of the earlier age this restrictive law took the form of local and finally papal legislation prohibiting members of established orders from leaving to form more rigorous groups. It will be remembered that the Cistercians had had their origin in just such a secession from the Benedictines. As the creation of new orders was discouraged, the claustration of the members of the old ones was more rigorously enforced. The secular clergy did not like them messing about in their world. The anonymous Premonstratensian cited above described their attitudes: 'For I have heard many priests or clerks praising such and such an order of canons but murmuring that those who have left the world should remit the care of it again to secular men, as though it were not worthy for them to deal with secular business.'[6]

In fine, extreme social pressure together with the desires of the new orders themselves, fattened by success, made it difficult for the

---

[3] *Liber de diversis ordinibus et professionibus* 2, in *PL* CCXIII, 814.
[4] *Ibid.*, 5, in *PL* CCXIII, 827.
[5] Letter 56 in *PL* CLI, 336.
[6] *Liber de diversis ordinibus et professionibus* 2, in *PL* CCXIII, 836.

monk or canon to expand his work in the world. Monks had been in the forefront of the intellectual developments of the eleventh and twelfth centuries—as is exemplified by the names of the jurist Gratian (d. about 1179) and the author and preacher Bernard of Clairvaux—but had fallen so far behind by the mid-1200s that, according to the Cistercian Stephen of Lexington, abbot of Clairvaux, the mendicants condescended to them as though they were rude ignoramuses. Even the gentle Robert Grosseteste, bishop of Lincoln and patron of England's Franciscans, used to tell the friars that, unless they studied at the university, 'it will surely happen to us as it has to other religious whom we see, alas! walking in the shadows of ignorance'.[7] Stephen attempted to rectify this unhappy state by founding the college of St Bernard at Paris in 1245–46. The Cluniacs followed in 1260 with their college, and soon similar establishments were endowed at other universities.

Although eventually providing many notable university teachers, these institutions had only a slight effect on the orders themselves. In fact, impeded by rules against participation in the life of the world and by their own vested interests, the older monastic orders had little to do with the creation of the new universities, schools, and hospitals. It was the canons who were interested in these new outlets, especially the canons regular, and who served as the intermediaries between the older and the newer types of religious, between the monks and the mendicants. During the twelfth century the outside schools of the canons regular of Nôtre-Dame cathedral, of Saint-Victor, and of Mont-Sainte-Geneviève constituted the original nuclei of what later became the University of Paris. The Dominicans and, somewhat more reluctantly, the Franciscans carried on the interest of the canons. Not only did the former erect *studia* in their more important convents, but they also sent their first master, Roland of Cremona, to teach at Toulouse and Paris around 1229, hardly fifteen years after their foundation.

The principal difference between these two great movements of the religious was that the mendicant orders were directly interested in the lay apostolate and therefore entered into the world in the fullest possible sense, by hearing confessions, by

[7] Thomas of Eccleston, *De adventu fratrum minorum in Angliam* 15, ed. A. G. Little (Manchester, 1951), 91.

regular preaching, and by sharing their services with the laity in a more intimate way than the religious had ever done before. This accounts for the curious layout of some Dominican churches in the 1200s, namely, the double nave with a central colonade, one nave being for the *fratres* and their services, the other for the laity and preaching. Another difference was in the circumstances in which the movements operated. Although the papacy in the Gregorian age, carrying on a struggle with the older state churches, was very permissive about the wide lay support elicited by the founders of many new orders, few were actively fostered by papal authority. In the thirteenth century, however, once the papacy had decided to embrace the new movements—Innocent III recognized the Humiliati in 1202—they were immediately associated with a centralized Church that had scarcely existed in the earlier age, one that, so to speak, forced their missions down the throats of the older orders and the secular clergy.

This is not meant to imply that there were more priests among the mendicants than there had been among the monks of the twelfth century, or that the monks of Cluny and Citeaux, as well as those of other orders, especially the canons regular, had not exercised real influence on the secular clergy. During and after the Gregorian age the monks and canons regular had revolutionized the life of the parish clergy by inculcating higher standards of literacy, and, most of all, by insisting on clerical celibacy. They had exalted the priesthood by enriching the liturgy with new ceremonies and feasts, by spurring the removal of the eucharistic cup from the layman's lips, and by reinvigorating the ancient teaching of transubstantiation, the priestly miracle of the mass. In connection with the ideas of the *pax dei* and the crusade, also, the penitential literature that had been largely monastic in the past had invaded the world and set the pattern for the court of conscience presided over by the secular priesthood.

There was an age of transition in the fifty or seventy-five years around 1200 when the monks and canons-regular still tried to lead. The Cistercians—partly through the military orders created on their model—were deeply involved in the crusades. They conducted the first preaching tours against southern French heresy and headed the movement that converted these into armed invasions or crusades. They were the order first chosen by the popes for missions in Greece after the Latin conquest of Byzantium in

1204. The canons were especially active in instructing the clergy in their duties. A renewal of parish work was stimulated by Peter Cantor. His book on cases of conscience is a monument to the growing significance of the sacrament of penitence and the expanding jurisdiction and activities of the court of conscience in his time. The life of Peter's student James of Vitry, a canon-regular of Oignies in Brabant, may serve as a symbol of this age. Not only was James a preacher who, as contemporaries said, moved France more than any other man, but he was also in close contact with the new movements of the Humiliati and the Franciscans, which he praised in a letter of 1216. In the very same year, he won papal approval for the Beguine movement, begun earlier around the Premonstratensians in the Low Countries and revivified by James's 'spiritual mother' Mary of Oignies, the famous Beguine of Liège. Moreover, James had a hand in bringing the ideas of the new Italian devotion to Liège, where it culminated in the final exaltation of sacerdotal authority, the feast of the *corpus Christi*.

During the thirteenth century the new orders moved ahead to take the lead. They enriched the liturgy, the Dominican Thomas Aquinas composing the order of service for the institution of the feast of the *corpus Christi* in 1264. They specialized in developing the mechanisms of the penitential system. The already lively debate between Franciscan laxists and Dominican rigorists anticipated the future evolution of casuistry in the practical life of the Church. By 1234 the Dominican Raymond of Peñafort had issued his great penitential *Summa*, the most extensive manual of casuistry. The mendicants were also the foremost preachers of the age. So important did preaching seem to some that they put it ahead of all the other duties of the clergy. General of the Dominicans from 1254 to 1263, Humbert of Romans remarked that the Saviour celebrated only one mass while here on earth and was not known to have heard confession; his life was spent in prayer and preaching, to the latter of which he gave most of his time.

To sum up this history, the religious had twice invaded the world and, in so doing, had twice remade the Church. In the course of these two revolutionary interventions the religious themselves had changed radically. Withdrawing from the world in the earlier age, the monks had sought to persuade men to share the purer life with them. Their ideal was expressed by Peter Damian when he reported that Romuald, founder of the Camaldolese monks (about 1012), preached near Orvieto 'as though he wished to convert the whole world into a hermitage and to associate the whole multitude of the people into the monastic order. And indeed he stole many there from the world whom he divided among many holy settlements.'[8] Later on, although there was still an accent on withdrawal, the monastic ideal seemed to be penetrating the world. The abbot Joachim of Fiore (d. 1202) proposed a new social structure suitable to the coming new age. One part was to be a monastic order composed of five oratories with different degrees of severity. There was also to be an oratory of the priests and clerks to work in the world, perform divine offices, visit and heal the sick, and teach Latin and the sacred text to the young. The third part was the oratory of the married laity, or *conjugati*, 'living the common life with their sons and daughters and using their wives for the procreation of children rather than for libidinousness'.[9] They were to share all in common, live by their own labour, and provide for the clergy and the monks. In short, Joachim proposed something not unlike Robert of Curzon's perfect society and close to Francis's dream for his Franciscans. In only one way did he prove to be a bad prophet. The sacerdotal and teaching functions largely absorbed the monastic and eremitical passions of the new orders. By invading both secular clergy and laity, the religious had converted the streets and marketplaces of the world into their monastery, a fact that posed a problem for monasticism in the later Middle Ages. When all men were to some degree monks, what need was there for the cloistered religious?

Ambivalence and freedom

At the time of the Gregorians, a somewhat inadvertent alliance between the Church and the aristocracies of town and countryside had resulted in the weakening of princely and monarchical authority throughout much of the west. Apart from this social circumstance the clergy propagated a particular idea of freedom. In part this was expressed by their insistence on their right to govern and finance themselves without excessive interference by

[8] *Vita beati Romualdi* 37, ed. Giovanni Tabacco in *Istituto storico Italiano per il Medio evo: 'Fonti per la storia d'Italia'* XCIV (1957), 78.
[9] *Dispositio novi ordinis pertinens ad tercium statum ad instar superne Jerusalem*, in Herbert Grundmann, *Neue Forschungen über Joachim von Fiore* (1950) 120–1.

lay authority or reliance upon it. Although this happened to coincide with the interests of the aristocracies in their battles with the
princes, it did not fire laymen half so much as did another aspect
of the idea of freedom that the clergy, especially the religious,
put before their eyes.

Derived from antiquity, the idea was both beautiful and
extreme in its terms and demands. St Paul had said: 'I wish you
to be without care.'[10] Neither property nor its management was
to be a source of care, of worry, anguish, and competition. The
ideal was the life of the apostles (Acts, 4:32–35): from each
according to his means and to each according to his need. The
common life was so essential a part of the religious life for Peter
Damian (d. 1072) that he asserted, 'those only are fit for the office
of preaching who possess no gain from earthly riches, and who,
having nothing individually, possess everything in common'.[11]
Preached widely, the praises of the life apostolic passed into
Gratian's *Decretum* and were thence constantly drawn upon by
later ideologues: 'Most unsuitably does he teach who announces
the poor man Christ with a fat belly and rubicund cheeks.'[12] Nor
should the golden wealth of letters and learning be misused.
Although, as John of Salisbury wrote in his *Policraticus*, every
profession has its *miles gloriosus*, its boasting self-seeker, learning
was to be used only for man's betterment and for God's glory.
Like other sources of power, learning could corrupt. Francis of
Assisi urged: 'Care not about books and knowledge but only about
good works; "learning puffs up but love builds!" '[13] And he
replied to a novice who asked permission to own a psalter: 'After
you have a psalter, you'll want a breviary. And after you have that,
you'll sit in your chair like a great prelate, and say to your brother:
"Fetch me my breviary!" '[14] Besides, learning was deceptive,
if only because it cannot tell one enough. Although sententious,
Bernard of Clairvaux was right when he wrote a young monk:
'Believe one who knows: you will discover some things more fully

[10] I Corinthians 7:32.
[11] *Contra clericos regulares proprietarios* 5, in *PL* CXLV, 490.
[12] Jordan of Saxony, *Liber vitasfratrum* 3, 8, ed. Arbesmann and Humpfner (New
York, 1943), 346, adapted from Gratian's *Decretum* I, 35, 4 in *CICan* I, 131. A
passage from Jerome.
[13] *Speculum perfectionis* 4, 7, ed. Paul Sabatier (Manchester, 1931) II, 13–4—a
collection of stories dated about 1311/12. The biblical passage is I Corinthians 8:1.
[14] *Speculum perfectionis* 4, 9, ed. Sabatier II, 14.

in forests than in books. Trees and rocks will teach you what you cannot hear from schoolteachers.'[15]

Moreover, when Paul said ' "I wish you to be without care", he was speaking about the solicitude of house and family that is incumbent upon those who have wives'.[16] Freedom from the cares of the flesh meant much in this age not only to the religious but also to both intellectuals and lovers. The two were combined in Abelard and Heloise. Preferring to be his strumpet than the wife of an emperor, Heloise refused at first to marry her middle-aged professor because she wished him to be without care as befits both the intellectual life and the relationship between true lovers. Even the married longed for this freedom, as is shown by the custom of willing beds to the monks or to the poor. In 1254 William Usclacan, a well-to-do Toulousan, willed that his bed should be kept in his house, there 'to be faithfully equipped with blankets, in which a poor man may lie in remission of my sins'.[17] The pauper was the Christ, and the sins were those that had engendered the dying penitent's family and his angers and worries in the busy life of the world.

And to be without care could sometimes even liberate a man from fear of death, a topic much discussed in medieval literature. Told of his approaching death, Francis of Assisi called brothers Angelo and Leo.

> And when these two had come before him, full of grief and sorrow, they sang with many tears the Song [in praise] of brother Sun and of all the other creatures which the saint had written. And then, before the last verse of this song, he added a verse about sister Death, saying:
>
> 'Be praised, my Lord, for our sister Bodily Death From whom no living man can escape. . . .'[18]

That the desire to be free and to transcend earthly care could sometimes be strained and self-destructive, however, is to be seen in the lives of the saints. James of Voragine recorded the story of the desert father, St Macarius, as particularly praiseworthy:

[15] Letter 106 to Henry Murdach, in *PL* CLXXXII, 242.
[16] Jordan of Saxony, *Liber vitasfratrum* 3, 8, ed. Arbesmann and Humpfner (1943), 345.
[17] Cited in J. H. Mundy, 'Charity and social work in Toulouse', *Traditio* XXII (1966), 209–10n.
[18] *Speculum perfectionis* 12, 123, ed. Sabatier I, 345–6.

'When he killed with his hands a flea that stung him, and much blood came out of it, he blamed himself for having avenged an injury to himself, and therefore remained naked for six months in the desert. Whence he returned wholly torn by scabs and bites', dying shortly thereafter.[19] Indeed, this great ideal of freedom from care, fathered by the insatiable yearnings of the religious mind, demanded the impossible of ordinary men. As a result, the higher and more impossible the goal, the greater was the ambivalence in men's minds and the more passionate their awareness of failure.

The religious viewed the work of the world with suspicion because it impinged on their freedom. Ideally, they were not even supposed to teach. From Jerome came the oft-repeated slogan that the monk does not have the duty of teaching but rather of grieving, of lamenting himself and the world. Francis of Assisi thought little of letters and of preaching, save by the living example of apostolic poverty. On the other hand, either because they secretly sought the power to be gained by proselytism or because they knew that their freedom depended on the support of the world, practical monks knew that they had to serve those who remained in the world. Writing before 1141, the Cluniac Orderic Vital lauded a Norman priory because local knights and nobles not only worked together with the monks in the cloister, helping them thrash out practical and religious matters, but also received instruction and aid in return, so that the convent became 'a school for the living and a refuge for the dying'.[20] In terms of practical ecclesiastical or secular politics, monks needed book learning. As Geoffrey of Breteuil (fl. about 1173) put it when asking a lay benefactor for books, 'a cloister without a library is like a fortress without an arsenal'.[21] No matter what Francis and some of his followers may have wished, the majority of his order wished to educate their members and to build churches in which to preach. And earthly fame was tempting. John of Salisbury shows how it can be obtained. 'Nothing appears wiser to me for a man striving for glory than the favour of honest writers.'[22]

The choices were not always clear and easy. Charitable work

---

[19] *Legenda aurea* 18, ed. J. G. T. Graesse (Bratislava, 1890), 102.
[20] *Historia ecclesiastica* 2, 5, 22 in *PL* CLXXXVIII, 447.
[21] Cited in Philippe Delhaye, 'L'organisation scolaire', *Traditio* V (1947), 237.
[22] *Policraticus* 8, 9, ed. Webb, II, 280.

and the care of the parish involved the clergy in the world. Such ecclesiastical services were supposed to be free, but customary fees had grown up and became subjects of debate between rigorists and laxists, and between laymen and clergy. Disputes like those between the parish priests of Toulouse and their parishioners in the 1230s over burial, marriage, baptismal and other fees were common, as were those among the clergy themselves over burial rights and other spiritually and materially profitable prerogatives. A popular preacher like James of Vitry could always be sure of winning his audience when he said that the religious gave a little to the poor in order to gain much for themselves, and John of Salisbury sourly remarked that Hospitallers often sucked up to the rich instead of embracing the *pauper Christus*. Certainly, there were many problems of conscience here. John of Flagy's late-twelfth-century version of the *Romance of Garin le Loherain* comments bitterly:

> When the *prud'homme* lies sick abed
> And has great fear of death,
> He does not look to his brother or son,
> Nor to his relatives or first cousins;
> He gives his lands, rents and mills
> To the black monks made by Saint Benedict,
> And neither daughter nor son gets anything.[23]

Far more important than any conscious deceit was the economic problem posed by charitable service. By donating to a monastery or hospital some money, a piece of property, or a rent-producing investment, individuals could assure themselves of pensions and care in old age or illness or could provide their children with education. Here was a mutually profitable arrangement but one that led to the slow accumulation of property by the Church, and that helps to explain lay seizure of Church property both in the Gregorian age and in the crisis of the later Middle Ages. When the work of the Church required fund-raising, it often disturbed the rich if only because it called their bluff. The Dominican William of Abingdon's sermons delighted his audiences until he began to build a house for his order. Henry III of England then

---

[23] Cited in Georg Schreiber, 'Cluny und die Eigenkirche', *Gemeinschaften des Mittelalters* (Münster, 1948), 117n.

remarked to him: 'Brother William, you used to speak so spiritually; now all you say is "Give, give, give!" '[24]

Attractive though it was, the ideal of the sparse communitarian life found only a partial echo in practice. Around 1200 the *Bible* of Guiot of Provins discussed the various groups of the religious in the sceptical and humorous tradition common in medieval letters. The Cistercians were miserable, he said, because the monks in the farms or granges who lived well deprived the rest of good food. The abstinence of sick Carthusians from meat was little more than suicide. As for recluses or hermits, they were simply mad. Best of all were the Augustinian canons, who ate, drank, and dressed well; Guiot would be happy to suffer with them. It may be argued, however, that a certain moderation or even ease was necessary for the successful pursuit of the celibate, collective life of a religious community. Robert Grosseteste told a Dominican that

> 'three things are necessary for earthly health: food, sleep and play (*jocus*).' Indeed, he enjoined upon a certain melancholy brother that he should drink a cup full of good wine for his penitence and, when he had drunk it, although most unwillingly, he said to him: 'Dearest brother, would you but take such a penitence frequently, you would have a much better ordered conscience.'[25]

Indeed, for a Christian even sorrow should be made to evoke joy. In William Usclacan's testament of 1254 he not only followed the usual tradition of endowing annual commemoratory dinners in hospitals for the poor, but also directed his heir to provide a feast, 'on the day on which I died, for the chaplain or rector of the church of the Taur, the subchaplain, and eleven poor, of bread, wine and meat faithfully and *plentifully* for the remission of my sins.'[26]

The ascetic urge so strong among the religious also posed problems for the secular clergy. The traditional practice of priestly marriage—concubinage, as Latin canon law had called it since antiquity—was attacked by the monks in the Gregorian age and after, thus providing an issue around which rigorists could

[24] Thomas of Eccleston, *De adventu fratrum minorum in Angliam* 10, ed. A. G. Little (1951), 46.
[25] *Ibid.*, 15, ed. Little, 92.
[26] Cited in J. H. Mundy, 'Charity and social work in Toulouse', *Traditio* XXII (1966), 209n.

mobilize lay support—make the teacher suffer!—in their campaigns for 'reform'. Although the Gregorian age marked a real revolution in the practices of the clergy, one that was observed with horror by Muslims in Spain, the old tradition was hard to uproot. The distinguished Ailred, who died as abbot of Rievaulx in 1166, was the son, grandson, and great-grandson of rural priests. Clerical concubinage remained customary, especially in northern England, Scandinavia, and parts of Germany, and was not infrequent in France and Spain. Of the 705 priests visited by Odo Rigaud, archbishop of Rouen, eighty-six were denounced to him as guilty of this fault. Although there are no figures for our period, in one semester of 1335, of the 207 papal dispensations for bastardy (*ex defectu natalium*) to allow entry into holy orders, no less than 148 were granted to sons of those in the *ordo sacer*. Below the level of the priesthood, clerical concubinage or marriage was even more widespread. The 'reformers' in the circle of Peter Cantor at Paris —somewhat half-heartedly, it must be confessed—wanted subdeacons and deacons released from the prohibition, partly because they often procured papal dispensations and partly because celibacy led them into 'perversion'.

For all their puritanism, medieval clerics were more free in their talk than religious men today. They joked about sex. Clement VI (1342–52), for example, is reported to have responded to the objections of his confessor to his relations with women by saying that it was a habit he had picked up in youth and engaged in now only on doctors' orders. He tried to quiet the murmurs of his cardinals and judges by producing 'a small black book in which he had written the names of different . . . popes who were lubricious and incontinent, and he showed from their deeds written there that they governed the church better and did many more useful things than others who were continent.'[27] They also described the prickings of the flesh with remarkable fidelity. The quasi-autobiography of the strange hermit Peter of Murrone (Celestine V) makes it abundantly clear that, for him, God's kindest miracle was to ease his conscience about the body's natural tumult, nocturnal emissions and dreams.

These remarks about clerical attitudes remind us that churchmen, especially monks, were members of an order that had a social

[27] From the chronicle of Melas cited by Johann Haller, *Papsttum und Kirchenreform* I, 121.

character of its own. Living in a society in which class distinctions were overlaid by those derived from membership in purportedly functional orders, men and women of this period were much more given to playing roles or to choosing their way of life because of the roles inherent in them than is true today. The physical courtliness, eruptive romance, and rage of the gentlefolk in arms and those emulating them contrasted sharply with the bookishness and often stubborn and maudlin emotionalism of the clergy. No brief description can describe the range and qualities characteristic of these or other medieval orders. They all overlapped, and few individuals were wholly fulfilled or contained by the choice of order they, their families and circumstances had made for them. Francis of Assisi was the son of an ambitious and successful cloth merchant. His flight from his father's business led him first to seek to shine in chivalry's martial glories among the gay and gilded youth of his town. Repelled there, he turned to poverty's wonders, building a migratory community of similar souls, there imbibing a distillate of the religious life with its sacrifices, humility, freedom and also its psychic ostentation and self-love.

Although it also appears to have attracted the hearty bachelor, the Church, and especially the monastery, offered a natural channel to men who had a larger share than most of womanly or motherly qualities. Correspondence between monks was often astonishingly warm and delicate. A thirteenth-century regulation for Franciscan hermitages will illustrate the quality of motherliness:

> Two of [the hermit friars] should be mothers and they should have two sons or one at least. . . . The two who are mothers should hold to the life of Martha and their two sons to that of Mary [Magdalene]. . . . And those brothers who are mothers should strive to remain remote from all persons and . . . should guard their sons . . . so that no one may speak with them. And the sons should not speak to anyone except their mothers . . .[28]

The existence of womanly warmth among communities of men does not imply that homosexuality was permitted or treated lightly when discovered. There is no doubt that it existed among clergy and monks. A poet, courtier, and archdeacon, Walter Map

---

[28] Heinrich Boehmer, 'Analekten zur Geschichte des Franz von Assisi', *Sammlung ausgewählter kirchen- und dogmengeschichtlicher Quellenschriften* IV, 46. I owe this reference to Kennerly M. Woody of Princeton University.

loathed the Cistercians. He reports that two Cistercian abbots were boasting to Gilbert Foliot (d. 1188), the bishop of London, about Bernard of Clairvaux's miracles. Perhaps desiring to increase verisimilitude, one remarked that he had even witnessed an occasion when the saint's powers had deserted him:

> A certain marquess of Burgundy asked Bernard to come and heal his son. We went there and discovered the child to be dead. *Dompnus* Bernard ordered the body taken to a private room, and, "everyone being excluded, he lay upon the boy," and then, having prayed, arose. The boy did not get up, however, but lay there dead. Then I [the incorrigible Walter Map] interjected: That *was* the unhappiest monk of all. For I've never heard of any monk who lay down upon a boy that did not straightaway rise up after him. The abbot blushed and they went out as many laughed.[29]

More than occasional homosexuality, what marked the monks was self-mortification or mutual mortification. The best example of this is the curious practice of penitential flagellation common among the religious, a practice that has obvious psychosexual overtones. The lash and the stick were known among the laity as forms of corporal punishment, but penitential flagellation was not practised by laymen until the spread of the religious vocation in the thirteenth century. Then it appeared in times of social stress in the form of mass flagellation. An early example was the flagellant movement in wartorn Italy in 1259. This secularization —if it may so be termed—of a monastic practice was to develop apace in later times.

A final demonstration of the ambivalence of the medieval religious mind is that, although it was ruled by a sense of oneness and of transcendency or otherworldliness, a curious result was that the cult, the faith, and indeed God himself, were brought into the world in a very tangible manner. On one hand, one sees a great monotheism; on the other, to speak like a Muslim, one perceives the polytheistic or pluralistic character of the local cults of the saints, not to speak of the cult of the B.V.M. In many ways that were quite beautiful the faith penetrated into daily living, in that earthly life emulated that of heaven. Eight knights and four

---

[29] *De nugis curialium* 1, 23, ed. M. R. James, *Anecdota Oxoniensia* (Oxford, 1914) XIV, 39. The miracle attempts to repeat the raising of the Shunamite's son by Elisha reported in 2 (Vulgate 4) Kings 4:34.

sergeants elected the grand master of the Temple, and thus there were twelve 'in honour of the twelve apostles. And the twelve brothers should together elect a brother chaplain to hold the place of Christ Jesus who is to busy himself keeping the brothers in peace, love and accord. And there will be thirteen brethren.'[30] Also, according to the theological masters appointed to examine the *Postilla* or *Lectura super Apocalypsim* of the Franciscan Peter John Olivi in 1319, Peter believed that, just as the Synagogue had been propagated by twelve patriarchs and the Church by twelve apostles, 'so the final church of the remaining Jews and gentiles is to be propagated by twelve evangelical men. Whence Francis had twelve associates or sons, through whom and in whom was founded the evangelical order.'[31] This image of the world as merely a mirror of what is in heaven or sacred history could be used for comic effect. Buoncompagno of Signa found the origin even of particular passages of Roman law in holy history. The invalidation of a contract because of fraud (*exceptio doli mali*) was prefigured in paradise, because, when the Lord asked, ' "Adam, where are you?" [Adam] straightway proposed the *exceptio doli mali*, saying: "The wife whom you gave me deceived me." '[32]

Being in the world, the objects of the faith could be handled very rudely. Take relics, for example. When Constantinople fell in 1204, the Latins ransacked it not only for gold and silver, but also for relics—and what a haul they made! Intelligent men were attached to these objects. James of Vitry wore a necklace on which was hung a finger of Mary of Oignies (d. 1213 and never canonized) encased in silver, which he finally gave 'to Pope Gregory IX of solemn memory to carry against the vice of swearing (*spiritum blasphemie*) by which he was atrociously tempted'.[33] Nor were readers of the time shocked by reading that Countess Theodora, the sister of Thomas Aquinas, 'asked for the right hand of the said holy body [of Thomas] from the abbot of Fossanuova, which he was not able easily to pull off the body, although it had lain for fourteen years in the earth, but was obliged to cut off with a knife, and which gave off a wonderfully sweet odour to those venerating

---

[30] *La règle du Temple*, ed. Henri de Curzon (Paris, 1886), 210.
[31] Published in Etienne Baluze, *Miscellanea sacra* (Lucca, 1761), II, 271b.
[32] *Rhetorica novissima* I, 14 in *BIMA* II, 254a.
[33] R. B. C. Huygens, *Les lettres de Jacques de Vitry* (Leiden, 1960), 1n and 72. The story itself comes from Thomas of Cantimpré's life of St Lutgarde.

it'.[34] Because of the mystery of the incarnation, the divine body itself was treated in much the same fashion. In 1178 Peter Maurand, a Cathar heretic at Toulouse, recanted his heresy and swore concerning the mass that

> the bread and wine which are placed upon the altar, are, after consecration, not only a symbol (*sacramentum*) but also the true body and blood of our lord Jesus Christ, and actually (*sensualiter*) and not only symbolically, but in very truth, [the body] is handled and broken by the hands of priests and ground by the teeth of the faithful.

And Peter was merely repeating the oath exacted from Berengar of Tours in 1059 at the time of the battle over transubstantiation.[35]

This peculiarly miraculous capacity of the priest created difficulties. Because their intention is evil, Peter Lombard remarks, neither heretics nor excommunicates can confect the sacrament and, for the same reason, a mass validly confected cannot be said to be eaten by an animal. Thence arises the question: 'What then does a mouse take or what does he chew? Only God knows.'[36] Furthermore, why did the Lord choose this particular kind of miracle? In part, it was 'lest the mind abhor what the eye perceives, because we are not in the habit of eating raw flesh or drinking blood . . . and lest the Christian religion be mocked by unbelievers'.[37] God was being tactful.

These illustrations and the tales of miracles abounding in contemporary sources sometimes make the clergy of this age appear to be merely obscurantist and manipulative and the believers who followed them merely foolish and superstitious. That miracles were always imaginary and frequently outright

---

[34] One of the lives added to James of Voragine's *Legenda aurea*, ed. Graesse, 919. The story derives from the more detailed account in chapter 11 of the *vita* by William of Tocco in *AA. SS.*, March 1, 678A-B.

[35] Unpublished charter in the Departmental Archives of Toulouse, series H, Fonds Saint-Sernin, liasse 688: XXI, lxxix, 1. The text was carried in Gratian's *Decretum* 3, 2, 42, *CICan* 1, 1328–29, and was obviously an easy way to nail a heretic of almost any kind.

[36] *Libri IV sententiarum* 4, 13 in *PL* CXCII, 868.

[37] *Libri IV sententiarum* 4, 10 in *PL* CXCII, 863. These articles of the Lombard were among those that were not believed by everyone, but it is notable that those of the missionary cast of mind, like Roger Bacon, were embarrassed by this spiritualized cannibalism.

frauds can hardly be doubted by those who place their reliance in natural reason. What were not fraudulent or imaginary were the functions, miracles and other like beliefs served, and the ensuing mental and physical satisfactions they gave their devotees. These functions were many. As we shall see, like today's street magic and astrology, they helped the individual who feared sickness and death or worried that his love was meretricious and untrue. Those of one religious order often mocked the saints of another, and the advancement of their programmes, revolutionary or reactionary, was bound up with the frequency and popularity of the miracles of their saints. Not that this differs much from the imaginary stories about our popular leaders, or men 'before their time', and all the other types of members of today's earth-bound pantheons. . . .

Where the medieval attitude differed from that of today was that, as the heir of a revolt against the earth-centred religions and reason of the Greek and Roman world, the Church and those who fostered and entered it favoured other-worldly modes of expression, one of which, the miracle, was an undisguised affront to natural reason. It was not that the mysteries of Christology or even the liquefying of the blood of Saint Januarius of Naples were more indemonstrable or irrational than contemporary—or, for that matter, modern—convictions about man's natural moral potential, about the necessary advantages of freedom for man's advancement, and about man's central role in the cosmos. It was merely that they were undisguisedly so. And to explain this what has to be examined is the function vested in the ecclesiastical order and those who supported it. At this time, churchmen could stand against all the hierarchs of the secular and lay world. Two institutions had been built in western Europe, the Church and the state, and it was characteristic of this time that there was no one word to describe the state, the institution that, because it operated in the real world and not in the imaginary heaven, was potentially the more powerful of the two. The claims of both the clergy and the secular hierarchs were implicitly total, but it was the good fortune of the men of this age that they could set them against each other, choose between them, and select the ways of acting and modes of thought now of one, and now the other. The two totalities did not add up to one totalitarianism. In this circumstance, the belief in miracles and in things indemonstrable often meant freedom.

Clerical hostilities

Although standing together against common foes, churchmen were not always united in advancing the Church. Deeper ideological issues as well as the relationship of the papacy to the rest of the Church will be treated later. What will be examined here are the narrow conflicts between the secular clergy and the religious and between the various orders of the latter.

The main duty of the secular clergy was to work in the world. They were therefore placed in the unhappy position of making concessions to it, actions that could easily be attacked by the more rigorous of the monks or mendicants. In spite of the general effort of churchmen to separate the Church from the state and the things of God from those of Caesar, these remained closely bound together and provided rigorists with plenty of ammunition. The prince-archbishop of Mainz paraded in full armour with bared sword borne before and was an archetype of the German prince-prelate—except the primate of Cologne, who exercised no civil jurisdiction. A Parisian clerk is reported to have joked that he could believe anything, but not that a German bishop could be saved. He reasoned thus because 'almost all German bishops wield both swords, spiritual and material. And because they judge *de sanguine* and wage wars, it is more fitting for them to care about paying soldiers than to bother with the salvation of the souls committed to their charge.'[38]

A result of the intermixture of state and Church was that many careers were both ecclesiastical and secular. The famous Poitevin, Peter of Roches (d. 1238), began as a knight under Richard Coeur-de-Lion, entered orders to become bishop of Winchester in 1205, and in 1213 rose to the chief civil office in England, that of justiciar. Not only was he active in English politics until his forced retirement in 1235, but he was also an excellent general, fighting in England, Wales, the Holy Land, and, in his last years, for Gregory IX in the papal states. Another Englishman, Gervais of Tilbury (d. after 1211), was raised in Italy, studied and perhaps taught at Bologna and, as a clerk, was in the service of England, Sicily, and the archbishop of Rheims before he became military commander of the kingdom of Arles for the Emperor Otto IV and there married. He apparently retired as a secular

[38] Caesarius of Heisterbach, *Dialogus miraculorum* 2, 27, ed. Joseph Strange, 1, 99.

canon in England. In 1215 France's host at the decisive battle of Bouvines was marshalled by Garin, a onetime canon and Hospitaller, then bishop of Senlis, later chancellor of France. The *mores* of government service penetrated the clergy deeply, as did those of the martial aristocracy. In 1298 the chapter of the collegiate church of St John the Evangelist of Liège authorized its members to participate in armed expeditions to protect their personal or family interests.

Such vitiations of the ideal were exceptional, and the blame for them could not always be placed on the shoulders of secular churchmen. The appearance of great numbers of new orders and devotions sometimes damaged established local churches. The parish clergy were hurt by the wave of religious enthusiasm that accompanied the early mendicant movements. One can understand the feelings of the ordinary clergy when one sees the occasionally spiteful jealousy of the orders with which they were competing. In the early 1300s the mendicants at Paris held up the theological degree of a Picard *plebanus* known to be hostile to them. The latter finally applied to master Hannibal of Ceccano, who persuaded the friars to let him pass the examination in exchange for his allowing them into his parish. Afterwards, during the usual festive dinner, Hannibal was called upon to praise the new licentiate, which he did, wittily (*budaice*) congratulating him upon his advanced age and closing with: 'Indeed, for a long time now did our bachelor expiate here in Paris a sin committed in Picardy!'[39] Even the cardinals, the princes of the church, occasionally evoke sympathy as they confronted the self-righteous rigorism of the regular clergy. When Pope Nicholas IV (1288–92) asked the prior general of the Austin friars for a penitentiary, he produced one brother Augustine, a former jurist and chancellor of King Manfred of Sicily who had joined the order after the defeat and death of his Hohenstaufen prince in 1266 and who had subsequently reestablished himself by winning fame for moral rigour and self-punishment. When the general led him before the pope and cardinals in consistory, the latter, 'seeing him despicable in dress and austere and rigid in visage, exclaimed to the general,

---

[39] Jordan of Saxony, *Liber vitasfratrum* 2, 6, ed. Arbesmann and Humpfner, 110–11. Hannibal Gaetani of Ceccano, archdeacon of Arras and university master, became archbishop of Naples in 1326 and cardinal in 1327.

"What woods did you drag him out of?" [40] But they were soon saddled with Augustine.

Nor were the religious often humble. Around 1160 Odo, prior of Canterbury and later abbot of Battle Abbey, taught his novices that the taking of the monastic vow was as much an advance over baptism as the latter had been over circumcision, and as that in turn had been over natural law. In their relations with prelates and the papacy the religious were so convinced of the superiority of their vocation that they frequently forgot the ancient injunction: 'Nothing quite so pleases God in a monk as obedience; for one obedience is worth more than all the virtues.' [41] The various orders were also jealous of each other, and this sentiment permeated the later mendicants. Sometimes it was harmless and even worthy 'regimental pride', but it could easily become much more vicious. The Franciscan historian Salimbene constantly impugned the Dominican John Schio of Vicenza's (d. 1260) saintly reputation, and even remarked that Dominic's (d. 1221) sanctity was a fabrication. He reports that John once threatened his brethren with exposure unless they put up with his overweening self-esteem: 'I have exalted your Dominic, whom you kept hidden twelve years underground and, unless you shut up, I'll vilify your saint and tell what you're doing.' [42] He also attributed the following remark to the cardinal who pushed the canonization of Dominic in 1234: 'Because the Franciscans have a saint, make sure you have one too, even if you have to fabricate him from straw.' [43]

Although they remade the Church in this period, the regular clergy fought not only with the seculars but also among themselves. This extended to combats within orders. This was partly the result of a conflict of ideals. The Franciscans initially wished to stay out of the world, teaching only by example. Eremitical in his own bent, Francis was against the building of churches and was not in favour of obtaining papal privileges that enabled the

[40] Jordan of Saxony, *Liber vitasfratrum* 2, 7, ed. Arbesmann and Humpfner, 117. Prior general from 1298 to 1300, Mathew of Termini took the name Augustine upon his conversion. He died in 1309.
[41] *Ibid.*, 2, 2, ed. Arbesmann and Humpfner, 78. Jordan was citing Hugh of Saint-Victor (d. 1141) who derived his thought from the pseudo-Augustine *Sermo de obedientia et humilitate*. The idea is also common in the *Vitaspatrum*.
[42] *Cronica* in *MGH. SS.* XXXII, 77.
[43] *Ibid.*, in *MGH. SS.* XXXII, 72. Francis had been canonized in 1228.

Franciscans to preach and hear confession by overriding the local ordinaries or bishops. Nor did he want his brothers to be prelates, in spite of a rather eloquent plea by the cardinal-bishop of Ostia, Hugolino de'Conti of Segni: 'In the primitive Church, the pastors and prelates were poor and fervent in love and not in cupidity. Why therefore do we not make your brethren bishops and prelates who by word and deed would avail to influence all the others?'[44] Francis is reported to have replied that he wanted his brothers to be 'minor' and not 'major', and that they would teach better by example than by governing. Like that of the monks before, this hope soon failed. While there were only two Franciscan bishops in 1245, fifty-six attended the council of Vienne in 1311. And there were disputes among the various grades within orders, especially among the Franciscans. The lay friars fell out with those in holy orders. The struggle came to a head during the second ministry of their general Elias of Cortona from 1232 to 1239. Himself a lay friar, Elias tried to have them run the order. In his *Book on Prelatry*, Salimbene describes the general's tyranny and bad manners (*rusticitas*) and delights in stories against the lay brethren. He especially enjoyed that of the priestly brother who, being made to take his turn at kitchen duty, was summoned to perform the mass for some passing French travellers. The priest replied: 'Go sing the mass yourself. I'm cooking which you've refused to do!'[45] One of the most fascinating results of the weakening of the lay friars and their gradual exclusion from the First Order was the secularization of Franciscan devotion in the latter half of the thirteenth century. It was during that period that the affiliated Tertiaries, or Beghard and Beguine organizations, really became significant.

---

[44] *Speculum perfectionis* 3, 43, ed. Sabatier I, 109–10. Dominic gave a similar reply. Hugolino was the later Gregory IX.
[45] *Liber de prelato* in his *Cronica*, in *MGH. SS.* XXXII, 103.

Clerks and laymen

Although generally harmonious, the relationship of the clergy with the laity was not always happy. Churchmen were especially censorious about merchants and soldiers. Everyone admitted that the soldier had a place in society. From antiquity the right of self-protection and the defence of family or fatherland was not only permitted to soldiers but even enjoined on them. In spite of the rules of the truce of God, they were not to cease fighting for these just causes even in Lent, lest—said Bartholomew of Exeter —they appear to tempt God by their unpreparedness. Nevertheless, rigorists went far in their condemnation of soldiers. John of Salisbury was harsh enough when he remarked in his *Policraticus* that there had hardly ever been a just war in the world, but he could not hold a candle to Bernard of Clairvaux. In his enthusiasm for the crusade, Bernard cheered the Templars on to battle with a perfervid prose appropriate to one whose lance was his pen:

> How gloriously the victors return from the battle! How blessed are the martyrs who die in the battle! Rejoice, stout champion, if you live and conquer in the Lord, but exult and glory even more if you die and join the Lord! . . . for if those who die *in* the Lord are blessed, how much more are those who die *for* the Lord?![46]

But for those at war in the secular world he shed no tears. Most of their killing was sheer murder, he said, because they were merely after the booty and self-advancement. Yet even Bernard was obliged to take up the question of self-defence, although he went about it with typical obliqueness and tried to make it more a crime than a virtue: 'Nevertheless, one there is who slays a man not with zeal for vengeance nor for pride in conquest, but only as a means to escape. But I would not call even this a good victory, since of two evils, it is easier to die in body than in soul.'[46]

Because of the complex interplay of the urge to religion or to the clerical life and family interests and conflicts, also, the clergy often trod on laymen's toes, often without intending to. Francis of Assisi's mother fought her husband's frenzied attempts to force her boy to advance in society and 'to be a man'. The autobiography of Peter, the hermit of Murrone who became Pope Celestine

[46] *De laude novae militiae ad milites Templi* i, i and 2 in *Sancti Bernardi opera III* (Rome, 1963), 214–15. The biblical passage is Apocalypse 14:13.

V illustrates the problem of a substantial peasant family. At the time of his father's death Peter was the youngest of seven remaining sons of twelve born to his parents. One was already a monk and his mother wished Peter to enter the Church also, but his brothers opposed the expenditure on his education, arguing that ' "it suffices for us to have one who does not work," for clerks did not labour in that village'.[47] Thomas Aquinas's aristocratic family trained him for the clergy, but they wanted him to remain close at hand at Montecassino where, we may guess, he could comfort his mother and probably be of use to the family. When, at the age of fourteen or fifteen, he determined to join the Dominicans, who intended to take him to Paris, 'so that he should be removed from his relatives',[48] his mother reacted by having him kidnapped and forcing him to reside with the family for over a year.

A striking example of this problem—one that reminds us how many of the 'reform' movements of the Church were linked to adolescent revolt—may be seen in Salimbene of Parma's description of his entry into the Franciscan order. Salimbene had it in for his family. He never forgave his mother for having first saved his sisters from the cradle when, in an earthquake, the baptistery in Parma threatened to fall on the house. After this, he reports, 'I did not love her so much, because she ought to have cared for me, a boy, more than for the girls.'[49] But there was obviously more to it than this. When he entered the order at sixteen, he did so under the influence of his older brother Guy, who had left the world when already established as a judge and married. Apart from an illegitimate brother named John who went away to Toulouse, Salimbene would be the last to carry on the family name, and his parents consequently fought bitterly against his decision, even enlisting the help of the Emperor Frederick II. His father's rage once led him to cry out to his boy against the friars: 'Don't you believe these *piss-in-skirts*!'[50] The youth had an unusually strong case of *mal du siècle*. He replied to the final overtures of his parents by comparing himself to the harlot Jerusalem, 'My father was an Amorite and my mother an Hittite',[50] though he forebore from continuing the verses: 'None eye

[47] *Tractatus de vita sua*, ed. Arsenio Frugoni, *Celestiniana* (Rome, 1954), 57.
[48] James of Voragine, *Legenda aurea*, ed. Graesse, 918–19.
[49] *Cronica* in *MGH. SS.* XXXII, 34.   [50] *Cronica* in *MGH. SS.* XXXII, 40 and 53.

pitied me . . . but I was cast out in the open field, to the loathing of my person, in the day that I was born.'[51] Although Salimbene was something of a social snob and liked to remember his distinguished family background, he obviously enjoyed having frustrated his parents: 'I, brother Salimbene, and brother Guy of Adam destroyed our family both male and female by entering the order so that we might build it in heaven'.[52]

If clerks trod on laymen's toes, the reverse was also true. Direct lordship over ecclesiastical offices was no longer common, but patronage rights were still very much alive and protected in canon law as well as civil practice. Society's commanding elements influenced the Church very considerably. In 1207 a letter of Philip II Augustus of France to his governors in Normandy regulated the adjudication of disputes between secular patrons and the Church over the presentation of candidates to the ordinary for rural parishes. Such conflicts were to be settled by a panel of four priests and four knights chosen by the parties, and its decision was to be binding in civil and canon law. What this and similar measures led to was that the clergy—especially the higher—were largely derived from aristocratic families or from those attached to their interests. Of about 314 German bishops of the thirteenth century whose social origins are known, only eighteen were of bourgeois or peasant origin. The effects of this social pressure were sometimes pernicious. Becoming abbot of Ardres near Boulogne in 1161, Peter Mirmet was shocked to find that almost all his Benedictines were lame, blind, deformed or illiterate. They were also almost all of noble birth, making it clear that the house had been used as a dump by the local aristocracy. Peter's experience was not unusual. Buoncompagno's manual of love letters begins a note sent to a nun with:

> The voice of the turtle or rather of the cuckoo has sounded and has been heard in our land, that you have proposed to put off the honour of this world and to receive the monastic garb, and to lead the life of the cloister together with hunchbacked, lame, hooknosed, and squinting women.[53]

---

[51] Adapted from Ezekiel 16:3–5, the text that was in Salimbene's mind.
[52] *Cronica* in *MGH. SS.* XXXII, 56.
[53] *Rota veneris*, ed. Friedrich Baethgen (Rome, 1927), 20. The biblical reference about the turtle is to the Song of Solomon: 2, 12. *Cucullus* is a cowl and *cuculus* a cuckoo, hence our *truffator* is punning, as Beatrice Gottlieb points out.

Since many clerks acquired office through family power, they owed favours in return. In his archiepiscopal visitation Odo Rigaud was not surprised to come upon an abbot who had dowered and married off his nieces and financed a nephew through the university, even giving him an expensive copy of the Corpus of civil law, all without the consent of the chapter. The clergy picked up many of the prejudices of the leisured classes. The old canons of the Church encouraged clerks who were insufficiently endowed to work at any occupation save that of the merchant or soldier. So pervasive was snobbery, however, and so well did it fit in with guild unionism, that a synod at Arras in 1275 also prohibited the crafts of weaving and dying cloth, cobbling and others. The Dominican doctor Hugh of Saint-Cher (d. 1263) fought the aristocratic bias of his own order but it was still strong enough to allow gentlemen novices to enter before the canonical age of fifteen. Snobbery was, however, most vigorous in older monasteries and cathedral chapters.

This vice was fought, and fought vigorously, during the period treated in this volume. The days were over when it could be said, as it had been at Cluny, that, save as a labouring *conversus*, 'no son of a villein will ever be in my cloister'.[54] Peter Cantor militated against nepotism and aristocratic prejudice in his widely read *Verbum abbreviatum*, calling them forms of simony. A series of thirteenth-century glosses on John of Garlande's *Morale scolarium* (1241) all point out that the author 'proves that nobles in spirit and word ought to be preferred to nobles of race in ecclesiastical benefices'.[55] Men in the universities and lay professions deprecated such aristocratic influence. The jurist and publicist Peter Dubois (d. 1320) lamented its hold on the Burgundian clergy, and the medical doctor and lay theologian Arnold of Villanova found it a vice that threatened the Church with extinction. He attacked clerks who considered themselves above their brethren because of their families, protesting that even 'those born of the most vile adulteries, if decorated by *mores* and cleanliness of life, are more noble than others, even to the degree that their parents gave a clearer example of vileness'.[56]

[54] Cited and discussed in Georg Schreiber, 'Cluny und die Eigenkirche', *Gemeinschaften des Mittelalters*, 83n.
[55] *Morale scolarium* 10, ed. L. J. Paetow (Berkeley, 1927), 208. This is the Oxford gloss but the teaching is the same in all of them.

Arnold's shrillness implies that the social rigidities that were to become marked in the later Middle Ages were already a problem. This change affected papal legislation. In 1232, when Gregory IX was informed that the chapter of Strassburg refused to admit anyone who was not noble on both sides of his parentage and most eminent in knowledge, he answered with considerable asperity in the letter *Venerabilis frater*. He disallowed the canons' claim not only because it was difficult to find men of great learning to fill the very highest dignities let alone canonries but also because

> purity of life and nobility of virtue, not that of lineage, make a pleasing and suitable servitor of God; for God chose for the government [of his church] not many noble or powerful according to the flesh but instead those who were non-noble and poor, in that God is no respecter of persons.[57]

Even the layman's adherence to the Church was not disinterested. That Francis of Assisi was beloved there is no doubt, but he was also a 'property', one that was to become exceedingly profitable as a focus of pilgrimages, what might be described as 'religious tourism'. When he was near Nocera and sick to death with dropsy, the news of his condition reached home. 'When the men of Assisi heard this, certain knights rushed hastily to that place to bring him back to Assisi, fearing that he would die there and that others would have his most holy body.'[58] Nor were all pious confraternities actuated only by pious motives, not even those of the poor and humble. In his treatise on statutes, Buoncompagno of Signa wrote:

> Likewise, inspired by charity, confraternities are created in many parts of Italy, called *confraduglie* in Italian, for which rather simple statutes are made, telling how much wine or grain each member ought to contribute. Indeed, I said, inspired by charity, because common folk join such confraternities here and elsewhere so's to fill their maws and swell their bellies. In the diocese of Florence, a fraternity of farmers exists for the utility of the church. As is usual among those who

---

[56] *Apologia de versutiis atque perversitatibus pseudotheologorum et religiosorum ad magistrum Jacob Albi*, ed. Henrich Finke, *Aus dem Tagen Bonifaz VIII* (Munster, 1902), in *CICan* II, 480–1, clxv.

[57] *Liber extra* 3, 5, 37.

[58] *Speculum perfectionis* 1, 22, ed. Sabatier I, 57. Also recounted in Celano's and Bonaventura's lives.

found such fraternities, the rectors were those who [arranged] no mean banquets for the members and, after the banquet, were to render account of all expenditures. Then one governor rose in the presence of all, saying: 'Blessed be the Lord who has performed a miracle in and through us, because nothing of that which we have given is lacking to pay the expenses and nothing remains save one ha'penny!'

—for the fabric of the church. Whence, says Buoncompagno, comes the Tuscan proverb: 'May what happened to the parishioners of the church of Saint Hilary happen to us.'[59]

Although men of this period were devout, whole parts of their lives were barely touched by the Church and its moral precepts. One of the most important of these was love. Although the literature of medieval love was partly compounded of themes, allegories and symbols taken from sacred texts and ecclesiastical writers like Bernard of Clairvaux, the Church itself plays only a small and rather negative role in it. The most religious of all love poems, *Tristan and Iseult*, proves that true love cannot exist here on earth but only in heaven, an idea whose inspiration is obvious. But, although the God who loves true lovers plays a very active role in the poem, the Church is represented by only one doddering character whose hopeless duty is to make the lovers re-enter society by encouraging them to surrender their love and resume their normal careers, one as queen and the other as a soldier. And who can forget Aucassin's speech in which he avers that he would sooner go to hell than heaven because in hell were to be found those who were lovesome, beautiful, and brave and whose lives were full of passion? Heaven was inhabited by a few prophets— Enoch and Elijah are the medieval stereotypes—and miserable priests, the old, decrepit and sickly.

In fine, medieval men seem to have felt toward their religion as most men feel toward ideologies and beliefs even now. They obeyed the precepts of their cult and Church, and yet they changed them to suit their tastes or, if that was impossible, avoided them altogether. Religion is a very complex thing, and it may be that no man has but one religion. In the twelfth and thirteenth centuries Latin Christianity was so successful that men saw no reason to take more than occasional or superficial exception to clerical leadership. One may measure the degree of their

[59] *Cedrus* in *BuF* I, 125.

adherence in a rather simple way. After fortifications, the building of churches and cloisters probably involved the largest investment of money and energy in this period.

But the beauty of these buildings should not permit us to forget how they threatened the clergy's hope for freedom. Fulk, parish priest of Neuilly, became a great preacher, and, at the beginning of his conversion to revivalism, he tore down the church at Neuilly over the opposition of his parishioners. His earnings enabled him to replace it with a sumptuous edifice. But, for all his preaching about voluntary poverty, against usury, and his plan to raise money to enable the poor to go on crusade, his career fell apart because men wondered where the money he had collected was going: 'And by the hidden judgment of God his authority and preaching began to diminish remarkably among men.'[60] Writing shortly before, Fulk's teacher Peter Cantor tells of Bernard of Clairvaux,

> weeping because he saw thatch-roofed shepherds' huts like the pristine cottages in which the early Cistercians had once lived [now converted] into star-strewn walled palaces. And for this disease of building, these monks, like others, are often punished by the instrument of their offence. For to protect them, even their farms are castellated and, lest they lose them, the Cistercians often hide the truth and leave unmentioned God's justice, fearing even to grumble against princes. For this reason they have lost their freedom of which 'tis said:
> 'An empty-handed traveller will sing before a thief.'
> [And this freedom they have lost] for the riches of their farms and fields, permitting dormitories and refectories to be built for them by plunderers and usurers as a sign and eternal memorial of their avarice.[61]

But who can make up his mind on a point like this? Caesarius of Heisterbach tells us that when a rich Parisian businessman or usurer came to repent, Peter Cantor told him to restore his ill-gotten gains to the poor and to those from whom he took them. His bishop, Maurice of Sully, who died in 1196 with the choir and nave of Nôtre-Dame completed, had wanted the money put toward his great church.

[60] James of Vitry, *Historia occidentalis* 6, Douai 1596, 288.
[61] *Verbum abbreviatum* 86 in *PL* CCV, 257. The quotation is from Juvenal's *Satires* 10, 22.

PART FOUR

Government

X

The Church

Popes and princes

In the age with which this book deals the clerical order and its elected chief, the pope, were generally assumed to stand above lay power. To canon lawyers, Christendom was a group of nations governed by princes or other lay authorities submissive to the presidency of the pope. In his decretal *Solitae* of 1198, Innocent III expressed this concept as follows: 'We do not deny that the emperor is superior in temporal matters to those who have received temporal things from him, but the pope is superior in spiritual matters, which, as the soul is to the body, are more

BIBLIOGRAPHY. This chapter intends to provide a balance for the well-known views of scholars such as Michele Maccarrone, *Chiesa e stato nella dottrina di Innocenzo III* (Rome, 1940), who maintains that what have been seen as assertions of political power by this pope dealt with scriptural or ecclesiastical questions and had no temporal applications. Although useful as an antidote to the very strong statement of the opposing position by such as Walter Ullmann, *Medieval Papalism: the political theories of the medieval canonists* (London, 1949), this position neglects the fact that the Church was not merely seeking to lead man to heaven by means of governing itself and man's spiritual life, but also was trying—as it saw it—to make the world a fit place for his preparation for heaven by means of calling on, supervising, and freeing itself from his lay governments.

The literature on the Church is vast and a reference to a few stimulating studies will have to suffice. Geoffrey Barraclough, *Papal Provisions: aspects of Church history—constitutional, legal, and administrative* (Oxford, 1935) will correct the impression that the papacy tyrannized over the local churches. Further information on the relationship of the papal and local churches may be found in Friedrich Heiler, *Altkirchliche Autonomie und päpstlicher Zentralismus* (Munich, 1941) and Victor Martin, *Les origines du Gallicanisme*, 2 vols. (Paris, 1939). Brian Tierney, *Foundations of the conciliar Theory: the contributions of the medieval canonists from Gratian to the Great Schism* (Cambridge, 1955) has expanded our knowledge of the conciliar idea. By reading the polemical literature of the time and by reviewing the legislation and frequency of the councils themselves, I have been encouraged to argue that this conciliar epoch was almost as lively as that of the fifteenth century. For the effect of the legislation at the councils, see the last two chapters of this book, and for the conciliar parallel in the parliaments of the secular state, see chapter XI.

worthy than temporal ones.'[1] Innocent concluded that the emperor, as the head of secular society, was to be judged by spiritual authority according to the virtue or vice of his government. After all, secular might merely advanced the earthly good of the multitude, enabling it to live in the virtue attainable by natural man. The higher end of spiritual power was that of eternal life and supernal virtue, attainable only by God's grace and through the Church.

To the clergy, the duty of secular government was to serve the Church. Defending ecclesiastical right in 1301, Giles of Rome discussed the use of coercion, the material sword. Because the Church could not shed blood, the state should act for it, but, in so doing, it did not develop a power of its own. To Giles, secular might was like the tongs in the hand of a smith, himself likened to the Church. Although this tool touched hot iron, which the smith could not, the smith moved it. There were also other images to express this idea of subordination. Minister of France's kings and abbot of their last resting place, Suger of Saint-Denis (d. 1151) wished the kings of France and England to cast themselves at the pontiff's feet, and urged the emperor to perform the service of groom (*strator*) for this prince of princes. To John of Salisbury, instigator and companion in exile of Thomas Becket, princes were merely the Church's ministers. He asserted that 'all law that does not bear the imprint of divine law is to be censured as inane, and a princely constitution that does not conform to ecclesiastical discipline must be considered harmful'.[2] When Innocent III told the archbishop of Ravenna in 1198 that 'ecclesiastical liberty is never better preserved than when the Roman Church obtains full power both in temporal and spiritual matters',[3] he had summed up the natural bent of the ecclesiastical mind to confuse the two swords, the material and the spiritual.

The source of this power was explained in various ways. To some churchmen, it rested on the Donation of Constantine (*Constitutum Constantini*). In 1207 Gerald of Wales congratulated this ancient emperor because the gift of majesty is worth more than a mere gift of property. But the Donation was an awkward document. It could be read broadly to mean the emperor had

---

[1] *Liber extra* I, 33, 6 in *CICan* II, 197.
[2] *Policraticus* 4, 3 and 6, ed. Webb I, 239 and 251.
[3] Letter no. 27 in *PL* CCXIV, 21.

given the Empire to the pope. But, like Accursius in his ordinary gloss (about 1250), civilian jurists could not but notice that, legally speaking, the emperor had donated what was not his to give. He was only the Empire's administrator, not its owner. He was called 'august' from the verb *augere*, and this gift certainly did not increase the Empire. When they rose against papal civil government in 1152, the Roman revolutionaries went further in a letter to the emperor:

> This lie and heretical fable in which Constantine is alleged to have simoniacally given the Empire to Sylvester is so thoroughly exposed in Rome that common workmen and washerwomen silence even the most learned about the subject and the pope with his cardinals does not dare to appear in this city for shame.[4]

Read narrowly, the Donation granted the popes only the territories of the ancient western Empire or even only Italy and the islands, a term generously glossed to include Spain and the British Isles. But this had nothing to do with the seat of real imperial power in the 1100s. It could also be argued that Constantine had been the giver, and that he who gives here on earth is greater than he who receives. Addressing the Emperor Otto IV around 1211, Gervais of Tilbury said in his *Otia imperialia* that God had founded the Empire and that the emperor was the source of the pope's glory. Because it provided too narrow a base for the pyramid of papal power, then, the Donation, although never repudiated, came to play a lessening role in ecclesiastical apologetics.

The Donation was reinforced and eventually partly replaced by another and equally old justification: the pope had received both earthly and celestial power from Christ himself through the blessed Peter. In 1080 Gregory VII had urged his prelates assembled in council:

> Act now, I beg, fathers and most holy princes, so that all the world should understand and know that, if you can bind and loose in heaven, here on earth you can remove from anyone and grant to anyone on their merits empires, kingdoms, principates, duchies, marquisates, counties, and indeed the possessions of all men.[5]

[4] The letter of Wenzel cited in G. W. Greenaway, *Arnold of Brescia* (Cambridge, 1931), 136.
[5] *Registrum* 7, 14a, ed. Ph. Jaffé, *Bibliotheca rerum Germanicarum: Monumenta Gregoriana* (Aalen, 1865, rprt.), II, 404.

When focused on the papal prerogative, this sentiment became a cornerstone of Rome's power structure. Congratulating John of England for admitting that he held his realm of Rome, Innocent III remarked in 1213:

> The king of kings and lord of lords Christ Jesus, 'priest forever according to the order of Melchizedek,' has so established the kingdom and the priesthood in the church that the kingdom is priestly and the priesthood royal . . . so that, as body and soul, both the kingdom and priesthood should be unified in the single person of the vicar of Christ to the great advantage and augmentation of both.[6]

This doctrine certainly gave scope for an ampler historical justification than the fragile Donation. Had not the popes transferred the Empire from the Greeks to the Franks at Charlemagne's crowning? And, as Albert Behaim, archdeacon of Passau, wrote in 1240, could they not therefore transfer it again to the French or the Lombards if the German princes were delinquent in providing the Church with a suitable protector? To these legalistic arguments may be added the appeal of the utopian dream of a unified Christian society. Jurists repeated the old text included in Gratian's *Decretum*: 'Whenever disputes arise between Christians, they should be brought to the church and there settled by ecclesiastical men.'[7] Although he wrongly assumed that his words would fit the future, Boniface VIII spoke truly of the past when, in the bull *Rem non novam aggredimur* of 1301, he called Rome 'the common court of all the nations of the Christian people'.[8] Even Peter Dubois, Boniface's enemy, who sought to unite Europe under the French king, envisaged the pope as the ultimate arbiter of Europe's wars and disputes.

Aided by the confusion of their spiritual and temporal powers, the popes fostered an awareness of their presidency. Functioning as both priests and judges, popes wrote to princes as though to children. The formula for a congratulatory letter to a newly elected German king (*rex Romanorum*) read: 'A mother derives great joy from the excellence of her son, and scarcely anything so

---

[6] Letter no. 131 in *PL* CCXVI, 923–4. The biblical passages are Ps. 110:4, Exodus 19, 6, and 1 Peter 2:9. The priest Melchizedek was also king of Salem (Genesis 14:18).

[7] *Decretum* 2, 11, 1, 7 in *CICan* I, 628.

[8] *Extravagantes communes* 2, 3, 1 in *CICan* II, 1256.

delights parents as the wisdom and probity of their offspring.'[9] Boniface VIII addressed Philip IV of France in 1301: 'Hearken, dearest son, to the precepts of thy father and bend the ear of thy heart to the teaching of the master who, here on earth, stands in place of Him who alone is master and lord.'[10] Buoncompagno of Signa, who knew that the pope liked to be addressed as 'prince of all princes', suggested that lawyers pleading in consistory would do well to begin with 'I have risen to speak before the father of all fathers, who obtains the plenitude of power on earth in place of Simon Peter',[11] or, 'I have risen to speak before him . . . who yokes the necks of kings and emperors, who crowns the worthy and uncrowns the unworthy . . .'.[11] Even enemies of the popes admitted their greatness. The imperialist publicist Alexander of Roes confessed that, at the second council of Lyons in 1274, 'not only did the Christian people and ecclesiastical prelates assemble at the feet of the Roman pontiff, but even the kings of the world, together with the Jews, Greeks and Tatars, confessed that the monarchy of the world [belonged] to the Roman priest'.[12] And, in 1321, the rabbi Todros ben Isaac casually referred to the pope as the 'king of nations'.

In the papal view, all secular princes held of the pope, even the emperor. At the imperial diet of Besançon in 1157 two cardinals, irked by the emperor's support of the church of Hamburg-Bremen against the Scandinavian see of Lund, voiced this curial ideal. They boldly asked, if the emperor did not hold the Empire from the pope, from whom he did hold it? In spite of hasty papal retraction, this was not mere bumptiousness. One of the cardinals involved was Roland Bandinelli, the later Alexander III, a noted canonist and, for five years previously, chancellor of the Holy See. The idea never died. Although he was in the imperial service, the jurist Roffred of Benevento (d. about 1243) wrote that 'vassals are those who receive anything from anyone in fief, as the emperor has the kingdom of Sicily from the pope, and many say the same about the Empire',[13] an opinion stated as a fact by the papal

[9] Baumgartenberg Formularius de modo prosandi in BuF II, 807.
[10] Pierre Dupuy, Histoire du différend d'entre le pape Boniface VIII et Philippes le Bel (Paris 1655, rprt.), 48.
[11] Rhetorica novissima 5 in BIMA II, 262b.
[12] Notitia seculi 8 in MGH. Staatschriften I, i, 154.
[13] Cited in E. H. Kantorowicz, Friedrich II—Ergänzungsband (1931), 26.

publicist Alvarez Pelayo in 1327. Nor was this juristic hyperbole. Distinguishing between the different ages in the history of the Church, Thomas Aquinas casually contrasted the time when the Roman emperors persecuted the Church with the present when they defend it, a time in which, he said, it is suitable for kings to be vassals of the Church. His younger associate, Ptolemy of Lucca, observed that the emperor was the servant (*minister*) of the Church, and that he received the Empire 'from the church under oath like a vassal of the church getting a fief (*sicut fidelis ecclesie sub titulo feudi*), and this is the reason that the Church can depose him more easily than it can any other prince'.[14]

Although the popes did not get far with this idea in the older central parts of Europe like Germany, France and northern Italy, they did better along her frontiers. By means of the crusade, the popes helped frontier powers mobilize for expansion. Furthermore, the relatively undeveloped peoples on Europe's periphery were often protected by the popes against the pressures of the more central powers. Papal suzerainty was momentarily acknowledged in Scandinavia, Hungary, Poland, Bohemia and Bulgaria, but the best known example is the British Isles, all of whose realms were at one time or other under papal lordship. William of Normandy conquered England under the papal gonfalon. Although it has been questioned, it seems likely that Adrian IV gave Ireland to England's king in 1155 so that he might propagate a 'reformed' religion there. In return Rome was to receive one penny annually from each hearth, a tax reminiscent of Peter's pence revived at the time of England's conquest in 1066. To help repulse a French invasion, John placed his realm under Innocent III's protection in 1213, and the pope was granted an annual tax of 700 marks from England and 300 from Ireland. Although papal suzerainty lasted only until the reign of Edward I, Peter's pence remained on the books until the time of Henry VIII.

Similar papal pretensions extended into the Mediterranean region. Since the eleventh century the Norman kingdom of Apulia-Sicily had been held of Rome. Aided by French immigration, the popes intervened in the Iberian peninsula, eventually taking Portugal (1179), Aragon, and even Leon under their

---

[14] *Determinatio compendiosa de iurisdictione imperii*, 30 in *MGH. Fontes iuris Germanici antiqui in usum scholarum*, 60. Thomas's remarks were contained in his *quodlibetum* 12, 13, ed. R. M. Spiazzi, *Quaestiones quodlibetales* (1949), 232a.

suzerainty. These nations used the link with the popes to help them conquer the Muslims and destroy the earlier unity of Iberia under the kings or emperors of Castile-Leon. In the eastern Mediterranean, ecclesiastical authority was for a time equally successful. In 1198 the pope was titled suzerain of Jerusalem, Cyprus and Armenia. In 1217 Peter of Courtenay, the second Latin emperor of Constantinople, was anointed and crowned at Rome. In 1217–21 an overly ambitious crusade against Egypt, the strategic base of Muslim power, was actually commanded by a clerk, the cardinal Pelagius Galvao.

In all cases the secular riposte was rapid, and led to a weakening of the papal position in the thirteenth century. As an excommunicate, Frederick II Hohenstaufen led a crusade himself and took the crown of Jerusalem and Cyprus in 1228–29. Once a papal fief, Aragon led the counterattack against the French allies of the popes in Sicily in 1283. In the central parts of Europe, also, the papal attempt to spread its hegemony was quickly defeated. An example is the Albigensian crusade of 1209, which began as a papal affair. From 1210 on, Rome sought to recoup its investment by a tax of three pence per hearth in the conquered territory, and, in 1215, Innocent III dictated what he hoped would be a definitive settlement. But a victorious uprising of the southern French against the crusaders forced the French Crown to intervene in 1226. After the Capetian victory in 1229, papal authority was excluded from this region, except for the Venaissin, which the pope was given as a consolation. In fine, the efforts of the Church to win direct dominion resulted either in merely nominal rewards or clear failure. It is nevertheless important to note that secular governments were on the defensive from the Gregorian age until well into the thirteenth century.

The indirect power exercised by churchmen through the court of conscience was more significant for their leadership than the direct exercise of political authority. The expansion of the penitential system has already been sketched, and it has been seen how much it affected even so stubborn a group as the businessmen. That the law concerning usury was partly inspired by the need to protect crusaders reminds us that the crusade was related to the penitential system. The crusade was a war launched by the pope, although it must be confessed that the popes avoided the word *bellum* in the promulgation of these enterprises. On the other hand, Bernard of Clairvaux frankly used the term *bellum* and the great jurist Hostiensis described the crusade as the *bellum romanum* because Rome was the capital of the faith. And even Pope Clement III (d. 1191) was obliged to describe the state of hostility between Islam and Christendom as a *guerra*. Whatever it was called, unless the pope proclaimed the war, clerical taxes could not be raised for it nor could soldiers be protected from their creditors. What constituted a crusader was also decided by the pope. A year after the conquest of Majorca from Islam in 1228, the pope granted Christian settlers of that island the same indulgence as that given a crusader. The system of papal indulgences (remissions of the temporal penalty for sin gained by penitents by performing good works) grew up in close conjunction with the holy war, an early plenary indulgence having been granted by Urban II to the crusaders in 1095. Soon, penitents unable to march against the infidel or unsuited for military service were allowed to perform a good work by buying a crusade indulgence. The system so developed, especially when the crusade against the infidel became less important, that churchmen associated the sale of indulgences with the financing of any worthy cause. When Maastricht's citizens had to rebuild a bridge that had collapsed, they turned to the Roman court to launch their fund drive. At Orvieto in 1284 foreign prelates joined with the pope and his courtiers to purchase a forty-day indulgence for this worthy cause.

Although clerical ideas about the war against the infidel were nearly totalitarian, the Latin Christian's obsession with the crusade helped both Church and society to limit warfare at home. Small wars at home were impeded by the truce of God and even large ones were discouraged by clerical harping on the doctrine of the just war. Derived from pre-Christian classical thought, the *bellum justum* was defined by a good cause, principally self-defence, and by the careful observance of certain procedures, such as a formal declaration and moderation in the actual fighting. As the crusade turned back into Europe, however, western wars began to take on the totalitarianism that had marred Christendom's campaigns against the infidel. This may be observed in the struggle between the popes and the Hohenstaufen in Italy. Describing the crusade waged against the March of Treviso and Ezzolino of Romano from 1256 through 1259, Rolandino of Padua

lamented the change in the character of war from the early part
of the century:

> *Ha Deus!* Then were the wars, if one may say so, good wars.
> Then . . . were one captured, he was not forthwith put to death
> or loaded with chains, nor was he instantly condemned to be
> horribly mutilated in his members but was instead sent where
> he wished honourably and with praise. But today Ovid's
> prophecy has been fulfilled[15]

and man's golden beginning is covered over with filth, treason,
and fratricide.

These grim circumstances were as yet hardly experienced outside Italy, and one may therefore emphasize that penitential
mechanisms were successfully used by the Church to control
princes and states. Once taken, for example, the crusader's oath
was irrevocable without papal dispensation. Obliged to swear to
go on crusade in order to be crowned by the pope in 1220, Frederick
II Hohenstaufen suffered excommunication for nonfulfilment in
1227 just as he was reinforcing the Empire's hold over northern
Italy and cementing his power in his southern Italian realm.
Clerical intervention for reason of sin was also applicable to
marriage and divorce, matters of consequence in an age when
international relations were closely bound to dynastic policy.
This was not of great moment until papal centralization had
grown to the point where Rome could intervene regularly. In the
days of the old state churches princes married or divorced whom-
ever they chose, and an episcopate largely appointed by themselves obligingly consented. This practice persisted. When Philip
II Augustus of France dissolved his unhappy marriage to Ingeborg of Denmark with her hopeless claims on the English throne
and set out to ally himself to the Hohenstaufen, a local council at
Compiègne was easily persuaded to annul the marriage. But
times had changed. The pope reserved Philip's case and, from
1193 to 1200, fought him to his knees. These princes had made
themselves liable to the charge that for reason of sin (*ratione
peccati*) they were not fit to govern and were unworthy of being
obeyed by their subjects.

To enforce the Church's will a whole battery of sanctions had
long been under development. Most ancient was personal ex-

---

[15] *Cronica . . . marchie Trivixiane* in Muratori, *RIS* (1905 edn.) VIII, i, 22.

communication, an act that severed a prince from communion with his subjects and thereby absolved them from their oaths of allegiance. From this evolved the interdict. This stricture withdrew all but the last sacraments from subjects whose apathy to 'spiritual' causes permitted them to live easy under recalcitrant leaders. Although individual and group interdicts had long been known, whole peoples were not placed under this ban until the pontificate of Alexander III, and its greatest triumphs were won when Innocent III used it against France in 1200 and England in 1208. Later, still stronger stuff was needed, and at the first council of Lyons in 1245 Innocent IV not only anathematized Frederick II Hohenstaufen as a heretic but also launched a crusade against him. After this grand fulmination, one that harked back to Europe's great civil war of the Gregorian age, there were no more secret weapons left in the papal arsenal.

The extension of the pope's direct and indirect powers was questioned by moderate or cautious churchmen. Writing between 1149 and 1152, Bernard of Clairvaux coined phrases to be repeated by many thereafter. He asserted the supremacy of spiritual power and the Church's right to use secular coercion. Had the material sword in no way pertained to the Church, 'the Lord would not have replied "It is enough" to the apostles who said "Behold, here are two swords", but rather, "It is too much." Therefore both the spiritual and material swords are of the church, but the latter is to be wielded for the church and the former by the church . . .'[16] But the pope's power should not encourage him to wear a crown or ride a white horse surrounded by soldiers. He who must imitate Peter ought not emulate Constantine. Besides, Bernard told the pope:

> You err if, as I esteem, you think your apostolic power to be the sole one instituted by God. If you believe this, you disagree with him who says, 'There is no power but of God . . .' Although he said this principally for you, he did not say it for you alone. For later the same [apostle] says, 'Let every soul be subject unto the higher powers'. He does not say 'the higher power', as though for one, but rather 'the higher powers', as though referring to many. Therefore your power is not the

---

[16] *De consideratione* 4, 3 in *Sancti Bernardi opera* III, 454. The biblical passages are John 18:11 and Luke 22:38.

only one to derive from God; so also do those of the middling and of the lesser.[17]

In essence, Bernard's teaching was prudential: all things were permitted to the pope, but not all things were expedient.

More vociferous were the clerks still attached to the fading majesty of Europe's state churches. To them, their princes were still vicars of God and of Christ, titles the popes had arrogated to themselves by the early 1200s. During the fury of the Gregorian wars the proponents of imperial and royal authority had expanded arguments that derived from the polemics of late Roman times. The monk of Farfa, Gregory of Catina, wrote about 1111 that God alone judged and transferred the *imperium*, which preceded the *sacerdotium*. The Saviour never gave the Church temporal power; Constantine had done that, and his action was inane. The Lord had recognized the authority of Pontius Pilate, the emperor's representative. Inspired by such views and by Roman law, jurists consistently repeated these ideas. The ordinary gloss on the *Decretum* (c. 1215–17) by John Teutonicus repeated the notion that the *imperium* derived from God alone, and in his *Summa* (1188–90) the canonist Huguccio of Pisa recalled that the Empire preceded the papacy in history. Publicists went further. In the 1280s Jordan of Osnabrück and Alexander of Roes maintained that, if the pope's was a royal priesthood, the emperor's was a priestly kingship. Although the pope had transferred the Empire from the Greeks to the Germans, this was no mere human initiative, but was instead part of heaven's unalterable design: 'Even before it happened, it had been traced out by divine prefiguration that the empire of the Romans must be transferred to the Germans at the end of time (*in fine seculorum*)',[18] there to remain until the coming of the antichrist. Furthermore, in 'multifarious ways, the Lord of all, Christ Jesus, deigned to honour the Roman empire in the days of his flesh . . . . Indeed, the Lord honoured Caesar or the Roman king when entering the world, living in it, and departing from it.'[19] The Saviour's coming signalled an era of universal peace, the *pax Romana*. The Lord submitted to the census,

[17] *De consideratione* 3, 4 in *Sancti Bernardi opera* III, 444. Romans 13:1 and 2.
[18] Alexander of Roes, *Memoriale* 36 in *MGH, Staatschriften* I, i, 147. Most of Alexander's arguments came from the earlier *De romano imperio* of Jordan of Osnabrück.
[19] *Memoriale* 4 in *MGH, Staatschriften* I, i, 94–5.

THE CHURCH

ordered tribute paid to Rome, and paid it himself. Finally, he admitted Pontius Pilate's jurisdiction over his body, thus confirming the emperor's right to wield the material sword. These arguments were to be summed up anew by Dante Alighieri in the early 1300s.

For a time these opinions did not elicit much support, largely because papal authority was backed by the majority of the Latins. Because the efficacy of ecclesiastical censure depended upon the cooperation of a prince's subjects, or the weightier or more active among them, papal political power was largely a reflection of the subtle and almost unconscious alliance of the Church with Europe's aristocracies against the princes. A substantial part of what there was of political liberty within any monarchy in this period derived from the fact that its subjects had two monarchs—the secular prince and the pope—and could shift their allegiance from one to the other as circumstance dictated, thus destroying whatever pretensions to absolutism either prince may have had. One aspect of this was that the pope was responsive to complaints about a 'tyrannical' prince. Speaking pragmatically but with inadvertent accuracy, John of Paris described this state of affairs around 1300:

> When a king sins in temporal matters, the judgment of which does not pertain to the Church, [the pope] does not have the right to correct him in the first instance, a right that instead belongs to the barons and peers of the kingdom. If these are not able or do not dare [to do this], however, they may invoke the aid of the Church which, requested by the peers as an aid to law (*in subsidium juris*), may remove the king and proceed against him in the aforesaid manner,[20]

that is, by excommunicating him so that the people is freed of its allegiance and can replace him.

What was involved here was the familiar doctrine of the need to remove a tyrant. Developed in extreme terms by a polemist like Manegold of Lauterbach in the Gregorian age and given a more moderate form by John of Salisbury in the twelfth century, the fundamental notion of this doctrine was that a prince who breaches his contract with his people for reasons of his own self-interest or intemperance may be overthrown and even slain. To

[20] *De potestate regia et papali* 13, ed. Jean Leclercq (Paris, 1942), 214.

the clergy, tyranny *par excellence* was interference with ecclesiastical freedom, but the popes and others were always careful to
remind their readers that tyranny affected the laity also. When
Innocent IV condemned Frederick II in 1245, he not only adverted to this prince's putative heresy, invasion of clerical freedom, and breaches of the peace, but also stressed the sad condition
of the kingdom of Sicily. According to the pope, many of the best
of the clergy and laity had been driven out, and the rest had been
reduced to poverty, exhaustion, and slavery.

In line with this, the Church generally favoured electoral over
hereditary monarchy, perhaps because it was itself an electoral
institution. The canonists frequently cited a passage from
Jerome where he describes the practice of the see of Alexandria,
whose priests chose one of their number to be bishop, 'even as the
army makes the emperor or as deacons choose one of themselves
whose industry they know and call him archdeacon'.[21] It is therefore not surprising that, in 1199, Innocent III militated against
the election of Philip of Swabia of the inimical race of the Hohenstaufen by contrasting freedom and hereditary succession:

> Whence it appears obvious that we should oppose him lest, if
> a brother should now immediately succeed a brother just as a
> son a father, the Empire should seem to him not to be conferred
> by election but to be owed to [dynastic] succession. Hence
> what ought to be free would appear to be hereditary.[22]

To the popes this provided a satisfactory way of aligning the
interests of the *populus* with those of the supreme pontiff as long
as the distinction between the jurisdiction and the agent was maintained. As Innocent IV said: 'The pope has the Empire from God,
and the emperor from the people.'[23]

The weakness of the papal position was that the divine origin
of the office and the election of the officer by the people could be
combined so as to exclude the pope altogether. Cino of Pistoia
wrote: 'Nor is it absurd that [the Empire] should derive from
both God and the people. The emperor is from the people but the
Empire is called divine [and derives] from God.'[24] Cino was not
being inventive. Writing around 1302–03 with the French
monarchy in mind, John of Paris had said the same about royal

[21] The text was carried in Gratian, *Decretum* I, 93, 24 in *CICan* I, 328.
[22] Letter No. 29 in *PL* CCXVI, 1028.
[23] Cited in E. H. Kantorowicz, *The King's Two Bodies*, 298n.

331

power. And behind him were writers like the moderate canonist Huguccio of Pisa, who had questioned papal claims by stating: 'However, I do not believe that the emperor has the power of the sword and the imperial dignity from the pope but rather from election by the princes and the people',[24] who represented divine power in this instance. John of Paris used this argument to undermine the historical base of the papal claim, namely, the transfer of the Empire from the Greeks to the Franks. This act was not performed by the popes alone, he asserted, but also by the Roman people, 'for a reasonable and necessary cause, namely, for their defence against infidels and pagans, since no other seemed able to defend them; which action they were able to take legally because the people makes the king and the army the emperor'.[25] As did other authors, John found ways to justify hereditary monarchy, as when he said that royal authority derived not from 'the pope but from God and from the people electing the king either in person or in dynasty (*in persona vel in domo*)'.[25]

Because papal power over the secular state rested on the consensus of the *populus*, the clergy was never able to impose its will wholly upon the laity. This was the case in the German Empire, the one state against which the popes mobilized the plenitude of their power. That Rome won much cannot be doubted. Although the electoral traditions of all other western monarchies faded in this period, the reverse was true in the Empire. If a general increase in the competence of the secular state was seen almost everywhere else, the Empire slowly weakened. But the papal victory was by no means complete. Rome viewed the creation of a German king (*rex romanorum*) as a sort of episcopal election. This helped to formalize the election by limiting the electoral body and by instituting the majority vote, a regulation that was not fully accepted in Germany until 1338 or even 1356. Still, the popes had wanted more. As with episcopal elections, they sought to intervene in disputed elections. They did so with partial success in the conflict between the Welf Otto IV and the Hohenstaufen Philip of Swabia in 1199 and again during the Great Interregnum with the bull *Qui coelum* of 1263 when the electors fell out over the choice of Richard of Cornwall and Alphonso of Castile. More significantly, the popes claimed that

[24] *Ibid.*, 322n.
[25] *De potestate regia et papali* 15, ed. Jean Leclercq 221–2, 199.

the final and decisive act in the elevation of a German king, or emperor-elect, was papal consent. In the letter *Venerabilem* of 1202, Innocent III presented the papal brief: 'But even were the princes, not in discord but rather in accord, to elect as king a sacrilegious person, an excommunicate, a tyrant or fool, a heretic or pagan, should we then unction, consecrate or crown a man of that kind? Certainly not!'[26]

Although the Germans welcomed the idea of electoral monarchy—apologists like Alexander of Roes finding it to be a mark of German natural freedom in contradistinction to Gallic or other servility—and although, in effect, they applauded the weakening of imperial government, they never accepted the rest of the papal programme. Eike of Repgow's *Mirror of the Saxons* (1224–32) refused to exclude excommunicates from the imperial office, a restriction that would have opened the door to unlimited papal intervention. The electors were certain that it was their action alone that made the German monarch and, furthermore, that their *electus* (the *rex romanorum*) enjoyed immediate administration of the Empire with or without papal confirmation. This doctrine grew from the 1199 Hohenstaufen Declaration of Speyer through Lewis of Bavaria's *Licet juris* in 1338 to full acceptance in the Golden Bull of 1356. Although the might of the Empire had been irreparably damaged by the papal king of kings, the principle of the ecclesiastical command of secular government was never accepted in Germany.

In order to defeat the Empire, the popes were obliged to reinforce the ideological justification of other European princes. Regional sovereigns were not likely to applaud Frederick I Barbarossa's remark that they were merely subordinate kinglets under the Empire. Many western nations subscribed to the fiction that, like Rome itself, they were founded by the Trojans. Like England and Castile, some nations had never been part of the Carolingian reconstruction of the Roman Empire and could therefore assert their freedom from imperial sovereignty. There the germ of the notion that each king was the emperor of his own kingdom early made its appearance. Castile recalled the Visigothic declarations of independence from Rome. Geoffrey of Monmouth in 1147 tells that a king of England requested Roman law from the pope early in the Christian era. Refusing, the pope

[26] *Liber extra* 1, 6, 34 in *CICan* 11, 80.

replied: 'You are the vicar of God in your kingdom. According to the royal psalmist . . . "Give the king thy judgment, O God, etc." He did not say, "the judgment or justice of Caesar".'[27] Areas once under Carolingian sway but no longer within the Empire went about it in different ways. During the twelfth century the Capetian kings of France propagandized themselves as Charlemagne's direct heirs, true rulers of the Franks. Germans like Alexander of Roes replied to this pretension by saying that the French were merely the by-blows of Frankish soldiers and Gallic women and spoke the tongue of the conquered. The popes came to the rescue of the French by first applying to them, in the letter *Per venerabilem* of 1213, the doctrine that regional kings justly recognize no superiors over their realms. This teaching had become a commonplace by the 1250s and 1260s, when Alphonso X of Castile composed his *Siete partidas*: 'Kings are vicars of God each in his kingdom placed above his people to maintain them in justice and truth as far as temporal things are concerned, just as the emperor is in his Empire.'[28] By means of this doctrine, the popes isolated the emperors and prevented the united front of secular princes for which the Hohenstaufen had hoped.

The political actions and ideologies of the papacy were therefore partly determined by expediency, the expediency of a monarch who divides in order to rule. In 1310 the French charged the dead Boniface VIII with having said: 'If between the kings and princes of the world there is not discord, the Roman pope cannot be pope; but if there is discord among them, then he is pope, because each one fears him for fear of the other, and he can rule them and do whatever he wants.'[29] And, in his famous letter *Ineffabilis amoris* of 1296 in defence of ecclesiastical liberty, Boniface himself came close to this. He asked the king of France, then already at war with England and at loggerheads with the Empire, what he thought would happen if he so offended the papacy that the see of Rome would join his enemies. Still it was not this opportunism but rather the support lent the papacy by the directing elements of local society that gave consistency to eccle-

[27] From the *Leges anglorum* of about 1200, a London gloss of the *Leges Edwardi Confessoris*, ed. Felix Liebermann, *Gesetze der Angelsachsen* (1901) 636. The psalms are 23:1 (24:1), 44:8 (45:7), and 71:2 (72:1).
[28] *Las siete partidas* 2, 1, 5 in Madrid 1807 II, 7.
[29] Pierre Dupuy, *Histoire du différend d'entre le pape Boniface VIII et Philippes le Bel* (Paris 1655, rprt), 335.

siastical leadership. Unified action by substantial elements of the English nobility and Church against his 'tyranny' made John Lackland capitulate to Innocent III in 1213. A similar combination of powers enabled Innocent IV, acting as suzerain of Portugal, to depose Sancho II and crown his brother Alphonso in 1245.

Secular government and the local clergy

The battle was not only over who should lead Christendom; it was also over who should direct the local churches. The basic issue was the freedom of the Church: the liberty of the clergy to guide the 'moral' life of laymen, to be judged by those of their own order, to choose their own officers, and to be exempt from secular taxation. This battle was waged in many ways. In general, the further the arena of conflict was from France or Italy, the more primitive was the nature of the struggle. In Scandinavia, for example, state churches of a more or less Carolingian pattern were still the order of the day. Courts Christian were barely separated from secular tribunals, and their jurisdiction over laymen was undeveloped. As late as 1247 in Sweden the *privilegium fori*, or right of clergy to trial in their own courts, was as restricted as it had been in Carolingian Frankland. During the time of Sverre of Norway (1182–1202), the king was excommunicated, deposed by papal order, and the land was laid under the interdict partly over the issue of the freedom of clerical elections. But Sverre was able to mobilize most of his bishops behind his declaration in 1199 that the royal appointment of prelates was traditional in his land. Elsewhere in Europe the old state churches were never completely forgotten—witness the complaint of the French bishops in 1247 to the pope in which they reminded him that Charlemagne had chosen supreme pontiffs and that the kings of France used to confer all bishoprics—but the principle of ecclesiastical liberty was almost universally accepted.

Principle is one thing, practice another. In principle, clerks were exempt from secular taxes. In practice, since many prelates held baronies, or even duchies or counties, they usually owed both service and taxes, just like other vassals. In spite of changes during and after the Gregorian age, most princes also retained substantial powers over their local churches. Among these was the *regalia*, the right to collect the revenues of a vacant see until a new prelate was installed. German and Spanish princes were often given a share in the Church's tithe in order to protect Europe's frontiers. Local practice varied widely. The customs of Milan in 1216 noted that 'although by canon law, [tithes] cannot be possessed by laymen, general custom allows laymen to acquire and raise them in effect (*in effectu*)'.[30]

More threatening was the introduction of direct taxes on income from real and movable property, a novelty first seen on a large scale in Italy. The first significant legislation on this subject, that of Alexander III in the third Lateran Council of 1179, was primarily directed against the town governments of Italy. Charged with imitating Pharaoh's plundering of the Jews, the towns were informed that such taxes were henceforward forbidden 'unless the bishop and clergy perceive so great a need or utility that, without any coercion, in order to assuage common purposes and necessities when lay resources do not suffice, they may esteem that aids ought to be given by the churches'.[31] So open to pressure were the local clergy, however, that Innocent III in 1216 made such grants contingent on papal approval. In 1260 Alexander VI applied the same legislation to French and other towns, and enlarged it to forbid the taxes on acquisition of property by the Church that were becoming common (statutes on mortmain). The capstone of this legislation was Boniface VIII's bull *Clericis laicos* of 1296, which extended the prohibition to all western monarchies, with special reference to France. Violent opposition obliged the pope to suspend the bull in the next year and to fall back on the position of Alexander III.

After this surrender the late medieval system of 'voluntary' gifts from the local clergy became more common. Nor could it have been otherwise. The Italian towns against which the papal legislation had first been directed were Rome's faithful allies in the war against the Hohenstaufen, and had therefore come to rely on papal grants of taxes on clerical real property and non-spiritual incomes. France, as Rome's mightiest single ally, was regularly granted clerical taxes assessed by the popes from the days of the Albigensian crusade. By the time of Philip IV the Fair France had come both to expect and to rely on this supplementary income. Around 1300 the king could count on about 260,000 pounds of

[30] *Liber consuetudinum Mediolani 1216/17* 22, 2, ed. Enrico Besta (1949), 115.
[31] *Liber extra* 3, 49, 4 in *CICan* II, 655.

Tours (about 160,000 florins) when the French clergy's tenth was assigned him. His revenue from the tallage raised on all properties other than military fiefs gave only a slightly larger sum, about 315,000 pounds of Tours. In short, as it had done with the Jews, the undeveloped but growing state found it easier to tax the Church than its own subjects, especially the aristocracies of town and countryside.

Another issue was that of the courts Christian. In part, this concerned the jurisdiction of the clergy over 'moral' cases among laymen. This aspect of ecclesiastical authority increased until the later years of the thirteenth century. An example is the Church's jurisdiction over testaments, or the parts of testaments which concerned the Church or the poor. Inspired by the ideal of individual moral responsibility and also by a desire for bequests, the Church had long encouraged the individual to settle his accounts in his last will or testament. Such documents were relatively rare until the late twelfth century, however, because individual action was restricted by the ties of vassalage, manorial bonds, and the communitarianism of the extended family. As these weakened, the testament slowly became more common. Clerical legislation multiplied, an example being the command of the council of Toulouse in 1229 that a churchman must be present at the writing of a last will, a practice that obviously discouraged heresy and encouraged restitution for usury and charitable donations. A whole series of practices grew up around the testament. An example is the endowing of obits or commemoratory masses to be said in memory of a dying penitent, a form of fund-raising that helped finance parish and other schools. This all led to increased litigation in the courts Christian.

More significant was the *privilegium fori*, or benefit of clergy. The right of clerks to settle disputes among themselves was generally admitted and will not be treated here. Moreover, the principle claimed by clerks was that of trial by peers, that is, by those of their own order. The implementation of this principle was expressed by the famous tag: 'The accusor pleads his suit in the court of the defendant (*Actor sequitur forum rei*).'[32] This worked well enough in regard to civil cases against the clergy, but it did not satisfy either lay princes or society in regard to criminal offences. The secular state rarely surrendered the prosecution of

[32] Repeated everywhere, the source of this phrase is *Code* 3, 19, 3.

337

crime, even in the case of national and religious minorities like the Jews. Besides, treason, or its medieval equivalents, was a criminal offence. Thus the criminal clerk was a principal issue in the long battle from 1164 until 1170–72 between Henry II of England and Thomas Becket, and the arrest of Bernard Saisset, bishop of Pamiers, in 1301 on a charge of treason precipitated the final, decisive struggle between Boniface VIII and Philip IV of France.

The Church wished to try its own criminals. Typical of its law was a letter of Lucius III in 1181 stating that clerks, 'especially in criminal cases, may never be condemned by other than ecclesiastical judges, even if royal custom should have it that thieves should be judged by secular ones'.[33] But the clerical extremists, with Becket among them, went beyond that. Henry was willing to let the trials be conducted in an ecclesiastical forum, but insisted on punishing the clerks found guilty. Becket argued that the king's programme invaded clerical immunity and offended God, who did not wish men to be punished twice for the same offence, that is, to be degraded from orders by the Church and then executed by the state.

The archbishop's position is difficult to understand unless one remembers that clerical idealists were hoping to remake the world on the model of the Christian community at this time, and that clerical justice was far more gentle than secular. From the days of John of Salisbury to those of the circle of Peter Cantor at the University of Paris, clerical leaders had been attacking the barbarism of the secular courts and their violent corporal punishments, especially those of the Plantagenet 'tyrants' of England. Bad in themselves, these punishments were even worse when applied to clerks. For John of Salisbury or Peter Cantor, degradation from orders supplemented by imprisonment amply sufficed for the punishment of crime. There is also no doubt that clerical justice was often quite soft. This may be illustrated by a curious use of the remedy of exile by an archidiaconal court of Rouen, in which archdiocese clerks still enjoyed the right to exculpate themselves by a personal oath and the oath of cojurors. In 1262 a judicial inquiry (*inquisitio*) had established the guilt of a clerk reported to have had relations with his brother's wife. The archdeacon, 'fearing that the said Thomas, appearing in his court with his compurgators, would lie, enjoined him to leave the country for two

[33] *Liber extra* 2, 1, 8 in *CICan* II, 241.

years and busy himself at the University of Paris or elsewhere'.[34]

Churchmen were never able to win the day completely. One reason was that some crimes so threatened the clerical order that the Church itself sought harsher penalties. In 1222 Stephen Langton, the archbishop of Canterbury, a student and exponent of the ideas of Peter Cantor, stripped a deacon of orders for Judaizing and handed him over to the Crown for punishment—he was burned—thus obeying the recommendation of the papal decretal *ad abolendam* of 1184 to call in the secular arm. And the clergy were often forced to bow before outraged public opinion. In Padua in 1301 a clerk condemned for theft, murder, and rape was protected against execution by canon law but was hung in a cage from the top of the commune's Red Tower until he expired a fortnight later.

But all cases were not as extreme as these, and the way in which churchmen won much of what they sought was by surrendering those activities that could lead them before secular tribunals for criminal or civil offences. Here the popes charted a tortuous course. On the one hand, with the exception of Pascal II's abortive agreement with the emperor at Sutri in 1111, they were unwilling or unable to divest the Church of the secular jurisdictions it had acquired, that is, principates and territories whose clerical lords were adjudicable by secular authority. On the other hand, the popes consistently legislated against clerks' exercising secular offices. As we have already seen in Chapter II, this effort led to the paradox that, although the Church increasingly regulated the life of the world *ratione peccati*, churchmen began to withdraw from the professions and from lay administrative posts. By 1215 clerks were prohibited from serving as procurators, advocates, judges, and public notaries for civil governments. The spirit of this law is shown by a letter Innocent III wrote to Richard Coeur-de-Lion in 1198 about Hubert Walter, archbishop of Canterbury and England's chief justiciar. The pope there ordered the king that 'for the sake of their souls, he should not permit the said archbishop to exercise secular administration any longer nor should he again admit the archbishop or any bishop or priest into secular government'.[35]

---

[34] *Regestrum visitationum archiepiscopi Rothomagensis. Journal des visites pastorales d'Eudes Rigaud*, 1248–69, ed. Th. Bonnin (Rouen, 1852), 432.

[35] Cited in Justus Hashagen, *Staat und Kirche vor der Reformation* (1931), 207.

This legislation was premature. Lay literacy was not yet developed enough to produce a large professional cadre from which state servants could be drawn, and the immaturity of public finance obliged lay power to rely on clerical benefices to pay many of its officers. In England, for example, the twelve members of the *curia regis* of 1195 included the chief justiciar named above, three other prelates, three archdeacons and another clerk who later became bishop of London. It is therefore not surprising that, after Hubert's resignation in 1198 in obedience to the pope, he soon resumed the justiciarship and held it until his death in 1205. Except for the layman Ralph of Glanville, who inspired the treatise on England's laws that traditionally bears his name, the authors of England's manuals of administration and law were churchmen. Among these were Richard FitzNeale, the presumed author of the *Dialogue of the Exchequer*, who died in 1198 as bishop of London, and the archdeacon Henry of Bracton, who died as chancellor of Exeter in 1268. England may serve as a paradigm of the larger continental monarchies in this respect.

The problem was exacerbated by what may be described as Rome's inadvertent Italian myopia. Papal legislation was suitable only for the urbanized regions of Italy where lay education and lay professionalism were more advanced than elsewhere. The attempt to withdraw the clergy from secular offices weakened the half-lay, half-ecclesiastical intermediary groups—the Gervais of Tilburys, for example—from whom the state had drawn so many servants in the past. Still, even north of the Alps positive results were already being achieved. As early as 1259, the composition of the *parlement* of Paris, France's highest court, was nearly half lay, and if in 1272 England's King's Bench (*coram regis*) was almost wholly clerical, it too was half lay by 1307. Although only the beginning of a process not to be completed until modern times, secularization was already the order of the day.

The use of clerks in secular government and of church benefices as payment for state service helps us to understand the third area of combat between secular and ecclesiastical authority, namely, the right to appoint to clerical office. During most of the period treated here the Church, heir of the Gregorian victory over Europe's state churches, increased the freedom of clerical elections and reduced princely power. This was particularly evident in the Empire, where the final struggle between the Welfs and the

Hohenstaufen in the early 1200s cost the emperors almost all the rights remaining to them after the *pactum Calixtinum* of Worms in 1122. In 1201 Otto IV Welf surrendered the *spolia*, the tax paid by a bishopric on the death of its incumbent. At Speyer in 1209, he gave up the *regalia*, or right to collect income from a vacant see and exercise the bishop's right to appoint to clerical benefices during the vacancy. More important, he withdrew his representation from episcopal elections and lost the power to intervene in case of a disputed election. These concessions were confirmed by his rival Frederick II Hohenstaufen in the Golden Bull of Eger in 1213. Although not implemented until after Frederick's death in 1250, Eger was a dividing line in the history of the German episcopate. From this time, the popes and local German princes became more important in limiting or defining episcopal freedom than the German kings.

Though less radical, a similar change took place in France and England. In the latter the kings kept a real measure of control over the Church after the battle over the *regalia* and elections in the conflict between Henry II and Becket. The biographer of William the Marshal reports that in 1194 Richard Coeur-de-Lion ordered the archbishop of Rouen to give the marshal's brother the see of Exeter as a reward for his loyalty. At the same time, the local church was increasing its freedom. When John Lackland fought his unsuccessful battle with Innocent III from 1208 to 1213, the bishops—who had usually supported the king against the pope in the past—sided with Rome. By 1209 only two of England's seventeen prelates remained at home and stuck by John. When the dust had settled, the king had been forced to admit the pope's right to install his own candidate in disputed elections. Stephen Langton, who was an enemy of the Plantagenets when serving as a professor at the University of Paris, was provided by the pope when there was a double election for archbishop of Canterbury in 1208. He occupied his see, England's primacy, in 1213.

If the power of secular princes declined, they still retained many rights. Bishops and abbots held important fiefs from princes and therefore could not take up their administration without their consent. Like the aristocracy generally, princes were patrons of churches and monasteries and could therefore, according to canon law, nominate candidates for the attached offices and livings.

Indeed, the laity as a whole had rights in this connection. The Gregorian age had seen the end of direct lay participation—other than princely—in episcopal elections, but in towns and even in villages parish associations began to grow in power, paralleling the rise of the economic and social corporatism examined earlier. Parishioners constituted organizations that elected officers, like the Venetian *procuratores* from around 1150 and the Florentine *operarii* in the 1180s, who controlled the building or charitable activities of their churches. The power of the purse and the lively pressures of popular devotion made these parish corporations into collective patrons, who presented their candidates to the ordinary or chose from those nominated by him. As described in Rolandino Passaggeri's *Summa* of the notarial art, a new *plebanus* was chosen by popular election. This sample document describes the assembled parishioners, who, after diligent inquiry and invocation of the Holy Spirit, 'unanimously and in full accord and consent agreed upon *dominum* Peter . . . among others there nominated, and by electing, they requested, and, by requesting, they elected him as priest and rector of the said church.'[36] Local election of parish rectors, a tradition derived from long before the days of the Gregorian revolution, was widespread not only in north and central Italy, but also in the new towns of central and eastern Germany. As a result, the principle was reflected in canon law. About 1311 William Durand the Younger remarked that, without prejudicing the authority of the ordinating officer, 'the opinion of the people is required in ordaining a priest' in order to find the best man, and that 'a bishop should not be installed without the testimony of the clergy nor clerks without that of the people'.[37]

Neither patrons nor parish organizations limited themselves to helping choose the clergy. Princes policed the morals of their subjects. So enthusiastic was Louis IX of France's campaign to eradicate blasphemy that he was censured for it by Clement IV in 1268. Princes often inspected their clergy. Ottokar II, king of Bohemia, deputized a *plebanus* and a layman to visit monasteries in the diocese of Passau in 1259. In 1234 Otto I, duke of Brunswick, removed all young and pretty nuns from the double monastery of Nordheim and prohibited the replacement of the rest

[36] *Summa artis notariae* I, 5, in Venice 1583 I, 126r-v.
[37] *De modo generalis concilii celebrandi* 2, 15, 2 and 38, 3 in *TUJ* XIII, 161ra and 165ra.

when they died, thus converting it into a male house. Parishioners were always eager to get their hands on parish administration. In 1296 those of the Dalbade church in Toulouse accepted an arbitral settlement of their disputes with the clergy. The arbiters provided that changes in the cost of services were to be made only 'with the assent and advice of all the parishioners or of a two-thirds majority of this body'.[38]

This capacity of laymen to act in matters ecclesiastical had various sources. They had always been permitted and even encouraged—as during the Gregorian purge of the Church—to interfere in order to reinforce the 'moral' or material fabric of the Church. And western princes, heirs of Constantine, persisted in thinking of themselves as God's vicars. At Pavia in 1160 and again at Avignon in 1162 Frederick I Barbarossa emulated his imperial predecessors by summoning councils to deal with the schism caused by the disputed papal election of 1159. Few rallied to him, however, and he eventually gave up and simply supported the 'antipopes' against Alexander III. Later on, Caesarius of Heisterbach recorded a debate at the University of Paris on the Becket case. As one who called clerical servility to princes worse than simony, the celebrated Peter Cantor declared the archbishop to be a martyr in the cause of ecclesiastical liberty. The opponent was the jurist Master Roger, who bluntly declared that Becket's punishment suited his crime of contumacy. That, for the time being, Peter's was the more sonorous voice is shown by the fact that Becket was the first saint whose jubilee was celebrated throughout Europe.

Proponents of ecclesiastical liberty were necessarily opportunist. The popes, for example, were never in a position to attack everywhere at once. From before the Gregorian age their prime target was the emperor, a fact which meant that Rome pressed less heavily on other western princes. Threatened by the Hohenstaufen imperial renascence, by the disputed papal election of 1159, and by Frederick I's pretended arbitration at Pavia in 1160, Alexander III fled to France and sought help from the greater princes, especially Henry II of England, then the coming man. In 1161 he canonized Edward the Confessor, thus confirming the Plantagenet dynasty so recently arrived on England's throne, a

[38] Cited in R. C. Julien, *Histoire de la paroisse N.-D. la Dalbade* (Toulouse, 1891), 138 and 151.

343

gesture countered by the imperialist pope Pascal III's canonization of Charlemagne in 1165. Because of Hohenstaufen ascendancy throughout most of the 60s, Alexander tried to rein Becket in and tone down his radical position in the conflict with Henry II. The archbishop's assassination in 1170 forced the pope's hand, but otherwise the battle could not have come at a better time for him. Not only did Henry II's domestic troubles increase during the 70s, but also the Hohenstaufen position weakened considerably. The pope sketched out an agreement with Henry in 1172, canonizing Becket only during the next year, and turned to devote his attention to the Empire. The emperor's defeat at Legnano in 1176 led to a temporary settlement. In sum, Alexander had dragged his feet in England in order to gain a sure footing in Italy. As a result, the English settlement had an air of compromise about it that caused much heartbreak among the Anglican spokesman for ecclesiastical freedom and reform.

Indeed, papal concessions to secular allies often offended local reformers. One theme of complaint that had long been voiced rose in volume during the thirteenth century as the popes mobilized their every resource to defeat the Hohenstaufen and the Italian Ghibellines. Writing around 1311, William Durand the Younger asserted that, not only should secular authority have no power over the clerical order, but also the Roman Church 'should not, as it appears *prima facie* that it can, concede this privilege to [princes], but rather revoke what has been granted'.[39] What William had in mind were the grants of clerical taxes to the English, the Aragonese, and especially the French kings. What papal diplomatic manoeuvring meant to local churchmen may be easily illustrated. As England and France gravitated towards war over Flanders and Guienne in the 1290s, clerical taxes were much sought after. This was why Boniface VIII tried to take the granting of them into his own hands. His bull *Clericis laicos* of 1296 was, in turn, a reason why Robert Winchelsea, archbishop of Canterbury, stood so firmly against his king Edward I. Because of the power of the French, however, Boniface attempted to appease them by his *Etsi de statu* in 1297, which permitted Philip IV the Fair to collect clerical taxes without papal consent in case of dire need. This had the effect of neatly cutting off the limb on to which Winchelsea had boldly ventured.

[39] *De modo generalis concilii celebrandi* 2, 3, 1 and 2, in *TUJ* XIII, 158vab.

William Durand's complaint also concerned the rights of appointment to clerical office. In the appeasement of 1297 Boniface granted Philip the right to provide one canon in every collegiate church of France and of the provinces of Lyons and Viviers. Typical of the later Middle Ages, this favour reflected not only the renascence of secular power over the Church but also the way in which the monarchical impulse, whether of popes or princes, was triumphing over electoral traditions. The crude bargaining between pope and prince over the filling of church posts that marked late medieval history was already clearly signalled in the relations of the French kings and their satellites with Boniface VIII. In the Neapolitan kingdom of the Angevin Charles II this issue came to a head around 1300. In 1302 a Catalan ambassador reported that Boniface, annoyed at the Angevin's refusal to appoint a member of his own family to an ecclesiastical post, called the king a common fellow and no gentleman. Charles replied that he had had enough of that kind of talk, and riposted with: ' "And if you look at the matter carefully enough, Father, those who are yours have enough and I've given them enough." Furious, the pope then said: "Don't you know that I can take your kingdom away from you?" And the king replied, "I do not!" '[40] As it turned out, Charles was right because of French power.

What this and other invasions of ecclesiastical liberty portended for the future was not yet understood. Generally speaking, the cause of ecclesiastical liberty was still supported by the *populus christianus* or its leading elements. The popes won their victories over secular princes because these same princes were those from whom the aristocracies of town and countryside sought their freedom. What made it difficult to see this alignment was that the popes, like all those who ostensibly lead other men, assumed that it was their slogans and commands that actuated the complex movements of the *populus*. In reality, such movements have usually been preparing for a long time, and also dictate the decisions and statements of individual officers, however high their rank.

[40] The diary of the priest Lawrence Martini for the bishop of Valencia, January to March 1302 in Heinrich Finke, *Aus dem Tage Bonifaz VIII*, XLV.

The government of the Church

As the jurist Lucas of Penna wrote ca. 1348, the Church was a state, and it may be added that it was the best organized and most ecumenical government in western Europe. The territorial organization of the Church had long been stabilized by Europe's division into archiepiscopal provinces and episcopal dioceses. The diocese was usually split up into a number of archdeaconries, which, in turn, consisted of units placed under a senior priest or chief officer, variously titled a rural dean, dean of Christianity, archpriest or senior *plebanus*. At the bottom were the parishes, headed by their rectors, chaplains or *plebani*.

This organization was not rigid or unchanging. From 1316 to 1334 John XXII created ten new dioceses and one new arch-diocese in Toulouse. There were also wide variations in size. In the diocese of Lincoln in the 1290s the archdeaconry of Stow consisted of four rural deaneries, that of Lincoln itself of twenty-three. There were poor and rich bishops. The bishop of Rochester had about a fifth of the income of the bishop of Winchester. Although these variations seem haphazard, they are explicable in terms of history. Dioceses created in antiquity were usually smaller than those created in the Middle Ages, and hence those of the Mediterranean basin were not so large as those of northern Europe. The bishop of Cavaillon in Provence ruled a territory scarcely as large as a northern parish, and enjoyed a revenue hardly a hundredth of that of the bishop of Winchester. These differences meant much. The petty size of Italian dioceses explains why so many officers attached to the papal court could boast the episcopal grade and why a wealthy prince-bishop from northern Europe, like Anthony Bek of Durham (d. 1310), could be looked upon as a man of a different order when visiting Rome in 1302.

Administrative changes created new offices and emptied old ones of their authority. Archdeacons, whose powers were outlined in ancient canons, impeded the centralization of authority within the diocese. Episcopal courts reached out to limit the administrative and judicial powers of these officers from about the mid-twelfth century. In thirteenth-century legislation, culminating in Boniface VIII's collection of decretals published in 1298, the bishop's judge (*officialis*), an office at once more powerful and with less tenure than the older archdeacon, gradually became the

346

second personage of the diocese. Not that archdeacons disappeared. Although weakened, their jurisdiction often remained, and archidiaconal revenues could be used to pay the new judges.

The larger units of the Church were also significant entities. Toledo's primacy evoked in Castilian minds the image of Iberia unified as in Visigothic days. The pretence of Milan and Palermo to a measure of freedom from Rome was useful to the emperors in their struggles with the popes. The renewed, if momentary, subordination of the see of Lund to that of Bremen in 1133 symbolized the thrust of German expansionism into Scandinavia. Because the see of York was 'statist' (and also expansionist at the expense of Scotland), and that of Canterbury 'reformist', York's vain struggle for equality with Canterbury epitomizes the defeat of England's state by its Church. From before 1300 the papacy recognized still larger entities, the nations. The sense of national identity was clear at the council of Vienne in 1311–12. There, matters to be voted on in council were first discussed by the clergy divided into six parts representing France, Spain, the British Isles, Germany, Scandinavia (Dacia), and Italy. Typical of the French and Italian leadership of the Church in this period, ten rolls of the records of these meetings are French, nine Italian, five Spanish, four German, one English and one Scandinavian. Later on in the letter *Vas electionis* of 1335, the popes imitated antiquity by dividing the Church into four great nations: France, Germany (including Scandinavia and the British Isles), Italy and Spain. This division had great appeal throughout the later middle ages, and it has the curious advantage of showing historians the geographical pattern of the Reformation long before the event.

The pope stood at the head of the Church. The jurists vied with each other in their efforts to describe his plenitude of power as analogous, though superior, to that of the emperor. The papacy adopted the insignia associated with ancient secular power, like the umbrella of the eastern potentate brought from Venice in the 1170s and the superimposed coronets that, by the early 1300s, made up the triple-tiered papal tiara. Some of the honorific ceremony and practice of the papal court had been stolen from that of the emperors. Writing in 1161–62, the reformer Gerhoh of Reichersberg remarked that the *curia romana* had previously— and more appropriately—been called the *ecclesia romana*, a caustic allusion to the adoption of the term *curia* around 1100.

The papal court in this age was prepossessing. Its highest officers were the cardinals, the 'brothers' of the pope. At first numbering about twelve but rising to about twenty in the early fourteenth century, the sacred college—bishops, priests, and deacons—did not form a true college until the twelfth century. The systematization was accomplished by the end of the reign of Alexander III (d. 1181). The meeting of the pope and his *fratres* in consistory had replaced the old episcopal synod of the Roman clergy and had become Christendom's highest court, wherein were promulgated the papal decretals. The cardinals were gradually elevated above the rest of the clergy, a process completed by 1245, when they were gratified with the red hat and given precedence over all other dignitaries. As befitted their status, the most important legatine missions were normally entrusted to them, although, since papal legates took precedence over all local clergy, lesser affairs could be given over to other clerks.

The judicial functions of the papacy had so expanded by the mid-thirteenth century that the consistory was supplemented by a group of chaplains specialized as judge-auditors. Having the right to hear cases involving matters below the episcopal grade, these judges constituted a tribunal later to be called the Rota. At about the same time a number of other officers, such as the papal penitentiaries in charge of cases of conscience, developed quasi-judicial functions. Finances were mainly entrusted to the chamberlain, the second officer of the papal court, endowed with his own semijudicial and scribal staff. The various types of scribes in the records section were under the chancellor, an officer almost invariably a cardinal until 1216 when the chancellorship was abolished and replaced by a vice-chancellorship, an office not held by a cardinal. All told, the number of papal courtiers was about four hundred in the late 1200s, not including the many apprentices and servants and about one hundred soldiers. The popes did not boast a regular messenger service, but were content to use the efficient couriers of the Italian merchant-bankers.

The papal letters, or decretals, embodied the judicial decisions of the pope taken in consistory; contemporaries were becoming aware that these established a normative law of precedents. They were not always happy about this and some argued that the only true legislative act of the pope was the issuance of decrees in council. Around the time of the official publication of the *Liber extra*, or decretals of Gregory IX, in 1234, Buoncompagno of Signa rather sourly described the difference between the two kinds of canonists:

> A decretist is so called from the decrees, as a decretalist from the decretals. . . . A decree is a holy canon promulgated by the authority of the highest pontiff with the assent of a council. . . . A decretal is the first born of the decrees, whence it is said: 'A decretal is named from decree and is its diminutive, but now it's trying to be equal to it.'[41]

But Buoncompagno was exaggerating. The new papal collections also included the canons, or decrees, of the general councils summoned by the pope. Indeed, it can be argued that the pope at no time stood as high in papal dignity as he did when heading the work of a council. More than anything else, the great councils, beginning with the first Lateran in 1123 and finishing with Vienne in 1311–12, illustrate the papacy's triumph over the Empire, whose ruler had been wont to call councils in the past, and testify to its hold on the loyalty of the local clergy. From the third Lateran Council of 1179 to Vienne, a general council met on an average of once every thirty-three years. By the fourth Lateran Council of 1215, metropolitans, bishops, mitred abbots, provosts of cathedral chapters, and even university masters of theology and law participated. Lay representatives of states and princes were entertained but did not participate directly.

Nor were papal general councils the only church assemblies where legislation was issued. Repeated papal legislation that reached its peak in the fourth Lateran Council required every unit from the rural deanery to the archbishop's province to hold yearly convocations or synods. Above these were the national or regional councils, such as those of the Scottish and English churches, as well as those of certain provinces that habitually worked together. After the Capetian conquest of Normandy the provinces that, together with the University of Paris, constituted the kernel of the *ecclesia gallicana* were Rheims, Sens, and Rouen, joined occasionally by Bourges and Tours. The meetings of these national synods, and even some provincial ones like Canterbury and York, tended to coincide with the great courts or parliaments

---

[41] *Rhetorica novissima* 2, 3 in *BIMA* II, 258.

summoned by princes. They therefore represent a developing sense of national identity among churchmen.

The tendency to increasing centralization was as manifest in each diocese as in the Church at large. The one exception was the religious, but it is an exception that proves the rule. New religious orders sought exemption from episcopal authority and looked instead to the papacy. The Cistercians, for example, were not visited by the ordinaries and, together with the Templars and Hospitallers, were exempt from the subventions raised for the crusades. The mendicants won exemption from the bishops' control, and were privileged to conduct the lay apostolate in spite of the opposition of the secular clergy. These exceptions to the centralization of episcopal authority contributed much to the centralization of authority in Rome. One reason the popes won such ascendancy over Europe's churches was that they could arbitrate in the struggles between the regular and secular clergy.

Nothing is more striking than the degree to which papal authority rose above that of the bishops in the twelfth and thirteenth centuries. Control of the penitential system developed partly out of the crusades and the papal monopoly of plenary indulgences, which were first granted in connection with the crusade. The appearance of the apostolic penitentiaries and of their college under a cardinal in the reign of Innocent IV (d. 1254) provided central control of this system. By 1153 the right to canonize had become a papal monopoly, of great importance in power politics—witness the cases of Edward the Confessor and of Charlemagne cited above—and in setting the moral tone of the Church. The authentication of relics was exclusively papal by 1215. The constitutional significance of this is obvious when it is recalled that every altar had to contain a relic. Also important was the growth of the appellate jurisdiction of the curia, bringing to Rome hundreds of cases already adjudicated in lower courts or reserved for the holy see, together with dispensations from the ordinary course of the law.

Papal control of the ecclesiastical hierarchy increased rapidly. During the twelfth century the popes developed their powers in regard to local prelates by insisting on their right to confirm elected candidates, by making visits to Rome obligatory for certain categories of prelates, and by controlling the transfer, or translation, of bishops from one see to another. Local elections were carefully scrutinized, disputed ones being invalidated and the rival *electi* replaced by papal appointees. The thirteenth century witnessed the growth of a system in which the filling of certain posts was reserved to Rome. Admitted as part of the papal prerogative even by those who, like Robert Grosseteste, questioned the actual practice, papal provisioning and reservations provoked many battles. They overrode local interests and, at the cost of local absenteeism, enabled the popes to finance the curial personnel at Rome and favour Italians and others wedded to their cause.

On the other hand, this system was not wholly unpopular outside of Rome. It appealed to the literate, for example, because it aided the universities, whose graduates otherwise found it hard to penetrate the serried ranks of the local clergy. Although well established before 1250, the first legislation on the subject included in the canonical collections was the letter *Licet ecclesiarum* of 1265, in which Clement IV unequivocally claimed a sovereign right over all ecclesiastical posts but went on to reserve to himself the provisioning of only those benefices that fell vacant when their incumbents were serving at, or visiting, the holy see. Thereafter, with some temporary retreats, papal intervention increased. Of the sixteen promoted to the episcopal grade in France from 1295 to 1301, only one was elected by a cathedral chapter in the old style; all the others were *in manibus papae*. In 1311 the bishop of Angers complained that, of the thirty-five prebends vacated in his diocese since 1291, he had conferred only five; the rest had been provided by the popes.

Papal taxation also grew. Providees or *electi*, for example, paid certain fees in return for papal confirmation, the amounts varying according to the wealth of the benefice and the amount of litigation involved. The fees usually included the common services (a tax equalling about a third of the first year's revenue of the benefice), the minor services (fees for the curial personnel), and several others, of which the largest was for a private audience with the pope. Wealthy prelates paid heavily. In 1302 the abbot of St Albans in Hertfordshire had his election confirmed at Rome at a cost of over 1,000 marks in common services, about 325 in minor ones, and about 1,200 for a private visit; in all, over 2,500 marks or just above 10,000 florins. As frequently happened, the abbot was obliged to borrow from the pope's Italian merchant-bankers, and in order to do that he had to buy a dispensation for having connived at usury. As we have seen, metropolitans and certain abbots were required to visit Rome at specific intervals. Some had won exemption, like the archbishops of Zagreb and Toledo because of their watch on Christendom's frontiers. Others had commuted this obligation to the sending of a deputy and a fixed payment. Around 1300 Rouen and Rheims each paid 2,000 florins every second year; Canterbury paid 1,500 and York 600 every third year.

In 1199 these and other fees were supplemented by the papal tithe, a percentage of the income of ecclesiastical benefices and installations. Like many taxes, it was initially small and designed to fill a specific need, the subvention of the crusade. It speedily grew. In 1199 it was set at a fortieth. In 1215 the fourth Lateran Council authorized the collection of a twentieth for three years. In the period from 1247 to 1274 a tenth was raised no less than twenty-one times. Moreover, because of the 'internalizing' of the crusade, the receipts were increasingly used at home. During the nine years of his pontificate, Boniface VIII (d. 1303) encashed about 1,800,000 florins, a sum largely spent in Italy against Sicily and the rebels in the papal states. Nevertheless, the secular state was already cutting heavily into this revenue, and the above figure does not include the allocation of tithes to the kings of Aragon, England and France and to lesser princes. In spite of this dangerous precedent, its regular and systematic collection made the papal tithe the most advanced form of medieval taxation except for that of the Italian urban republics.

Local churchmen often reacted against the growth of papal government. They even complained about the general councils, on the grounds that the new laws were too numerous to be obeyed. Peter Cantor describes a bishop of Chartres exhorting the fathers in the Lateran Council of 1179 to issue no more new laws, saying, 'let it rather be ordered and striven for that evangelical teaching be observed, which now only few obey'.[42] Peter then refers to two canons of that council which, he claims, have been forgotten at Rome: one dealt with the recuperation of tithes from laymen and the other prohibited the assignment of benefices before they were actually vacated (expectative graces). Writing around 1150, Bernard of Clairvaux bewailed the frequency of appeals to Rome, attributing their increase to nothing other than curial avarice.

[42] *Verbum abbreviatum* 79 in *PL* ccv, 235.

Everywhere rigorists deplored papal dispensations permitting pluralism, that is, allowing a single clerk to hold several benefices. Peter Cantor compared the practice to having a single general command both the right and left wings of an army. He also said it weakened discipline:

> I have even heard that when there were two canons [holding benefices] in two churches and one was dean in one and the other in the other, it was asked which was the spiritual father of the other, and which the obedientiary. The answer was that, when they were in one of the two churches, he who was the dean of the church where they were was the spiritual father of the other, and the other his obedientiary.'[43]

The same author concentrated his attack on papal exemptions, whereby abbots were freed from the authority of their bishops or bishops from that of their metropolitans. Peter was able to cite a rare case of agreement between those two rivals, Bernard of Clairvaux and Gilbert of La Porrée, bishop of Poitiers, attributing to the latter a belief that exempt abbots were clearly schismatics. In his *On Reflection* Bernard complained to the pope that, by granting such exemptions, 'you prove that you have the plenitude of power, but perchance not that of justice. You do this because you can, but the question is whether you ought',[44] and he drew a picture of the Church as a disordered body with fingers attached to its head. During the thirteenth century criticism was also directed against papal reservations and provisions, a practice that obviously defied ancient canons like those listed by William Durand the Younger: 'A bishop from another city ought not to be elected. Foreign clerks ought not to be preferred to those raised in their own churches.'[45]

Such authors clearly sought to limit papal authority. To be repeated for centuries, the basic sentiments were to be found in Bernard's *On Reflection*. The apostle Peter gave Rome what he himself had been given,

> solicitude, as I have said, over the churches. Did he not give domination? Hear him. 'Not ruling over the clergy, he says, but being examples to the flock.' And lest you think this to be

[43] *Verbum abbreviatum* 31 in *PL* CCV, 116.
[44] *De consideratione* 3, 2 in *Sancti Bernardi opera* III, 442.
[45] *De modo generalis concilii celebrandi* 2, 15, 2 in *TUJ* XIII, 161ra.

said solely out of humility and not in truth, the word of the Lord is in the Testament: 'the kings of the gentiles exercise lordship over them; and they that exercise authority upon them are called benefactors.' And he concludes: 'But ye shall not be so.' It is clear: domination is forbidden to the apostles.[46]

Bernard was also convinced that all Church offices were of direct divine ordination, not just that of the pope. He concluded that

> your power is therefore not the only one to derive from God. So also do those of the middling and of the lesser. . . . Above all, reflect that the holy Roman Church . . . is not the mistress but the mother of the churches. You are not the lord of the bishops but rather one of them. Indeed, you are a brother of those who love God and a sharer with those who fear him.[47]

Using these passages and interpolating an historical basis fitting the Aristotelianism of their age, John Quidort of Paris, Marsiglio of Padua, and William of Ockham later argued that episcopal power derived directly from God and not mediately through the pope.

Resistance to papal centralization grew slowly. One reason was that the excesses attributed to Rome were also characteristic of the local churches. Pluralism was common. Before his election to the see of Durham in 1283 Anthony Bek held no less than five benefices other than his archdeaconry. Nor, even if it did cause absenteeism, was pluralism always vicious. Laws regulated the holding of posts *in absentia*, and suitable vicars had to be provided. Thus controlled, the system was hardly more than a special form of taxation. And the revenues derived from absenteeism not only paid for the upkeep of some curial officers but also financed university education by paying the professors' salaries. Papal reservations and provisions were advantageous to the university-trained clergy, and the local clergy itself often took the initiative in seeking papal action in order to resist what were called the 'armed prayers' (*preces armatae*) of princes and nobles. To uncover the motives behind many of the antipapal diatribes, one need do no more than cite the complaint of the Gallican Church in 1247, commonly called the *Protestation of Saint Louis*. A

---

[46] *De consideratione* 2, 6 in *Sancti Bernardi opera* III, 418. The biblical passages are 1 Peter 5:3 and Luke 22:25–6.

[47] *De consideratione* 3, 4 and 4, 7 in *Sancti Bernardi opera* III, 444 and 465–6.

passage notable for its candour tells us that papal provisions were prejudicial 'to the lord king and to all the nobles of the kingdom, whose sons and friends were accustomed to be promoted in the churches'.[48]

Rome's critics were hard put to find a programme of action. The rise of Rome to supremacy in the west had paralleled the growth of clerical liberty and prestige, and her majesty was therefore blinding. Peter Cantor objected to many things about the papacy, but when forced to face the fact that he would have to question Rome's authority, he could only stammer:

> Am I not allowed to ask the lord pope, 'Why do you do that?' It is only a sacrilege when one contradicts or vituperates his work. True, I do not see the solution of these problems or how they may be obviated, but I know that the divisions and exemptions of this kind in the Church do not derive from its canons, old or new, but rather from the special authority of the apostolic see that God will not permit to err.[49]

The lamentable result, Peter says, is that Caesar governs everything and his consuls and proconsuls govern nothing. Like many who accent moral rigorism because they lack practical programmes, Peter and his ilk blamed others than themselves. The Church's problems came from either the pope or his court, especially the latter. It was they who made, as the Saviour had said in the Temple, 'my house, the house of prayer, into a den of thieves and a house of commerce'.[50] To such minds, Roman corruption became a standard theme, one that rapidly became popular throughout Europe. Thus the biography of William the Marshal tells us that when the 'sly' king of France prepared to rob 'honest' England at the Roman court, he sent the relics without which one never succeeds there, that is, money for greasing palms. Few indeed avoided this easy escape from responsibility. In his *Policraticus* John of Salisbury records a conversation with Adrian IV in which he told the pope that everyone knew the Roman curia to be, not the mother, but the plundering stepmother of the

---

[48] The *gravamina ecclesie Gallicane* published in the *additamenta* of Matthew Paris, *Chronica majora*, in the *Rolls Series* LVII, vi, 105. The correct dating is given by Geoffrey Barraclough, *Papal Provisions*, 11.

[49] *Verbum abbreviatum* 44 in *PL* CCV, 139.

[50] *Verbum abbreviatum* 36 in *PL* CCV, 123. Adaptations of Matthew 21:13 are repeated *ad nauseam* by rigorists in this and later periods.

Church. Adrian asked John what he thought, and John weaseled: it was common report, he said. The pope smiled and told about the revolt of the limbs of a body against its stomach, which, the limbs complained, did nothing but devour what their labour had gained. Likening the belly to a prince, Adrian reminded John that a body will die without nourishment.

In spite of the popularity of the Roman cause throughout the period covered in this volume, the rise of the pope and of the *ecclesia romana* to the leadership of Christendom had left them dangerously exposed. In the pre-Gregorian days of the state churches, rigorist reformers could and did attack the vices of prelates and of particular parts or members of the Church, but it did not occur to them to attack the whole as subsumed in its head. In the later age there was no one else to attack—except oneself! As generals are blamed for the defeats of their armies, so Rome was to be blamed for the failures of the Church or of Christendom, the society it headed. To be the head of all is to be held responsible for all. Until around 1300, however, occasional failures were more than compensated for by great victories.

Papal monarchy and the conciliar or republican impulse

The increased centralization of Church government resulted in a parallel growth of the clergy's desire to participate in that government. We have already seen that, in the ecumenical and local churches, the papacy actively fostered the renewal of the old conciliar traditions. Another source of the conciliar, or republican, impulse is to be found in the regular clergy.

Whereas the older monasteries of the Benedictines, including Cluny, were somewhat monarchical, the newer orders were more conciliar. The *Carta caritatis* issued by Stephen Harding in 1119 for the newly founded Cistercian order was a significant step in this direction. It proposed an annual chapter general under the chairmanship of the abbot of Citeaux to regulate the discipline of the new order and perform legislative and judicial functions. Although the constitutional structure became more complex as the order grew and although it was not always successful in operation, the consequences of this innovation cannot be overestimated. The Cistercian rule formed the basis of the constitution of the Templars and of most of the other military orders founded in the twelfth century, and it strongly influenced the organization of the Augustinian or regular canons. In the fourth Lateran Council of 1215 similar assemblies meeting triennially in each province or kingdom were imposed on the many houses of the old Benedictine order by conciliar decree.

The culmination of this movement, however, awaited the mendicant orders. Although the Franciscans and some lesser groups were more socially democratic, in that they initially gave the laity within the order a greater voice, the Dominicans provide the best example of a republican constitution. Formulated between 1220 and 1228, with some later additions, their constitution distinguished three levels: the individual convent, the province, and the whole order. The basis of the Dominican organization was the convents, whose members elected the conventual priors and controlled their legislation and actions. The provinces and their priors were controlled by an annual assembly of the conventual priors and another group of spokesmen elected by the convents called the diffinitors. On the highest level, an annual chapter general, composed of provincial priors every third year and at other times by provincial diffinitors, elected and controlled the master general of the order. With the exception of the masters general, whose tenure was life, all other officers were elected for a limited term, and all, including the master general, could be removed by one or another of the various assemblies.

There was much debate about the constitutions of the different mendicant orders. Within the Dominicans, Hugh of Saint-Cher spoke out in 1257 against the annual change of officers, whereas Humbert of Romans pleaded at the Council of Lyons in 1274 for the easier removal of tyrannical or incompetent officers. The latter point of view had been argued at length by the Franciscan Salimbene of Parma in his treatise *On prelatry*, in which, inspired by the conflict within the order over the 'tyranny' of the minister general Elias of Cortona, he proposed the abolition of lifetime office in all regular orders. His model was the Italian urban republic:

> For do we not observe that, in the cities of Italy of our times, the captains [of the people] and the *potestates* are changed twice yearly, and that they give good justice and rule well? For, when they come into office, they swear to observe the statutes that have been promulgated by the wise of the city to which they

357

have come. Furthermore, they have judges and learned men with them who are governed by the law of the ancients [the *ius commune* or Roman law], in consulting which they do everything. For if 'the number of fools is infinite', so also 'is the multitude of the wise the health of the earth'. Therefore, if laymen rule their cities excellently by means of officers elected for short terms, how much more would the religious, who have their rule, the statutes of their predecessors, conscience and God before their eyes, be able to improve their government. And so for the aforesaid reasons, the conservation of the regular orders of clergy is the frequent change of prelates.[51]

Although Salimbene's suggestion was not accepted except for the limitation of the terms of local officers in the mendicant orders, it is nevertheless clear that, as the orders of the regular clergy had become more centralized, they had also become more republican or conciliar. A similar process occurred in the central government of the Church as a whole. The issues were the election and deposition of the pope and his obligation to take the advice of assemblies or councils in weighty matters. Because he was an elected monarch, there was no problem about election *per se*, but the question of the resignation or deposition of a pope was much more difficult. Although there was much debate, informed opinion generally agreed that a pope could resign. This issue came to the fore for the first time in the Church's long history when Celestine V stepped down in 1294. As for deposition, most canonists agreed that a heretical or wholly incompetent pope could be deprived of his office, largely because the rights of a prince must sometimes be overridden in order to assure good leadership for society. Necessity knows no law, went the legal tag, and necessity, in this case, was the good of the Christian people. Furthermore, it had long been recognized that, since the world is a bigger place than Rome (*orbis maior est urbe*), a collegiate body or assembly, not to speak of the whole Christian people, was superior to any one officer, no matter how high, in its capacity to formulate or defend the faith. The central problem was finding the agencies that could control or depose the elected monarch and claim an authority equal or even superior to his.

There were two such agencies in the Church, the sacred college

[51] *Chronicon* in *MGH. SS.* xxxii, 156. The biblical passages are Ecclesiastes 1:15 (Vulgate) and Wisdom of Solomon 6:24.

of cardinals and the general council. The cardinals had long claimed the right to remove a heretical pope. The claim had been formally stated in the days of the struggle around Gregory VII, when his dissident cardinals tried to remove him and looked into history to authenticate their act. In juristic terms—arguing from the superiority of any college over its elected head—a similar formulation was made by John Quidort of Paris in the early 1300s: 'I however believe that the college of cardinals suffices for a deposition of this kind because their consensus, standing for the whole of the Church, elects the pope, and it would therefore seem likely that it could depose him.'[52] On the whole, such extreme positions were not much favoured even among the members of the sacred college. In the twelfth century the cardinals, divided by the continuing conflict between the Empire and papacy, limited their efforts to the 'schismatic' creation of 'antipopes'. Later, as in the case of the Francophile cardinals in the court of Boniface VIII around 1300, they specialized in sabotaging a pope's programme. Far more significant in practical terms was the requirement that the pope needed the consent of his *fratres* of the sacred college when taking actions of great moment for the Roman Church. In a constitution of 1234 Gregory IX ordained that 'there be no alienation of the papal patrimony without the common advice and consent of the brethren, and that each one of these should possess the faculty of freely opposing his veto for a legitimate reason'.[53] In 1262 Urban IV rescinded his predecessor's recognition of Richard of Cornwall as *rex Romanorum* on the ground that he had acted without the consent of all the cardinals. In principle, though not in fact, the cardinals possessed the right to veto papal acts.

The case of the cardinals, however, was not strong. They were as visible as the pope and, unlike him, did not command as much loyalty from local churchmen. The clergy often believed that the 'vices' of the *ecclesia romana* were not attributable to the papal 'little white father', but instead to the 'corruption' of his court. Furthermore, the cardinals were faced by a practical difficulty: the failure to find a foolproof way of electing a pope. It seems simple: the pope was chosen for life by his brethren of the sacred

[52] *De potestate regia et papali* 24, ed. Leclercq, 254.
[53] Cited in Harry Bresslau, *Handbuch der Urkundenlehre* (2nd edn., Berlin, 1931) II, 58n.

college. Of the thirty-five popes and 'antipopes' who were elected from 1145 to 1334 no more than eight were from outside this college—a testimony, one would think, to the solidarity of this group. Yet, because of the immense pressures on the cardinals, the election of a pope was more easily described than done. Efforts were made to create an expeditious and safe method of election, but all failed in the long run. Although the right to elect a pope had become a monopoly of the *ecclesia romana* in the eleventh century, the equality of the votes of the different grades of cardinals (bishops, priests and deacons) was not established until the later twelfth century, nor was the participation of the larger mass of the Roman clergy eliminated until the final triumph of the consistory at the same time. Until these changes had been completed and the rule of a two-thirds majority in papal elections had been imposed by the third Lateran Council of 1179, there were recurrent disputed elections of much use to secular power in its struggles with the Church. During the long reign of Alexander III (1159–81), there were no less than four imperialist popes, one of whom, Calixtus III, was in office for ten years.

The problem then became one of obtaining the required majority when the cardinals could not agree on a candidate. Sometimes the result was vacancy. From 1241 to 1305 the periods of vacancy totalled about ten years, one being no less than two years and nine months. In an attempt to correct this, a new electoral procedure, that of the conclave, was borrowed from Italian urban elections. First heard of in 1216 and used intermittently thereafter until it was made obligatory at the second Council of Lyons in 1274, the conclave meant that, once the election began, the electors were locked up until they made up their minds. Even this draconian method did not obviate vacancies, because the cardinals postponed elections until they were forced into conclave by public pressure. A still higher agency seemed necessary to force the cardinals to serve the presumed common good of the Church. The conciliar theorist William Durand the Younger therefore proposed that if the Roman see were vacant for more than three months the sacred college should be deprived of its right of election, and this right should devolve on metropolitans, bishops, and other suitable clergy—in short, on those churchmen who traditionally made up a general council. Although nothing came of William's suggestion until the Council of Constance in 1417, it is clear from his attitude and from that of John of Paris that the only group in the Church that was thought to possess higher authority than the pope was a body more representative of the *populus christianus* than the pope's cardinals, namely, a general council.

As noted earlier, general councils summoned by the popes partly represented the victory of Rome over the local and older state churches. At the same time, the conciliar movement was also a reaction of the local churches to the centralizing force of the papacy. Its needs in the struggle with the Hohenstaufen made the papacy give in more than it normally would have done to the power of the prelates arrayed in the general councils of Lyons in 1245 and 1274 and Vienne in 1311. At Vienne the complaints of the clergy against aspects of papal centralism make up much of the extant record of that assembly. The bishops and other prelates in these councils slowly forced the papacy to adopt some of their hostility to the mendicant orders. These religious were allied to papal centralism by the privileges of foundation and the licences to preach granted by the supreme pontiffs. Torn between the mendicants and the prelates, the papacy oscillated, veering now to one side and now to the other. In the first half or two-thirds of the thirteenth century the popes generally supported the mendicant innovation. Innocent IV, who called the first Council of Lyons as a move against the Hohenstaufen, was a notable exception to this policy. At the second council of Lyons and at Vienne the prelates got their way, and the legislation passed there against the expansion or foundation of new orders and for the policing of those permitted to continue was accepted by the popes.

Theory paralleled the growth of the actual power of general councils. Perhaps the most systematic theoretical discussion was that of William Durand the Younger, bishop of Mende, who, at the time of the Council of Vienne, wrote a tract on councils and the reformation of the Church. Not only did his work put the need for reform in the strident terms of the episcopal opposition to papal centralism, but it also formulated a clearly defined conciliar constitution. As William expresses it, counsel is salubrious for a republic and for the administrators who govern it. Especially when acting against previous conciliar decisions or against generally approved law, a pope or a secular prince should never use his plenitude of power without the express consent of his cardinals or equivalent secular counsellors or magnates. Indeed, no ecclesiastical or secular prince should be 'able to edict or concede [dispensations or exceptions] against such councils or laws *de novo* unless a general council has been convoked, since, according to the rule of both laws, what touches all should be approved by all'.[54] William then proposed a system of local councils not unlike that already encouraged by papal legislation, but added as a capstone 'that the pope should issue no general laws from now on unless a general council has been convoked, which council should be called every ten years'.[55] And, although William did not think in the political terms that made the later Marsiglio of Padua's vision so striking, there is little doubt that, perhaps adding a few words about the inspiration of the Holy Spirit, he would have agreed with that author's definition of the role of a general council in his *Defensor minor*. There Marsiglio tells us that, as long as a council's edicts do not contradict Holy Scripture,

> the faithful in Christ are obliged to obey the precepts and human statutes of a general council as long as they have not been revoked. For the reason that they are human law and because they have been issued for the common utility of man either simply or for a time, none of Christ's faithful may rise or act against such laws without incurring mortal sin. And therefore we assert that these laws must be obeyed for the attainment of eternal salvation.[56]

Given the rich practical experience of western churchmen in general councils and other assemblies, the appearance of William's conciliar constitutionalism must have seemed to some to point the way to a conciliar Church. After all, the canon lawyers generally held that, at certain times, councils were superior to the popes. Alan had taught in early-thirteenth-century Bologna that 'in a question concerning the faith a synod is superior to a pope. . . . Whence it happens that for such a reason [heresy, for example] a synod can condemn and judge a pope'.[57] It is therefore not surprising that, using similar arguments, John of Paris later proposed

[54] *De modo generalis concilii celebrandi* 1, 4, 4, in *TUJ* XIII, 155va. William is referring to the rule *quod omnes tangit ab omnibus comprobetur* that derives from Roman law and is in canon law. See Code 5, 59, 5, 2 and *Sexti decretalium* 5, de regulis juris 29 in *CICan* II, 1122. The rule itself is not to be found in the title *de diversis regulis juris antiqui* of *Digest* 50, 17 in the Mommsen, Krueger edition.
[55] *De modo generalis concilii celebrandi* 1, 4, 4 in *TUJ* XIII, 176va.
[56] *Defensor minor* 5, 20, ed. C. K. Brampton, K. Brampton (Manchester, 1922), 16.
[57] Cited in Tierney, *Foundations of the Conciliar Theory*, 67n.

362

that a defective or heretical pope 'should be warned to step down, and, if he does not wish to, can be removed, and a general council can be called and he can be summoned before it. And if he is discovered to be pertinacious and violent, he can be removed by the advocate of the secular arm, lest the sacraments of the church be profaned.'[58] As we shall see in Chapter XV, ideas like these were used in the French attack upon Boniface VIII and in the imperialist polemic against John XXII. In spite of this, the conciliar movement faltered in the early fourteenth century. Boniface VIII may have been defeated by the French, but the monarchical principle triumphed in the Church. No more general councils were called after the Council of Vienne until the fifteenth century, and in many ways papal monarchy reached its culmination in the pontificate of John XXII.

This was how it looked on the surface, but the conciliar movement was not dead. If there were no more ecumenical councils, those of the regional and national churches—the *ecclesia gallicana*, the *ecclesia anglicana*, etc.—continued to meet. Wedded now to the developing nations of the later Middle Ages, these councils provided churchmen with continuing practice in conciliarism and were the training grounds from which the conciliar fathers of Pisa, Constance and Basel came.

[58] *De potestate regia et papali* 22, ed. Leclercq, 248.

XI

The Monarchies

The Empire

Parallel with the expansion of Europe's economy in the twelfth and thirteenth centuries, the western state began to grow and to become more centralized. The process was not completed until the emergence of the nation-state in modern times, but fundamental steps were taken in this period. Such being the case, it is curious that the Empire which had been Europe's greatest state

BIBLIOGRAPHY. Although heavy going, the best survey of the western monarchical and feudal state is Heinrich Mitteis, *Der Staat des hohen Mittelalters: Grundlinien einer vergleichenden Verfassungsgeschichte des Lehnszeitalters* (Weimar, 1948, transl. 1975), and, for the relations of government to society, Emile Lousse, *La société d'ancien régime: organisation et représentation corporatives*, vol. I (all published, Louvain, 1943). The emphasis of this chapter is placed on an implicitly comparative approach to the institutions of the individual states. This even extends to the use of titles and rubrics. The parliamentary movement of the thirteenth century is often described as a conciliar movement in order to emphasize its similarity with the comparable movement in the Church. More strange to Englishmen's ears is the use of viscount for sheriff and of count for earl, but the reader is reminded that these officers were so described in the Latin and French they were in the habit of speaking. Lastly, it is to be regretted that the Iberian peninsula, southern Italy and Sicily, and Scandinavia are not given much attention in these pages. The excuse is that one cannot do everything and that, with the exception of Sicily, Apulia and Calabria, the forms of government in Iberia and much of southern Italy were not too dissimilar to those of either France or England. Scandinavia (and Hungary and the bordering Slavonic states, for that matter) and its institutions are to be likened more to those of Carolingian times than to those described in this volume.

On France, see the very uneven sections of Ferdinand Lot and Robert Fawtier, eds., *Histoire des institutions françaises au moyen âge: I: Institutions seigneuriales; II: Institutions royales; III: Institutions écclésiastiques* (Paris, 1957–64), Charles Petit-Dutaillis, *The Feudal Monarchy in France and England* (London, 1936, trans. from the French of 1933), and P. E. Schramm, *Der König von Frankreich* (Weimar, 1960). A good survey—a trifle too straightforward—is to be found in Robert Fawtier, *The Capetian Kings of France—987–1328* (London, 1962, trans. from original French ed., 1958).

For England see the latter part of Frank Barlow, *The Feudal Kingdom of England —1042–1216* (2nd edn., London, 1961), J. E. A. Joliffe, *Angevin Kingship* (New of the eleventh century, whose ample territories extended into north and central Italy and penetrated deeply into the area of modern France and the Low Countries, began to fall apart in this same period.

This did not seem to be the case around the mid-twelfth century. After the long civil war of the Gregorian age from the 1070s through the 1120s, a time when most of the later German princely lines made their appearance, a period of pacification and renewal began before the death of Henry V (1125) and continued through the crowning of the Hohenstaufen Frederick I Barbarossa (1152). This recrudescence of the central state was partly caused by the desire of the local church, now somewhat freed from imperial control, to avoid being dominated by the new local princely dynasties, partly by the resistance of smaller Italian towns to greater ones, like Milan, that grew at their expense, and partly by society's need to stop constant civil war by means of regional ordinances for the reestablishment of the peace (*Landesfrieden*).

York, 1955), J. C. Holt, *Magna Carta* (Cambridge, 1965), and F. M. Powicke, *The Thirteenth Century: 1216–1307* (2nd edn., Oxford, 1962). Holt's book is rich in comparisons with the rest of Europe.

On Germany and the Empire, see Geoffrey Barraclough, *The Origins of Modern Germany* (2nd edn., New York, 1947), Geoffrey Barraclough, ed., *Medieval Germany: essays by German historians*, 2 vols. (Oxford, 1938), E. H. Kantorowicz, *Frederick II* (Princeton, 1957, trans. from his *Kaiser Friedrich der Zweite*, 2 vols., Berlin, 1927–31). The last is a work of great importance not only for the history of the Empire and for the Hohenstaufen state in southern Italy and Sicily, but also for the elitist ideology (Bildungsaristokratie) in Weimar Germany.

On political theory and the conception of the state in this period see R. W. and A. J. Carlyle, *A History of Medieval Political Theory in the West*, vols. II to V inclusive (Edinburgh, 1902–36). O. Gierke, *Political Theories of the Middle Ages* (Cambridge, 1913, a translation by F. W. Maitland of part of the author's celebrated *Das deutsche Genossenschaftsrecht*, 3 vols., Berlin, 1861–81), C. H. McIlwain, *The Growth of Political Theory in the West* (New York, 1933, rprt), and such special studies as Sergio Mochi Onory, *Fonti canonistiche dell'idea moderna dello stato* (Milan, 1951), Gaines Post, *Studies in Medieval Legal Thought* (Princeton, 1964), and Michael Wilks, *The Problem of Sovereignty in the Later Middle Ages* (Cambridge, 1963). On the limits imposed on princely power, see Ennio Cortese, *La norma giuridica: spunti teorici nel diritto comune classico*, 2 vols. (Milan, 1962–64), Marcel David, *La souveraineté et les limites juridiques du pouvoir monarchique du IXe au XVe siécle* (Paris, 1954), and the useful but preliminary work of Antonio Marongiu, *L'istituto parlamentare in Italia dalle origini al 1500* (Rome, 1949, translated in 1968). A book of special value to all these subjects is Fritz Kern, *Kingship and Law in the Middle Ages* (Oxford, 1948, trans. from his *Gottesgnadentum und Widerstandsrecht im früheren Mittelalter*, 1914, and his *Recht und Verfassung im Mittelalter*, 1919), an imaginative work that suffers only from its neglect of medieval doctrines of conciliar government and teaching concerning the issuance of new law.

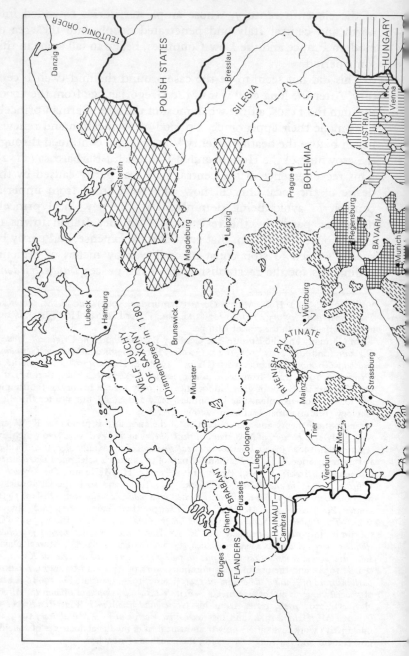

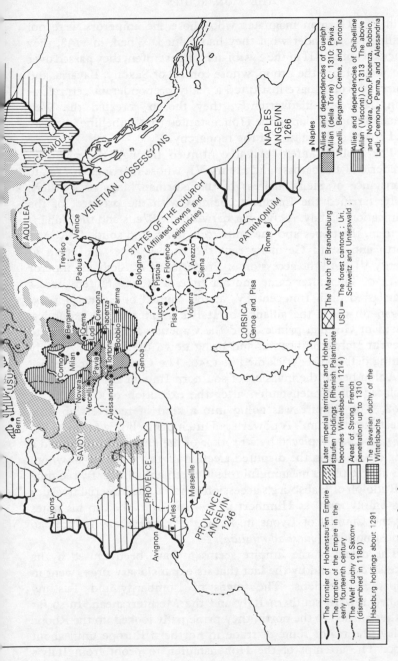

Legend:

- Alies and dependencies of Guelph
  Milan (della Torre) C. 1310: Pavia.
  Varcelli, Bergamo. Crema, and Tortona
- Alies and dependencies of Ghibelline
  Milan (Visconti) C. 1313 The above
  and Novara. Como.Piacenza, Bobbio.
  Ledi, Cremona. Parma. and Alessandria

- Naples

- The frontier of Hohenstaufen Empire
- The frontier of the Empire in the
  early fourteenth century
- The Welf duchy of Saxony
  (dismembred in 1180)
- Habsburg holdings about 1291

- Later imperial territories and Hohenstaufen holdings (Rhenish Palantinate
  becomes Wittelsbach in 1214)
- Areas of Strong French
  penetration up to 1310
- The Bavarian duchy of the
  Wittelsbachs

- The March of Brandenburg
- USU = The forest cantons ; Uri,
  Schweitz and Unterswald :

5. The Empire and Italy about 1300.

Still, the German magnates who chose the emperors were not willing to surrender what they had gained. When, in 1138, they elected Conrad III of the Swabian Hohenstaufen, they passed over the Welf Henry the Proud, whose control of Saxony, Bavaria, and Tuscany would have instituted a really preponderant centralization. However inadvertently, they thereby created the Welf (Guelph) opposition to the Hohenstaufen (or Ghibelline) dynasty and ensured the failure of the monarchy.

The Hohenstaufen revival continued through the reigns of Frederick I Barbarossa and Henry VI, whose marriage in 1194 to Constance of Sicily, heiress of the Norman kings of southern Italy, terrified the Empire's enemies with the prospect of the unification of Italy. A civil war between the Welfs and the Hohenstaufen, the popes and the emperors, north and south Italy, and north and south Germany rent the Empire after the death of Henry VI until the accession of Frederick II of Sicily as emperor in 1220. Thereafter came another time of Hohenstaufen success that lasted until Innocent IV, at the council of Lyons in 1245, began to weave the alliance of Italy's greater urban republics, dissident German princes, and the Capetian French that was to prevent Italy's unification and bring down the Empire. Already tasting defeat, Frederick died in 1250. The Capetian cadet house of Anjou began the invasion of southern Italy in 1265 and finally replaced the Hohenstaufen after the execution of Conradin in 1268. The Empire was going into a kind of receivership—the 'great interregnum'. A powerless Dutch princeling was elected in 1245, and was replaced by a brother of the king of England and a king of Castile in the disputed election of 1257, neither of whom was able to play a meaningful role in German politics. By the time of Rudolph of Habsburg's accession in 1273, the imperial treasury was empty, and, as Humbert of Romans remarked in his notes for the Council of Lyons in 1274, the Empire was reduced to almost nothing (*quasi ad nihilum*).

The defeat of the Empire seems to have been caused by its excessive size and by the fact that its expansionary urges went in disparate directions. The towns of Lombardy and Tuscany pushed toward southern Italy and the Mediterranean. In so far as they turned to the north, they principally looked up the Rhone valley, the major route of trade to northern Europe until about 1300. The attempt of the Hohenstaufen to profit from Italy's commercial and industrial growth by defeating the Lombard League was largely foiled by 1183. The second stage of the Hohenstaufen war was based on southern Italy and failed with the collapse of Frederick II's attempt to conquer northern Italy, the fragmenting of the southern Italian state in 1282, and the consequent economic subordination of that region to northern Italy.

In Germany, guided by the flow of her rivers toward the North and Baltic seas and by the eastward-leading reaches of her great plain, growth was to the north and the east. This expansion exerted a pull on the older southern, western, Rhenish and northern centres. Whereas in the past the Germans had looked towards Italy and France, the twelfth and thirteenth centuries saw many of them turn to expansion at the expense of the Slavs and the Scandinavians. By that time, German intervention in Italy was largely Swabian or Austrian, and was far less vigorous that it had been earlier. Far from being protected against the French, the left bank of the Rhône and parts of the territory along the Rhine gradually fell away from the Empire, and Provence went to Charles of Anjou of the Capetian line in 1245. French culture and military prowess penetrated and fragmented the political structure of the Lorraines and the Rhineland and profoundly influenced Franconia, Thuringia and Swabia. What the schism between the concerns of northern and eastern Germans and the imperialist ideas of many southern Germans and some Italians meant is shown by what happened at the battle of Legnano in 1176: the emperor was defeated by the Lombard League because the Welf of Saxony, Henry the Lion, had refused him his support.

The failing of the Empire was accompanied by a shift of its centre. In 1281 Alexander of Roes lamented that the imperial office had been lost by the Franks and Saxons to the weaker *Alemanni* of Swabia. Although not longsighted enough, he was looking in the right direction. If the northern and eastern Germans had lost interest in France and Italy, those of Swabia and Austria had not. The need to control the popes who, as in the Gregorian age, aided the drive for independence of local German princelings and of Italian towns made the Swabian Hohenstaufen look towards Italy in the traditional manner. To rule the Empire at home they had to go south and hold or capture the financial and ideological resources of the Italian cities. By the thirteenth century the focus of Empire had gone still farther south. Frederick II was the *puer Apuliae*, and, although south Germany still played a role in Italian politics, the real basis of imperial power lay in southern Italy. From the imperialist point of view, the disadvantage was that in moving southward the Empire had to alienate its authority in the relatively undeveloped economy of Germany in order to acquire rights in the more expansive economy of the Italian republics and princely states. The emperors weakened their state by selling cheap to buy dear.

The Empire's failure did not mean that its subjects suffered. Italy was rent by a great civil war in the thirteenth century, but it rose to lead large areas of the west's economy, and an Italian papacy ruled the Latin and even the Greek communions. Italy's lawyers looked back on the treaty of Constance as the moment when the Italian city republics came to recognize no temporal superiors on earth. The custom of Milan of 1216 stated that the emperor had then granted full jurisdiction to the Milanese and other Lombards. Albert of Gandino tells us in his treatise on statutes of 1289 that the same treaty permitted the Lombards to legislate as sovereign peoples. Later, Alberic of Rosate of Bergamo opined that, in strict law, cities did not possess the right to tax, except for those of Lombardy, who had won it at Constance. He added that, 'in fact, however, all [Italian] cities have usurped this right'.[1]

Much the same was true of Germany. The Hohenstaufen defeat of the Welf Henry the Lion in 1180 did not end Saxon expansion but rather split the duchy among aggressive local magnates and gave increased independence to the new princely states along Germany's frontier. In the twelfth century the rulers of Holstein, Meissen, and Brandenburg raced the Saxons to open land for German settlements. In 1212 Bohemia became a kingdom, and in 1220 the Teutonic Knights joined with the Knights of Livonia to conquer the eastern Baltic shores. German town liberty also grew. Leagues, such as the *Confoederatio pacis rhenana* founded in 1254 by the princes and townsmen of Mainz, Cologne, Worms, Speyer, Basel and other communities, served to make life tolerable in a decentralized political structure. A combination of free towns, local princes, and seigniors smashed the Baltic empire of the Danes from 1227 and began the heavy commercial and

[1] *De statutis* 3, 19, 4 in *TUJ* II, 57va.

cultural penetration of the Scandinavian peninsula. Rural leagues were also to be seen, the *Eidgenossenschaft* of Uri and Schwyz being founded in 1291. Intense decentralization made townsmen and rural gentry band together to maintain the peace and punish crimes, as in the initially informal system of the *Vehmgericht* in Westphalia, nominally ruled by its largely powerless duke, the archbishop of Cologne.

Within the Empire, the first Hohenstaufen effort had been to tighten central controls. Frederick I Barbarossa wanted dynastic succession to replace the elective monarchy, and this was proposed at the diet of Würzburg in 1196. Lacking that, Frederick had associated Henry VI in his government and titles, and Frederick II did the same with Henry VII and Conrad IV. In Italy the diet of Roncaglia (1158) asserted the Empire's right of taxation and legislation in the towns, which were to be governed by imperial *potestates*. In imitation of the tight administration of southern Italy, Frederick II tried to govern Italy's provinces by his vicars and her towns by his *potestates*. In Germany the period of success was that of Frederick I, who forced even the greater princes to surrender offices held in freehold and receive them back in vassalage. The old system of the *ministeriales*, the quasi-servile knightly and administrative elite, was extended and made especially efficacious along the major arteries of communication. There was the usual feudal monarch's attempt to ally with the townsmen against their local princes and with the ministerial service cadre and gentry against the nobility, *liberi* or *Freiherrn*. This had results. In 1241, for example, the towns provided two-thirds of Germany's revenues.

Yet all these efforts failed. A Rhenish prince-bishop and Saxon notables repulsed the attempt to found a dynastic monarchy at Würzburg. In the mid-thirteenth century the electors chose foreigners as emperors, always a sign of a failing monarchy. Although not complete until the fourteenth century, the slow exclusion of the lesser princes and magnates from the electoral college reinforced the power of the greater ones and their dynasties. This was already clear in Eike of Repgow's law code, the *Mirror of the Saxons* of the 1220s, according to which the greater princes —the Wittelsbach Rhenish count palatine, the duke of Saxony, the margrave of Brandenburg, and the king of Bohemia (who first actually voted in 1237) together with the ecclesiastical princes of Mainz, Trier and Cologne—voted first, though they could be overridden by the lesser magnates, with this important reservation: 'He whom the *illustres* (*vorsten*) have chosen unanimously, [the lesser magnates] will name to the kingship before any other.'[2] Eike's idea was very different from that obtaining at the election of Philip of Swabia in 1199, in which twenty-six magnates first voted, and their vote was then confirmed by twenty-four others.

In Italy the imperial renewal announced at Roncaglia in 1158 was largely abrogated by the peace of Constance in 1183. The spread of the office of *potestas* (*podestà*, in Italian), or head of state, elected by the townsmen just after this treaty illustrates this fact. Need for money and allies led to the alienation of other imperial rights. In 1162 Pisa bought the administration of its county. By combining money and a promise of loyalty Florence had won self-government by 1187. So independent had even the Empire's allies become that in 1256 Pisa supported Alphonso of Castile's candidacy for the kingship of the Romans, rejecting the vote of the German electors for Richard of Cornwall by arguing that the whole Roman people should vote for the head of state.

In Germany the links of vassalage forged by the Hohenstaufen were speedily circumvented. The Saxon magnates who helped Frederick I defeat Henry the Lion in 1180 demanded and received an immediate distribution of the properties and rights taken from the Welf, a precedent reflected in a later legal doctrine that the emperor could not hold great fiefs for longer than a year. The tendency to use Germany to support expensive policies in Italy resulted in the wholesale loss of imperial rights north of the Alps. Already in the late twelfth century imperial ministers were being freed or given hereditary rights, and they were thereafter increasingly titled *nobiles viri* or *liberi*—a policy pursued with abandon by Otto IV. In the Golden Bull of Eger in 1213 and the *Confoederatio cum principibus ecclesiasticis* of 1220 Frederick II surrendered his remaining controls on the election of German prince-bishops, as well as his *regalia*, tax rights, and jurisdiction, in return for their support. The greater secular imperial fiefs— for example, Austria in 1156 and Bavaria in 1180—were already becoming hereditary *de facto*, but the surrender of tax rights and jurisdictions within the states of the local princes (*domini terrae*) awaited the *Statutum in favorem principum* of 1232. Weakly sup-

[2] *Sachsenspiegel* 3, 57, ed. C. W. Gärtnern (Leipzig, 1732), 449.

ported by the towns, *ministeriales*, and gentry, reaction against this policy was crushed by Frederick II's defeat of his son Henry VII in the same year. By the time of Conrad IV in 1251, Italian expeditions were being mounted by means of the massive sale or pledging of remaining royal properties and rights in Germany. Even these were not much. In spite of one brief effort to reverse the trend, German juristic tradition reduced the exercise of almost all imperial rights to the moment when the emperor appeared in person to exercise them. The town of Bern elected its own *Vogt* (imperial governor or *potestas*) in 1268, in 1271 and again in 1291. The latter election was held to be valid by its inhabitants until the emperor visited in person, and the *potestas* was held to be replaceable only if the citizenry, as Roman citizens, agreed to the election of the emperor. In 1290 Besançon sought letters of confirmation from the pope for the election of Rudolph of Habsburg before asking that prince to confirm their ancient liberties.

Since they were gaining freedom hand over fist, it is no wonder that the Germans had to be bribed to support either side in the later wars between the Hohenstaufen and the popes. It was not, as Alexander of Roes said in his *Pavo* of 1285, that the papal peacock and the French cock had joined to bring down the imperial eagle; it was rather that the eagle had settled on the ground himself. By the end of the thirteenth century the Empire had been shaken to its foundations, and contemporaries knew it. Meir ben Baruch of Rothenburg on the Tauber, a rabbi who had officiated all over Germany, remarked that 'now every prince is like a king in his land and who would dare to tell him what to do'.[3] In 1274, Humbert of Romans recommended the following course to Gregory X:

> That the king of Germany should not be elevated by election but instead by [dynastic] succession, and that he should thereafter be content with his kingdom that he may be the more feared there and that he may better serve justice in the German kingdom. That, likewise, Italy should be provided with one or two kings bound by laws and statutes based on the consent of the towns and prelates. And they [one in Tuscany and the other in Lombardy] should rule by [dynastic] succession in the future, and may in certain cases be deposed by the apostolic see . . .[4]

[3] Cited in S. W. Baron, *A Social and Religious History of the Jews* (New York, 1957–67) VIII, 152.
[4] Cited in A. Hauck, *Kirchengeschichte Deutschlands* (8th ptg, Berlin, 1954) V, i, 49n.

Other projects for dismemberment went further. In 1280 Nicholas III is reported to have proposed to Rudolph of Habsburg that the Empire be divided into four independent kingdoms: Germany, Arles, Tuscany and Lombardy. What was visionary about these ideas was that no united kingdom could be established in Arles, Tuscany, or Lombardy, not to speak of Germany.

In fine, in looking for the growth of state apparatus and the state's centralizing agencies in response to economic pressures, one would have to turn one's attention from the fading imperial superstructure to the German and Italian princely states and urban republics. This does not mean that the Empire was dead by 1300. Germany's local princes did not become sovereign in public law until the Treaty of Westphalia in 1648, and there were revivals of the imperial idea and institutions before, and even after, that time. Furthermore, the weakening of the Empire in the period here considered was punctuated by periods of renascence, some of which, like the reigns of the Hohenstaufen Henry VI and Frederick II, made the failing Empire seem to an outsider's eye to be at its apogee. Indeed, to Dante and others, the memory of these reigns left a legacy of hope for a universal state that meant much for the political theorists of the later Middle Ages.

England

Perhaps the most striking contrast with the Empire was to be found in England. Although there were other centralized governments, such as that of the Normans and Hohenstaufen in southern Italy, England was one of the few areas where the lineaments of the modern nation-state might be discerned before 1300. This was partly because England was a relatively small area endowed with a relatively small population, so that the economic centralization of the time could effectively work toward political centralization. But not all relatively small areas in western Europe repeated England's experience; there were other elements as well.

It used to be customary to attribute much of England's precocious centralization to the Norman conquest of 1066. The conquest gave the Crown greater fiscal and feudal resources and a greater portion of the unoccupied lands, such as the forest, with which to remunerate servitors than was true of most continental monarchies. The fact that the fiefs granted to any single individual

were not often concentrated in a single region may also have helped
the monarchy for a time. On the other hand, the conquest was not a
single event, nor should too much be made of its recasting of basic
English institutions. Although its monarchy was weakening,
England was a quasi-Carolingian state before 1066, and its conquerors inherited many unitary institutions, such as the shire
administration and the royal courts in the subdivisions of the
shires called the hundreds. These institutions were reinforced by
the succession of invasions. After 1066 the penetration of England
by foreign cultures, institutions and population diminished in
vigour, but it continued. The second cycle of penetration ran from
about 1135 to 1154 and ended with the accession of Henry II. A
later military invasion was repulsed, that of the Capetian French,
which occurred in 1216–17. Even after this final invasion a
noteworthy thing about the English Church and government was
the degree to which Frenchmen and other foreigners played a role
in building the central government and filling its offices, as they
did in the reign of Henry III (1216–72).

It is of course true that the baronial opposition to the king was
also led by foreigners. The greater magnates and the leaders of
the rural and urban aristocracies were French in origin, and so was
the law under which they lived. Noteworthy leaders, like the
baronial King Stephen of Blois (d. 1154) and the baronial rebel
Simon of Montfort (d. 1265), came from France. Yet the main
effect of foreign intervention was to enhance centralization. Not
only did the conquest crush the indigenous culture and language
of the English, but it also set the conquered and conquering
peoples apart, in a manner not dissimilar to the Norman and
later Angevin-Capetian conquests of southern Italy, whose
native cultures, however, resisted the French with more success.
The separation lent a measure of solidarity to the French minority
and the English population suffered for long under laws that
punished it more severely than its masters. Although England's
monarchs were princes in France, where, by the time of Henry II,
their domains were ampler and richer than their island kingdom
and where, until John, they spent most of their time, this did
not weaken their desire to centralize England. Indeed, they looked
upon England as a mine from which to finance their expansionist
policies on the continent. This rational exploitation of England
was one of the reasons why the retention and then expansion

of royal justice in that land was peculiarly fiscal and brutal. Until at least 1278 even the accidental killing of another man involved a threat of hanging and confiscation of property that had to be bought off. And the royal courts were notorious for levying extraordinarily heavy fines. No wonder that Gerald of Wales flattered the French by claiming England to be the home of tyranny.

The idea of rational exploitation led England's princes and their officers to use any tool that came to hand. Naturally, most were French. The influence of Franco-Norman 'feudal' law was profound, as was that of French town law. Equalled only by the Empire in Italy, England recruited administrative personnel from places as far away as Sicily. A Bolognese, the son of the great Accursius, Francis Accursius (d. 1293), served Edward I as an ambassador and jurist from 1273 to 1281. Far more than either northern France or Germany until the latter half of the thirteenth century, England was open to the influence of the Italian schools of Roman law. Doctrines reinforcing the tendencies of a centralizing monarchy, such as that of the inalienability of royal property and rights, were speedily picked up. The late-twelfth-century justiciar's manual ascribed to Ralph of Glanville used Justinian's *Institutes* to define the majesty of England's king, and the anonymous author of the lawbook called *Fleta* (1290–1300) copied in his prologue both this earlier source and the Roman style panegyrics accorded Frederick II Hohenstaufen. As significant is the fact that the first centre of Roman legal studies outside of Italy and adjacent southern France was that of Vacarius in mid-twelfth-century Oxford. Although humble, it began a university tradition of civilian studies that persisted into modern times. If Stephen of Blois expelled Vacarius not long after his arrival in 1149, it was not effective, as a royal prohibition in 1234 against the teaching of Roman law in London's practical schools clearly shows.

Overt English hostility to Roman law also preceded that of northern France—as when Glanville both used and attacked the *canones legesque Romanorum*—showing that England's jurists knew more Roman law than their counterparts in the Capetian monarchy. Both in his case book and in his treatise on the laws, England's most famous legal writer, Henry of Bracton, made extensive use of Bologna's celebrated jurisconsult Azo, especially when insisting on the use of prior judicial decision as legal precedent. Bracton's masterpiece was itself modelled on the *Institutes*, the first three books being devoted to the substantive law of persons, things and contracts, and the fourth and largest—as befitted the essentially fiscal nature of England's courts—to procedure. In fact, from the days of Vacarius's civilian manual called the *Liber pauperum* England's jurists emulated the Italians by codifying or summarizing the law of their land, a royal law that, when contrasted to England's local customs, was considered to be the *ius commune* of the kingdom, just as Bologna's Roman law was the *ius commune* of decentralized Italy. This is different from northern France where, from 1200 onward, legal manuals strongly influenced by Roman norms appeared but were there issued as the local customs of the various provinces. Besides, no French author had the stature of a Glanville or a Bracton until Beaumanoir wrote his customs of the Beauvaisis in 1283.

Not only did the French gallicize English towns in the first generations after the conquest, but the expansion of the production of raw wool for export in the twelfth century seems to have been partly due to the pressure of northern French and Gascon merchants. Until the mid-thirteenth century the role of a French-derived Jewry was to enhance the monarchy, since the Jews were the king's, and it illustrated the dependence of England's major raw material producers on foreign economic elements. This was reflected in the consistent anti-Judaism and hostility to foreigners of the merchants of the English towns. By the latter part of the thirteenth century England's economy had become somewhat 'colonialized', her monarchy being closely bound up with the Flemish wool manufacturing towns, the wine trade of Guienne, and the Italian merchant-bankers (as well as some Germans) who expedited this three-cornered traffic. The need for centralized controls to protect England's producers was evident.

In spite of the need for central government, England was not unlike many continental powers. Her Church sought freedom and usually had its way up to the beginning of the thirteenth century. Her service aristocracy was restive and troublesome, seeking to build centres of local power based on private castles and on the possession of once-royal courts and offices. In the early twelfth century about one hundred families possessed palatine counties, monastic advocacies and county administrations in hereditary right. England's frontier barons consistently disturbed the monarchy. The Anglo-French of Ireland and southern Scotland were ever ready to intervene in England. Palatine counties, those of the prince-bishop of Durham and the earl of Chester, were like little kingdoms. Local administration of the county, or shire, had, as in Normandy, tended to become hereditary. The magnate Geoffrey of Mandeville (d. 1141) was granted hereditary right to the shrievalties of London, Essex, Middlesex and Hertfordshire, a veritable principality immediately adjacent to the very heart of the monarchy. In spite of earlier royal efforts to control the baronage and retain the local organs of government, it seemed as if England, at the accession of Henry II in 1154, might undergo the same decentralization that the continental monarchies had suffered.

Such was not to be the case; the reigns of Henry II and his sons brought about greater centralization. The fact that Richard was rarely in England and that John was driven to desperate expedients because of the collapse of his French domains did not halt the process. Apart from the reasons given above, namely the need for centralized controls to defend the kingdom against foreign pressure, there were others related to specific institutions within England.

Unlike some continental churches, the Church of England was unable to serve as a leader of the magnates' opposition to the Crown. Headed by Canterbury, the Church tried to play this role. Stephen Langton's leadership of the baronial opposition at the time of *Magna carta* in 1215 is one of several attempts, as is the close relationship between Robert Grosseteste, bishop of Lincoln, and the mendicants whom he fostered with Simon of Montfort in the mid-thirteenth century. Other than the traditional loyalty to the Crown on the part of the clergy who had careers in government, a principal reason for the Church's failure was papal policy, a policy dictated by Rome's desire for England's friendship while struggling against the Empire, a nearer and more threatening enemy. We already know how Alexander III dragged his feet at the time of Thomas Becket's combat with Henry II over clerical judicial immunity. Innocent III was initially more severe with John, probably because that prince formed an alliance against the Capetians of France with the Emperor Otto IV Welf, then threatening Rome. The issue was one of moment because, as we know, Innocent had appointed Langton—thought to be an enemy of the Plantagenets—to the see of Canterbury. John capitulated in 1213, admitting the suzerainty of the pope over England and Ireland. Throughout 1215 Langton and his bishops fought John, but their policy was defeated when Innocent released his royal vassal from his oath to maintain *Magna carta* and subsequently suspended Langton for refusing to excommunicate the baronial leaders. A similar conflict between the pope and the local Church occurred during Robert of Winchelsea's (d. 1313) tenure as archbishop. Winchelsea obeyed the bull *Clericis laicos* (1296) against clerical taxation even after the pope had found it expedient to withdraw the bull *de facto* and to make peace with England. The pontiff then suspended the primate. In brief, the inadvertent and never wholly satisfactory alliance of pope and king weakened the opposition of the English Church. The king's hold on his Church was reinforced, and, in return, the pope was able to finance the *curia romana* by providing Italians with English posts, and by extending the payment of common services to all of England's prelates.

The barons (*barones*, *divites*, *tenentes in capite*, etc.), a by no means unified group that had emerged by the twelfth century from the somewhat undifferentiated military service cadre that came to England during and after the conquest, were the principal servitors of the king but also his principal opposition. Since the barons had won hereditary title to their fiefs by the early twelfth century, the desire of the knights of the shire or gentry (*milites*, *vavasores*, or *liberi homines*—the gentry eligible for the knightly dignity) to enjoy not dissimilar tenure and privileges inadvertently led to an increasingly conscious alliance between them and the Crown. From the assize of Clarendon in 1166 onward, royal writs provided means whereby knights could appeal from the barons' seigniorial courts to those of the Crown to protect hereditary right and to curtail 'unjustified' expropriation. A royal procedure of this kind, being a sworn inquest (*inquisitio*) into the law or the facts of the case, gave the knights or gentry an advantage by providing a jury of their peers. By the mid-thirteenth century the struggle between the king and the baronage had so instructed the nation that the distinction between the magnates and the gentry or knights was understood everywhere. Prompted by the future King Edward I, a body called the *communitas bacheleriae Angliae* (bachelors were not yet enfeoffed knights) proposed what became the provisions of Westminster in 1259, which further limited baronial seigniorial courts and repeated a passage from the earlier provisions of Oxford requiring that sheriffs be chosen from among the vavasours of the county in which they were to serve. Later on, in 1316, the knights spoke for the *communitas Angliae* and, among other things, requested that those who acquired the shrievalty should expressly surrender alliances with the greater magnates. The knights and, to some degree, the rest of what was coming to be termed the 'commons', had come to think of themselves as representing the whole body of the realm.

The idea of the commons (the commune) reminds us of another interest group, the citizens of the cities and burghers of the boroughs. Although town growth was slow in England and small in comparison with Flanders across the Channel, English towns were active and growing constituencies. As the barons began to attack the policies promoted by Henry II, his successors Richard and John made both money and friends by granting town charters. By 1216 no less than seventy cities and boroughs had gained their liberties, and it is obvious from the care with which London was treated in *Magna carta* that the barons knew the importance of placating the townsmen. On the other hand, one cannot separate the interests of some towns and especially of many small boroughs, really villages, from those of the barons who aided and promoted their growth. Of about 160-odd new towns founded in England from 1066 to 1370—about forty per cent of them being planted between 1151 and 1250—only twelve per cent were royal foundations while seventy-eight per cent were seigniorial, either ecclesiastical or lay. When this figure is considered together with the thirteenth-century spread of village and borough liberties and the baronial attack on the restrictions of the royal forest, it is evident that the inhabitants of small towns and villages had more to gain from the barons than from the king. Much the same may be said of the knights of the shire, or lesser nobility. Many of these were attached to the greater lords by common local interests, and their actions cannot be understood purely in terms of class conflict.

Reservations aside, it was the arbitration of conflicting interests that encouraged the growth of royal centralism, and the concurrent growth of a sense of the community of the realm. The first express conceptions of this kind come from John's reign, and are a development of the idea of the peace. In 1205 John promulgated a sworn commune of England for the defence of the realm and the maintenance of the peace. A peace brotherhood was also implied in London's laws of about 1210, wherein the prince stated that 'all free men of our realm are brothers sworn [to uphold] our monarchy and our kingdom'.[5] The other side of unity's coin was the prince's demand for service, especially of a fiscal kind. As early as 1166 Henry II had found ways to collect scutage—a traditional tax in lieu of personal military service—from knights' fiefs held of his tenants in chief. The Saladin tithe of 1188 was a further step to taxing everyone in the kingdom, although, being for a crusade, it could not set precedent. The unsuccessful wars with the Capetians obliged the monarchy to develop new taxes and fiscal mechanisms. In 1198 Richard required an aid of five shillings from each hide, to be assessed by the sheriff and knights or other county worthies. The feudal aid had become so extended by 1207 that John required a shilling on every mark of rent and personal property from everyone no matter from whom he held his land. Together with the appearance of a nation-wide customs system, this shows the precocious centralization of England's government.

England's unity built a machinery of central government that was more advanced than any other in Europe, save for the *curia romana* or the Norman and Hohenstaufen kingdom of southern Italy. Most of the principal bureaux of the *curia regis* were established in the reign of Henry II. The second person of the realm was the chief justiciar, an office analogous to that of vizier in an Islamic state and one of extraordinary importance under an absentee monarch like Richard. For this office one of England's first great legal treatises was written, the account of the laws that went under the name of the chief justiciar Ralph of Glanville. Although their personnel was interchangeable, the courts he supervised began to specialize in the early thirteenth century. That called of Common Pleas, sitting in Westminster, dealt with the suits between private litigants normally brought to the Crown. That of the King's Bench (*coram rege*) dealt with criminal cases, royal rights, and by the 1260s monopolized the right to investigate charges of failure of justice in all other courts, thus further penetrating the free ones of the great magnates. Besides the courts and

---

[5] *Willelmi articuli Londoniis retractati* 9 in Felix Liebermann, *Gesetze der Angelsachsen* I, 490. A compilation of 1210 attributed to the Conqueror.

the justiciarship there were the offices of the treasury, the chancery, and the exchequer. A semijudicial body, the latter dealt with the crown's income. As noted earlier, the *Dialogue of the Exchequer*, written between 1177 and 1179, is one of the earliest secular administrative manuals in Latin Europe.

On the local level, centralization resulted in the loss of the hereditary character of the office of viscount, or sheriff; this officer was now to be recruited for a year's term from among the local knights. More important were the means used by the royal government to supersede and police the shire administration. Itinerant justices were sent out from the king's court from about 1166 onward. Because their functions were initially investigative as well as judicial, there was little that was new about this institution. It had been seen before in England under Henry I, and there had been analogous institutions in France as far back as the Carolingian *missi*. What is important is that this institution of justices in eyre did not fade away after its revival. Reflecting the norms taught in the Roman law of the schools, the justices pried into local administration and pursued crime without waiting, as had been traditional in many cases, for an accusation by a harmed party. This active uncovering of crime not only interfered with local independence but was also profitable for the Crown. This explains the sour comment by Becket's partisan, John of Salisbury, about these errant justices: 'And indeed the word error, although it does not fit their offices, nevertheless fits the persons of those who wander from the path of equity to follow the train of avarice and rob the people.'[6]

Royal offices would have had no future if the gentry had not supported royal initiative. The role of the sheriff as a judge would not have diminished if the Crown had not been able to count on three knights of the shire and a clerk to protect the pleas of the Crown for judgment by the justices in eyre, as in the articles issued in 1194, or, as in the next year, to entrust the investigation of infractions of the peace in each county to local knights. From the assize of Clarendon in 1166 the discovery of crime or malfeasance was generally put into the hands of four to twelve knights or other worthies, a method that was to develop into the jury system after the Church's prohibition of ordeals in 1215. A typical example of the early inquest is to be seen in Glanville:

[6] *Policraticus* 5, 15, ed. Webb, I, 344.

Whether he die testate or intestate, all the property of a usurer is the king's. When alive, however, no one is normally charged or convicted of the crime of usury, but, among the other *inquisitiones* of the king, it ought to be inquired and proved by twelve legal men of the neighbourhood on their oath if someone has died in this crime.[7]

Led by the baronage, England's aristocracy fought to control the growth of the Crown. Henry II's later years (d. 1189) were embittered by rebellions, and a major revolt coupled with foreign intervention battered the irrepressible John (d. 1216) into momentary submission and disturbed the first years of Henry III's reign. The barons rose again in the 'fifties of the thirteenth century, initiating a period of constitutional crisis and war that ended around 1267. A renewed period of troubles began in the later years of Edward I's reign, leading to the confirmation of charters in 1297 and culminating in the assassination of Edward II in 1327. In saying that the barons rose against the king, one must be careful to point out that the majority of the magnates never acted at any one time. In 1215, for example, central England's baronial families and those of the Welsh marches were not as exercised as those of the north, who had more unified territorial and jurisdictional possessions, or East Anglia. Only about forty-five barons holding thirty-nine baronies out of a total of 197 forced John to bow at Runnymede in 1215. Although the barons may be said to have won much of what they fought for during the thirteenth century, it was at considerable cost. They had to admit, and even invite, the gentry and the townsmen of the commons to participate in government. Although soon replaced, the early great families also wore themselves out in the struggle. By the early fourteenth century only seven of the twenty-three great families of the twelfth-century peerage still remained powerful.

What the barons and their followers sought was to limit the service owed the prince to what they thought traditional and right. They insisted on their right to be consulted concerning all *nova iura*, that is to say, about war and peace, about new taxes, and about any statute or ordinance that might impair their status. They also argued for trial by their peers in order to protect themselves from individual persecution. In Europe's past history, attempts

[7] *De legibus et consuetudinibus regni Angliae* 7, 16, ed. G. E. Woodbine (New Haven, 1932) 112.

to control monarchy had led to decentralization of the state, to the splitting of a once unified body politic into independent entities, as in France, where even counties had been subdivided into castellanies or baronies. A pale reflection of this was seen in England also. We have noted how royal jurisdiction invaded the seigniorial courts. Even as that was taking place, parts of the apparatus of royal government fell into the hands of prestigious local families. In Wiltshire, for example, the Crown controlled about two-thirds of the courts in the hundreds in 1194. By 1275 it controlled slightly less than a third, and in the northern and western regions the magnates' gains were even greater. In spite of this, old-fashioned decentralization was not the primary path the English baronage followed. For the reasons advanced earlier in this chapter, they as much as anyone else needed centralized government.

The magnates devolved power on themselves by trying to seize the royal government. Although their local authority was their base for action, they did not try to weaken the central offices of the monarchy, but instead to run them. This was done in two ways. The first was the creation of advisory councils to control the Crown's officers and even to appoint them. The second seems to have been inadvertent. As the monarchy wavered under attack, the Crown's judges began to emphasize the law as against the king. Whereas the early *Dialogue of the Exchequer* echoed the ancient sentiment that the king was of God and above the law, the later Bracton repeated the equally hoary notion that, although the king ought not to be subject to any other man, he was certainly under both God and the law. This idea that royal judges were administrators of something transcending the royal person may have been a reason why the powerful office of chief justiciar was allowed to lapse in 1232 and finally disappear after 1268. Instead of the old great offices of the *curia regis*, the central government's new offices were those that grew out of the king's personal household. For example, the keeper of the wardrobe, Peter of Rievaulx, was instrumental in removing Hubert de Burgh, the last real chief justiciar, in 1232.

Like the judges, the barons who opposed the king began to think of themselves as men who had sworn to uphold the abstract entity of the Crown but not necessarily an unsuitable prince who wore it. The barons' declaration against Edward II in 1308 stated:

Our homage and oath of allegiance are more significant and bind us more by reason of the crown than by reason of the king's person. . . . When, if it happens that the king does not behave reasonably with regard to the crown, his liege men, by the very oath they have taken to the crown, are justly bound to restore the king [to reason] and to repair the estate of the crown, otherwise their oath is violated.[8]

An interpolation of the time of Simon of Montfort in Bracton's famous text argued that the earls (*comites*) of England were the associates (*socii*) in government of the king, and concluded that he who has associates has a master. But this measure of participation had advantages for the Crown, if not for the monarch who wore it. Owing to the growth of the parliament, the national tax system developed from the feudal aid that had been limned in the reign of John had become relatively permanent, more so than in any other reasonably large monarchy in Europe.

On the other hand, there is little doubt that, headed by the barons, the relatively aristocratic elements who met in parliament were not granting the monarchy sufficient subsidies to meet its domestic and foreign responsibilities. Increasingly, therefore, the king was forced to rely on external resources and revenues. Involved in the wool trade, the Italian merchant-bankers helped carry the burden until the economic crises of the early fourteenth century. Edward I's debts to the relatively modest firm of the Riccardi of Lucca alone aggregated 392,000 pounds from 1272 to 1294, while the ordinary revenue of the English Crown in 1318 was only about 30,000 pounds yearly. Because of its customs on the export of wine and raw wool, the crown could still rely on the three-cornered traffic among Guienne, England, and Flanders. So significant had this become that, in the constitutional crisis of 1297, the earls, or counts, complained—with some exaggeration —that the export duty on raw wool—raised in 1275 and again in 1294—equalled about a fifth of the value of all the land of England. In 1318 the Crown drew slightly more revenue from Guienne than it did from England. As long as the baronial opposition effectively starved the Crown at home, the ties with Flanders and Guienne meant everything to England's kings. From the late thirteenth century onward, their increasing involvement abroad was a kind of institutional emigration of the monarchy that led to

[8] Cited in Kantorowicz, *The King's Two Bodies*, 365n.

the later Hundred Years War. A nation may need centralization, but it may not wish to pay the price.

France

The monarchies of England and France had been elective in their early days. As the rights of heredity and primogeniture grew among the barons, or greater officers of state, both monarchies became completely hereditary principates. The steps in this direction were taken at almost the same time in both kingdoms. Henry III at his accession in 1216 was England's first king not to be elected or designated as heir by his predecessor; in France, it was Louis VIII in 1223. The first princes to assume governance immediately upon their predecessors' deaths were Philip III of France in 1270 and Edward I of England in 1272. In spite of such similarities, the French monarchy was stronger. As long as the electoral tradition was alive, the Capetians associated the eldest heir in the kingship or designated the chosen successor as king-to-be during the life of the incumbent. This system worked in France but not when it was tried by the Plantagenets. The designation (1155) and association in kingship (1170) of his son Henry by Henry II was a disaster because the young king immediately allied with his father's enemies. To compare France with the Empire, the French monarchy suffered from minorities—a five-year one in the eleventh century and a ten-year one after the accession of Louis IX in 1226—but, unlike the ruinous minority of Henry IV in eleventh-century Germany, the French minorities were easily passed through. Popular support enabled the regent, Blanche of Castile, to give her son Louis IX a stronger government when he took over in 1235 than she had received at the beginning of the minority.

Paradoxically, the strength of the Capetian house was what seemed to be its weakness, the small size of the royal domain. There was certainly nothing unique about the Capetians. An active man, Louis VI had put some order into the Ile-de-France. His son, Louis VII, had married France's greatest heiress, Eleanor of Aquitaine, and thus seemed to have started the monarchy on the way to success. Louis's divorce in 1152 and Eleanor's subsequent marriage to Henry II of Anjou and England, however, reduced the Capetians almost to their nadir. Not only were Brittany, Champagne, Flanders, the Midi—in short, all the greater duchies and counties independent *de facto*—but Henry held Guienne and adjacent regions in south-central France, as well as Anjou, Poitou, Touraine, Maine and Normandy, and was thus France's most powerful prince. Even the Church, over which the Capetian kings had retained much authority, seemed more Plantagenet than Capetian. Of the seventy-seven prelates in the kingdom, twenty-seven were Plantagenet nominees and twenty-six Capetian. Comparing the kingdoms of Christendom, Louis VII knew where he stood:

> The emperor of Byzantium and the king of Sicily may boast about their gold and silken cloth, but they have no men who can do more than talk, men incapable of war. The Roman emperor or, as they say, the emperor of the Germans, has men apt in arms and warlike horses, but no gold, silk or any other wealth. . . . Now your king, that is, the king of England, lacks nothing and possesses everything, men, horses, gold, silk, jewels, fruits, and wild beasts. And we in France have nothing except bread, wine and joy.[9]

Weakness was really strength, because the movement toward ecclesiastical and aristocratic liberty continued in France. The Capetians did not differ from other princes in their policies: they were hard masters towards the church, towns and baronage of their domains. Their advantage lay in the fact that they did not have too big a church, too many towns, or too large a baronage under their sway. Louis VII won the support of France's local churches by confirming the liberties of churches and monasteries ruled by other French princes. Although Philip II fought Innocent III over his divorce from Ingeborg of Denmark, these hostilities faded between 1200 and 1213 when the Capetian emerged as the enemy not only of the Plantagenet John, but also of the dangerous Otto IV Welf, whose armies were decisively beaten at Bouvines in 1215. Thereafter, although Philip was at first reluctant to join the Albigensian crusade and Louis IX refused to aid the popes against the Hohenstaufen, the Capetian house became the papacy's principal ally in Italy and Germany. Moreover France was the refuge of the popes when Italy became too hot for them, and of the

---

[9] Walter Map, *De nugis curialium* 5, 5, ed. M. R. James (1914), 225. The story is told and improved on in Gerald of Wales, *De principis instructione* 3, 30 in *Rolls Series* XXI, viii, 317–8.

Plantagenet clergy at the time of Becket and Langton. Leading schoolmen at Paris, such as Peter Cantor, were celebrated defenders of Becket's cause, and Gerald of Wales, resident in Paris on and off from 1165 to 1180, wrote his book *On the Instruction of Princes* there, a major polemic comparing the tyranny of England's kings with the pacific glories of those of France.

Under Louis VII and Philip II the Capetian court delighted to hear complaints from the subjects of France's other great princes. The decisions of the Capetian court and the privileges granted by the kings tended to support the subjects of these princes. In the Plantagenet domains the Capetians supported the baronage. In Burgundy, where the barons ruled, they supported the knighthood. Everywhere outside of the royal domain the Capetians encouraged towns like Rheims, Soissons, and Dijon to gain their freedom at the expense of the local princes. Sometimes, as in the Laonnais, the king buttressed a movement of villages to combine in order to win liberty. In short, Louis VII and Philip II gave away what was not theirs to give and could thus profit from the desire for freedom or independence of those who held of their great feudatories. It is no wonder that by the accession of Louis IX in 1226, the Capetian monarchy was looked upon by many as a fountain from which freedom flowed.

France's other princely houses, like the Plantagenets in their ample lands along the Atlantic shores, suffered from taking the first serious steps towards governmental centralism. The Capetians profited from the resistance of the subjects of these houses, and their state expanded with extraordinary rapidity in the early decades of the thirteenth century. Shortly after 1200, campaigns marked by little resistance cost the Plantagenets Normandy, Anjou and Poitou, leaving only Gascony or Guienne in their hands by 1226. After Bouvines in 1215 royal garrisons were invited into Flanders, whose barons and towns swore loyalty directly to the king in 1226. Military promenades by Louis VIII made Languedoc prostrate and ready to sign the peace of 1229, by which all of the province but the counties of Toulouse and Foix was surrendered to the royal domain. By 1245 Charles of Anjou, a Capetian cadet, had taken over the imperial territory of Provence, and, at about the same time, the nominally independent county of Champagne was all but run from Paris. This sudden growth meant much to the monarchy. A reliable contemporary estimated that the income of the Crown had nearly doubled from 1180 to 1223, and, by the death of Louis IX in 1270, France was Latin Europe's richest monarchy. More, the once restive seigniors and knights of the Ile-de-France and other parts of the old royal domain had found outlets for their energies by becoming the officialdom of a rapidly expanding state. Contemporaries were awed by these developments, and Gerald of Wales, that hater of the Plantagenets, knew what to tell them. Normandy fell so easily, he said, because

> at the time of the dukes, before the kings had oppressed the Normans, as they did the English, with violent government and insular tyranny, [the Normans] were high and strong in liberty and most lively and undaunted in arms to repel injury. With, however, the necks of the nobility bowed down by the oppressions of these tyrants, how could they arise with daring arms and spirits to resist the freemen of France? For there is nothing that so excites and raises up the hearts of men to virtue as does the joy of liberty; and there is nothing that so depresses and lessens them as does the oppression of servitude.[10]

The hand of the Capetian state at first rested lightly on the lands brought under its rule. More than in England, the basic unit of government was the rural or urban seigniory. When the jurist Beaumanoir used the word 'sovereign' he tells us that it refers to the king when he is expressly mentioned, 'but that, in all the places [in my text] where the king is not named, I am referring to those who hold in barony, for each baron is sovereign in his barony'.[11] The monarchy was reluctant to intervene in the affairs of these quasi-independent entities. Writing in 1283, Beaumanoir tells royal officers that 'at no time whatsoever does one strike or push free communes [*viles de commune*] as one does a minor child'.[11] His father, writing the *Book of Justice and of Pleas* around 1259, had recommended that, before a royal officer could be elected as a town mayor, a two-thirds majority of the voters be required. It was in these particularistic entities, in fact, that much of the development of state apparatus took place. In towns, for example, we see the beginnings of the professions of lawyer and notary, at first in the area of the Midi open to the influence of the Italians but, by the end of the thirteenth century, spreading

---

[10] *De principis instructione* 3, 12 in *Rolls Series* XXI, viii, 258.
[11] *Coutumes de Clermont-en-Beauvaisis* 34, 1043 and 50, 1524, ed. Salmon II, 23 and 270.

northward, to the Châtelet of Paris and elesewhere. The office of the *potestas*, or professional and elected head of a city-state, was copied from Italy, especially in Provence. Professional political leadership spread even to the towns in northern France. The burgher John of Champbaudun began as royal provost of Crépy-en-Valois in 1246, moved to Paris, and then completed his career by being elected as mayor of Montreuil-sur-Mer, Compiègne, and Crépy.

The Crown penetrated these jealously independent local entities reluctantly, by providing special services or by purchase. Whereas in England almost all new towns were founded by seigniors or princes alone, in France sharing (*paréage*) of capitalization and lordship was the order of the day. In Gascony forty-three per cent of the new towns and villages founded from about 1250 to 1350 were planted by seigniors aided by princes, such as the count of Toulouse and the kings of France and England. The royal 'conquest' of the Dauphiny between 1274 and 1333 consisted in the Crown's acquisition of two of the larger baronies, a sharing in the erection of two large villages, or *villeneuves*, and the purchase of a part of the lordships of Gevaudan and Viviers from their bishops.

The monarchy often waited for an invitation before intervening in local society. Because of the conflict between the humbler and the wealthier, and because of pressures imposed by growing centralization, many towns were in financial difficulties after 1250. To oversimplify, lesser citizens preferred a tallage based on an individual's real property or his income, whereas the rich preferred sales and similar taxes. The conflicts between the two, and the consequent reluctance of oligarchies and plutocracies to allow the people a share in government, made town finance a hit-or-miss affair, based largely on loans or sales of communal property. Constant appeals to the Crown to adjudicate conflicts between the parties led to the royal auditing of town accounts. The records of thirty-five northern French towns were examined in 1254, and by 1262 all were being threatened with investigation. The Crown claimed impartiality, but this impartiality necessarily militated against the patricians, under whom the towns had gained their liberty. As Beaumanoir saw it:

> We have seen many struggles in the good towns of one group against another, as of the poor against the rich. . . . and the rich

seek to put all the expense [of the government] on the community of the poor. . . . [A town governor must therefore] assess the tallage in his town by loyal inquiry, on the rich as well as the poor, from each according to his means.[12]

To effect this, moreover, required a change in government because 'we see many good towns in which the poor and middling folk hold none of the administrative offices of the town, so that the rich have them all and are feared for their wealth or lineage',[12] and appoint their relatives to be the tax assessors. This explains why the Crown was warmly supported by the people against the patricians and why the monarchy not only began to tax the towns from about 1285, but also to take over their governments.

Even though the central government had begun to grow, France was still a profoundly decentralized, provincial nation. Private war was one of the principal problems faced by the central government, far more so than in relatively centralized England. Blanche of Castile had outlawed such wars in the royal domain, but the attempt to legislate for the whole of the kingdom by Louis IX in 1258 caused a general outcry. This attempt to suppress what had long been considered the rightful practice of the seigniors, of free towns, and even of villages, was not very successful. Quasi-independent provinces like Brittany paid no heed at all and sometimes the central government was itself obliged to grant exemptions from its own rules. In 1278, for example, the count of Foix refused the orders of the royal seneschal of Toulouse to cease campaigning because he had royal letters authorizing him to make war.

Much of what took place on the national level in the smaller country of England took place in France on the provincial level. Annual assizes, or *grands jours*, performed judicial and even legislative functions in many provinces. In the 1250s the regional assembly of the Agenais consisted of the proctors of the towns and of four gentlemen speaking for the barons and knights of the province. In 1254 the Crown ordered the convocation of a council of prelates, barons, knights, and two representatives to consider an embargo on the export of wine in the seneschalsy of Beaucaire. Regional or provincial custumals, or codes of local law, began to appear. The first such books were issued in Normandy in 1194

[12] *Ibid.*, 50, 1520, 1522 and 1525, ed. Salmon II, 267, 269 and 270–1.

Bruges
FLANDERS
Ghent
Arras
Cambrai
Amiens
Rouen
Beauvais
Rheims
Bayeux
NORMANDY
Chalons
Paris
CHAMPAGNE
MAINE
Troyes
BRITTANY
Sens
Le Mans
Orleans
Angers
Tours
Nantes
ANJOU
Bourges
BURGUNDY
Poitiers
Chalons
POITOU
Lyons
MARCHE
Angouleme
AQUITAINE
AUVERGNE
Le Puy
Bordeaux
TOULOUSE
Albi
Avignon
GASCONY
Montpellier
PROVENCE
Toulouse
Arles
Marseille
Narbonne
NAVARRE
ARAGON
CATALONIA

Direct royal (Capetian) government	Plantagenet house lands	Catalonia - Aragon
Northern episcopal domains closely linked to the monarchy	Plantagenet dependencies and aquisitions	French and imperial dependencies of Catalonia - Aragon
Cambrai: Area of French preponderance within the Empire	House of Toulouse-Saint Gilles	Frontier of the Kingdom of France

6. France in the 1180s.

and 1204 and in the Vermandois in 1254-58. Thereafter, in sharp
contrast to the predominance of the royal *ius commune* of England,
provincial customary law served as the basis of French jurisprudence.

Provincial separatism also figured in the way the monarchy
treated its inheritance. It will be recalled that Henry II of England

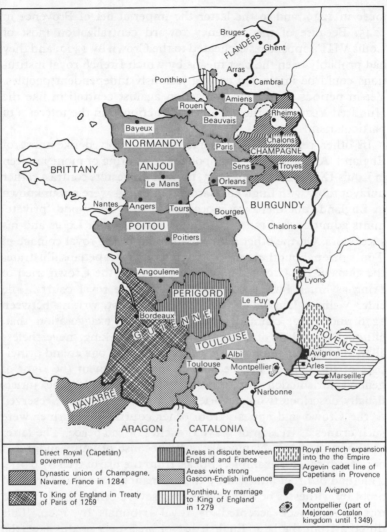

7. *France about 1310.*

Legend:
- Direct Royal (Capetian) government
- Dynastic union of Champagne, Navarre, France in 1284
- To King of England in Treaty of Paris of 1259
- Areas in dispute between England and France
- Areas with strong Gascon-English influence
- Ponthieu, by marriage to King of England in 1279
- Royal French expansion into the the Empire
- Argevin cadet line of Capetians in Provence
- Papal Avignon
- Montpellier (part of Majoraan Catalan kingdom until 1349)

made desperate attempts to divide up his continental realms to his sons' satisfaction. The same practice was known to the Capetians and was especially important at the death of Louis VIII in 1226, when his recently expanded domains were divided into appanages among his sons. The important ones were those of Poitou and Anjou; to the former was added the county of Tou-

393

louse in 1249, and to the latter the imperial fief of Provence in 1245. Because of the tendency toward centralization most of Louis VIII's appanages escheated to the Crown by 1300; and they had probably been the best means by which French royal institutions could be implanted among jealously independent peoples. Yet in periods of provincial reaction against centralism like the Hundred Years War the appanages functioned in the interests of particularism.

In other respects France's institutions evolved like those of England. An attempt to monopolize the minting of money is seen in Louis IX's ordinance of 1263, though the results contrast rather unfavourably with England. Baronial mintings were not unknown in England, but there was nothing like the thirty-odd 'private' mints admitted in France even after the efforts of Louis and his successors. On the other hand, the spread of the royal coinage of Tours throughout the areas conquered by the Capetians illustrates the gains of the Crown. As in England, also, the Crown tried to bring as much business as possible into the royal courts. The elder William Durand, a famed encyclopedist, writing between 1276 and 1287, claimed with considerable exaggeration that, although many held of the barons and not of the king, 'nevertheless all men in the kingdom of France are under the power and principate of the king of France, and he has over them the right of general jurisdiction and power'.[13] Dreams aside, the jurists usually described two categories of Crown cases: those reserved to the Crown and appeals from other courts. The former were such crimes as treason or grave breaches of the peace. The latter were appeals from seigniorial courts because of faulty judgment or procedure—for example, appeals from the use of trial by battle, a method of proof attacked by the ordinance of 1258 in favour of proof by witnesses or documents. For severe crimes Italian-style torture had been accepted by royal tribunals by 1300. This differed from the later English use of an aspect of this law (the *peine forte et dure*) in that torture was used in France as a partial proof confirming the results of a sworn inquest (*inquisitio*), whereas in England it was used to make a defendant submit himself to the judgment of an inquest jury. The English system was known in France, but principally in seigniorial courts.

[13] *Speculum juris*, tit. de feudis, n. 28, cited in Lot and Fawtier, *Histoire des institutions françaises* II, 220n.

Another similarity with England was the attempt of the Crown —as early as 1181—to require service from all the nation's inhabitants, whether or not direct vassals of the king. Here the monarchy fell back on a tradition derived from Carolingian times and sanctified in most regional customs, namely that in a *defensio patriae* the prince could call on the service of everyone. The later Capetians and the early Valois tried to use this tradition to force those who did not serve to pay a compensatory tax. Until the scheme collapsed in the 'feudal' and provincial reaction against the central government of the early fourteenth century it seemed so useful that, as in modern states, every war, no matter how aggressive, was described as a defence of the fatherland. Furthermore, the close relationship between service and taxation reminds us that, from the 1290s on, the Crown tried to foster two tax resources, sales taxes (*aides*) and tallage in lieu of service. The general principle was stated in the *Book of Justice and of Pleas*: all men owed service for reason of the common profit and the defence of the whole kingdom.

As government grew, governmental machinery became more complex. From the mid-twelfth century, when most local administration was given over to hereditary provosts or to provost-ships farmed out to towns such as Paris, the change toward centralized control was spectacular. Emerging from *missi*— an imitation of the Plantagenet itinerant justices—sent out to strengthen local administration and to police the provosts, the non-hereditary *baillis*, first mentioned in an edict of 1190, became the provincial governors of France in the course of the early thirteenth century. As other regions were conquered from Poitou through the Midi, similar functions were given to officers called seneschals in imitation of Plantagenet titles. From 1229 these provincial governors had judges associated with them who, by 1270, had become almost independent of their chiefs, so complex had the law become. The investigative functions of the early *baillis* were now carried on by officers, some clerical and some lay, sent out from the king's court to report on provincial administration. These were the *enquêteurs* (*missi, inquisitores*) made celebrated by Louis IX's inquiries of 1247. The grandeur of this government is shown by the fact that France's *baillis* and seneschals were far more highly paid than comparable officers in England. There were also family traditions of such service. Son of a knight and *bailli* of the Gatinais, Philip of Remi, lord of Beaumanoir, served as *bailli* or seneschal in Clermont-en-Beauvaisis, Poitou, Saintonge, Vermandois, Touraine, and Senlis.

The king's court likewise grew, later than that of England, although eventually more rapidly. Until 1295 the treasury was entrusted to the Templars of Paris. The 'men of the accounts' or exchequer, slowly emerged and began to exercise their judicial powers from about 1285. By 1306 the *chambre de comptes* had sixteen members, more than the English exchequer. By the middle of the thirteenth century, the mixed ecclesiastical and lay tribunal of the king (*parlement*) had become resident at Paris and had begun to grow rapidly. By 1296 there were fifty-one resident judges, and by 1319 sixty-nine, numbers that compare strikingly with the four or five justices of the Common Pleas and the three on the King's Bench across the Channel. Especially significant was the size of the Chamber of Inquiries, the part of the *parlement* that investigated cases brought to the Crown from lesser courts. It indicates the degree to which the king was asked to intervene and arbitrate in the quarrels of French local society. Of the sixty-nine judges of the *parlement* in 1319 forty were in this chamber. The procedures of this court were more complex than comparable ones in England. The investigation into the provisions of local law was made by a judicially summoned inquest of sworn residents (*inquisitio in turba*); the investigation into the facts of the case and the final judgment were made by an *inquisitio* conducted by a board of these professional judges.

The level of legal professionalization surpassed that of England by 1300. For the first time in western history a school of Roman law developed beyond the Alps that had much to teach the Italians. The work of James of Revigny (d. 1296) and of Peter of Belleperche (d. 1308), both teachers at Toulouse and then at Orléans, was strongly influenced by the systematic and dialectical approach of the philosophers at Paris. This method was transmitted to Cino of Pistoia, the teacher of the most celebrated lawyer of them all, Bartolo of Sassoferrato. In France as in England, there was also a strong reaction against Roman law. Elicited from the pope by Philip II, the decretal *Super specula* of 1219 forbade its study at Paris. But, as in England, the study of this normative jurisprudence could not really be stifled. French juristic doctrine on this point is summed up in a royal edict of 1312:

Our kingdom is especially ruled by custom and *mores*, not by the written law; although in certain parts subject to this kingdom, by the permission of our progenitors and selves, the written laws are used in many cases, they do not bind as written law, but as a custom introduced in the [local] *mores* following the model of the written law. Furthermore, as the study of the liberal arts introduces a student to the science of theology, so does the teaching of the *leges* and the written law perfect reason's understanding . . . and prepare [the mind] for the understanding of local customs . . . ; it therefore pleases us that[14]

Roman law should be taught in places other than Paris.

The result was that provincial customary law was deeply influenced by Roman legal norms. The custumal of the Orléanais called *The Book of Justice and of Pleas* was not only modelled on Justinian's *Digest*, but 195 of its 342 titles were lifted from that book, and thirty-one others from the decretals of Gregory IX, although these foreign sources were camouflaged as enactments of French princes or judgments by French judges. Yet French law was not like the normative Roman law taught in the Italian schools or even the procedural *ius commune* of the English. It was a provincial law. The French governors were not merely jurists or administrators, they were also French gentlemen. Beaumanoir was a great jurist not only because of his knowledge of law, but also because he brought to his *Customs of Clermont-en-Beauvaisis* of 1283 a mind schooled in poetry and therefore interpolated into his lawbook wonderful tales and striking exemplars. A recruit from the aristocracy of the old domain, like others in French service, Beaumanoir believed he could judge the actions of his king. He refused to record a royal edict in his book because it contravened the public interest. A *bailli* must obey all the commands of his lord, he says, save for those

for which he may lose his soul if he does them, for the obedience he owes is to be understood as doing right and maintaining loyal justice. Nor will a *bailli* be excused before God if he wrongs his own conscience following the command of his lord, and it is better for such an officer to leave the service than that, because of a command or anything else, he wrongs his conscience.[15]

[14] Cited in Emile Chénon, *Histoire générale du droit français publique et privé* (Paris, 1926), I, 510n.
[15] *Coutumes de Clermont-en-Beauvaisis* I, 18, ed. Salmon, I, 22.

397

Lest too idyllic a picture be conjured up, it should be remembered that many offices were farmed out to their occupants in the same manner as was the office of sheriff in England. In France this was not true of the great officers like the *baillis*, seneschals, and their judges, but the lesser ones were often sold or farmed. Moral rigorists railed against this practice, one that the republican Brunetto Latini said was characteristic of all monarchy. Even those who excused it, like Thomas Aquinas, thought that it was a bad habit and one that could be indulged in by a prince only 'if it can be presumed of those [to whom the offices are sold] that they are suitable for the exercises of such offices and that the offices are not sold at so high a price that [the investment] cannot be recovered without burdening your subjects'.[16] The reports of Louis IX's *enquêteurs* record many complaints concerning the extortion and tyranny of these lesser officers. A curious example is the complaint of a farmer named Durand from the village of Langlade in the seneschalcy of Beaucaire. Harassed by a royal officer, he determined to depart from the village, together with his mother and his brother. Meeting them at the gate, the officer told them that they could go, but that he would get them. Durand made the mistake of replying: 'You'll get what you deserve. I want to leave this town and quit it, because I can't live in peace with you who bedevil me night and day.' The officer exploded: 'Wouldn't it be fine if the mouths of you and your brother were stuffed *de merda* so that you couldn't bellow or breathe *nisi per anum*,'[17] and, sweeping a cowflop off the ground, he suited his actions to his words at the expense of the open-mouthed farmer. The *enquêteurs* found for the peasant.

On the whole, France was the happiest monarchy of thirteenth-century Europe—one reason for the canonization of Louis IX in 1297. But the motive for John of Joinville's 1309 biography of the sainted king was partly to condemn the monarchy of Philip IV the Fair (1285–1314). The honeymoon of the Capetians and the French people was suddenly ending. French society needed the arbitrative and centralizing functions of the Crown but had thought it would cost less than it did. Like the English earlier, the French wanted the functions but did not want to pay for them.

[16] *De regimine Judaeorum* 5, in R. M. Spiazzi, *Opuscula philosophica* (1954), 250b.
[17] Cited in Robert Michel, *L'Administration royale dans la sénéchaussée de Beaucaire* (Paris, 1910), 88.

In spite of France's great success, the air resounded with complaints about maladministration and illicit taxes by the time of Philip IV. The king, said Joinville and Peter Dubois, should live of his own, but the old domain and tax structure were not enough to finance the new services required of the state. If the crown was richer than it had been before, it was far poorer in terms of its needs. In 1203 its income is estimated to have been 179,000 pounds of Paris and its expenses 95,000. In 1292 it took in 589,000 pounds and spent 687,000, and was in debt to everyone. The hand-to-mouth financing characteristic of the later medieval age of crisis had begun.

So hard put was the monarchy to make ends meet that it began to kill the geese that laid the golden eggs. The repeated expropriations of the Jews and of the Lombards are examples of this. The Templars, like the Lombards great creditors of the monarchy, were attacked and their properties held by the Crown from 1307 to 1313. The Crown tried to float forced loans throughout France, and, in 1295 in a desperate attempt to raise money, began to debase the coinage stabilized by Louis IX. Even the urge toward freedom was mocked by a desperate government. The farmers on the royal domain—indeed, anywhere within reach of the government—were forced to buy their freedom at the cost of their land and other means of livelihood.

If the real attack on the structure of the new monarchy awaited the reaction by the provincial aristocracies and free towns at the accession of the Valois dynasty in 1328, the beginnings of disintegration were already being seen. In so far as it worked—and it was growing—royal taxation was successful only because local society shared in the proceeds. In 1296 the princes of great fiefs like Flanders and Burgundy were given half of the subvention raised, a hundred-odd great barons were given a third, and lesser seigniors were given a quarter. Reaction against royal centralization was everywhere to be seen. The *parlement* of Toulouse began to develop independently between 1278 and 1303. In 1302 the seigniors and towns of the Auvergne supported the Crown's attack on the Roman Church but demanded in exchange the confirmation of their local customs and the local recruiting of Crown officers. This reaction against the new monarchy was partly expressed in an estates movement, similar to that in England. What was most typical of France, however, was provincial separatism, which revived the appanage with far more detrimental effect than in the past and invited the intervention of the English into French affairs during the Hundred Years War.

Monarchs and councils or parliaments

Intellectuals had much to say about monarchy, arguing for and against a prince's prerogatives. Cino of Pistoia remarked that there was no clear consensus among the lawyers even on the *lex regia*, which stated that the people had surrendered to the prince its right to make the law, and that what pleases a prince has the force of law: 'John [Bassianus] said that today the Roman people cannot make law . . . Ugolino said the opposite. The ordinary gloss approves John's opinion . . . Certain moderns hold with Ugolino . . . Now, choose which of these opinions pleases you, because I don't care.'[18] Opinions were as much divided among the philosophers and theologians as among the jurists. They rarely committed themselves wholly to one form of government, that is —to use the Aristotelian terms of the thirteenth century—to monarchy, aristocracy, or democracy. Some, like Giles of Rome, were primarily monarchists. Others, like Ptolemy of Lucca, were primarily republicans. Wiser than either, Thomas Aquinas was of many minds, depending on his audience. Addressed to a prince, his tract on monarchy does not praise electoral government. In his other works, however, he praises it.

Monarchy was the principal form of government in the period with which this book deals and it had been the only form of government in the early Middle Ages. In spite of that, the earlier age had willed to the men of the late twelfth century a rich political tradition. Monarchy was often elective in the early Middle Ages, and law was often issued by the prince with the express consent of the 'people', as in the Carolingian assembly at Pîtres in 864. To the tenth century Hincmar of Rheims not all monarchies were of divine foundation. He cheerfully conjectured that many princes had been elected and removed by their citizens and soldiers. Leaning on Augustine, he opined that princes were under the law

---

[18] Cited in Cortese, *La norma giuridica* II, 130. John Bassianus (d. 1197) and Ugolino (d. about 1233) both taught at Bologna. The ordinary gloss was by Accursius (*c.* 1259). The *lex regia* and its variants are to be found in the *Digest* I, 4, 1, 1, the *Code* I, 17, 1, 7, and in the *Institutes* I, 2, 5.

and not above it. It was with such doctrines—all basically derived from Jerome and Augustine—that the Gregorian revolution had been waged. Manegold of Lauterbach (d. about 1103) had argued that words such as 'king', 'duke' and 'count' were names of offices not necessarily transmissible by nature or dynasty; and he maintained that the persons who held these offices could and should be removed if they broke their contract (*pactum*) with the people to serve and protect them. This tradition was later expressed by the canonist Rufinus: 'Whence when a king is instituted, a certain tacit pact is initiated between him and the people, so that the king governs the people and the people remember to honour the king with established tribute and services'.[19] A child of revolution, Manegold had gone further, likening the prince to a hired swineherd who could be dismissed for incompetence or dishonesty.

During the twelfth and thirteenth centuries much was added to this tradition. The revival of Roman law amplified the number of texts of use to monarchists and to their opponents. The republican tradition was strengthened by the study of Aristotle, whose *Politics* was translated in 1260, and whose thought had been echoed in some of the Arabs translated earlier. Furthermore, by the early thirteenth century the contrast between monarchism and republicanism was much clearer than it had been before. The centralization of the economy was strengthening the monarchies that, with the exception of the Empire, were becoming frankly hereditary. On the other hand, there were real working republics in Italy and a form of government of a republican character was to be seen in almost every western town. The expansion of Europe had widened the horizons of Latin thinkers and they were consequently able to think of political institutions or systems comparatively. Brunetto Latini compared the institutions of monarchy and the republics in his *Tresor*. When writing his continuation of Thomas Aquinas's *On the Rule of Princes* around 1305, Ptolemy of Lucca not only did the same but also exhibited an understanding of comparative institutions. Ptolemy treated the Church as one of the types of monarchy, distinguished between electoral and

[19] *De bono pacis* 2, 9 in *PL* CL, 1617c. Germain Morin, 'Le discours d'ouverture du concile général de Latran 1179', *Atti della pontificia accademia romana di archeologia*, ser. 3, Memorie 2 (1928), 124ff., identifies this Rufinus with the canonist who became archbishop of Sorrento in 1180. Migne and others hold to an Italian bishop who wrote in the 1060s. The question is not of much significance here.

hereditary monarchy, and noted that in Hungary and Spain kings were bound by the law of the land and were not infrequently overthrown if they disobeyed it. He also digressed to describe the government of Egypt and its importation of slaves to constitute an administrative and martial élite. In these circumstances the institution of monarchy and thought about that institution matured rapidly.

To thirteenth-century thinkers monarchy was a form of government in which the people delegated their powers to one man for life. Writing on prelatry in 1283–84, Salimbene of Parma employed an often cited passage of Gregory I: 'Indeed, man by nature is a ruler over brute animals, but not over other men, and he is therefore taught that he is to be feared by animals but not by other men, because it is a crime against nature to wish to be feared by an equal.'[20] From this and other assertions about the natural equality and freedom of men evolved arguments as to the nature of the monarchical magistracy. One question was about whether a prince should be feared or loved by his subjects. Obsessed with Plantagenet tyranny, Gerald of Wales asserted that a true prince must be loved and not feared. Although known for his gentle personal manners, Roger II, king of Naples and Sicily (d. 1154), was proud to be feared by his subjects.

More consequential, however, was the argument about whether a prince should be elected or succeed dynastically. On this the theorists divided, but the central tradition of the ecclesiastical intellectuals who addressed themselves to this question was in favour of electoral monarchy. In his general textbook, the *Summa theologiae*, Thomas Aquinas proposes that law can be made either by the multitude or by the agent representing it. Elsewhere in the same work he praises the ancient constitution of the Jews, who were governed by a prince aided by a group of elders or seigniors (*seniores*), all chosen from the people.

> For this is the best of all polities, being a mixture of monarchy, in so far as one leads, of aristocracy, in so far as many rule according to virtue, and of democracy, that is, of the power of the people, in so far as the rulers are to be chosen from the popular elements and the election of these rulers pertains to the people.[21]

[20] *Liber de praelato* in his *Cronicon* in *MGH. SS.* XXXII, 120.
[21] *Summa theologiae* I–II, 105, I, c.

In short, Thomas thought the ideal monarchy was an elective one.

There were also those who supported the Germanic national and imperial tradition, however weak the actual Empire may have been. In his *Otia imperialia*, Gervais of Tilbury noted a vice of hereditary monarchy, one that was also mentioned by the later Ptolemy of Lucca, namely, that the subordinate officers of a hereditary prince tend to be hereditary also. Gervais praised Tiberius Caesar for telling provincial governors who wished to increase taxes that good shepherds shear their sheep but do not flay them. He then went on:

> For surely the Roman republic was far more wisely defended when the government was obtained by election and not by succession, and the governors of each of its provinces acted in a much more restrained manner when they ruled for a term because they feared to lose the power committed to them relatively easily (*de facili occasione*). But now paternal succession calls to government immature infants, inconstant, harsh, impious fellows, and authors of all sorts of levity, who do not believe themselves to rule as a duty imposed by God, but rather as a right owed to them by nature.[22]

Useful for helping to define the government of the Church and for the ruling of the urban republics of the time, these electoral traditions were not of much use in the monarchies which were, as we have seen, becoming more openly hereditary in this period. This was not only because economic centralization fostered the development of the stronger, hereditary form of the institution of monarchy, but also because the counterpoise of ecclesiastical power made it unnecessary for men to seek freedom by replacing monarchy by the republican form of government. It is to be noted that in western Europe the monarchies were not transformed into republics until several centuries after the Reformation, when the Church no longer existed as a viably independent institution. In the monarchies of the thirteenth century, therefore, the problem was not that of doing away with monarchy, but rather that of controlling the powers of the prince.

The debate over princely power took many forms. It was asked whether a prince had a monopoly of all the power delegated to him by the 'people' or—as William Durand the Younger put it—

[22] Published by G. C. Leibnitz, *Scriptores rerum Brunsvicensium* (Hannover, 1707), 902.

was merely a person of superior authority, like Scipio in the Roman republic, who, although he surpassed all other members of society, was not more powerful than the people as a whole. The theorists usually held that the wisdom of the whole people was greater than that of any individual. There were, however, some like Peter of Auvergne, rector of the University of Paris in 1275, who never missed an opportunity of pointing out how vicious or incapable the people were. Besides, the jurists found that the *lex regia* sanctified the notion that, once surrendered, the power of the people was forever lost to the prince, and hence his judgments could not be questioned. Other jurists expatiated on the *lex digna* (*Code* 1, 14, 4), in which the prince confessed himself to be bound by the law. And if the definition of the *lex regia* held that a prince was not so bound, it was usually admitted, as it was by Frederick II Hohenstaufen to the inhabitants of Rome in 1238, that a prince was bound by the mother of law, that is, by natural reason. To sum up this interminable debate, it was generally admitted in theory that in case of grave necessity the people could recover their power and an unsuitable prince be removed.

To be given reverence a prince must be fit, that is, defend the faith, possess moral and practical capacity, and serve the commonweal. If he is tyrannical, serving only his own interest, he robs his subjects of life, liberty, property and position, thus precipitating the withdrawal of obedience so pithily described by Jerome long before: 'For the phrase of the speaker to Domitian is well known: "Why should I," he said, "treat you as a prince when you don't treat me as a senator?" '[23] And the matter could be expressed even more strongly. John of Salisbury declared that sacred Scripture teaches us that it is licit and even glorious to kill a tyrant. Thomas Aquinas said that a revolt against a tyrant was not a mortal sin or sedition:

And so the upsetting of this kind of government cannot be considered sedition unless by chance the government is so inordinately disturbed that the subject multitude suffers more from the ensuing disturbances than from the tyrant's government. For a tyrant who nourishes discords and seditions among the people subject to him that he may more safely rule them is really more seditious.[24]

---

[23] The text was carried in Gratian's *Decretum* 1, 95, 7 in *CICan* 1, 334.
[24] *Summa theologiae* II–II, 42, 2, ad 3.

Certainly, no individual should be permitted to seize power illicitly. Speaking of the assassination of Caesar, Thomas says:

> For Cicero is talking about the occasion when someone violently seizes the government when the subjects do not want that to happen or when they agree to it only because they are coerced, and when there is no recourse to a superior by whom he may be judged to be a usurper; then whoever kills a tyrant to liberate the fatherland is to be praised and to receive the reward.[25]

Things rarely reached the point of tyrannicide, however, and therefore practical mechanisms by which the incidence of princely power could be regulated were of much greater importance. One of these mechanisms was trial by peers. In its application to the relationship between a prince and his subject or a lord and his vassal the principle was based on a combination of ancient ideas, namely, that no more than any man should a prince be the judge of his own case, and that when a freeman is defending his rights he should be judged by his equals. This principle was embodied in England's *Magna carta* of 1215 and was also common on the continent. In France, for example, the *Establishments of St Louis*, a compilation of customary law in 1272–73, admitted the right of a gentleman to be judged by his peers when sued by the king in a royal court concerning his inheritance.

On a grander scale, the institutional development that enabled a prince and a whole social order or group to settle their disputes was the emergence out of the old royal or princely court of large assemblies representing society's powerful elements. These invariably exercised judicial functions. In the *cortes* or parliament of Benavente in 1202, for example, the king of Leon reported that 'the content of the case both of my party and that of the knights and others having been heard, judgment was rendered between me and them' by the prelates, vassals, and representatives of the towns there assembled.[26] Decisions of this kind could also be entrusted to a special officer whose decisions were to be submitted to an annual judicial review. From 1265 on the king of Aragon chose an officer called the *justicia mayor* from among the lesser nobles. This officer tried the cases in which the interests of the

[25] *Commentum in quatuor libros sententiarum Magistri Petri Lombardi* 2, 44, 2, 2, ad 5 in A. Passerin d'Entrèves, *Scritti politici*, 93–4.
[26] Juan Beneyto Perez, *Testos politicos españoles de la baja edad media* (Madrid, 1944), 202, No. 532.

Crown and its principal subjects conflicted, and he could not be removed save by a vote of the *cortes*. By the Golden Bull of 1222 in Hungary, the lesser nobles assembled in the annual general meeting were to review the actions and decisions of the king and of his chief justiciar, the *comes palatii*. Princely resistance to this kind of examination led to statements maintaining the subject's right to withdraw his allegiance. Celebrated examples are the final chapter of England's *Magna carta* or the thirty-first chapter of the Golden Bull mentioned above.

But the judging of disputes is secondary to the promulgation of the law by which judgments are made. Here, too, the older medieval tradition helped. Princes had traditionally issued new law with the assent or advice of the officers and magnates assembled in their courts. This procedure needed only some institutional development to be useful in the new context of the centralizing state. The conciliar character of princely legislation was based on contradictory motives, however. The prince's dream was to communicate his commands to as large a number of his subjects as possible: the subject should come to hear and go home to obey. When Roger II of Naples and Sicily (d. 1154) met his notables at Ariano he informed them that 'we therefore wish and command that you will receive faithfully and obey expeditiously the sanctions we have caused to be shown to the present assembly'.[27] The subjects were of a different opinion. Princes sometimes voluntarily recognized this. In his great assemblies at Foggia in 1225 and 1234 Frederick II invited the participants to submit their complaints (*gravamina*) against the royal administration or its officers. The position taken by the subjects was based on the concept of most political philosophers that a prince should not make new laws without consent. Sometimes the consenting court was a small body. Writing on the daily actions of popes and princes, William Durand the Younger remarks that 'it appears to be wise for the republic and for the administrators of the republic that they should limit their power under reason, and that, without the council of the lord cardinals, the lord pope and, without the council of other prudent men, kings and princes'[28] should not use their plenitude of power to abrogate old law or issue new law. A more generous formulation is seen in the first book of the

[27] Cited in Cortese, *op. cit.*, II, 235n.
[28] *De modo generalis concilii celebrandi* 1, 4, 4 in *TUJ* XIII, 155va.

Siete partidas of Alphonso X of Castile, where a prince is forbidden to issue new laws without the consent of the 'people'. What this meant in practice may be instanced by the *cortes* of Barcelona in 1283, when the prince confessed that 'if we or our successors should wish to make any general constitution or statute in Catalonia, we will do this with the approbation and consent of the prelates, barons, knights, and citizens of Catalonia or of the larger or saner part of those summoned [to the *cortes*]'.[29]

A variety of matters was dealt with in such assemblies. Humbert of Romans says that kings held great courts several times a year to handle important business requiring broad advice, to hear accounts rendered by those who served the Crown, and to issue what edicts were necessary for the good of the realm. More specific was the concession made by Alphonso IX of Leon at his accession in 1188. He informed his subjects that he would not make war or peace or hear important suits without the consent of the bishops, nobles, and worthy folk of the towns. Avid exponents of councils for other princes, the popes had a keen eye in these matters. In 1267 Clement IV regretted that the king of Naples and Sicily had raised heavy taxes without the advice and free assent of the prelates, barons, and notable inhabitants of his cities and towns. In his commentary on the Decretals of Gregory IX, Innocent IV maintained that princes should not debase coinage without the consent of the people or its major part. In 1228 the patriarch of Aquileia, prince of the March of Friuli, refers to fortifications, public works, and roads constructed on the advice of his assembly of prelates, nobles, *ministeriales* (lesser nobles), and the citizens of the towns. When a dynasty became extinct, the change to a new house came under the purview of the magnates or the 'people'. Rarer, because under the emperor, was the right won by 1300 of the *ministeriales* of Styria (there, the great nobles) to determine who was to replace the local prince were the dynasty to run out. In general, then, what was treated in such assemblies was new dispositions or enactments—in the medieval phrase, *nova jura*. This was stated in the imperial decision of Worms that preceded the *Statute in favour of the princes* of 1231–32. The assembly meeting at Worms was asked to consider the following question:

[29] Perez, *op.cit.*, 304, No. 542.

If any of the princes of the land (*domini terrae*) can make constitutions or new laws without the consent of the better or more important people of the land? With the consent of the princes, it was so defined concerning this question: that neither princes nor anyone else can make constitutions or new laws unless the better and more important people of the land have first agreed.[30]

The conciliar or parliamentary movement of the thirteenth century not only defined *nova jura* with increasing exactitude but also created formal systems of representation. Since not everyone could attend, representatives whose action bound the electors at home were everywhere known by about 1250. Within the assembly the principle that a majority vote bound the whole body came to be accepted, with the support of Ulpian's famous statement to this effect in the civil law's *regula juris*. More significant than either of these necessary but almost automatic mechanisms was a more mature grasp of social differentiations. In the past it had been customary to refer to the action or advice of the magnates or, alternatively, of the 'people'. In the thirteenth century distinctions were made between the nobles and the commons, and even among subdivisions of these groups. Simple terms took on more complex meaning. An example is the word 'people'. A canonist of the early thirteenth century tells his reader:

Note that there is a difference between the people (*populus*) and the *plebs* which is the same as that between an animal and a man or between a genus and a species. For nobles and non-nobles collected together constitute the *populus*. The *plebs* is where there are no senators or men of consular dignity. . . . Those senior in birth are defined in three ways, by nobility, dignity, or antiquity.[31]

The prelates and greater barons had always been members of the kings' courts and were naturally fitted into the new assemblies. Sometimes, as in Castile and France, all gentlefolk, baronial and knightly, formed one body. Elsewhere the lesser nobility or gentry were distinguished from the greater, presumably because

---

[30] *MGH. Legum sectio IV* II, 420, No. 305.
[31] *Summa 'antiquitate et tempore,'* cited in Post, *Studies in Medieval Legal Thought*, 374–5n. The unknown jurist is commenting on a phrase of Isidore of Seville in the *Decretum* 1, 2, 1 in *CICan* I, 3. The remote source of this distinction is *Institutes* 1, 2, 4, and, in regard to antiquity, Aristotle, *Politics* 5, 1.

the latter were traditionally members of the prince's court or because they possessed important courts and jurisdictions of their own. This was the case in England, where two representative knights were drawn from each county to sit in the Commons as that house began to take shape in the later thirteenth century. This sense of being representatives of a collectivity was presumably the reason why the polemical author of the early-fourteenth-century *Modus tenendi parliamentum* felt that the knights (as well as the representatives of the boroughs and the proctors of the lesser clergy) represented the community of England, whereas the barons and prelates were there only for their own persons. In parts of Spain this sense of their order's importance was earlier and more vigorously expressed by the *caballeros*, or knights, and by the townsmen. At the assembly of Barbastro in 1192 Catalonia's knights were constituted as a separate arm (*brazo*), distinct from the magnates (*ricoshombres*) and the citizens of the towns. This also happened in Aragon and in Friuli in Italy. In Aragon the clergy did not constitute a *brazo* until the fourteenth century. There, as in England, the lesser clergy usually met in their own convocations or synods, while the prelates having jurisdictions, and therefore considered to be barons, always met with the national assembly.

Representation from towns was also varied. In England the formula of two representatives for each borough appeared for the first time in 1265. In Frederick II's parliaments of Foggia the cities and fortified villages (*castella*) each sent two representatives in 1232, and in 1240 each city sent two and each *castellum* one. Decentralized France had a late start, and rashly attempted to get everybody into its early general parliaments (forerunners of the estates general). The parliament of 1307–08 contained prelates, barons and representatives of no less than 558 towns and villages in northern France.

There was no uniformity about how often assemblies met. Emulating old princely courts and the general assemblies in Italian towns, some assemblies hoped to meet four times a year. This was impracticable for general assemblies, but smaller select councils often did meet three or four times yearly, as in England's constitutional crises of Simon de Montfort's time. In Catalonia a *cortes* at Barcelona in 1283 decreed an annual great assembly, but a later meeting at Lerida in 1301 wisely determined that once every third year would be enough, save in case of public necessity. The need to follow up decisions taken in parliament involved choosing councillors to sit with the prince. Even before there was a parliament in England, twenty-five notables (of whom four were to remain permanently beside the king) were elected by the barons at Runnymede to check on the implementations of *Magna carta*. In the troubled time of the baronial wars from 1258 to 1265 more elaborate arrangements were made. An interlocking system of councils of four, twelve, and fifteen members, partly chosen by the king and partly by the barons, policed the working of the 'reforms' and the issuance of *nova jura*. The chief officers of state —the treasurer, chancellor and chief justiciar—were to be chosen jointly by the king and barons and were to participate in the work of these councils. These revolutionary arrangements did not last in England, but they show which way the wind was blowing. In 1287 the king of Aragon conceded that the *cortes* of Saragossa should meet yearly and that it, together with the proctors of the town of Saragossa, should choose the king's councillors, 'with whose council we and our successors will govern and administer the realms of Aragon, Valencia and Ribagorza'.[32] Warring with Venice over Trieste in 1283, the patriarch of Aquileia called his parliament of prelates, nobles (*liberi*), *ministeriales*, and townsfolk. Together they chose a commission of twenty-four members, six from each group, and the prince bound himself to carry out whatever it determined about the waging of the war and the condition of the land.

The parliamentary trend is also evidence of the degree of centralization achieved by 1300. The movement was most successful in the smaller, less populous realms of Latin Europe. In the larger or more populous monarchies the impulse toward conciliarism had a provincial or particularist character. In France provincial assizes and assemblies like those of Agen appeared early and were more systematized than the national assemblies, which had hardly begun before 1290. In Italy particular realms, like Friuli, the kingdom of Naples, and Sicily under the Catalans after 1282, were the centres of conciliarism. In Germany similar institutions were to appear in the local principates. Except in territories to the north and east, however, notably in Brunswick-Lüneburg, Pomerania, and Bohemia, where there were assemblies

[32] Perez, *op. cit.*, 249, No. 453.

of the clergy, nobility and townsfolk in the 1280s and 1290s, German conciliarism moved slowly. There the towns and knightly families sought to escape the princes' control in a more traditional way, by claiming that they held directly of the emperor.

In 1300 no one could have guessed that the parliamentary trend would weaken. It had grown rapidly in the thirteenth century and was to continue growing well into the fourteenth. But weaknesses were already evident. The early years of Frederick II Hohenstaufen's reign in Naples and Sicily were notable for the number and importance of the parliaments assembled, but as the war with Rome and northern Italy became more intense Frederick ceased calling them, presumably because they might have opposed his heavy drafts on their resources. But this is not the whole story. In the latter half of the fourteenth century, the time of Latin Europe's general social crisis, the parliamentary trend began to weaken almost everywhere. Increasing warfare required a hard, strong government that could trammel people's rights in order to protect the people. The crisis also evoked intense internal social wars. What was needed was the creation of a separate estate, the estate royal, to subdue and arbitrate social conflict by coercion. This estate—the prince or dynasty—was an agency created by society having as its advantage the fact that its interest was only itself and not that of any one other group, class or part of society. Except for a final burst of effort in the fifteenth century, and except in relatively small or peripheral areas like England, parts of Spain, southern Italy and eastern Germany where aristocratic resistance was able to contain the monarchy or principate, the parliamentary or conciliar trend was to fail everywhere. Frederick II Hohenstaufen was a foretaste of the monarchy to come just as, as we shall see, the seigniors of the Italian towns were a foretaste of the future principate.

In spite of what the future was to bring, most western Europeans of around 1300 would have patted themselves on the back and have applauded the sentiment of Marsiglio of Padua when he wrote that, unlike the monarchies or tyrannies of the servile peoples of the east, 'royal monarchy is a temperate form of government in which the ruler is a single man deferring to the common good and to the will or consensus of his subjects'.[33] And even the monarchist Giles of Rome opined that a prince must

[33] *Defensor pacis* I, 8 in *MGH. SS. in usum scholarum* I, 38.

have counsel to determine great questions and affairs—law, war, taxes, public safety and the supply of food. Because, he said, one man cannot know as much as many and because one is more easily corrupted than many, a good prince must associate many counsellors with himself in a kind of partnership (*societas*), thus becoming 'one man with many eyes, many hands, and many feet'.[34]

[34] *De regimine principum* 3, 2, 4 in Rome 1607, 460; see also 3, 2, 4 and 3, 2, 17–19.

XII

Seigniory and Town

Village and town

Writing his *Reconquest of the Holy Land* in 1306, the French
publicist Peter Dubois complained that Europe was divided
among rival princes, and, far worse, among warring towns, led by
those of Lombardy and Tuscany. He asked the question: 'But
since these cities and the many princes that do not recognize any
superior on earth . . . will zealously stir up disputes, before whom
will they litigate or proceed in law?'[1] Dubois answered that a

[1] *De recuperatione terre sancte* 12, ed. C.-V. Langlois (Paris, 1891), 10.

BIBLIOGRAPHY. For the medieval village and small town, see the bibliography to
chapter VII above and K. S. Bader, *Studien zur Rechtsgeschichte des mittelalterlichen
Dorfes*, 2 vols. (Weimar, 1957–62). On the towns consult the same bibliographical
note and recent reprints of M. V. Clarke, *The Medieval City State: an essay on
tyranny and federation in the later Middle Ages* (Cambridge, 1926) and Henri Pirenne,
*Early Democracies in the Low Countries: urban society and political conflict in the
Middle Ages and Renaissance* (London, 1915, trans. from French original dated
1910). Because the republican form was most developed in north and central Italy,
most attention has been given to that region. Daniel Waley, *The Italian City-
Republics* (London, 1969), provides a good introduction to the subject. The
treatment in this chapter has been designed to find the mean between the classical
class analysis of political events typified by Gaetano Salvemini, *Magnati e popolani
in Firenze dal 1280 al 1295* (Florence, 1899, reprinted in 1960 without the appendix
of published documents) and the prosographical analysis of Niccolà Ottokar,
Il comune di Firenze alla fine del dugento (Florence, 1933) by making use of the
testimony of contemporary jurists and theorists. Two of these have been seen
through others' eyes, Mussato through those of Nicolai Rubinstein, 'Some ideas on
municipal progress and decline in the Italy of the communes', D. J. Gordon, ed.,
Fritz Saxl, 1890–1948: a volume of memorial essays (Edinburgh, 1957), 165–83, and
Remigio through those of C. T. Davis, 'An early Florentine political theorist: Fra
Remigio de' Girolami,' *Proceedings of the American Philosophical Society* CIV (1960),
662ff. Other than primary sources, guidance in the relationship of law to constitutional matters was acquired from the study by Cortese mentioned in the
bibliography of the preceding chapter, Georg Dahm's distillation of his larger work
on criminal law in his small *Untersuchungen zur Verfassungs- und Strafrechtsgeschichte
der italienischen Stadt in Mittelalter* (Hamburg, 1941) and from Ernst Salzer's
irreplaceable *Über die Anfänge der Signorie in Oberitalien* (Berlin, 1900).

council of Europe should order all conflicting parties to cease from making war. Their disputes were to be put before arbiters elected by the parties, with a possible appeal to the pope if arbitration proved unsatisfactory. To Dubois, the enemies of peace, the enemies who prevented Europe from uniting to crush Islam, were independent princes, lords and towns. Like Dante he had in mind what had happened to the Empire. It had been destroyed by the German princely states—independent in fact, if not yet in law —and by the Italian urban republics. The latter were his particular bane. Beaumanoir had a similar view. The Empire had collapsed in Lombardy, he said, because urban patricians, men of high lineage, had plotted against the emperor. Both thinkers hated those who disrupted the unitary structure of monarchy.

Happier with the political structures of his time and perhaps inspired by Aristotle—himself a man who examined a highly decentralized society—Ptolemy of Lucca had a different view. Completing Thomas Aquinas's *On the Rule of Princes* around 1305, Ptolemy not only changed the whole bias of the work, but also described with sympathy and understanding the kind of decentralized political structure that existed in Italy. In most of northern and central Italy government took the form of urban republics, whose officers were elected for short terms:

> In the regions of Liguria, Aemilia and Flaminia, which are today called Lombardy, no lifetime government is to be found unless by way of tyranny, with the exception of that of the Doge of Venice who nevertheless has a temperate government. Whence government by short-term office is the one most suitable for these regions.[2]

Even where the imperial tradition still meant something,

> counts and other princes, unless perhaps they tyrannize by violence, must rule in the republican style [*more politico et civili*]. There are to be found among them, however, certain titles of dignity depending upon imperial right by which they have jurisdiction over their subjects, although today this authority is diminished or almost wholly eliminated because of the power of the cities.[3]

[2] *De regimine principum* 4, 8, ed. Spiazzi, *Opuscula philosophica*, 336a. By temperate government, the author means that the Doge was elected for a life term. Ptolemy or Bartholomeo Fiadoni was a Dominican associate of Thomas Aquinas who died in 1327 as bishop of Torcello.
[3] *De regimine principum* 3, 22, ed. Spiazzi, *op. cit.*, 325a-b.

In some parts of Italy, for example Sicily, Sardinia and Corsica, there was despotic or tyrannical government. But, as a northern Italian, Ptolemy believed that Apulia and Sicily—the nurse of tyrants, as the ancient historians told him—were more Greek than Italian.

What could be described analytically could also be a matter of pride or even religious devotion. We have already seen how the baronage could confuse its prerogatives with the liberties of a 'people', hallowed tradition, or the health of the state. With their fiefs held of the 'sun', or 'sovereign' fiefs, as they were termed in the later Middle Ages, great baronial families were convinced of the quasidivine right of their lordship. Two mottoes from northern France will demonstrate this point:

> Roi ne puis, prince ne daigne, Rohan suis.
> King I cannot.
> Prince I deign not.
> I am Rohan.

> Ne suis ne roi ne duc ne prince aussi,
> Je suis le sire de Coucy.
> Neither king nor duke nor prince either
> I am the lord of Coucy.

Even more exaggerated were the pretensions of urban republics. From 1212 onward, the town of Marseilles was led by rich bourgeois who organized the 'people' into a peace association called the confraternity of the Holy Spirit. From before 1212, and rapidly thereafter, the lordship of the various parts of Marseilles was acquired through suasion or purchase by this confraternity. In 1214 a town seal appeared. In 1218 the town won the right to mint the coins it needed for its extensive commerce. By 1220 the counts of Provence had recognized the community's right to self-government. Thereafter the political role of the confraternity was surrendered to an elected *potestas*, or head of state. The period from 1220 to 1230 was Marseilles's greatest age of real freedom and self-government. Just before this happy time the rectors or the consuls of the confraternity built a system of alliances with nearby cities. In 1218 the preamble of one of the treaties reads:

> Through God, we proceed to all our councils and acts because, through his aid, we have won the liberty of our city, decorated our republic, increased the profit and right of our city, and,

through him, we preserve the peace of our city, and, with his will, will preserve it in the future; wherefore, God alone governing our city of Marseilles, we, having in mind the profit of our city and wishing to provide for it in the future,[4]

form a firm and perpetual alliance with the town of Nice. A similar sentiment was expressed more succinctly by the Venetians. Their ducats bore the legend: 'Sit tibi Christe datus quem tu regis iste ducatus' ('Be this duchy, which you rule, given to thee, O Christ'). The significance of this kind of idea is not that it rests on faith. It is this: to be ruled by God is to be ruled by no other, certainly by no earthly power. Formulated in inscriptions on coins and seals and symbolically expressed in the cults of hundreds of patron saints of great families and towns, a restive sense of independence was the mark of the political entities characteristic of the high Middle Ages, the rural seigniory and the free town.

It has already been noted that there was no sharp distinction between town and village and that almost everything in the town had a counterpart in the village. Settlers of unoccupied land were not infrequently called *burgenses*, or bourgeois, in the twelfth century, presumably because they inhabited *bourgs* or *burgi*, terms that originally meant fortified enclosures. Although this practice died out in the thirteenth century as *burgensis* began to be limited to a social class among townsmen, well-to-do villagers frequently used the term to set them apart from the lesser members of their communities. The distinction seen in town between artisans and tradesmen on the one hand and the bourgeois on the other appeared in the villages as well. In thirteenth-century Switzerland and Savoy the neighbours (*vicini*) who were called to judge cases, bear witness to local customary law and property rights, and perform other duties of worthy citizens were called not only 'the elders' (*seniores villae*), 'the better and more ancient parishioners' (*parochiani meliores et antiquiores*), and good men (*probi viri*), but also—in emulation of Rome's distinction between the *honestiores* and *humiliores*—*viri honesti* or *honorati*. That these were not fixed or rigid distinctions, however, is shown by the customs of Ville-franche-de-Lauragais in 1280. There adultery was proved when the adulterer 'was taken naked with a naked woman or clothed with a clothed woman but lying on the ground by any inhabitant

---

[4] L. Méry and F. Guindon, *Histoire analytique et chronologique des actes et des délibérations des corps et du conseil de la municipalité de Marseille* (Aix, 1873) I, 272.

of the said town having with him two consuls or any other two good men, or, indeed, *any two others* or more, whencesoever they may come, worthy of trust'.[5]

Villagers certainly liked to think of themselves as possessing urban institutions. Some village or small-town customary codes spread widely; for example, that of Lorris in 1155, an important code in the *villeneuve* movement of northern France. Usually, however, villagers liked to think of themselves as governed by town law. Two charters of 1159 issued by the archbishop of Magdeburg to *locatores*, or town planners, are evidence of this. In the village of Pechau, south-east of the archiepiscopal city, the settlers were to have the *ius burgense*. This was, in fact, the usual northern German settlers' law, that is, Flemish law. In the village of Grosswusterwitz, north-east of Magdeburg, they were also to have the same law, but there it was called the law of the town of Schartau. In Grosswusterwitz, moreover, the market was to be organized according to the law of Magdeburg.

Many titles of office, like mayor and *scabini* (*échevins*), had long been common to village and town, and now villages sought to emulate the new town styles as well. One of these was 'consul', a title for those who served as members of the executive and judicial boards that governed towns in late twelfth-century Italy, southern France, and parts of Spain. By the later thirteenth century almost all northern Italian villages had consulates, or boards of elected consuls. The spread of such institutions was sometimes very rapid. In the Lauragais around Toulouse, a city with a proud and independent consulate, about nine villages boasted consulates in 1256. Sixteen years later, just under a hundred small towns and villages possessed governing boards using this elevated style. This was not so everywhere. An Austrian Cistercian of Baumgartenberg remarked that Austrians did not have to know how to address letters to townsmen or villagers: 'Besides, because there are no consuls of cities, fortified villages or open ones (*castellorum seu villarum*) in our country, we therefore don't have the habit of writing to them'.[6]

Emulating the practice of the larger towns, some of these boards of governors combined knights and commoners. In 1282 the consuls of Cordes-en-Albigeois were half knights and half

[5] J. Ramière de Fortanier, *Chartes de franchises du Lauragais* (1939), 706.
[6] *Formularius de modo prosandi* in BuF II, 741.

417

boni homines. Although many baronial families began to protect seigniorial rights by limiting what could be inherited by females and even, through primogeniture and other systems, by males, their lordly rights were often subdivided. Just after 1150 the lordship of the village of Montferrier outside of Montpellier was held by seven lords, the sons of four fathers, and in 1207 no less than thirty-five co-seigniors held the large barony of Mirepoix at the foot of the Pyrenees. What this meant is obvious. The courts may have been the lords', but many lords were scarcely more than yeoman farmers themselves. Where seigniorial rights were subdivided among families habitually living in town, special arrangements had to be worked out. In 1216, for example, the family of the lords of Cerrato, a village outside Siena where this family resided, arranged for the exercise of its jurisdiction: 'We will elect one of us *rector*, who will be held to bear the government of the *castellum* and to inhabit the castle three days each month and there to decide the suits brought before him in the established court of the men of the castle.'[7]

Like towns, villages formed alliances to further their ends. Chapter IV described the attempt of villages in the Laonnais to make the king of France intervene against their lord, the bishop of Laon. In 1320 the *parlement* of Paris voided the election of a proctor in law by Villeneuve-Saint-Georges and four other villages because they had no officially recognized commune, but the ruling stated that if their lord, the abbot of Saint-Germain-des-Près, did not appoint such an officer, the villages would be allowed to elect him. In the early fourteenth century the thirteen villages of the *baillage* of Mas-Saintes-Puelles near Toulouse customarily acted as one unit in law. In a charter of 1314 the hamlet of Aigne in the same region was joined to the large village of Cintegabelle and was to elect one of the eight consuls governing the joint community. Perhaps the best-known example is the alliance of the small towns and villages of the seigniories of Uri, Schwyz and Unterwald in 1291. The alliance was renewed in 1315 to remain in existence for centuries.

The difference between the villager and townsman was in the degree of liberty attained. In Roman law and pure theory, every *universitas*, or whole, had the right to make its own law. As

[7] Cited in Johan Plesner, *L'émigration de la campagne à la ville libre de Florence au XIIIe siècle* (1934), 56n.

418

thirteenth-century commentaries on Italian statute law invariably show, this freedom was limited by seigniors or by larger communities that exercised seigniory. Most village rights embodied in customary law were, so to speak, negative. They set limits to taxation, military or other services, rents, fees, and fines for justice. When positive they usually defined the personal freedom of the inhabitants, principally by giving them the right to move away. Quite frequently, however, villagers won a measure of jurisdiction or even of self-government. They usually participated in the judgment of civil cases, and often had full jurisdiction over them, as was the case in most southern French *bastides* during the thirteenth century. More rarely, as in parts of Italy, Swabia and southern France, rural consulates won the right to try criminals, a matter of significance because the punishment of criminals involved death, confiscation of property and heavy fines. Costs and fines were usually shared between the community and the lords. Relatively rare were the rights accorded to Villefranche-de-Lauragais in 1280, which gave its consuls full jurisdiction over thieves, homicides, adulterers and all other criminals. Control over the raising of taxes was rarer, but by no means unknown. Village governments frequently had the right to control how taxes were to be raised, to raise their own, or to have a share of the amount collected. Permission to refuse taxes imposed by the lord, however, was rare indeed.

Since consuls and mayors controlled such important matters, their choice was obviously of great importance. The law of Beaumont-en-Argonne of 1182—it eventually spread to 500 towns and villages—gave the inhabitants the right to elect the mayor and *jurati*, officers who had powers of justice, administration and finance. Rural consuls in Italy and France were elected, sometimes by all freemen in the community, sometimes through cooptation by an outgoing consulate, thus creating a village oligarchy. Even where there was great freedom this right of election was usually shared with the seigniors. In most southern French or Gascon *bastides* the community presented a slate of candidates to the lord, who chose the four or so consuls for the year. In Pasignano, a village outside Florence owned by a Cistercian monastery, the consuls or *potestates* were chosen half by the monastery and half by the inhabitants. This did not always assure the lord of the officers' subservience. In 1173 one of the consuls of Pasignano was the largest landed proprietor in the village, a contentious fellow involved in lawsuits against the abbot. Sometimes the consuls were elected by the inhabitants and merely confirmed by the lord. The 1254 statutes of Vidigulfo outside of Milan have as their first article: 'First, the inhabitants (*vicini*) of this place ought to choose the consuls, the smiths, the guards of the fields, and the swineherds; and the aforesaid lords or, in their name and power, their agents ought to invest and confirm them.'[8]

In the thirteenth century (although not thereafter) the areas where a measure of political freedom was possessed by villagers were either those that needed settlers, like Germany east of the Elbe, or, like parts of France, Italy, and southern and western Germany, where seigniorial or urban particularism made it necessary for lords to buy the loyalty of their subjects. England had a strong new-town movement, quite as vigorous as the somewhat later one of the *bastides* in Gascony, but it was typical of England that substantial political liberties were rarely accorded the settlers of planted communities. In the Gascon *bastides* these liberties were very common. The Gascon subjects of England's king could turn their loyalties, if they wished, to the king of France.

At the best, however, and in spite of the fact that villagers both sought and attained some of the freedom that townsmen were winning, village liberties, especially political ones, were restricted. Save for relatively primitive areas where seigniorial and urban institutions had barely penetrated like parts of Scandinavia, the swamps of Frisia and Schleswig, and the lands of the Baltic Slavs, villagers everywhere seem to have known that they needed to be affiliated with a lord or a larger community. A charter of 1172 records the action of the inhabitants of a Swabian village that had become or remained wholly free:

> With unanimous consent, the inhabitants (*villani*) of Bernheim have subjected their town of Bernheim, which they have possessed up to now freely and properly free of all lordship, to our power, on these terms, namely that they and all of their posterity will pay the empire twenty-five measures of wheat each year in order that, from now on, they will remain secure from all tyranny under the protection of our imperial highness.[9]

[8] Statutes published in P. S. Leicht, *Storia del diritto Italiano : le Fonti* (2nd edn.), 334.
[9] Cited in Otto Gierke, *Das deutsche Genossenschaftsrecht* I, 204n.

In an age when the ideal unit of power was the barony or free town, villages were too small to stand alone. Many clustered for protection below a seigniorial castle. Although many villages were fortified—the frequency of the suffix *bourg* in many French village names attests to this, as does the astonishing number of 205 *castella*, or fortified villages, in the *contado* of Florence in 1200 —few villages could stand a regular siege. Although rural power collectively meant much in the economy, villages did not have enough industry or commerce to stand alone. Self-sufficiency could be found only in a large town or in a substantial barony that united many villages. Observant men of the time recognized this. According to Ptolemy of Lucca, it seemed probable that princely government was best for very large areas with discordant interests and traditions. The republican form was ideal for substantial cities. Very small communities, however, lacked a quality that cities had, namely,

> the community of the multitude, without which a man cannot live decently; and how much more true is this [the possession of such a community] of a city than of a village, in that there are many arts and crafts in a city to provide a sufficiency for human life, by which arts and crafts, indeed, a city is constituted.[10]

To craftsmen and tradesmen may be added a personnel with political and military training whose experience of life was different from that of the farmer busy tilling his fields. In Italy and many parts of Latin Europe this personnel was provided by towns. More commonly it was the baronial families and, on a somewhat lower level, the rural gentlefolk who not only constituted that personnel themselves and trained their sons in the arts of war and government but also used the resources of a number of villages to recruit and pay for the soldiers, lawyers, bailiffs, clergy and other specialized persons. One may not say that the farmer had no conception of freedom or political rights; yet, considering the time at his disposal and the size of the social and economic units characteristic of the age, it was more profitable for him to entrust political functions to seigniors, gentlefolk, or townsmen. The characteristic political form of the village was therefore monarchical: the intimate monarchy of the rural seigniory. At the same time, it is to be noted that there were not only

---

[10] *De regimine principum* 4, 2, ed. Spiazzi, *op. cit.*, 328a.

monarchical elements in the political life of the village and small town, but also oligarchical and democratic ones, that is to say, republican ones.

Town liberty

A standard type of town seal had walls or towers engraved on it. Townsmen were proud of their walls and spent more money and time on them than on any other kind of monumental architecture. The walls were not built because the society in which these towns existed was especially given over to war. That was the case in the period before 1150 and that after 1300, but the period treated in this volume was relatively pacific. In terms of the history of warfare, the development of defensive fortifications—both urban and, for that matter, seigniorial—was the technological counterpart of a series of institutional restraints that gave the defensive a great advantage over the offensive in this period. As we have seen above in the chapters of Parts One and Three, these restraints were various. With some success, the ecclesiastical order had tried to limit war at home and to project it abroad by means of the crusades. The increased liberties of the aristocracy of the sword, townsmen, and even villagers, had limited the service they owed and impeded or made more expensive the raising of armies for offensive warfare. On the other hand the institution of the *defensio patriae* enabled defending powers to call on the service of all available freemen. As basic as these technological and institutional limitations was the solidarity built within each social order and class during this time of increasing liberty and somewhat beneficent economic circumstances. It was this that gave the militias of gentlefolk and townsmen the unity needed to defend their walls and the cohesion needed on the field of battle. That this solidarity was never complete or these institutions always efficacious is obvious, and that they were already weakening before 1300 has already been shown in these pages. For most of the period treated in these pages, however, the townsmen's militias and fortifications and those of the martial aristocracy joined with the ecumenical authority of the Church to limit war.

In terms of the towns themselves—and, to a lesser extent, of the villages of the seigniories—the wall meant freedom. In this relatively pacific age, the wall, so to speak, was not so much needed as wanted. Not only is the capacity to defend oneself the *sine qua non* of liberty, but also the possession of this capacity by towns and rural seigniories was an essential expression of the decentralized political structure of this age. Decentralization helps to explain the relative indifference of many of Latin Europe's inhabitants to the fact that they were ruled by kings and emperors. These princes and the political entities they ruled were at a distance. The real, or intense, political life of the 'people' took place in their towns and villages. It is worth remembering that the people moved to limit or destroy Europe's monarchies only in the modern period when both the seigniory and the free town had all but disappeared.

In the years being considered here towns everywhere sought liberty from their princes, but this does not mean that urban liberty was always opposed by princes. Towns were profitable and princes founded them and tried to attract inhabitants to them. Ecclesiastical or other, princes were convinced that spiritual advancement required a material foundation. Founding a small town or village, a bishop of Meissen wrote in 1154:

> Although, with Mary, one must choose the good or, rather, the better part of intimate quiet in the sweetness of the contemplative life, we are nevertheless generally obliged, with Martha, to be busy in the bitterness of the active life and to be disturbed about many things. For the tabernacle of the covenant and the ark of the Lord's witness would not shine with such brilliance were they not protected from storm and rain with haircloth and rams' skins died red and blue. Whence the Church of God is not only to provide the Lord's flock with a good teacher in those things that are spiritual and eternal, but also sagaciously to succour it by a provident shepherd in those things which are carnal and temporal.[11]

Since in relatively unsettled areas a town was the origin and head (*exordium* and *caput*) of a whole province, as the archbishop of Magdeburg said when founding Jüterbog in 1174, towns demanded even more of a prince's solicitude. Besides, there was political advantage in granting a town liberties. Under Henry II, Rouen had been given a limited measure of self-government, and in 1199 and thereafter the law granted to Rouen was extended to the towns

---

[11] Rudolf Kötzschke, *Quellen zur Geschichte der ostdeutschen Kolonisation*, 28, No. 10. The biblical references are Luke 10:38–42 and Exodus 25 and 26.

of Poitou and Guienne. These towns were among the few centres that remained loyal to the Plantagenets during the Capetian conquests in the early thirteenth century.

Towns usually aimed to rule themselves, however—an ambition that brought them into conflict with their princes. Northern and central Italy's towns were the most successful in achieving independence, some in 1183 at the time of the treaty of Constance, the rest, *de facto* if not *de jure*, during the collapse of the Hohenstaufen cause in the thirteenth century. Almost as free were the towns in Flanders and the immediately adjacent regions. The control of the counts-of Flanders weakened after the strong reign of Philip of Alsace (1169–91) and failed almost altogether as the Capetians supported the towns against the princes in the unhappy reign of Guy of Dampierre (1280–1305). The counts retained some jurisdiction, however; only Tournai, freed from its bishop in 1188 by its own efforts and those of the French crown, could be said to be a real republic in the Italian style. Suitably enough, its belfry was the tallest in Flanders. In the rest of modern Belgium, that is, in Brabant and the Liègeois, urban liberty was not so extensive. Other areas notable for liberty were the Lorraines, the Burgundies, and the adjacent regions in the western marches of the Empire and along the valley of the Rhine at its confluents. During the collapse of the Hohenstaufen dynasty, towns in Swabia, modern Switzerland and along the upper Rhine and Danube advanced greatly. To the west and south, as the dynasty of the Raymonds weakened, Toulouse and to a lesser degree other towns in Languedoc gained a brief hold upon independence, as did towns in Provence and along the Rhône as imperial power faded. But in these southern French regions town liberty weakened by the 1250s as Capetian power penetrated southward.

That towns sought to govern themselves and that their political form was a kind of collective lordship or republic was widely recognized. Ptolemy of Lucca observed 'that in every region, whether in Germany, Scythia or France, cities live politically [*politice* = as republics], but [elsewhere than in Italy] they are bound by laws under the limiting power of a king or emperor'.[12] Although the desire was common, a glance at the map of Europe indicates the principal circumstances that limited the measure of self-government attained. The areas notable for urban liberty lay

[12] *De regimine principum* 4, 1, ed. Spiazzi, *op. cit.*, 326b.

along the frontiers of the principal power blocs or in regions characterized by intense political fragmentation. The most important of these were the western and southern marches of the weakening Empire, extending from the North Sea through the Lorraines and Burgundies and down the Rhône to Provence, thence swinging across northern and central Italy.

In many of these regions local dynasties were being pushed to the wall by nearby greater powers. Among these was the house of Saint-Gilles in Languedoc and Provence, squeezed by the kings of Aragon, the Plantagenets, and the finally triumphant Capetians. The counts of Flanders also weakened under Capetian pressure, but when the French seemed about to take over in the early 1300s the Flemish, with English help, resisted them. In addition to these political circumstances, Flanders and northern and central Italy had one other great advantage. As the most highly urbanized parts of Europe they had industrial and commercial resources that allowed them to have their way to a degree unknown elsewhere in Europe. Since these regions needed to import food and raw materials, however, their industrial and commercial specialization would not have been an advantage had not Europe's political structure been as decentralized as it was.

The formation of leagues of towns helped the drive toward urban independence. In Italy these date from the later eleventh century. In the next century the greatest one was the Lombard league formed after the destruction of Milan in 1161 by the Hohenstaufen. In 1167 and 1168 ten major towns (including a reconstructed Milan) that extended from Lombardy through the Romagna, joined with some lesser allies to defeat Frederick I Barbarossa in 1176 and forced him to capitulate at Constance in 1183. Thereafter, although leagues were common enough in Italy (Milan headed a league of seventeen cities in 1226), the tight oath association of the league was replaced by something similar to a modern system of interlocking alliances. During the thirteenth century Germany became famous for its leagues, a necessary corollary of the 'feudal' decentralization taking place within that realm. From 1226 onward the emperor, who wished peace at any price within Germany and hence supported the local princes, legislated against such leagues, notably against seven Franconian towns led by Mainz that were fighting the prince-archbishop of that city.

The slow dissolution of the Empire made such efforts nugatory. A *consortium* for the peace was started in 1254 and eventually included as many as a hundred towns stretching from Basel to Cologne and from Zürich to Bremen, a league briefly joined by seven ecclesiastical princes, the count palatine of the Rhine and many counts and lesser lords. This league arranged for assemblies to maintain the peace, meeting four times annually at Cologne, Mainz, Worms, and Strasbourg. Another and more durable league was that of Germany's seaports, eventually known as the Hanseatic league. It began in 1210 when the burghers (*burgenses*) of Lübeck and Hamburg granted each other the protections of mutual citizenship. By 1285 the king of Norway observed that, when one dealt with the thirteen towns extending from Bremen, Hamburg and Lübeck in the west over to Wisby, Riga and Revel in the east, one was dealing with one *universitas*. There were other kinds of town leagues, small and large, temporary and durable, in Germany during the latter half of the thirteenth century. The village and small-town confederation of the Swiss of 1291 has already been mentioned. A great town like Cologne was a member of several leagues, being allied with Franconian and other Rhenish towns, with those of the Netherlands, and with Bremen and Hamburg on the North Sea.

A characteristic of town liberty was the election by the citizens of boards possessing judicial and executive powers. In twelfth-century Italy the members—numbering anywhere from four to twenty-four—of these boards were usually called consuls. The origin of this term has been much debated, but it was probably a reminiscence of the consuls who headed the Roman republic, as well as a reflection of the practice of counts and dukes—like the counts of Toulouse and the dukes of Benevento—who called themselves by this title. The consular institution was widespread in Italy by the end of the eleventh century. Florence's creation of its consulate in 1138 was somewhat behind the times. The institution spread throughout southern France to western Languedoc and penetrated into south-western Germany. Because of the tendency of the emperors to import grandiloquent terms from Italy, the members of the governing board of Lübeck were called consuls by the emperor in a charter of 1188, and the same was true in Utrecht in 1192. This spread to the far north of the term consul meant very little. Lübeck's consuls did not have the powers of

Italy's consuls, and in fact were merely the usual northern town councillors or *scabini* by another name.

Another office that had its origins in Italy and spread to Provence and parts of Burgundy and Swabia was that of the *potestas*. As the word itself shows, the *potestas* was one who exercised supreme power or was the head of state. Initially the office that exercised imperial jurisdiction in Italy's towns, it became elective after the peace of Constance, and spread as Italian towns became independent either of the Empire or of local bishops and other seigniors. The elected *potestas* was accorded the honours accorded princes. Greeted with processions when he entered the town, he was acclaimed and seated upon a throne, the see of glory (*solium gloriae*) as the manuals for this office called it. At first the *potestas* was elected from a town's own inhabitants, as was the first *potestas* of Pisa in 1190, but later he was chosen from another town, as happened at Pisa in 1208. Foreigners were elected because they were less involved in the conflicts within the town. There was legislation that prohibited a *potestas* from marrying within the town where he served and even from dining privately with its citizens. A more important reason for choosing a foreigner was the Italian's fear of princely government—which, after all, had just been overthrown. *Potestates* were usually prohibited from summoning general assemblies of the people (*conciones, arengae, parlamenta*) on their own initiative, lest they establish themselves as tyrants by working on the passions of the community. They were strictly controlled by elected town councils and had to undergo a public examination (*sindicatio*) at the end of their term of office.

The potestarial office also reflected the growing professionalization of Italian political life. Elected for a year or half a year, the *potestas* was a salaried officer who brought with him a retinue of jurists, notaries, and squires to help him govern and to judge important cases. Although invariably a knight, so that he could head the town's army, a *potestas* was a professional governor. A good practitioner of this craft often enjoyed a distinguished career. In four decades of the thirteenth century, twenty such officers are known to have served in at least six towns each. Writing in 1282, Bonvesino of Riva praised William of Pusterla, a fellow citizen of Milan, because he had been elected *potestas* sixteen times in nine cities from 1190 to 1224, and no less than four times in Bologna. So wise was William that 'when he was *potestas* of Bologna, there, among the jurisconsults, these latter, seeing a man without Latin [*illiteratus*] to be so wise, called him antonomastically the Wise Layman'.[13] The Franciscan Salimbene expresses the Italian's respect for this office by complaining that Elias, the general of his order, failed to rise when receiving Gerald of Corrigia, the *potestas* of Parma, accompanied by his two sons, themselves occupants of many *potestariae*. In the course of time a literature about the government of cities appeared. Written in the 1240s, John of Viterbo's *On the Rule of Cities* was the best known manual of this kind.

The Italian-style *potestaria* rarely spread beyond the peninsula. There were other officers at the head of towns in the north. The mayor was one of these. Professional mayors were known in northern France around 1300. The difference between the *potestates* and these mayors was that the latter were usually royal officers employed or elected to serve in this capacity, an indication of town subordination to royal or princely authority. With the exception of some towns in Flanders, the non-professional mayors were also somehow subordinate to a prince. In the laws of Rouen that spread so widely throughout the Plantagenet domains the mayor was chosen by the prince from a slate—in Rouen's case, a slate of three—presented to him by the electoral body or the citizens. Another partial analogue to the *potestas* was the *burgomaster* (*magister civium* or *magister concilii*). This office was seen as early as 1224 in Strasbourg but did not spread widely till around 1300. The burgomaster served as the head of the governing town council. What the *Bürgermeisteramt* lacked that the *potestaria* had was that the *potestas* had the power of heading a community free of a lord's authority, that burgomasters were natives of the towns where they served their yearly terms, and that they lacked the professional quality that was so striking in Italy—a reflection of the relatively simple professional development north of the Alps. Well before 1300 Italy's towns boasted professional associations of lawyers and judges, not to speak of the humbler notaries. There was little to equal that in the north save around the courts of the kings of England and France.

Another difference between Italy and northern Europe was in

[13] *De magnalibus urbis Mediolani* 19, ed. F. Novati in *Bollettino dell'Instituto Storico Italiano* xx (1898), 147–8.

the degree to which princely power was able to change the social composition of a town and its expansion at the expense of the neighbouring countryside. Ideally speaking, a northern town was the capital of a province and therefore housed not only merchants and artisans, but also members of the old service cadres that were slowly becoming knightly. Save for a few late foundations, like Freiburg in the Breisgau (1120) and Lübeck (1157–58), from which *ministeriales* or knights were expressly excluded, such groups generally lived in or near towns and initially took part in their political life. Until 1112, for example, *ministeriales* were leaders of communal activity in Cologne. In Mantes on the Seine it seemed normal as late as 1150 for a common council of knights and burghers to be formed to maintain the peace and protect the poor.

This old pattern changed where princely power was fairly strong, and it changed in two ways. Either the knightly or ministerial aristocracy was excluded from active participation in town politics, or town and countryside were separated. In northern and central Italy the fading Empire could not seriously impede knightly participation. This was also the case in Languedoc, until just after the mid-thirteenth century, and in Provence. The participation of knights or ministerial groups was known in Germany as far north as Alsace and Franconia. Cities like Mainz, Worms, Strasbourg and Zürich were famed for their active ministerial or knightly aristocracy. To add to what we have seen above in chapter VII, in 1198 the town council of Worms was composed of twelve *ministeriales* and twenty-eight burghers. Elsewhere, as in Cologne and Regensburg, not a few ministerial families, faced with the choice of being knights outside the community or burghers within, simply transferred to the status of burgher and helped shape the developing patriciate.

The effect on a town's political structure of the exclusion of knightly elements was unmistakable. It sometimes created what may be described as double towns. In a Capetian charter given to Saint-Quentin in 1195, for example, the knights and to some degree the clergy had their own court, that of the count. The viscount's court, on the other hand, handled most of the legal business of the burghers, who in 1215 won the right to elect its judges (*scabini*). The mayor and the sworn men of his council (*jurati*) exercised the general right of government, other than judicial, over the burghers. A similar pattern can be seen in Liège, where the old *civitas*, or early town nucleus, remained in the hands of the archbishop-prince, his knights, and their *scabini*, who also exercised what we would call criminal justice over the whole town, and the *portus*, or new town, was ruled by its burghers whose *jurati* judged its civil cases. The Liège type was common in what is today eastern Belgium and adjacent regions, including Brabant, in the thirteenth century. In Flanders the pattern was somewhat different. There the *scabini* split into two bodies, a town board initially presided over by the count's bailiff, and another board that served as the count's court for the rural districts. Starting in 1194 in Arras in Artois and spreading to Flanders in 1209, the town *scabini* were elected by the burghers for a year's term. Although the larger Flemish towns dominated the surrounding countryside by 1300, this jurisdictional split was rarely obliterated and was to be reinforced in the later Middle Ages.

A corollary of the divisions within the town was the split between town and countryside. In Italy the towns established their sway over whole provinces of the Empire. There was nothing to equal this north of the Alps. Not that towns there did not have similar ambitions. From 1202 through 1204 the consuls of Toulouse led expeditions against twenty-three rural seigniors and communities. Although successful at first, the effort failed because of the Albigensian crusade and the subsequent reimposition of princely control. This does not mean that northern towns did not possess jurisdictions extending beyond their walls. Even a modest town like Provins in Champagne had eight villages under its administration, and their inhabitants had a vote in town affairs. In Germany the disintegration of the Empire offered opportunities that towns were quick to seize upon. Because territorial princely states were only in process of formation, towns used their link with the Empire as a method of winning their freedom. New recruits hastened to join their ranks. The idea of the imperial city was already clearly expressed when Lübeck in 1226 was described as a 'free city' (*libera civitas*) and an 'imperial place' (*locus imperii*). A similar status was granted to Vienna in 1237. The emperor recorded that 'we have received this city and its citizens in our protection that they shall never be removed from our power or from that of the Empire'.[14]

[14] Cited in Hans Planitz, *Die deutsche Stadt im Mittelalter*, 418n.

Wherever they were located in Germany—most were in its western and southern regions—cities of this kind had extensive rural circumscriptions under their sway. So also did some towns in Swabia, Burgundy, and Lorraine that were not imperial cities. Metz eventually had over 150 villages under its rule. Great though northern Europe's cities were, however, they were not in a position to do what Italy's republics had done, that is, conquer whole provinces. Italians were proud of the success of their towns. Remigio de' Girolami wrote about his native Florence:

God has granted this city seven extraordinarily good gifts by which man, if he uses them evilly, as often happens, will be blinded, but, if he uses them suitably, his path will be lighted. These gifts are the abundance of money, the nobility of the money itself, a multitude of people, a civility in style of life, the woollens industry, the armaments industry, and the command of the countryside in the county or district . . .[15]

The rise of the 'populus'

In the twelfth century many newly founded towns were somewhat democratic because the settlers were relatively undifferentiated as to class. In older cities with established social differentiations the need for solidarity in opposing the power of lords or princes engendered associations that proclaimed the equality of their members. In Italy this equalizing tendency was also expressed in architecture. The restive knightly clans that often led communal movements were ordered not to build higher towers than their neighbours. In 1164 the consuls heading the *compagnia*, or peace society, of Pisa took the following oath: 'I . . . will cause . . . the master-captains of the walls of the city of Pisa to swear that they will not build any tower . . . higher than the measure previously constituted.'[16] Revolutions against lordly authority, moreover, stirred up and mixed together all the social classes of a town. When the commune of Le Mans was formed in 1070, individuals with disparaging names like Dope (*Pauper sensu*), the Bear, Three Balls (*Qui dicitur habere tres testes*), and Mohammed briefly

---

[15] Cited from his *De bono communi* in C. T. Davis, 'An Early Florentine political theorist: Fra Remigio de' Girolami,' *Proceedings of the American Philosophical Society* CIV, (1960), 668a.

[16] Cited in Edith Ennen, *Frühgeschichte der europäischen Stadt* (Bonn, 1953), 285n.

appeared. A kind of equality therefore characterized many towns in the early twelfth century.

As towns grew, so did social differentiation. Where knights had always been in a town, the developing conception of nobility in the thirteenth century separated them ever more sharply from other social groups. More important, an urban patrician aristocracy emerged, and, consequently, oligarchies and plutocracies monopolized office. At Bruges in 1240 only members of the Hanse of London, the rich merchants' association, could hold public office. In the late twelfth century the laws of Rouen granted by the English kings stated that the mayor and the twenty-four *jurati* (twelve *scabini* and twelve councillors) were to be chosen only from the Hundred Peers. At Freiburg in the Breisgau the twenty-four *conjuratores*, called consuls after 1218, held office practically for life, and were recruited only from the merchants or knights of the patriciate (*Richerzeche*). Cooptation was common. At Ghent three bodies of thirteen members each served in rotation as boards of governors, advisers, and electors. Accurately enough, their members were termed the *viri hereditarii*. Sometimes patrician associations played a direct role in government. An act of 1297 from Cologne lists the officers of government in order of their importance. These were the judges, *scabini, officiales de Richerzecheit* (the patricians' association) and the consuls. In Italy similar phenomena were everywhere to be seen. One example will suffice. In Genoa all important business had been brought before the *concio*, or general assembly of the citizenry, until 1157. Thereafter a relatively aristocratic small council monopolized the town's business, even electing the first *potestas* in 1190. Oligarchic monopoly of office served a useful function for a time. By limiting the group involved in politics it tightened the solidarity of those who dealt with a prince or lord when fighting for town liberty.

Even as they were being cemented oligarchies came under attack. Part of the attack came from outside the town, and took the form of intervention by princes. Princely policy was opportunistic. Where weak, princes frequently supported oligarchies, as did the French kings in Flanders in order to weaken their powerful feudatory, the count of Flanders. Where strong, they generally aided the *plebs* as the Capetians did during Stephen Boileau's provostship of Paris from 1261 to 1269 and during the later thirteenth century in the northern French communes. Since most towns had won a measure of freedom while under patrician government, the princes largely intervened on the side of the middling or lower elements—at least until self-government had been weakened or destroyed. One of the few truly democratic constitutions in Languedoc was that of Nîmes, for example, a constitution granted by the count of Toulouse when he restored there the power of his representative, the vicar. The charter of 1207 reads:

> The whole people of the city or its larger part shall be summoned by crier and trumpet with our vicar to create consuls, and, when they have been assembled, they shall elect five good men from each of the quarters into which the city is divided, which twenty electors shall swear to elect four consuls as best they can.[17]

Hohenstaufen policy, tailored to fit the situation in Italy, was essentially the same: divide in order to rule. To split a town's ruling group, the imperialists often supported knightly privileges. Elsewhere, as in the march of Treviso where Ezzelino of Romano was imperial vicar from 1239 to 1259, they supported the humble many by insisting on real equality in law to the detriment of the rich and powerful.

In Italy the attack on oligarchical leadership was sparked by the great war against the Hohenstaufen, a war requiring heavy taxes and militia service. What was suffered most acutely in Italy was common to all of Europe as the increasing centralization of the state demanded heavier expenditures of effort and money. The burden of military service may be illustrated by the *Book of Montaperti*, the military archives the Florentines left on the field of battle when their army was routed by the Sienese in 1260. Composed of a mixture of professional and militia soldiery, the army was large. There were pioneers and a siege train, and elaborate care was taken for the provisioning of the host and even for medical service. An order of the day tells us that a doctor had been chosen 'to cure and visit the sick in the army burdened with fever or other sicknesses, which Master Roger had been chosen and elected in the city of Florence as a doctor with certain others to treat those wounded in the present army'.[18] Apart from the town's

[17] Cited in P. M. Viollet, 'Les communes au moyen âge', *Mémoires de l'Académie des Inscriptions et Belles-Lettres* XXXVI, ii (1901), 436.
[18] *Libro de Montaperti*, ed. Cesare Paoli (1889), 75.

lion keeper and some others, every category of the population seems to have been involved in this unlucky expedition.

Taxation was perhaps more burdensome than personal military service. Sales taxes and duties on imports were widespread and were favoured by the rich, but they were difficult to expand according to need and were unpopular with the mass of the people. Around 1300 the sale of *rentes* or income from a city's revenue, began in northern Europe. This was effective and was popular with the well-to-do, who bought them and collected the interest, but it enraged the poor. The sale of *rentes* was one of the malpractices attacked by the popular party in Liège when it rose against the patricians in 1302. In Italy a different system designed to achieve the same objectives had sprung up much earlier, one that was to develop into the funded debt of the communal *montes*. Starting in the Italian maritime cities—in Genoa in 1164 and in Venice by 1171—citizens were 'forced' to lend money to the government, for which service they were allotted a share in the income from an established source of revenue. In the course of time the state debt was divided into negotiable shares that could be willed, sold, or otherwise alienated. Businessmen, the rich, and ecclesiastical institutions often found them to be profitable investments. They also tried to get a hand in their management. In Genoa, where the tax on salt provided the basic revenue for the *compera salis*, the principal *mons* of that town, shareholders had direct control. Reorganized in 1274, the *compera* was managed by officers appointed by a representative of the town government, the captain of the people, and by a council of the larger shareholders. Even where their control was not so blatant town councillors who were shareholders were obviously subject to conflict of interest when they set the rate of return on what was nominally a forced loan but was actually an investment that brought anywhere from four to fifteen per cent annually.

If those with means preferred such methods of raising money, the middling and lesser folk favoured taxes based on property and income. The doctrine of the French *bailli* Beaumanoir, namely, that the tax should vary according to the wealth of those taxed, was the common one in this period. In Pisa as early as 1162, such a tax had become a yearly imposition. At Volterra shortly before 1214 the tax was limited to three shillings annually per hearth or head of family except in case of war. The ways in which such taxes were collected were many and various. One system involved three stages. The first stage was the determination of the total tax to be raised. The second was the estimate, or *extimum*, of the wealth of each household by a more or less careful public examination under oath. The third stage was the actual collection of the tax based on this estimate. At Volterra in 1239 the officers making such estimates and collecting the taxes were to swear 'in good faith and without fraud to impose the tax upon the men in their quarter, the rich according to their wealth, and the poor according to their poverty, by examining carefully the equity and convenience and inconvenience of each inhabitant'.[19] There were, of course, problems. For a time the knightly elements—at Pistoia as late as the mid-1280s—were less severely taxed than others either because of their military value or because of ancient privilege. It also took time to extend the application of such a system. Only in 1240 did the popular party in Milan impose this kind of taxation on the rural areas where so many of its patricians and knights had property. The greatest problem was how to live up to the principle of taxation according to wealth. Then as now the rich had many ways of hiding property and income.

Quite as impelling as these practical matters were the people's hopes and dreams. Whether fitted for it or not, everybody wanted a higher place in society. Just as the bourgeois wanted to be a gentleman, so did the artisan want to be a bourgeois. However oligarchical government may have become, the fiction of the equality of all citizens was part of a town's public propaganda, and the role of the 'people' was never entirely obliterated. If for no other reason than to read through the statutes, general assemblies of the people (*conciones* or *parlamenta*) were held three or four times yearly. There was also a vague tradition that *nova jura* needed the consent of the entire citizen body. Oligarchies took care to try to suppress this tradition by controlling the calling of public assemblies as we see at Arles around 1200:

> If any public assemblies are to be held during a consulate, if any changes in the consulate are to be made, or improvements, augmentations and diminutions in the law are to be introduced, or taxes for the common utility are to be raised for a war or re-

---

[19] Cited in Enrico Fiumi, 'L'imposta diretta nei comuni medioevali della Toscana', *Studi in onore di Armando Sapori* (Milan, 1957) I, 332.

prisals, the consuls should provide that these things are to be done for the city and consulate with the better and saner council of the consulate and of the archbishop.[20]

What gave muscle to these ambitions and memories was the rise of the guilds of tradesmen and craftsmen. If individuals were too poor to exercise political leadership, they could insist on their guild's participation in government as a corporation.

The popular or democratizing movement was first seen in Italy. Starting with Milan in 1198, almost all Italian towns witnessed the creation of a political organization designed to give the *populus* a larger voice in government. This effort also produced a new office within the republic, with special jurisdiction to protect popular interests and enforce the laws that the popular party had forced through. This was the office of the captain of the people. Like the *potestas*, the captain had a large and a small, or special, council and was elected. Unlike the *potestas*, the captain was often a citizen. The great victories of the popular party stretched from the peace of Saint Ambrose in Milan in 1258 to the Most Sacred Ordinance of Bologna in 1282 and the similarly named ordinance of Florence in 1293. By that latter date, moreover, the state had become corporate; the basic electorate had become the guilds together with some sort of regional representation of the quarters of the town. Typical of the new arrangement was the creation of new officers to enforce new and special legislation, officers like the Florentine standard-bearer of justice (*gonfalonarius* or *vexillifer*) and lesser standard-bearers of guilds and militia companies. Frequently there appears a group of six to twelve ancients (*anciani*) or priors, chosen by lot or elected from the leading guilds. Serving brief terms (two months in Florence in the 1290s), this group stood above all the other magistrates of the republic and was therefore analogous to the prytany of ancient Athens. The corporate state had made the Italian urban republic hydra-headed.

The advance of the 'people' necessarily led to an increasing formalization, or brigading, of non-popular elements. In Italy these were headed by the knightly group, or *magnati*, a group that defined itself, or was being defined, during this social struggle. In Pisa during the 1280s the knights—both of old lineage and new

[20] Published in Fritz Kiener, *Verfassungsgeschichte der Provence* (Leipzig, 1900), 195.

436

creation—constituted a *commune militum* with its captains, marshals and notaries, thus paralleling the structure of the *commune populi*. In the second half of the thirteenth century Pavia had three *potestates*, each with his council—one for the knights, one for the people, and the other for the notaries and jurists—all subordinate to the *potestas* of the commune and his council.

At the same time, the rise of the guilds led to attacks on the power of the *magnati* and to an attempt to exclude them from holding popular offices and even from having a meaningful share of the political life of the community. The quasifamilial associations (*consorteria*) of this group had been abolished in Bologna in 1252, the carrying of sidearms in town was prohibited, and not a few towers had been demolished. There was also an attempt to exclude the *magnati* from public office. By 1282 in Bologna and 1293 in Florence, a person representing the people or sitting in the general council could not be one 'who has not worked in [a] craft with his own hands'.[21] This exclusion of the knightly aristocracy was sometimes extended to the professional aristocracy of lawyers and judges, and frequently to celebrated commoner families. A Bolognese law of 1288 allowed the *potestas populi*, as the captain of the people was there titled,

> uninhibited and free will to exile those of the magnates of the city and district of Bologna and those of the great commoner families [*de magnis caxalibus popularium*], whenever and however often it may be necessary for reason of any crimes, rumours or rixation which they may or can commit, which God avert, or which they may be suspected of being able to raise up.[22]

This exclusion of the wealthier or more educated was designed to establish a society in which the 'people' could live in peace. As the Most Sacred Ordinance of Bologna put it in 1282, 'wishing and intending that rapacious wolves and gentle lambs should walk with equal step',[23] the gentle lambs obliged ninety-two persons of the aristocracy to put up a monetary guaranty for their own good behaviour and that of their families. In a similar period of Florence's history, from 1293 to 1295, it is estimated that members of seventy-three magnate and great popular families were exiled,

---

[21] Cited in Dahm, *Untersuchungen zur Verfassungs- und Strafrechtsgeschichte der italienischen Stadt im Mittelalter*, 33.
[22] Cited in Dahm, *op. cit.*, 39n.
[23] Cited in Salvemini, *Magnati e popolani in Firenze* (rprt, 1960), 327.

just under half of all the families in this category.

That this extreme legislation could not succeed is obvious. There were grave divisions among the guildsmen themselves, notably between the wealthy entrepreneurial guilds and those of the crafts and trades. Even when the guilds had won representation in government, moreover, there were still simple workers whose crafts were so humble that they were frequently denied the right to form guilds. When the humble followed tradition and sought to participate in political life, a problem typical of democracy was posed: should the majority make concessions to what was in terms of social power and probably even of numbers a minority? In this kind of struggle the old aristocracy could always find a way to get its foot in the door. Also, coherent political leadership proved to be impossible without using persons from the aristocracy. The leader of the Florentine popular party in 1293 was a knight, Giano della Bella, and the leaders of most of the democratizing movements were also knights. The laws excluding magnates and rich popular families from political life were therefore either formally repealed or informally subverted. After the failure of Giano's popular movement in 1295, the priors were to be chosen only 'from the more prudent, better and legal artificers . . . continuously exercising their profession or who are recorded in the book or matricule of any profession of the city of Florence, so long as they are not knights'.[24] But a gentleman of Dante's knightly grade was soon thereafter enrolled in the apothecaries' guild.

Limitations aside, the *populares* were triumphant. Writing around 1277–79, Giles of Rome flatly stated what he believed to be the reality of the Italian city:

For in the cities of Italy the many, as the whole people, commonly rule. The consent of the whole people is required in establishing statutes, in electing the *potestates,* and even in correcting the *potestates.* For although there is always found a *potestas* or lord who rules the city, nevertheless the whole people rules more than does the aforesaid lord, because it pertains to the whole people to elect him, to correct him if he acts badly, and even to establish the statutes which the lord is not permitted to go beyond.[25]

[24] Cited in Dahm, *op. cit.,* 33.
[25] *De regimine principum* 3, 2, 2, Rome 1607, 455.

Giles certainly exaggerated, but no more so than someone who calls a western European state or the United States a democracy. In Florence in the 1290s, leaving aside the banner-bearer of justice and the six priors elected by the twelve major guilds, there were three principal councils, one with 100 members in charge of finance, a second with 300 to serve with the *potestas*, and a third with 150 to sit beside the captain of the people, all elected by or from the twelve major guilds and the twenty-one minor ones. Since the terms for these councillors were for a half year without the possibility of reelection to the same council, and since the councils were elected at different times during the year, well over 1,000 citizens out of a total population of 40,000 to 50,000 were called upon for service each year. Nor was Florence extraordinary. Lucca, a city with a population around 15,000, had a main council of 1,550 members.

Although anywhere from twenty-five to fifty years behind Italy, a similar 'democratization' took place throughout Europe and was particularly marked in the industrial towns of Flanders and nearby regions. The changes sometimes paralleled the Italian experience strikingly. In Swabian, Burgundian and Alsatian towns there was the office of the captain of the people, or guild *Obermeister*, which first appeared in Basel in 1280. In Freiburg in the Breisgau a revolt of the 'people' against the patricians made the twenty-four consuls into an annually elected board, and basic financial power was given to another annually elected council of twenty-four. In 1293 this council was chosed from the eighteen trade and artisan guilds and its meetings were presided over by the guild *Obermeister*. Elsewhere the systems varied. At Liège, the sixty governors of the crafts moved into the government beside the two burgomasters and their council of *jurati*. From 1313 onward the general assembly of the people policed the issuance of *nova jura*, an act of 1311 having stated the principle that new taxes could not be raised without the express consent of all citizens whether big, middling or humble. Already weakened in 1297, the thirty-nine 'tyrants', or *viri hereditarii*, at Ghent were replaced by a council recruited from three 'members'. The first 'member' was the *poorters*, a group that soon became a new aristocracy and contained no less than twenty-six families of the old *viri hereditarii*. The second 'member' was the lesser crafts, and the third was the weavers in the cloth industry. The great victories of

439

the *populares*, or guild parties, in these regions did not come until the fourteenth century.

The above remarks on the rise of the popular party may give the impression that medieval republicanism was similar to modern in being organized around a system of two or more parties. It is true that opposing parties alternated in office from time to time, and it is also true that they had different social objectives within the community and different attitudes toward foreign policy. The Flemish oligarchy was pro-French, and the popular party was in favour of Flanders's counts and England's kings. Italian Guelphs favoured the papacy and town self-government, while the Ghibellines supported the unity of Italy within the Empire and the subordination of the city to imperial monarchy. Italian parties also developed machines or organizations and, like modern ones, tended to be captured by elements that had little to do with their initial ideological bent. In the late thirteenth century, for example, the Guelph party of Florence, once the party of the 'people', fell into the hands of the aristocracy. By labelling all opponents Ghibellines, the party exercised an extraconstitutional power of great efficacy. The fewer Ghibellines there were in fact, the more mighty was this party machine. A further similarity to modern parties may be seen in the party idea around 1300. As Bartolo of Sassoferrato (d. 1357) remarked in his tract on parties, Guelph and Ghibelline had become ideologically meaningless terms after the fall of the Hohenstaufen. To him, a man could be of either party depending upon where he was living or serving as an officer. Indeed, parties had nothing to do with causes:

> Take the case of a city that has a tyrant, who, with his party, is called a Guelph, then any good man is opposed to this party because he is opposed to this tyrant. And in that country he will be called a Ghibelline. And say also that in another city . . . there is a Ghibelline tyrant, certainly this same good man will oppose that tyrant, and there he is Guelph.[26]

In spite of these similarities with modern politics, medieval town politics were not based on the two-party system. Even where two parties were allowed to coexist, as in Todi, the offices were evenly divided between the two parties, a practice that has

[26] *Tractatus de Guelphis et Gebellinis* 3, in *Concilia, quaestiones et tractatus Dom. Bartoli a Saxoferrato* (Lyons, 1550), 154rb.

PARTY SYSTEMS

little relation to modern party methods. The medieval ideal was
clearly a one-party town. The reason for this is difficult to ascer-
tain. It is likely that the ideal of a unified Christian community—
one church, one state—was influential here. In spite of the fact—
to be briefly explored in Chapter XV below—that medieval political theorists often denied the parallel between the ecclesiastical
and secular communities, one is inclined to this argument because
modern party systems did not emerge until the eighteenth century
and then first in those societies, like the United States, where
ecclesiastical pluralism or disunity was most advanced.

Apart from the possible influence of the ecclesiastical model,
it also seems that circumstances were not propitious for the
development of a two-party system. The nearest the Italian city
republics came to this system was in the days of the struggle
against the Hohenstaufen when, to overstate the case somewhat,
the Ghibellines favoured unity and monarchy and the Guelphs
favoured decentralization and the republican form of government.
The frequent exiling of the leaders of defeated parties may here
inspire one to argue that the ideological gulf between monarchism
and republicanism—so much greater than anything seen in
eighteenth-century North America and Britain—was too broad
to be spanned by an open, public compromise. Furthermore, at
the time when, owing to the defeat of the Hohenstaufen, the
parties were becoming ideologically weaker, the 'people' and its
guilds had arisen, spreading a corporate form of social organization
that eventually reached from the top to the bottom of society.
Party adherence was not enough to guarantee political participation; a citizen had to be a member of a guild, a professional association, or an order like the *magnati*. These entities therefore became
the loci of real politics. Politics was reduced to the determination
of how much representation in the body politic each group was to
have, and what groups were to be allowed to constitute themselves
members of this body. In this society, it seems, the corporations
had taken over the role of the parties. This does not mean that the
parties disappeared. From the beginning, they had always had to
do with 'foreign affairs', that is, the relation of the city state to the
Empire, the papacy, and other powers. In the practical absence of
the Empire, they were still of use in describing Italian diplomatic
alignments. Thus, for example, Florence's rivals in Tuscany were
Siena and Pisa. Florence being Guelph, Siena and Pisa were

441

Ghibelline. Were a merchant to move from Florence to Siena, he would give up being a Guelph and become a Ghibelline.

Italian republicanism

The political circumstances described above evoked much debate among contemporaries. Some of the participants were northerners, such as the scholars at Paris fortified by their Aristotle or Avicenna. One northern chronicler, John of Hocsem at Liège, was inspired by the revolution in his city when the popular party won power in the early 1300s to discuss Aristotle's teaching and to favour democracy somewhat over oligarchy. On the whole, however, those most interested in these problems were Italian. Italians had before their very eyes living independent republics, both oligarchical and democratic, as well as working monarchies. They were therefore in the best position to make comparisons and to defend or attack the institutions of republicanism.

To such thinkers the republic, or *civitas*, was a community of citizens sharing civic burdens and reaping the benefits of civic peace. Although citizenship (*civilitas, cittadinantia*) was heavy with religious or patriotic overtones, it sometimes became rather casual, even vulgar. In Pisa in 1286 naturalization required twenty years of residence. Because industry needed labour and the treasury wanted money, however, this had been reduced to three years by 1319, and all rural inhabitants with an *extimum* above fifty pounds were obliged to enrol as citizens. In theory, all citizens were equal before the law and equally free. In theory again, all citizens could hold office. Discussing Aristotle's description of the Cretan and Spartan constitutions, Ptolemy of Lucca rejected the oligarchical system of Crete in favour of the Spartan one, in which the king

> was elected by the wise, chosen from all the grades of the citizenry; and this appears consonant with reason, that a king should be raised up to rule the people by the consent of the whole council, as the cities of Italy commonly do today. For this is what the word city means, being, according to Augustine's *City of God*, 'a multitude of men bound together by a certain bond of society'. Whence a city is the unity of the citizens.[27]

[27] *De regimine principum* 4, 18, ed. Spiazzi, *op. cit.*, 347a. The passage from Augustine is from *De civitate dei* 15, 8 2.

The theorists thought that this form of government was better for the city than a monarchy. Monarchy had many weaknesses. It led to tyranny, for example, because, like Saul, a man raised to kingship puffs up with pride. John of Paris explained that 'because of the great power that is conceded to a king, a kingdom easily degenerates into tyranny'.[28] Monarchy was also inefficient because some men are good as subjects but, when raised up, are incapable of ruling. Bonaventure repeated the old saw that ship captains are made, not born, and, like Ptolemy of Lucca, he noted that Rome rose under elected leaders and fell under hereditary emperors. Answers to these telling points were provided by Giles of Rome in his *On the Rule of Princes*. Human nature makes fathers want their sons to succeed to their place, hence dynastic succession is natural. If an heir is defective, Giles argued, monarchy is not just a prince, but instead a whole system that holds the body politic together.

> We may therefore say that it is useful for a realm for a son to succeed in the government of his father, and, if there is any defect in the royal child to whom the royal care should come, it can be supplied by wise and good men whom the king should join to himself in a kind of society [*in societatem*] as his hands and eyes.[29]

At about the same time Humbert of Romans was arguing that counsellors were often more important to a monarchy than the king himself.

Putting the shoe on the other foot, Giles and those of his persuasion argued that elections and the participation of many in legislation led to sedition. Ptolemy replied that, according to Valerius Maximus and practical experience, the appetite for honours inheres in all men and they will be seditious if that appetite is never sated. As for legislation, men best obey a law they have proposed for themselves. In addition to these arguments it was stated that no one man, however wise or instructed, is superior to the whole population. As Peter John Olivi said in his defence of the mixed constitution of electoral monarchy plus conciliar government:

---

[28] *De potestate regia et papali* 19, ed. Leclercq, 237.
[29] *De regimine principum* 3, 2, 5 in Rome 1607, 237.

That regime in which the subjects participate in certain elections and councils is more acceptable to them, and, because of this, is better advised, more honourable and more authoritative, because it would be difficult, indeed incredible, that one acting together with many could err as much as one acting alone.[30]

Monarchists believed that hereditary monarchy was the best system after the fall of man from grace. Even Giles confessed that

speaking absolutely, it is better to choose a prince by election than by hereditary succession. Nevertheless, because men have corrupt appetites, and because of the actions and conditions of men which we perceive by experience (*experimentaliter*), it seems more suitable to a realm or a city that its lord be raised up by heredity than by election.[31]

This was a difficult point to get round, because of the *experimentaliter*. But the argument from history could be reversed. Ptolemy of Lucca adverted to the often cited case of the ancient constitution of the Jews, whom God had ordered to elect their leaders. He then turned to Rome itself, the perfect paradigm of a successful republic, a government that had even been praised in the first book of *Maccabees*. For him, God and history together confirmed the licitness and usefulness of the republican form of government.

In arguing from human experience, the analysts compared and contrasted monarchy and republicanism. One distinction was election of officers for a term (*ad tempus*) as against hereditary succession. There were also life terms of office. As has been seen when the Franciscan Salimbene discussed prelatry, these were usually not favoured by those of the republican tradition. They were favoured, however, by those who championed the mixed constitution with its elected prince, and even by some republicans who found a model in the doge of Venice. Under these differing regimes there were also differences in lesser officers. Ptolemy of Lucca noted that great officers in kingdoms generally held their charges hereditarily. Writing in the early 1260s, Brunetto Latini contrasted France and Italy, saying that there was one kind of office

as they are in France, and they are perpetual, and they sell the provostships and give them to those who buy them at the highest

[30] Cited from his *De renunciatione papae* in *Archivum Franciscanum Historicum* XI–XII (1918–19), 354–5.
[31] *De regimine principum* 3, 2, 5 in Rome 1607, 461.

price (and then look after their own good and not the profit of the bourgeois); the other is in Italy, where the citizens, bourgeois and commons of the town elect their *potestates* (*poeste*) and their lords as they wish, and these are more profitable to the common good of the town and of all their subjects.[32]

Within a republic, the difficulty was in determining who should participate in the government, whether the rich or the poor, the young or the old, the learned or the average citizen. Writing in the 1240s, John of Viterbo counselled against choosing *potestates* simply because of nobility or wealth, but he stated that, other things being equal, the wealthier man was preferable to the poorer because of the latter's need for money. The anonymous *Pastoral Eye*, another thirteenth-century manual on town government, noted that towns

> choose many people for the councils of their land, adhering perhaps to these rules that 'what touches all should be agreed to by all' and '*ubi bonum, ibi emolumentum*'. And even Scripture (*auctoritas*) says that omnipotent God 'sometimes reveals to the humble what he hides from the powerful'. . . . What is asked from many is more easily discovered, and truth is revealed more clearly by many men.[33]

Following Aristotle and perhaps common sense, the general opinion looked upon the middling folk as the ideal political class. According to Ptolemy of Lucca, those fit for office and council were 'the middling folk of the city, that is, not those who are too powerful for they easily tyrannize over others, nor yet those of too low a condition for they straightway level everything (*statim democratizant*)'.[34] Experience at Liège seems to have taught John of Hocsem the same lesson. Although favouring democracy over oligarchy, John thought that the weakness of popular government was its attempt to achieve an absolute equality of all the citizens, since some were obviously of more value to the community than others. In theory, however, according to Ptolemy, all should have a chance at honours: 'Praiseworthy therefore is that policy in which office and honours are distributed to each in turn according

---

[32] *Li livres dou tresor* 3, 73, ed. F. J. Carmody (Berkeley, 1948), 392.
[33] A composite quotation from the *Oculus pastoralis* 6, 5 and 2, 3 in L. A. Muratori, *Antiquitates Italicae medii aevi* IX, 856 and 806. For the source of the *quod omnes tangit* phrase, see p. 362n. The other commonplaces have not been identified.
[34] *De regimine principum* 4, 8, ed. Spiazzi, *op. cit.*, 336a.

to merit, as did the ancient Romans and as even Aristotle recommends.'[35]

In fact, although the perfect citizen was often a noble in reality, there clearly was an idea of natural equality in the Italian republic. According to Salimbene, John Barixellus, the liberator of Parma, was the perfect political success—a man of humble origins who rose to the top of the heap. His fellow citizens rewarded him well: 'First, because they made him rich, who had been poor. Second, they gave him a wife of noble lineage, namely of the *Cornacano*. Third without election he was always to be a member of the council because he had common sense (*sensum naturalem*) and the gift of public speaking.'[36] Bonvesino della Riva described Hubert della Croce, a Milanese military hero of around 1215. A fine soldier, a great eater (he once devoured thirty-two fried eggs), he was a man whose mistress bore him a daughter of wondrous strength. Still, Hubert was always polite (*curialis*): he never displayed his strength without reason, nor injured anyone without cause. He was the ideal soldier of a republic.

A second major distinction between republicanism and monarchy was the way in which laws were formulated. Although the theorists knew that many kings were in fact bound by the law, something that led them to distinguish between good royal government and despotical or tyrannical rule, they often stressed the prince's freedom to make law. Both Giles of Rome and Ptolemy of Lucca emphasize his arbitrary power (*arbitraria potestas*) or free will (*liberum arbitrium*) in issuing law, a law found in the inmost recesses of his heart (*in pectore*). Although a republican, Ptolemy found this princely capacity to be an almost godlike quality:

> A king, who is the artificer or architect of society, ought not be lacking in answering the needs of the realm, those that pertain to the conservation of human social life, but instead ought to supply every defect for this society. And we must therefore conclude that, in this case, princes can impose legitimate exactions, tallages, or tributes, just so long as they do not transcend the bounds of necessity.[37]

Unlike a prince, the elected officer of a republic was bound by the

[35] *De regimine principum* 4, 7, ed. Spiazzi, *op. cit.*, 335a.
[36] *Cronica* in *MGH. SS.* xxxii, 374–5.
[37] *De regimine principum* 3, 11, ed. Spiazzi, *op. cit.*, 311b–312a.

laws of the community in which he served, and changes or innovations in those laws had to be made with the will of the people (*ex arbitrio populi*). Furthermore, since a retiring magistrate's record was examined at the end of his term by a process known as *sindicatio*, his execution of his office was reviewed by the 'people'.

In republics the problem was to determine how the people make the law. Summing up the tradition of the commentaries on Italian statute law, Alberic of Rosate stated that the law was made by the people acting as direct legislators or indirectly by their judges. The judges created precedent by rendering interlocutory or definitive sentences—subject to revision by a public review (*sindicatio*) at the end of their terms. Direct legislation took place in three ways. The first, relatively rare, method was to summon the people, or *universitas*, in a public parliament and there have it act on a proposal (*propositio*) of the rector or magistrate of the city. The second and usual method was that the officers and the 'councillors . . . should be convoked in the accustomed manner, and among them there should take place the proposal (*propositio*), discussion (*consultatio*), and enactment (*reformatio*) or the issuance of statutes'.[38] A third method was to have the *universitas* or councillors choose experts and give them the power of issuing statutes, a system naturally favoured by the good lawyer himself. The three stages of *propositio*, *consultatio* or *deliberatio*, and enactment were known before Alberic wrote. Borrowing much of his material from Albert Galeotti (fl. 1250s–72), Albert of Gandino described the process in the following words:

> And note that councillors (*decuriones*) have to be there to make a council, and that a resolution be there proposed (*propositio*), and that there may be proposed in a council whatever its members think ought to be enacted, the *potestas* being present, because it is his right that resolutions can only be introduced in his presence . . .; second, that anyone may speak (*sit arengatum*) to what is proposed by the *potestas*; third, that such a resolution shall be discussed (*deliberatio*) by the members of the council to determine whether or not they wish it made into law (*sit statutum*).[39]

There were difficulties attending the legislative debates. Alberic cites a question posed by the earlier Bolognese doctor Martin

[38] *De statutis* 1, 4, 3–6 in *TUJ* II, 2va-b.
[39] *Quaestiones statutorum* 2 in *BIMA* III, 157–8.

Syllimani (d. 1306): in order to abrogate or change a law, could a *potestas* summon both his own council of the six hundred and the *concilium populi* of the captain of the people? The answer is no,

> because, if the council of the people is mixed together with the council of the six hundred, the councilmen of the people, for reason of fear or reverence, will not dare to speak their minds as freely as they would were they by themselves, and they are therefore often drawn to follow the councilmen of the council of the six hundred.[40]

The normal method was therefore to summon the councils separately and to take their votes individually.

The question was asked whether the law handed down by the judges or proclaimed by the 'people' necessarily obtained currency. It did, so long as it did not conflict with the law of nature or divine law. Some professors believed that the Roman law taught in the schools embodied enough of nature's law to relegate to second place the statutes of the city states. This opinion was not generally received by Italian lawgivers. Both the monarchical state of Naples and Sicily and Italy's many republics asserted that superiority of statute law over Roman law and sometimes, as at Salerno in 1251 and Amalfi, in 1274, insisted that 'if the [Roman] laws were, are, and will be holy, good customs are even more holy, and, where customs speak, there ought the law be wholly silent'.[41] In fact, the superiority of local statute law had long since been a commonplace. Buoncompagno of Signa commented drily on this in the early thirteenth century: 'Civil [Roman] law ought not be much commended because not a hundredth part of the earth is ruled by it, and because it is vituperable, in that statutes of mere peasants make it immediately vanish, and popular plebiscites tear from it its authority and favour.'[42] Notwithstanding the superiority of statute law, the Roman law of the schools had an important function in divided Italy. It gave the peninsula the equivalent of an international law and a normative jurisprudence of equity with which to accord the laws of the independent states. As a result, the laws of Rome were generally considered to be the common laws (*iura communia*) of Italy, a role they were also to play later on in the German Empire.

[40] *De statutis* I, 120 in *TUJ* II, 17va.
[41] Cited in Ennio Cortese, *La norma giuridica* (1954) II, 139.
[42] *Rhetorica novissima* 7, 3 in *BIMA* II, 289b.

Another difference between monarchy and republicanism was the emotional tone of the two systems. Ptolemy of Lucca was aware of this, saying that a king or prince has something divine about him, because in his architect's hands is the care of everything. This is not so of a person elected for a year or a half year, one who is paid for serving in an office or on a council. He is a 'mercenary' and seeks gain. Like the newly rich, politicians quickly become enraged at those who threaten them, and, since they fear losing office, they use the public treasury to buy friends. Elected heads of states, or *potestates*, were sometimes disrespectfully treated. A Paduan chronicle in 1302 described one such officer as a malicious fellow, and in the next year called another one an imbecile. The great advantage of mercenary politicians or salaried officers over princes was expressed by Ptolemy as follows: 'Usually, however, the way of governing those places where the government is republican is mercenary: for the lords are hired for a salary. Where, however, salary is the objective, the officer does not concentrate so much on ruling his subjects, and therefore the rigour of the law is tempered.'[43] This temperance was one of the reasons why Salimbene recommended the elective system of the Italian republic to the Church for its prelates, and it allows us to understand why Brunetto Latini, roundly contradicting his source in Aristotle's *Ethics*, claimed that 'Seigniories are of three kinds: one is of kings, the second is of the aristocracy (*des bons*), and the third is of the commons (*des communes*), which is the best of all three'.[44]

But not all peoples are equally suited for the republican form of government. Moved by the natural history of the time, Ptolemy of Lucca believed that, because of the influence of the stars, climate and geography, there were naturally servile peoples. To this northern Italian, the Sicilians and Greeks were among these. To Marsiglio of Padua, all Asiatics favoured hereditary monarchy because of their natural servility. Reading Vegetius, John of Hocsem of Liège discovered that all southern Europeans were servile, but not the good northern folk of Liège. Still, Ptolemy confessed that, certain unhappy peoples excepted, cities every-

[43] *De regimine principum* 2, 8, ed. Spiazzi, *op. cit.*, 285a-b.
[44] *Li livres dou tresor* 44, ed. Carmody, 211. The comparison with the *Ethics* comes from Nicolai Rubinstein, 'Marsilius of Padua and Italian Political Thought of his Time,' in J. R. Hale ed. *Europe in the Late Middle Ages* (Evanston, Ill. 1965), 51.

where tended to have the republican form of government, whereas large regions tended to have the monarchical form. But his careful analysis did not really satisfy him. He summed up his argument:

> Republican government (*regimen politicum*) flourishes best in cities . . .; large regions (*provinciae*) appear to pertain more to royal government, as is seen in many cases, except for Rome, which governed the world by its consuls, tribunes, and senators . . . and except for certain other Italian cities [of today] which, although they rule whole provinces, are nevertheless ruled by the republican form of government (*politice*).[45]

Having thrown his sociology out of the window, Ptolemy then reverted to patriotism:

> Certain regions are servile by nature, and such should be governed by despotical government, and I include in despotical royal as well. Those, however, who are virile in mind, bold of heart and confident in their intelligence, such men cannot be ruled except by a republic (*principatu politico*), which term I extend to include aristocratic. This kind of government flourishes best in Italy.[46]

Buoncompagno had put it more succinctly. Italy, he said, 'neither can nor ought live under tribute, because liberty has placed its principal seat in Italy'.[47]

The principate and oligarchy

Although not easily discernible until the fourteenth or even the fifteenth century, most of the changes that were to mark the dawn of modern times were under way in the late thirteenth century. The unit of political mobilization was becoming larger. Most clearly in England, but also visibly in France, the national state was being born. In the Empire the territorial states of the *domini terrae* were beginning their consolidation. Even in Italy larger political entities were beginning to assemble, and a few centres like Milan, Venice, and Florence were beginning to move ahead of and absorb their smaller neighbours. Everywhere the jealous independence or striving toward independence that marked the medieval town was beginning to wane.

[45] *De regimine principum* 4, 2, ed. Spiazzi, *op. cit.*, 327a.
[46] *De regimine principum* 4, 8, ed. Spiazzi, *op. cit.*, 336a.
[47] Cited from his *Liber de amicitia* in Carl Sutter, *Aus Leben und Schriften des Magisters Boncompagno* (Freiburg i B., 1894), 5. This is a curious reminiscence of the tax exemption of Italy under the Roman empire.

It was also in the later thirteenth century, when the popular parties were winning their victories and Italy's towns approached their most democratic moment while those of northern Europe were beginning to move toward theirs, that two contrasting institutional forms began to appear: princely government and stable oligarchy. The first was perhaps more important. In France and most of northern Europe the building of princely government, or what Ptolemy of Lucca called despotical government, took place by the reimposition of the power of traditional monarchies or princely states upon erstwhile free towns. To some degree this occurred in Italy as well, where the vestigial powers of the Empire were enlivened again by changed circumstance. On the whole, however, Italy's peculiar destiny was to invent entirely anew the institutions of monarchy and principate.

The ways in which this invention took place are clear. With the exception of Venice with its lifetime doge, officers in the Italian cities held their posts for short terms, six months or a year. They were also strictly limited in their powers. This began to change in the latter half of the thirteenth century. Azzo VII of Este was elected *potestas* of Ferrara in 1242, again in 1244, for three years in 1247, and again in 1258. At his death in 1264, his heir Obizzo was elected governor, rector and perpetual, or lifetime, lord of the town. In Parma Gilbert of Gente became captain of the people and of the guilds for a five-year term and took over the office of *potestas* as well. In 1254 he was elected for a ten-year term, with the provision that if he died in office the remainder of his term would go to his son. In 1303 a relative, Gilbert of Correggio, was elected perpetual defender of the peace and protector and defender of the merchants, arts and guilds. The grant to Albert della Scala at Verona in 1277 is an example of the new kind of magistracy. Albert was given full, general and free authority to govern the city, change the statutes, alienate the town's properties, decide all cases, and generally handle all other matters

> by his free will (*suo libero arbitrio*) and wish as it may appear to him to be useful and better . . . and whatsoever may be done, acted or decreed by him or by his command . . . will persist unchanged as if it had been done, acted or decreed by the *potestas* . . . , *anciani* . . . , and general and special council and by the whole people of the city of Verona.[48]

[48] Cited in Salzer, *Über die Anfänge der Signorie in Oberitalien*, 173.

451

A similar grant to Guido Bonacolsi, captain of Mantua, in 1299 added that the captain should make war and peace, choose and remove *potestates*, judges, and other officers, summon councils and general assemblies, refuse permission to summon the same bodies, and generally do anything 'with council or without, at his full, pure and general choice and will, no solemnity of law, custom, reform, decree or statute being observed'.[49] Although the development of true dynastic succession awaited the fourteenth century, the Scaliger of Verona associated their heirs in their offices in the 1290s. In fine, three changes were taking place in the old republican magistracies: terms of office were lengthening, the areas of competence were being enlarged, and the beginnings of dynastic succession were visible.

It seems to have been rare for the old office of the *potestaria* to be converted into the new and extraordinary magistracy, the basis of the later principate. A reason for this is that the *potestas* had appeared at a time when the then aristocratic republics had recently broken free from imperial or local princely power. Fearful of a renewal of monarchy, the citizenry had carefully circumscribed the powers of the new head of state. Although *potestates* sometimes enjoyed *liberum arbitrium* to impose sentences on criminal offenders, even this power was customarily limited. For example, the *potestas* of Bologna in 1250 was able only to enlarge pecuniary fines. He could not reduce them. And similar provisions are seen in a Pistoian statute of 1296. Unlike almost all the extraordinary magistrates, *potestates* were rarely elected in general assemblies of the people, and at Bologna a *potestas* or his family was not even permitted to be praised in that body. Nor could *potestates* generally summon general assemblies themselves except under certain conditions, as at Siena, where this action required a two-thirds vote of the council. Although new towns were sometimes named after popular *potestates*—as was Pietrasanta in 1255 after Guiscard of Pietrasanta, *potestas* of Lucca—anything that smacked of the hero on horseback, as the equestrian statue of Oldrado da Tresseno, *potestas* in Milan in 1233, was viewed with great alarm. Of the Lombard towns that have been studied, only Ferrara seems to have evolved the principate from the *potestaria*.

At Milan, Verona, Mantua and Padua the later princes derived from the captains of the people (*capitaneus populi*, or sometimes

---

[49] Cited in Leicht, *Storia del diritto Italiano: le Fonti* (2nd edn), 338, No. 30.

potestas populi), an office that appeared around 1244 and that had been generalized by the rise of the popular party and the movement toward democratization by the 1270s. Extraordinary powers were granted to the captaincy. The captain's principal function was to defend the legislation of the *populares* and, in the manner of a Roman tribune, protect them from their enemies. Being an enforcement agency, the captain usually had a semiprofessional elite corps of soldiers chosen from the militia. Having appeared during the democratic movement, in short, the captaincy was not hampered as much by the safeguards that had been placed around the *potestas* when the principal enemy was monarchy. It seemed more important when this office was invented to give it extraordinary powers to enforce the will of the people. And this was even more true of the other popular and extraordinary magistracies that were invented after the captaincy of the people.

There was also a vigorous martial tradition, one stimulated by the struggle between the Hohenstaufen and the republics. Salimbene remarked that Italy's little states were like children piling their hands atop each other's. The one who last slipped his hand out from below and slapped it on top felt happy. There is no doubt that, much as in ancient Athens, the popular parties were in favour of war and expansion in order to weaken rival towns, exploit the countryside and spread the good word of ideological belief. Under Della Torre leadership from the 1240s to the end of the 1270s, Milan's popular party conquered Como, Lodi, Bergamo, Novara, and Vercelli. It would therefore seem that military leaders had the best opportunity of becoming extraordinary magistrates or lords. It is certainly true that the leaders of all parties, popular and aristocratic, derived from the knightly elements, and the ascendancy of particular families was built on ability in war. The hero of the resistance at Milan after the great defeat by the Hohenstaufen at Cortenuova in 1237, Pagano Della Torre, set his family up to lead the popular party for the rest of the century. On the other hand, warfare alone does not explain the rise of the seigniors. War captains—indeed, temporary dictators in the Roman sense—like Humbert Pallavicini in 1259 and William of Montferrat in the 1290s at Milan had moments of great puissance but did not found principates.

Because war with one's neighbour is sometimes an expression of internal social conflict, the social conflicts within the Italian towns were probably more significant than war itself in creating the new magistracy. The fear of social war had become a common literary theme around 1300. Although the sanguine Ptolemy of Lucca asserted that despotical or royal government had no place among the naturally free men of Lombardy or Tuscany, he often added the quiet caveat: except by way of tyranny. Bonvesino della Riva warned that division within the city was the only thing that would permit foreign princes or tyrants to establish their sway over the free Milanese. Albertino Mussato cautioned the Paduans against the rising tyranny of Can Grande della Scala by likening him to Ezzelino of Romano. Just after the arrival of Can Grande to power in 1313 Mussato wrote several other works to explain that—to him—unhappy event. Borrowing from the astrological and determinist teaching of Peter of Abano, he proposed a cycle of senescence in which the spirit of liberty failed and tyrants arose.

The notion that tyranny derived from oligarchy was a commonplace, to be found in Thomas Aquinas's *On the Rule of Princes* and in Aristotle. What seemed harder to explain was how tyranny arose from democracy. As Mussato put it, Padua had begun as a mixed government of knights and *populares*, had become an oligarchy of the rich ('the fat people', *pinguis populus*) oppressing the *plebs*, and had then become a plebian democracy from which, in 1313, tyranny had arisen. Leaning on the ancients Mussato conjectured that, like the human body, the body politic held together in sobriety and duty into its forties. Thereafter, fat, lustful, envious, insolent, the political body sickened for twenty years, until finally freedom died, wasted by tyranny. This likening of the growth of the principate to a sickness of a democracy was an enlargement of a Platonic conception earlier stated by Thomas Aquinas. In his *On the Rule of Princes*, Aquinas argued that 'the government of the many has almost always ended in tyranny, as was clearly shown in the Roman republic'. And he went further than this to state that 'if one studies past and present history one will discover that tyranny has been more frequently exercised in lands ruled by the many than in those that are governed by one'.[50] Here he appears to have stood midway between his colleague Ptolemy of Lucca—who feared only the very rich and the very poor and put his faith in the middling persons—and Peter of Auvergne who was convinced that where the many dominate, there is

[50] *De regimine principum* I, 6, ed. Spiazzi, *op. cit.*, 263a.

tyranny: 'Where the multitude rules, it does violence to the rich by confiscating their goods in the manner of a tyrant, and it is therefore obvious that the multitude is a tyrant'.[51]

That the struggle was partly one between the rich and the poor was evident. Remigio de' Girolami preached that the cause of one of the divisions rending Florence was

> because the artisans speak evil of the rich (*magni*), namely that they are being devoured by them, that they commit treason, that they protect the property of their enemies, and such like things; and, on the contrary, the rich say that the artisans wish to dominate and do not know that they are spoiling the country, and similar things.[52]

All the moderates could do was to repeat Ptolemy of Lucca's recommendation to exclude the extremes of wealth and poverty from the management of the republic. In the mid-fourteenth century Bartolo of Sassoferrato, in his tract *On the Government of Cities*, still argued that cities of modest size, like Siena and Perugia, should be ruled by the multitude (*multitudo*), but he carefully excluded the mighty (*potentes*) and the very poor (*vilissimi*).

There can be no doubt that these elements were for the most part excluded from full participation. In Florence, for example, the regulations of entrepreneurial or industrial guilds like the *Calimala* not only exploited the humbler artisans economically, but also exercised a limited criminal jurisdiction over them. The growth in thirteenth-century law of the Roman distinction between the *honestiores* and the *humiliores*, emphasizing pecuniary punishments for the former and corporal punishments for the latter, indicates a brutalization of social relationships. The attack on the magnates and the rich *populares* allied to their cause was also pushed with great severity. Bolognese statutes in 1282 and Pisan statutes in 1286 provided that magnates could be proceeded against in law on the basis of simple presumption or rumour and could be condemned in certain cases on the basis of likelihood, as if the case had been fully proved. Torture as a method of proof

---

[51] *VIII libri politicorum seu de rebus civilibus* 3, 8 in *Thomae Aquinatis opera omnia* (ed. S. E. Frette) XXVI, 234a. I have been led to this commentary on Aristotle's *Politics* and this passage by Alan Gewirth, *Marsilius of Padua* (New York, 1951) I, 200n and *passim*.

[52] Cited in Davis, 'An early Florentine Political Theorist,' 667a.

had been introduced into the Italian courts during the early thirteenth century. Although not received everywhere, its value as a partial proof (*semiplena probatio*) had been widely recognized as useful in cases involving grave criminal offences, including the crime of treason, during the period that witnessed the rise of the democratic ideology. Torture was used in the social wars, because the offences were necessarily those that involved rixation and even treason. Both the *plebs* and the magnates were especially open to charges of these kinds. In Parma in 1316, for example, torture could only be applied to commoners in the presence of the *anciani*, the heads of the popular party and the guilds:

> and this should be done and observed in order that the said citizens may not or should not be seriously oppressed or harmed, saving and reserving that the *potestas* and the captain and their judges may torture magnates, nobles and powerful men, if need there be, without the presence of the *anciani* of the people. . . . Against all others of whatsoever condition one must proceed and should proceed rationally and with such moderation of torture that none should fall into danger of death from the severity or damage of torture.[53]

The significance of this legislation is not that gentlemen were handled with special brutality in Parma, but rather that ideological and social conflict had exacerbated the relationships of people in different classes and styles of life to the point that anything seemed permissible. In this context, the lengthening of the terms of office characteristic of the captains of the people and the extension of their areas of competence may be seen as nothing more than the granting of sufficient time and authority to accomplish the policies regarded as beneficial by ideologically inspired parties. It seems unsatisfactory to say, moreover, that the later principates were instituted by either the rich or the poor, the aristocracy or the *plebs*. The extremes of both these groups were disenfranchised, and they tended to increase the disaffection that distempered the body politic whenever defeat in war or economic difficulties supervened. Although the majority ruled, it could not hope to be always successful, and its solidarity was therefore often badly shaken.

Blame or praise for the development of the principate cannot

[53] Cited in Dahm, *op. cit.*, 38.

be put on any one group. The Milanese *principate* was established by the Visconti family. The first sign of that family's coming to power was the assumption of the lordship of the town by archbishop Otto in 1277. This was followed by repeated five-year terms as captain of the people granted to Matthew V Visconti from 1310 onward. There is little doubt that the Visconti initially represented a relatively aristocratic constituency in Milan and its dependent regions. Yet the restraints on the old magistracies had already been weakened by the popular party, whose leaders, the Della Torre, played the role that the Gracchi did in the Roman republic. The popular party of the association, or *credentia Sancti Ambrosii*, had created for Martin della Torre the extraordinary magistracy of the *potestas populi* in 1256, had appointed him lord (*dominus*) in 1259, and granted his brother Philip a lifetime term as head of the *credentia* and lord of Milan in 1264.

And Milan epitomized the aspirations of many Lombard and Tuscan towns. It had led the battle to free Italy's towns from the Empire. In the thirteenth century its popular party had been among the first and most vigorous in Italy. Between 1250 and 1300 it was already starting to pioneer the development of the principate and the large-scale territorial state. The history of this greatest of Italy's cities illustrates something else as well. No matter what its social origins or initial party affiliation, a principate—that complex composed of a prince, his family, and his agents— belonged to no one part of the polity it was called upon to rule. Until no longer needed and weakened, the advantage of this form of government was that it drew its sustenance from all social groups, permitted no parties, and favoured no one member of society at the expense of his neighbour, save only the prince himself. Writing in 1324 Marsiglio of Padua spoke of the sovereign people as the legislator and defender of the peace. In the sense that the people were choosing the principate he was right; but in that system the *legislator* and the *defensor pacis* were to be not the people but the prince.

To these political or social reasons may be added another. It has been remarked above that the unit of political mobilization was becoming larger, and it is evident that this process involved the relationship of the greater towns to the small towns and villages of the countryside. In northern Europe, monarchs were to use the resistance of the countryside to urban domination to control, or take power in, their towns. Something similar took place in Italy and, just as in the case of the movements within the towns, those of the countryside generally aided the growth of the principate. Sometimes, in times of economic hardship or those of rapid industrial growth, the countryfolk flooded into town, there to swell the disenfranchised groups disrupting the political balance of the community and ready for any extreme course of action. Not a few of the later princely lines derived from families whose power was based not only in the town itself but also in the villages and small towns of the countryside. A notable example is the authority of the marquesses of Este in Verona, Mantua, and Ferrara. In the latter city the Estensi had won out over the rival family of the Torelli with whom they had long shared office to become Ferrara's hereditary *potestates* in the late thirteenth century. The Estensi remind us of other great families that built loose alignments of towns and rural areas, ones that intimate the later principates. Of such a kind was the da Romano family in the Trevisan march with its centre in the Venetian Alps near Bassano and that extended its power to Verona, Vicenza and Padua. This proto-principate fell apart in the late 1250s. Southern Piedmont and Lombardy saw the rise of the Montferrat family in Alessandria and Acqui whose leaders held offices in towns as far apart as Ivrea, Como and even Milan in the 1260s and '80s. At the same time, it is to be remembered that, although there were important rural or small town elements in their constitutions, the durable principates were built around the greater cities such as Milan.

Not all Italian republics evolved into principates, and there were limits to the powers of the princes even in the ones that did. Others were slowly converted into relatively closed and stable oligarchies. Venice was the only one in which this process could be clearly discerned around 1300. The abolition of the general assembly, or *arenga*, the closing in 1297 of the group from which the grand or governing council was recruited, the defeat of a popular revolt in 1300 and a patrician revolt in 1310, and the creation of a secret council cemented the oligarchy in power. Although this history pertains to the fourteenth century, it may be noted here that the problem is to explain why Venice and, to some degree, Florence and other towns were able to build stable oligarchies when elsewhere this effort faded rapidly as the principate rose. What seems to have been peculiar about Venice and Florence was the extraordinary strength of their international connections, connections that freed them more than other towns from the pressures exercised by the small towns and villages of the surrounding countryside. Venice already had a maritime empire, and it was the governing cadre of this empire and of the fleets binding it together that constituted the oligarchy. In Florence it was the aristocracy of her international merchant-bankers, so much more successful than those of any other city and so closely linked to the papacy and its financial structure, that was to form the base of her oligarchy.

Whatever the source of the peculiar strength of these groups, there is no doubt that they were oligarchies. We have seen that Bartolus of Sassoferrato argued that cities of modest size were best ruled by the multitude. Very large regions, he thought, were best governed by a king or prince, preferably one who was elected. Large cities should neither be ruled by a king nor by the multitude.

> These should instead be ruled by a few, that is, by the rich and good men of the city. . . . For Venice and Florence are ruled in this way ... and in these the said suspicions [against oligarchy] play no role. For although they are said to be ruled by the few, I say that they are few with respect to the multitude contained in these cities, but they are many with respect to any other city. And since they are many, the multitude does not refuse to be ruled by them, and, because they are many, they cannot easily be divided against themselves in that many middling folk remain who uphold the law of the city.[54]

A deceit surely, but a deceit necessary for the successful maintenance of aristocratic or oligarchical republicanism.

[54] *De regimine civitatis* 20 in *Concilia, quaestiones et tractatus Dom. Bartoli a Saxoferrato* (Lyons, 1550), 156rb.

PART FIVE

Thought

XIII

The Intellectuals

The academy and the academics

However inefficiently the system works, intellectuals are produced by education and their interests and casts of mind are formed by educational institutions. As is obvious, these institutions were primarily ecclesiastical in the period with which this

BIBLIOGRAPHY The standard history of the university is that of Hastings Rashdall, *The Universities of Europe in the Middle Ages*, 3 vols. (2nd edn. by Powicke and Emden, Oxford, 1936) and the reader with less time may also consult a useful paperback by Gordon Leff, *Paris and Oxford: Universities in the Thirteenth and Fourteenth Centuries* (New York, 1968). The most convenient general survey of theology is André Forest, F. van Steenberghen, M. de Gandillac, *Le mouvement doctrinal du XIe au XIVe siècle* (Paris, 1951) and to this may be added two very easily read books by M.-D. Chenu, *La théologie au douzième siècle* (Paris, 1957) and *La théologie comme science au treizième siècle* (Paris, 1957) and Beryl Smalley's lovely *The Study of the Bible in the Middle Ages* (Oxford, 1952, now in paperback). Philosophy and science can perhaps best be approached by means of standard manuals such as F. C. Copleston, *A History of Philosophy*, vols II and III (London, 1950–53), Martin Grabmann, *Die Geschichte der scholastischen Methode*, 2 vols. (Freiburg, 1900–10), and A. C. Crombie, *Medieval and Early Modern Science*, vol. I: *Science in the Middle Ages* (2nd edn., New York, 1959). A good guide to utopian thought may be seen in S. C. Easton, *Roger Bacon and His Search for a Universal Science* (New York, 1952). Special attention has been given to the problems of academic freedom, the idea of progress, and the autonomy of human morality. These topics are not usually treated as central by intellectual historians but are given more weight by those whose bent is social or cultural. Work on Joachim of Fiore, for example, is still dominated by the name of Herbert Grundmann and his *Studien über Joachim von Floris* (Leipzig, 1927), and *Neue Forschungen über Joachim von Fiore* (Marburg, 1950). But see also Marjorie Reeves, *Influence of Prophecy in the Later Middle Ages* (Oxford, 1969), and Henri de Lubac, *Exégèse médiévale*, rols. III and IV (Paris, 1961–4).

There are also several books that convey both the enthusiasm of modern minds for this period and also the enthusiasm of their medieval forebears. These are Henry Adams, *Mont-Saint-Michel and Chartres* (a book constantly reprinted since its publication in 1905), C. H. Haskins, *The Renaissance of the Twelfth Century* (Cambridge, Mass., 1927), and Erwin Panofsky's paperback titled *Gothic Architecture and Scholasticism* (New York, 1957). This enthusiasm can sometimes go quite far. Johan Nordström, *Moyen-âge et Renaissance* (3rd edn., Paris, 1933), finds nothing basic in the Renaissance that was not known in Gothic France.

book deals. And it was of great importance for the recruiting of the educated classes that, although most intellectuals derived from fairly substantial and even gentlemanly families, the Church was pledged to free education. Around 1300 William Durand the Younger summarized papal legislation dating from 1179 through 1215 and thereafter, wherein it was proposed that

> the bishops should provide masters in their cathedral churches and major parish churches who should teach poor students without cost . . . , and that a tenth part of all ecclesiastical benefices, both secular and regular, should be assigned to poor scholars in the individual faculties of the university by whom the Church of God will be illuminated.[1]

In regard to the university students, this system was amplified with the foundation of residential colleges ostensibly or initially for poor students, the earliest such institution being created at Paris in 1180. The effects on lower school education of this effort and of the fund-raising that went along with it were also impressive. Although none were known before, testamentary bequests mention five parish schools in the somewhat backward town of Toulouse between 1234 and 1257.

People of means rarely used these schools. Family chaplains taught the scions of the nobility, and the children of ordinary gentlefolk or burghers were instructed by notaries or lesser clerks, some of whom may have doubled in the parish schools mentioned above. Middle-class testaments sometimes set aside income or property for the education and maintenance of children by ecclesiastical orders until they reached their majority. Perhaps reflecting the formalization of the university structure to be discussed shortly, more elaborate systems of lower schooling were growing up in the thirteenth century. These sometimes came close to modern systems. Although his figures may be questioned, John Villani's early fourteenth-century chronicle of Florence delineated the educational structure of a large city. In Florence, he claimed, 8,000 to 10,000 boys and girls were learning to read and write. On the secondary level (one that clearly overlapped the university, as is shown by the fact that Thomas Aquinas had completed six years in the faculty of letters at Naples at the age of six-

---

[1] *De modo generalis concilii celebrandi* 2, 4, 16 in *TUJ* XIII, 165rb. In Durand's text, what is translated as 'major churches' is 'baptismal churches', showing that he is referring to the northern and not the Italian practice.

teen), Villani reports that 1,000 to 1,200 students attended six abacus schools to learn arithmetic and business, and that four great grammar schools housed 550 to 600 students of Latin and logic. Bonvesino of Riva, a teacher himself, states that Milan had about seventy teachers of elementary letters and eight professors of grammar in 1288. As we learn in 1316, also, to these masters of Latin grammar must be added an undetermined number of professors of the abacus.

Conflicts between ecclesiastical and secular authority over education were frequent. In 1253 the town government of Ypres settled a controversy with the chapter of St Martin, agreeing that the staff (a rector and his masters) of the three great schools should be provided by the chapter, and that these schools, whose costs were to be regulated, should enjoy the monopoly of secondary education. Little schools, those that taught reading and writing, were exempted from the settlement and could be opened by anyone under town licence. Dating at least from 1195, this long conflict between town and chapter reminds us that the Church often tried to monopolize teaching, and that it was sometimes slow to catch up with growing needs. As a result, secular government regulated and even invaded and secularized the schools. More advanced in the greater towns of Italy, this process was to be seen everywhere. In 1253, for example, Lübeck's town fathers founded a longlived municipal Latin school.

Overlapping but ascending beyond these schools were the universities. These initially informal groups were formalized during the twelfth century. Perhaps the earliest was the school of law at Bologna, privileged by the authentic *Habita* issued by the emperor in 1158 and shortly confirmed by papal authority. Because the town of Bologna provided the teaching staff of the *studium* the students, who were usually not citizens, organized under their rectors to control and regulate the service sold them, and eventually won a decisive hand in choosing their instructors. In Paris, where the masters were churchmen and not town citizens, the king recognized their association and that of their students as an exempt and special jurisdiction in 1200. Although the students were also organized in Paris, the masters' association, divided into faculties or nations within the large faculty of arts, was in many senses the real university. Perhaps for this reason, it was more consistently inventive, disturbed, and torn by problems about academic liberty than was the law school at Bologna. In spite of this, the two institutions had much in common. Both came under general papal legislation, such as that issued at the Lateran Council of 1179 which regulated the licence for teaching, and the requirements for the degrees in both institutions were formalized in the 1220s.

The university system expanded rapidly during the thirteenth century. Masters' associations similar to that of Paris had appeared in twelfth-century England and, as at Paris, were constituted into universities early in the thirteenth century, at Oxford in 1214 and at Cambridge in the 1230s. Southern France also created a university. The groups of doctors assembled in Montpellier created a faculty of medicine in 1220, to which the lawyers added one of law in the 1230s. In the north, Orléans, long famed for its *dictatores*, evolved into a university in the same decade, and became northern France's most important centre for the study of law. This was because, in order to encourage the study of scripture and theology, work in civil law was forbidden at Paris in 1219 by a papal letter, thereby disrupting one of the four original faculties (law, medicine, arts and theology). A still more interesting experiment was the foundation of a university at Toulouse in order to attack heresy at the end of the Albigensian crusade in 1229. Oddly, this university's early propaganda tried to woo students away from Paris by promising to teach Aristotelian natural philosophy at a time when that subject was temporarily banned in Paris. Although at first attracting teachers of the quality of John of Garlande the grammarian (d. 1252), and Roland of Cremona (d. 1250), the first theologian of the Dominican Order to teach in France, this university initially faltered before the hostility of the southerners and the poverty of the counts of Toulouse. After the victory of the Inquisition in Toulouse during the 1230s, however, the university began anew.

In general, it was in Italy, the greatest centre of medieval town life, that the growth of *studia* was most marked. Between 1204 and 1248 no less than nine were created, six in northern towns and three in Rome and southern Italy. Although the other faculties played a role there too, the northern ones were notable for their accent on law. Those in the south were the first quasinational universities in western history. One was the university founded in 1224 at Naples by Frederick II Hohenstaufen, an institution servicing the whole of this prince's southern kingdom and not licensed or owned by the town in which it was located, as were most *studia* in northern Italy. To supplement this centre of arts and legal studies, Latin Europe's most ancient school of medicine at Salerno was given additional privileges in 1231 by the same prince. Elsewhere than Italy and areas of French culture, the university system did not evolve quite so rapidly. Although princely initiatives date from as early as 1208–09, the Spanish universities do not seem to have got under way until around 1300, although the *studium* of Salamanca flourished from 1254 until its collapse in the '80s. In Germany there were no universities, although important *studia* such as that of the Dominican Order at Cologne were almost of this level.

With the exception of Paris and Bologna, these institutions were not large. In 1262 a chronicle was read before the masters or doctors (the terms are synonymous in this period) and before the bachelors and scholars of the liberal arts—the arts faculty—of Padua's *studium*. There were two professors in physics and natural science, one in logic, and six in grammar and rhetoric. The ideal foundation erected by Alphonso X at Salamanca in 1254 provided for one civilian jurist with a bachelor as assistant, three canonists, two logicians, two grammarians and two physicists. Small though these institutions were, their academic ceremonies were already like those of modern times. In 1215 Buoncompagno of Signa read his *Rhetorica antiqua* before the professors in canon and civil law and the other doctors and students of Bologna. At the end of his reading he was acclaimed and crowned with laurel. University curricula had also taken definitive form by the mid-thirteenth century. At Salerno the young doctors studied logic for three years and then devoted five years to Hippocrates, Galen and practical surgery. They were licensed after one final year of practical experience under an experienced physician. The standard schedule at Paris for a theology degree began with six years in the arts faculty, the last two as a bachelor attaining the M.A. To become a master or doctor of theology, the student spent eight years in the theological faculty, devoting four years to biblical exegesis and Peter Lombard's *Sentences*, and four years to serving as a bachelor disputant and teacher. In fact, this group of *baccalaurei formati* of theology was to emerge as the basic teaching staff in the later Middle Ages.

Naturally the curriculum was sometimes changed, and careers were rarely so regular. Most secular clerks dropped out of the theological race after about two years of higher study. Still, this meant much for the literacy and training of the clergy, even rural clergy. In the deanery of Stowe in the diocese of Lincoln, a territory provisioned by Cambridge University, only nine per cent of the rural priests had the M.A. in the period from 1205 to 1235, but by 1258 to 1279 twenty-one per cent boasted this distinction. Great careers took longer. Thomas Aquinas did his arts study at Naples and, between visits to pick up degrees at Paris, spent over ten years with Albertus Magnus in the Dominican *studium* at Cologne. Thereafter he taught and wrote regularly at Paris, with periods at the papal curia, Bologna and Naples. As a celebrated professor he also counselled popes, princes, bishops and ecclesiastical courts, dying on his way from Naples to attend the second Council of Lyons in 1274.

The *magistri* developed many of the professional qualities associated with modern academic intellectuals. Although long impeded by bishops or by officers such as the episcopal chancellor at Paris and the archdeacon at Bologna, the masters' real power was their monopoly of the right to examine students and thereby to control access to their profession, that is, to teaching or to practice. A royal edict of Melfi of 1231 expressed the balance of powers in regard to the doctors of Salerno:

> We order that in the future no one seeking the title of doctor shall dare to practise or otherwise heal unless he should first be approved at Salerno by the judgment of the masters in a public examination (*conventus*). He should then enter our presence [or that of our regent] with letters concerning his faith and sufficient learning both from the masters and other doctors, and then receive from us [or our regent] the licence to heal.[2]

The power of the masters to conduct examinations was firmly established even in universities like Bologna where the students were powerful and chose or had a hand in choosing the teaching staff.

The *magistri* were expected to publish as well as to teach. One of Thomas Aquinas's claims to attention was that, as one of his

---

[2] Cited in Paul O. Kristeller, 'The School of Salerno', *Studies in Renaissance Thought and Letters* (Rome, 1956), 528.

biographers remarked, he had written nearly one hundred books. Even the radical Franciscan Ubertino of Casale found it suitable to defend the famed Peter John Olivi before the papal court with the following admonition: 'And your Apostolic Wisdom should know that the quantity of books of brother Peter . . . is twenty-seven times greater in quantity of letters than the text of [Peter Lombard's] Sentences.'[3] Famed for its academics, the Dominican. Order produced historians such as Bernard Guy (d. 1331), a large part of whose history of his Order was devoted to listing the intellectual accomplishments and literary productivity of its famous scholars. Not that the doctors were always or slavishly respected. William of Auxerre was a distinguished Parisian theologian active in implementing the papal revival of the study of Aristotle's metaphysical and natural philosophical works in 1231. About him the Franciscan Salimbene casually remarked that, although a great logician and disputant, William, in his sermons, did not even know what he was saying.

Although chastened by a still vigorous tradition of Christian humility and anonymity, academic scholars habitually signed their works, just as did many of the artists and architects of the time. This was partly for reason of intellectual policy, in that an author must be responsible for what he has written, but it was principally motivated by professional pride. Few authors, however, went as far as the jurist Roffredus Epiphanii of Benevento (d. after 1243), the first letters of each chapter of whose *Quaestiones sabbathinae* spelled out *Roffredus Beneventanus juris civilis professor factor operis*.[4] This curious example brings up the problem of plagiarism. Of course, both juristic and scholastic treatises cited authors, ancient and modern alike, by name. This was because learned pieces were directed to an audience already in the know, and because these sources were authorities whose opinions had to be attacked or relied upon. It was different when the audience was broader. Careful in his technical works, Thomas Aquinas did not bother to footnote his debts to Vegetius in the second book of his *On the Rule of Princes*, a work addressed to a lay audience. There

[3] Cited in Decima L. Douie, *The Nature and the Effect of the Heresy of the Fraticelli* (1932), 95. It is not as bad as it sounds. Ubertino was objecting to the examiners' sampling of Peter's works.
[4] Friedrich Carl von Savigny, *Geschichte des römischen Rechts im Mittelalter* (Heidelberg, 1829), v, 186. I owe this reference to Domenico Maffei of the University of Siena.

were other motives also. Fearing to set his readers' teeth on edge before all of his argument had been ingested, the secular master Henry Goethals of Ghent (d. 1293) quoted but did not identify Aquinas when attacking his doctrine of original sin. The Dominicans, of course, identified it straightway, and quickly sprang to the defence of the *doctor communis*. Earlier authors were shaved even closer than this. The modern editor of John Quidort of Paris's (d. 1306) *On Royal and Papal Power* has asserted that at least a third of this inventive and radical work was lifted from recent authors like Aquinas and even from some living colleagues at Paris. Unlike modern authors who are impeded by literary copyright, medieval ones were not limited to borrowing or plagiarizing ideas, but could save themselves time by copying another author's text as well.

Especially among the theologians, the professors slowly built a corporate tradition that made them an institutional force to be reckoned with. However, intellectuals are always famous for internecine battles, and were so in the Middle Ages. Roger Bacon asserted that scholars like Alexander of Hales (d. 1245) and Albertus Magnus (d. 1280), whose training had taken place before Aristotle's natural history was fully accepted and who had had little language and mathematical instruction, were incapable of understanding philosophy and true theology. Albert, in turn, appears to have opined that Roger looked upon Aristotle as a God who could never err. The distinguished Franciscan theologian Peter Auriole (d. 1322) was notorious for his acidulous views about any and all of his contemporaries and teachers. Later on William of Ockham (d. about 1349) turned the tables on him by observing —possibly falsely—that he only just dipped into Peter's works, having wasted barely a day's worth of reading him in his whole life.

There was more here than intellectual backbiting. Outside ideological issues to be discussed later, institutional pressures made for conflict. When, as we shall see, the new mendicant orders invaded the parishes and dioceses of the secular clergy, they were much resisted at Paris by the secular masters. Nevertheless, supported strongly by the popes, they forced their way into the faculties at Paris from 1229, when the first Dominican, Roland of Cremona, began teaching there. The battle was fought on every level, occasionally erupting into great explosions such as that of the 1250s, when the career of the secular doctor William of St Amour (d. 1272) was ruined and he himself rusticated from Paris in 1260. In the intense ideological combats in and after the 1270s, moreover, the mendicants themselves split apart. Led by the English, the Franciscans attacked Thomas Aquinas, asserting the superior authority of members of their own order such as Bonaventure. In 1287 a general chapter of the Austin Friars reminded the brethren of their duty to defend the opinions of their great spokesman, Giles of Rome (Egidius Romanus, d. 1316). Delayed consistently since the Parisian condemnation of 1277 that attacked certain propositions expounded by Thomas Aquinas, the canonization of this great Dominican in 1323 and the revocation of the articles ostensibly attacking him by the University of Paris in 1325 left no doubt as to the efficacy of the Dominicans' protection of their major thinker. Not that all mendicants agreed with their own order's positions . . . But that is another story.

In spite of these often grave divisions, the *magistri* of the faculties of arts and theology did constitute an order, one able to withstand and defeat the power of bishops and other ecclesiastical authorities. Putting aside the bureaucratic struggles over who had the right to confer degrees or licences for teaching, the issue was largely that of who had superior competence in theological and philosophical matters. Aided by able theologians, Bishop Stephen Tempier of Paris condemned a series of Averroist and naturalist Aristotelian propositions, some Thomist, in 1277. Soon to be chancellor of the university in 1280, the theologian Geoffrey of Fontaines called this act scandalous because, as he said (quite without regard to the facts of the matter), those in authority were ignorant.

The academics were not slow to take on even higher authority, the pope. Recalling William of St Amour's debates with the mendicants in the 1250s, the poet John of Meung called the university the guardian of the key to Christianity, far superior in this authority to the popes. When the issue of the mendicants' privilege to preach was attacked again in 1290, the secular masters took up the cudgels under Henry of Ghent. Henry asked why, since the masters could discuss sacred Scripture, they could not question the mendicants' position in the Church. Famed for intemperate courage, the papal legate Benedict Gaetani (the later Boniface

VIII) summoned the professors to meet with him because 'they ought to know of a certainty that the *curia romana* does not have feathered feet, but instead leaden ones'. When the masters came before the council of the northern French clergy, Benedict addressed them:

> You sit in your chairs and you think that Christ is ruled by your reasons. . . . Not so, my brothers, not so. Because the world has been committed to us [at Rome], we ought to think not about what will humour you clerks, but about what is advantageous to the whole world. . . . You believe that you have great glory and commendation with us at Rome. On the contrary, we judge you to be fatuity and blather (*fumus* = smoke). . . . I have seen your arguments, and they are true, but they can be answered. And this is the answer (*solutio*):

that there be no more questioning of the mendicants' privileges. Warming to his material, the legate added:

> And I tell you truly that before the *curia romana* will remove this privilege from the same brethren, it will rather confound the University of Paris. For we have not been called in order to be learned or appear glorious, we have instead been called to save our souls. And because the life and teaching of the said brothers saves many souls, their privilege will always be preserved.

After this peroration, one of the masters sourly observed: 'Lo! So valid and firm were the arguments of the masters built up over ten years that they have all been shattered by the *dictum* of one cardinal. What do you think they will say [at Rome] when the university of masters established in their chairs was not able to answer one cardinal?'[5]

The curial party won this battle because both the mendicants and many of the French bishops stood behind it, and because the university had obtruded into a matter of church organization. It lost a later combat because the pope intervened in the sphere of theology, and because of basic institutional changes. By this time, as we shall see, the papacy had been defeated by the French state, the mendicants were divided and hostile to the papacy, and the

[5] Heinrich Finke, *Aus den Tagen Bonifaz VIII*, Anhänge, v–vii. The reference to leaden as against feathered feet is a play on the notion of fear in *Digest* 4, 2, 6: Sufficient fear is that which falls upon the constant man, not that which affects the timid one who, as birds take to flight, is moved to flee by any and everything.

conciliar idea of ecclesiastical government—often led by the bishops and Parisian professors of the *ecclesia gallicana*—was clearly threatening the papal monarchy. In an attempt to assert the independence of the papacy at Avignon from the northern French, John XXII supported the opinion of a papal commission of masters of theology on the beatific vision, enunciating a doctrine now generally thought to be orthodox. This was in 1333. In 1334, amid much excitement, twenty-nine masters of Paris informed the king that the pope's opinion was a personal one, having no other significance than that he held it. The king then supported his university. Shortly thereafter, the pope retired from the fray and withdrew his declaration. Even in the midst of it, the usually peppery John XXII was very defensive indeed. He wrote to the king: 'And because perhaps someone will tell you that we are not a master of theology, hear what a wise man says: "Give ear not to who speaks, but rather to what he says." '[6] And this embarrassed wise man held an office whose doctrinal infallibility had been asserted at the second council of Lyons in 1274!

Freedom is power, and the academics had a substantial measure of that.

Learning and intellectual freedom

The intention of the clerical intellectual was to educate man towards Christ. Because most thinkers of this time assumed that man's natural reason was capable of comprehending some part of the cosmos and even of glimpsing the nature of the divine principle itself, knowledge was almost idolized. This Christian 'naturalism'—if so it may be termed—suited an age of social growth and intellectual confidence. It enabled the Latins to plunder the wealth of ancient and Islamic thought, breathing the heady air of intellectual exploration. It was useful to a Church that, leading the world, was obliged to build rational institutional structures based on natural law and the principles of human behaviour. At the same time, this philosophy was inadequate. Like all naturalist systems, it did not enable man to predict his tomorrows or obviate his death. Because it was based on experience in time, it could not penetrate nature's mysteries, the origin of the

[6] Heinrich Denifle and E. Chatelain, *Chartularium universitatis Parisiensis* (Paris, 1889), I, 436–7, No. 978.

world or the meaning of eternity. Nor did it help solve human quandaries such as whether behaviour is based on natural determinism, free will and moral responsibility. Since a philosophy derived from man's experience in nature was unable to provide him with ultimate hope or consolation, thinkers of the time were also bound to insist upon those traditions that stressed the importance of what could not be understood or predicted by natural reason. Of these traditions, many were embodied in the teaching of the Church concerning the miraculous interventions of divine grace for man's good. Around this, in turn, had been built a different, non-rational way of looking at the world, one that had marked the theology of the Church from the days of its earliest reaction against the relatively naturalist thought of the Greco-Roman world.

Most intellectuals did not conceive of themselves as walking a tightrope strung between the pure naturalism of a philosophy of reason and the religious imperatives of man's need as expressed in theology. Some did, but the more typical way was to attempt to use philosophy and theology together in order to allay doubt and persuade men of the validity of Christian doctrine. To Roger Bacon philosophy was needed in order to make man believe in the glory of the eucharist, which, as he said, many deny, many doubt, and many receive with repugnance. Earlier, writing before 1230, Roland of Cremona explained his programme: 'Since there are many who believe that the human soul is corruptible and dies together with the death of man's organs, nor are there many who doubt this, and of those who say that this is not so, some are buttressed by faith alone . . . it has therefore seemed useful to me . . . to adduce the reasonings of philosophy.'[7]

What Roland and Roger shared with most of the intellectuals of their time was the belief that philosophy could aid the church, and that, although miracle, grace, and indeed the whole panoply of the non-naturalistic teaching of the faith were necessary to fulfil man on earth and in heaven, man's natural reason and his experience in nature were almost enough to enable him to see God and understand the cosmos. Aquinas taught:

> The gifts of grace are added to nature in such a way that they do not do away with it, but rather perfect it. Hence the light of the faith that is freely infused into us does not destroy the light of

[7] Cited from his *Expositio in Job* by Chenu, *La théologie au douzième siècle*, 28

natural knowledge implanted in us naturally. For although the natural light of the human mind is insufficient to show us these things made manifest by faith, it is nevertheless impossible that these things which the divine principle gives us by faith are contrary to those implanted in us by nature. Indeed, were that the case, one or the other would have to be false, and, since both are given to us by God, God would have to be the author of untruth, which is impossible. . . . For just as sacred doctrine is founded on the light of the faith, so is philosophy founded on the light of natural reason. Whence it is impossible that those things which are of philosophy can be contrary to those things which are of the faith.[8]

even though, of course, the things discovered by philosophy are merely imperfect imitations of the perfect. At the same time, the philosophy discovered by natural reason could lead to the discovery of higher things. As Roger Bacon put it:

The objective of all philosophy is that the creator shall be known by the knowledge of what he has created (*suae creaturae*), which creator . . . is to be served by an honourable cult, beauty of *mores*, and the honour of useful laws, that man should live in peace and honesty in this life. For speculative philosophy has as its end the knowledge of the creator through his creatures.[9]

These opinions did not mean that, in regard to the faith, reason or philosophy were considered superior to authority or theology. It was generally believed that reason and knowledge invariably buttressed the faith and that, indeed, although reason's function was ancillary, it was useful for the work of describing God and defending the faith. Bonaventure reminded his readers that good authority supported the use of philosophy for this end.

And to speak briefly, the [modern] masters have put little or nothing in their writings that you will not find in Augustine's books. Read Augustine's *De doctrina christiana* where he shows that Holy Scripture cannot be understood without the skills of the other sciences, and even where he shows that Israel's sons carried off Egypt's vases, just as the theological doctors have appropriated philosophical doctrine.[10]

[8] *In Boetium de trinitate* 2, 3, cited in Chenu, *La théologie comme science au treizième siècle*, 88
[9] *Opus maius* 2, 7, ed. Bridges, III, 51.
[10] *Epistola de tribus quaestionibus* 12 in *Opuscula varia* (Quaracchi, 1898) VIII, 336ab.

Following Augustine, it was asserted that reason and its dialectical tools were necessary to confound heretics and unbelievers. To those who advanced the dictum of Gregory the Great (d. 604) that 'faith to which human reason lends proof has no merit',[11] Abelard had long before had a ready answer. A man might claim that an idol was the true God and assert that there was no need to prove the proposition because you cannot argue about faith, thus confounding the Christian irrationalist by using his own defence. When dealing with this question, Aquinas stressed the function of persuasion. Reason must be employed to teach the faith. Certainly, if only doubt is to be removed, authority may be used. But if auditors, especially students, are to be persuaded 'then it is necessary to lean on reason to investigate the root of the truth and to show how what is said is true. If the master determines the question by naked authority, the auditor is indeed told what is the truth, but, acquiring nothing of knowledge, he goes away empty'.[12] Bonaventure said that one should even study the enemies of the faith:

> And perhaps certain [intellectuals] who are really studious (studiosi) appear to be over inquisitive (curiosi). But if someone should study the writings of heretics that he might better comprehend the truth by refuting their opinions, he would neither be a curiosus nor an heretic, but instead a Catholic.[13]

What lent these often silly, casuistical statements a special meaning for intellectual freedom was not only the belief that the knowledge derived by reason accorded with the faith, but also the conviction that knowledge grows. Priscian's ancient tag (quanto iuniores, tanto perspicatiores) was often quoted, although John of Salisbury and Peter of Blois used the more modest notion that, if moderns can see further than the ancients, it is because they are dwarfs on the shoulder of giants. There was a belief that there was much to be discovered. Roger Bacon argued that, men being what they are, past knowledge was not perfect. Earlier thinkers serve to fire us to go beyond them. There had already developed a controversy between the ancients and the moderns. In the early

---

[11] From his *Homiliae in Evangelia* cited in Martin Grabmann, *Die Geschichte der scholastischen Methode* I, 144. Abelard's answer is to be found in his *Dialogus inter philosophum, judaeum et christianum* in PL CLXXVIII, 1639.
[12] *Quodlibetum* 4, 9, ed. Spiazzi, *Quaestiones quodlibetales*, 83b.
[13] *De tribus quaestionibus* 12 in *Opuscula varia* (Quaracchi), 336a.

1200s the often vulgar Buoncompagno of Signa was told that he could not invent a new rhetoric because there was nothing new under the sun and the ancients had done it all. He replied that Aristotle knew nothing of rhetoric and Cicero not much more. He reminded his readers that, although the old saw 'nihil est recens sub sole' is true in general, it is not true in specifics: God daily creates new souls and infuses them into new bodies, and, working with the primordial hyle, a common artisan works it into new shapes at will. Indeed, the renovation of grace given us by the incarnation shows that man, God's creation, can perceive things with new eyes, whence the apostle Paul 'ordered him who came first to be silent when something has been revealed to him who comes after'.[14] There was also a psychic dimension to this feeling, one expressed by Joachim of Fiore among others:

> For when Scripture says, 'the eye is not satisfied with seeing nor the ear filled with hearing,' what else does it mean but that full and unending pleasure is to drink not what has been tasted but instead what is yet to be tasted, nor to hear what has been heard and interpreted by the fathers, but rather to hear something new from God's inexhaustible treasure, something we lack of divine wisdom.[15]

A problem about new knowledge was that it was often non-Christian. Preaching at the time of the prohibition of the study of natural history at Paris, James of Vitry counselled scholars to avoid Plato and Aristotle, partly because, as he said, theologians need no natural science and partly because Plato erred in saying that the planets were gods and Aristotle erred in asserting that the world was eternal. General of the Dominicans from 1254 to 1263, Humbert of Romans complained of the ostentation of professors who forever cite Plato, Aristotle, Algazel, Averroës, Alfarabi, and other 'unworthy' philosophers.

Most intellectuals did not share this attitude. Abelard acclaimed Plato to be the greatest of philosophers, and John of Salisbury stated that Aristotle had awakened the Latin mind from sleep or death. Writing in the late twelfth century, Daniel of Morley, that worshipper at the shrine of Arabic scientism in Toledo, condemned the teachers of Oxford and Paris for their hostility to, and

---

[14] *Rhetorica novissima*, prologue in *BIMA* II, 252.
[15] *Tractatus super quatuor evangelia*, ed. Ernesto Buonaiuti (Rome, 1930), 195. The biblical passage is Ecclesiastes 1:8.

ignorance of, natural science. After the reinstitution of Aristotelian studies at Paris, Roger Bacon attacked Alexander of Hales (d. 1245) on the same grounds. Bacon was concerned not only with natural science and metaphysics, but with moral philosophy as well. In his *Opus maius* Roger excerpted whole sections from Seneca, and defended his action.

> For although we are able to understand from our Christian faith what those philosophers did not know about the virtues that lead to grace, that is, faith, hope and charity, nevertheless we are less efficacious in works and do not equal them in elegance of statement about the virtues which are commonly required for honesty of life and the community of human society. . . . It is therefore essential that Christian philosophizers should study attentively the great glory created by these [pagan] philosophers.[16]

Nor was he being particularly inventive. Cicero and Seneca had been both praised and used in a practical treatise on town government written in the 1240s by John of Viterbo in Italy.

There were various ways to work the ancient and modern non-Christian philosophers into the Latin tradition. Just as civil law could be 'canonized' to include it in canon law, so could a philosopher's views be slipped into philosophical and even theological traditions. Abelard's attempt in his *Introduction to Theology* to liken Plato's *anima mundi* to the third person of the Trinity on the grounds that Plato sensed the nature of the godhead but was speaking in a disguised manner (*per involucrum*) was much discussed by thinkers of the later twelfth century. Later on Roger Bacon explained away the polytheism and sacrifices of his Roman favourites by asserting: 'Whence these philosophers busied themselves with such because of civil law and because of the multitude, not because of their truth, as Seneca says in the book he composed about superstition.'[17] Another way was to limit the area in which the teaching of the ancients and of the modern Jews and Arabs applied, a method to be discussed later in this chapter. Whatever the way, these sources seemed so useful that everyone employed them even to help prove theological propositions. In his theological *summa*, Alan of Lille tells his reader that he will prove

[16] *Baconis operis maioris pars septima seu moralis philosophia* 3, 5, *proemium*, ed. Eugenio Massa (1953), 132.
[17] *Ibid.*, 1, 8, ed. Massa, 132.

the unity of the Trinity 'first, by proving the unity of its essence by reasoning, second, by the varied authorities of the philosophers of the gentiles, and, third, by using the authorities of the holy fathers, both of the Old and New Testaments'.[18] He then proceeded to cite anything that came to hand—ancient philosophers, hermetic writings, Arabs like the astrologer Albumazar, as well as a mass of ancient and modern Church fathers and commentators.

Even when non-Christian and contrary to the faith, therefore, past intellectual tradition had a certain authority. This authority did not lie in the texts themselves so much as in the group that specialized in explicating them, the *magistri*. Earlier on we have examined this group and its autonomy with regard to the rest of the Church. The attainment of this autonomy required self-policing, that is, ideological solidarity. Albertus Magnus, for example, did not agree with Peter Lombard on original sin, but admitted that he would uphold Peter's view out of respect for the master. There were, of course, dissenting spirits. A more contentious man, Roger Bacon thought that the Lombard's book should be replaced in theological training by the study of sacred Scripture, history, natural philosophy and mathematics. But in important matters a rough solidarity existed. The revival of Aristotelian studies was pushed just as avidly by Albert and Thomas Aquinas as by the extremist naturalist school at Paris, those known to modern literature as the Latin Averroists, after the great Arabic commentator Averroës. That the *magistri* thought of themselves as authorities, even Church fathers, may be seen in a twelfth-century collection of excerpts called the *Liber Pancrisis*, a book 'that is all gold, because herein are contained the golden sentences and questions of the holy fathers Augustine, Jerome . . . and of the modern masters William of Champeaux, Yves of Chartres, Anselm of Laon'.[19]

The problem of intellectual freedom for the *magistri* cannot wholly be described in the familiar terms of the conflict between authority and reason in theology and philosophy. In the first place, those who defended reason were not merely disinterested intellectuals who were convinced that man's natural endowment

[18] *Quoniam homines* I, I, prologue, ed. Pierre Glorieux, *Archives d'histoire doctrinale et litteraire du moyen âge* XXVIII, (1953), 122.
[19] Cited in Chenu, *La théologie au douzième siècle*, 358, who dates the book in the second third of the century.

with reason enabled him to describe the godhead and the nature created by the deity, they were also those whose claim to attention rested on their capacity to utilize ancient and other non-Christian sources or authorities to buttress their arguments. Theirs was, in short, the authority of the learned professions, especially the academic. In the second, reliance on authority was a very complex thing. James of Vitry and the others of Peter Cantor's circle were certainly opposed to Plato, Aristotle, natural philosophy and all the rest, but they were not the less revolutionary because of that. Merely by trying to realize here on earth the teaching of the Acts of the Apostles—whatever the remote Platonic source of this social utopianism may have been—James and his colleagues could and did turn the world on its ear. And the same may be said of the later radical Franciscan Peter John Olivi, who stoutly maintained that Aristotle and the other philosophers had nothing to do with Christ. In sum, those who loved biblical authority were often revolutionary.

And authority itself required constant redefinition. Although much was said about the fact that no one was permitted to doubt dogma, few, if any, basic doctrines were not susceptible to interpretation. At the time of the controversy over the Eucharist in the late eleventh century, contemporaries had noted that Augustine differed from Ambrose. The attempt to reconcile these contradictory authorities obliged the intellectuals to employ their reason, however tortuously. Later on Aquinas perceived that the doctors who preceded the Arian heresy did not speak as clearly about the unity of the divine essence as did those who followed it. On another point, this Dominican noted that Augustine had changed his mind: 'For in his books written after the birth of the Pelagian heresy he spoke more cautiously of the power of free will than in those he wrote before the said heresy.'[20] Long before this, Alan of Lille had stated the problem more generally: authority, he said, has a nose of wax that can be bent in any direction, an opinion that was also applied to sacred Scripture, the source of all authority. Written in the first quarter of the fourteenth century, the *Mirror of Human Salvation* told its audience of preaching friars and parish priests that 'Sacred Scripture is a soft wax that takes upon itself the disposition of the form of the impression of

[20] From the *proemium* of his *Contra errores Graecorum*, in *Opera omnia* (ed. Pietro Ficcadori, 1853, rprnt.) xv, 239a.

every seal',[21] now of the lion, now of the eagle, now of Christ, and now of the devil. Authority, in fine, was much like reason, being largely texts and traditions interpreted by men, members of institutions who used their reason to advance their own and their institutions' causes.

The *magistri* or *divini* of the thirteenth century enjoyed a real measure of autonomy and rarely had their opinions suppressed by the rest of the Church and society. In spite of the death penalty so freely imposed on heretics in the thirteenth century, no *magister* was executed for his views before 1300. Not that theirs was always an easy road. Some, like William of Saint-Amour and Siger of Brabant (d. 1281–84), were silenced and even rusticated from Paris. Several had to trot down to Rome for clearance. Siger was on his way there when he died. Peter John Olivi had substantial parts of his works repeatedly condemned from 1284 onward but, in spite of formal submission, appears to have gone on writing as he saw fit until his death in 1298. Amalric of Bene (d. about 1205–06) suffered the graver obloquy of being anathematized after his death, and the sect that formed around his teaching, like that of the later Olivites, was hunted down. Books were burned, but none of the professors were killed: no *magister* before the astrologer Cecco of Ascoli in 1327, and no *divinus* before John Hus in 1415.

Although the opinions described above roughly represent the central position of the intellectuals of this age, the mainstream of thought oscillated between—to choose one aspect only—those who stressed the usefulness of natural philosophy and the power of reason and those who adopted the opposite position. This oscillation was most marked during crises in the Church's institutional life. Being static, somewhat antihistorical, and inclined to justify things as they were, the naturalist position was not of much help in founding new institutional bases for the Church in periods of revolutionary effervescence. At such moments the utopian urge of Latin society called upon the irrational or religious side of Christian hope. Once the old impediments were demolished, the philosophers of reason were the only ones who could erect a solid building by bringing into harmony all the conflicting viewpoints. An illustration of this is the development

[21] Prologue of the *Speculum humanae salvationis*, ed. J. Lutz and P. Perdrizet (1907), 3.

481

of the doctrine of transubstantiation. It seems suitable that in the Gregorian revolution, when the Church underwent institutional recasting and rose to lead Latin Europe, the rationalist defenders of the symbolic interpretation of the eucharist were defeated by the spokesmen of the miraculous interpretation. Symbolizing clerical power, the priest enacted a miracle that daily renewed the incarnation, binding God to man and to his institutions. In the course of this battle the rationalist Berengar of Tours (d. 1088) was castigated, but by the 1130s and 1140s, the Church's need for system and organization had led to the victory of those interested in rational dialectics and even natural science. In the long run Bernard of Clairvaux had lost out to Abelard. But here these names are freighted with too much meaning. Few individuals were wholly on one side or the other; depending on the specific polemical issue, most shared a bit of both.

A similar crisis occurred at the end of the twelfth and in the early years of the thirteenth century. The repression of the great popular heresies, the opening of the Church to new forms of monasticism and to increased lay participation, and the insistence on economic and social utopianism set the intellectual community afire. Not only was anything that smacked of intellectual systematization questioned, but also not a few of the utopian extremes—the beliefs of those, one might say, whose devotion to good causes had led them to go too far—came under attack. Although basically similar to the pattern seen in the late eleventh and early twelfth centuries, there was far more to align one's sights on in the developed philosophy and theology of this later time, and the cone of fire was consequently broader. Arabic Aristotelianism was attacked at the University of Paris in 1210 and 1215. The Platonic or pantheistic naturalism of Amalric of Bene was repudiated at Paris in 1210, as was that of the Carolingian philosopher John the Scot Erigena at Rome in 1225. The utopian and inevitabilist historical thought of Joachim of Fiore was rebuked at the Lateran council in 1215. Later these traditions sprang up again, their currency renewed either by institutional affiliations, as that of the Franciscans to Joachitic thought, or by a spate of new translations, as in the case of Aristotle and his commentators, ancient, Jewish or Arabic.

The last crisis to be considered here took place around 1300. The Church attacked the pullulation of the mendicant orders and their utopian extremism. Divided within itself, the Church was attacked and its leadership seriously questioned by lay society and the secular state. As exemplified in the work of Peter John Olivi, Joachitic utopianism and historicism were condemned. Aristotelian naturalism, and especially the Averroistic interpretation of that philosophy, had been questioned at Paris in 1270, and again in 1277, by the celebrated commission of Stephan Tempier, the bishop of Paris. In Italy the extreme positions of the determinist astrologers Peter of Abano, professor of medicine at Padua, and of Cecco of Ascoli, professor of astronomy at Bologna, were attacked with great vigour. An age of reaction or pacification followed, as is shown by the retraction of the articles against Thomas Aquinas in 1325.

Somewhat parenthetically, it may be noted that a not dissimilar struggle rent the Jewish intellectual community. A principal issue was the penetration into Latin Europe of Maimonides's *Guide to the Perplexed*, an attempt to find accord between the revealed religion of Jewry and the somewhat Platonized Aristotle of Arabic philosophical circles. The reaction of the Latin rabbinate was vehement, especially that of northern France and Germany. Although less successful than its counterpart in the Latin Christian tradition, the defence of the new thought was similar to that used by Latin philosophers at the time of the Parisian condemnation of the 1270s. A medical doctor from Barcelona and Rome, Seraiah ben Isaac ben Salathiel, said about the rabbi Nachmanides of Barcelona: 'Nachmanides was a Talmudist and understood nothing of philosophy and therefore attacked Maimonides in his commentary on the Pentateuch. . . . Now, he would certainly have done better to keep silent because if anybody wants to render a judgment he must first understand what he is judging.'[22] Nachmanides was actually a moderate in the matter and his defence of Maimonides is similar to that used to defend the Parisians who studied Aristotle and Averroës. Nahmanides asked the Talmudists: 'Has then Maimonides sought to disturb your greatness in Talmudic studies when he wrote a book that is intended to be a refuge against the Greek philosophers, against Aristotle and Galen? Have you ever read these books, or have you

[22] Cited in Moritz Güdemann, *Geschichte des Erziehungswesens und der Cultur der abendländischen Juden* (Vienna, 1880–84), II, 157–8.

been seduced by your own arguments?'[23] The struggle was as violent as anything seen among the Latins. Led by Rabbi Solomon ben Abraham, the Jews of Montpellier denounced the *Guide* to the Dominican inquisitors, who burned it in 1233.

Human history and natural history

Men of the time thought history was important. Sacred history was considered essential to the study of theology, and history generally was recommended as a means of educating man toward the good. Gerald of Wales outlined its advantages for a prince:

> And so the careful reading of the histories of the ancients is of no mean advantage to a prince because he is there warned of the chancy outcome of war, of difficult and fortunate circumstances, of hidden traps and precautions, and, history teaching, may examine as though in a mirror past actions to see what is to be done, what avoided, what fled, and what pursued.[24]

Godfrey of Viterbo addressed his versified and abbreviated history to the Emperor Henry VI with these words: 'It is impossible for an emperor . . . to attain . . . the glory of his office if he does not know the course and origin of the world. . . . For an emperor who is learned in philosophy is thought to stand before all other men, but, if he be ignorant of wisdom, he appears to err or stray rather than to reign.'[25] Godfrey then proceeded to repeat the mythical history of how the Trojans moved to Europe and founded the kingdom of the Franks.

This tendency to fuse myth with history is also shown by Martin of Troppau (*Polonus*, d. 1279) who blandly repeats the story that Charlemagne had visited Jerusalem and that Pope Sylvester II (Gerbert of Aurillac, d. 1003), famed in his time for mathematical and scientific knowledge derived from the Arabs, had, like Faust, sold his soul to the devil in return for knowledge and power. And Martin, a papal penitentiary, prelate and counsellor of princes, was a principal source of historical information for intellectuals of the stature of Marsiglio of Padua and William of Ockham! It is therefore evident that, in this period, history was popular, intended to catch the eye, and, above all, programmatic

[23] Cited *Ibid.*, I, 72.
[24] *De principis instructione* I, II in *Rolls Series* XXVIII, viii, 42–3.
[25] *Memoria seculorum*, prologue in *MGH. SS.* XXII, 103.

or polemical. Godfrey's tale about the Trojans and Franks was a programmatic statement. From the time of the Carolingian Franks onward, the inheritance of the presumed brothers of the Trojan Aeneas who founded Rome was their natural right to govern other peoples, and the story of the Franks, unconquered by Rome, was the *locus classicus* of the idea of the natural freedom of the German race. Like the later Marsiglio of Padua, John of Paris used history polemically to argue against those who put the Church and papal power above the state. History tells us, he says, that in the days of the sainted Emperor Henry III, no pope could be elected without imperial assent, and that ecclesiastical unction, although mentioned in the Old Testament, is nowhere to be found in the New. Besides, he added, unction was not used everywhere in his own day, notably not in the monarchies of Spain. In France royal power had clearly preceded ecclesiastical authority.

> 'Therefore royal power is not from the pope either intrinsically or in terms of its exercise, but instead from God and from the people electing the king either in person or in dynasty. . . . To say then that royal power derives immediately from God and afterward from the pope is utterly ridiculous.'[26]

History was conceived of in a variety of ways. From Abelard onwards, those of the philosophical or dialectical tradition viewed it as something static, as, in a sense, something in which great changes were not likely to take place until the end of time. Times change, it was said, but not the faith. Little things are mutable, but great things unchanging. Christian historicism recognized, of course, that there had been different ages and that the world was to end, but this perception could be robbed of its attraction for an enthusiast by a division of ages such as that propounded in the work of Otto of Freising, the great historian of the mid-twelfth century. Otto divided history into three ages: that of the Old Testament and the law, the present age of the New Testament and the sacraments, and a third age, the end of time, or the end of the world. The second or contemporary age was a dry chronicle of the histories of the successive empires. It was a time of senescence, awaiting the antichrist and the sound of the last trump. Thomas Aquinas's view of the past was more complex, but he too likened the age in which moderns lived to that of old age. And senescence was more or less ageless:

[26] *De potestate regia et papali* 10, ed. Jean Leclercq (1942), 199.

The last age is the present *status*, after which there is no further age of salvation's [history], just as there is no further age after old age. For, although there is a determined number of years in the other ages of men, there is not in old age, because old age begins at the sixtieth year and some people live for 120 years, and so it is not determined how long this status of the world will last.'[27]

This resigned passivity did not find universal favour. There were many who found the modern age superior to preceding ages. As expressed by the Roman grammarian Priscian, an ancient tradition asserted the superiority of modern learning over that of the past. Aquinas himself asserted that man's successive generations ever better comprehended both the speculative and practical sciences, a conviction received with especial sympathy by those intellectuals whose bent was practical or technical. This has already been seen in Buoncompagno of Signa and, in spite of the authority of Roman law, it was part of the legal tradition as well. Writing before 1256, Rolandino Passaggeri introduced his section on contracts with the following words:

And because it is true that those who are more recent are more perspicacious and because our age brings with it new and more subtle *mores* in matters contractual as in other things, it is fitting that, ancient rites being omitted—not that we should judge them wrong or contrary to law, but rather that they are somewhat foreign or suitable to few or none of the subtleties of modern men (*modernorum*)—we should imitate the character (*forma*) of our age in the dispositions and modes of contracts, just as we do in other things, and we should employ the customs of our own time in order that the quality of our life should be improved (*observantia vitae reformetur*).[28]

This straightforward idea of man's advancement failed to appeal to enthusiasts and utopians, who required something stronger, a religious dimension or an image of moral progress. Such a tradition had also long existed in the west. The Parisian canon regular and teacher, Hugh of Saint-Victor, distinguished the character of each succeeding age in the history of the faith. Not only did the earlier ages differ from those that followed in

---

[27] *In epistolam ad Hebraeos* 9, 5 in *Opera omnia* (Parma, 1852–73) XIII, 744b, cited in Chenu, *La théologie au douzième siècle*, 76.
[28] *Summa artis notariae* I, *praefatio*, in Venice 1583, I, 2v. See *Code* 3, 38, 3.

their spiritual character, but also each age had within it a few spokesmen of the following one, the prophets of what was to come, the men before their time. This insight—if such it may be termed—was enthusiastically picked up by many followers.

Still stronger notions of progress were to be seen in the writings of the Premonstratensian Anselm of Havelberg, who died as archbishop of Ravenna in 1158. Defending the multiplication of new orders in the Church, he said that spiritual progress was the essential quality of the Christian faith. Although he believed that men were living in the last of three ages, that initiated by Christ's coming, there was progress within that age. Seven seals, or periods, were delineated, of which men were then in the fourth, and, in spite of persecutions, each age was one of fulfilment through which the Church moved on its upward course. Praising the new orders—the Vallumbrosans, Cistercians, and others—Anselm said: 'Succeeding from generation to generation, God's wonderful dispensation causes the youth of the Church to be ever renewed by a new order (*religio*), just as the youth of the eagle which seeks to fly higher in contemplation.'[29] Nor should it cause surprise that an unchanging God allows the Church to change the forms of its devotion,

> because it is necessary that, according to the progression of time, the signs of spiritual grace should increase and increasingly declare the truth. Thus, together with the desire, the knowledge of the truth will grow in the course of time, and so first there have been published good things, then better, and lastly the very best.[30]

And Scripture revealed itself progressively. Commenting on Revelation 6:5 Richard of Saint-Victor (d. 1173) glossed the text: ' "And when he had opened the third seal," that is, when according to the progress of time, the effect of the divine promise and the progress of human salvation more and more had begun to be discerned and known in sacred Scripture, "I heard the third beast saying, Come and see." '[31]

By the latter part of the century these ideas had been elaborated into many schemes of history. Some were non-utopian. Writing

[29] *Dialogus* I, 10 in *PL* CLXXXVIII, 1157.
[30] *Dialogus* I, 13 in *PL* CLXXXVIII, 1160.
[31] Cited in Wilhelm Kamlah, *Apokalypse und Geschichtstheologie : Die mittelalterliche Auslegung der Apokalypse vor Joachim von Fiore* (Berlin, 1935), 118.

shortly before his death in 1202, the dean of Saint Paul's, Ralph of Diceto, divided history into three ages: the ancient age (*vetustissima*) that ended with the incarnation, the past age (*vetera*) of redemption, and the contemporary age (*moderna*) beginning in the mid-twelfth century. For such schemes to become utopian or revolutionary, however, they had to be tied up with the unfolding revelation of an ever purer faith in the procession of the three persons of the Trinity. Conceived of in time, this inevitable procession of the divine gave the enthusiast something analogous to modern secular fervours in that all he had to do was to tape down the actual history of this ineluctable progress to make sure that he mounted the right bandwagon before, so to speak, it galloped off. For this the enthusiasm of innocence—a quality often possessed by the learned—was needed. Such a one was Joachim of Fiore. This abbot envisaged the successive ages of the Father, the Son, and the Holy Ghost. In the final age the slow evolution from the slavery of the Mosaic law through the lighter burden of the law of Christ was to be fulfilled in the full spiritual freedom of the Holy Spirit. Then were all men to receive and live on earth some part of the monastic vocation. Echoing contemporary social movements like the children's or youth crusades and the exemplification of childhood's innocence in the life of saints like Francis of Assisi, Joachim replaced old age with youth as the distinguishing mark of the age to come. In the first age of the Old Testament the maturity of the aged (*maturitas senum*) had taught man to shun the transitory and cleave to the lasting. In the second age of the New Testament the patience of youths (*patientia iuvenum*) became man's teacher. In the third age leadership was to be surrendered to the sincerity of children (*sinceritas puerorum*), unspoiled by property and the corruptions of the flesh.

To this was added a conviction that the history of the faith had always been marked by the increasing perfection of its institutions. Joachim insisted that this inevitable spiritual progress was to be embodied in ever new orders and devotions. The sanguine abbot not only believed that the older orders, including Peter's see and its priesthood, were soon to be replaced or purified by spiritualized monks, but also that they would trip over themselves in their haste to foster and protect the new order.

For just as the old man Simeon lifted up the boy [Christ] in his arms, so the successors of Peter . . . , seeing this order which

488

follows Christ's footsteps in spiritual virtue, will sustain it by [their] authority . . .

Indeed, the old order of things should rejoice that it will be replaced:

> nor should it grieve over its own dissolution since it knows that it will remain in a better succession . . . and, if it knows that it will be succeeded by such a fruit, what order can grieve that its own particular perfection is lacking in itself, when a universal perfection succeeds it?[32]

Although Joachim preached ineluctable progress, the victory he foresaw was not to be won easily. Before the angel pope came to usher in a new earthly paradise, an apocalyptic upheaval complete with antichrist and Armageddon was to afflict mankind. Even before this frightening consummation, much had to be fought out by his followers. Perhaps influenced by the followers of Gilbert of La Porrée, bishop of Poitiers, Joachim attacked the static image of trinitarian unity found in Peter Lombard and insisted on his own view of the historical procession of the three persons. Showing that the old order was not quite so willing to step down as the abbot envisaged, this view was roundly condemned by the pope and the bishops meeting at the Lateran Council in 1215. Perhaps Joachim had suspected this unwillingness. Although he hoped that Rome would support the new order and thereby become a spiritualized Church purveying spiritualized sacraments, he not infrequently referred to the Church in the world as the great whore (*meretrix magna*), a view avidly developed by his followers. Indeed, although Joachim himself was vague about details, Joachitic sectarians in Italy and elsewhere, like the earlier Amalricians at Paris, proclaimed the abolition of the Church as it was. William the Breton (d. 1224) reported that the Parisian groups had argued

> that the power of the Father lasted as long as the Mosaic law; and, because it is written, 'the old shall be cast out when new things come in', after Christ came, they abolished all the sacraments of the Old Testament, and then the new law flourished up to this time. In this time therefore they said that the sacraments of the New Testament are come to an end and the time of the Holy Spirit has begun, in which they said that confession,

[32] *Tractatus super quatuor evangelia*, ed. Buonaiuti, 80. For Simeon see Luke 2:25ff.

baptism, the Eucharist and other sacraments without which salvation cannot be had have no longer any further place, but each man inwardly merely through the grace of the Holy Spirit can be saved without any exterior act.[33]

The Parisian Amalricians were convinced that the age of the Holy Spirit had already begun or would within five years, but Joachim of Fiore, according to such supporters as the Franciscan Hugh of Digne (d. by 1257), never actually named a time, although he thought of it as imminent. Both his enemies and the later Franciscan Spirituals, however, were sure that he had. In the condemnation of Joachitic views at Anagni in 1255, a judge stated:

> So much for the words of Joachim, by which he strives in a bizarre and incredible way to exalt I know not what order that will come, as he says, at the end of the second age, of which there now remain only five years, . . . by which, I say, he seeks not only to exalt [this order] over all other orders, but indeed above the whole Church and the whole world, as is clearly stated in many passages of the above work.[34]

Explaining to his brother Franciscans why the abbot's doctrines had failed to elicit broad support, Hugh of Digne put his finger on the truth. Like most utopian theories, Joachim's asked too much of ordinary mortals. History was on the side of the believers, but it was not going to be easy. 'The second impediment that prevented the abbot Joachim from being believed was that he predicted future tribulations. This was the reason why the Jews had slain their prophets. . . . For carnal men do not willingly hear about future tribulations, but instead about consolations.'[35] Lastly, if Joachim had not named a date, his followers certainly had.

Moved by a not dissimilar conception of progress, with its promise of material and moral improvement, modern man is apt to exaggerate the revolutionary or heretical possibilities of such an idea in the Middle Ages. It must nevertheless be remembered

[33] Cited from his *De gestis Philippi II* by Herbert Grundmann, *Religiöse Bewegungen im Mittelalter*, 365–6. The biblical passage is an adaptation of Leviticus 26:10.
[34] The second article of the protocol of the commission at Anagni, ed. Heinrich Denifle, 'Das Evangelium aeternum und die Commission zu Anagni', *Archiv für Litteratur- und Kirchengeschichte des Mittelalters* II, (1900), 112.
[35] Recounted by Salimbene in his *Cronica* 15 in *MGH. SS.* xxxii, 238.

that the idea of restoring a primal bliss, now long since lost, was just as useful in stimulating 'reformist' and revolutionary action in this period. Robert of Curzon envisaged the reform of society and the Church in terms of a return to the primitive community of the apostles. Imitation of the apostles or of the Saviour was attempted not only by possessed individuals like Francis of Assisi, but also by whole movements, like the extremist wing of the Franciscans. Nor did the notion of restoration necessarily conflict with that of progress. Man's capacity to restore a spiritual perfection that had been lost shows that God can make man perfectible, and this idea could be combined with the humbler notion of mundane advancement or progress. All that was needed to combine the two was to settle upon a great historical event, as did Bonaventure when discussing the origin and advancement of the Franciscan order:

> Does it not move you that the brothers were simple and un-learned in the beginning? Indeed, this ought greatly to confirm your faith in the order. I confess before God that it is this that has made me love the life of Francis so greatly, that it is like the beginning and perfection of the Church, which first began with simple fishermen and afterward advanced to famous and learned doctors. And this is what you will see in the religion of the blessed Francis, namely, that God shows that it was not invented by man's prudence, but instead by Christ; . . . for it shows that this work was divine since learned men did not disdain to descend into the company of simple ones, bearing in mind the apostle's message: 'If there is a wise man among you, let him become a fool, that he may be wise.'[36]

Much in vogue in the thirteenth century, especially in Franciscan circles, this type of thought was not without its difficulties. It could not be seriously proposed that Francis was the equal of Christ or the Franciscans of the apostles. This impediment, however, could be sidestepped. Borrowing heavily from Peter John Olivi, Ubertino of Casale, the leader of the spiritual Franciscans, agreed in 1305 that Francis and his brethren were certainly not Christ and the apostles. Nevertheless, there had been something imperfect or unrealized about the apostolic age. Because of the

---

[36] *De tribus quaestionibus* 13 in *Opuscula varia* (Quarachi), 336ab. The biblical passage is 1 Corinthians 3:18.

perfidy of the synagogue and because the gentiles were then incapable of understanding so spiritual an idea,

> the Holy Spirit showed the apostles that the state of the perfection of the evangelical life was not at that time to be transferred to the multitude of the people. Whence the apostles did not require this state to be observed in the churches they ruled, that state, that is, that they had accepted when it was imposed upon them by Christ and which they [as individuals] had fully obeyed.[37]

Referring to Joachim of Fiore, Ubertino goes on to observe that the true or fulfilled apostolic mission was not to be spread till a later time—the sixth seal of the seventh age, by his calculation. As John the Divine had prophesied in Revelation 7:2, that age was to see the coming of the angel ascending from the east, bearing the sign of the living God. To Ubertino and those of his persuasion this angel was Francis of Assisi, and he noted in passing that Bonaventure had asserted this identity when preaching at Paris. In short, Francis was not Christ nor were the Franciscans the apostles, but Christ's full apostolate was to be made real only by the Franciscans in their own age.

In spite of all its fancifulness and bizarre complexities, as well as the repressions that this type of thought provoked, the Christian idea of progress never lost its appeal. Linked to a utopian view of the world and of man's relation to his neighbour, to the attack on usury, to the growth of economic corporatism, and to the exaltation of poverty and communal living, it was an essential part of the psychic enthusiasm and hopefulness of the age. It flourished in a final burst of glory at the end of the thirteenth century when, in the work of Roger Bacon and others, this historical vision was combined with the natural history and moral sociology of the Aristotelians. In Roger, mechanical inventions like flying machines and optical devices, astral and geographical influences, the correct ordering of law and society, the abolition of sexual and moral irregularity, and the reform of education, were all necessary to defeat the Tatars, the Saracens, and the soon-to-appear antichrist.

---

[37] *Arbor vitae crucifixae Jesu Christi* 5, 1 in Venice 1485 (rptd), 422a. Ubertino's debt to Peter is seen in his repeated story of Bonaventure mentioned below. For this see article 20 of the condemnation of Peter's *Postilla in apocalypsim* as condemned presumably in 1325 published in Ignaz von Dollinger, *Beiträge zur Sektengeschichte des Mittelalters* (Munich, 1890) II, 540.

I do not wish 'to set my mouth against the heavens', but I know that if the Church would study Holy Scripture and sacred prophecy and the foretellings of the Sibyl, of Merlin, of Aquila, of Joachim and many others, and also the histories and books of the philosophers, and would order the ways of astronomy to be studied, a sufficient suspicion or even a certitude of the time of the antichrist will be discovered. . . . And it is believed by all the wise that we are not far from the times of the antichrist. . . . And because individuals, cities and whole regions can be changed for the better according to the aforesaid, life should be prolonged as long as necessary, all things should be managed functionally, and even greater things can be done than are mentioned in this book not only in the natural sciences, but also in the moral sciences and arts, as is evident in Moses and Aristotle.[38]

Although the religious idea of progress could not readily be applied to the world of nature, men felt hopeful as they dealt with natural history in this period. Borrowing from Aristotle, intellectuals accepted the notion that, since nature begins with less perfect forms, the later the time, the more perfect was the natural object. More important in setting the mood of the age, this was a time when men were everywhere clearing forests and swamps, when architecture and metalwork had surpassed in quantity and technical quality the achievement of the ancients and of other contemporary cultures, and when the development of transportation was taking the decisive steps forward that were eventually to give western Europe a crushing superiority over all its neighbours. Not that the twelfth and thirteenth centuries saw technological innovation on a scale comparable to that of modern times. Still, men could imagine that nature was beneficent and that it could be conquered and put to man's use. Just as the Latins plundered Greek and Islamic society economically, so also did they intellectually. The spate of new translations of Arabic, Jewish, Byzantine, and classical sources mentioned briefly in the first chapter attests the Latins' ability to use the conceptions of other peoples. Albertus Magnus may not have been an inventive thinker, but his encyclopedic interest in the sciences—indeed, in

[38] A composite quotation from the *Opus maius* 4, 16, sections on Mathematics and Astrology in ed. Bridges I, 269 and 402. The biblical paraphrase is from Psalm 72 (73):9. The prophecies mentioned above were largely composed in the thirteenth century.

all kinds of subjects and all kinds of authors—is an example of the aggressive confidence of the Latin mind.

There was a wide gap in the natural science of this age between the theoretical sciences propounded by the schoolmen and the practical applications of artisans, architects and others, but the width of this gap can be exaggerated. As the occasional act ennobling or granting privileges to architects or master of works especially in Italy shows, the higher practical arts were no longer rigidly separated from the liberal arts around 1300. A distinction was made between practice and theory but their necessary relationship was recognized in contracts of apprenticeship recorded in Rolandino Passaggeri's *summa* of the notarial art of 1256. Neophytes were to be instructed in both the *practica* and *theorica* of their art or craft. Perhaps the best example of the wedding of theory and practice was the medical profession. The translator Dominic Gundisalvo, archdeacon of Segovia (d. after 1190), had said, paraphrasing Alfarabi and the ancients:

> The royal virtue is composed of two virtues, one of which consists in the knowledge of universal rules and the other in the use of observation and the assiduity in working and testing, just as a medical doctor does not become a perfect physician unless he has knowledge of universal rules, which is called *theorica*, and unless he demonstrates assiduity in healing and in experiments with medicines with the sick, which is called *practica*.[39]

There were humanists who played with science. Essentially a literary man, Alexander Neckham, who had taught at Paris and who died as abbot of Cirencester in 1213, compiled not only a moralized account of natural history, but also a dictionary of tools and domestic implements. The great mathematician of the age, Leonard Fibonacci of Pisa, whose own work, although theoretical, was not philosophical or speculative, kept in touch with those who were. He dedicated his manual of geometry and measurement to the imperial astronomer Dominic the Spaniard and his *Book of the Abacus* to the noted translator and astrologer Michael Scot.

Still the gap was wide. More than the 'religious' nature of the age or the clerical character of its intellectuals, the lack of a general,

---

[39] *De divisione philosophie, de partibus practice philosophie,* ed. Ludwig Baur, *Beiträge zur Geschichte der Philosophie des Mittelalters* (Münster, 1903), IV, ii-iii, 135.

efficacious technology of science explains this gap. The inability to do much with what knowledge there was led theoretical minds interested in natural science toward teleological and metaphysical speculations and vulgar practitioners and some intellectuals to the deceptive, if remunerative, satisfactions of magic. The difficulty here was not that such men postulated a necessary interlinking of all of nature's parts from the stars to the earth and a common quality, or essence, within all of the elements composing the cosmos. It was rather that neither the natural scientists nor the street magicians could use their possibly valid theories for the purpose of transmuting metals, predicting the course of nature, or, save for the most obvious phenomena, showing the effects of the movements of heavenly bodies on man's life. Both common sense and anti-intellectualism lay behind the widespread mockery of the theoreticians and the magicians, popular though the latter sometimes were. To Buoncompagno of Signa alchemy was pure futility, whose adepts were never able to accomplish anything, because, as he put it, their subject contained nothing, and about nothing nothing is true. What is more, 'intelligent sailors know more about the changes of the weather that astrologers by their learning'. Nor was it only what moderns call the pseudo-sciences that elicited his mirth. He felt the same way about mathematicians, to whom he said, 'you really have little or nothing to boast about because you merely count other people's things, and in this you're like common moneychangers. So don't boast about the science of numbers because there's hardly anyone so stupid that he can't count his own money.'[40]

On the other hand, the vulgarities of common sense were combated not only, so to speak, by the needs of the popular market, but also by strong traditions among the intellectuals. One wonders why, for example, since most of Aristotle's works of importance to natural philosophy had been translated from the Greek by the 1160s, some minds were ever drawn to Arab translations and pseudo-scientific works, especially to those laden with overtones of natural determinism. Other than the obvious facts that anything is grist for somebody's mill and that some things are intrinsically interesting, there seem to be two motives for this. One is that some intellectuals were what their enemies claimed them to be, *curiosi*: lovers of the foreign, prone to hide or obfuscate the clear expres-

[40] *Rhetorica novissima* 8, 3 in *BIMA* II, 289b.

495

sion of obvious ideas by inserting turgid phrases culled from often appalling translations. The second is more consequential. However true and useful, the Aristotelian tradition was too secularist, too hostile to dreams and revelation. By that is meant that it was psychically too narrow to encompass man's moods, to inspire utopian hope or feelings of certitude. What drove some men away from Aristotelian natural history and drew them to Arabic astrology was much the same impulse that attracted them to Platonic or Platonizing thought: Aristotle's monotone intellectualism as against Plato's emotional melodiousness.

Platonic and other ideological fancifulness nevertheless sometimes led to useful scientific work. There was, for example, the study of optics by the English school of Robert Grosseteste and his followers through Roger Bacon, its great popularizer. Seeking to harmonize the illuminative mysticism of Platonic Augustinianism with the naturalism of the Aristotelians, these latter day Boethians linked together dialectics, the experimental, or experiential, side of the natural sciences, and mathematics to create a scientific method. Bacon summed it up:

> There are two ways of knowing, argument and experience. Argument demonstrates and makes us concede conclusions, but it does not certify or remove doubt . . . unless the truth is discovered by experience. . . . When arguments do not certify these [propositions about natural phenomena], abundant experiences are to be carefully examined by means of instruments . . . and so in such matters no opinion can give certainty, for all depends upon experience.[41]

And what lent experience or experiment certainty was the employment of mathematics:

> In mathematics we can reach the full truth without error and certitude without doubt in all things because mathematics provides a demonstration by means of its own necessary cause. And a demonstration in turn tells us the truth about things. . . . But in the other sciences without benefit of mathematics, there are so many doubts, so many opinions, so many errors on the part of man that they cannot be explained, as is obvious, since a demonstration by its own necessary cause is not in them of their own power, in that in natural things there is no necessity

---

[41] *Opus maius* 6, 1 and 12, ed. Bridges II, 166 and 201, a composite quotation from several chapters.

because of the generation and corruption of their own causes and therefore of their own effects. . . . And therefore in mathematics alone is there certitude without doubt.[42]

Natural science, like history, posed a problem to the philosophers and theologians of the time, that of determinism. In Albumazar's *Introduction to Astronomy*, which John of Seville translated around 1133, the great Arab astrologer argued:

Just as the planets portend a man's possible range of choice, they likewise show that a man can choose only what they prognosticate because his choice of a thing or of its contrary is made by the spirit of reason which is implanted in the individual's living mind by means of the influences (*significationes*) of the planets.[43]

As John of Salisbury repeatedly stressed in his *Policraticus*, this emphasis on the role of nature or the stars in determining man's and nature's history subsumed God into nature and deprived both him and man of free will—a quality certainly necessary for civil and moral order, for who—one might ask—can justifiably hang a man who is not responsible for his actions? Nevertheless, John reserved his real hostility for the magicians, and his opposition was moderate. Like Thomas Aquinas afterwards, he saw value in astrology:

Although I assert that no trust should be put in auguries, I nevertheless trust and do not deny the value of those signs which divine disposition has given to educate God's creatures. 'For in many places and many ways, God instructs his creatures, and . . . makes clear what will happen now by the voices of the elements, and now by the evidences of sensible and insensible things'.[44]

Such accommodations aside, fears inspired by theories of astrological and other natural determination helped provoke the assault on Aristotelian naturalism at Paris in the early 1200s.

In spite of this opposition, all sorts of astral, geographical and climatological theories of determination invented by the ancients and elaborated by the Arabs became part of the intellectuals' dis-

[42] *Opus maius* 4, 1, 13, ed. Bridges I, 105–6.
[43] Cited in Richard Lemay, *Abu Ma'Shar and Latin Aristotelianism in the Twelfth Century* (Beirut, 1962), 128n.
[44] *Policraticus* 2, 2, ed. Webb I, 417a. John garbled the biblical passage from Hebrews 1:1.

497

course during the thirteenth century. So familiar were these by 1300 that they were used to explain the natural liberty of one's own people, as by Peter Dubois for the northern French, and the slavishness of others, as by Ptolemy of Lucca. One could accept much if, like Aquinas, one restricted determinism of nature to man's lower nature. Even men's *mores* and morals could be determined by the climate or the stars, but this was limited by man's free will, God's grace, the devil's temptation, and even, as Bacon quaintly added, good or bad advice, especially in childhood. Both Albertus Magnus and Roger Bacon thought one could avoid the practical weakness of astronomical naturalism and assert its present and future value by broadening its focus. Bacon expressed this as follows:

> It is clear from these and similar writings that it was not Ptolemy's intention for the astrologer to render a sure judgment in individual cases . . . but he can render a limited judgment not in every case but instead in a general matter (*universali*), a judgment midway between the necessary and the impossible.[45]

Even this relatively sage advice was only sometimes able to restrain those whose theoretical inclinations were totalitarian or who responded to man's need for comfort and predictability. Bacon's own utopianism led him not only to believe in wholly undemonstrable relationships between astronomical conjunctions and past historical events, such as the children's crusade, but also to predict that astrology would be a necessary tool in the forthcoming war against the infidel and the antichrist.

'Scientia' and 'sapientia'

A teacher at Paris, Henry Goethals of Ghent observed about the relationship of divine and natural law to positive law that 'it is our design to live according to nature'.[46] An Augustinian critic of Thomistic Aristotelianism, Henry did not quite mean what a modern or an ancient stoic would by this phrase, but there is little doubt that he conceived of a world in which it was both profitable and possible to link God, nature and man. Even more vigorous

[45] *Opus maius* 4, *judicia astronomiae*, ed. Bridges I, 245.
[46] *Quodlibet* 2, question 17, cited in Georges de Lagarde, *La naissance de l'esprit laïque au déclin du moyen âge*, III, 253.

were the opinions of Thomas Aquinas and others who expanded the sphere of natural theology in the thirteenth century. From man's experience in nature, philosophy could prove the existence and even define some of the attributes of the deity, who, through revelation, explained nature's meaning and guided the hopes, passions and institutional structures of mankind. Thomas argued that philosophy was useful and necessary for the faith. It confounded those who combated the faith by showing that their arguments were either false or unnecessary. More significant were two other functions of philosophy:

> First, to prove those things that are the preambles to the faith, that are needed in order to know the faith, or those things proved by philosophy that faith presupposes, that is, those things proved by natural reason concerning God, namely, that God exists, or that God is one, or similar things concerning God or his creatures. Second, to make known things of the faith by means of analogies (*similitudines*), just as Augustine in his book *On the Trinity* used many analogies taken from philosophical doctrines in order to explain the Trinity.[47]

Naturalist theologians and philosophers were, however, faced by real quandaries. Perhaps because of the influence of Platonism, those who sought to elevate nature and the natural world stressed the role of the divine spirit or its immediate manifestations in providing man with his intellect and matter with its individuality and particular form. To judge from the excerpts collected by their enemies, this was the root of the varied pantheisms attributed to Amalric of Bene and David of Dinant in the early 1200s, and also of the doctrine described as the unity of the intellect, which was attributed to Averroës and to the Latin Averroists, especially Siger of Brabant (d. about 1284). Such doctrines not only weakened the Christian's conviction of corporeal and personal immortality, but also, by making both individuation and the individual's capacity to think dependent on the emanations of a necessarily uniform divine spirit, threatened individual responsibility. Writing in 1323, Thomas Aquinas's quasi-official biographer, William of Tocco, congratulated his hero:

> For quite apart from the said great volumes . . . in which he

---

[47] From his *In Boetium de trinitate* cited in Chenu, *La théologie comme science au treizième siècle*, 89.

confuted the ancient heresies, he . . . destroyed the heresies appearing in his own time, of which the first was that of Aver-roës, who said that there was one intellect common to all men. Which error encouraged the crimes of the wicked and detracted from the virtues of the saintly, since, if there is but one mind in all men, there is no difference between men nor distance between merits. And this even penetrated strongly into the minds of the ignorant and thus spread so dangerously that when a certain knight was asked in Paris if he wished to purge himself of his crimes, he answered: 'If the soul of the blessed Peter is saved, I will be also, because, if we know everything by means of one intellect, we will share the same fate.'[48]

To defeat the Platonizing Aristotelians, Thomas turned to Aristotle himself. He followed the great naturalist in locating his source of individuation and cognition in the matter initially created and then enlivened by the divine spirit. Since no two things in nature are exactly alike, this seemed to resolve the problem of individuation and intellection. It required, however, that Thomas and those like him play again a game that had been played in antiquity and in Islam. The perception given to an individual by his material corporeality had somehow to be linked to the uniform divine intellect that had sparked the matter into being. This was done by postulating a series of intermediary intellects—active, possible, etc. Not only was this intellectually cumbersome, but it also indicated to some that the Thomistic solution did not differ fundamentally from that of the Averroists. From the time of Bonaventure through the condemnations at Paris in the 1270s and thereafter, the so-called Augustinians and their allies confounded the two in a common attack, tarring the Thomists with the brush used on the Averroists.

The Augustinian critics were willing to do more than merely attack, and honestly looked for ways out of the quandary. Although for a time retaining much of the descriptive apparatus connected with the idea of the active and possible intellects, thinkers of this general persuasion simplified matters and based their principle of man's intellectual endowment on God's intervention through a special illumination. When pushed far enough, the cure was as bad as the malady. On the one hand, the direct application of God's illumination to seemingly random and partic-

[48] *Vita S. Thomae Aquinatis* 4, in *AA.SS.*, March 1, 664BC.

ular cases had the advantage of freeing a theologian from having to explain the unexplainable by means of reason, but it left him with two worlds, that of divine intellection and that of the human or natural perception, linked only by an unpredictable divine initiative. This was of little assistance in justifying the human institutions of Church and government: it is perhaps lovely that God loves sinners, but it is ugly when he does not necessarily love those who, in human terms, do good. Confounding the regularities of divine illumination with the arbitrariness of grace, this teaching principally served to comfort those curious spirits who believed that they had found in the history of particular institutions—as did the Joachitic Franciscans—or even in their own lives —as did Francis of Assisi and not a few heretics—the traces of a direct divine intervention that had not illuminated neighbouring institutions or persons existing in darkness.

On the other hand, to use the other side of the illuminist argument brought the philosopher theologian back close to where he had come from. To assert that God had so illumined man that all men possessed a sufficient measure of synderesis—the capacity, that is, to understand and live according to moral and even religious truths—was equally unsatisfactory. Practically, this sense of man's innate capacity for goodness seemed to be at variance with the record of man's behaviour here on earth. Theoretically, the weakness of this position was that, since everyone had the capacity to be good and yet only some exercised it, the individual's free will was the agent of his choosing to be good. As the polemicists of the fourteenth century were to claim against Ockham, this opinion smacked of the Pelagian heresy because it weakened the primal motivating force of divine election or predestination. God may have been free and may have endowed man with a capacity for freedom, but, like the Aristotelian deity, he had left it up to man to make the choice.

The question could be put in different ways. One of these was the necessary attempt—necessary because, to the monotheistically minded men of this time, God was the all pervasive source not merely of life but also of all lovable things like freedom, truth, and beauty—to define God's freedom and to see if it is possible to describe it in human terms. God's freedom had always posed insoluble problems, problems so weighty and frightening that they were sometimes humorously phrased. The Latin father

Jerome, the great monk and cardinal Peter Damian, Alan of Lille, one of the most prolific of the twelfth-century doctors, and Thomas Aquinas all debated whether God could restore the virginity of a girl so that it could be said she had never been violated. Although titillating, the discussion was not absurd. It raised the question whether God could undo what he had done, and the related question whether he could act in defiance of the principle of noncontradiction, that is, Rome either was or was not, but could not have been both. In other words, were man's conceptions of why and how things are done capable of describing God's ways of acting? An Augustinian of Damian's stripe was to reply that, although the deity generally seems to have acted in a predictable way, he could do what he chose. Most intellectuals, however, accorded the victory to those who built the naturalist tradition. Some maintain, said Alan of Lille, that God can abrogate what he has done, because having to bow to a necessity imposed by the passage of time (*fluxus temporis*) is offensive to divine omnipotence. But Alan himself felt very differently:

> In opposition to this, we say that God cannot change what has taken place, because, if he did, he would obviate his own will and his orderly arrangement of things (*ordinatio*). For since he willed that there be a world, if he now wishes that there never had been one, he would go against his own will, which God forbid![49]

That is, God's will was so strong that he could not change his mind!

To bind the principle of divine freedom to what had been created in the past satisfied many a natural theologian and Aristotelian naturalist, but it seemed to justify everything that had ever happened, including some things that churchmen disapproved of. Writing around 1310–13, Dante Alighieri, who elsewhere heaped praise on both Thomas Aquinas and the Averroist Siger of Brabant, sought to reverse Augustine's celebrated attack on the moral basis of the Roman state in order to justify secular authority in his own period. He applauded the virtue of the Romans, the spread of whose empire was, in his opinion, divinely ordained. There was little new in his argument.

[49] Quoniam homines 1, 2, 4, ed. Pierre Glorieux, *Archives d'histoire doctrinale et litteraire du moyen âge* XXVIII (1953), 233.

Derived from ancient sources, the thesis that God had justified the role of the Romans had been stated at length by Jordan of Osnabrück around 1281, and Ptolemy of Lucca had dilated on the natural virtues of the Romans shortly thereafter. But Dante's philosophical bent inspired him to add nature to the equation. For him the will of God was expressed in the world by the principle of right. Rome's capacity to conquer and to govern proved that its empire was in accord with nature's right order.

> Hence it is clear that nature ordains things with respect to their capacities, which respect is the basis or right placed in things by nature. From this it follows that the natural order cannot be conserved in things without right, since the fundamental principle or right is annexed to [nature's] order. . . . The Roman people was ordained by nature to govern.[50]

What was, then, was right.

This was an awkward doctrine. Since the past constitutes the precondition of the present, the creator is bound to his creation as it stands at the present moment. As the Averroists were said to have put it, God cannot but produce and create, and that creation is necessarily good by definition. Although this description of God and nature could be greeted with a certain complacency in a time when circumstances and institutions seemed beneficent, it has the weakness of relying on a limited vision of man's experience. It was not only dualist sectarians like the Cathars who knew that not everything in creation was good. Many orthodox Christians were not convinced by the familiar arguments that evil was merely the absence of good and that human misery was a punishment for man's sins. In his manual of love letters, Buoncompagno of Signa repeated a theme common in popular literature. Replying to a nun who charged her correspondent with proposing to commit adultery at the expense of the Lord of Hosts, the persistent lover replied that he would 'much rather violate the bed of him who has slain my parents and relatives, and who visits us with storms, hail and tempests, than that of any earthly man who can harm few or none'.[51]

Furthermore, to describe the divine principle as bound to its creation and to its prior ordinances fails to account for the seem-

---

[50] *De monarchia* 2, 6, ed. Gustavo Vinay (Florence, 1950), 148.
[51] *Rota veneris*, ed. Friedrich Baethgen (1927), 21–2.

ingly accidental, the unpredictable, and, from the point of view of each mortal man, the unknowable in life. There was much conjecture about the inexhaustible surprises provided by nature itself, but the traditional way of dealing with unpredictable events was through the conception of the miracle, an act transcending the 'common course of nature', performed by the deity or even by Satan. So important were such unpredictable events to the 'religious' mind that they had been built into the foundation of the Christian faith from its earliest times. The thinkers of this period —with some notable exceptions—insisted that, since God created all of nature, miracles were not to be considered unnatural. Also, Augustinians like John Duns Scotus (d. 1308) argued that, since God is the first cause, were he bound by any internal necessity derived from his own nature and were he subject to any external pressure derived from his own creation, all freedom and judgment of merit among men would be destroyed. God must be free for man to have any hope of freedom.

Whether Averroists or Thomists, the adherents of Aristotelian naturalism were aware of the insufficiences of the teaching they espoused. The Thomists especially endeavoured to escape its limitations by emphasizing in different ways God's freedom to perform miracles—in short, to insist on the free will of both the deity and man. Their Augustinian critics dismissed these exceptions and kept their eyes glued on the general implications of the system. What made it worse for Thomas Aquinas and the other innovators of natural theology was that there were conflicts between the faith and the doctrines of Aristotle and his followers. Most of the conflicts derived from different ways of looking at the world. Opposed to the Christian's historical view, with its creation, its incarnation, and all the other clear demarcations of human and divine history, was the static view of the Aristotelians' human and natural history. The Aristotelians insisted upon the eternity of the world or cosmos. Having neatly extended an analogy derived from present experience back into eternity, their position was ostensibly the stronger of the two, but it clearly contradicted the faith. With his usual discretion—for he was never one to insist on theory to the exclusion of commonsense—Thomas Aquinas recognized the problem in several of his quodlibets. There he said that the creation of the world at a given moment in time is one of those things that must be believed and cannot be demonstrated by human reason (*cadunt sub fide, non sub demonstratione*), and that a Christian who insisted on trying to prove otherwise would make himself the laughingstock of unbelievers.[52] That one could poke fun at revelation's historical scheme is shown by John of Jandun (d. 1328). Commenting on the Christian idea of the *creatio ex nihilo*, he wrote:

> The gentile philosophers did not know this method of creation. Nor is this astonishing because it cannot be known from sensible evidence . . . especially because this way rarely happened. Indeed, it never occurred except once, and it is now a very long time since that happened. Those therefore who understand this kind of creation know it by another way, that is, by the authority of the saints, by revelation, and by things of the sort.[53]

And John elsewhere went on to assert about a similar matter that this kind of belief or credulity is best learned in childhood by dint of repetition.

There were other problems that aroused curiosity and doubt. Siger of Brabant asserted that the whole world of philosophers could not convince anyone of personal immortality, and Thomas Aquinas confessed that no one could say in what the beatitude of the future life consisted. Since these were dogmatical questions, they did not deny that the afterlife existed or that heaven was bliss, but merely opined that no proof or definition could be offered by unaided human reason. To judge from the condemnations at Paris in 1277, however, some of the artists at the university had asserted that bliss was to be found only in this life, and that bodily death was itself so terrible that there was no point in worrying about the Christian's hell.

There were other types of incredulity, some of which affected the institutional structure of the Church. Since the days of the Gregorian revolution, clerical celibacy had been prized and enforced. It had, indeed, become the mark of the whole ecclesiastical order. Yet the lively attack it had elicited around 1100, in such tracts as the Rouen or Norman Anonymous, was never stilled. It echoed through the Platonic school of Chartres and came

---

[52] *Quodlibetum* 12, 6, 1 and *Quodlibetum* 3, 15, 2, 2, ed. Spiazzi, *op. cit.*, 277b and 68b–69a.
[53] From his *Quaestiones super libros physicorum* cited in Stuart MacClintock, *Perversity and Error: studies on the 'Averroist' John of Jandun* (Bloomington, Ind. 1956), 91–2 and 173–4n.

down into the thirteenth century, by that time becoming popular primarily among the laity, or whoever wrote what laymen read. The type of argument employed is to be seen in Andrew the Chaplain's *On Love* written in 1184–86, a work condemned by Stephan Tempier's commission of theologians in 1277, and thereafter translated with enthusiam from its rather learned Latin into the vernacular tongues. Andrew says:

> Nevertheless I believe that God cannot be gravely offended by love, for what is done because nature obliges us to do it can easily be purged by expiation. Besides, it does not seem fitting to count as a crime that [act] in which the greatest good in this life has its origin and without which no one on earth can be considered worthy of praise.[54]

From love comes virtue—a sentiment that, suitably spiritualized, once delighted the heart of Bernard of Clairvaux, though Andrew's context would have horrified him. Besides, as seen in an earlier chapter, the idea that celibacy was impossible or unnatural was very widespread, especially among the laity. It is also true that a poet of the quality and popularity of John of Meung—a man much influenced by Parisian intellectual circles—found, in his *Romance of the Rose*, that almost all the institutional virtues of clerical society were unlovely: poverty was ugly, abstinence and chastity unnatural, and humility and obedience refused man his high place in nature's order. But here one has begun to delve into the vast literature of satire and incredulity, a subject to be touched on later.

Faced with the insufficiencies of the basic system of thirteenth-century thought, the critics of Averroist Aristotelianism and Thomistic natural theology tried to find ways to release God from bondage to his own creation. From the Augustinians of Bonaventure's persuasion through John Duns Scotus to the *via moderna* of the later Ockhamists, one way this was done was to criticize the Thomist attempt to demonstrate the existence of the deity or first cause and define his basic attributes by means of analogies derived from the world of nature. Although it did not win universal support, this destructive effort was generally successful. To cease to argue from effect to cause was costly, however. What appeared good to man could no longer be said to be necessarily God's good. Only those moral injunctions and ecclesiastical institutions that were based on revelation—that is, on

[54] *De amore* 1, 6, G., ed. Amadeu Pages (1930), 162.

sacred Scripture—were to be regarded as valid. And, since the Bible offered little more than the Deuteronomic code, Christ's laws of love, and Paul's recommendations, not too many of the practical institutions of the Church were directly bolstered by this authority. How this threatened the institutional structure of the Church and its claimed superiority over the secular state was already clear in John of Paris's tract *On Royal and Papal Power* of 1302, and Marsiglio of Padua's *Defensor pacis* of 1324.

The excision of the accretions of natural theology took time and care. It was impermissible to assert, as did a proposition condemned at Paris in 1277, 'that nothing can be known about God save that he exists or has being',[55] since revelation not only told the faithful that God existed but also described many of his actions and qualities. Sometimes, in their desire to attack what they thought to be the dangerous innovations of natural theology, the proponents of the freedom of the deity could get pretty close to this condemned proposition. They usually stated it more carefully and, in so doing, could fall back on a long tradition of Christian thought. In the canon of the Lateran Council of 1215 in which the unorthodoxies of Joachim of Fiore and of Amalric of Bene were castigated, it had been found necessary to limit the area of natural theology by asserting that 'there is no similarity to be discerned between the creator and his creatures that is not over-topped by a discernible dissimilarity'.[56] Even Alan of Lille, who had been among the leaders of those expanding the role of reason in theology, opined that the terms with which we describe God differ from those with which we describe men. There is, therefore, no true similitude of God and man. Man may be rational, but God is reason itself. Such distinctions certainly appealed to the moderate Thomas Aquinas, but the Augustinians and Duns Scotus used them to weaken Thomistic natural theology irreparably. Although we know much from the faith and from immediate divine illumination, Scotus said, unaided human reason can know no more than the fact that both God and man have being. Our analogies from life in time, derived from our limited and sensory intelligence and will, cannot be applied to that most wilful, all-perceiving, and eternal principle of freedom.

[55] Heinrich Denifle, *Cartularium universitatis Parisiensis* I, 553. This is error No. 215 of item No. 473.
[56] *Liber extra* I, I, 2 in *CICan* II, 6–7.

In many ways the men of the later thirteenth century were turning back to the antirationalism of earlier churchmen, to views like those of Bernard of Clairvaux. Attacking Abelard, Bernard had said:

> Since he was prepared to use reason to explain everything (*de omnibus reddere rationem*), even those things which were above reason, he presumed against both reason and against the faith. For what is more hostile to reason than to try to transcend reason by means of reason? And what is more hostile to the faith than to refuse to believe what cannot be attained by reason?[57]

To Bernard, as to the later Augustinians, to believe was an experience, an experience deriving from direct divine infusion and therefore productive of certitude. Against the rationalists' belief that theology had to lean on the crutch of philosophy for its proofs, Bernard asserted in a much cited passage:

> We know [the truth]. But how do we think that we understand it? Disputation does not understand it but holiness does, if, in some way, the incomprehensible can be understood. But unless it can be comprehended, the apostle would not have said, 'that we be able to comprehend with all the saints.' The saints therefore understand. Do you want to know how? If you are holy, you understand and know. If not, be holy, and you will know by experience.[58]

Bernard's opinion about Abelard's misuse of reason won the support of others than mystics and irrationalists. Solid philosophers agreed with it. Describing the interminable debates in the theological faculty of Paris about the character and origin of the human intellect and other matters, the 'Averroist' John of Jandun wrote in 1323: 'Of what use this is, and how such a school advances the catholic faith, God alone knows. And anyone can learn this for himself from the officious strivings [of these divines], anyone, that is, who [honestly] seeks ... from them the rationale of their

---

[57] *Contra quaedam capitula errorum Abaelardi* 1, 1 in *PL* CLXXXII, 1055.

[58] *De consideratione* 5, 14 in *Sancti Bernardi opera* III, 492. The biblical passage is an adaptation of Ephesians 3:18.

[59] From chapter ii of his *Tractatus de laudibus Parisius* in the edition by MM. Taranne and Leroux de Lincy (Paris, 1856). The text is defective: 'Quid autem utilitatis et qualiter religioni catholice conferat tale gignasium Deus novit; et ab ipsorum sedulitatibus poterit hoc addiscere qui ab eis hujuscemodi processuram [?] ... expetet ratione.'

arguing in this way.'[59] John was repeating what many had said before. In his *Opus minus* Bacon had remarked that theologians overstepped their bounds when they discussed matter, species, being, ways of knowing, etc. These problems were not their business. They should merely accept the solutions propounded by philosophers. But John of Jandun was saying much more, namely, that each discipline, theology and philosophy, was autonomous, not in terms of the truths it discovered but in its presuppositions, methods, and results. He would have agreed with the earlier Boethius of Dacia, some of whose opinions had been questioned in 1277 by Stephan Tempier's commission at Paris. In his *On the Eternity of the World* Boethius had separated the spheres comprehensible by means of philosophy or natural reason from those comprehensible by means of faith or theology. Debating the familiar difference between the Christian creation in history and the philosopher's eternity of the world, Boethius concluded that 'two things are apparent: one is that natural [philosophy] concerning the eternity of the world is not able to contradict the Christian faith, and the other is that natural reason cannot prove the world or the first movement of the world to have been new.'[60] There were, he might have said, two truths, one in theology and the other in philosophy.

Although the idea of a double truth was looked upon as an Averroist heresy, the separation of the disciplines was going on apace. Even the attack of 1277 at Paris upon natural theology and Averroist thought appears to have had the inadvertent effect of strengthening this separation. Some thought that the means of separating the disciplines was by defining the terms or languages appropriate to each, and by giving to one, notably theology, the possession of a higher truth. The Parisian theologian Peter of Poitiers (d. 1205) observed that an opinion of the ancient Boethius, a philosopher rather than a theologian, reflected probability more than truth. Earlier, Bernard of Clairvaux had chided Abelard for applying philosophy's probabilities (*aestimationes*) to theology, in which only certitude reigned. Since his view was based on the psychic experience of certitude implanted in an individual by the deity, Bernard's opinion was similar to that of the later Bonaventure and was used in the attack on Thomistic natural theology. In fact, the majority of the academic intellectuals around 1300

[60] Cited in MacClintock, *Perversity and Error*, 100.

limited natural philosophy to the production of probable propositions.

But natural science could not be deprived of a measure of certitude. The astrologer and medical doctor Peter of Abano stated
forcefully that he and other natural scientists dealt with things
that could be described by means of human certitude (*per humanam
certitudinem*) and not, as the theologians did, with things to be
held by simple credulity without reason. His view, much disliked
by both the Augustinians and those of the *via moderna*, had a
tradition behind it. Alan of Lille had stated before that, 'properly
speaking, there is no science of God. For when it is said that it
[*scientia dei*] is known or understood, reference is being made
rather to the knowledge of the faith and of belief (*credulitas*) than
to the knowledge of certitude (*ad scientiam certitudinis*).'[61] Besides,
the results of Robert Grosseteste's repeated experiences or
experiments in optics had given him a feeling very similar to
Bernard's illumination by divine light. Galileo's insistence upon
certitude wherewith he fell foul of Cardinal Bellarmine finds its
origins in this early debate.

Nor could theology dispense with probabilism. Even the rising
tide of biblicalism around 1300 that sought to cut away all other
authorities, ancient or modern, merely encouraged theological
probabilism, that is, the weighing of one authority against another
and of one historical precedent against another. Arguing from
Scripture against Bernard of Clairvaux's stand that the secular
sword was to be used at the behest of the Church, John of Paris
blandly remarked that the great Cistercian's opinion had relatively
little weight. When the same Dominican's treatise on the eucharist
was being examined by the bishop and theological doctors of Paris
in 1305–6, they summed up his position:

> It was asserted in the presence of the college of the masters of
> theology that John [of Paris] holds that either way of assuming
> the body of Christ to be on the altar is a probable opinion, and
> that he approves both by means of Holy Scripture and the
> opinions of the saints. Furthermore, he says that nothing has
> been determined by the Church, and that nothing therefore
> falls under the faith, and that, if he had said otherwise, he would
> not have spoken correctly. And he who would pertinaciously

[61] *Quoniam homines* I, 1, ed. Pierre Glorieux, *Archives d'histoire doctrinale et litteraire du moyen âge* XXVIII (1953), 136.

assert either one of these options of itself to fall under the faith should incur condemnation or anathema.[62]

The attempt to separate philosophy from theology—*scientia* from *sapientia*, as the Augustinians put it—by giving the latter the superiority of certitude and the former the inferiority of probability was bound to fail in the long run. That it was already questioned is an index of the degree of autonomy already accorded *scientia*. And certainly those who worked in philosophy had long since been aware that, whatever the ultimate objective of learning was, *scientia* differed from *sapientia*. In his glosses on Plato's *Timaeus*, William of Conches (d. 1153–4) had repeated a traditional distinction between the work of the creator and the work of nature. The former created *ex nihilo* and performed miracles; the latter created only according to the rules placed in it at its creation. The proponents of natural theology were also aware of this. Albertus Magnus observed in his commentary on Aristotle's *De coelo et mundo* that the business of a philosopher was not to discuss God's omnipotence or his miracles but rather what happens in nature by reason of the causes inherent in it.

Such distinctions became truly significant when they touched on sensitive areas. One such area was that of man's moral life here on earth. In his *On Monarchy*, Dante defined man's objectives:

> Unerring providence has ordained two objectives that man must seek: the bliss of this life which consists in the utilization of his own powers and is configured by the terrestrial paradise, and the bliss of eternal life which consists in the enjoyment of the divine vision to which his own powers cannot ascend unless aided by divine illumination, and which is made understandable by the celestial paradise.[63]

Like his master Thomas Aquinas, Dante believed that the former objective was attained by means of the exercise of moral and intellectual virtues and the latter by means of the theological virtues and spiritual teaching that transcends human reason. Unlike the heavenly objective, the earthly objective could never be perfectly achieved. Writing shortly before 1310, Engelbert of Volkersdorf, abbot of Admont, said: 'And so the objective and reward of the present felicity of the temporal kingdom is to labour

---

[62] Denifle, *op. cit.*, I, 120, No. 656.
[63] *De monarchia* 3, 16, ed. Gustavo Vinay, 280–2.

continuously with zeal and joy in building its peace and that of its subjects even if it can never really obtain that peace fully.'[64] The objectives, then, were clear, but the problem was to determine whether moral and political virtues were valid of themselves or only in terms of their relation to celestial ends.

The general tradition of thirteenth-century thought was to allow a limited autonomy to man's natural moral virtues. Ever moderate, Thomas Aquinas opined that the political virtues were not morally indifferent but were intrinsically good, and that they could be meritorious if informed by God's grace. The argument could be put far more strongly. An anonymous commentary produced in the arts faculty at Paris just after 1277 advances the case that God helps those who help themselves. The author contends that felicity derives both

> from a divine cause and from a human cause. Felicity derives from a divine cause or originally from God as a primal and remote cause. In an immediate sense, however, this same felicity is from a human cause. Whence happiness is not from God immediately, but instead from God if man works with him (*homine cooperante*). Whence it appears that felicity consists in human actions, because it is necessary for man to labour and act if he would be called happy.[65]

An even stronger statement was to be found in John of Paris. Acting as *cooperatores dei*, men, pagan or Christian, are able to acquire moral virtue and 'it must be said that the moral virtues acquired [here on earth] can be perfect without the theological virtues, nor, except for a certain accidental perfection, are they made more perfect by [the theological] virtues'.[66] A secular morality independent of Christianity had begun to make its appearance and, with it, the hope of discovering a firm link between God and man, between heaven and earth, began to fade. Although often revived, the teaching of the Thomistic proponents of natural theology did not appeal to the major intellectuals of the later Middle Ages or of modern times.

The mystics and utopians, however, did not give up easily, and

[64] From his *De ortu et progressu et fine regnorum et precipue regni seu imperii Romani* 18 in Vinay's edition of Dante's *De monarchia*, 284–5n.
[65] Unpublished Paris manuscript quoted in MacClintock, *Perversity and Error*, 165n.
[66] *De potestate regia et papali* 18, ed. Leclercq, 229.

the years around 1300 witnessed the assault by their last forlorn hope. It seemed to the utopians that a universal scheme of knowledge that possessed certitude could be discovered. The innate certitudes of mathematics were thought capable of lending natural philosophy and theology certitude. Raymond Lull's scheme of unified knowledge was based on this supposition. So was Roger Bacon's: 'Since therefore it is shown that philosophy cannot be known unless mathematics is known, and everybody knows that theology cannot be known unless philosophy is known, it is necessary for a theologian to know mathematics.'[67] And this unity of knowledge will indeed be useful. By means of it

faithful Christians will attain the reward of future blessedness. . . . the republic of the faithful shall so dispose its temporal goods that all things useful both to individuals and to the multitude for conserving bodily health and the wonderful prolongation of life shall be effected in material and moral goods and done in discretion, peace and justice. . . . All nations of the infidels predestined to eternal life shall be converted to the great efficacy and glory of the Christian faith. . . . Those foreknown (*praesciti*) to be damned who cannot be converted shall be restrained by the ways and works of wisdom rather than by civil wars.[68]

But man's natural endowment with reason was really not up to the task. Direct divine illumination was needed. Bacon confessed 'that, through his own industry, man cannot know how to please God with a fitting worship nor in what way he should deal with his neighbour or even with himself, but is wanting in those things until the truth is revealed'. What was needed was a magic monarchy:

that a revelation should be made to one man only that he ought to be the mediator between God and man and the vicar of God here on earth, a man to whom the whole human race should be subject and who ought to be believed without contradiction . . . and he is [to be] the legislator and the highest priest, who has the plenitude of power in spiritual and temporal things, as

[67] *Opus maius* 4, 4, *mathematicae in divinis utilitas*, ed. Bridges 1, 175.
[68] *Compendium studii philosophiae* 1, ed. J. S. Brewer, *Opera Fr. Baconis hactenus inedita*, 395. Bacon believed that churchmen should rule the world and therefore used the phrase 'civil wars of laymen (*laicorum*).'

a 'human God', as Avicenna says commenting on the tenth book of the Metaphysics, 'whom it is licit to adore after God'.[69]

This conjuring up of an angelic pope and priest-king who would enable the Latins to defeat antichrist and convert all mankind to Christ—an institutionalization of the miraculous or of direct divine illumination—was not merely a curious politico-religious vision. It was also evidence that many intellectuals around 1300 found the natural theology and philosophical naturalism that had culminated in the Thomists to be insufficient. Others, like John of Jandun and the Ockhamists, found them faulty. The utopians tried to force God and nature to be one; the others were resigned to thinking that this was impossible. From whichever side they approached the problem, however, they had one thing in common. The men who created late medieval philosophy and theology were no longer confident that unaided human reason could build a workable Christian synthesis. The Christian naturalism that had inspired thinkers from Peter Abelard to Thomas Aquinas was beginning to fail.

[69] *Baconis operis maioris pars septima seu moralis philosophia* I, I, ed. Massa, 8.

XIV

Heresy and Enthusiasm

Doubt and heresy

Quoted by the cardinals gathered at Anagni in 1255 to examine the works of Joachim of Fiore, Gratian's *Decretum* defined heresy as occurring when 'each man chooses for himself that teaching he thinks to be the better one. Whoever therefore understands Holy Scripture in a manner other than is required by the judgment (*sensus*) of the Holy Spirit, by whom it was written, is to be called an heretic even if he does not leave the Church.'[1] And what the

---

[1] *Decretum* 24, 3, 27 in *CICan* I, 997–8, based on Jerome and Isidore of Seville.

BIBLIOGRAPHY. The standard general history of heresy and enthusiasm is that of Herbert Grundmann, *Religiöse Bewegungen im Mittelalter: Untersuchungen über die geschichtlichen Zusammenhänge zwischen der Ketzerei, den Bettelorden und der religiösen Frauenbewegung im 12. und 13. Jahrhundert* (2nd edn., Hildesheim, 1961). There are good monographs on every major sect. Examples concerning the Cathars are Arno Borst, *Die Katharer* (Stuttgart, 1953), and Christine Thouzellier, *Catharisme et valdéisme en Languedoc à la fin du XIIe et au début du XIIIe siècle* (Paris, 1966). A good refutation of the purportedly antisocial aspects of heresy, especially Catharism, is to be found in Paul Alphandéry, *Les idées morales chez les hétérodoxes latins au début du XIIIe siècle* (Paris, 1903). The history of heresy has been bedevilled by the conflict between those who believe that it is essentially a religious phenomenon and those who feel that it is essentially social and economic in origin. I avoid this either/or position. Since it is likely that few or no human activities lack a religious dimension—'religion' meaning here ideologies, thoughts, and actions based upon an appeal to, or use of, indemonstrable propositions and conceptions —and few or none lack an appeal to the world of reason or to what can be known, or projected to be likely on the basis of man's experience in the world, I am not inclined to feel that, simply because a monk wrote a commentary on the Book of Job, he was only or necessarily writing about religion, or that, because a guildsman spoke for his craft monopoly, he was only or necessarily speaking about probable profit. The result of this conviction is that 'my' medieval believers and heretics can be expected to be both religious and economic men.

The social analysis of heresy also often suffers from the fault of linking heresy and enthusiasm to specific entities—the town or urbanism, for example—or to limited social classes, such as the poor. With all its limits, this work is interesting. See A.

515

Holy Spirit had inspired was the Church militant, that is, the popes, the bishops, and the theologians here on earth. As could be expected in the area of Latin culture whose basic definition was lent it by the Church, Gratian accented the need for religious unity and condemned divergence from the Church's traditions, difficult though these were to define.

Gratian's stress on intellectual categories meant much. All heresy began in questioning accepted beliefs. The men of this age tended to view all thought in terms of heresy and orthodoxy. Although some hated the practice (Peter Cantor, for example, cited Abelard, Bernard of Clairvaux and Gilbert of La Porrée as though they were all on the same side), not a few learned professors of the schools commented frequently that their rivals' opinions smacked of heresy. Yet from 1150 to 1300 no ecclesiastical intellectual was more than censured, rusticated, or briefly imprisoned for divergent opinions. This contrasts sharply with the burning or perpetual immurement meted out to members of heretical sects.

Although, then, the charge of heresy was thrown about very generously, ideological divergence on the part of single individuals or intellectual groups rarely drove ecclesiastical authorities

---

P. Evans, 'Social aspects of medieval heresy', *Persecution and Liberty: essays in honor of G. L. Burr* (New York, 1931), 93–116 and Norman Cohn, *The Pursuit of the Millennium* (2nd edn., New York, 1961). Recent Marxist analysis may be exemplified by Ernst Werner, *Pauperes Christi* (Leipzig, 1956) and Bernhard Töpfer, 'Die Apostelbrüder und der Aufstand des Dolcino,' *Städtische Volksbewegungen im 14. Jahrhundert* (Berlin, 1960), 62–84. On the role of women, see Gottfried Koch's excellent *Frauenfrage und Ketzertum im Mittelalter: Die Frauenbewegung im Rahmen des Katharismus und des Waldensertums und ihre sozialen Wurzeln* (Berlin, 1962). A sort of popular small history principally useful for transcribing into French some of the results of this and earlier German research is Taddeusz Manteuffel, *Naissance d'une hérésie: Les adepts de la pauvreté volontaire au moyen âge* (Paris, 1970, from a Polish original). Indispensable for studying the ideologies of those who have dealt with heresy up to 1950 is the first part of Arno Borst's book on the Cathars cited above.

I am tempted to include here H. C. Lea's standard *A History of the Inquisition of the Middle Ages*, 3 vols. (New York, 1888), but prefer to suggest to the reader that, if he wishes a taste of this astonishing man's perceptiveness and wit, he read instead his *A History of Auricular Confession and Indulgences*, 3 vols. (Philadelphia, 1896). Although sometimes close to the Know Nothings who influenced him in his early adulthood, Lea was one of the few great American historians.

In the last part of the chapter, the principal departure from the usual subjects treated under the rubric of repression is my attempt to link the growth of governmental authority, legal 'reform', and the movement toward republicanism and even democracy in the towns to the development of the Inquisition.

to serious efforts of persuasion or repression. In his life of Louis IX John of Joinville tells us that a bishop of Paris comforted a university teacher who doubted the sacraments by likening the professor to a soldier at the front and himself to one at the home base. It was safer back there: one was less assailed by doubts. The heresies that elicited attention were those which caused substantial numbers of believers to secede from the orthodox community. How extensive such a secession could be was seen in western Languedoc in the early 1200s. In 1207 at Montréal near Carcassonne a papal legate and his companions were obliged to debate publicly with a group of Cathar heretics and to have the debate judged by the arbitration of four laymen, two knights and two burghers. In the early days of his episcopate at Toulouse from 1206 to 1231, Fulk of Marseilles was told by a 'wise knight' that it was impossible for a gentleman in his position to act against the Cathars 'because we have been raised with them, and we have kindred among them, and we see them live virtuously'.[2] The withdrawal from the Church had become so general that Languedoc was visited by a repressive crusade in 1209.

Secession from the orthodox Church must, however, be carefully defined. The heretics—even those widely diverging from the traditional faith, like the Cathars—thought of themselves as the only true Christians. There is also evidence of doubt, scepticism, and simple disbelief among the majority that adhered to the Church. How widespread this was cannot be determined, but it must have been pervasive. As an example, men of the time were ambivalent or in conflict about miracles. A common lament was that there were no miracles any more, that the age of miracles was forever gone because of the 'corruption' of the Church or some similar reason. At the same time miracles were constantly being seen by some, and religious literature and ecclesiastically inspired chronicles were crowded with references to these events. Anti-Hohenstaufen in his convictions, Caesarius of Heisterbach is happy to tell stories against the King of the Romans Philip of Swabia. On being fed some typical ecclesiastical war propaganda to the effect that a formation of Templars had been miraculously hidden from the Saracens who surrounded them by singing a verse from

[2] The chronicle of William of Puylaurens, ed. by Beyssier in the *Bibliothèque de la Faculté des Lettres de l'Université de Paris* XVIII (1904), 127–8. This is found in chapter seven of this work and the incident of 1207 is recorded in chapter 9.

Psalm 26, Philip is said to have sourly observed that, had he been there, he would have dropped that psalm and run for it. Salimbene records how Buoncompagno of Signa made fun of the popular Dominican miracle worker and preacher John Schio of Vicenza at the time of the alleluia of 1233, a widespread popular 'religious' movement against the Hohenstaufen. As a counterattraction, Buoncompagno announced at Bologna that he would fly. When the crowd had assembled, he drily congratulated its members on having seen him, and dismissed them with his blessing. He had worn wings, but he had not flown. When the Florentines heard that John was about to visit their town, the local wiseacres said: 'For God's sake, let him not come here. We've heard that he raises the dead, and we are already so numerous that our city can't hold us.'[3]

To scepticism may be added moral rigorism as a source of hostility to miracles. Joinville tells us that King Louis IX of France praised Simon of Montfort, the commander of the Albigensian crusade, because he refused to stop his work in order to witness a miracle going on near at hand. The body of the Lord had become flesh and blood in the hands of a priest, thus confuting the heretics. Simon's faith, the king said, was so secure that he had no need of proof. But there was more here than Louis thought, namely the conflicting functions and characters of the clergy and the laity. What soldier enjoys the excited cries of the ideologues who, at one and the same time, urge him to risk *his* life in combat and draw attention to *themselves*?

The Franciscan Salimbene may be taken as illustrating the mixture of credulity and disbelief typical of the time. Although he was not really interested in sanctity, Franciscan saints were sound in his opinion. So were most saints of the larger mendicant orders, except that he was happy to record stories against the rival Dominicans and the new order of the Friars of the Sack. Saints fostered by the secular clergy, however, were invariably frauds. Politically a Guelph and a gentleman by birth, Salimbene was especially hostile to plebeian holy men. Speaking of one Albert, the standard-bearer of the lion banner for the wine-porters' guild of Cremona, he ascribed Albert's success and the spread of his cult to Parma and Reggio around 1279 'partly to the hope of the sick to become well, partly to the desire of the curious to see

[3] *Cronica* in *MGH. SS.* xxxii, 83.

spectacles (*novitates*), partly to the secular clergy's envy of the new religious (*moderni religiosi*) and partly to the profit to be gained by bishops and canons from such a cult'.[4] He then added a final reason: the desire of gentlemen exiled because of their adherence to the imperial party to return home during a wave of plebeian good feeling precipitated by the elevation of a working-man to sanctity. Salimbene is clearly referring to the struggle between the Guelphs and Ghibellines and to the kind of social alliance between the top and bottom of society that often threatened the mixed aristocratic and middle-class Guelph *populares* who were gaining control of many Italian town republics around 1250.

The teachings of the faith were also sources of doubt. As an example, the idea of predestination always tormented its believers. Joachim of Fiore likened doubt on this point to one of the devil's temptations of Christ during the forty days. It was especially hard on the monk, who had given up so many pleasures:

> If therefore you are not elected, you exhaust yourself in vain by sustaining such labours, for no one can be saved who is not chosen; and if, however, you are chosen, even if you spare yourselves so that you are idle at the moment [when the Lord comes], you will be saved, because no man of the elect can perish.[5]

Joachim's solution was dour. If you seek to profit from your faith, you breach the law of Matthew 4:7, 'Thou shalt not tempt the Lord thy God.' The abbot then went on to sound what he thought was a more hopeful note: 'For although we cannot be certain in this life whether we are reprobate or chosen, nevertheless just as the sign of election (*signum electionis*) is to act strongly and to be strengthened, so is the sign of reprobation to fall from rigour with one's power of justice enervated.'[6] Even with this Calvinist doctrine of the external means to salvation, there was still a burden on the believing man to show by his dogged happiness that he did not despair. God, so to speak, was keeping mum. As the early

---

[4] *Cronica* in *MGH. SS.* XXXII, 503–4.
[5] *Tractatus super quatuor evangelia*, ed. Buonaiuti, 159. The 'at the moment when the Lord comes' translates the phrase *ad horam* because Joachim was either thinking of Matthew 24:42–50 or Apocalypse 3, 3—or both. Note the similarity to Calvin's response to those who urged him to cease working in the late days of his life: 'Would you that God will find me idle when he comes?'
[6] *Tractatus super quatuor evangelia*, ed. Buonaiuti, 160.

fourteenth-century manual for preachers and parish clergy called the *Mirror of Human Salvation* put it: 'No man should presume to investigate why God wished to create men who he knew would fall or why he wished to create those angels whose fall he certainly foreknew. . . . These works of God and others like them are beyond human understanding.'[7]

To those needing greater mental security these solutions did not appeal, their insufficiency in this regard being one of the great sources of both heresy and doubt. The anti-Cathar tract called the *Liber antiheresis* produced between 1184 and 1207 by Durand of Huesca's Waldensian circles remarked that the dualist or Cathar sects argued that the orthodox teaching on predestination meant that, since God created everything and foreknew what he was creating, God had created evil. An extremist Lombard Cathar stated the same point in relation to the history of Lucifer and the other fallen angels. Between 1241 and 1250, his *Book on the Two Principles* queried how the moderate Cathars could assert that the angels were good before they fell from heaven when their own reasoning obliged them to confess that

> God from the beginning knowingly and by knowing created his angels and made them of such an imperfection that they were in no way able to evict evil. And thus God, who is good, holy, just, wise and fair, and who is greater than any praise . . . is altogether the cause and beginning of all evil, which must be denied most strongly. Wherefore it is necessary to confess that there are two first principles, one, namely, of good, and the other of evil, which is the head and cause of all imperfection of the angels and likewise of all evil.[8]

Both orthodox Christians and moderate dualists countered this argument by asserting—with some exaggeration—that it deprived man of free will, thus inducing psychic despair and destroying the individual responsibility upon which society and the church are based. Yet the doctrine of the extreme dualist was not as destructive of man's optimism as might seem at first glance. From the point of view of mental comfort there was not much to choose between orthodoxy and heterodoxy. Even the most optimistic Christians were resigned to a substantial measure of sorrow.

---

[7] *Speculum humanae salvationis* 1, prologue, ed. Lutz and Perdrizet, 5.
[8] *Liber de duobus principiis*, ed. A. Dondaine (1939), 84.

When discussing the number of those predestined to salvation, Thomas Aquinas wrote:

> It may be said that a good proportionate to the ordinary state of nature is found in many and is lacking only in very few. But a good that exceeds the ordinary state of nature is discovered only in very few. For just as it is evident that there are many men who have a knowledge sufficient for the government of their own lives, and very few, who are called fools or idiots, who lack this knowledge, so there are very few indeed with respect to those others who are able to attain a profound knowledge of intelligible things [that is, of philosophy]. Since, therefore, eternal blessedness, which consists in the vision of God, exceeds the ordinary state of nature—especially because grace has been weakened by the corruption of original sin—there are very few who are saved.[9]

It is therefore not to be wondered at that certain groups of dualists such as the Rhenish Luciferians lauded the fallen angels, proposing that their souls would eventually return to heaven, and some even asserted that Lucifer was himself the brother of God who had been unjustly cast down from heaven. God, they thought, was too cruel to be worshipped.

Aquinas's analogy of the attainment of philosophical learning with the attainment of salvation reminds us that talk about predestination was very close to talk about death. Paralleling the Luciferians' condemnation of God because of his unjust damnation of Lucifer was the orthodox Buoncompagno of Signa's cursing of God because he condemned man to death. There is a story told by Caesarius of Heisterbach about Landgrave Lewis II of Thuringia (1140–68). Literate and therefore especially hard on the clergy, as Caesarius puts it, he loved to cite Psalm 115:16: 'The heavens, even the heavens are the Lord's: but the earth hath he given to the children of men', drawing thence the principle that there was no connection between heaven and earth. He was wont to say that, if he was predestined to salvation, no evil deed would cost him heaven; and, if foreknown to damnation, no good one would gain it for him. When urged to repent lest he die in sin, he replied: 'When the day of my death comes, I will die. I cannot put it off by living well nor bring it closer by living evilly.'[10]

---

[9] *Summa theologiae* I, 23, 7, ad 3.
[10] *Dialogus miraculorum* I, 37, ed. Joseph Strange I, 33.

This kind of doubt or scepticism was anything but the exclusive possession of those who joined heretical sects. Constant anti-Christian polemic reinforced natural scepticism. Jewish literature on this theme has been discussed in Chapter III above, and Muslim propaganda condemned such things as monogyny, clerical celibacy, and trinitarian polytheism. It is true that much of the evidence about this kind of thought, at least that which concerns princes and prelates, comes from the mouths of their enemies. Gregory IX's letter of 1239 condemning Frederick II Hohenstaufen was widely distributed. The pope saw fit to close this lengthy missive by asserting that Frederick enjoyed repeating that three impostors, Moses, Jesus and Mohammed, had deceived the world, and that two of these had died in glory but Jesus had been hanged. The emperor, the pope went on, did not believe in the Virgin Birth because none is born save of the carnal commerce of man and woman, 'and a man ought not to believe anything that he cannot prove by the meaning and reason of nature'.[11] According to two hostile witnesses deposing before Clement V in 1310–11, Boniface VIII when still a cardinal observed that, although the mob (*vulgus*) might think otherwise, an educated man (*literatus*) simply could not believe in the Trinity, Virgin Birth, or the real presence in the mass. These questions had come up in a discussion concerning the relative validity of Christian and Muslim law, wherein the cardinal had maintained that

> no law is divine, but all laws have been invented by men, and many eternal penalties are there included for one reason only, namely that men [on earth] shall be restrained from evil deeds by fear of punishment. Therefore the laws have no [absolute] truth except that, because of fear of punishment, men will live civilly and peacefully.[12]

It cannot be said that these ideas were merely the fabrications of polemists or malevolent tongues. Anent Frederick II's incredulity, the Muslim historian Sibt ibn al-Jauzi of Damascus (d. 1257) remarked that the emperor made it perfectly clear in his speeches that he was an atheist who poked fun at Christianity.

[11] J. L. A. Huillard-Bréholles, *Historia diplomatica Friderici Secundi* v, i, 350.
[12] Pierre Dupuy, *Histoire du différend d'entre le pape Boniface VIII et Philippes le Bel* (Paris 1655, rprt), 531 (testimony No. 7 quoted above) and 534 (testimony No. 12).

Besides, such scepticism even had a popular base. In 1288 the harangue of a Bolognese statute read:

It often happens that the barkeepers and those who play at dice in the streets and public squares of the commune of Bologna burn with rage and utter ignominious words against God and against his mother which is truly detestable and horrible, and, because of their tumult, put many difficulties in the way of the preachers who announce the word of God in these squares, wherefore . . .[13]

In 1299 a student at Bologna reported to the inquisitors that he had heard a burgher or farmer from a nearby village assert that Merlin was the son of God and that he could prove that proposition just as easily as he could prove it about Christ. The extremist naturalism of the statements attributed to Frederick II and Boniface VIII finds its parallel in the denial of the afterlife by certain heretics in Tuscany or the Romagna mentioned by Buoncompagno of Signa in the early 1200s. They imitated, said this author, the ancient Athenians, 'who mendaciously asserted that, because such things can be shown demonstratively, all things proceed from the elements and all individual things individually revert back into their elements'.[14]

More fundamental and, in a way, more beautiful is doubting disbelief. Caesarius of Heisterbach tells us of a female recluse who, pressed by a visiting abbot to recover her faith in God, asked: 'Who knows if God exists or if there are with him angels, souls or the kingdom of heaven? Who has seen them? And who has returned from there and told us what he has seen?'[15] One has the impression that the Church was powerless against this kind of doubt. Attempts to face it directly either leaned on miracles—and a miracle itself required an act of belief—or on some rather vulgar reasoning. Alexander Neckham praised dialectics and the university of Paris where this subject was taught. He told of a young scholar who lay dying and confessed that he could not believe in personal resurrection unless persuaded of it by reason (*probabiliter*). A fellow student came to him and argued in this wise:

[13] Cherubino Ghirardacci, *Della historia di Bologna*, Part One, Book 9, p. 279. 'Streets and public squares' is a free rendering of the original's *in scalis et in platea* (for *plateis?*). 'Barkeepers' for *incisores casei* is taken from DuCange, s. v. *incisor*, from whose reference this statute was looked up in Ghirardacci.

[14] *Rhetorica novissima* 8, 1 in *BIMA* II, 278b.

[15] *Dialogus miraculorum* 4, 39, ed. Strange I, 207.

If you believe in the future resurrection, this resurrection will either be or will not be. If you believe it will be and it is not, this belief will not harm you. If you believe it will be and it is, this belief will be of advantage to you. Now, if you do not believe and there should be a future resurrection, eternal woe will fall upon you. It is therefore better to believe than not to believe.[16]

According to Alexander, the youth closed his eyes in happy belief.

If he did so, his awakening must have been rude, at least according to the moral rigorists. John of Joinville tells us of the old woman of Acre who carried a brazier of coals and a bucket of water. She wished, she said, to burn heaven and put out the fires of hell so that man would act not for reward but rather for love of God. The famous verse of Jacopone of Todi, that wild Franciscan (around 1230–1306), said that he did not care if he were saved or damned, just so long as God would tell him what he could do for Him. And Jacopone's message was not an easy one. Like his parts or manifestations such as human love and freedom, God sometimes seemed to help man but at others to harm him. A man then, says Jacopone, who loves either love or freedom should resign himself to loving them for themselves and not for any good they may do him or his world. To both the elegant seneschal of Champagne and the onetime lawyer of Todi Alexander's Parisian scholar had broken the law: 'Thou shalt not tempt the Lord thy God.' There was to be no '*do ut des*' in their religion.

It is obvious that doubt and scepticism were significant parts of the Latin view of the world. What held them in check, one feels, was not the capacity of churchmen to prove personal resurrection, free will, man's freedom to make moral choices, and other like propositions. These things can be hoped for or believed in, but, as not a few of the theologians and philosophers of the time stated, they cannot be proved. The matter must be put in a different perspective, a comparative one. First, the teaching of the Church was no less capable of gaining the trust of its adherents than the other metaphysical systems that had preceded it or were to follow it. Second, the period from 1150 to 1300 was one in which the relatively beneficent material conditions of life combined with the newness of many of the Church's institutional and mental

[16] *De naturis rerum* 2, 73 in *Rolls Series* XXXIV, 297.

mechanisms to reinforce the Latins' sense of cultural confidence, and, for a time, bemused and delighted the many who wished to believe or who wished not to disbelieve.

The relationship of doubt and scepticism to heresy is difficult to define. It is true that the genesis of an heretical idea and sect had much to do with these feelings about the faith. Since, however, most heretical groups replaced orthodox theology with variant forms of the same metaphysical character, doubt and scepticism could help orthodoxy just as much as they could heresy. An instance of this is to be seen in the Franciscan chronicler Salimbene. Initially a Joachite, he was persuaded by his eschatologically minded brethren that the new age would be ushered in in 1260, the date on which they prophesied the death of the one they called the antichrist, Frederick II Hohenstaufen. When Frederick suddenly died ten years before the projected date, Salimbene, already shaken, one may presume, by the obsessive enthusiasm of these sectaries and by their revolutionary doctrine of the sudden transformation of the Church, dropped his belief in the Joachite teaching, and resolved that, from then on, he would not believe anything he did not actually see. Besides, although some heretical sects mocked miracles, some were tempted to use them. Around 1320 a Cathar preacher tried to prove the truth of metempsychosis, or transmigration of souls, by telling of a Perfect who, 'while standing next to a fountain, said to the believers that he recalled that, when he was a horse, he lost the shoe from one of his feet in the bed of the said fountain while drinking there. And he caused the said horseshoe to be looked for and it was found there.'[17] Even the orthodox could not get much lower than that. It is therefore probable that, since both orthodoxy and heterodoxy suffered from the same 'fault', the doubting or sceptical parts of men's minds did not lead them to favour one over the other. The heretic was not one who believed too little, but rather one who believed too much.

As were the orthodox, heretics were influenced by ideas coming from Byzantium and Islam. Several sects of the Waldensian type show Judaic influence, and one such, the Passagians of around 1200, were clearly judaizers, defending circumcision, the Jewish sabbath, and the primacy of the Mosaic law. The partial parallel

[17] Depositions before the Inquisition at Carcassonne, 1319–20 in Ignaz von Döllinger, *Beiträge zur Sektengeschichte des Mittelalters* II, 217.

between Cathar teachings and those of the Kabbalah, strong among Mediterranean Jews at this time, with its metempsychosis and its dualism, has often been noted. Since the Kabbalah often reinforced the attack upon Maimonidean rationalism by the Spanish and southern French rabbis, it paralleled the doubts about Aristotelian natural theology so strongly expressed by many Christian utopian enthusiasts, both orthodox and heretic. Of closer contacts between the Jews and the Cathars little is known except that the orthodox claimed that there were many. The principal influence on the Latin Cathars was clearly Byzantine. Before 1167, for example, the westerners held to the Bogomil or Bulgar doctrine that Lucifer, cast out of heaven by God, was the founder of evil. In that year, however, Niketas, the Cathar bishop of Constantinople, visited the Lombard churches and assembled a council of the prelates of southern France and Champagne at Saint-Félix-de-Caraman near Toulouse. Ordaining bishops in both areas, he persuaded the Latin Cathar clergy to adopt the rigorous dualism of his Church whereby Lucifer was regarded as coeternal with God and as the creator of the material world.

Most Christian enthusiasts who leaned toward heresy were antisacerdotal. Hugo Speroni of Piacenza asserted around 1177 that merit and not office gave the priest his power. And merit was hard to come by. Writing between 1179 and 1202, Alan of Lille remarked that the Waldensians 'strive to prove with various authorities that the power to bind and to loose was given only to those who preserve and live both the teaching and the life of the apostles'.[18] So far, thought some, had the clergy fallen from the apostolic life that all the sacraments of the Church were vitiated. According to the ex-heretic Buonacorso of Milan, writing between 1176 and 1190, this was the opinion of the Arnoldists, a pre-Waldensian sect deriving its name from Arnold of Brescia, the companion of Abelard, radical 'reformer', and leader of Rome's revolt against the temporal dominion of the popes, who was slain in 1155. This view turned the enthusiast into a heretic: so corrupt is the Church that the true believer had to attack it to cleanse it, or, if that failed, secede to found a pure church.

---

[18] *Quadripartita editio contra hereticos, Waldenses, Judaeos et paganos* 2, 6 in *PL* CCX, 383. The heretics were the Cathars and the pagans the Mohammedans. The tract is also called *Contra hereticos*, and will be referred to under this title in subsequent notes.

Such assaults could be nipped in the bud, the orthodox believed, by insisting that the merit of the officiant was not the basis of sacramental validity. An argument that appealed to the ordinary penitent was expressed by Alan of Lille:

> To this we reply that all priests have the power of binding and loosing, but that those only who adhere to the life and teaching of the apostles use this power worthily and justly. And this, namely the phrase worthily and justly, is what the aforesaid authorities [quoted by the Waldensians] are to be understood to be referring to when they say that an unjust priest neither binds or looses. Absolutely speaking, however, the remission or retention of sins is also performed by those who are not holy, for God gives his blessing to the worthy seeker even by means of an unworthy minister.[19]

This and similar arguments were codified in the time of Innocent III in the doctrine *ex opere operato*, wherein grace was considered to be conferred by a sacrament irrespective of the merit or demerits of the persons administering or receiving it.

A variety of reasons made this seemingly simple solution unacceptable. One was that, since the moral quality of the priest had no relation to the validity of the sacrament (as long as the words were correctly recited), the doctrine was destructive of individual responsibility and hence of social and ecclesiastical organization. Something was therefore needed, and that turned out to be the idea of intention. In the moralistic excitements of the Gregorian revolution, this ancient idea had been revived, being expressed, for example, in Peter Abelard's *Ethics*, where he asserts that the merit or demerit of an individual did not lie so much in what he did as in his intentions. As early as Hugh of Saint-Victor, this teaching had been applied to the sacraments: the priest must intend to perform them for them to be efficacious. By the time of the great scholastics the matter had become complex. Some, like Bonaventure, opined that God would supply man's deficiencies; others, like Aquinas, that habitual or virtual intention, that is, the lack of a positively perverse intention, was enough. But few indeed there were who cared to maintain at length that, even with God supplying, one who did not believe in the faith and was a heretic could perform or receive a valid sacrament. In short, however hard the

---

[19] *Contra hereticos* 2, 7, in *PL* ccx, 383–4.

doctors tried to lock the door, it always came unlatched again: the problem was, as of old, to define what was a heretic.

This definition was important, because the enthusiasts could always find a way of damning the clergy who had made their accommodation with the world. One way employed by both orthodox and heretical enthusiasts was to attack the crime of simony as heresy. The attitudes of these men derived from the Gregorian age when the 'reformers' had dusted off this ancient weapon in order to beat the clergy loyal to the old state churches. Simony was a good target: it was capable of almost infinite expansion. It occurred not only when a sacrament was purchased or an office bought, but also when a sacrament or an office was obtained by means of, or exercised under the shadow of, family influence, favour, moral vice, or even hypocrisy. Hence, as Alan of Lille says, the Waldensians could use a passage of Pope Gregory I wherein he observed that the true priest must not only conserve the teaching but also live the life of the apostles—a task well nigh impossible.

The failure to observe this ideal could be embraced in the ample reach of the charge of simony. Since simoniacs were heretics, the enthusiasts could make use of the old belief that a believer should not attend heretical conventicles and use the notion that such heretical sacraments were invalid. And there were good precedents deriving from the age of the Gregorian revolution. Had not, as Peter Damian reported, the Vallumbrosan radicals of the mid-eleventh century Florence asserted that, because of simony, there was no pope, no king, no archbishop, and no priest, and that, therefore, thousands of men, deceived by the 'trumpery and incantations' of false masses, had died without a valid sacrament? And there were textual authorities in plenty for the radicals' views. In 1218 two branches of the Waldensian movement, the Lombard Poor of Christ and the French Poor of Lyon, tried to heal their differences in a colloquy at Bergamo. The French more or less accepted the orthodox position on sacerdotal authority; the Lombards refused, alleging that a Christian must obey God, not man. Although admitting that God would supply human deficiencies, they asserted that simony obviated the orthodox arguments. To prove their point, the Lombards cited authorities culled from so orthodox a source as Gratian's *Decretum*. Among these was one attributed by Gratian to Gregory I in which the pontiff stated that simoniacs 'cannot be priests, whence it is written: damnation of the giver, damnation of the receiver. And this is the heresy of simony. In what way, therefore, can they who are not holy and are damned sanctify others? How can they transmit or receive the body of Christ? He who is cursed, how can he bless?'[20]

From this it was a short step to propose that only good men, indeed, only those predestined to salvation, could be true priests, that, in short, there was a priesthood of all true believers (the *praedestinati*), lay and clerical alike. This view was attributed to the Arnoldists and to later similar groups among the Waldensians. Stephen of Bourbon says that he learned from his experience as an inquisitor in the Rhône valley between 1232 and 1249 that some Waldensians held that good women could be priests. Indeed, at the conference of Bergamo in 1218 the Lombard Poor charged that the extreme views of their French associates on this point would lead them to admit not only women but even whores—*praedestinatae*, one hopes!—to the priesthood.

This vigorous, lay antisacerdotalism was restrained by several things. One was that the movements of orthodox and heretical enthusiasts took place in the traditional pattern of the Church where, until after 1300, lay religious passions were normally channelled into monastic or quasimonastic groups. To these groups the sacraments were of only limited importance; the way of life was almost everything. Thus, for example, the French Waldensians at Bergamo accepted the sacerdotal authority of priests ordained by Rome. Really important things, such as their preaching and exemplaristic living with all in common like the apostles, they entrusted only to their rectors and ministers, who were laymen. As in the monastic and mendicant orders, the leaders were to be elected by the community. The compromise reached at Bergamo by the Lombard and French sectaries provided that the community 'gathered together in one body . . . may jointly choose provosts for life or rectors for a set term whichever seems more useful to the community or for the maintenance of peace'.[21]

[20] *Decretum* 2, 1, 1, 12, *CICan* 1, 361. Friedberg notes that Cardinal Deusdedit had attributed this passage to Pope Pascal I. The Waldensian source is the *Rescriptum heresiarcharum Lombardie ad pauperes de Lugduno qui sunt in Alamania* published in Giovanni Gonnet, *Enchiridion fontium Valdensium* (Torre Pellice, 1958), I, 181–2.
[21] *Rescriptum heresiarcharum Lombardie* in Giovanni Gonnet, *Enchiridion fontium Valdensium* I, 171–3.

This principle of the lay direction of important matters usually seems to have faltered as time went on. In orthodox movements, this is exemplified in the Franciscan order—a matter to be examined in chapter XV below. Among the heretics, the larger sects seem to have evolved toward hierarchy and sacerdotalism, and would certainly have gone further in that direction had they been able to grow freely. The Cathars were early divided into simple believers (*credentes*) and Perfects (*perfecti*). Hierarchies of offices appeared—bishops, for example, as early as 1164. These officers were initially chosen by the *perfecti*, but in the thirteenth century by their hierarchical superiors. The *perfecti* were celibate, and women, although permitted into this grade and even into the diaconate, were never chosen for higher office. Among sects of the Waldensian type this evolution did not always take place. Still, when Bernard Guy codified the available information in his inquisitor's manual of 1323–24—a source amply verified by depositions before the Inquisition at Carcassonne in 1318–20—he noted that the sect had a self-perpetuating and celibate cadre of bishops, priests and deacons from which women were excluded. Although clearly a reflection of the orthodox model, this tendency must also have reflected a practical need. Perhaps, just as such varied sources as the Latin father Jerome, the Norman Anonymous of the late eleventh century, and Marsiglio of Padua said about the growth of the Catholic hierarchy in antiquity, the experience of schism dictated this development. All heretical movements, including the Cathars, suffered from constant scission. Hierarchy based on priestly magic and sociosexual differentiations was one way of combating the self-defeating tendency toward heresy within heresy.

The movement toward hierarchy and sacerdotalism was, however, slowed by the enthusiasts' belief that they had a way of living or a way of knowing that made them, as individuals or as a sect, superior to others. This gnostic élitist feeling was readily reinforced by the western monastic tradition, in which monks thought of themselves as already citizens of the supernal Jerusalem. Of special importance was the teaching of Joachim of Fiore and the later Joachites. In their dream of progress in history, the monkish *viri spirituales* of the third age yet to come were to live the contemplative life and enjoy a spiritual intellection of Holy Scripture granted them by the Holy Spirit, an understanding far

above that of the clergy of the second age who, bound to the compromises of the active life, could enjoy only a rational understanding. This sense of personal or group gnosis frequently made the
theology or philosophy of such sects somewhat inconsistent. The
Amalrician sect that was crushed at Paris in 1210, one similar in
some ways to the Joachites, was inspired by a Platonic pantheism
presumably taught by the Parisian master Amalric of Bene and
derived from John the Scot Erigena. Although believing that God
was everywhere and in everything, they did not conclude as one
would expect that all men were morally or spiritually equal but
rather that he who knows with the Apostle Paul that 'God
worketh all in all' cannot sin. Most such sectaries thought of
themselves as God's special vessels into which the Holy Spirit or
the Saviour had already been poured.

The conviction that there was a way or gnosis possessed by
some had interesting results. The Roman clergy always claimed
that it led to moral antinomianism, and this was the case sometimes. Garnier of Rochefort wrote in 1208–10 that the Amalricians were wont to say: ' "He who knows that God does all
would not sin even were he to fornicate for he ought not to attribute all the things that he does to himself, but rather to God." O
shameless opinion. And why do they hold it? In order more
easily to persuade girls to fornicate.'[22] The notion that a soul
annihilated in God's love may do anything it wants without re-
morse was among the opinions for which the Beguine Margaret,
called Porrette, was condemned in Paris in 1310. The risk or the
charge of moral antinomianism was used at the council of Vienne
in 1311 in the canon *Ad nostrum* as a reason for policing the Beguines and Beghards.

Antinomianism was not the only result of this kind of gnostic-
ism. Religious conceptions were spiritualized in a way that made
them more intellectually satisfying to some. The Amalricians
held that 'hell is nothing other than ignorance and paradise
nothing but the knowledge of the truth, which they say they have,
. . . and this full knowledge is the resurrection nor is there any
other kind of resurrection to be expected'.[23] Deriding physical

[22] *Contra Amaurianos* 2, ed. Clemens Baeumker, *Beiträge zur Geschichte der
Philosophie des Mittelalters* XXIV (1926), v/vi, 12. The attribution to Garnier is
putative but likely.
[23] *Ibid.*, 3 and 7, ed. Baeumker, 13 and 21.

resurrection after death, these sectaries prized the intellectual resurrection to be experienced in this life. Other kinds of spiritualizations are to be seen among the Cathars. The onetime heretic and later inquisitor Rainier Sacconi tells in 1250 that John of Lugio of Bergamo—one of the few Cathar intellectuals known by name—asserted that

> the primal principle of evil is known by many names in Holy Scripture, for it is called evil, iniquity, cupidity, impiety, sin, pride, death, hell, calumny, vanity, injustice, perdition, confusion, corruption, and fornication. And he even says that all the aforesaid vices are gods or goddesses which have their being from the evil he asserts to be the primal cause, and that this primal cause is ever signified by these vices.[24]

The gnosis, or knowledge of the way, was sometimes more generous than orthodoxy to non-Christians. It has been noted that the Latin utopian tradition was strongly anti-Judaic, but heretical utopian movements were always minority ones, and were therefore often mildly pro-Judaic. The Amalricians were convinced that, were a Jew to have their knowledge of the truth, he would need no baptism, and Prous Boneta, a later Olivite, added the Saracens as further beneficiaries of her dispensation. Some Joachites shared these views. In 1254 the antimendicant professors of the University of Paris examined the *Eternal Evangel*, a compilation of Joachim of Fiore's tracts introduced and glossed by the Franciscan Gerald of Borgo San Donnino. To this friar, the *Eternal Evangel* was to replace the New Testament in the age of the Holy Spirit now nearly ushered in. Among the propositions the professors purportedly found, and certainly condemned, was the following: 'However greatly the Lord will afflict the Jews in this world, he will nevertheless reserve some to whom he will impart benefits at the end, even to those who remain Jews, so that in the end he will liberate those remaining in Judaism from the attacks of other men.'[25] It may be noted parenthetically that, curiously enough, William of Saint-Amour, the leader of the secular professors, was himself an eschatologist. He believed that the disorderly enthusiasm evidenced in the mendicant movement

---

[24] *De Catharis et Pauperibus de Lugduno* in Dondaine, ed., *Liber de duobus principiis*, 72.
[25] Denifle, *Chartularium universitatis Parisiensis* I, 273, No. 243.

and its affiliates was a sign of the coming of the antichrist whose appearance initiates the end of time.

The gnostic philosophy of this period was of two kinds, one stressing the inherent goodness of the material world and the other stressing its malevolence. Proponents of the former, the Amalricians accented the natural moral purity of those who know the way, and they linked this to the idea of progress. In five years, according to them, since God was everywhere and in everything, the world would become a sinless paradise of man in nature. The Cathars, especially the rigid dualists among them, opposed this view. They contrasted the unalterable sinfulness of the material world created by the primal principle of evil with the sempiternal bliss of the spiritual world, the two being linked together only by the slow ascension of purified souls to heaven. Both extremes were somewhat unconvincing. The Amalricians erred by saying, in effect, that whatever is is good, or is shortly to be so. Writing thirteen years after the eradication of their sect, Caesarius of Heisterbach pungently remarked that the five-year term was long past and that things had not come off as foretold. The Cathars went to the other extreme. The material world was all bad: eating meat was impermissible because born of carnality, marriage no better than fornication, sin so pervasive that those consoled (a ceremony combining the effects of baptism and extreme unction) in sickness had best commit suicide (by an *endura* or fast) if they showed signs of becoming well, and charity was of advantage only when given to those of the faith. In 1246 a gentleman's wife from Avignonet, south of Toulouse, told the inquisitors that she turned away when the Cathars preached that 'a man could not be saved if he slept with his wife (*habendo rem cum ea*)'.[26]

As in orthodoxy, however, doctrine was one thing and life another. The Amalricians may have been libertinist, but the Ortliebians, an Italian sect that shared many of their views, were morally rigorist. The advantage of the Cathar separation of the *credentes* from the *perfecti* was that the former were not expected to eschew marriage or the other things of the material world. And, dour though they were, the Cathars were not devoid of heart. Burned in 1321, the Perfect William Belibasta is said to have taught that 'it was a good work to give charity to anyone, so much so that, if a man gave charity to the devil because of God, God

[26] Toulouse Municipal Library MS. 609, 130r.

would remunerate that act', and that, if a man had fallen, he could remember that 'God will indulge all the sins of men, except the sin of desperation, that is, when a man despairs of God's having pity'.[27]

Heresy and society

Orthodox or heterodox, the enthusiasts felt that there were things wrong with the world. One widespread belief was that sexual *mores* and institutions were unsound. Almost everything was criticized, and attitudes were everywhere in conflict. Secular letters, we have seen, often expressed views about love and sexuality contradicting those of the Church. What was true of orthodoxy was also true of heresy: the heretics held conflicting views. Some were libertinist or opposed to institutional restraints. An interrogation of the Inquisition at Bologna in 1299 reports that Gerald Segarelli of Parma, head of a quasi-Franciscan sect called the Apostles or Poor of Christ, taught that, regardless of marriage, nude necking and even copulation could be performed without sin. Others were violently opposed to sexuality, although few went as far as the Cathars who, in their hatred of it, thought marriage evil because it made concupiscence legitimate. One of their arguments, however, appealed to others besides moral rigorists. According to Alan of Lille, 'they even say that marriage obviates the law of nature, because natural law dictates that all should be in common, and marriage appropriates to one what ought to be common in natural law'.[28]

Varieties of sexual expression were also involved here. A Bolognese statute of 1259 directed the *potestas* and other officers of the republic to aid the captains of the Society or Confraternity of the B.V.M. in their war on sodomy and heresy. These two crimes were frequently linked in the literature, both practical and polemical. This does not mean that homosexuals were more than usually heretical: they are not long for the world who make more risky what is already risky in itself. What the literature shows is that men saw all crimes or deviations as analogous. The charges against Boniface VIII peddled by the French party after his

---

[27] Protocols of the Inquisition of Carcassonne, 1319–20 in von Döllinger, *op. cit.*, II, 182 and 198–9.

[28] *Contra hereticos* I, 63 in *PL* CCX, 366.

death in 1303 include heresy, simony, usury, the more common sexual 'faults', and a purported defence of masturbation.

The role of women came into question. Like certain groups among the orthodox monks, Cathar and Waldensian heretics placed women slightly higher than did the orthodox Church. There were also female sectaries who attracted small followings from time to time. Such a one was Willelma of Milan, whose cult attracted the monks and aged pensionaries of the Cistercian monastery of Chiaravalle near Milan, but whose followers—this annuity set included a Visconti—went off the deep end and were charged with heresy after her death in 1281. Another was Prous Boneta of Montpellier, a woman condemned for her own peculiar version of the Olivite heresy in 1325. Her way of emphasizing the female principle in Christianity was to propose that she was the spiritual Mary through whom God would send the Holy Spirit to the world. She was a commentary on Christian guilt and female hope. The Lord said to her, she reported, that 'just as Eve, the first woman, was the beginning and cause of the damnation of all human nature and of all the human race through the sin of Adam, so "you will be the beginning and cause of the saving of all human nature and the human race by means of the words I make you say, if they are believed"'.[29]

Many had the conviction that Christian life was failing because of man's sinfulness. According to a Toulousan enemy of the Inquisition in the early 1230s, one who later hereticated and was burned, the Christian's life was not very noble. 'Sirs, hear me. I am not an heretic because I have a wife, and I lie with her, and I have children, and I eat meat, and I lie and I swear, and I am a faithful Christian.'[30] The sectaries blamed the pervasiveness of sin on the corruption of the Church. Equally important, also, is the fact that the attack on heresy evoked campaigns within the Church in which churchmen, from the popes down, condemned other churchmen for neglecting their mission, for deserting Christ's path, and for personal avarice and lubricity. The problem is, therefore, to discover what all this shouting was about.

The motives for self-condemnation among churchmen are reasonably evident. Self-criticism was a practical way for the

[29] W. H. May, 'The confession of Prous Boneta', *Essays in Medieval Life and Thought Presented in Honor of A. P. Evans* (New York, 1955, rprt), 29.
[30] Guillaume Pelisson, *Chronicon*, ed. Charles Molinier (Aniché, 1880), 17.

Church to mobilize itself for the combat with heresy. More significant was the fact that, by blaming individual clerks for their failure to attain the Christian ideal, churchmen directed attention away from the Church as a whole and away from the need to examine the practicality of that ideal. The reasons for sectarian criticism, both orthodox and heretical, were not wholly dissimilar. As in the criticism of the papacy for its immersion in worldly affairs, to blame others was to avoid blaming oneself, and anxiety about the inherent impossibility of attaining the ideal could be allayed for a time by believing that one's failures were caused by others.

Much of the polemic was misdirected or untruthful, sometimes deliberately so. The polemists maintained that the clergy of Languedoc were luxurious and rich. A few were, but most were not: Languedoc's church was a poor one. In the key diocese of Toulouse the bishop was so indigent that, in 1206, he was hounded by his lay creditors and even by his own cathedral's canons. Papal letters and even public opinion claimed that heresy was victorious in Languedoc because there was no living Christian devotion in that region. This was nonsense. The rise of heresy everywhere paralleled the growth of orthodox enthusiasm and the building of the Church. The rector of the Dalbade church in Toulouse alleged that his parish revenues had fallen off 'both because of the heretics whose perverse sects abound in the area of Toulouse and because of the newly built churches in the parish [of the Dalbade] to which almost all of our parishioners go during festivals and other days'.[31] And the Church could hardly be expected to reform itself to meet the objections of its critics, since their demands were themselves contradictory. Clerical celibacy is an example. On the one hand, the clergy were constantly being condemned for failing to live up to this ideal. On the other, many sectarians, especially the heretical Waldensians, saw clerical celibacy as a vice and a requirement that had no authority in sacred Scripture.

This polemic represented the ambivalences, contradictions and difficulties of the Christian vision. There was no unified teaching of what the Church itself should be. There had always been those whose conception of the Christian republic was founded on the

[31] See J. H. Mundy, 'Charity and social work in Toulouse', *Traditio* 11 (1966), 237n.

idea that men were neither perfect nor perfectible. They accepted the endowment of the Church with property and even wealth so that it could carry out its mission efficiently. Some went even further to insist that, directly or indirectly, the Church should rule men for their good by exercising jurisdiction and coercion. Spokesmen for this point of view were somewhat sorrowing, because they knew the dangers and possible corruptions inherent in this course. One such was Gerhoh, the provost of the Augustinian chapter of Reichersberg, a noted reformer but also a defender of ecclesiastical property and jurisdictions. Using the image of Jesus standing before Pontius Pilate successively clad in the white robe of the priesthood and the purple of empire, he sadly observed:

> I answer that it would indeed please me if the things which are Caesar's could be rendered to Caesar and the things which are God's to God, but with this caution, that the Church be not ravaged or stripped of its white robe if the purple is taken off too incautiously.[32]

Against these may be set those who tried to free the Church from the contaminations of the world. Moderate spokesmen would have the Church rest lightly upon it. Peter Cantor praised Bernard of Clairvaux for his dislike of expensive churches, and he lauded Peter Abelard who insisted that the gifts given by the count of Champagne to his monastery called the Paraclete should come from pure and not tainted income derived from usury or violence. Others, like Peter Waldes, who converted in 1173, and Francis of Assisi, composed what may be described as the utopian wing of the Christian republic. Naked to follow the naked Christ and, like the apostles, having all in common, they were moved by the primitive communism described in the Acts of the Apostles. Poverty was to rule. They were to have no property and there was to be no saving for the morrow. They would earn their bread by preaching, begging and working.

Many, perhaps most, of those inspired by these ideals were laymen. This does not mean that the clergy were not in such movements. One heretical sect, the Amalricians, was led by secular clergy from in and around Paris. Of its thirteen leaders, at least three were masters at the university, and all but two had studied

---

[32] *De novitatibus huius temporis* of 1155/6 12, in *MGH Ldl* III (1897), 296–7.

arts or theology there. Among them were four parish priests, and all the others were clerks in minor orders. More frequent was leadership by members of the monastic or mendicant orders. In general, however, most leaders—such as Waldes and Francis mentioned above—were laymen, inspired by texts and ideas from the clergy, but laymen nonetheless.

There was little new about any of this. Most of the ideas of the enthusiasts, both orthodox and heretical, had been heard during the Gregorian revolution before 1100. What kept the enthusiasm relatively orthodox around 1100 was the same as what did it later on: the immense expansion of the number of monastic orders and of the types of life and work to which the new religious and their associated layfolk devoted themselves. In the twelfth century, however, frictions increased. Remembering the Gregorian disorders, the secular clergy fought throughout the century to claustrate the monks again and to limit laymen's participation in preaching. Once established, the orders of the religious themselves prized *stabilitas*, which was guarded by preventing the members of their orders from going off to found new and more exciting ones. The result was increasingly restrictive legislation issued in general councils, legislation that reached its peak in the third Lateran of 1179 and was repeated at the fourth in 1215. To use political terms, the aristocracies of the Church had combined to repress the people, and it is probable that the crisis of popular heresy arose in the late twelfth century, partly because of the repression of monastic and lay religious passion.

But the policy changed: the prince of the Church came to the aid of his people and derived great profit thereby. Although placing him firmly under episcopal command, Alexander III embraced Waldes in 1179, and, in 1180–01, Waldes swore loyalty to the Church. The decisive change took place during the pontificate of Innocent III. Negotiations starting in 1198 led to the papal promulgation in 1201 of a rule for the Lombard Humiliati. Some of the Waldensians, Durand of Huesca's Poor Catholics and Bernard Prim's Poor Lombards, were accepted as legitimate groups in 1208 and 1210, thereafter leading the fight against the Cathars and other heretics. In 1216 James of Vitry persuaded Honorius III to licence Mary of Oignies's Beguines, a movement she had begun at Liège around 1207. The Franciscans received verbal approval in 1209 and a rule in 1223. The Dominicans received a rule in 1216. These and other orders were privileged by Rome to perform sacramental, penitential, and preaching services throughout Europe. They opened the channels for lay enthusiasm and, by so doing, cut the ground from under the popular heresies that seemed so flourishing around 1200.

This expansion was to continue until the counterattack of the secular clergy and the older orders clamped the lid on again in the late thirteenth century. Before the reaction took effect, however, the spread of the Church's mission by preaching and the formation of lay devotional groups associated with the new orders had brought about a religious literacy among laymen that has its equal in Christian history only during the Reformation of the sixteenth century. Writing on the Lombard Humiliati whom he visited in 1216, James of Vitry praised their preaching and remarked that almost all of their male members were literate, by which he meant that they had some Latin. But those who had only vernacular tongues also knew much religion. An example is Prous Boneta of Montpellier. She not only had an elaborate vision of Christian progress, but she also had views on the ideological roles of ecclesiastical intellectuals. Commenting on the earthly paradise soon to come, then briefly held up by Pope John XXII, who was the antichrist in her opinion, she noted that the new Church of the Franciscans and Dominicans had prepared its way. But this Church, which she likened to a spiritualized Eve, was temporarily torn asunder. From Eve's church God, a spiritualized Adam, had had two sons, Cain and Abel. Abel was the Franciscan Peter John Olivi, and Cain the Dominican Thomas Aquinas, 'who was recently canonized. And just as Cain slew his brother Abel in the flesh, so did this brother Thomas slay his brother, namely the said brother Peter John, spiritually, that is, in his writings.'[33]

Exceptions aside (these were most noticeable in Italy), the linguistic culture of the enthusiasts was vernacular. Waldes employed a priest to translate sacred text and commentaries. We also hear of translations of Jerome, Augustine, Gregory I, and Bernard of Clairvaux. The Church early began to investigate this work, and, by the end of the 1230s, papal letters, local conciliar legislation, and the activity of the Inquisition had begun to control and

[33] W. H. May, 'The confession of Prous Boneta', *Essays in Medieval Life and Thought Presented in Honor of A. P. Evans* (1955), 24.

even to prohibit these translations. What offended churchmen was that almost all heretical sects had forms of biblical criticism and interpretation that conflicted with the orthodox ones. Many rejected not only the modern doctors of the church but even the Latin fathers in order to base their arguments on sacred Scripture alone, thus obviating many of the institutions of the contemporary Church. Lastly, not a few were hostile to Latin, partly because ordinary layfolk could not understand it, but also partly because it was the language of the ecclesiastical order and the world of learning. The idea that Latin slavery was opposed to vernacular freedom, an idea that was to be part of the Reformation, was already known.

In 1178 a cardinal examining heretics at Toulouse was horrified to have to discuss the faith in the vernacular. He feared that, as an Italian, he would not understand what they were saying. Mainly, however, he was upset by having to give up Latin, the language of the liturgy and religious thought of the western Church since the days of the German invasions so many centuries before. The cardinal's fears were well founded, more so than he could have known. The replacement of Latin—at first by the vernacular poetry and literature of the aristocracies and those who emulated them, and then, after an initial period when the lay scribes and notaries revived and popularized a vulgarized Latin, in legal documentation—portended the defeat of the ecumenical Church by western Europe's regional states, and the subordination of the clerical order to the magistrates and princes who headed them. Heresy failed, but the extremists really won the battle. To defeat them, churchmen were obliged to get over their repugnance and to use the vernacular, thus broadening immensely the vernacular religious culture by 1300.

The history of the Church as a social institution does not alone explain the growth of religious utopianism and heresy. The ideals and angers of these movements both reflected society's needs and permeated society. It is true, however, that, in comparison with both antiquity and modern times, the conception of distinct social orders, such as the clergy and laity, each with its character and function, was strong. As long as monasticism was expanding to admit new devotions and functions, lay utopians could express their dreams by entering the Church without too greatly disturbing civil society and its private property, coercion, and other equally necessary but unpleasant institutions. Churchmen often said that they alone could live according to natural and divine law, that is, in true freedom and equality, and with the communal sharing of property. Out in the world, the laity were obliged to live by the *ius gentium*, the law that instituted slavery, contract, and private property. Perhaps because they could exist alongside and not within secular society, the Humiliati, Beguines, and mendicants were able to erect relatively durable institutions, relatively durable, that is, when compared to the short-lived ancient or modern utopian settlements or revolutionary societies.

All the same, there were limits to the discreteness of the social orders; indeed, they were already beginning to break down. As has been several times seen, the spread of the monastic vocation to the laity had begun to enable a man to live religiously in the cloister of his own heart while inhabiting the world and going about its business. The essence of secularism or the lay spirit had therefore already been born although the institutional effects of this were not to be seen until nearly two centuries had passed. Another limit to discreteness, and one that made itself felt sooner, was the analogousness of ecclesiastical utopias to secular ones. Although a major tradition among churchmen insisted upon the distinction between things ecclesiastical and things secular, some, especially the utopians, went pretty far in the other direction. Examples are legion, but there is a curious one about the ideal form of government by Peter Cantor. When discussing the sin or heresy of simony, Peter says that princes derive their authority from ecclesiastical consecration. Can then, he asks, the churchman who consecrates commit simony? 'When someone is too young, like a boy to whom as heir a kingdom should fall, or someone is insufficient in life and merit, does the prelate sin who grants him the service of consecration? It seems so. For does he not consent? He can and he ought to resist . . .'[34] Since justice is a sacred thing, it is simony to sell it or to buy its exercise. It is simony to buy a kingdom or a duchy because princes have the care of souls (*cura animarum*). And the heresy of simony could be introduced by more than money; the exercise of family influence and favour was also simoniacal.

---

[34] *Summa de sacramentis et animae consiliis* III, 2a: *Liber casuum conscientiae* 185, ed. Dugauquier (1963), 102.

One asks whether the royal dignity should be conferred by election. For it appears iniquitous to some that, as though forced by necessity, men should be obliged to receive unjust princes by reason of succession. And Jerome says: 'Joshua the son of Nun is chosen from another tribe that it may be known that the government of the people is to be conferred not because of blood but because of life.'[35]

Is then hereditary monarchy heretical? Not necessarily, Peter only asked a very loaded question.

That enthusiasts had beliefs that extended into the political and social realms is therefore not surprising. War and coercion were to be abolished in the Christian community of the utopians. Economic exploitation was condemned and economic brotherhood prized. At the least, all men should labour honestly and not live off the sweat of others. Better yet, the primitive communism of the apostles was to be the basis of Christian organization. Most sectarians did not attack the institutions obeyed by others, but some were more aggressive. The late twelfth-century Passagians, for example, preached Micah 4:3 seriously. Christians should beat their swords into ploughshares and the nations should not learn war any more. Nor should there be any princes: 'That for which a king appears to have been created, namely to wage war, to wield the material sword, and to administer punishment, should have no further place among Christians.'[36]

More widespread than pacifism was the idea of economic brotherhood. It will be recalled that craft and trade guilds were only beginning to be organized in the later twelfth century, and that the full flood of this movement was reached in the late thirteenth century. Although few guilds were directly affiliated with the new orders of the Church, the spectacular growth in the number of charity hospitals—some created by the Waldensian-style movements of the Poor of Christ—and of confraternities offering burial and other charitable services shows how close this explosion of religious passion was to the emergence of a guild economy. Burial and medical services are among the first needs of working-

---

[35] *Liber casuum conscientiae* 185, ed. Dugauquier, 101. The passage from Jerome is found in Gratian's *Decretum* 2, 8, 1, 6 in *CICan* I, 591.
[36] *The Summa contra haereticos ascribed to Praepositinus of Cremona* 21, ed. J. N. Garvin and J. A. Corbett (Nôtre-Dame, Ind., 1957). This is a composite quotation of two passages on pp. 225–6.

class people, and charitable institutions evoke less resistance than economic ones. In northern France in the two decades after 1200, Robert of Curzon's utopian message and the propaganda against usury of his contemporary Stephen Langton provided arguments for economic brotherhood useful to guildsmen in their attacks on exploitative entrepreneurs and rich masters. Although many were founded by nobles or town patricians, the early Beguine settlements in the Low Countries and the Rhine valley attracted female workers in the cloth industry, women who continued to work when brigaded into these semiclerical groups. Widespread in northern and central Italy, the Humiliati at first were largely industrial workers. Crafts that were exploited by entrepreneurial merchants had an unusual affinity for religious enthusiasm. Foremost among these were the weavers, whose very name—*textores* —became a popular synonym for heretics.

To such working-class groups doctrines about the poverty of Christ or the apostles had a natural appeal. Almost all such doctrines asserted the moral superiority of the poor. This teaching was often somewhat strained, but few went as far in this direction as William Cornelis. A secular canon of Antwerp, he resigned his prebend, preached poverty, and died with the reputation of a saint in the early 1250s. On his demise, his sect was charged with heresy. According to their enemies, the canon and his followers maintained that the poor were automatically saved and the rich damned. Being in a state of grace, the poor could fornicate without sin and a poor woman commit prostitution. More moderately, the working-class commitment to religious enthusiasm emphasized the purifying force of labour, an idea exemplified by the Waldensians, Humiliati, Beguines and early Franciscans. Although begging, or mendicancy, was good for the soul because it inculcated humility, Francis of Assisi's original idea—embodied in his rule of 1221—was that his friars should also work at the trades they knew. James of Vitry reported enthusiastically in 1216 that the early Franciscans, male and female, worked with their own hands. Later on, Bishop Robert Grosseteste of Lincoln preached to the Franciscans at Oxford and, after praising mendicancy, went on to observe that there was a still higher stage, 'namely, to live from one's own labour. Whence he observed that the Beguines are the most perfect and holy of religious because they live of their own labour and do not burden the world with exactions.'[37]

543

Several things, however, combined to minimize the stress on labour and, as in the case of the Franciscans, replace it with mendicancy. One was an argument concerning function. Early on, the *Liber antiheresis* argued against the Waldensian doctrine of the necessity of labour by noting that the Lord had exempted his apostles from manual work because he wished them to spend their time preaching, praying, and saving souls. Another was more subtle and gradual: the decline of this kind of religious economic utopianism coincided with the rise to power of economic corporatism and artisan guilds. As the guilds won their place in the world, they no longer needed the aid of the utopians and therefore actively discouraged the competition provided by congregations of celibate workers. Not all churchmen were happy about the replacement of work by begging. William of Saint-Amour, the famous enemy of the mendicants at the University of Paris, complained that the world was crowded with people who did no productive labour and had harsh words to say about the Beguines and Beghards of his time:

> Please note that what I have said above concerning mendicity I have said especially because . . . of certain youths who are called Good Workers, and because of certain young women, who are called Beguines, who are spread throughout the whole kingdom, and who are all perfectly capable of working but instead wish to do little or no labour and to live from alms in bodily sloth under the pretext of praying.[38]

Other evidence of the relationship of utopian enthusiasm to social corporatism is the assault on usury. Just as sodomy was linked to heresy in the religious mind, so was usury, the crime against economic brotherhood. The attack on usury and heresy by the White Confraternity established in Toulouse in 1209 under Bishop Fulk of Marseilles mentioned earlier, may stand as a paradigm of ecclesiastical propaganda and action. Caesarius of Heisterbach reports that around 1200 some heretics from Montpellier came to preach in Metz. They were there protected by

---

[37] Thomas of Eccleston, *Tractatus de adventu fratrum minorum in Angliam* 15, ed. A. G. Little (1951), 99. For James of Vitry, see R. B. C. Huygens, *Lettres de Jacques de Vitry* (1960), 76. His letter No. One not only describes these orders but also uses all the biblical texts on manual labour, Ephesians 4:28, 1 Thessalonians 4:10–21, and 2 Thessalonians 3:7–12.

[38] Cited in Paul Alphandéry, *Les idées morales chez les hétérodoxes Latins*, 12–3n. 'Good Workers' is *boni valeti, valetus* meaning journeyman.

some patricians (*potentes*) who hated the bishop because he had refused burial to one of their relatives who was a usurer. Were then usurers usually inclined toward heresy? It seems not. The heretics responded to orthodox charges by charging churchmen with usury. Picked up by the Inquisition in Bologna in 1299, one such claimed that the Dominicans were especially notorious because they buried usurers and received usuries as charity, all to keep their concubines in style! The only community where this question has been studied, Toulouse in the early thirteenth century, shows that some usurers were heretics and some not. Two usurers were unusually faithful Christians—Pons David, an important donor to the Hospitallers, and Pons of Capdenier, whose testamentary gifts began the foundation for the mother house of the Dominican order. As with sodomy, so with usury: usury was risky enough without adding heresy.

Usury, with its entrepreneurial overtones, had a class connotation. This is because a usurer was not merely one who lent money at interest, but one who became well-known. Obviously, the poor lent both commodities and money, but what preserved them for virtue was their incapacity to be vicious on a sufficient scale. Although not a few patricians or gentlefolk were notorious usurers —for example, the great families of Metz or the merchant-bankers of Tuscany—their relatively established wealth, their interest in public office, and their hostility to the new rich diluted their economic aggressiveness. Ideally, therefore, the usurer was a bourgeois making his fortune. Especially in the twelfth century, when bishops who were lords of cities were charging the proponents of urban liberty with heresy, it is probable that some of these burghers were heretics. On the other hand, in the literary sources and inquisitorial registers of thirteenth-century Languedoc, the burghers, although there, are not heavily represented.

Gentlefolk and town patricians seem to have been rather more involved. An example is Hugo Speroni, consul of the town of Piacenza and a onetime schoolmate of the celebrated jurist Vacarius at Bologna, who wrote against the Church around 1177 and whose sect was still alive in the 1220s. Another was Peter Maurand of Toulouse, who was forced to confess and undergo penitence in 1178, a matter involving a trip to the Holy Land, restitution of usuries, and restoration of tithes to the Church. A member of a patrician clan, one line of which regularly produced

Cathar heretics, Peter owned a towered town house and substantial rural properties including a castle or fortified village. Later an inquisitorial register of 1245–47 clearly shows that the mixed rural and urban aristocracy of the Toulousain was deeply implicated in heresy. One may conjecture that those of high social level who turned towards heresy added to the usual motives their discontent with the way their economic position was threatened by new wealth and their political leadership by the rise of the *populares*. This tinctures with truth the common Guelph charge that Italian Ghibelline gentlefolk were heretics. But one must tread with care. The most that can be said is that the imperialist party in Milan, Brescia, and Bologna had heretical overtones, and that Ghibelline chiefs in Lombardy, like Humbert Pallavicini and the proto-tyrant Ezzolino of Romano in his lordships of Treviso, Padua and Vicenza, actively protected heretics against the Inquisition.

Although specific class or order affiliation was significant in given places and at given times and although the urban middle classes were perhaps not strongly given to it, no class was exempt from heresy. At the same time, heresy was strongest and most inventive where urban life was vigorous and growing. Northern and central Italy were its most vibrant centres, and Milan, the very symbol of town industry and self-government, was often described as heresy's capital. Other lively areas were Languedoc and adjacent regions, the Rhône valley, the Rhine and its western confluents, and the relatively heavily urbanized region extending from Liège through Brabant to Flanders. But these were also the regions where Gregorian enthusiasm had been liveliest, where most of the monastic innovations were first introduced, where the mendicant movements had their first success, and where orthodox enthusiasm and learning flourished most brightly. In other words, the regions marked by relatively heavy urbanization were in the forefront of everything, orthodox or heterodox.

Not that rural populations were slow to adhere to heresy. Villagers picked up from the towns whatever was exciting and meaningful. Rural Flanders and the villages of Champagne, whose fairs were visited by southern Frenchmen and Italians, were influenced by Catharism. Languedoc and adjacent regions offer the best examples of rural heresy. Around 1210 there was scarcely a family of seigniorial grade there whose members did not play with Catharism, and it had even penetrated the local princely houses of Foix, Béziers, and possibly Saint-Gilles-Toulouse. Rural heresy in Languedoc shows a pattern that was to be repeated in the later Protestant movement in that region. Whereas Catharism flourished among gentlefolk in the early 1200s, the crusade of 1209–29 and the repression by the Inquisition through the decades of the mid-century confined it to the humbler farming population. From the records of the confiscations of property for heresy it would seem that this had to do with the fact that a leadership cadre is more visible and hence more exposed. Gentlefolk were also more directed to careers in civil and ecclesiastical office than ordinary farmers, and the first things hit by repression were these outlets for family ambition. Oliver of Termes, member of a heretical family and a gallant soldier against the crusade and against the Inquisition in Narbonne during the 1230s, gave up, went on crusade with Louis IX in 1248, and entered the royal service.

When successfully attacked, heresy lost its hold first in the richer areas. In Italy and southern France Catharism was strongly implanted in both town and countryside in the early 1200s. After the mid-century it weakened rapidly in the towns and in the more populous and heavily cultivated plains. This affected its intellectual quality. The historian Matthew Paris reported that the Lombard and Tuscan Cathars sent members to study at the University of Paris, and we know of the condemnation or exile of at least three such students in 1241 and 1247. By 1300 Catharism had long since ceased to grow intellectually and had sunk to a somewhat primitive dualism not unrelated to diabolism and witchcraft. It was also pushed out of the plains into isolated pockets in Piedmont, the Alps above Lake Como, and the Pyrenees. A similar move took place in the heretical wings of the Waldensians and in the later offshoots of mendicant extremism. An example of the latter is Gerald Segarelli's sect called the Apostles, a curious mixture of Franciscan poverty, Joachitic optimism, and Catharist dualism. Starting in Parma and the Romagna about 1260, the sect spread throughout Lombardy. By 1308, when its leaders were slain, it was strong only in a few villages in the foothills of the Alps above Vercelli.

The fact that a local seignior hostile to the town of Vercelli initially aided the Apostles shows that there was more to this process than mere flight. Inhabitants of marginal lands, especially uplands, seem to have leaned toward extremist beliefs. Early in its history, Waldensianism spread from the Rhône valley to the hills of Dauphiny, Savoy, and Piedmont. In 1210 the bishop of Turin launched against them the first of a series of intermittent small wars that lasted throughout the thirteenth century. In the meantime the Waldensians spread through the Alps to Austria, Moravia, and Bohemia (where Peter Waldes died in 1216). In the early 1300s they began moving down the Apennines to southern Italy. The endemic social conflict between hillfolk and plainsfolk seen in much of Italy and the Pyrenean region in the later Middle Ages was already developing. This was an aspect of the combat between town and countryside, between settled agriculture and herding. The hillfolk resisted the building of ecclesiastical and secular government, with its tax collectors and repression of smuggling in the interests of a regulated and corporatized economy. A not dissimilar phenomenon was earlier seen in the forested plains and marshes around the Weser River in northern Germany. The primitive rural population called the Stedingers was charged with heresy and defeated in 1234 by a crusade launched by nearby towns, seigniors, episcopal authority, and papal pronouncements. Vestigial paganism and a reluctance to pay tithes there may have been, but no real heresy. The Stedingers were really resisting commercial penetration, expanding government, and a measure of urban centralization.

Heresy could also sometimes demarcate a cultural frontier. An example was the Catharism or Bogomil heresy proselytized from Byzantium through Bulgaria into the south-east marches of Latin Christendom. In Bosnia this heresy became the religion of the local prince or *ban* in 1199, a status it was to hold until well after 1300 in spite of campaigns launched by the Hungarians, Venetians and popes throughout this period.

To conclude this brief section on the regional history of heresy, it may be said that, although rural populations rarely invented doctrine and never developed it to its highest intellectual pitch, they were as much given to heresy as urban ones. And if one looks at the geographical distribution of heresy it is clear that urban growth does not wholly explain the incidence of heresy. Heresy was far stronger in relatively less urbanized Languedoc than in heavily urbanized Flanders. Something other than urbanization must also have counted.

It has been remarked that the area of modern Belgium, the valleys of the Rhine and the Rhône, Languedoc, and northern and central Italy generated most of the new enthusiasms for orthodoxy as well as for heterodoxy. These were the regions where the devolution of political power into small principalities, urban republics, and petty scigniories was most marked. Areas in which the older monarchies had held on better and were renewing their power, such as England, royal and Plantagenet France, Aragon, Castile, and Norman and Hohenstaufen southern Italy, were not famed for heresy or for inventive orthodoxy in the early 1200s. Although ecclesiastical liberty had everywhere increased since Gregorian days, the princes of these regions had retained greater power over their local churches than did small princes, seigniors, and town councillors. The greater princes therefore had a greater interest in defending an institution that was still useful to them in governing their subjects. Where the link between secular power and the Church was less strong, the religion of the Latins was both more inventive of new forms of orthodoxy and more liable to the danger of heretical secession.

Repression

Other than profiting from the generally happy circumstances of the age, the principal way the Church defeated the popular heresies was by opening its gates to the initiators of new devotions, new enthusiasms, new utopianisms. However dangerous these movements were, their success in undermining heresy is evident. Contemporaries understood this. When Bishop Fulk of Toulouse visited northern France and the Low Countries in 1212 to raise money and men for the Albigensian crusade, he was impressed by the successes against heresy of a group to which he was introduced by Robert of Curzon and James of Vitry. This was the Beguines. Four years later James of Vitry, on his way to Rome (where he had his Beguines approved) and to the Holy Land, stopped off in Milan,

> which is the womb of the heretics, where I remained for some days and preached. . . . One can scarcely find anyone in the whole city who resists the heretics except for certain holy men

549

and religious women who are called Patarines [that is, heretics] by malicious and secular men, but who are called Humiliati by the pope from whom they have received the right to preach to fight the heretics, and who has confirmed their order. These are they who, leaving all for Christ and assembling in diverse places, live from their own manual labour, frequently preaching the word of God. . . . And so greatly has this order multiplied in the diocese of Milan that they have founded one hundred and fifty conventual congregations, men in some and women in others, not counting those who remain in their own homes.[39]

One may conclude from this that the Church in part defeated the popular heresies by means of persuasion, that is, by providing what appeared to be attractive alternatives and by preaching.

Many churchmen believed that persuasion was the only just way. Coerced belief was not considered true belief. The question was whether persuasion alone would succeed. At first preaching was employed in Languedoc. Bernard of Clairvaux went there in 1145, and, although his tour was much lauded, he was hooted down at Verfeil near Toulouse and his mission had no lasting result. Later Cistercian missions were equally abortive. As a result, preaching was slowly supplemented or reinforced by coercion. The third Lateran Council of 1179 asked laymen to help and promised them the rewards and protections given crusaders. Two years later Henry of Marcy, abbot of Clairvaux and recently appointed cardinal and papal legate, raised a small force while preaching in Languedoc and captured the town of Lavaur. In 1209 the Albigensian crusade was launched, at first under the command of the legate Arnold Amalric, abbot of Citeaux. There was a similar change in the activity of the Dominicans, whose founder, Dominic of Osma, had preached in Languedoc without much success from 1206 to 1208. In 1221 the pope instructed them to combat heresy. In 1231 they were referred to as inquisitors in a law applicable in Rome that passed into imperial legislation the next year. Thereafter the Dominicans (and occasionally the Franciscans) produced not only famed preachers but also inquisitor-judges. From the 1230s onward Dominican tertiarics, or associated layfolk, were brigaded into confraternities of Jesus

---

[39] Huygens, *Lettres de Jacques de Vitry*, 72–3, No. 1. *Patarinus* was the old word for almost any kind of heretic in Lombardy. The phrase translated as 'secular men' is *seculares homines*, and it may mean the secular clergy, who sometimes hated orthodox enthusiasts almost as much as they did heretics.

Christ or the B.V.M. to help hunt heretics, and Dominican generals and inquisitors denounced as unprofitable the public debates with heretics and Jews that had been so common around 1200. Persuasion without some coercion had failed.

The penalties for heresy were found in Roman law. As summed up by Gratian's *Decretum*, these were mainly exile and confiscation of property. Gratian and the other canonists also borrowed from Roman law the notion that heresy was a crime against the state, an idea given added significance in this period because of the general conviction that the common good (*salus populi*) required the sturdy defence of the *respublica christiana*. War was permissible to defend this entity, and the canonists therefore allowed the death penalty for pertinacious heretics.

Not all were happy about this revival of ancient law, but it gradually won out. An example of changing attitudes may be seen in the comments on the execution of Arnold of Brescia at Rome in 1155. At the time his execution was attributed to the civil prefect of Rome and not to the pope. Although this was legally accurate, contemporaries saw through it. Gerhoh of Reichersberg wept: 'How I wish that he had been punished for his admittedly evil doctrine by exile or imprisonment or by any other penalty besides death, or, at least, that he had been killed in such a way that the Roman Church or its court should not bear the responsibility for his death.'[40] By the time the canonist Huguccio of Pisa (d. 1210) wrote, Arnold's case was no longer being bewailed, but instead used as an example. To be tried, degraded, hanged and then burned on order of the pope, as Huguccio describes it, was justifiable punishment and shows that heretics 'are not to be punished for heresy alone . . . but, when incorrigible, they are to suffer the extreme penalty, as was done in the case of Arnold of Brescia'.[41]

As canon law tightened, so did secular law. The law itself was old, but publication and enforcement were required, and here local princes took the lead. Other than profiting from the confiscation of property, their motives were various. Those who dominated their local churches fought to protect those profitable institutions. Others desired to appear more catholic than the pope.

[40] *De investigatione Antichristi*, in *MGH Ldl* III (1897), 347–8.
[41] Cited from his *Summa* in Henri Maisonneuve, *Etudes sur l'origine de l'Inquisition* (1960), 88.

England was off to an early start. In 1165–66 some Flemish or German Cathars were condemned by a local synod at Oxford, 'relaxed' to the secular court, and there branded and exiled. The Constitutions of Clarendon of 1166—one of Henry II's unsuccessful attempts to impose a settlement on Thomas Becket—ordered prosecution of those aiding such heretics. In the meantime the kings of Aragon were moving ahead. They imitated Roman law by assimilating heresy to treason, and ordered exile, confiscation, and in 1197 death by fire. More useful to the popes were the laws of Frederick II Hohenstaufen. In edicts issued from 1224 to 1239-Frederick extended the death penalty from Lombardy to all his dominions. His laws were accepted into canon law by Innocent IV in his *Cum adversus haereticam* of 1254, thus making ecumenical and normative what had been local and inconsistent.

Some churchmen still resisted the trend to severity, but they had to lower their sights. Before heresy had become widespread, such men could afford to be tolerant, largely because the people and their princes traditionally and almost thoughtlessly slew those who had been expelled from the Church. Thus Bernard of Clairvaux had been able to say with inadvertent cynicism that 'We approve the zeal [of the people], but we do not persuade them to do it because faith is a matter of persuasion and is not to be imposed by force.'[42] Long before the time of Innocent IV, this position was untenable, and reformers like Peter Cantor were reduced to insisting on due process and easier punishment. Peter blamed a prelate for condemning as Cathars women who had refused the advances of a priest. Perhaps he had in mind an occasion in the late 1170s when Gervaise of Tilbury started the persecution of a sect in Rheims upon being refused by a maiden who asserted that the loss of her virginity would be tantamount to immediate damnation. Still, Peter did not want heretics to circulate freely and corrupt others. Imprisonment, he thought, was the answer, but, if death had to be imposed, a heretic should be given time to think it over. The Romans, he thought, were gentler than the judges of his day.

> Even the infidels used to allow a delay of thirty days to a Christian . . . that he might think over whether or not he

---

[42] Cited in Maisonneuve, *op. cit.*, 105n.

wished to sacrifice to the idols. . . . Why then does the Church presume to examine men's hearts with this strange and foreign judgment? And why are Cathars immediately burned and not given legitimate delays to think the matter over?[43]

A system of clerical police clearly had to be instituted. Previously heresy had been pursued and punished by the bishops and secular authorities. Reliance on the latter was unsatisfactory because it gave laymen too much power even over the clergy, and because laymen were either indifferent or excessive in their severity: action against heretics in Northern France, for example, being like lynchings. Effective episcopal action was impeded by bishops who were recruited from local society and reflected local interests and moods, something obviously harmful to the Church in Languedoc, where the gentry were often heretical. Even the forced replacement of bishops by the popes could not be efficacious: a local man was eventually bound to be elected as successor. With inquisitors appointed by the popes in the 1230s, however, systematic and consistent pressure could be applied. Direction of the various missions was eventually regulated by the appointment in 1262 of a senior inquisitor resident at the papal court.

The inquisitors usually came from the mendicant orders or were associated with these new groups. Armed with papal letters instructing them 'to reform the Church' as well as to purge the heretics, their missions initially evoked much popular support and, one imagines, got caught up in local issues and hysterias that had little to do with heresy and orthodoxy. Aided by some mendicants, Conrad of Marburg, *scholasticus* of Mainz, spread fire and death in much of western Germany from 1227 until he and three of his companions were assassinated in 1233. The Dominican Robert, called the Bugger because he was a converted Cathar (Bulgar), was active from Flanders to Champagne. The peak of his career was reached in 1239 when he is said to have burned just under two hundred inhabitants of the village of Montwimer in one day. He was shortly thereafter arrested and sentenced to life imprisonment by the Church. Occasional excesses, however, were not the principal reason for opposition. The heretical minority resisted being rooted out and the relatively orthodox majorities wearied of the disruption of their communities by probing in-

43 *Verbum abbreviatum* 72 in *PL* ccv, 320.

vestigations. The history of Peter of Verona may stand as an example of the curious ambivalences with which this problem was fraught. The first inquisitor at Milan, this Dominican was assassinated in 1252. Within ten months of his death, he was canonized as Saint Peter Martyr—an example of the same strange parallelism by which slain crusaders in arms were compared to the Holy Innocents of Bethlehem slaughtered by order of Herod the Great.

To these normal human motives must be added political and jurisdictional ones. Although often grateful for help against the heretics, the secular clergy were rarely enthusiastic. Meeting in councils, French and German bishops helped to arrest the missions of Conrad of Marburg and Robert the Bugger. The papacy, however, had its way, and the mendicant inquisition was introduced along with mendicant preaching, teaching and parish work. Princes and self-governing communities also often resisted the papal inquisition. Frederick II Hohenstaufen promulgated the harshest laws against heresy, but his Ghibelline supporters actively impeded the inquisitors. Furthermore, where heresy was weak and where the state's power over the local church was strong, the papal inquisition never really penetrated. This was the case in Castile, England, and much of central, northern and eastern Germany. Inquisitors were to be found in France, but they were much busier in autonomous or frontier provinces like Flanders, Champagne, and Languedoc than in royal or north-western France. Indeed, the repression of heresy was clearly tied to political power. Around 1250 the inquisitor Rainier Sacconi estimated that there were about 2,500 Cathar Perfects in northern and central Italy as against some 200 in southern France. But the crusade was launched against Languedoc, not against Lombardy. The popes were tempted to attack Milan, but dropped the idea when the Emperor Frederick II actually proposed it. The reason is obvious. Milan headed the towns who were the popes' best allies in the struggle against the Empire. All the same, Italy's urban republics slowly allowed the inquisitors to come in. Although townsfolk everywhere fought the first introduction of the inquisitors in the 1230s (as late as 1256 in Genoa and 1289 in Venice), the frequency with which their advent was hailed by the Guelph, or popular, parties shows that the leading elements and even the majority of the inhabitants favoured the inquisitors.

In the course of time, the inquisitors became specialists. To the vast literature against heresy they added their own type: manuals of procedure. Partial manuals appeared in the 1240s, but the first full-scale one was written around 1256, an anonymous work that was subsequently expanded by the Franciscan David of Augsburg (d. 1272). In 1178 it was still possible for a council headed by a papal legate to have the Cathar Peter Maurand of Toulouse recant by repeating the oath taken by Berengar of Tours in 1059 in favour of the real presence in the sacramental host. This worked because Cathars also did not believe in the real presence, but it was rough and ready. With the manualists came sophistication: the basic beliefs of each sect were described and lines of questioning suitable to each were suggested. The almost surgical tenor of this literature is illustrated by Bernard Guy's discussion of what to do about a heretic who suddenly asks to retract when being led out to execution. Unless a recidivist, he is to be received into penance, and for two reasons: mercy is to be preferred to rigour, and, adds the experienced policeman, the fainthearted would be scandalized if the penitent were refused. The sincerity of the penitence, however, must be tested. A prompt and voluntary confession of all those associated with him in heresy was this test.

But these were surgeons who had the policeman's hatred of crime and were angered by what they thought were the diseases of the body social. Inquisitors were often onetime heretics, and some, like the Bugger, were driven insane by their work. Even Bernard Guy, perhaps provoked by the Franciscan Bernard Délicieux's (d. 1320) attacks on the Dominican inquisitors, deserted judicial calm to record with gruesome joy the slaughter of Dolcino of Novara and Margaret, the last leaders of the Italian Apostles in 1307. Margaret was cut to pieces before Dolcino's eyes, and he himself suffered the same fate immediately afterward.

These punishments should not leave the impression that the inquisitors were especially brutal. Awful corporal punishments were normal in medieval practice. They derived from German and Roman traditions and were reinforced by the infrequency of imprisonment in the early Middle Ages and the wide publicity given to public executions as a mean of repressing crime. By replacing the death penalty with imprisonment, indeed, the inquisition was 'progressive'. Two great inquisitorial campaigns broke the back of the Cathar heresy in the large diocese of Toulouse, those of 1245–46 and 1256–57. The first was directed against a heresy still widespread and was more gentle than the second, which pursued persistent and stubborn remnants. In the year 1246, 945 heretics were sentenced. None were killed; 11 per cent were imprisoned, and 89 per cent were given various penitences. In 1256–57 about 15 per cent of 306 sentences were levied against those who had previously died in heresy or were in flight, 7 per cent were death penalties, and 78 per cent were sentences of imprisonment. Although one can see how heavily the Inquisition weighed on local society, it is clear that the hopes of Peter Cantor for legal reform had become real.

What Peter and his contemporaries among the Italian jurists meant by legal reform involved more than the substitution of imprisonment for the death penalty. Among these was the replacement of the early medieval modes of proof normally employed in cases where the charge against a putative offender was not wholly provable, that is, oath, battle and ordeal. Oath and battle long resisted the assault of the jurists. The clergy had a traditional right to compurgation by their peers and kinship groups used the same method to protect their members, thus forcing a case to arbitration by invoking the threat of vendetta because of family solidarity. Battle obviously appealed to the martial *mores* of the aristocracy. The ordeal was less resistant. Largely a method of condemning one against whom there was suspicion but insufficient proof, the ordeal—although it could sometimes be avoided by exile—was both brutal and led to frequent abuses, especially in the case of those foreign to the communities in which they were judged. Clerical participation in the administration of the ordeals was formally prohibited by canon eighteen of the fourth Lateran Council of 1215, an act which caused it to be replaced throughout much of Europe by the procedure known as the *inquisitio* supplemented by torture.

Another aspect of legal reform was caused by the fact that the social utopianism of people like Peter Cantor joined with the professionalism of the jurists to insist on a more active prosecution of crime. Accusation by the injured party (*accusatio, appellatio*) was supplemented by other procedures, especially by the old but now vastly extended judicial inquiry initiated by a deposition of substantial evidence against a putative wrongdoer (*inquisitio*).

The attack on the old modes of proof and the lively prosecution of justice were favoured by those institutions and communities that had a strong sense of the individual's responsibility and his citizenship or membership. Such entities were not only opposed to the protection of putative wrongdoers by family and local interests, but were also convinced of the advantage to be gained by making all members or citizens equal in rights or obligations, save for differences allowed to individuals in return for special functions or services. As is known, the modern nation-state was to carry this jurisprudence to its highest point, and it is to be noted that the signs of this future development were already visible in Norman and Hohenstaufen southern Italy, Plantagenet England, and late thirteenth-century Capetian France. Typical of the period treated in this book, however, the political and institutional entities that took the lead in inventing and developing the new jurisprudence—new in the sense that it was an adaptation to contemporary circumstances of the norms defined in Roman law —were the ecumenical Church and the small state or community, of which the best and most developed examples were Italy's urban republics. A brief examination of the new law will therefore reinforce the description of the growth of governmental power already given above in Part Four. More to the point here, it will also enable us to see why the majority of contemporaries did not consider the judicial procedure of the Inquisition to be monstrous; indeed, why it was even popular.

The new law was more learned and sensitive than the old. Written procedure replaced verbal. Civil courts and prisons were separated from criminal ones. A system analogous to bail (the *fidejussores*) was introduced, and custodial or pre-trial imprisonment of those suspected of grave crime was distinguished from imprisonment as punishment. Personnel became increasingly professional. From the mid-twelfth century the old diocesan board of laymen and clergy under an archdeacon was replaced by the bishop's judge (*officialis*). In Italy lay consuls were replaced by professional jurists for important cases. Opposition to these changes was constant. Churchmen lamented the replacement of synodal justice by what they called Justinian's laws. Gentlemen insisted on their right to defend themselves with their swords, thus beginning the evolution of the trial by battle into the private duel. But the new law was winning out.

There were several ways of controlling the professional judges. In Italy many were elected and an examination of their decisions (*sindicatio*) by an elected council or even a general assembly took place at the end of their terms. By Roman and canon tradition, a judge did not sit alone but was required to have counsel. This was sometimes political. Albert of Gandino tells us that at Cremona the *potestas* could not sentence a criminal for high crime without the consent of the *anciani* or of four elected members of the council. Usually a judge had to choose professionally trained assessors to aid him (*consilium sapientum*). William Durand described Italian practice in civil cases: 'If indeed there is no assessor at the trial with whom the judge can deliberate, then, according to the general custom in Italy, learned men should be elected jointly by the litigants so that the judge should pronounce according to their opinion.'[44] Ecclesiastical inquisitors invariably chose a group of *jurisperiti* or other notables to help them judge.

As the new system developed, lawyers appeared, evolving from the old advocates who represented the Church and the judicial assessors elected by the litigants who had sat among the judges. They now stood before the bar to speak for their parties. The use of lawyers created some problems. The twelfth-century code called *Peter's Excerpts* recommended that counsel be equalized to aid the poor, and John of Viterbo noted that a *potestas* was obliged to provide advocates for the powerless or poor. Another problem was lack of agreement about the role of the lawyer in the courtroom. Buoncompagno of Signa argued that a lawyer's duty was to defend the law, prepare a client's case, and help his party answer questions put to him. Other theoreticians sought to protect the serenity of the court by enabling it to question a defendant without a lawyer's interruption—*sine strepitu advocatorum*. Theoretically, a lawyer defended justice and therefore only helped a litigant who, he thought, was in the right, but a wit like Buoncompagno knew better. Lawyers were out to win and to make money. More learned jurists argued that even an excommunicate or one banished for treason should be represented by a lawyer in order to protect the law and public interest. In both canon and Italian urban law, however, the less liberal interpretation of the lawyer's role was usually applied in case of grave crime: treason, habitual

[44] Cited from his *Speculum juris* 2, 2, 1 in Guido Rossi, *Consilium sapientis judiciale* (1958), 37.

violence and heresy. As a result, *Ad extirpanda* of 1252, the basic papal legislation on the pursuit of heretics, forbade legal counsel for heretics. Even when sometimes permitted, as it was both before and after that date, counsel was limited to giving the defendant general advice.

These severities derived from the nature of the inquisitorial procedure. Roman law had it that a defendant did not have to prove his innocence, but the excellence of a well conducted *inquisitio* inadvertently reversed this rule. A suspect was arraigned or an investigation begun when persistent reports reached the ears of a judge, a report obtained from many worthy and honest men, or, as Hubert of Bobbio (dead by 1245) put it, one that 'was not doubted by the people or by a majority of the people'.[45] As a result, trials of usurers, traitors, violent criminals and heretics were usually founded on public opinion. Like their secular counterparts, clerical inquisitors first summoned local parishioners or townsmen to give testimony or created boards of these persons to start an inquiry. Once sufficient indications of guilt had been assembled to begin a trial, such report or *fama* was converted into manifest proof, principally by means of witnesses or voluntary confession. Given the efficiency of the *inquisitio*, substantial evidence was often accumulated early in a trial or even before it had begun, a fact that made it difficult for a lawyer to protect or even to serve a suspect who was in all probability guilty.

Two other qualities marked trials for heresy. The first was that a defendant was rarely given the names of those who testified against him, although he could prepare a list of his known enemies. As Albert of Gandino tells us, this impediment to the defence was known in Italian criminal law when witnesses were thought to need protection against a defendant famed for violence and evil life. The second was the use of torture. Adapted from Roman law, the *quaestio* was introduced into Italian urban jurisprudence as early as 1228 (at Verona). In theory its employment was limited. The crime had to be of unusual gravity, the torture moderate, and, as John of Viterbo wrote in the 1240s, it could be used only when a suspect was very probably guilty. Besides, what was elicited by the *quaestio* had to be repeated voluntarily to qualify as a confession, and was then accepted only as a partial proof to be supplemented by

[45] Cited by Albert of Gandino, *Tractatus de maleficiis* 17, ed. Hermann Kantorowicz, *Albertus Gandinus und das Strafrecht der Scholastik* (1926), II, 100.

other proofs. There is no doubt that there were excesses in the employment of torture. The manual on town government called *The Pastoral Eye* has Justice complain against *potestates* that, without sufficient care and 'when proof is lacking in a criminal case, you turn straightway to torture; . . . nor do you consider how much trust should be put in such procedures'. Some withstand torture better than others who will say anything, 'and therefore confessions thus extorted from defendants should not be considered as sure evidence of crime unless afterwards, having been free [from torture] for a time, they should persevere in their confessions'.[46] And the torture of a suspect could also be used to implicate others. As the papal letter *Ad extirpanda* put it in 1252:

> A *potestas* . . . is required to force all heretics . . . short of breaking limbs and danger of death . . . , as . . . murderers of souls and robbers of the sacraments. . . . expressly to confess their errors, to accuse all other heretics whom they know . . . and their receivers and defenders, just as thieves and robbers of temporal things are forced to accuse their accomplices and to confess the crimes they have committed.[47]

In short, the procedures of the Church's inquisitorial tribunals were modelled on, or were similar to, those of the Italian secular courts as these changed during the rise of the popular parties in the urban republics. In this age of social utopianism and democratic hope, an ever more intense insistence on the welfare of the community made social, political, and religious crime appear so heinous that the search for evidence and the clear establishment of guilt were subordinated to the desire to elicit a confession from the criminal or suspect. By such a confession he confirmed the validity of the community from whose laws or beliefs he had diverged. From being passive and protective, justice had become active and penitential.

But no more than the functional egalitarianism of the state and the social totalitarianism of the popular parties did the Inquisition wholly have its way. The latter half of the thirteenth century saw the rise of the bishops assembled in their councils. Just as the conciliar fathers usually attacked the mendicants, their preaching

---

[46] *Oculus pastoralis* 6, 5, *Invectiva justitiae* in L. A. Muratori, *Antiquitates Italicae medii aevi* IX, 853–4.
[47] Cited in Piero Fiorelli, *La tortura giudiziaria nel diritto commune* (Milan, 1953), I, 80.

and teaching, so also they attacked the Inquisition. This resulted in the 'reforms' of Boniface VIII—provision of legal aid, publication of the names of witnesses, etc.—and the gradual subordination thereafter of the Inquisition to the national or local churches. In the meantime, however, the popular heresies of 1200 had been broken—some, like the Cathars, nearly extirpated, and others, like the Waldensians and the Illuminist sects, gravely weakened.

But the nature of divergent or secessionist belief was undergoing change. Future heresy was to be more moderate—the dualist Christianity of the Cathars, for example, never again played much of a role. Its origins were to be more priestly or more academic and therefore less monastic and less popular than before. There were many advantages to this. The theological probabilism of the schools disguised the dangerous thrust of new ideas. The academic or sacerdotal grades of the spokesmen of what seemed to be a reformed orthodoxy made it possible for them to build a lay and clerical party before they could be silenced. In the post-monastic age of the later Middle Ages, the true successors of Peter Waldes were John Wycliffe, John Hus, and Martin Luther. The final chapter of this book will attempt to describe the beginning of the great transition, one in which the lay and clerical constituencies of the later Reformation were first beginning to identify themselves.

XV

Unam Sanctam

France and the great events

The issues in the struggle between ecclesiastical and secular authority were ancient and they had a double aspect. On one side was the struggle of the Church for ecclesiastical liberty against the desire of secular governments to appoint, tax, control and judge the local clergy. On the other was the desire of the Church, especially of the papacy, to judge and regulate the actions of secular governments. The first great struggle was largely a contest between King Philip IV of France and Pope Boniface VIII, and continued intermittently from 1296 until the election of the Frenchman Clement V in 1305 and the settlement of the papacy at Avignon on the Rhône river in 1309. The second began in the teens of the fourteenth century, involved a civil war in Germany and resulted in the election of an imperialist antipope. It reached its peak in the 1320s and dragged on until 1347. The two principal

BIBLIOGRAPHY. The reader should consult the bibliographies to chapters II, III, IV, IX and XIV above. On the question of the Franciscans and other mendicants and associated devotions, read Gordon Leff, *Heresy in the Later Middle Ages : the relation of heterodoxy to dissent*, vol. I, part I (New York, 1967), and M. D. Lambert, *Franciscan Poverty : The Doctrine of the Absolute Poverty of Christ and the Apostles in the Franciscan Order, 1210–1323* (London, 1961). D. L. Douie's *The Nature and the Effect of the Heresy of the Fraticelli* (Manchester, 1932) is elegant and indispensable and Ernst Benz's *Ecclesia spiritualis : Kirchenidee und Geschichtstheologie der franziskanischen Reformation* (Stuttgart, 1934) is inspiring and even great but also drives one mad by its lack of footnotes. A Protestant eschatologist, Benz had the genial idea of relating the weakening of the Church to the collapse of the Franciscan and Joachite *ecclesia spiritualis*. Here and elsewhere I have tried to place this particular event in the context of general social and institutional movements. The best statement of the ideological conflict between church and state is Jean Rivière's magnificent *Le problème de l'église et l'état au temps de Philippe le Bel* (Louvain, 1926), to be supplemented and broadened by perusing the books mentioned in the bibliographical note to chapter II. I have avoided summarizing all the polemics by concentrating largely on John Quidort of Paris and Giles of Rome.

protagonists were John XXII and the emperor (or, rather, king of the Romans) Lewis of Bavaria. The details of this protracted combat are narrated in the next volume of this series.

In the public eye, the Church emerged relatively unscathed from these great struggles. Save in constitutional theory, that with the Empire was almost a victory. At the end of Lewis of Bavaria's life, the emperor's pope had long since disappeared while the pope's imperial candidate remained firmly on the throne. But there is no doubt that Rome was defeated by the Capetian Philip. The French party triumphed in the Roman court and brought the papacy to Avignon. In spite of this, the Church had not formally surrendered any basic institutional power to the secular state, and even the effect of the French seizure of the Roman court was soon to be dissipated by the collapse of France during the Hundred Years War. What Philip's victory meant in the long run could not be perceived by contemporaries. Who, in 1300, would have believed that, following the lines of Europe's secular, national diplomatic alignments, the Latin Church was to be split into two or more obediences during the Great Schism, and that, in the Conciliar Age, it would begin to surrender institutional powers to secular authority? What a contemporary could see, however, was that the papacy was stumbling badly in its attempt to handle the Capetian, and he would compare this with its earlier victory over the Hohenstaufen.

As Alexander of Roes and other Germans confessed, the Empire had fallen before the attack of Rome and France. When Conradin was executed in 1268 the Hohenstaufen cause seemed obliterated. Rome and ecclesiastical liberty seemed triumphant. Many knew, however, that the Hohenstaufens had left a legacy. Many of their institutional objectives appealed to other secular governments, and the polemical literature of the time of Frederick II was merely temporarily shelved. Rome was well aware of this and even invented the verb 'to frederickize' (*fretherizare*) to describe it. One lively centre of fretherization was the court of Philip IV the Fair.

A reason that the French Capetians had become the heirs of the Hohenstaufen was that, from the latter days of Philip II Augustus, France was Rome's principal ally. The alignment of the Capetian cadet house of Anjou-Provence with the popes and the Guelph popular parties of Italy had not only enabled the French to conquer southern Italy and Sicily, but had spread French influence throughout the peninsula. Although many had second thoughts as the Angevins cemented their power, most Italians thought highly of the French, of their manners, arts, and even institutions. Another reason was that France was at the peak of its power. The Plantagenet threat seemed defeated, and Louis IX had even been invited to arbitrate England's civil troubles at the Mise of Amiens in 1264. The same prince bore the burden of the crusades from the 1240s until his death at Tunis in 1270. Although he suffered one severe defeat and gained no territory, his efforts helped to stabilize the Latin frontier against Islam until his death. The might of France is best seen in the reign of this prince. Somehow, although often unsuccessful in what he undertook to do, Louis exemplified the greatness and glory of monarchy for all of Latin Europe. We have already seen that the Florentine Dominican Remigio de' Girolami stated around 1300 that, in comparison with France's king, all other western princes were mere kinglets. And even France's heretics—those, at least, in northern France—were unusually loyal. According to Caesarius of Heisterbach, the early thirteenth century Amalricians believed that the Latin peoples would be ruled by the king of France in the forthcoming age of the Holy Spirit.

So useful were the French to Rome that the pontiffs converted almost all Capetian and Angevin wars into crusades, thus enabling them to be financed by clerical taxes. The popes also reinforced within the French mind the conviction that the French were a special people. Although the title *rex christianissimus* had been liberally bestowed on other princes before the thirteenth century, Innocent III declared in 1215 that this title was a special mark of the French king. Alexander III had told the archbishop of Rheims in 1171 that the kings of France had always helped St Peter in his hour of need and possessed unshatterable faith. What exalted the prince could also glorify the people. In 1239 Gregory IX wrote that, on earth as in heaven,

> the son of God . . . according to the divisions of tongues and of races . . . has constituted diverse kingdoms, among which, as the tribe of Judah was granted the gift of a special benediction among the sons of the patriarch, so the kingdom of France is distinguished from all the other peoples of the earth by the privilege of honour and grace.[1]

[1] J. L. A. Huillard-Bréholles, *Historia diplomatica Friderici secundi*, v, i, 457–8.

As a gesture of peace between the already embroiled monarchy and papacy, Boniface VIII canonized Louis IX in 1297.

As France aided Rome, the number of cardinals representing the French and Angevin southern Italian interest gradually increased. Of the thirteen popes who reigned from the accession of the Frenchman Urban IV in 1261 until that of Clement V in 1305, four were French, the first breach of the Italian monopoly of that office since 1159. For years—since the decretal *Per venerabilem* of 1213 concerning the king of France—the popes had argued that a king is emperor in his own kingdom, thereby contradicting Frederick I Barbarossa's observation that Europe's kings were mere *reguli* under the emperor. In 1303 Rome suddenly reversed its position. Shortly before he was seized at Anagni by France's Roman allies, Boniface VIII remarked anent his tentative alliance with the German king Albert I of Habsburg that all kings, and especially the vainglorious king of France, should be subject to the emperors. But this attempted diplomatic revolution had no morrow. The brief pontificate of Boniface VIII's Italian successor was followed by that of the Frenchman Clement V, who moved the papal court from Rome—actually from Italy because the court had spent much time in Viterbo, Orvieto, and elsewhere— to Avignon. There new troubles began. The renewed marriage between French and papal policies helped to precipitate the battle between John XXII and Lewis of Bavaria. French influence had long been penetrating southern and western Germany, and the Capetian court was dreaming of having its king elected emperor. Although not without reservations, John XXII was an advocate of that policy.

But French power was not alone in causing these conflicts. The beginnings of the changes that precipitated the crises of the later Middle Ages also played a role, and one of these changes was the weakening of France and the failure of its expansion. The loss of Constantinople by the Franks in 1261, the collapse of the union of the Byzantine and Roman Churches in 1282, the fall of Acre in the Holy Land in 1291, and the general weakening of the *d'Outremer* in the face of Islamic and Byzantine attacks affected the French with peculiar intensity. They had led the crusades and the crusades were failing. Faced by these failures, the French blamed not only the Order of the Temple but also their great ally at Rome. And almost all the issues that exacerbated the relationship between the secular powers and Rome were directly linked to the arrest of French expansion and to the domestic crises that foreshadowed the internal breakdown of France in the later Hundred Years War. In 1296 the issue contested between Boniface VIII and Philip (as well as the king of England) was the secular government's right to tax the clergy without papal approval. The French Crown needed money to suppress the revolt of the Flemish cities and engage in the struggle with England over Flanders and Guienne. The Crown's penury was made worse by the resistance of France's provincial aristocracies, rural and urban, to financing the growth of the central state.

To Boniface VIII, the growing rivalry of France and England was threatening because it drew ecclesiastical revenue away from causes dearer to Rome's heart and, he thought, closer to the interests of the *civitas christiana*. Foremost among these was the hope of resuming crusades against the infidel, a cause still believed in, at least formally, by most of the Latin population. But priorities differed. The pope wanted to get on with the crusade, but he first had to settle Italy. The French wanted the same, but they first had to settle the Anglo-Flemish question. Another conflict of interest concerned Catalonia-Aragon. The revolt of the Sicilians against the Angevin French in the Vespers of 1282 had established a Catalan dynasty in that island. By the early fourteenth century, Catalan fleets and armies were penetrating the Aegean regions of the French *d'Outremer* and weakening southern French commerce, especially that of Angevin Marseilles, in favour of Barcelona and Valencia. The rise of Catalonia-Aragon also encouraged the still lively separatism of the barely or newly absorbed provinces of southern France extending from once imperial and now Angevin Provence to Capetian Languedoc.

The increased importance of Catalonia-Aragon in Europe's affairs encouraged Boniface VIII's desire to escape from the French alliance. The repulse of repeated Angevin attempts to reconquer Sicily and the failure of the Capetian wars against the Catalans led this pope—who had earlier fostered these efforts because of the link between the Hohenstaufen tradition and the Sicilian Catalans—to think in terms of a detente or even an alliance with Catalonia-Aragon. At least one Catalan spokesman, Raymond Lull, had plans for the renewal of the crusade that must have been more attractive to the pope than the French one. It was not Lull's strategy that appealed to Rome; indeed, it must have seemed rather strange to a Roman. Whereas the French and Italians usually suggested the conquest of Egypt or Syria as a start for the defeat of Islam, Lull preferred to start the attack at Granada in Spain, and thence move to North Africa and through Egypt to Syria. What did appeal to the pope was the institutional side of Lull's scheme. While the French talked about uniting the military orders of the Church under their king, Lull proposed that they should be unified under the Church, to be used as the shock troops of the great attack. Even more enticing was his proposal 'that the pope and the cardinals should assign the tithe of the whole Church to the crusade until the Holy Land is conquered, the tithe which they now give to Christian kings. For this tithe has its origin in, and is contributed by, those who labour in order that the church should be honoured and sustained, but the kings divert it to secular causes, which is wicked'.[2] The pope's attempt to work out something with Catalonia-Aragon and the unrest in Languedoc precipitated Philip IV's most threatening attack on the papacy and on ecclesiastical freedom. This was the arrest in 1301 of Bernard Saisset, bishop of Pamiers and papal legate, and the request to Rome that, instead of being judged at Rome, the bishop be degraded and handed over to the royal courts to be charged with high treason and collusion with the dissident southern French and the Catalans. The pope refused and, after several other letters, issued the famous bull *Unam sanctam*, on which more anon.

At the time of Lewis of Bavaria, too, the pope's adhesion to French policies redounded to the disadvantage of the papacy. Even before the 1290s the radical Franciscans of southern France had come to share the ideologically inspired politics that had emerged earlier in Italy, where, as the Hohenstaufen cause failed and that of the Angevins rose, the radicals had come to view the alliance of the French with the papacy as the principal danger to the spiritual freedom of the Church. Being hostile to the crusade as an intromission of material force into religion, they had even prayed for the defeat of Louis IX's crusades. When the Catalans revived the Hohenstaufen dream in 1282, the Franciscan radicals joined that camp along with other enthusiastic sects. In southern France this ideology was tied up with regional separatism. In

[2] *Disputatio Raymundi christiani et Hamar saraceni* 2 in *Beati Raymundi Lulli opera* (Mainz, 1729, rprt) IV, 477b.

Languedoc radical Franciscans like Bernard Délicieux and the townsmen who supported them intrigued with Catalonia-Aragon, and were consequently pursued by both the pope and the king in the 1320s. It is not surprising that the leaders of the radical Franciscans were on the side of Lewis of Bavaria.

There was more here than the particular situation of France. France merely experienced more intensely what was happening in all the well-developed parts of Europe. All were affected by the cessation of western expansion and the beginning of the Islamic counterattack. But because the German frontier continued to expand, and because the full extent of the Turkish threat was not yet apparent, it was hard to read the signs. Men could not see where they were, and followed the same old routes, blaming others when they led nowhere, as Boniface blamed the French and as the French blamed Boniface.

Clerical indecision

The clergy found themselves incapable of acting with solidarity during these great conflicts. Although the clerical order had always been divided during past struggles with secular authority, it had always supported ecclesiastical liberty and the papacy more than it did around 1300. The problem is to find out why.

It is perhaps not surprising that, although somewhat unwillingly, the prelates of France adhered to the cause of Philip the Fair in the northern French assembly of 1302. The secular clergy and the older regular orders had fought for nearly a century against the invasion of their parishes and prerogatives by the mendicant orders fostered by the popes. Also, as noted earlier, the secular clergy and the older orders were closely linked to local interests. They had long resisted Roman centralization, whether this favoured appointment to local posts of university-trained clergy or of Italian absentees. It did little good for Cardinal Matthew of Aquasparta to argue in a consistory of Boniface VIII that the French had no reason to complain because only two of France's prelates were Italian, and these were men with great reputations (one of them was Giles of Rome) who had spent much of their lives in France. The bishops of the secular clergy, the abbots of the older orders, and the provosts of the cathedral chapters who were summoned to general councils also tended to favour a conciliar policy, whereas the pope stood for the monarchical element in the Church's constitution.

The secular clergy's shaky loyalty would not have been decisive, however, had not the mendicant orders failed to help the papacy. One reason for this, as we know, was that the growth of the mendicant movement and its lay affiliates was being slowed by the clergy assembled in the ecumenical councils to which the popes were being forced to bow. The squeeze had already been felt at the first Council of Lyons in 1245, but the legislation of the second Council of Lyons in 1274 was much more drastic. Several of the newer orders of friars were there abolished, one of them being the Friars of the Sack, an order founded in Provence in 1248 and granted a rule in 1251, which boasted about eighty houses at the time of its abolition. The culminating legislation was the canon *Cum de quibusdam mulieribus* at the Council of Vienne in 1311 which cut off any further expansion of the Beguines. By the time of these councils, what had once seemed progressive had come to be viewed as disorderly and dangerous. And there was something to be said for this opinion: monasticism was laicizing with a vengeance. In 1310 Augustine Trionfo, an enemy of Peter John Olivi, inveighed against the rather strange world of lay enthusiasts, perhaps having in mind such examples as the Franciscan tertiary, philosopher, missionary, and social utopian Raymond Lull and the medical doctor, divinator, and lay theologian Arnold of Villanova: 'For when we see certain of these fellows to be mobile and fluctuating in their status, so that they are now married, now continent, now secular, now monks, now overseas, now at home, now spurning the world, now belonging to it, this is a sign that the visions of such people are not divine revelations but rather diabolical illusions.'[3]

But the conciliar fathers would not have had their way had not the mendicants themselves been gravely divided. Not only were there conflicts between the orders, especially the Dominicans and Franciscans, but there was also an increasingly intense battle within the Franciscan Order. By far the largest of the mendicant orders, this was also the most unstable and tumultuous one, partly because it was the closest orthodox equivalent to the extremist wings of the Waldensians and Humiliati described in

---

[3] *Tractatus contra divinatores et sompniatores* I in Richard Scholz, *Unbekannte kirchenpolitische Streitschriften aus der Zeit Ludwigs des Bayern* (Rome, 1914), II, 483–4.

the last chapter. Francis and his early companions differed from the other extremists simply in their determination to obey the authority of the bishops and the popes—thereby inadvertently playing a successful 'counter-revolutionary' role. The initial domination of the laity within the order and the express desire to imitate the life and presumed poverty of Christ caused the Franciscan order to attract many passionately utopian spirits who would have otherwise leaned toward heresy or toward remaking the world *ad instar Jerusalem.*

In the early days of the order, the principal conflict concerned lay leadership. Francis was a layman and so was Elias of Cortona who, having served as the mothering and practical Martha to Francis's spiritual Mary until the latter's death in 1226, assumed the office of General Minister at that date. Elias tried to maintain the predominance of the lay brethren. As these slowly lost out to the clerical brethren, the general was forced to become increasingly arbitrary in his government during his second generalship beginning in 1232. The lay principle was enough to protect him among the Italian brethren, but the opposition was led by those from outside Italy where there was at first no mass base of lay recruiting. The pressures were so great that the pope was obliged to depose him in 1239. Although the life of Francis and his close companions provided an admirable example of the eremitical life and of personal fulfilment, only the brethren in orders possessed the literacy, the education, and the ability to provide sacramental services that were necessary for the success of the Franciscan mission among the laity.

As in early Christianity, moreover, spontaneity and equality were lost in the emphasis on the mission. How things changed may be seen from one example. Francis was suspicious of learning and education because he feared that they created invidious distinctions between those who were spiritually equal. His rule of 1223 therefore stated that those who were *illiterati* should not officiously busy themselves becoming Latinists. And he insisted in his testament of 1226 that the rule should never be glossed, but instead obeyed—because it was the word of God—*ad litteram, ad litteram, ad litteram.* Like most of his secular counterparts in the popular parties of the Italian city republics who tried to protect their statutes from manipulation by trained jurists by using the legal counterpart of Francis's injunction, Francis was deceiving himself. A law without a commentary is one that nobody has ever bothered to read. Commenting upon Francis's rule in the middle of the century, Bonaventure shows how the rule could be interpreted in such a way as to reinforce a social hierarchy which put *those in orders* at the top. For, says he, 'the rule does not prohibit study for those with letters, but only for the unlettered and lay. Following the apostles, [Francis] wants each one to remain in that vocation to which he has been called so that no one should ascend from the laity into clerical orders. But he did not want clerks to become laymen by refusing to study.'[4] Although the spectre of lay rule faded with the fall of Elias, it is noteworthy that the lay brethren and the associated tertiaries of the laity were often very radical in the later thirteenth century.

The growth of the Francisan mission had other consequences. Few laymen could follow the eremitical and wandering life of a Francis. What most of them wanted were the preaching, sacramental, burial and charitable services the order could offer. To provide such services the Franciscans invaded the spheres of the parish clergy and of the other mendicant orders. And their sense of their own peculiar fitness to perform these services led them to allow themsleves to be appointed bishops and cardinals, led them, in short, to play ecclesiastical politics. This had horrified the Order's founder during his own lifetime, but it is fair to say that his own friendship with its cardinal protector, Hugolino of Ostia, the later Gregory IX, was of great value to both himself and his Order. Francis also revealed a remarkable ability to manipulate men politically. He stilled the opposition of the brethren to his second rule by claiming that the deity had intervened directly, so that he appeared to be another Moses on another Sinai or indeed a veritable Christ. His insistence on promulgating his own rule—unlike the founders of other orders, including the Dominicans, who settled for a version of the so-called Augustinian rule—served to foster the aggressive sense of the Order's peculiar fitness for its mission. This vigorous sense of the all-important mission led the later brethren to use the papal privileges to fight their battles with the secular clergy, thus disobeying the injunction of Matthew 10:23, 'And when they persecute you in this city, flee into another', a passage repeated in Francis's testament of 1226.

---

[4] *Epistola de tribus quaestionibus* in *Opera omnia* (Quaracchi) VIII, 334b. The idea is an adaptation of Paul, I Corinthians 7:24.

It might also be argued that, the more 'counter-revolutionary' the role of Francis and his Franciscans was in defeating the popular heresies by channelling lay utopians into the order, the more vehement did the Franciscans become in pushing their mission.

A mission requires sustenance. The early Franciscans sought to rest lightly on the world, asking or earning only a day's ration of food and a minimum of dress and housing. Eventually, after the middle of the century, the idea of Franciscan poverty split into two doctrines, that of the *usus pauper* and that of property. The former meant that, however acquired, a minimum of material goods should be used. This was dear to the rigorist ascetics who crowded into the order, although they remained a minority within it. Like Bernard of Clairvaux, Francis would have been mortified by the magnificent convents and churches erected in his name, starting with the basilica raised over his tomb in Assisi by Elias. It is probably true, however, that the austerity required by John of Parma, general from 1247 to 1257, or by the Spiritual Franciscan, Ubertino of Casale, not only alienated the majority of the brethren but also encouraged a veneration of exceptional ascetics that denied the teaching of the Acts of the Apostles: from each according to his means and to each according to his needs. The Dominican Thomas Aquinas's teaching that love or charity (*caritas*) was the source of all virtues did not appeal to the intolerant devotees of the religion of poverty.

The teaching on property was more complex than the *usus pauper* because it provided a way to avoid real poverty. Ideally, the Franciscan was to acquire, by begging or working, only enough for the day, without accumulation for the morrow. Neither the member nor the order was to have any property, that is, the predictable or controllable use of a good derived from or produced by the earth. But predictable use was exactly what the Franciscan mission required. Without it there could be no regular maintenance of churches or of libraries, no regular preaching, sacramental services or charity. The mission also required a necessary specialization of personnel, and specialization is a question of the allocation of time, and time has to be bought or endowed by property's fruits. Workingmen were sometimes wise and often inspired, but they had little time to think inventively and less to teach. Behind Prous Boneta stood Peter John Olivi, whose *Postilla in Apocalypsim* she had read (or had had read to her) in a widely diffused vernacular translation, and behind Salimbene's stammering day labourer of Parma named Master Benvenuto stood those who had translated or had read him sections from the Bible, Joachim of Fiore, Michael Scot, and the anonymous prophetical works being produced at the time.

The Franciscan problem was therefore to reconcile the forwarding of an aggressive mission with an ideological refusal to endow it. Starting with Gregory IX's *Quo elongati* of 1230 and continuing intermittently throughout the century, papal intervention provided this endowment by finding ways around the rigour of Francis's rule and testament. The basic teaching of papal legislation was that the predictable use of the fruits accrued to the Franciscans, but that the ownership of the property from which the fruits derived was vested in Rome's hands, two proctors in each province, etc. Writing shortly after 1312, the conservative Bonagratia of Bergamo argued that, 'since by natural and divine law the use of all things pertaining to human life ought to be common to all men, and, since it came about by iniquity that this is said to be mine and that yours',[5] the Franciscan's right to use nature's fruits was a modern fulfilment of the natural communism of the apostolic community. And since Nicholas III had been inspired to issue the decretal *Exiit qui seminat* in 1279, in which it was declared dogma that Christ and his apostles had owned nothing severally or in common, it appeared to believers that the Franciscans were indeed the fulfilment of Christian hope.

After the defeat of the lay brethren, poverty became the central, almost obsessive, issue in the Franciscan order. It is possible that it became so central and so exaggerated because the defeat of the lay principle made the order very much like the other mendicant orders. Poverty was the Franciscan substitute for the radicalism of the early order, its special claim to attention, and its way of endeavouring to contain the enthusiasm of its eremitical and laic wings. Although there were serious battles about poverty as early as the 1240s, the split over this issue between the minority radicals, soon to be called the Spirituals and the Fraticelli, and the majority, or Community, awaited the end of the generalship of Bonaventure in 1272. Most of the early radicals' charges concerned the *usus*

---

[5] Cited in Douie, *The Nature and Effects of the Heresy of the Fraticelli*, 158. Bonagratia was using Gratian's paraphrase from Augustine and from a letter attributed to Clement in his *Decretum* 1, 8, 1 and 2 and 2, 1, 2 in *CICan* 1, 12–3 and 676.

pauper. They correctly asserted that the majority was nothing like as austere as the founder had wished. The radicals then moved on to a much more telling point. The distinction between use and ownership, they said, was deceitful, because he who enjoys the predictable use of the fruit of a good is surely the moral owner of the good in question. Composing his *Sanctitas vestra* just after 1312, the Spiritual Ubertino of Casale observed:

> Certainly the blessed Francis did not wish to ask from the pope that the possession would be the pope's and the use ours. Quite the contrary, he wanted the ownership to be vested in the hands of the prelates, donors, or communities, so that no tenure be given to the brethren that they might not be expelled if it pleased the owners of the property. This he shows in his testament and legend when he says that the brethren should not inhabit their poor homes as their own, but as pilgrims and strangers living in the homes of others.[6]

Especially during the pontificates of Boniface VIII and John XXII, the usual policy of the popes was to aid the Community and crush the Spirituals—sometimes with the aid of the Inquisition. The spirit of this effort may be seen in a famous phrase from John's bull *Quorundam exigit* of 1317: 'Great is poverty, but greater still is blamelessness, and the greatest good of all is obedience.'[7] The radical Franciscans were therefore indifferent to the cause of Boniface VIII, and they actively sided with Lewis of Bavaria against John XXII. But there was more to come. The glory granted the Franciscans displeased both the secular clergy and other mendicants, none of whom enjoyed the privilege of poverty. Besides, the weakness of the Community's position on use and ownership was self-evident and involved the papacy in upholding a dubious cause at the cost of some bloodshed and constant turbulence at the papal court and elsewhere. In the decretal *Ad conditorem canonum* of 1322 John cut the Gordian knot and used the Spirituals' argument to weaken the position of the Community. The pope there denied that there was any substantial difference between the predictable use of fruits and the ownership of the property whence they derived. With some exceptions, therefore,

---

[6] Cited in Leff, *op. cit.* I, 148. The latter part of this quotation derives directly from Bonaventure's *Legenda S. Francisci* 7, 2 in *Opera omnia* (Quaracchi) VIII, 523b.
[7] *Extravagantes Johannis XXII* 14, 1 in *CICan* II, 1223. Cf. chapter IX above, note 41.

the Franciscans were to hold property in the same way that other orders did. Following the teaching of Thomas Aquinas, he asserted that not poverty but charity was the basis of a perfect life. Spurred on by the Dominicans, the same pontiff issued his *Cum inter nonnullos* in the next year, which declared that it was heresy to assert that Christ and the apostles did not own and have free use of property. Their order having been stripped of its peculiar claim to attention, it is therefore no wonder that the leaders of the Community, or conservative Franciscans, went over to the side of the Bavarian, there to rest in uncomfortable proximity to their enemies of the radical wing. One must conclude that the largest and most popular of the new orders actively harmed both the papacy and the cause of ecclesiastical liberty in the struggle with the secular state.

And the loss was more than tactical, of forces arrayed for battle. Bonaventure reports that when Francis came to ask Innocent III for what was to become the privilege of poverty, Cardinal John Colonna said:

> If we refuse the request of this poor man as being too hard and too unheard of . . . we must avoid offending Christ's Gospel. For if anyone should say that there is in the observance of evangelical perfection or the vow of this man anything that is strange, irrational, or impossible of performance, he is to be convicted of blaspheming against Christ, the author of the Gospel.[8]

By 1300 it no longer seemed possible to convert this dream into reality. Furthermore, as the problem of poverty had become central in the order and its partisans had become aware of the difficulties they faced, they had begun to seek the assurance that their cause was inevitably going to win—and that shortly. In the 'thirties, and even more so in the 'forties, the Joachitic idea of spiritual progress permeated radical Franciscan circles, so that each crisis over poverty was accompanied by one over Joachitic historicism. The first of these occurred during the generalship of John of Parma when Gerard of Borgo San Donnino published his *Introductorius Evangelii Aeterni*, a glossed compilation of Joachim's historico-theological works. As we have seen, Gerard thought that these were to replace both the Old and New Testaments in the

---

[8] *Legenda S. Francisci* 3, 9 in *Opera omnia* (Quaracchi) VIII, 512a.

forthcoming age of the Holy Spirit. The storm provoked by this publication resulted in a hasty condemnation of Joachim's teaching by a papal commission at Anagni in 1255, the resignation of John of Parma in 1257, and a period of quiet repression under Bonaventure.

The lid on the Spirituals was lifted when Raymond Gaufridi became general in 1289, and they had high hopes until Celestine V resigned in 1294 and was replaced by Boniface VIII. Thereafter things worsened for them. The Olivites of Languedoc were wiped out in the 1320s and Peter John Olivi's *Postilla in Apocalypsim* was condemned in 1326, perhaps because of the exaggerated doctrines the Franciscans and Tertiaries had derived from his teaching. Their belief was that Francis and his twelve companions had founded the Church of the third and final age. The constitution of this new evangelical Church or order was composed of Francis's rules and testament together with the bull *Exiit qui seminat* on the poverty of Christ. So evangelical were these precepts that no authority, whether that of the pope or of a general and ecumenical council, would ever be able to change them. If the inquisitor Bernard Guy's understanding of what they had to say is correct (and there is no reason to doubt it), they were asserting that a self-designated élite could controvert the opinions of the majority of the Church in the name of spiritual progress.

The reaction of the Church was not merely to deny that the radical Franciscans were the vehicle of spiritual progress, but also to question the idea of progress itself. A secular clerk who had been silenced in 1279 at the time of *Exiit qui seminat*, John of Anneux, sprang up to defend the pope in 1328, tripping over his own words in his haste to damn the Franciscan dream:

> How could this witless fellow Francis discover a new way of living which so many doctors, Augustine, Gregory, and other doctors and saints inspired by the Holy Spirit didn't know, and which the Church that had lasted before him for a thousand years did not have, and then it was more perfect and the men of the time were a hundred times more perfect than they are now, nor can the way of life of this Francis be lived except by hermits in the desert.[9]

Others more moderate than John said the same in effect, and it is therefore probable that the failure of the Franciscans marked a

[9] Cited from a Bodleian MS by Douie, *op. cit.*, 170.

recession of the hope of spiritual progress that had fired so much of the life of the Church from the Gregorian period until the time of Avignon. Thereafter the hope was not lost, but gradually became attached to the secular state—as in the time of Cola di Rienzo (d. 1354)—and then in later times flowered again to become the obsession of modern secular intellectuals and dreamers.

The failure of the Franciscan radicals' doctrine of poverty also served to advance the process of secularization, to bring nearer the moment when all true Christians, whatever their worldly vocations, were equal to the religious. In his *Ad conditorem canonum*, John XXII had argued that, without charity, the member of a religious order derived no spiritual advantage or freedom from his vow of poverty unless he was free of the solicitude or care incumbent on those who seek to use or acquire property. And such was clearly not the case of the Franciscan or, indeed, of any monk. In 1334, Ockham described the pope's position in these words:

> This error opposes all the religious who profess to live without their own property (*sine proprio*). According to it, if monks . . . are solicitous to acquire, conserve, and dispense temporal goods after taking their vow of poverty . . . their [personal] surrender of goods . . . confers no advantage on them as far as [spiritual] perfection is concerned. And from this error there follows a certain ancient error . . . : namely, that it is not better to do good works with the vow than without the vow.[10]

Ockham was right. John XXII had taught that there was no spiritual or moral advantage to being in a religious order. And the doctrine of charity or love could be fitted into this context. A later defender of John XXII's position, John of Celle, a Tuscan gentleman who retired to a hermitage in 1351, told the Fraticelli that they had made poverty their idol and lost sight of mercy and love. In urging the elders of Ephesus to be charitable, Paul had reminded them of Christ's injunction (Acts 20:35): 'It is more blessed to give than to receive.' John drew from this the corollary: 'And if this is true, and it certainly is true, the rich man who gives deserves more than the poor man who receives.'[11] If motivated by

[10] *Tractatus contra Joannem* 23, ed. H. S. Offler, *Opera politica* (Manchester, 1956), III, 89.
[11] Felice Tocco, 'L'eresia dei fraticelli e una lettera inedita del beato Giovanni delle Celle', *Studi Francescani* (Naples, 1909), 460. This reference is owed to Douie, *op. cit.*, 236.

charity, a wealthy lay donor, then, was more blessed than a poor monk who received. Perhaps this was a recognition of the fact that a utopian hope that had threatened to penetrate all society at the time of the Humiliati and the preaching of Robert of Curzon had been channelled into the mendicant orders and especially the Franciscan. And it had there failed once again.

Lay pressures

Clerical solidarity would not have failed had not the laity pressed hard upon it. And laymen did so because Latin society was already in difficulties. Overpopulation had led to the cultivation of marginally productive land and its attendant problems. By 1300 social and economic corporatism had maximized rights and profits in agriculture, industry and commerce, and had divided society into clearly demarcated interest groups who tended to fly at each other's throats in order to realize their ambitions. As a result, men responded with excessive angers and utopian fancies to the first *rallentando* of the realization of their dreams. The potentiality of social and economic corporatism to mobilize larger units of production and government was known, but was not yet able to win full support. To give such support, people had to be convinced by the harsh experience of domestic and foreign war that private right and property had to be diminished and that the liberties and privileges of localities and groups had to be restricted. But they were not yet ready to surrender their hopes or advantages in order to set up the unitary monarchies and principates that were to harness and police their passions in early modern times.

Certainly these monarchies and principates were already emerging around 1300. The conception of the *arbitraria potestas* or *liberum arbitrium*, which enabled princes to act without the constraints of prior law and without being bound by councils was already well defined by this time. In spite of this, the princely prerogative was everywhere impeded by local and particularist elements. Nor was it to be set free—and then never wholly so— until the last effort of ecclesiastical conciliarism and secular estatism or parliamentarianism had been defeated by the princes in the fifteenth century. Still, the restraints on the powers of the princes and their unitary states were already beginning to weaken. Before 1300 Latin Europe had been ruled by the alliance of the ecumenical power of the Roman Church with the local rural and urban aristocracies. At the time of Boniface VIII this combination faltered and the aristocracies, hard pressed by the rise of the plebs beneath them and by the growth of princely power above, sought to escape their dilemma by sacrificing the Roman Church to their enemies.

There were many reasons for this reaction by lay leadership. Men of the time saw the matter in terms of their resistance to ecclesiastical domination. The thirteenth-century growth of the Church's mission pressed heavily upon laymen. The attack on usury, the exercise of tighter controls over marriage and the family, and the regulation of just war in the forum of conscience were paralleled by the Church's desire to police the relationships of Europe's states, its call for service against the heretics, and for crusades against the infidel and even against Latin powers whose actions were thought to impede the crusade. The Church's call not only provoked lay participation in devotional life, but also inspired a revival of those traditions that summoned lay magistrates and princes to examine, and intervene in, the workings of the Church. Laymen were not merely meretricious in their desire to control the behaviour, services, and appointments of the clergy. Having been called to serve, their consciences, their fears and other passions, were as deeply involved in the affairs of the Church as were those of the clergy. As we know, also, laymen were more capable of acting than they had been before. The growth of lay literacy and professionalism had begun to give laymen the ability to intervene in the clerical sphere and the spread of the monastic vocation to the laity living in the world had begun to give them the conviction that they were the spiritual equals of ecclesiastics.

And the consciences of men are often very closely related to their interests. Responding to petitions from Languedoc in 1301, Philip the Fair complained to the bishop of Toulouse about the inquisitors, then actively pursuing the Spiritual Franciscans. He charged these Dominicans with not fearing to commit the most inhumane and abhorrent crimes under the guise of protecting the faith. (Later, as we know, he changed his tune when he learned that the Spirituals were in contact with Catalonia-Aragon.) In 1308 the same prince mounted his campaign against the Templars and asked the theologians of Paris if laymen could not proceed against heretics without ecclesiastical permission. The theologians said no, 'except when evident and notorious danger threatened, in which case the secular power could arrest them if it had the sure hope of ecclesiastical confirmation'.[12] The king's hope for confirmation speedily became sure because of pressure on the pope at Avignon and because of the severity of the torture inflicted on the Templars. Nor were princes the only ones to act in this way. All sorts of groups adopted policies designed to limit ecclesiastical power and to intervene in the affairs of the Church. Typical was a synod held in 1258 at Ruffec (between Poitiers and Angoulême) where the clergy complained about leagues combating ecclesiastical jurisdiction created everywhere by 'knights, communities and barons, farmers and townsmen (rustici et burgenses)'.[13]

Quarrels between towns and churchmen were frequent and concerned all the issues that embroiled Rome and the larger states. An extreme but revealing example is a complaint against the knights (ministeriales) and citizens of Eichstätt brought before an archiepiscopal council held at Mainz. The bishop reported that these townsmen, aided by some great magnates, had remained almost a year under excommunication, plundered the Church's treasure, continued burial services, and, 'with heretical and diabolical presumption and perversion, had cruelly and violently expelled the bishop together with the clergy who supported him, and had chosen laymen to serve as bishop, provost and dean', thus neatly continuing the administrative services of the Church.[14] There was nothing particularly new about such actions, but they intensified as the century went on. Describing the divisions that rent Florence in the early 1300s, Remigio de' Girolami noted that the clergy called laymen 'traitors, usurers, perjurers, adulterers, robbers, and it's true of many. On the other hand, laymen say that clerks are fornicators, gluttons, idle fellows, and that the religious are vainglorious robbers, and it's true of some.'[15]

Apart from the clergy's right to trial in its own courts, what angered the laity was the extension of the papal right to appoint to

[12] Heinrich Denifle, Chartularium universitatis Parisiensis I, 126, No. 664.
[13] Cited in Georges de Lagarde, La naissance de l'esprit laïque au déclin du moyen âge I, 169n.
[14] Annales erphordenses fratrum praedicatorum in the Monumenta Erphesfurtensia of the Scriptores rerum Germanicarum in usum scholarum 44, 97.
[15] Cited in Charles T. Davis, 'Remigio de' Girolami', Proceedings of the American Philosophical Society CIV (1960), 667a.

posts in the local churches, the increased control of local church courts over testaments and bequests, the consequent appeals to Rome, and Rome's taxation of the local churches. On the lowest level, the bone of contention was money. It had long been a commonplace that Rome was avaricious. When Louis IX in 1245 complained about the taxes paid by the French Church to Rome, he said that his kingdom was being impoverished and foreigners were being made rich from its spoils. A despatch in 1301 from an Aragonese ambassador at Rome noted that the French embargo was bringing the pope to his knees. The French had ordered, he reported, that

> no one shall take from the kingdom gold, silver, cloth, wool, horses, and money even in letters of exchange or deposit contracts. And thus the French prelates who have been summoned by the pope have been wholly prevented from coming. Whence you should know, famous lord, that fear and tremors have gripped not a few, especially if the way of gulping or drinking the gold of France should be closed to them.[16]

The pope combated this charge. Boniface VIII remarked in consistory that Capetian revenues had more than doubled since the days of Philip II Augustus because of taxes and other favours granted by Rome. An argument that might have carried more weight—but did not—was that the communities and seigniors who were losing business to the ecclesiastical courts were losing far more cases to the royal tribunals. In regard to taxes, the French Crown had been assigned substantial ecclesiastical subsidies by the popes in every year from 1284 until 1296, and it was Boniface's attempt to stop this that precipitated the first crisis between him and Philip. And the reason for this was that the monarchy had not yet been able to impose a system of regular and sufficient taxation upon France's notables and communities. Nor was it to be able to do so until the latter part of the Hundred Years War. Even so, what can be said of that later time can probably be said of 1300: the fiscal demands of the secular state were growing more rapidly than those of Rome. Unused to the costs and constraints required of them and threatened by the quasidemocratic urgings of the plebs, the leading elements of town and countryside did not wish to pay for the growing central state but were nevertheless obliged

[16] Heinrich Finke, *Aus den Tagen Bonifaz VIII* (1902), p. lv.

by circumstances to favour the growth itself. For a time, then, they joined the prince and the people in seeking a 'religious' justification for making the Church pay.

One way of providing a different focus of 'religious' loyalty from the Church was to develop the idea of the nation or the people. Here one does not refer to the traditional division of Europe into four great peoples: the Germans, the French, the Italians and the Spanish. What is more pertinent is the idea of nationhood that arose from several deeply felt and somewhat primitive elements. In the letter of Gregory IX of 1239 cited above, these were fundamentally two: language and race. When Edward I summoned the archbishop of Canterbury to the model parliament in 1295, he—a French speaking prince—cited the threat of an invasion from France, whose king, he said, intends to obliterate the English tongue (*lingua Anglica*). Race consciousness may be seen in the Rhinelander Alexander of Roes. Italians, he thought, were ruled by the love of acquisition (*amor habendi*), Germany by that of ruling (*amor dominandi*), and Frenchmen by the love of knowing (*amor sciendi*). Their natural qualities determined the different kinds of government: in Italy the people rule, in Germany the soldiery, and in France the clergy, an arrogant and lustful crowd. The word Gaul comes from the word for cock, and the French share the weaknesses and strengths of that bird. The Frenchman is 'handsome of body, but handsomer feathered than plucked, that is, clothed than naked'. The French are wrong to say that Gaul comes from *galla* in Greek which means milk, and that they are so called because their bodies are so white. 'It is true that, in comparison with the Spaniards or Moors (variant: Greeks), they do stand out as being white in body, but, in comparison with other adjacent regions, namely those of the Saxons and English, they cannot be said to compare in whiteness in any way.'[17]

Moral and institutional qualities were added to these basic definitions. Peter Dubois insisted that, by geographical and astral determination, northern France was the only natural cradle of those capable of ruling other men. Stealing his text from the Hohenstaufen propaganda of Godfrey of Viterbo (who had indirectly taken it from its sources in Carolingian Frankland), John of Paris found that the French, heirs of the ancient Trojans, had never been subject to the Romans or anyone else and hence were

[17] *Memoriale* 15 in *MGH. Staatschriften* I, i, 107.

naturally free. Assembled in 1247 to protest against ecclesiastical policies, the French baronage, headed by such notables as the dukes and counts of Burgundy, Brittany, and Saint-Pol, used arguments that prefigure those of the Monarchomachs of the sixteenth century. They insisted on the slavery of Roman institutions and the freedom of those of the Franks, that is, of the French aristocracy of the sword, and there is even a hint that they suspected their own Gallo-Roman plebs.

> Because the superstition of clerks does not consider that the kingdom of France was converted from the error of the gentiles to the Catholic faith by the wars and by the blood of not a few under Charlemagne and other princes ... they have so absorbed the secular jurisdiction of the magnates that sons of slaves judge according to their laws the children and sons of freemen; and because they ought rather to be judged by us according to the laws of the first victors, the customs of our ancestors ought not to be superseded by [their] new constitutions ... ; we, barons of the kingdom, perceiving with attentive mind that the kingdom was not acquired by the written law nor by the arrogance of clerks, but by the sweat of soldiers, declare[18]

that, except for marriage, usury and heresy, no case shall go to an ecclesiastical tribunal. And the reclamations of urban patricians often excluded usury as well, at least in so far as the enforcement of testamentary restitution was concerned.

In France the monarchy for a time embodied the sentiments of the nation. The conceptions of the king as emperor in his kingdom and as most Christian and ever orthodox were repeated *ad nauseam* in the manifestoes issued by Philip's ministers William of Nogaret and William of Plaisans. So faithful a vicar of Jesus Christ was this prince that a sermon delivered at the court during the Flemish war congratulated the Flemish people on the opportunity of being defeated, thus to be brought back to the ways of Christ and of right reason. Indeed, to this perfervid sermonizer, the king's interests were identical to those of the faith: 'Whoever inveighs against the king works against the whole Church, against

[18] Matthew Paris, *Chronica majora* in *Rolls Series* LVII, iv, 595–3. See the discussion of this and other texts cited later on in Georges de Lagarde, *La naissance de l'esprit laïque* I, 161 and *passim*. For parallels with Hohenstaufen polemics see Helene Wieruszowski, *Vom Imperium zum nationalem Königtum* (1933), especially the references given in her Verzeichnis, 222ff.

Catholic doctrine, against sanctity and justice, and against the Holy Land.'[19]

In his address to the French clergy in 1303, Nogaret asserted that such a prince had the duty of reforming the Church if it required it. This was not new. In 1239 Frederick II Hohenstaufen had proposed to reform the Church (*reformare in melius*), and, combating his condemnation by the Council at Lyons in 1245, his *Illos felices* of 1246 described his reason for this programme. The prince 'most especially intends this, that the prelates and the clergy should be returned to that state of poverty in which they were at the time of the primitive Church. . . . For clerks such as those contemplated the angels, and, coruscate with miracles, cured the sick, raised the dead, and subjected kings and princes to themselves by sanctity and not by arms.'[20] By 1247 the northern French barons had borrowed this imperial rhetoric to justify reducing the powers of the Church. They acted, they said, in order that 'our jurisdiction thus revived should breathe again, and that they, up to now enriched by our impoverishment . . . , should be reduced to the state of the primitive Church, so that then, living in contemplation while we, as is fitting, lead the active life, they will perform miracles, those miracles that have so long departed from this earth'.[21]

The *civitas christiana* had many defenders, each of whom wished to defend it by first purifying the others. In 1301 Boniface VIII issued two bulls, *Ausculta, fili carissime* and *Ante promotionem*, in which he summoned a council of French prelates and masters of law and theology. To reconquer the Holy Land, ecclesiastical liberty had to be restored in France, and royal policies, such as the debasement of coinage, had to be rescinded. What the pope had in mind, he said, was to discover what could be done 'for the augmentation of the Catholic faith, the conservation of ecclesiastical liberty, the reformation of the king and of the kingdom, the correction of past excesses, and the good government of the kingdom'.[22] The rage of the French court may perhaps be gauged

---

[19] Cited and its context explored by E. H. Kantorowicz, *The King's Two Bodies*, 254.
[20] H. L. A. Huillard-Bréholles, *Historia diplomatica Friderici secundi* VI, 393 and Eduard Winkelmann, *Acta imperii inedita* II (Innsbruck, 1880), 50. A discussion in Ernst H. Kantorowicz, *Friedrich II*, Ergänzungsband, 231–2.
[21] Matthew Paris, *Chronica majora* in *Rolls Series* LVII, iv, 593.
[22] *Les registres de Boniface VIII*, III, 336, No. 4426: *Ante promotionem*.

from this tract of Peter Dubois: 'You, noble king, by inheritance above all other princes defender of the faith and destroyer of heretics, can, ought, and are obliged to require and so arrange that the said Boniface be held and judged as an heretic . . .'[23] In June 1303, the court adopted and publicized widely a plan already suggested by Frederick II in 1239: a general council would be convened to examine and judge the crimes attributed to Boniface VIII. Even with the grave split in the college of cardinals, the adhesion of the French clergy to the crown, and France's diplomatic power, it is unlikely that this council would have carried more weight than the one summoned later at Rome against John XXII by Lewis of Bavaria. In the meantime Boniface had been seized at Anagni by France's Roman allies. He was shortly thereafter released by his own friends, but died suddenly in October 1303. Before these events, however, he had issued in November 1302 the great bull *Unam sanctum* and it is to the polemics around that bull that our attention must be turned.

John of Paris and Giles of Rome

The literature produced during this time of crisis was rich and varied. Utopians such as Roger Bacon and Raymond Lull looked for an angel pope to mobilize the Latins against the antichrist, to launch the crusades again, and to convert the infidel, Jew and pagan. Lull even thought in terms of the conquest of the world. Afraid that the vast realms of the Tatars would be converted to Islam or to Judaism, he urged the Latins to convert this people and told them that God was on their side: 'He has given the Latins the power to acquire the whole world, if they wish to.'[24] The opinions of another Catalan, Arnold of Villanova, sometime doctor of Boniface VIII, were close to those of Lull. Like Lull, his politics were anti-French and he was an even more forthright adherent of the cause of the radical Franciscans. He also believed in an early version of the secular idea of progress in which the new Church or spiritual order of the Franciscans' imagination was all mixed up with mystic dreams about medicine and natural science.

---

[23] *La suplication du peuple de France* cited in Michael Wilks, *The Problem of Sovereignty in the Later Middle Ages*, 236. The tract was probably written in 1303.
[24] *Disputatio Raymundi christiani et Hamar saraceni* 3 in *Beati Raymundi Lulli opera* (Mainz, 1729; rprt) IV, 477a.

Other utopians favoured secular leadership. In the Norman lawyer Peter Dubois's *Recovery of the Holy Land*, the Church was to
be reformed and lessened in size, and its members were to receive
a stipulated income from properties entrusted to the management
of secular men. Latin Europe was to be unified under the king of
France, who was to direct the conquest of the Holy Land, indeed,
of the whole Near East. As a first step, the pernicious freedom of
the Italian city republics and the resistance of the Catalans and
Sicilians to French power were to be obliterated.

Several things limited the appeal of the utopians. As can be
seen above, their politics were in conflict: some favoured clerical
leadership, some secular; some favoured the French, others their
enemies the Catalans and Aragonese. Besides, they were all looked
upon as mildly mad. Although Lull's work was approved at Paris
in 1310 and was to influence later figures like Nicholas of Cuşa,
clerical intellectuals were reserved about his work. Suspected of
being a Joachite, Roger Bacon was shunted aside in his later years,
perhaps imprisoned. An ardent defender of the losing cause of the
Spiritual Franciscans, Arnold of Villanova was convinced that the
clergy had it in for him because, although married and a medical
doctor, he wrote about theology. He was probably correct, but the
churchmen's reserve is also partly explained by his own lack of
moderation. Responding to attacks on his own earlier tract pro-
claiming the immediate coming of the antichrist, Arnold asserted
that churchmen had been warned by two divine messengers, and
that,

> just as they had rejected John [the Baptist] and Christ by
> different defamations, so do they now defame these two modern
> messengers. For they said of him who [the Lord] first sent to
> them, namely, Master R. Lull, that he was an illiterate or an
> idiot and ignorant of grammar. And then he sent them the
> second aforesaid messenger [Arnold himself!], not only a true
> and splendid expert in the Latin language, but admirable in
> many subjects, and they said that he was a rash fantast, and a
> magician or necromancer.[25]

[25] *Tractatus quidam in quo respondetur obiectionibus que fiebant contra tractatum
Arnaldi de adventu Antichristi*, ed. M. Batllori, *Analecta Sacra Tarraconensia*
XXVIII (1955), 68. *Illiteratus* and *idiota* essentially meant that Lull knew no Latin.
I owe this reference to J. N. Hillgarth of Boston College.

The utopian schemers obviously did not direct their attention to things as they were, but there were others who did, and it is these who shall be considered at greater length. They did not seek to lay a new foundation for the world, but instead sought to modify the structure already built. Two principal questions were argued in this literature. The first of these was the conflict between monarchism and conciliarism. It is noteworthy that both Boniface VIII and Philip IV tried to summon councils in which to condemn each other. This conflict of political ideologies has been rehearsed in the chapters of Part Four above and will be referred to here only in so far as it concerns the second theme. The second theme is the familiar one of the relationship of the Church to the state, the prospects of the independence of the latter from the former, and the assertion by many churchmen of the necessary subordination of the state and the laity to the Church and the clergy. Of these writers the two greatest, Marsiglio of Padua and William of Ockham—not to speak of lesser figures like Dante and the papalist Augustine Trionfo (d. 1328)—escape the scope of this volume. The two on whom attention is centred here are John of Paris, whose *On Papal and Royal Power* appeared in 1302, and Giles of Rome, whose *On Ecclesiastical Power* was written in 1301.

To John Quidort of Paris, the Church had to keep the mean between the Waldensians and the Herodians. The former wished it to surrender all property, indeed, in a sense, to leave the world. The Herodians—Herod had mistakenly thought that Christ was a *rex terrenus*—wanted the Church to rule the world. Following Bernard of Clairvaux, John argued that the pope is not a lord with dominion, but rather a steward of souls for which he is accountable. Just as Christ ruled men's hearts and not their possessions, so does the pope 'accept the keys of the kingdom of heaven, not because of power in possessions but because of his power over [moral] crimes'.[26] Whatever temporal authority the Church enjoys was given it by the people or their governments. The very fact that Constantine gave the Church the Italian empire (*imperium italicum*) and that the Church accepted the gift proves that it did not have civil dominion *de jure*. Nor can the pope dispose of lay properties. Like the later Marsiglio, although not with the same vehemence and clarity, John argues against Henry of Cremona's assertion in 1302 that 'those who say that the pope

[26] *De potestate regia et papali* 10, ed. Leclercq, 197.

587

does not have power in temporal matters are to be judged as heretics because what they are saying is that the Church cannot coerce heretics by the secular arm'.[27]

The Church does have powers, said John, but they are wholly non-coercive. It has the power to consecrate, the medicinal power of the keys in the forum of conscience, and the power to teach or to preach. As with the other powers, this power is not a lordship (*potestas dominii*), but rather a right or capacity to teach authoritatively (*auctoritas magisterii*). The Church's fourth power, the authority of judging and punishing, concerns the cases of moral law that come under its purview and the exclusion of heretics from its community. The latter is, of course, a justifiable action, but here again the only coercive authority is that of the secular state. Even the moral offences that are to be examined by ecclesiastical courts are to be kept to a minimum. Unless there is firm scriptural precept, especially in the New Testament, the Church should not even render a moral judgment. Usury can therefore be adjudged, but the larger issue of private property cannot. In practical terms, John says, it is known that the common possession of property leads to civil strife among men, but moral and natural law favour it. The Church is not to interfere here, following Augustine's recommendation: 'Remove, [Augustine] says, the law of the emperor and one cannot say that this thing is mine. For in natural law there is one liberty for all and the common possession of all things.'[28] But, after man's fall, private property became necessary: heaven is not for this earth.

Two parenthetical observations may be made here. John is nothing like as daring as he may seem at first glance. There had always been a strong tradition among churchmen justifying secular authority, even that of pagan or infidel states, and there is nothing in John that can equal the rhetoric of earlier churchmen such as Peter Damian in the eleventh century. In his anti-Gregorian mood, insisting on the difference between spiritual and material things and enraged by a summons to arms to protect the Church and its properties, Peter had exploded:

If therefore for the faith by which the universal Church lives it is never allowed to take up arms of iron, how then do armoured

[27] *Ibid.* II, ed. Leclercq, 207.
[28] *Ibid.* 13, ed. Leclercq 213. This is a rough quotation by John from Gratian's *Decretum* I, 7, I in *CICan* I, 13.

hosts rage with their swords for the earthly and transitory riches
of the Church? Indeed, when the saints prevail [in the world and
Church] they will surely not destroy heretics or the worshippers
of idols, but will instead not flee being slain by them for the
Catholic faith![29]

With some exaggeration, it might indeed be argued that John had
merely returned to the position of the clergy of the earlier Middle
Ages when the state had dominated the Church. The second observation is that, being an Aristotelian, John allows an exception
to the Church's abstention from the employment of coercion
described above: the case of dire necessity, when any good man
must transcend his normal role and act as the agent of equity or
epiky. The pope may never dispose of lay properties 'unless by
chance in the ultimate need of the Church, in which case he acts
not as a *dispensator* [with ordinary jurisdiction], but rather as one
who declares the law (*declarator juris*)'.[30] But so can any good man.

The secular state, then, is independent of the Church. Although
the Church is more worthy, the *regnum* preceded the *sacerdotium*
in history. 'Whence the empire is from God alone. . . . And because the pope does not have the [spiritual] sword from the emperor, neither does the emperor have the [temporal] sword from
the pope, [as is shown in Gratian's *Decretum* 1, 93, 24]: "For the
army makes the emperor." '[31] And the forms of the organization of
Church and state were different. Contradicting the tradition that
led Dante to plead for a universal monarchy, John maintains that
God's ordinance was that the faith must be one and unified, but
that the same is not true of civil society.

> The lay faithful do not have it from divine law that they must
> be subject in temporal matters to one supreme monarch. Of
> their natural instinct which comes from God they have it rather
> that they should live in a civil manner and in a community, and,
> as a result, that they should choose diverse kinds of governors
> in order to live well in common according to the diversity of
> their communities.[32]

There are many reasons for this difference. Religion can be more

---

[29] Book Four, Letter 4 in *PL* CXLIV, 316a. It is worth noting that the later scholium
or commentary on this letter went mad at this point.
[30] *De potestate regia et papali* 7, ed. Leclercq, 189.
[31] *Ibid.*, 10, ed. Leclercq, 197. Cf above p. 331 for this idea of Jerome's.
[32] *Ibid.*, 3, ed. Leclercq, 180–1.

unified than civil dominion because the word of persuasion travels more quickly and easily than the sword of coercion. John also fell back on Augustine who had argued that the history of Rome and of other empires did not show that a universal state was necessarily beneficial. John concluded that, although the rule of one man is probably best for any one state (a point later contradicted by Marsiglio of Padua who thought that unity consisted of the oneness of a community and not in the number of its elected magistrates), 'it is nevertheless better that many should rule in many realms than that one should rule the whole world'.[33] But the fundamental reason for John's argument was that, in the natural sphere in which the state operates, varieties of tongues, peoples, and climates make it obvious that 'what is virtuous in one people is not virtuous in another'.[34]

In terms of the origin of their authority the two forms of government were similar. Ideally, for John, each nation is possessed by its inhabitants, who entrust government to elected or permitted magistrates—an example of the latter being the hereditary monarchs of France. So also is the Church an assembly of the faithful who continue to possess its government while attributing the use or exercise of it to ecclesiastical magistrates. Although, for example, the papacy is of divine foundation, the person holding the office is not to be considered divine. God's rule of the world

> does not exclude our work, for we are his co-workers (*co-operatores Dei*). Although the papacy is of itself from God alone, it is nevertheless placed in this or that person through human cooperation, namely, by the *consensus* of the elected and of the electors, and, as a result, it can cease to be vested in this or that particular person by human *consensus*.[35]

A pope or other magistrate can therefore be removed, and the question boils down to how and for what reasons. Everyone agreed that the reasons should not be minor. Writing in 1295, Peter John Olivi opined that we must defer somewhat to princes: 'Thus minor mistakes or frauds (*fraudes*) may be committed by a monarch as long as he is obliged to use the advice of the many and the better in important matters.'[36] Real monarchists went much

[33] *Ibid.*, 21, ed. Leclercq, 247.
[34] *Ibid.*, 3, ed. Leclercq, 181.
[35] *Ibid.*, 25, ed. Leclercq, 255.
[36] *De renuntiatione papae*, in *Archivum franciscanum historicum* XI–XII (1918–19), 354–5.

further than this. An anonymous defender of Boniface VIII in a tract of about 1308 commented on a report that the pope had asserted that he, being theoretically both emperor and pope, could not commit simony on the grounds that everything was his anyway. Taking Boniface's as a probable proposition (*est ut sic, est ut non*), the author argued that, if Boniface had said it, 'it must be agreed that he should be understood in the good sense and not in the bad, especially because, when we do not know with what intention (*quo animo*) things are done, we ought always give a man the benefit of the doubt'.[37] Accepting the more moderate form of this kind of permissive thought, John stated that the removal of such an officer requires that he be mad, heretical, or totally inept.

Following one side of canonistic tradition, John spelled out how a pope should be removed. Like Peter John Olivi, John thought that if a pontiff were willing to resign and had good cause the cardinals could stand for the people and accept his resignation. Were he unwilling, his deposition required a greater *consensus populi*, and John therefore followed Gratian's chapter *Nunc autem*, 'where it is said that a general council was convoked to depose Pope Marcellinus'.[38] And if the pope violently resists deposition, a secular prince is to be called in, 'nor does he act against the pope as pope, but against his enemy and the enemy of the republic'.[39] John then goes on to praise the Emperor Henry III for removing the three rival popes and replacing them with another at Sutri in 1046—an action that had infuriated the Gregorians of the past. John even thought that the cardinals could invite secular intervention themselves if a pope were notoriously heretical or simoniacal, and then '*in subsidium juris* . . . the emperor, requested by the cardinals, ought to proceed against the pope and depose him'.[40]

Employed together with the teaching of the king as emperor in his own kingdom, John's doctrine was obviously useful to the king of France, just as it was to be useful to the conciliar fathers in the fifteenth century. Its weakness is also obvious. The Church was made dependent on the coercive power of the secular sword. It

[37] Heinrich Finke, *Aus den Tagen Bonifaz VIII*, p. LXXIV.
[38] *De potestate regia et papali* 24, ed. Leclercq, 254 and again in chapter 2, p. 248. Nunc autem is in *Decretum* I, 21, 7 in *CICan* I, 71. Marcellinus was a pope suspected of capitulating to the pagans at the time of Diocletian's persecution.
[39] *De potestate regia et papali* 22, ed. Leclercq, 250.
[40] *Ibid.* 23, ed. Leclercq, 215.

turned out that the prince or secular magistrate would require a heavy price in the form of the reduction of ecclesiastical liberty in return for his services. It is true that, unlike Marsiglio, John tempered his advocacy. He viewed the accidental power *in subsidium juris* as a double edged sword, one that could be employed by the Church as well as by the state. Just as a prince requested by the cardinals could act against a pope, so could a pope, requested by the barons or peers of a realm, act against a prince. In John's imagination, everything depended upon the people:

> For an ecclesiastical judge cannot impose a corporal or monetary penalty for a crime as can a secular judge, or only if the criminal wishes to accept it. And if he does not wish to accept it, the ecclesiastical judge can compel by excommunication or other spiritual penalty, which is the most that he can do, and he cannot do anything more. Now I say that the pope acts *per accidens* because if the prince is heretical, incorrigible, and a contemner of ecclesiastical censures, the pope can do something among the people so that he will be deprived of his secular office and deposed by the people. And the pope does this in ecclesiastical crimes, which cases pertain to him, by excommunicating all those who obey the prince as a lord, and thus the people depose the prince [directly] and the pope indirectly (*per accidens*).[41]

But the good Dominican John, who was so wise about princes, had forgotten the people, and did not perceive that their affections had shifted. From the Gregorian age until about 1300, the *populus christianus* and the popes had judged, limited, and even deposed princes. From 1300 onward the *populus* and the princes were to judge the popes.

John of Paris, Dante and Marsiglio all insisted that temporal ends and virtues were distinct from spiritual ones and were good in themselves. We recall that John said that 'moral virtues acquired [here on earth] can be perfect without the theological virtues'. And from this John went on to draw the corollary that, here on earth, 'without Christ governing, there is a true and perfect justice', that is, a true and perfect government.[42]

The defenders of ecclesiastical liberty and of the popes thought otherwise. Cardinal John Lemoine defended the bull *Unam sanctam* by noting that there were four ends in life: physical

[41] *Ibid.* 13, ed. Leclercq, 214.
[42] *Ibid.* 18, ed. Leclercq, 229.

health, moral virtue, the good of the multitude or society, and the good of the supernatural soul. These ends are in ascending order, and without the last the others are of no consequence. Giles of Rome was more subtle. He followed Thomas Aquinas in admitting that man's and nature's goods—health, a sufficiency of wealth, education, and peace—were intrinsically good. But, in Augustinian fashion, he argued from human experience that things beneficial in themselves are not necessarily good for man, who is incapable of using them to his own advantage. Without God's grace, therefore, they are of no value to man. He concluded: 'If therefore neither our end nor our bliss is to be found in temporal things but only in spiritual ones, it follows that temporal things are good only in so far as they are directed toward spiritual objectives.'[43] And it follows from this that, although the secular state is necessary to provide the peace in which the Christian may be educated toward blessedness, there is no just state unless the ultimate objective rules within its frontiers:

> For we say with Augustine (*De civitate Dei* 2, 21) that true justice cannot be found except in that republic whose founder and governor is Christ. Now, the pagan Romans appear to have talked much about justice and to have pontificated about the republic, but that republic, as Augustine says . . . , was not alive in *mores* but merely painted in colours. . . . Hence Augustine asserts (*ibid.* 19, 21) that the Roman republic was not a true republic because true justice was never there.[44]

In 1302 James of Viterbo not unfairly caricatured the thought of his master Giles by substituting the clergy for the more generous idea of the Church. 'No community can be called a true republic save the ecclesiastical one, because true justice, utility, and community exist in it alone.'[45]

It is true, says Giles, that secular power derives from God, and directly from him. But then so do fire, water, men's bodies and men's learning—indeed, everything in the natural world. But, since good things may be put to evil use, the thing itself is not the same as the use that is made of it. The search for salvation alone justifies all natural things, and, for that, the sacraments of the Church are required. Therefore 'because none are worthy of

[43] *De ecclesiastica potestate* 2, 4, ed. Richard Scholz (Leipzig, 1929, rept), 49.
[44] *Ibid.* 2, 7, ed. Scholz, 73.
[45] *De regimine christiano* I, 4 cited in Michael Wilks, *The Problem of Sovereignty*, 18.

honour, dominion, power, or, indeed of any other good except by ecclesiastical sacraments through the Church and under the Church, what our chapter heading said was well said, namely that, although there is no power except from God, no one is worthy of having any power unless he becomes worthy under the Church or through it'.[46] Giles then contradicts an argument already stated by John of Paris and much developed by William of Ockham, stating that secular princes or laymen should not complain about the yoke placed on them by the Church, because this yoke is not servitude, but instead liberty:

> Since faithful Christians are redeemed by the Church from the power of the devil, they ought to confess themselves to be ascript slaves of the Church. . . . But this servitude is to be considered meritorious because it is a servitude more of love than of fear, of devotion than of coercion. By this servitude nothing is lost, but much is gained because those things given by faithful men to the Church will be returned a hundred times over and they will also possess eternal life.[47]

As Ockham and Marsiglio were to point out, to Giles and his followers the practical Church of the world was not merely an institution of divine foundation but also a godlike one.

So immense is the power of the Church in this conception that it might be wondered what was left to laymen. According to Giles, the Church has obeyed the injunction to render to Caesar what is Caesar's by attributing to the laity a particular and lower form of lordship or ownership, while reserving to itself a superior and universal form. Anent the power of the secular state, Giles somewhat cynically applauds the view that, since all power is really vested in the spiritual sword, it was a good idea to invent the material sword in order that 'a certain dignity in [the exercise] of government should be given to the laity lest the lay people should perceive themselves to be totally contemptible in government which would cause murmurs and quarrels between the laity and the clergy in the Church'.[48] And here, glossing over Bernard of Clairvaux's earlier careful caveats, Giles asserts that the Church exercises both the lord's right (*dominium jurisdictionale*) and the tenant's right (*dominium utile*) in all temporal things. Still, as is

---

[46] *De ecclesiastica potestate* 2, 9, ed. Scholz, 85.
[47] *Ibid.* 2, 10, ed. Scholz, 95.
[48] *Ibid.* 2, 15, ed. Scholz, 136.

evident, the Church grants to laymen much of the tenant's right, that is, the right to raise fruits from temporal things, and this for good reason: in payment for the care of their souls, the laity will support the clergy. This is especially advantageous because sacred Scripture teaches us that, in order to occupy themselves wholly with spiritual solicitude, the apostles were enjoined to avoid earthly cares. 'It was therefore the glory of the apostles that they possessed nothing at all in so far as responsibility or anxiety (*sollicitudo*) are concerned, but everything in so far as lordship.'[49] And the clergy are the heirs of the apostles.

Deprived of its commander, an army is nothing and cannot wage war. By analogy, the good of the Church is embodied in the pope. 'The Church must be feared and its commands obeyed, and the highest pontiff, who holds the apex of the Church and who can be called the Church, must be feared and his commands must be obeyed, because his power is spiritual, celestial, and divine, and is without weight, number and measure.'[50] Lay or ecclesiastical, all other offices have weight, number and measure, but, like God (Wisdom of Solomon 11:21), the papal office and its plenitude of power could not be weighed or measured. This vision of the pope as *quasi-Deus* or *imago Christi* infuriated both Marsiglio and Ockham, and had already elicited much opposition. In 1295 Peter John Olivi—a relatively moderate figure in regard to practical papal power—had remarked: 'They say that he is uncreated, immense, impeccable, infallible, and prescient in all things, like Christ, an opinion which no one would state or even hint at, except a lunatic.'[51] Giles tried to circumvent this objection by employing the traditional separation of office and person. A truly spiritual man (*spiritualis homo*) can judge all others and never be judged. There are two kinds of spiritual man. One is spiritual because of his personal perfection; another, like the pope, because of his status or position. 'He who is spiritual according to his status and perfect in the highest degree according to the jurisdiction and plenitude of his power, he will be the spiritual man who judges all things and cannot be judged by anyone.'[52]

To believe otherwise, as was said in *Unam sanctam* and by

---

[49] *Ibid.* 2, 1, ed. Scholz, 37–8.
[50] *Ibid.* 3, 12, ed. Scholz, 209.
[51] *Epistola ad Conradum de Offida*, in *Archivum franciscanum historicum* XI–XII (1918–19), 368.
[52] *De ecclesiastica potestate* I, 2, ed. Scholz, 6.

John Lemoine and many others, is to substitute a Manichaean and heretical duality for a divinely ordained unity. It is therefore, as Giles says, 'indeed well said that the power of the supreme pontiff is that sublime power to which every soul should be subject.'[53] Or, as the princely Boniface VIII put it in *Unam sanctam*: 'We declare, state, decide and pronounce that it is altogether necessary for the salvation of every human creature to be subject to the Roman pontiff.'[54]

It has long been known that there was nothing original about *Unam sanctam*, and it has often been observed that both John of Paris and Giles of Rome depended heavily upon Thomas Aquinas. Yet from the teaching of Aquinas, central to the thirteenth century, two very different doctrines were derived to serve the need of institutional conflict. One, that of John of Paris, was to lead to the endless queries or *dubia* of William of Ockham and to the secularism of Marsiglio of Padua. It thus served to open the way for secular magistrates and lay philosophers to replace churchmen and theologians as the vessels containing the fundamental religion of western man. The other, that of Giles of Rome, so hardened a once somewhat flexible doctrine that, in spite of its occasionally very perceptive cynicism about laymen, it no longer rang true to life. To use the ancient monastic image, Giles' clerical Marys were to be supported by an unnaturally subservient group of lay Marthas. As we know from the case of the order of Grandmont, the attempt to deprive the Marthas of some exercise of leadership had never really worked even within the ecclesiastical order. When applied to monarchies and republics and to their subjects and citizens (all fired by the spread and laicization of the monastic vocation and ethos), this deprivation was not likely to fare half as well.

But perhaps the problem should be put differently. Perhaps one should emphasize the fact that the laity or the people only support the intellectual or religious leaders who sing the tune they wish to hear; and that, as the lay spirit became more powerful and capable, laymen threw the priests and monks onto the dump of vestigial minorities. It can be argued against this assertion that there is

[53] *Ibid.* I, 4, ed. Scholz, 11.
[54] *Extravagantes communes* I, 8, 1 in *CICan* II, 1246.

such a thing as 'true religion,' that is, intellectual and spiritual freedom, and that its spokesmen can lift man up and tear him free from his mundane concerns, even against his will. And that it was there that the clergy failed. Yet there are difficulties here too. When discussing the question of voluntary poverty, Thomas Aquinas remarked that he who seeks to live virtuously with no means of his own and who depends on the kindness or generosity of others has a problem:

Freedom of the mind is most especially required for the attainment of perfect virtue, for, if this is weakened, men very easily become 'partakers of other men's sins' either by agreeing expressly, or by being adulatory, or even by hiding their true feelings. And therefore this way of living is prejudicial to this freedom because there is no man who does not fear to offend him from whose kindness he lives.[55]

Aquinas' answer to this question was that those who give themselves to voluntary poverty are of such perfection (*homines in virtute perfecti*) that they could not be suborned by the little they need in order to live. But 'little' is a relative term, and it would seem from the history of the church in this period that the objection the saint thus hastily disposed of was the more probable or safer opinion. Even among the best, even among the Franciscans, there were few or none who were perfect and, consequently, few or none who were free.

This quandary was much discussed at the time. There had seemed to be a solution, one that had twice been tried, once at the time of the attack upon heresy and usury around 1200 and once again among the Franciscan rigorists around 1300: the utopian solution. When discussing 2 Thessalonians 3, 7–12, Peter Cantor urged the clerks to follow Paul:

When preaching in Achaia, the Apostle accepted no charity from [the people], partly because they were covetous and hated him to whom they gave, . . . and partly because he did not want the *curiosi*—who, seeing Paul labour with his own hands and eat the bread of his own labour, were no longer able, as had been their wont, to eat the bread of sloth [that is, the bread of other's labour]—to appear to have bought impunity by thinking: 'We

[55] *Contra gentiles* 3, 132, 4, 4 in Rome 1934, 386b. The biblical passage is 1 Timothy 5:22. Thomas's reply to this objection is 3, 135, 4, 4, on p. 391b.

have filled Paul's hands, and now we can do what we want.'[56]

But the whole history of the Church and indeed of society had shown that the ascetic's or utopian's solution, although possible for an individual—and then only momentarily—was impossible for the many. In Latin Europe, the attempt to realize this ideal had twice failed, once in the world at large and once within the narrower confines of the Franciscan order, and with this failure the solidarity of the Christian republic and the hope for a Christian society under ecclesiastical leadership had begun to weaken.

It serves no purpose to put the matter in the judicative or moralistic terms so often favoured by the historians of religion, and to declare that churchmen had failed because they were corrupt. These terms distort reality because they overlook the obvious fact that churchmen, although they seemed to lead, were only one group, one part, one nation within the Christian republic whose citizens permitted or created their leadership. They are also untruthful terms because they encourage us to forget that, although much of the Christian ideal was useful because it helped men both to develop their talents and to reconcile themselves to their misery, some part of the ideal—given man's character and history—was impossible of attainment. To dilate only upon the beauty of the hope of living the *vita apostolica* or of creating here on earth a perfect society on the model of the supernal Jerusalem obscures one of the principal functions of asserting impossible social and religious ideals. That function is a way of enabling men to condemn their neighbours for failing to live up to what they could not reasonably be expected to. An aspect of this social idealism is, then, an instrument for personal aggrandizement and social warfare because it deprives one's neighbours of rectitude and therefore even of their rights. A utopian dream, untinged by resignation, soon becomes a nightmare. An historian should therefore eschew judgment and instead try to understand, viewing those neighbours of the past, not as those others, but rather as his brothers. Concerning a special aspect of utopian hope, Peter Cantor once remarked: 'In nature's law, all things are in common —the earth for treading, the air for breathing, the water for drinking and bathing. Why then do princes and the Church hold as

[56] *Summa de sacramentis et animae consiliis* 3, 2a: *Liber casuum conscientiae* 3, 50, ed. Dugauquier, 342.

private goods what should be in common?' But in spite of his utopian hope, a thousand unspoken arguments from experience echoed in Peter's mind and finally made him say: 'It is difficult to advise princes on this matter; and it is hard indeed to condemn the whole Church.'[57]

That their world had begun to fall apart was not because churchmen were corrupt, but rather because they, just like their lay fellow citizens of the Christian republic, were not perfect. In judging them, the historian is to follow the rule:

Semper in dubiis benigniora praeferenda sunt.[58]

---

[57] *Ibid.: Liber casuum conscientiae* 3, 2, ed. Dugauquier, 162, para. 208.
[58] *Digest* 50, 17, Num. 56 de diversis regulis iuris antiqui.

Index

Abelard, Peter, 18, 19, 38, 217, 296, 476–8 *passim*, 485, 514, 516, 526, 527, 537; and Bernard of Clairvaux, 482, 508–9; *Dialogus* 92, 96

Abraham ben Samuel Abulafia, 83, 108

Abraham of Posquières, 86

Accursius, 11, 162, 242, 264, 277, 320, 400

Adam de la Hale, 215, 223

Adrian IV, Pope, (1154–9), 53, 324, 355–6

Aegidius Romanus, *see* Giles of Rome

Agriculture, 111–19; *see also* Manorial system

Ailred of Rievaulx, 38, 300

Alan of Bologna, 362

Alan of Lille, 13, 21, 253, 478, 480, 502, 507, 510, 526–7, 534

Alberic of Porta Ravennate, 179

Alberic of Rosate, 31, 33–4, 157, 241–2, 370, 447

Albert I, King of Germany (1298–1308), 565

Albert Behaim, 322

Albert della Scala, 451

Albert Galeotti, 447

Alberti, Florentine merchant bankers, 163

Albertino Mussato, 454

Albert of Cremona, 518–19

Albert of Gandino, 3, 11, 250, 264, 370, 447, 558, 559

Albertus Magnus, 84, 468, 470, 479, 493, 498, 511

Albigensian crusade, 16, 44, 71, 171, 180, 187, 192, 325, 336, 387, 430, 466, 517, 549–50, 554

Albumazar, 479, 497

Alexander III, Pope (1159–81), 4, 98, 178, 323, 328, 336, 343–4, 348, 360, 378, 538, 564

Alexander VI, Pope (1254–61), 336

Alexander Lombard, 10

Alexander Neckham, 127–8, 494

Alexander of Hales, 27, 470, 478

Alexander of Roes, 58, 323, 329, 333, 334, 369, 373, 582

Alexandria, 120, 130, 136, 155

Alfarabi, 477, 494

Alice of Montfort, 215

Almohades, 60

Alphonse of Poitiers, Count of Poitou

and Toulouse, 117, 161

Alphonso II, King of Aragon (1162–96), 5

Alphonso III, King of Portugal (1245–79), 335

Alphonso VI, King of Castile (1072–1109), 80

Alphonso VII, King of Castile (1126–57), 46, 56

Alphonso VIII, King of Castile (1158–1214), 80, 98

Alphonso IX, King of Leon, 407

Alphonso X, King of Castile (1252–84), 9, 38, 48, 80, 97, 108, 268, 332, 334, 372, 407, 467

Alvarez Pelayo, 324

Amalricians, 489–90, 531–3, 537, 564

Amalric of Bene, 481, 482, 499, 507, 531

Ambrose, St, 480

Andreas Capellanus, *see* Andrew the chaplain

Andrew, canon of St Victor, 14

Andrew II, King of Hungary (1205–35), 80

Andrew the Chaplain, 39, 211, 215, 220, 265, 266, 267, 506

Andronicus II Paleologus, emperor of Byzantium (1282–1328), 107

Anselm of Havelberg, 289, 487

Anselm of Laon, 14, 479

Anthony Bek, bishop of Durham, 346, 354

Aquinas (Thomas of Aquino), 27, 53, 176, 293, 303, 311, 324, 398, 400–5 pass, 464, 468–71 pass, 479, 483, 514, 539; *De regimine principum*, 18, 414, 454; *In Boetium de trinitate*, 474–5, 499; and Jews, 84, 86, 92, 94–5, 188; theological questions, 476, 480, 485, 499–500, 502, 504–5, 507, 512, 521, 527, 572, 575, 596

Aristocracy, 56, 58, 147–8, 265–82; rural, 123, 258; urban, 243–50, 274, 429, 432–3, 436–8; *see also* Knights

Aristotle, 84, 267, 401, 408, 414, 442, 445, 449, 477, 482, 483, 493, 495–6

Armenian Church, 77

Arnold Amalric, 550

Arnoldists, 526, 529

Arnold of Brescia, 526, 551

Arnold of Codalet, 170

Arnold of Villanova, 20, 41, 108, 313,

600